THE CHATFIELD STORY

Civil War Letters and Diaries of
Private Edward L. Chatfield
of the 113th Illinois Volunteers

THE CHATFIELD STORY

Civil War Letters and Diaries of
Private Edward L. Chatfield
of the 113th Illinois Volunteers

Terry M. McCarty
with
Margaret Ann Chatfield McCarty

Georgetown, Texas, 2009

Cover Image: Civil War Map #261, courtesy US Library of Congress

Library of Congress Catalog Card Number: 2008904102
ISBN: 1-4196-9722-6
ISBN-13: 9781419697227

Printed in the United States of America
BookSurge Publishing
North Charleston, South Carolina, 2009

DEDICATION

To the memory of Edward Livingston Chatfield and the boys of the 113th Illinois Infantry, young men principally from Kankakee, Illinois, soldiers who battled to preserve the integrity of a young nation, torn in half by an economic and moral calamity. One hundred fifty years later, we see some evidence of the wounds healing. Edward Chatfield witnessed, documented, and endured pivotal events in the preservation of our nation—westward expansion and the correction of abhorrent cultural practices—two of the most significant milestones of our history. But beyond that, Edward should also be remembered for his uncommonly tenacious grip on life, his resilient capacity to prevail in circumstances so grim that death might be welcomed, his combination of nature and nurture that maintained life's spark under the worst imaginable odds. Finally, Edward should be remembered for his dedication and commitment to the "we" that makes all civilized forms of life possible: his family, his comrades-in-arms, his church, his communities—Middlefield, Kankakee, and Littleton—and his nation. Edward's impressive, improbable and inspiringly well-connected life merits this book.

To the living Chatfield descendents who trace their trees back to Isaac and Lucy Tomlinson Chatfield of New Haven, Connecticut—early pioneers of Middlefield, Ohio. You are kin. Thrive in good health, do well for the world, and enjoy the read.

To the guardians of our community and national histories, especially the curators, genealogists, and historians of Middlefield, Ohio; Kankakee, Illinois; and Littleton, Colorado; your noble efforts have spun golden threads.

To our dear children and grandchildren, so very special to us, not only are you the trusted guardians of the Chatfield-McCarty heritage, you are among the critically important and manifestly sound people who will continue the healing started so long ago.

Terry and Peg Chatfield McCarty

ACKNOWLEDGEMENTS

When we began with our initial transcription work on Chatfield's letters in January 2006, we had no idea that our project would spiral outward, eventually involving the help of so many. It seems that this wonderful three-year project has taken on a life of its own, and with it, a great deal of time and effort from many people, both inside and outside of our family.

Our immediate family, of course, bore the brunt of it. There was always "The Book" that had to be considered when planning family time, and there was always something about "Chatfield" that inevitably worked its way into family conversations. The support and enthusiasm of our children and grandchildren played no small part in keeping this project alive. To our daughter, **Kimberly McCarty Mori**, who, despite your full-time responsibilities to your husband, three children, and frenetic schedule, you somehow found the time to nurture this book. You read each of our ongoing drafts, providing sound editorial corrections and critical feedback. You went far beyond what we had the right to ask. Thank you! To our son, **David McCarty**, who, while also unbelievably busy, you read our early drafts and offered key suggestions that found their way into this book. Thank you!

Our extended family also deserves special thanks. To **Catherine Clemens Sevenau**, our fourth cousin and the great-granddaughter of Isaac Willard Chatfield, thank you for your enthusiastic correspondence, your vast reference knowledge of the Chatfield family, and your critical reading and suggestions for improving this book. And to **Gordon Clemens**, Catherine's brother, and another fourth cousin to us, your knowledge and feedback on photo content and family ties has been extremely helpful. To **Susan Juza,** wife of the great-grandson of Charles Henry Chatfield (Edward Chatfield's youngest brother), thank you for helping us with the details of Charles's fateful story. And to **Elton and Lowell Chatfield**, you provided us with a complete history of the Chatfield genealogy dating back to 1450. Thank you, all of you. What a fine family you are!

We want to thank two neighborhood friends for helping out on this project, volunteering their proofreading skills. **Karin Sparks** and **Duane Benell**, your keen eyes have improved this book. Thank you.

Several community historians, researchers, and service providers have helped make this book possible. We want to give special recognition to **Lorena Donohue**, Deputy Director and Curator of Collections at the Littleton Historical Museum. Your assistance in making Edward's three Civil War diaries available to us is greatly appreciated. **Lee and Curt Eakin**, the photo and history you provided us on Riley Vincent Beach, Curt's great-granduncle, made it possible to tell his story in Appendix III, and we are most grateful. Many thanks to **Nancy Arsenean**, researcher for the Genealogy and History Department of the Kankakee Public Library, your assistance and enthusiasm in helping us find details on the Chatfield family in Kankakee is much appreciated. Three resourceful folks helped us research Colorado land records on the Chatfields. Thank you, **Heather Maricle,** of Arapahoe County's Recording Division, you went the extra mile! Your assistance with the old land books was terrific. **Shaun Boyd**, Archivist of Douglas County Library's History Research Center, thank you for helping research Douglas County land records. And many thanks to **Mary Amerine**, Supervisor of Jefferson County's Record Room; you helped us identify many of the various Chatfield land purchases. Thank you to **Matt Atkinson**, Park Ranger at Gettysburg National Military Park (formerly at Vicksburg Military Park). Your timely review of our draft and maps helped assure a more accurate telling of what took place in Vicksburg so many years ago. And thank you, **Audrey Bringelson** and **Don Goin;** your help in locating family burial plots at Kankakee's Mound Grove Cemetery and your interest in Civil War families from Kankakee proved vital to substantiating family historic details. To **Kevin Frye**, Historian of the Andersonville Historic Site, thank you for your information on the O'Dea Lithograph and for sharing with us the excellent DVD you produced on Andersonville. To **Rick Seyer,** former Mayor of Middlefield, Ohio, thank you for sharing your photos and vast knowledge of your town's history. Your street directions successfully guided us to Isaac and Lucy Chatfield's Middlefield home site. To **Keith Delfs**, Engineer, Geauga County, Ohio, we thank you for pulling out the 1837 plat map showing Isaac and Lucy Chatfield's "Batavia" lot #40 and allowing us to take photographs of it. To **Norman Stevens**, Executive Director of the Kankakee County Museum, thank you for your soldier photos and the Adjutant Daniel S. Parker letters and for setting aside your valuable time to share with us your interest and research in Civil War history. Special recognition is also deserved by **Edwina Carpenter**, Curator for the Brice's Cross Roads Visitor Center. Thank you for your time and effort in locating, scanning, and forwarding to us the accurate battle-line maps showing Union and Confederate troop positions on June 10, 1864.

We acknowledge a debt of gratitude to all of the above, whose enthusiastic help and support have carried us forward, adding interest and accurate detail not otherwise possible. Any errors or omissions of fact are, of course, our own.

Terry and Peg McCarty
June 2009

TABLE OF CONTENTS

TABLE OF ILLUSTRATIONS, MAPS AND PHOTOS

INTRODUCTION

"Terry, I need your help." Margaret Ann Chatfield ("Peg," my fiancée) was kneeling on the floor, peering beneath the bed, the edge of the blue and white comforter brushing her cheek. The carpeted floor of the small Yuma, Arizona, home was covered with hairballs and dust. Had Peg seen a shadow of something in the far corner underneath the bed? She lifted her head and took a breath, then bent down to look again. "I don't think I can reach it."

The year was 1964. Peg's cousin, Edaline Chatfield Rhea, had passed away earlier that summer. She was the only child of Edward Livingston Chatfield, the namesake of this book. Edaline had hidden something for safekeeping before she died, and the secret of its location was lost with her. The executor's phone call invited Peg's family to retrieve personal family items, and the two of us made the long hot drive from Los Angeles in earnest.

Peg was a high school history teacher, and it had been Cousin Edaline's wish that Peg would be responsible for the family's historical documents. Before her death, Edaline had bequeathed her father's Civil War diaries to the historical museum in the city of Littleton, Colorado, where "Chatfield" names a state park and recreation area, a dam and reservoir, a high school, some local housing developments and businesses, and a few streets, avenues and lanes. A treasure trove of war tales and family history still awaited discovery, as we would soon find out.

I moved the bed away from the corner, allowing Peg to reach down between the mattress and the wall with both hands, her feet dangling off to the side of the bed as she stretched across it on her stomach. She emerged with an old shoebox, its lid bound by a string of red yarn. Carefully slipping off the yarn, her eyes widened. Underneath the bed, inside that aged shoebox, was the treasure that Edaline had hidden so many years before—a collection of Civil War letters written by Edaline's father and other members of his family. Peg had never seen them before; she had only been told about them. Edaline's safe hiding place had finally been found.

Only a few of the letters were still in their original envelopes, their 3-cent Union stamps cancelled in Memphis. One envelope lacked a stamp and read, "Due 3". Some envelopes had no cancel marks whatsoever, having been hand-carried to their destination by friends. The bottom of one such envelope read, "Care of

Mr. Parker."* All envelopes had been addressed to the members of the Chatfield family c/o the Grand Prairie Post Office, Kankakee County, Illinois. The letters—over 100 of them—had been written in handsome cursive on paper of varying quality. Some were in excellent condition, easy to read and transcribe. Others had badly faded, written on cheap paper, frail and worn, their contents requiring delicate care and magnification to decipher. The letters were a special treasure. The diaries that Edaline had donated to the Littleton Historical Museum constituted a fine account of Edward's daily activities during 19 of his 34 months in the Union army, but his letters provided a window to his character and soul, his words chosen with care and written from the heart. Edaline had saved the letters for Peg, her historian cousin, the great-granddaughter of her father's younger brother, James Herrick Chatfield. Peg understood the compelling responsibility of such an inheritance, even then.

Inside the shoebox and beneath the letters lay a black timeworn binder, its two inch red spine rendered useless by missing brass screws, the outer edges of its 40 pages tortured, frayed by use. This was a copy of Riley Beach's *Recollections and Diary Extracts*. Riley had been one of "the boys" of the 113th, alongside Edward. Against the back wall of the slender bedroom closet stood a rolled 40" X 60" lithograph of Thomas O'Dea's famous picture of the Andersonville Prison—a bird's eye view of the stockade and its surroundings, with perimeter pictures depicting prison events, including, in one of them, six men hanging from a beam. On the nightstand beside the bed, two brass-clasped, leather-bound family albums held sepia photographs, the handsome portrait of uniformed Private Edward L. Chatfield in one of them. Other than what we saw in the picture, we knew very little about Uncle Edward back then.

Astonishment comes close to describing what we felt as we transcribed Chatfield's letters, his life as a Union private unfolding with each successive note, the Western Theater of the Civil War presented from a Northern farmer's point of view—always a keen eye on the soil conditions, the weather, and the height of the crops. Chatfield enlisted at the Kankakee Fairgrounds on August 5, 1862, training there until transferred to Camp Hancock (directly adjacent to Camp Douglas, Chicago) to be mustered into Company "B" of the 113th Illinois Volunteers and to march with General William Tecumseh Sherman's Right Wing of General Ulysses Grant's army. Chatfield's letters guide us to most of the well-known and pivotal sites of the Western Theater: Cairo, Memphis, Holly Springs, Coffeeville, Oxford, Chickasaw Bayou, Arkansas Post, Milliken's Bend, Young's Point, DeSoto Point, Steele's Bayou,

---

* Adjutant Daniel Sanford Parker of the 113th was an officer who had the occasional privilege of home leave. He had also been managing editor for a local newspaper, the *Kankakee Gazette,* when he enlisted. He served as the Regimental Adjutant until after the fall of Vicksburg, resigning on July 26, 1863, and returning to his editorial job.

Grand Gulf, Vicksburg, Corinth, and of course Brice's Cross Roads, where disaster awaited him.

Edward Chatfield loved his family—his mother, father, five brothers and sister—each of his letters expressing warmth and devotion. He was well educated for a farm boy, a community schoolteacher in Pilot Township before enlisting at the age of twenty. His penmanship was unusually elegant. Highly observant, he was a fluent writer who showed a willingness to experiment with words as he matured through the course of the war. His letters leave us little doubt as to his point of view regarding the purpose of the war: Edward saw himself as fighting to protect and defend the Union. Abolition, slavery, and "slaves' rights" were not his concern—a disappointment to us from today's standards. He honored the Sabbath, valued a good Protestant sermon, doubted his strength to be a worthy Christian, championed fairness, blistered at the rebellion, and despised the war's unending cruelty. He wanted the war to end and railed at the "Copperheads" for their protests against what they called "Lincoln's War." With their interference, Chatfield feared, the Copperheads would effectively extend the war. He would have been happy to see them all jailed.

His letters revealed a man of principles, a likable man who cared about others and the world around him. Nonetheless, Chatfield failed to reach today's standards for racial consciousness, acceptance, and sensitivity. Twelve letters and four diary entries include racial references that simply would not be written today, challenging us with the dilemma: Should we reprint the words of a young man raised in a racist nation, or shouldn't we? To omit any content seemed intellectually dishonest—another revisionist attempt to correct America's embarrassing and troublesome cultural past. Yet, to include the offensive language would have other consequences, including the likelihood of preventing this historical work from reaching a substantial section of its intended audience—school youth who would wish to explore Civil War history in greater depth. With this in mind and out of respect for all humankind, we've edited out the offensive racial references in this general publication.[*]

About half of *The Chatfield Story* comes directly from the letters and Edward's diary entries. The other half is background narrative, informative content about the war and surrounding events. Transcribed word for word in their original spelling and syntax, and edited as noted above, the letters span the interval from September 25, 1862, to June 15, 1865. Punctuation and bracketed information have been added here and there to enhance readability. Chatfield's three diaries are the property of the Littleton Historical Museum, not ours to copy and distribute at will. We received permission to paraphrase their content, and that is what you will read here. As a rule, we merely extended Chatfield's phrases into complete sentences and

---

[*]   Researchers may obtain an unedited transcription of Chatfield's letters in CD format at our website: http:// www.chatfieldstory.com

added proper punctuation. Occasionally, in some single entries, we re-sequenced the order of his thoughts. Although we have made every effort to preserve his original meaning, readers wishing to see Chatfield's exact diary entries may do so by appointment at the Littleton Historical Museum in Colorado.

This story begins with Edward Chatfield's birth in Ohio's Middlefield Township in 1842. His first seventeen years of life there trained him to be a prosperous farmer in an area with harsh and prolonged winters, lessons that would afford him survival in unforeseen circumstances. By the time that his family moved to Kankakee, Illinois, in 1859, Edward had become an able partner to his father, allowing for a successful transition to Illinois farming. Although he was too young to vote, Edward possessed the physical skills, strength, and industry to run his own farm, an eventuality that came uncomfortably close to never happening. Beginning in 1862, after the war's first year, Edward's letters and diaries take us with him on an amazing and perilous journey, providing an inspiring and powerful story that has become deeply meaningful to us. — *Terry and Peg McCarty, Georgetown, Texas*

PROLOGUE

Raccoons survived in Ohio's Middlefield area, industrious creatures known for their resourcefulness. Perhaps that's why the county was named Geauga, the Native American name for the furry masked bandits. Middlefield (Batavia, as it was originally named) was truly a backwoods area in 1820, when Isaac and Lucy Chatfield and their seven children (Lucius Napoleon, 1807; Lucy Almira, 1809; Albert Alonzo, 1811; Levi Tomlinson, 1813; Nathan Stoddard, 1816; Ruth Ann, 1817; and Charles Henry, 1819) ventured forth, leaving their New England Connecticut roots and settling on lot #40.[1] They chose to move to Geauga County because the Connecticut Western Reserve communities there had been built upon the culture, character and spirit of their New England Protestant ideals. Moreover, Lucy was acutely aware of the vast opportunities available there for young families—Lucy's father, Levi Tomlinson, having pioneered that area. Tomlinson had purchased land in Burton Township, Geauga County, way back in 1799 and had often resided there. It is quite likely that little Lucy had lived there, from time to time, as a child.

The folks in Middlefield considered 27-year-old Isaac Chatfield to be wealthy; he had purchased in cash nearly 300 acres of land.[2] Geauga's landscape was breathtaking, a combination of rolling hills and rich farmland, its elevations ranging from 844 feet to nearly 1,400 feet, a part of the Appalachian plateau. When the Chatfields arrived, full grown panthers roamed about, quick to pounce upon discarded chicken bones and other table waste, startling the inhabitants. Most of the important local industries revolved around land clearing and the selling of furs, grains, cheese and the precious commodity, black salt.[*]

Testing Isaac and Lucy's talents, snow blanketed Middlefield on average seven months every year, more than a foot per month decreasing to a half foot, January through March. For the farmer, the volatile climate was a formidable foe November through April, a fickle worry in May and October, and a dependable friend June through September. The region demanded hard work and seasonal vigilance to planting, sowing grains, and harvesting crops, and the family's survival hinged on meeting nature's mercurial predilections. But survive the resilient Chatfields did. Lucy delivered four more children, raising her birth total to eleven: Maria Antoinette "Maryetta" (1824), Gilbert Lafayette (1826), Charlotte Ann (1828), and Georgianna A. (her final child) in 1829, coincidentally the year that Middlefield's first church

---

[*] Much of northern Ohio sat above extensive underground salt beds laid down by ancient seas eons earlier. Black salt contained impurities of iron and sulfur and was valued for its medicinal and taste-enhancing properties.

edifice was built, an Episcopal Church sponsored by Isaac and other prominent community leaders.

Middlefield remained an economically isolated frontier until the 1832 Ohio Canal between Cleveland and Akron opened the area to extensive development. Prior to that, Middlefield had sat vastly undeveloped, its muddy roads turning to stagnant pools after the frequent flooding, and Pittsburgh, Pennsylvania, serving as the nearest market, a week's travel by wagon. Progress came slowly, even after the opening of the canal. It wasn't until 1901 that Middlefield had its own bank.

Farming proved difficult and costly, the winter of 1831-1832 especially harsh, the lack of thaw through May severely delaying spring planting and minimizing the summer harvest. Long winters were not the only hazard; early October freezes too often wreaked havoc on crops and fruit trees. By 1833, 46-year-old Isaac had grown weary of trying to manage so much land. With the opening of the canal and the inflow of many new settlers, he was able to sell off half of his estate, allowing him to concentrate his efforts on the remaining 150 acres. The sale also gave him more time to maintain his large two-story home, work as a county official, and assist at the church by reading sermons, conducting services in the absence of the minister and teaching school during severe winters.[3] As it turned out, Isaac had sold his property just in time. The great frost of 1834 devastated many of Middlefield's fruit trees, rendering them lifeless before the May thaw. The loss proved to be a disaster for many of the Middlefield farmers; nonetheless, the little community continued to grow. When 1841 arrived, Middlefield's population was over 770, Isaac was still a major landholder, and Isaac and Lucy's son Nathan was 25 years old—and about to marry.

Nathan had met Margaret Prudentia Herrick in nearby Twinsburg, her family having arrived from Worthington, Massachusetts. Smitten by her charm—a mixture of intellect, compassion, resilience, and beauty—Nathan asked David Herrick, Margaret's father, for her hand in matrimony. The couple exchanged vows in Middlefield's Episcopal Church on August 19, 1841, and began their wedded life together on farmland gifted by Isaac. Nathan was 25 and Margaret, 23. A year would pass before the young couple would welcome their first baby.

The August summer of 1842 ushered in Middlefield's season of hope and promise— the time when farmers would inspect the height and condition of their warm-season grasses in hopes of a good winter's forage. The fourth day of August would have been typical for the season, a warm and sultry day, partly cloudy with only a trace of wind. The temperature's high would fall somewhere in the mid-eighties, light showers briefly falling in the afternoon. It was on such a day that Nathan and Margaret

Chatfield greeted Edward Livingston, their first-born child, his birth[*] on such a promising day timed, as fate would have it, to place him among the generation of male infants in his country to face risk of mass annihilation within 20 years.

For conscientious parents in the 1840's, child rearing was not a task to be left to chance, the child's mind a "slate" to be written on by experience, as taught by John Locke a century and a half earlier.[†] Familiar with Locke's teachings, Nathan and Margaret believed that proper child rearing required careful planning and sound instruction using the best available secular and religious sources. Not only did they want to ensure that baby Edward would grow into a man of high character, they also believed that it was crucial to orient him for proper passage to the afterlife. To help articulate these values, Margaret turned to Edward Merriam, a trusted and respected friend from the church. Merriam agreed to compose an encomium.

Encomiums took the form of flowery compositions, their style prescribed in ancient Greek rhetorical exercises. Used by the ancients to extol heroes and nobility for their accomplishments, the encomium had become a script of sorts for the proper raising of children.[‡] Edward was ten months old when Merriam wrote his tribute, a welcoming salute to young Edward that must have been reread many times. When we first inspected this treasured writing in 1964, it had already been opened and refolded so many times that one of the eight sections had fallen away, lost forever from our view—at least, that's what we thought at the time. While sifting through the James Herrick Chatfield family *Bible* during the summer of 2008, we discovered a handwritten copy of the encomium. Margaret Prudentia Chatfield had penned a copy to present to her son, James Herrick Chatfield and his wife, Annie, to celebrate the 1876 birth of their second child. James and Annie had named their son, "Edward Livingston Chatfield Jr.," in honor of James's oldest brother Edward, a family hero and a person of sound character who had truly been *trained up* in *virtue* and *knowledge*, a *youthful pilgrim on the road*, a man who, in spite of all odds, had, indeed, been *crowned with length of days*.

---

[*]   Wishing to be with her mother for the birth, Margaret delivered Edward in her parents' home in Twinsburg, Summit County, Ohio, 27 miles south of Middlefield.

[†]   Experience was the great teacher, according to John Locke in his 1690 work, *Essay Concerning Human Understanding*.

[‡]   The 1860's was a time when nearly all social behavior of middle class Americans was heavily scripted by mid-17th century Christian doctrine, including the proper way to live, the proper way to evaluate weighty decisions, the proper way to be a friend, and especially, the proper way to die. For a fascinating discussion on the "Good Death" during the American Civil War, see Drew Gilpin Faust's book, *This Republic of Suffering, Death and the American Civil War.*

Encomium to Edward Chatfield - June 13, 1843

Mrs. Margret Chatfield
    Ma'am,

    Last winter, I inconsiderately made a promise to you which I feel myself incompetent to fulfill; but remembering the following rule of George Washington, ("Never make a promise without due consideration, but having made a promise, never fail of a punctual performance of it if it be in your power") I shall do the best I can.

Like as the opening flowers of spring
Or homeless songsters as they sing
That rise exulting on the wing
Is Livingston your boy
Or as the morning of the day
Or the opening flowers of May
Which do their promised fruits display
Your promised hope and joy

An opening flower just in the bud
A youthful Pilgrim on the road
A precious change on you bestowed
Is Livingston your boy
There is hopes and fears not realized
A character in youth disguised
By all your mind is exercised
For life train up your boy

Youth is the time to serve the Lord
His tender mind may then be stored
With virtue knowledge richest hoard
Your Livingston your boy
Then train him up in early years
And save many regretful tears
Which might come in after years
For Edward L your boy

Don't criticize on what I've penned
But to the sentiment attend
In what I have written as a friend
On Livingston your boy
May he be crowned with length of days

And may he walk in wisdoms ways
And to his parents be a praise!
Your child your hope your joy

That when Heaven and earth shall roll
And pass away like parchment scroll
We with the blest may meet his soul
Your darling son your joy
So now farewell may love abound
And faith and patience grow around
Till all at last in joy be found
With Livingston your boy

Edward Merriam.

Edward was three years old when brother David Avery came along, his November 1845 birth providing little Edward with his first sibling companion. His second brother, William Stoddard, arrived in 1847, just eight days before Edward turned five. Edward would embrace four more siblings before turning seventeen: Isaac Newton, when Edward was one month short of seven, James Herrick at age nine, Charles Henry at age thirteen, and when sixteen, his only sister Mary Margaret, the last born, on February 4, 1859.

As Edward gained siblings, his father (Nathan) was losing them—five passing away between 1848 and 1859—only six of Lucy and Isaac's children remaining alive after that: Lucius, Nathan, Ruth Ann, Charles Henry, Maryetta, and Lafayette. It was also during this period that Nathan acquired much of his wealth. On July 15, 1854, Nathan purchased 80 acres of public land in Kalamazoo, Michigan, the favorable price of $1.25 per acre set by the Land Act of 1820.[4] He couldn't pass it up, making full payment for it as required by law, $100.00 in "hard currency"—gold or silver.[5] But he didn't move there, and for good reason. The weather off the lake seemed too hazardous, with untimely freezes jeopardizing every crop and a growing season no longer than Middlefield's. More importantly, his parents were still in Middlefield and needed his support. They were advancing in their years, and every winter seemed to be more difficult for them. Beyond these considerations, Nathan probably hoped that he would be able to profit from his investment on some future day. Geauga County was not where Nathan wanted to stay, but until he could find something better, stay he would.

A golden opportunity presented itself in 1858—affordable farmland with a growing season nearly 30 days longer than Middlefield's, offering more sunshine, less
snow, and ample rain—a place in Illinois called Kankakee, Potawatomi for "Beautiful
River." Nathan and Margaret may have heard the news from their cousin, William
A. Chatfield, who had settled in Momence Township, Illinois, in 1844. Long before
the appearance of white settlers, the Potawatomi had made the Kankakee region
their home, a rolling, largely treeless prairie landscape with a beautiful river thickly
bordered with groves of oak, hickory, maple, cedar and black walnut. Fertile soil
sloped gently to the water's edge in some areas, giving way to sheer limestone
bluffs in others, abundant wildlife nearly everywhere. By 1858, Kankakee—60 miles
south of downtown Chicago—had blossomed into an exceptionally large county of
16 townships, a population exceeding 13,000,[*] and the site of a depot on the *Illinois
Central Railroad*. Nathan had found what he had been looking for.[†]

The timing seemed right. Lucy and Isaac had reached their early seventies, the
burden of the hard, stark winters in rural Middlefield increasingly troublesome,
making a more urbanized location attractive. They wanted the luxury of being able
to travel south by train, if need be, to avoid the harsh winters. North Ridgeville,
55 miles west of Middlefield, seemed ideal; the *Lake Shore and Michigan Southern
Railroad* had reached North Ridgeville by 1853. The two Chatfield families would
leave Middlefield within the year.

Nathan and Margaret, with their seven children, were the first to move, departing Middlefield after the 1859 summer harvest, young Mary Margaret then barely
eight months old. They arrived in Kankakee just in time to prepare for the coming
winter. A year later, in the fall of 1860, after 44 years, Lucy and Isaac bid goodbye to
Middlefield and set out for their new home in North Ridgeville.

The farmland Nathan had purchased on December 27, 1858, sat in Kankakee
County's Pilot Township, 172 acres of fertile soil about eight miles west of Kankakee
City along what is now Highway 17.[‡] Sheltering his family in a small wood-framed
building, Nathan began construction of his two-story home, his sons, Edward and
David, assisting him, and a variety of laborers, quarrymen, masons and carpenters
arriving to help assemble the building stone by stone. A full basement had to be
hand-dug before the walls could be erected. The walls consisted of hand-quarried
stone, hauled by wagon from the Wiley's Creek area nearly eight miles north of the
building site. The massive outer walls would taper from 22 inches at the base to 18
inches at the roof beams. The upstairs area would hold four bedrooms, three mea-

---

[*]   1860 US Census data.

[†]   According to the *1854 Gradation Act*, also known as the *"Bit Act,"* the price of public lands in Illinois had
      been reduced from $1.25/acre to 12 ½ cents/acre to encourage settlement.

[‡]   Lots 1 and 2 of NW ¼ and west half of the SW ¼ of Section 1 in Township 30 North of Range 10 East.
      (Kankakee County General Index 3, Grantee, 1860, Book 25, p. 593)

suring 15 x 15 feet and the fourth 11 X 9 feet, as well as the stairway and interior hallway. The downstairs area held two bedrooms, a living room, a sitting room and a bath.[6] When the stone house was completed in 1860, the original wooden structure became the kitchen, and one of the second-floor bedrooms of the home became a country schoolroom where Edward would teach local children. A testament to its sturdy construction, the Chatfield house still stands today, its driveway bordered by massive tall trees that were planted by Nathan and his sons 150 years ago.

The Chatfield Stone House
February, 1951

Courtesy of:
Daily Journal, February 21, 1951, p. 22, and
Kankakee Public Library Archives

CHAPTER 1: ESCALATION INTO WAR

"… to his mother's relief, he would wait until 1862 …"

As the 1860 elections drew near, the nation had reached a crisis. The question of whether western territories should be admitted as free or slave states polarized the nation. Upon the passage of the *Kansas-Nebraska Act of 1854*, allowing territories to decide to become slave or free states, the spirit of compromise steadily withered. Georgianna "Georgia" Robb, the oldest daughter of Nathan Chatfield's sister, Maryetta, wrote to her Uncle Nathan, Aunt Margaret, and cousins—at one point in her letter gently chiding her cousin Edward to write more often. Georgia penned her letter just eight days after the May 18, 1860, "upset" at Chicago's Republican National Convention. After four ballots, Abraham Lincoln, with his centralized political-economic policies and restrictive slavery platform, had dethroned the frontrunner from New York, William H. Seward. At the moment, the Democrats still had two candidates: John Breckenridge, popular in the South, and Stephen A. Douglas, favored in the North. If the Democrats couldn't decide on one or the other before the November election, they risked losing the election by a split vote, which for the rich and powerful in the South, meant certain disaster.

But Georgia Robb made no mention of any of this, and perhaps that's understandable. She had no voice in American politics; her right of suffrage would not come for another 60 years. Even so, Georgia and her family would have been cognizant of the ongoing dispute between South and North—of "states' rights" versus the immorality of slavery.

Letter - May 26, 1860
Middlefield [Ohio]
May 26th / 60

Dear Uncle Aunt & Cousins,

I now seat myself in the Hall with writing materials before me to Pen a few lines to you. As you see we have got this Box of articles packed and Grandpa is giving [it] to Burton immediately. I thought it would save the postage on a letter to drop it in the box, and it will of course be all the same to you when you get it. We are all well at present and life kind. Providence still watches over you all the same. Pa & Ma arrived home on Sat — the 19th. Pa has not purchased any place yet for certain. He found one in the south part of Illinois he liked very well containing 400 acres for $6,000 or $15 per acre or 17 and have it divided. It had excellent Bearing fruit and a great deal of every thing of not bearing, just set out. It had only a small log house on. But the man had got timber, Lumbir, shingles, every thing ready to build a house this Summer. He would give us if Pa would buy it. Pa has gone with his Brother Harvey Robb. Started yesterday morning to Buy or look out around Louisville or Mintor again, and so I guess he has given up Buying out West. They both liked the southern part better than the northern for several reasons it was much warmer and earlier. There was some soft water and a good fruit growing region. I Don't see how you can get along with Hard water to use. I know we could'ent, without looking pretty greasy at least. I received Auntes letter and Edwards while our folks were gone, and I assure you the perusal of it afforded me much happiness. I am glad to hear Edward that it did not strain you so bad the first time as I was in fear of, and that you are improving so fast in writing and wording also. I know that it was nothing that would if you tried become easier and you know it is only by practice we can make perfect. You must write often and I will do the same, and try and improve myself as I think there is need enough of it Don't you? Yes, I can hear you say.

Mother said you wished I could come out and go to school this Fall. I would like to very much but do not think I will or can, so don't look for me. You must excuse last poor writing. The reason I write with this Lead Pencil is because my Pen is up to Mrs. Gilmores, and I can write faster. Good By. Write soon. My love to all. Charlotte [Georgia's sister] is now writing a letter to David [Edward's brother], the first time she ever attempted to write one. You must all excuse her. No more at Present.

From your affectionate Cuz & Niece.

Georgia A. Robb Esqs

Edward L Chatfield*

---

* Customary letter-writing practice, in the 1860's, specified that the name of the intended receiver be placed below the sender's signature.

P.S. I hope you will not eat so much Pork as to make you all sick, as Grandma said it must taste good. You had not had any for so long. Edward you must write and tell us all how the Clothes fit you. Good afternoon. Ma came home and said what a multitude of work you had to perform. ——— We have made and sent this just as soon as we could and I hope they can help you a little.

Georgia*

When November arrived, the Democrats had not yet agreed upon a single candidate. Although the Democrats garnered the most votes—almost 48% overall—the ballots were split between Douglas and Breckenridge, who received 29.5% to 18.1% respectively of the popular vote. John Bell, representing the Constitutional Union Party, captured 12% of the vote. It was Abraham Lincoln, whose name wasn't even on the ballot in nine of the southern states, who carried the election with only 39% of the popular vote. The southern states viewed Lincoln's win as an irreconcilable affront to the concept of states' rights. Within 35 days of the election, South Carolina announced its secession from the Union. Six more states followed suit and seceded in January and February. Lincoln would not be sworn into office until March 4, 1861.

Following the Confederate firing on Fort Sumter on April 12, 1861, President Lincoln, sworn to protect the Union, had the justification he needed to call for a 75,000-man militia to put down the "Rebellion," a task he thought could be accomplished handily until four more states seceded between mid-April and June. At that, Winfield Scott, the Union General-in-Chief, advised Lincoln that the country appeared to be on the verge of what could become a long and arduous war. He explained to Lincoln that winning would depend upon the Union's ability to choke the South of its sources of supply by encircling and dividing it with an overwhelmingly strong network of blockades and fortifications. When the papers picked up on Scott's long-term plan, they ridiculed it as an overly extravagant strategy and dubbed it the *Anaconda Plan*, supporting their imagery with various sketches of an anaconda boa encircling the South. A decorated war hero, Scott had many years of war experience, having commanded troops as far back as the War of 1812, multiple wars with various Native American tribes, and the Mexican-American War. He knew what it would

---

*   "Grandpa," referred to Isaac Chatfield. (John Robb, Georgia's paternal grandfather, had died in 1832.) "Burton" named a little town 3.5 miles west of Middlefield. "Ma" and "Pa" were, of course, Jackson and Maryetta Robb. Edward's mother, Margaret Prudentia, wrote "Auntes letter." "Grandma," in the P.S., was Grandmother Lucy.

take. Those who were less informed argued that one overland Union invasion would bring the Rebels to their knees.

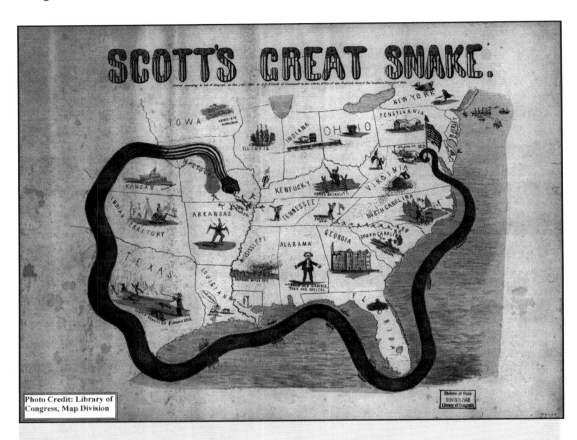

Photo Credit: Library of Congress, Map Division

Cephas Williams, the man who would later recruit young Edward Chatfield, was among the first wave of Kankakee men to volunteer after the firing on Fort Sumter. Williams entered as First Sergeant of Company "G" of the 20th Illinois Infantry in mid-June, 1861. As the 20th Infantry waged on in battle, his leadership skills and apt attention to detail advanced him to 2nd Lieutenant in a mere five months.

Edward Chatfield was a strong boy and not afraid of a fight, and, like many young men in his community, he was not one to shirk responsibility. Almost nineteen years old in June of 1861, Edward taught school in the upstairs room of his family's stone house during the winter months and worked ably, side by side with his father, during the growing seasons. He may have wanted to serve Lincoln's call in 1861, but to his mother's relief, he would wait until 1862 when he would turn twenty. He remained on the farm as the second wave of 125 Kankakee volunteers stepped forward in August of 1861 to muster into Companies "D" and "H" of the 42nd Illinois Infantry.

As it was, that first year of war was a catastrophe. By June of 1862, the combined Union/Confederate death toll was over 100,000, an astonishing 43,000 losses resulting from two battles in Tennessee: one at Fort Donelson, in February, and another at Shiloh, in April. In the latter event, Confederate States (CS) General Albert Sidney Johnston, sensing victory ahead, led his eager troops into battle. The savage bloodbath erupted near a church in Shiloh on April 6, 1862, and ended the following day. The losses were astounding: 23,746 men killed, wounded, and missing—a harsh lesson for both sides. While directing his troops from the front lines, General Johnston himself had lost his life on the first day—mistakenly shot, it is believed, by his own men. He was the highest-ranking officer killed in the Civil War, his death sending Confederate morale plummeting. The battle came to an end when CS General Pierre Gustave Toutant Beauregard, second in command to Johnston, withdrew his exhausted and disorganized troops to the command-center at nearby Corinth, a small Mississippi town astride a major railroad junction. The Army of the District of West Tennessee, commanded by U.S. Major General Ulysses S. Grant, did not pursue Beauregard, Grant having been satisfied with his recovery of the field taken by the Rebels the preceding day.[7] Injured at Shiloh, Lieutenant Cephas Williams nearly died of his battle wounds, his injuries severely impeding his speech and forcing him to resign and return home.[8]

Almost twenty years old by May of 1862, Edward likely would have seen the death numbers in the papers and would have been just as stunned by the losses as everyone else. But the papers went on to suggest that the worst was probably over. The Union boasted of its winnings in the West. No sooner had Beauregard retreated into Corinth, a strategically important rail center, than had U.S. Major General Henry W. Halleck's forces arrived and placed the city under siege. After Beauregard had managed to sneak out of the city in a deceptively ingenious withdrawal, Halleck occupied Corinth on May 30—a huge victory for the North. Although some Northern papers criticized Halleck for not pursuing Beauregard—"a lost opportunity to crush the enemy"—most praised him for taking the city and predicted that Union victory in the West was near. Indeed, even Jefferson Davis expressed dismay, unleashing severe criticism on Beauregard for abandoning Corinth.[9]

By this time, the horrific slaughter rate had staunched the flow of both Southern and Northern volunteers to a trickle, prompting the first Confederate draft in April of 1862. If the Northern citizens failed to heed Lincoln's July 2, 1862, call for 300,000 three-year volunteers, he, too, would consider a draft. The populace wanted the war to end. After all, they had been fighting for over a year.

By the 1862 summer harvest, Edward had grown very strong and bore the look of a man. David, at 16½, had matured into an adept worker capable of 15-hour workdays. William and Newton were not far behind in skills and endurance, nearly 15 and

13 years old, respectively. Each had the strength and size required to do much of a man's work, and there was a great deal of daily work to be done. By then, not only would the brothers help with the crops, they would also assist with the feeding and management of as many as 75 cattle.[10] The talk was that the war would soon end, but the papers made it clear that it wasn't over yet and warned readers that all able men who sidestepped military service would be viewed as cowardly. Lincoln's July call for volunteers would have been difficult to ignore. Even Cephas Williams, who had recovered from his injuries, responded to the call and accepted a promotion to captain in charge of recruiting and training in his home county, Kankakee. On Tuesday, August 5, 1862, having celebrated his twentieth birthday the previous day, Edward sat facing Captain Williams in a white tent on the Kankakee Fairgrounds. Familiar with the war's catastrophic losses, Edward, while returning the quill to the well, may have mused about how simple the act of signing a three-year enlistment then seemed.

Captain Williams personally trained the men he recruited, his tent-count increasing daily at the Kankakee Fairgrounds. Easing his boys gently into the army, Williams allowed their parents evening visits. He even allowed Edward's father to spend the night with Edward after serving jury duty in the city on Friday, August 15.

Back home, the hard life of a farming family continued, the shadow of death never far away. Edward's mother had taken ill. In her heartfelt letter to Grandmother Lucy (whom she called "Mother") Margaret revealed her struggle with illness, the limits of 1862 medical care, and the stoic suffering of a strong woman.

<u>Letter</u> – [August 15, 1862 - date estimated]

Ever dear Mother,

I am yet a probationer of time. We was made glad by the reception of a letter from Mother name ever dear to me. William went to Kankakee to carry his Father. He is one of the jury it sems. Lonesome to sit down in the evening without him. He sits morning and eving and plays on the melodion.* The boys all sing. Its is just as good as ever and Its musac as sweet. We cook Edwards victuals and send to him. His Father will board with him. He wears the coat he wore 10 years ago. You know he is careful of his cloths. It is without a brack. Here set four boys closely examining the papers Grandma sent. Magga is in the kichen washing dishes. I have a girl that does all my work. Don't expect anything of my help. Charles and Mary are fixing for bed. David says they have got 120 acre plowed. They have 62 bushels of wheat sowed, has not got done sowing wheat, are sowing 40 acres of flax. We have sold rising of 400 bushels of wheat for seed at one dollar per bush. The boys do all plowing and draging we have. We have a good Minister. I have not been able to hardly go out this winter. My real health is better but I spect I have something a comeing that we think is a cancer in the center of the brest. I thought at first it was a tumor but It comenced paning me. Applied Egg and salt shred to a salve, then applied Cranberry poultice. In three days it comenced runing watery substance. It became so painful that I left off poulticing now for 2 days. If I can have any doctr root found I shall apply that. The Doct Macks [Dr. Joel Mack said] I had better have it burnt out, but I fear I could not endure it.†

I fear I shall have you in reading so much of so little account.

Good Night

Edward was still encamped in Kankakee when his brother David wrote the following letter, its sauciness providing us a glimpse of David's style. This is the only letter in the collection from David. Tragically, his life would come to an end within twenty-five months.

---

* The melodeon, or cabinet organ, was among the more popular musical instruments of the era.

† Dr. Mack diagnosed Margaret's lump as possibly breast cancer just two months before he enlisted as the Regimental Surgeon for the 113th Illinois Volunteers.

Letter - August 21, 1862
Kankakee City
Thursday 21ˢᵗ, 1862
[Back of letter addressed as follows:]
To Mr Edward L. Chatfield Esq
If you dont Believe it
Then just Aply To
David A Chatfield and find out
To your satisfaction

Dear Brother,

As I have a few spare moments I will improve them in writeing you a few lines to let you on how we are getting along. We are all well at the present time and hope that thes few lines will find you enjoying the same blessings.

But I have some news to tell you. Miss Mary Egelston died yesterday Morning at 5 oclock a.m. she had ben [ill] only just about 5 days. she died with the Typhoid Fever. Her Funeral takes Place Tomorow and woodruff and all of his school expects to attend. I dont no whether I shall go or not. I shall go home Saturday if nothing happens.

I am geting along with my studyes finely with my book keeping in paticular, haveing got through single entry and got Pretty well started in Duble Entry, like the best of any thing studyed, and if I can only go the next term or 2 I thin that I should no as much about Book Keepin as any other Man.

Which do you think that you would like best. Going to school or going to War. For my Part I believe that I should prefer going to school. What kind of effect does it have on a fellow to shake. I wonder if it dont make him think of home. Say why dont you Enlist you again and get that big Bouty and that 60 days Furlough which Would be why fine. Father has got that Carriage of Grand Mothers, so when you Come home you will have some thing to ride in ~~The~~ O I forgot, how do you like the Darkeys? Don't — you thin that they are sweet? If you dont — I do. Oh no (I don't.) They are not fit to be treated like white soldyiers? Dont you think so? Say Ed what do you think of my writeing? a Which stile do you like best? I guess you will say that you will say the blooting [blotting] stile. Well the bloots cant be helped. So You must make the most of it. Oh, say you just inform old Mr. Grant that if he will forward me a Brigadier Generals Comission I will Accept it. Or, it make much Difference, if he can make it convenient, he can just send me a Major generals Commission. I am not paticular.

Father sold his land up in Mishigan for the sum of $5 an Acer for ½ of it and 5 ½ the other. He had a very good time. We are keeping Cattle for Mr. Spring for which we receive $3.00 a head. We are also keeping a darkey for Uncle Sam for which give his board [and] a girl for the Farm for which we receive her work.

Well, I guess that you will thin my thoughts are scatered, and so they are. One thing more and I close. Every Friday we have to write Compositions, and while I write this, Miss Barney thinks that I am writing Compositions. Good by for the present.

— D.A Chatfield

From today's vantage point, it is tempting to cast the Union side of the conflict as unified in opposition to slavery, and by extension, unified against racial prejudice. The reality was that a rigid class system existed, even in purportedly "free" Northern states, and racial prejudice was culturally ubiquitous. The fact that the Chatfields sheltered a black man, for pay, represented quite a change. Only two years earlier, no blacks lived in Pilot Township, where the Chatfields resided, and very few blacks lived in Kankakee County. With its 16 townships totaling more than 13,000 people, Kankakee County had only 18 blacks in 1860, seven of them under the age of 18, all of whom lived in three townships: Aroma, Kankakee City, and Momence. One labored as a master carpenter, two were his apprentices, three were barbers, and one worked as a servant in a white household. The rest were wives and children.[11] Before the war, Illinois state law did not allow blacks to testify against whites in court, and a black traveler who stayed in Illinois for more than ten days could be charged with a misdemeanor offense.[12] The war brought issues of race and freedom into general public discourse, and David's letter to Edward affords a view of white misgivings about the changing times.

CHAPTER 2: CAMP HANCOCK

"I am as hearty as a buck, never felt better than I do now."

Captain Williams soon had enough volunteers to form a company, just ten short of the prescribed 100, but close enough to receive regimental training and formal muster. His company reported to Camp Hancock in Chicago, Illinois, directly adjacent to Camp Douglas, where the first major test of the *Dix-Hill Cartel* was about to occur. The *Dix-Hill Cartel* was an agreement between the North and South which enabled the exchange of prisoners of war and sidestepped having to pay for costly prison camps.

Dix-Hill Prisoner of War Exchange Equivalencies[13]

    1 general = 46 privates
    1 major general = 40 privates
    1 brigadier general = 20 privates
    1 colonel = 15 privates
    1 lieutenant colonel = 10 privates
    1 major = 8 privates
    1 captain = 6 privates
    1 lieutenant = 4 privates
    1 noncommissioned officer = 2 privates

Both sides consented to abide by the agreement—a naïve and ill-conceived compact based upon trust between warring opponents. A Confederate victory at Harper's Ferry, mid-September 1862, would return more than ten thousand defeated Union soldiers to the North to be stripped of all duties until "properly exchanged." It must have seemed like a strange turn in logic to Chatfield—that fit and ready, well-trained soldiers were required to sit idly and wait around until the promise of "a proper exchange" had been carried out. One had to question the capability of warring belligerents to keep such promises.

Letter - September 25, 1862
Camp Hancock Sept 25th

Dear Folks at home

It was with pleasure that I rec'd a letter from home this morning and stating that you were getting along so well, and that David was getting better. Does Mary miss me much and do the boys say any thing about me when I am away? Your kind letter stated that you intended to go east. I will be at the depot when the excursion train comes in if you come on that. I will be there and meet you. I hope that you will have a nice journey. We have not been mustered in yet. We expect to be mustered every day. We got all formed in line once but, we were disappointed in our expectations. There is one company that is not full and we have to wait until the company is full. The country round here is very down and level. Our camp ground is on quite a ridge about 200 rods from the lake. The soil of the camp ground is a coarse gravel mixed with soil, so that it may rain ever so hard it will never get muddy. The companies that we joined here are a fine set of men. We go down to the [lake] every day and go in bathing when it is not to rough. There is ten regiments encamped at camp Douglas and thereabouts. 25 prisoners were brought into camp Douglas two days ago, and it is said that ten thousand are expected shortly. I have not been down to town since I came here. One reason was that I had no money, which was a very good excuse. When I get my money I will send it to you, and you can lay it out or use it as you choose think best. —— I suppose that Pa will come up here with you when you come. You must lay over one train and come down to camp and see us. The boys are all well, as usual. I am as hearty as a buck, never felt better than I do now. Camp life agrees with me first rate. Only I should like to see some of my friends from home once in a while. Mr. Schoby was here yesterday. He left this morning for home. It is time for me to quit to go on dress parade, so please excuse my poor scribbling until the next time.

Direct your letters to camp Hancock, Chicago Ill 113th Reg't Ill Vols.
Care of Cap't Williams.

This from E L Chatfield

N S Chatfield

K K K [Kankakee]

On October 1, 1862, Chatfield and his neighborhood friends mustered into Company "B" of the 113th Illinois Infantry, a regiment known as the Third Chicago Board of Trade. Chatfield's mother witnessed the ceremony presided over by Captain T.O.

Barry, whose dog-eared script contained the reassurances that mothers wanted to hear: "... the Rebellion would be crushed out in 60 days."

Letter - October 2, 1862
Camp Hancock Oct 2nd /, 62

Dear Folks at home,

As Mr. Jeffcoat*was going down our way I thought that I would take this oportunity to write you a few lines. Mother was here yesterday. She got here about 9 AM. Was very glad to see one [of] our dear folks. She was quite smart. She did not seem to be very tired. She stayed until about 7 PM when I went down to Chicago and saw her [off] all right. Got her ticket for her to Cleveland. It seemed pretty hard to part from my dear Mother. It may be never to see her more, but it must be. We were mustered into the U.S. service yesterday By Cap't T.O. Barry. A.G. Tuller was present. He said that he thought the Regiment a very fine one. He said that he thought that Rebellion would be crushed out in 60 days. I hope that it may be so. He said that we should be paid, armed and Equiped in a few days and sent right into the field. He said that we should go to Kentucky. I expect that we shall go the fort beginning of next week. I suppose that we shall [go] to Louisville Kentucky in the first place. We expect to recieve our pay in a day or two. There is about 11,000 paroled prisoners in Camp Douglas that were taken at harpers ferry. They are a pretty hard looking set. They are from V't, NY, Ohio and Indiana. And one Reg't, this state, the 65th. Some of them had not been in the service but two months. Well, I should have written more but Mr. Jeffcoat is ready, and so I must close for he is ready to start.

My love and respects to all inquiring friends,

E L Chatfield

N S Chatfield

PS - There will be something for you at Koones some time next week in the shape of a picture. Please pay the express.

Without knowing that he was foreshadowing his own future tattered condition, Chatfield had described the Northern boys as "...a pretty hard looking set." For the next month Chatfield's regiment would help guard Southern prisoners at nearby Camp Douglas, where, under the provisions of the *Dix-Hill Cartel*, thousands of Northern soldiers captured at Harper's Ferry were also housed, waiting until they could be "properly exchanged."

---

* Second Lieutenant John Jeffcoat, 26, was Chatfield's neighbor from the nearby township of Limestone in Kankakee County, the first of many neighborhood friends to be mentioned by Chatfield in his letters and diary entries.

Diary - October 25, 1862

Camp Hancock. It's very cold and snowing. We had battalion drill and stayed close to the tents.[*]

Diary - October 26, 1862

It's clear and cold. I was detailed for guard duty. Two companies were ordered to a funeral.

Diary - October 27, 1862

I got off guard duty at 3:00 a.m. and was then detailed to cook for the coming week. Our company got a good review. Captain Williams was taken sick and was out of his head.

Evidently, Captain Williams had a high fever; he could have been suffering from any number of conditions. It may have been a bout of malaria contracted while at Shiloh; then again, it may have been severe dysentery accompanied by delirium, a common occurrence during the war.

Writing on newly-purchased Union stationery decorated with soldiers marching forward into battle and a verse from James Sloan Gibbons's *We are coming Father Abraham* underneath, Chatfield conveyed an understandable mix of pride and trepidation, reassuring himself near the close of his October 27 letter by recounting his successful use of arms to help quell an uprising of Southern prisoners.

---

[*]   This was Chatfield's first diary entry, one of more than 400 separately dated observations logged in three individual volumes.

Letter - October 27, 1862
Camp Hancock Oct 27th /, 62

[Verse imprinted on stationery]

We are coming, Father Abraham, Six hundred thousand more,
From Mississippi's winding stream, And from New England's shore.
We leave our ploughs and workshops,
Our wives and children dear, With hearts too full for utterance,
With but a silent tear.
We will not look behind us, But steadfastly before.
We are coming, Father Abraham, Six hundred thousand more!

Dear Mother,

I got your letter that you wrote when you was in Ridgeville, and I have been waiting to see where you went to from there. But have not got a line since. I suppose that you must have had a pleasant visit with our friends and relatives. I hope that you have had a pleasant time. I am as well and hearty I could wish for, except that I have a pretty bad cold. The boys [from] our neighborhood are all usually well and they send their best respects. I got a letter from Father day before yesterday. He said that he and the rest of the family were well.

We got have got all of our 40 dollars now and all of our guns and equipments. We got our dress suit a few days ago. The coat is of a dark purple blue and the pants are of a light sky blue. We have got every [thing] that we want now. We expect to get marching Orders every day, but there is no telling how soon we shall go. We may [go] tomorrow, and we may not go for a month. If you should come back before we leave, you must give us a call, and I think that you would be very thankfully received (you would be on my part at any rate.) When I think that I may never see any of your dear faces, it makes me feel ———. But if we should never meet here on earth I hope to meet you where there will be no more parting and, no more sighing forever.

Yesterday morning my thoughts were all in a whirl. I will relate to you the circumstances. At about 5 oclock, was we were awakened by hearing the [long roll] which means that every man must turn all ready to fight. We had some ammunition given us, and then we marched to camp Douglas. When we got there, the cap't told us that every man must look out for himself. We marched down in front of one of the barracks and ordered the monsters to come out. They finally came out, and we took them prisoners, which amounted to just this, that we marched to Camp Douglas and took 1000 prisoners before breakfast. We were highly complimented afterward by the colonel [Colonel George B. Hoge.] Well, I guess that I will have to bring this to a close. From your affectionate son.

Please write soon,

E.L. Chatfield

Chatfield may have received an 1861 Springfield rifle musket this day. If so, he received an amazingly deadly weapon. The rifling of gun barrels greatly improved both accuracy and range. In contrast to a smoothbore musket with an effective range somewhere near 300 feet, the rifled musket was effective at nearly 2,000 feet. Given the smoothbore's limited accuracy, prior armies could march to close distances on the battlefields without greatly increasing their own risk of injury. It was the advent of rifling that turned Civil War battlefields into places of brute slaughter.

Diary - October 28, 1862
The Captain is a little better. I received a letter from Sarah Titcomb. The stars are shining bright tonight.

Sarah was Sergeant John S. Titcomb's sister. Since the stars were "shining bright" after reading her letter, it's possible that Chatfield may have been somewhat smitten by her. He mentions her several times. Sergeant John Titcomb, one of Chatfield's friends, enlisted in Salina and was later promoted to Captain of the 88th U.S. Colored Infantry.*

Diary - October 29, 1862
I was relieved from cooking after breakfast. James Henry returned from home and brought Mr. Cattle along with him. I wrote a couple of letters.

Diary - October 30, 1862
This was a pleasant morning. I went to the lake and washed my clothes in the forenoon. Then we had battalion drill.

Diary - October 31, 1862
We were called to leave camp and go into the city to be presented to the Board of Trade today.

---

* Beginning in December of 1862, blacks were allowed to enlist in the Union Army, but they were not allowed to command.

Diary - November 1, 1862

I got a letter from Mother and David today and attended a first rate Lodge meeting. Sixteen were initiated.

Diary - November 2, 1862

I had hoped to visit home today but was disappointed.

Diary - November 4, 1862

I had a first-rate visit with Mother this forenoon while visiting Kankakee. Then I started back to Camp Hancock.[*]

Heavy Confederate guns atop the bluffs of Vicksburg tightly blocked all passage south. The Union needed control of the Mississippi River to win the war; and Vicksburg, for President Lincoln, was "the key."[14] The 113th, with Chatfield and his fellow soldiers, would play an impressive part.

---

[*]   A year later (in his November 1, 1863, letter) Chatfield explains, "It will be one year, day after tomorrow, since I was at home from Chicago to attend the Election." Evidently, he received his pass home on Monday, November 3, 1862.

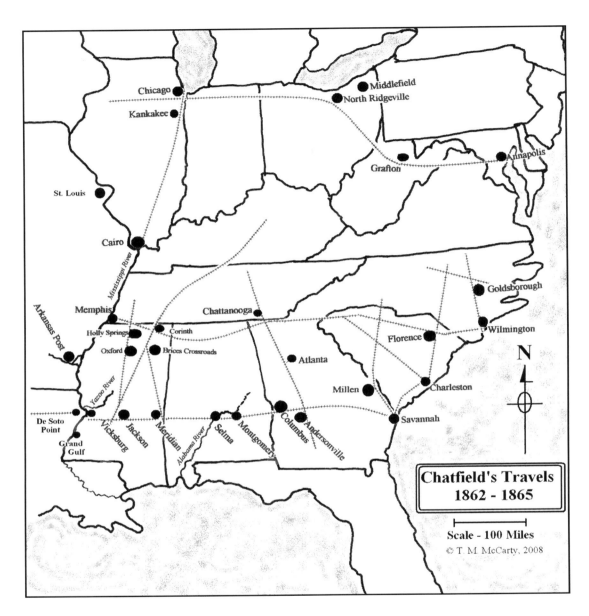

Chatfield's Travels – Starting out from Kankakee, Illinois, in August of 1862, Chatfield's Civil War tour would take him north to Chicago and then south to Cairo to steam down the Mississippi River to Memphis, Tennessee, on what would become the most perilous three years of his life.

CHAPTER 3: REAL SOLDIERS OFF TO WAR

"At daylight Sunday morn we heaved anchor and started on down the river."

Diary - November 6, 1862

The order that came this forenoon is that we are to leave for Cairo at 3:00 p.m. The 113ᵗʰ was escorted to the depot by 3 regiments. We headed south at 9 p.m. and reached Kankakee at 10:00 p.m. where the King inhabitants treated us with a meal.

First Sergeant Kellogg (often referred to as the orderly) joined the regiment at the Kankakee Station and vividly described the excitement of the train's departure.

> As the train came wheezing up to the platform, the perfect shower of goodbyes, farewells, Godspeeds and kisses, hugs and hand pressures were hastily enacted, the locomotive toiled mournfully for a brief space, the conductor shouted, "All aboard," the engine began to wheeze and cough, and the train crawled slowly away into the shadows of the night. The citizens cheered the vanishing cars, and we sent back an answering cheer, which hardly rose above the rumble of the receding train. We watched the lights of the old home town until

they were finally quenched in the thick midnight gloom, as we were whirled away toward the scene of conflict. — Orderly Kellogg[15]

Heavily traveled rails from Chicago to Cairo, Illinois, rarely rested, railroad depots on the Chicago Central clogged with many to witness war's despair.

… Under the dim light of the station lamp we saw the weeping mother hold her soldier boy close to her aching heart as they kissed the last long good-bye…. Those affecting scenes so often re-enacted before us contributed in no small degree to intensify the solemnity of that hour. At one station standing on the depot platform was an ominous looking box, and in the few minutes we were delayed there we learned from an old gentleman that it contained the remains of his boy which he was taking back to mother and the old northern home for burial. His soldier boy had been killed in a skirmish with the Rebels down in Missouri. — Orderly Kellogg[16]

The 113th reached Cairo late Saturday evening, November 8, 1862. An unbroken line of campfires glowed in both directions along the docks. High-water lines on the sides of buildings explained the necessity for sidewalks seven feet above the ground throughout the downtown area, a city of tough people contending with seasonal floods at the confluence of two mighty rivers, the Ohio and the Mississippi. On that day, the rugged port town was beset with commotion and noise from all directions: slamming train cars, blaring boat whistles, clattering cargo cranes, and the loud voices of mule drivers cursing and berating their teams while liberally applying the lash. Chatfield's regiment splashed through the muddy roads toward the boat that would carry them down the Mississippi River. Single story brick warehouses, converted to overnight military barracks, expelled odors of burnt potatoes and aging grease, a malodorous record of prior cooking for hungry troops passing through. Distant bands played music in reverberating swells. Black horse-drawn ambulances slowly worked their cargoes of sick and suffering down the crowded tracks. By the time Chatfield's regiment finally boarded, it was late at night, and no onlookers cheered the boys good-bye. The *C.E. Hillman* simply blew its whistle and steamed away.

Diary - November 8, 1862

We reached Cairo at 11:00 p.m. and marched to the boat. We were all on board by 2:00 a.m. I slept on the upper deck. I awoke at 4:00 a.m. and found that we were near Columbus, Kentucky, where we stopped 4 hours, then continued on toward Memphis. Now and then a Darkie would come down to the shore and wave his hat, and our boys would give him a round of cheers.

Diary - November 10, 1862

We passed New Madrid at 4:00 p.m.

Diary - November 11, 1862

We stopped due to fog. Several boys went ashore but only brought back a few ears of corn. We passed a few steamers with any quantity of contrabands* and arrived at Memphis at 8:00 p.m. We slept aboard this evening.

Dockworkers never stopped toiling below the bluffs of Memphis, unloading all things of war, including the trunk-like boxes used to bury the fallen. General Sherman assigned the 113th, under Colonel George B. Hoge, to Colonel Giles A. Smith's 1st Brigade, under Brigadier General Morgan L. Smith's 2nd Division of the Right Wing to General Grant's Thirteenth Army Corps. The two Smiths were related—Giles was Morgan's younger brother.

Chatfield's first letter from Memphis is missing its front page, its date estimated from corresponding entries in Chatfield's diary. Of note in the letter is Chatfield's comment on his riding as a wagon guard. This would prove to be a salient event, as this first experience may have set him up for a permanent position as a wagon guard later on—an assignment that may have played a role in sparing Chatfield's life.

Also of note in Chatfield's letter is his mention of Fort Pillow, Tennessee. Under Union control when Chatfield's transport passed by, Fort Pillow had originated as a Confederate fort, its 1861 construction supervised by the Confederate General Gideon J. Pillow. Three lines of entrenchment surrounded the fort, and tiers of heavy cannon faced the water in broad rows. Although believed to be invulnerable, the Confederates abandoned Fort Pillow in June (along with the city of Memphis)

---

*   Technically, any enemy property subject to seizure was "contraband," but Chatfield was using the popularized Union adaptation, meaning "freed slaves."

following their loss of Corinth, Mississippi. Within 17 months, the fort would become the site of the murderous carnage of 204 black Union soldiers. In his letter dated April 17, 1864, Chatfield would bristle at the travesty. In November of 1862 when he first reached Memphis, however, Chatfield was no crusader for racial equality. It would take a war to help change that.

Letter – [November 12 or 13, 1862 - date estimated]

[Letterhead: in green block-print, a picture of a mother with daughter, and the words: *"None but the Brave deserve the Fair"*]

[At 4:00 A.M. Sunday morning, November 9, near Columbus, Kentucky] at dark, we cast anchor, the Colonel [Col. George B. Hoge] fearing that if he went on in the night, that the boat might run on to a sand bar or run against a snag, of which there is a great many. At daylight Sunday morn we heaved anchor and started on down the river. I had forgotten to state that during the night I had a very refreshing sleep on the upper bunk on the soft side of the floor. [On Tuesday, November 11] at 7 AM a dense fog [was] comeing up. The transport had to tie up. When, a lot of the boys went ashore where they found a Rebel cornfield and some cattle. They shot a fine heifer, but she finally got away and ran into the woods. The boys brought a lot of corn on board. When, we started on in the course of the forenoon, we passed several steamers and gunboats. In the afternoon we passed Fort Pillow which is a very strong position, but no guns could be seen. Things begin to improve through this part of the country with frequently fine plantations, but we found a great many that were deserted except by a few stray Negroes.

Well, to go on with my story, we finally got to Memphis at 8 oclock Sunday* evening after a long journey of some 600 miles which took 3 days and 4 nights. And, during the whole way down the river, hard[ly] a white man cheered or raised his hat & fewer women. But among the darkies there seemed to be a plenty of whom feeling, for nearly every one we met would cheer and swing his hat or her hankerchief. So much for the darkies.

On Monday morning [sic]† we got our baggage of [off] from the boat and loaded it on to large wagons drawn by 6 mules. When, the Colonel formed the Regiment, and we marched to our present encampment (all except my worthy self included who rode as a guard on the top of the baggage.) Our present encampment is a very good one situated in the woods. It is quite hilly around here. The soil is a very fine clay which is very easily converted into dust. I think that would [be] a good country to raise wheat & fruit and may be corn. Memphis is quite a pretty town situated on a high bluff which is, as near I can judge, about 100 feet above the river.

---

*   (sic) According to Chatfield's diary, he arrived Tuesday evening, November 11.

†   The next day would have been Wednesday morning, November 12.

I have not seen the fort at this place yet, and so I cannot speak, our encampment being about 2 miles from town and in a different direction from the fort. John Titcomb is rather unwell, but is not serious. I have been rather unwell today but think that I will be better shortly. I should be much pleased if you could send me some stamps as I have not got a single one. We left Chicago so suddenly that I did not have time to do anything. Well, I will weary your patience, So I will close, adding that we have some darkies for cooks, so we are relieved from that duty. Give my love and best respects to all inquiring friends.

    your affectionate son

    Edward

N.S Chatfield

Postage stamps—the lack of them—constituted a major worry to most Union soldiers. The Union government wouldn't deliver letters for free. Chatfield seemed forever in need of stamps, the single item most routinely requested in his letters.

The typical horse or mule-drawn wagon measured roughly 10 feet long, 43 inches wide, 22 inches high, and most would carry about 2,536 pounds, the equivalent of 1,500 rations of hard tack, coffee, sugar and salt. A regiment required one rations-wagon for each day of travel—about 1.7 pounds per man.[17] The wagoner's challenge was to ride atop the wagon while protecting the soldiers' supplies and staying out of range of snipers.

Diary - November 12, 1862

I was detailed for guard duty. It was a pleasant day, and I hardly felt like standing.

Diary - November 13, 1862

I was relieved from guard duty at 9:00 a.m. I fired my gun in the forenoon. Brigadier General Morgan Smith reviewed us. The Colonel cancelled his order to stand guard, bringing us joy. We had a grand soiree in camp this evening.

Diary - November 16, 1862

John Fundy is quite sick this morning. We had a grand review this afternoon by General Sherman and Division Brigadier General Smith.

Private John Fundy was a 21-year-old Limestone Township farm boy who had emigrated from Canada with his parents. He was one of Chatfield's good friends and messmates.[*]

Diary - November 17, 1862
We had heavy rain today while I was on picket guard duty.

Diary - November 18, 1862
We had more heavy rain in a.m. Then I visited the cemetery.

Diary - November 19, 1862
Again, we had more heavy rain. We had company drill in the forenoon and battalion drill in the afternoon.

On Thursday, November 20, 1862, Generals Grant and Sherman met in Columbus, Kentucky, to finalize their plans on how to conduct the Central Mississippi Expedition. Grant would move on to Holly Springs and Abbeville, Mississippi, from Grand Junction, Tennessee. Major General James B. McPherson would march from Corinth and join Grant at Holly Springs. Sherman would advance to the Tallahatchie River, on Grant's right, with plans to confront CS General Sterling Price's front across the river from the small town of Wyatt, Mississippi, on December 2. There, a force under Brigadier-General Alvin P. Hovey, arriving from Helena on the west, would attack Price from the rear. If all were to go as planned, the boys of the 113th would fight their first battle at the Tallahatchie River.

---

[*] In his diary entries and letters, Chatfield mentions men from as many as twelve of Kankakee townships, including: Aroma, Bourbonnais, Essex, Ganeer, Kankakee, Limestone, Momence, Norton, Otto, Pilot, Salina and Yellowhead.

CHAPTER 4: THE CENTRAL MISSISSIPPI CAMPAIGN

"We are now truly in an enemies country…"

Diary - November 24, 1862
We received confirmed marching orders. I remained on duty for 38 hours.

On November 26, 1862, the 113th marched out of Memphis and headed toward the small town of Wyatt, 30 miles southwest of Holly Springs in Mississippi. Only a cemetery and a crossroad mark the vanished town today. Sardis Lake, created by a mammoth earthen dam, would not be built for another 78 years. Winter floods, customary events in the Yazoo basin back then, would soon complicate their march. Holly Springs, a major stop on the *Mississippi Central Railroad*, was Grant's chosen supply base, a thriving center of cotton trade mingling Southern with Northern interests, and, before the war, a vacation getaway for the Northern moneyed class—where the little city's classic architecture, tree-shaded streets, proud courthouse and town square conveyed a sense of refined aristocracy. The actual control of Holly Springs switched back and forth between opposing armies throughout the war.

With CS General Price's Second Corps of the Army of the West withdrawing from Holly Springs toward the Tallahatchie River in early-November,[18] the town's warehouses would soon be converted to Union arsenals with countless kegs of powder, rifles and cartridges. The vast store of supplies required by an army would be stockpiled throughout the city—covered wagons, blankets, pots, pans, tents, medical supplies, cots, stretchers, coffee, flour, barley, corn, onions and more. Several train cars loaded entirely with bacon would sit on the sidings, and hundreds of bales of cotton would narrow the streets awaiting shipment north. And, courtesy of the rapidly withdrawing Confederates, two large buildings already held unimaginable quantities of whiskey and cigars.

General Grant's wife, Julia Dent Grant, and their youngest child Jesse, along with Julia's servant slave (also named Julia)[19] would soon locate in the Holly Springs home of CS Colonel Harvey Walter.* The ultimate safety of Grant's family, the town, and its supplies would depend upon the protection provided by the garrison of 1,500 men commanded by Colonel Robert C. Murphy of the 8th Wisconsin Regiment—and also upon the genial mixture of Northern and Southern wealth and common interests.

Diary - November 26, 1862
We were up at 3:00 and had our tents struck and goods packed before sunlight. We were on the march at 7:00 a.m. and passed through Germantown at dawn. We marched 20 miles, and I felt a little tired. We camped beside a creek a little after dark. Supper was hard crackers and bacon. I lay myself down to rest beneath the grand canopy of Heaven.

By Saturday evening, November 29, 1862, the 113th had marched nearly 50 miles and camped "On the road to Holly Springs"—probably about 18 miles southwest of that town on what is now Old Highway 4.

---

* Gentlemen's agreements between opposing officers were surprisingly common during the Civil War. In return for the use of Walter's home, Grant would ensure its protection.

Letter - November 30, 1862
Nov 30th 1862
On the Road to Holly Springs

Dear folks at home,

As I have a few spare moments I will address you a few lines to let you know that I am still well and hearty. We have now been four days on the march and have traveled near 50 miles. We are now truly in an enemies country, and to see the destruction that is made of Rebel property is truly distressing. A great many of the houses that we pass are set on fire and the fences are used the same way. I hear that within two days march there is under General Grant nearly 200,000 men and they are all pouring in toward this place. Well, I must close in order to get my breakfast. I think that we have a great battle just before us, for the Rebels must fight or run. Well I must stop.

Direct your letters to Co. B, 113th Reg Ill Vols Via Cairo. Now do write. I have not received a single line yet.

Give love to all inquiring friends,

Edward

Mr. N S Chatfield

Diary - November 30, 1862

We left at 10:00 a.m. and marched 17 miles, then halted at 4:00 p.m. Our regiment served rear guard. Heavy rain drenched us at 9:00 p.m. We did not return to camp until 10:00 p.m. and had to pitch our tents in the rain.

The plan for December 2 was to engage and annihilate CS General Price at the Tallahatchie, squeezing his forces between Sherman, on the north, and General Hovey, arching up from the southwest. But when Sherman's three divisions converged on the little town of Wyatt on the northern banks of the Tallahatchie, Price was gone, having received ominous reports of Hovey's presence. Price's departure spared his army from a very costly fight. Only a hastily destroyed bridge and a lengthy string of freshly constructed earthworks remained, leaving Sherman little choice but to camp for the night and set about constructing a replacement bridge in the morning. While Price retreated southwest toward Grenada, Mississippi, Chatfield helped to build the bridge, a two-day project made vulnerable by heavy rain and flooding.

Diary - December 3, 1862
I was sent to the river and set to build a bridge.

Diary - December 4, 1862
We marched 5 miles to a high ridge.

In the woods on the high ridge about five or six miles north of Oxford, Mississippi, the boys in the regiment made camp in the miserable rain. That sort of life contrasted starkly with the conditions enjoyed by many of the officers, judging by Adjutant Parker's description of his circumstances that evening.

> December 4, 1862: Gen Sherman has gone over to Oxford today to see Gen Grant and confer with him as to our further progress. It has rained today and I am by a comfortable fireplace, on an easy chair writing on a book. My clerk occupies the desk copying orders. A dozen are about discussing various topics. I endeavor to confront the fireplace to advantage. I had a most delightful nights rest last night on the floor of this secesh* domicil. Our mess chest arrived all right yesterday and we are again faring sumptuously. We have just had a good meal of fried pork, potatoes, hominy & molasses and honey. My man Charlie Frith is one of the best. — Adjutant D.S. Parker[20]

Private Charlie Frith was a 32-year-old married farmer from Otto Township who enlisted in Chebanse Township on August 13, 1862. He was assigned to Company "H" of the 113th. An educated family man who was a dozen or so years older than most of the boys in his regiment, Frith had the writing skills and talent necessary to serve Parker well. Unexpectedly, Frith would elect to desert the army while at Young's Point, Louisiana, on April Fools' Day of 1863—a decision that would greatly damage his reputation and may have played a part in Parker's later decision to resign.

---

*   "Secesh," (si-sesh') meaning "secessionist," was the slang term commonly used by Northerners at the time.

On December 5, CS General Price watched for any opportunity to upset the Union army pursuing him from the north. Grant's advance cavalry, under the command of Colonel Theophilus Lyle Dickey (4th Illinois Volunteers) pressured and pushed Price into Coffeeville, 40 miles south of College Hill (Chatfield's "high ridge"). The single road had stretched Dickey's column to a thin thread two miles long. Three-fourths of Dickey's lead cavalrymen had dismounted, every fourth horseman guiding all horses to the rear, leaving those afoot vulnerable if rushed by attackers. Even worse, Dickey had left his flanks unprotected, making his troops an ideal target from either side, as his column marched toward cannon concealed on a small hill just north of the city. A masterful routing lay in wait, about to ensue.

Stationing his batteries on a knoll facing Dickey's column and flanking him on either side, Price opened on him at 2:00 P.M. with as many as six pieces of artillery. Within two hours, Dickey's cavalry, nearly six times Price's size, had fallen into disarray and retreat, so badly disorganized that they could not regroup until well into the evening.

Price's victory at Coffeeville, Mississippi, deeply troubled Grant, the effectiveness of his Central Mississippi campaign called into question. Grant could ill afford a major upset. The newspapers had already reported that General John Alexander McClernand—a rival of Grant whom most considered to be more of a politician than a military man—had been tapped by President Lincoln to challenge Vicksburg from the water. To Grant, Lincoln's action cast unwelcomed doubt on the authority of his Army of the Tennessee to do the job.

Compounding the situation, CS General John C. Pemberton, responsible for defending Vicksburg, would relish the use of strategies—some risky and improbable—that would cause Lincoln to doubt Grant's ability to manage. Grant could have safely assumed this. What Grant did not yet know, however, was that a Texas cavalryman had, in fact, just sent a brilliant proposal to Pemberton, his plan explaining in detail how to entirely shatter Grant's Central Mississippi Expedition with a minimum of force. Several weeks would pass before Texas CS Colonel John S. Griffith's suggestion would be put into action.

Unaware of any of this, Chatfield wrote home from atop the ridge near College Hill, using Union stationery decorated with an antebellum scene and inscribed with a verse from *The Girl I left Behind Me*, an old Irish song and popular regimental ballad.

Letter - December 6, 1862

[On Letterhead: A Picture of an antebellum scene, with inscription]
The girl I left behind me.
He turn'd and left the spot — O! do not deem him weak —
For dauntless was the soldier's heart, though tears were on his cheek
Go, watch the foremost rank, In danger's dark career;
Be sure the hand most daring then has wiped away a tear.

December 6th, 1862,
On Picket

Dear folks at home,

Here I am, lying flat on the ground, trying to write a few lines with some ink that I have just manufactured. I am as hearty and well as ever, and feel first rate after our marching as far as we have. The boys from our neighborhood are all well and hearty as bucks. They all send their best wishes and respects hoping to hear from home soon. There has not been but very few letters received by any of the boys from home, and as for myself, have not rec'd a single one from any one. Can it be that all of you have forgotten me, or that the letters misscarry. We reached the Tallehassie [Tallahatchie] 4 days ago, and found that Price had burned all the bridges and obstructed the roads as much as possible. So we had to stop to Rebuild the bridge. The stream is about 200 feet acl across and quite deep, and besides all that, the water runs very swift. It took them two days to build it. When, a heavy rain coming up came near washing it away and the army was obliged [to] move immediately. So we all moved out yesterday and marched about 5 miles to our present encampment which is a good one on a high hill in the woods. We had not been in camp but a little while, when our company was thrown out as pickets. Price had calculated to make a stand amd on the Tallehatchie and had thrown up long chains of breastworks and fortifications, some say as much as 15 miles. It is certain that he had a good position. But, when he found that he was likely to be caught in the trap that we had, he skedadaddled. With Grant coming in from the east with a heavy army and Sherman with our forces of about 35 or 40,000 which came from Memphis, which is in a northwest direction from here, he would be placed between two fires which he thought was to much. Several deserters have come in and they say that his soldiers are leaveing him every chance that they can get. If you were to travel through the country in our path you would [see] but very little of any thing. The houses are all robbed and fences, a great many of them, burned. The fences burned and destroyed. Corn & cotton taken for the use of the government. Yesterday we passed a large sawmill gristmill & cotton gin all combined which was lying idle [and] which was immediately set to work. There is lots of cotton through the country which is just picked and a good deal which is not picked yet.

About ½ mile from where I am now, there is an old fellow which ran away on our approach who had about 200 bales about half of which is already baled. Each bale being worth in Memphis about $150.

We live first rate as long as there is any thing to live on. This morning our boys went out and brought in about a bushel of sweet potatoes, a couple of pails of molasses and a pail of corn meal, all of which very soon disappeared, & the hogs and cattle around here have a curious way of shedding their hides, and, all put together, we make out to live. Well I must bring this irregular scribbling to a close. I wish that if you could you would send me a few stamps for I cannot get any here. Now do not fail to write as soon as you receive this, for I have not got a line from you yet, and it seems rather lonesome away down here in Mississippi.

I remain ever your son,

Edward L

To N.S. Chatfield

Direct Company B, 113th Regt. Ill. Vols., Via Cairo / Care of Capt. C. Williams

Price had successfully withdrawn to Grenada, Mississippi, beyond Grant's reach, his victory at Coffeeville raising eyebrows in Washington. But Grant was already in trouble, and he knew it, his position continuing to be challenged by General McClernand, a long time Democrat and the founder of the *Shawneetown Democrat*. McClernand was an influential man, having served as a representative at both state and federal levels. What's more, McClernand, a successful recruiter of Northern Democrats to the Union cause, was Lincoln's hope for keeping at bay the Peace Democrats, strong opponents to the war who identified themselves with pennies affixed to their lapels—people whom the papers called "Copperheads." McClernand's support proved so critical to Lincoln that the president had elevated him to the position of Major General by March of 1862. But Grant had little use for McClernand, unimpressed by his performance at Shiloh and earlier battles.

Incredibly, without consulting General Halleck, in top command of Union troops, and without Grant's knowledge or agreement, President Lincoln had given McClernand authority to command an independent army to take Vicksburg. Grant learned about the appointment in the newspapers.[21] Troops recruited by McClernand were already on their way to Memphis, while McClernand remained in Illinois awaiting final orders. Having not received "official" notice of McClernand's assignment, Grant submitted a plan for an attack on Vicksburg to General Halleck on the third of December and again on Sunday morning, the seventh.

Grant would divide up his forces, sending Sherman back to Memphis. There, Sherman would assemble a flotilla and proceed down the Mississippi with all available infantrymen—including McClernand's recruits. Speed was essential. If Sherman were to move too slowly, McClernand would reach Memphis first, and Sherman would be obligated to answer to McClernand, not Grant. But if the timing were right, Sherman would proceed down the river fortified with McClernand's recruits and would attack Vicksburg from the Yazoo River just north of the city, Grant holding Pemberton in place at Grenada. The plan looked good on paper. Grant received an answer from Halleck on Sunday evening.

> The capture of Grenada may change our plans in regard to Vicksburg. You will move your troops as you may deem best to accomplish the great object in view. You will retain, till further orders, all troops of General Curtis now in your department. Telegraph to General Allen in St. Louis for all steamboats you may require. Ask Porter to cooperate. Telegraph what are your present plans. — H.W. Halleck [22]

Grant had received Halleck's tacit approval. From his headquarters in Oxford, Mississippi, just five miles south of College Hill, Grant urgently summoned Sherman. They met on the morning of December 8 and set the details. Sherman would command an expedition from Memphis down the Mississippi with a force approaching 40,000 men. He would land above Vicksburg, cut the railroad to the west, move inland via the Yazoo, and cut the rails to the east. Then, together, Grant and Sherman would take the city. Until then, Grant would remain near Oxford, using his cavalry to draw out Pemberton's forces near Grenada.

Sherman selected Brigadier General Morgan L. Smith's division, the 113th Illinois within it, to accompany him back to Memphis via the shortest route—roughly 70 miles. They left College Hill for Memphis on December 10. In the meantime, the Federal navy received special orders to secure the Yazoo River, above Vicksburg's northern bluffs, where Sherman and his forces were to disembark within 16 days.

Diary - December 12, 1862

We had a 20-mile march today. We were 25 miles from Memphis in the morning and 5 miles away by night. Drizzling rain came in the afternoon. George Van Valkenberg is quite sick tonight.

No one knew it at the time, but Chatfield's good friend, Indiana-born George Van Valkenberg, had come down with the smallpox. Nearly six feet tall, Van Valkenberg was a 20-year-old married farmer from Kankakee's Limestone Township.

As the boys marched their way back to Memphis on December 12, it was already known that their intended landing place on the Yazoo River above Vicksburg's northern bluffs wasn't secure. The fate of a mighty ironclad, the *U.S.S. Cairo*, would play out at noon in the midst of its attempts to make the waters safe.

The USS Cairo as she appeared in October, 1862, while being re-outfitted for use by the Navy. Within two months, a devastating explosion would sink her to the muddy floor of the Yazoo where she would remain for 103 years. Reclaimed in 1965, the mighty Cairo is now on display at the Vicksburg National Park--the only "City Class" warship in existence. (1862 photo courtesy of Vicksburg National Military Park. Inset of reconstructed bow taken by authors.)

The December 12 Saga of the U.S.S. Cairo

Following Grant's decision to send Sherman to Vicksburg, the navy received orders to ensure that the Yazoo River north of Vicksburg, where Sherman would disembark, was free of hidden explosive devices once he arrived. On Thursday, December 11, two tinclads found and destroyed one of the deadly contrivances about 20 miles up the Yazoo near Haines' Bluff. On the following day, Friday, December 12, while Chatfield was returning to Memphis, five additional naval ships pushed slowly up the Yazoo in search of more hidden killers, the "infernal machines" known at the time as "torpedoes."

The eyes of sentries carefully examined the silt-green water for any sign of the silent and motionless devices secreted beneath floating logs or pieces of what might seem to be long-abandoned flotsam. A single contrivance was capable of blasting a cavernous opening through the hull of a ship, engorging it with water, and plunging it to the river bottom within minutes. The ingenious mechanisms had been fashioned by the Rebels to defend against the superior size and number of Union vessels plowing the central Mississippi waters.

The order of the ships had been predetermined. The *Marmora*, a tinclad, led the procession, followed by a second tinclad, the *Signal*. The *Queen of the West*, a ram,[*] held the middle position; the sister-ship ironclads, the *Cairo* and the *Pittsburgh*, protected the rear.[23] Lieutenant Commander Thomas Selfridge, a young, brash and ambitious Annapolis graduate, both skippered the *U.S.S. Cairo* and commanded the flotilla. His naval future depended upon his projecting the right reputation, an image that Selfridge had never left to chance. The son of a prominent naval officer, Selfridge had been raised to adopt the navy's important values as his own: adherence to regulation, leadership, bravery, intelligence, and success under fire. These were the tools by which he regularly measured his own actions. His efforts to distinguish himself won him no friends from enlisted ranks and occasionally raised the eyebrows of his superiors. His call for the elimination of all profanity, for example, seemed ludicrous to nearly everyone, and his occasional showy displays of "bravery" triggered compliance concerns from above. This mission would prove to be no exception.

Mindful of Selfridge's tendency towards overzealousness, Fleet Commander Captain Henry Walke ordered caution and carefully structured the mission with six specific orders:[24]

- *The fleet was to avoid the channel where the mines were set.*
- *Only the tinclads were to approach the shore and were to use small boats to remove and destroy the infernal machines.*
- *No boats were to proceed upriver until the area below them had been cleared.*
- *The ram should hold the intermediate position between the tinclads and ironclads and defend against all approaching enemy vessels.*
- *The two ironclads were to bring up the rear and were to shell all enemy positions encountered.*
- *If the execution of these orders were to place Selfridge or the flotilla in danger, he was to abandon the project and return the flotilla to the mouth of the Yazoo for further planning.*

---

[*]   A ship with a sharp metal beak affixed to its prow used to batter enemy vessels.

Selfridge sat in the cabin of his mighty *Cairo* as she slowly plowed her way behind The *Queen of the West*. It was 10:00 A.M.; his fleet had been underway for three hours yet was nowhere near the place where the torpedoes had been sighted the day before. The 2-knot-per-hour pace seemed needlessly slow, an unwarranted gift of time to the enemy. Stepping outside the helm, Selfridge hollered at Captain Edwin Sutherland, commander of the *Queen of the West*, to increase his speed and close up on the *Signal*. No doubt the order seemed abrasive to Sutherland, but the intent was clear. Speed and efficiency were important to Selfridge. Allow the Rebels no benefits and make them pay dearly for this war. And Selfridge had plenty of firepower: three army 42-pound rifles, three navy 64-pound smoothbores, six navy 32-pound smoothbores, and one 30-pound Parrott—a modern rifled gun named after its inventor, Robert Parker Parrott.*

Aware that Fleet Commander Walke expected high levels of caution, Selfridge was nonetheless committed to maximizing the use of his ship's vast reservoirs of power. There is no way to determine if Walke's sixth rule irritated Selfridge—but it may have. *"If the execution of these orders were to place Selfridge or the flotilla in danger, he was to abandon the project and return the flotilla to the mouth of the Yazoo for further planning."* Then again, Selfridge was familiar with the navy's way of running things, and he may have regarded the rule as merely a protective caveat for his superiors if something went wrong. Besides, Selfridge seemed to operate on two rules of his own:

1. *Always do more than you are asked to do.*
2. *Bravery is always forgiven; cowardice never is.*

The wheel of the giant *Cairo* rumbled a lapping thunder as black soot belched from the two 44-inch stacks to mingle with the Yazoo's overhanging tangle of dogwood, cypress and water oak limbs. The pungent odor of burnt coal and sulfur trailed in the ironclad's wake. The *Cairo* sat low in the water, an inverted griddle of plate-iron 2½ inches thick, her appearance thoroughly intimidating. She was a massive and powerful craft, 175 feet long and 51 feet wide, with a highly vulnerable wooden underbelly well hidden six feet below 512 tons of displaced water. Two steam engines drove the wheel recessed between two protective casemates. A small-bore, two-cylinder engine known to the crew as the "Doctor" delivered the prescribed quantities of water to five thirsty fire-tube boilers that, in turn, devoured 330 pounds of coal every ten minutes and produced 140 pounds of steam per cubic inch of cylinder. The second engine—an inclined Western Rivers engine—used boiler steam to heave two 22-inch pistons a distance of six feet with each half-revolution to propel the wheel. The force was comparable to a team of 600 horses pulling all at once.[25]

---

*   Many guns were named after the weight of their projectiles; a 64-pound smoothbore fired a 64-pound shell.

Having sped up its pace, the marvelous *Cairo*, a triumph in wartime engineering, propelled its way up the river, one mile in ten minutes.

At about 11:20 A.M., the flotilla was 18 miles upriver from the mouth of the Mississippi when the first hints of danger appeared. Musket pops sent Selfridge scurrying from his cabin to the top deck. The *Marmora*, ahead of the *Queen*, was reversing its wheel, backing up after having just rounded a turn in the river, musket smoke engulfing her starboard deck. Selfridge may have concluded that his lead boats were under attack and in need of his ship's protection. The next order he gave, "Ahead full! Guide between the *Marmora* and the banks!" arguably violated Commodore Walke's fifth order requiring that the two ironclads should bring up the rear. Selfridge had moved the *Cairo* out of position; he was no longer guarding the rear of the fleet. Believing that the *Marmora* was under fire, Selfridge must have deemed the move justified.

But Selfridge had it wrong. No gunshots were reported to have come from the banks. When reassured that the *Marmora* had simply been firing at a suspected torpedo, Selfridge did not return to the rear position. Instead he ordered First Master Robert Getty, in command of the tinclad *Marmora,* to cease fire and to lower a boat to examine the device, Selfridge sending a small cutter of his own to help investigate.[26] As the *Marmora's* sailors lowered their small cutter to the water, Selfridge commanded the *Cairo's* starboard batteries to open fire on the banks, justifying his position. The time was about 11:45 A.M.

The combination of shelling and slow current shifted the *Cairo's* bow toward the shoreline, aligning the back of the ship with the center of the river. Meanwhile, the men in the cutter probed the wooden block and found it to be debris from the torpedoes that had exploded the day before. But on their return to the *Marmora,* the sailors sighted, cut loose, and towed what turned out to be a live torpedo missed a day earlier. It was 11:50 A.M.

Perhaps the Yazoo's slow current should be blamed for causing the violation of Walke's second rule *("only the tinclads were to approach the shore...").* The *Cairo's* bow gently settled into the Yazoo's muddy southeastern bank, its nose wedged on the shore. She was downstream from the *Marmora,* an area that had not yet been cleared. At the helm of the *Marmora,* First Master Getty felt certain that more torpedoes were near, and he was right.[27] Two undetected deadly devices lay torpid in wait, their construction remarkably simple. Both had been made of demijohns, 5-gallon glass bottles covered with reed. Each had been filled with cannon powder. It is likely that friction wires entered their necks,* tightly sealed by wood, beeswax,

---

* A controversy still exists on the fusing of the torpedoes. Did electric current from the shore trigger them, as originally suggested by Admiral David Porter? Or were friction primers used to detonate the devices, as suggested later by historian John Wideman?

beef tallow, and lead carbonate. Strapped to logs by lines that ran to shore through pulley-weights below the bottles on the river floor, the devices hovered about 5.5 feet below the water's surface. The first torpedo sat about 30 yards from shore and 20 yards upriver from the *Cairo*. The second lay nearly parallel to the first, 37 yards out from the shore. Both were connected to a trigger-wire that would bring the devices against the sides of any passing boat. When snagged, the forward motion of the boat would pull the friction wires. Selfridge's 11:55 A.M. order to back away from the shore and slowly pull ahead to the right of the *Marmora* sealed the *Cairo's* fate.

Had the *Cairo* been four yards closer to shore, the tragedy may not have occurred, one of war's many unnoticed near misses. But she wasn't. Following its realignment with the shoreline and after the *Cairo* wheel churned the ship forward a half-length, the left side of her V-shaped bow bumped the wicker reed bottle closest to shore, propelling it forward and tightening the trigger-wire. The massive explosion convulsed and shattered the *Cairo's* vulnerable hull at her port quarter, tipping her top decks three feet starboard while sending her anchor high above the vessel before splashing its return, the ship's underside crushed into unrecognizable splinters. The outer torpedo was next to explode, its concussion and wave violently rocking the devastated vessel amidships, while precipitously pitching and drenching the *Marmora*, First Master Getty standing helplessly astonished on its bridge. Torrents gushed past the *Cairo's* bulkheads across searing furnaces, forcing roaring steam through all forward ports. In less than a minute, the left forward deck of the colossal *Cairo* dipped below the waterline.

Selfridge, stunned by the unimaginable event, shouted for assistance from the *Queen of the West* while ordering the *Cairo* to be driven ashore and moored to a willow tree. Within three minutes, the *Cairo's* forecastle overlooking the bow had dropped below water. Twelve minutes later, the mighty *Cairo* rested 30 feet under the water's surface, only her stacks and flag mast remaining above to tell her tale. Remarkably, there were no deaths. Yet the *Cairo* was gone—a mighty platform of war had sunk.

CHAPTER 5: TO VICKSBURG BY WATER

"I have my gun cleaned, my knapsack packed, and I'm ready to go."

On December 12, the same day that the *Cairo* had been sunk, a Confederate cavalry-man prepared to move out of Columbia, Tennessee, with orders to destroy the railroad communication from Central Mississippi to Memphis, Tennessee. His name was General Nathan Bedford Forrest.

Diary - December 13, 1862
We reached Memphis today.

The Union plan to take Vicksburg seemed relatively simple—at the time. Sherman would attack Vicksburg from the west; Grant would draw Pemberton's forces in the opposite direction by attacking him from the east, in the vicinity of Grenada, Mississippi. With the enemy drawn to separate battles, the city was expected to fall rather quickly. Adjutant Parker had been briefed on the battle plan and was highly confident of a positive outcome in his December 13 letter to his wife.

> ….We leave [Memphis] on Wednesday or Thursday on what is called the "Castor Oil Expedition." Some 40,000 men under command of Gen Sherman, with the gun-boat fleet to accompany us. Set sail on

either Wednesday or Thursday of this week. Our division will take habitually the center of the army. I think we will have a grand time. It is thought our first destination is Jackson, the capitol of Miss, and the home of the "rebel chief" Jeff Davis. We will have considerable land travel, as we go from Jackson to Vicksburg. We may, however, go from here to Vicksburg direct and essay the capture of that rebellious city first. You may Set it down that we will take it if we Start for it as the force will be a large and effective one.... — Adjutant D.S. Parker [28]

Diary - December 14, 1862

Lieutenant Colonel John Paddock returned to camp from home today.

A family friend from Kankakee, John W. Paddock mustered in when Chatfield did, October 1, 1862. Chatfield would remain a loyal supporter and friend, their final parting one of war's capricious misfortunes. Not only was Paddock a friend of the Chatfield family, he was a friend of Adjutant Parker, who a day earlier had written to his wife:

> I think Col Paddock and my clerk [Private Charles Frith] will form with me a mess. I will write you more in detail about my arrangements before we start. I know just how to prepare for the trip having been out once. I am bound to do the full fair thing by Col Paddock. I will befriend him to the uttermost, as I know he is a fast friend of mine. "With all his faults I love him still." He is looking finely and our boys are happy to see him back. — Adjutant D.S. Parker [29]

Diary - December 17, 1862

I have my gun cleaned, my knapsack packed, and I'm ready to go. The boats are arriving very fast.

Chatfield's knapsack contained several pouches for carrying about his worldly goods, its multiple compartments distinguishing it from the single-pouched haversack. The useful bags served the soldier as the custodian of all his personal belongings: his comb, toothbrush, wallet, harmonica, eating utensils, tobacco, writing paper, family photos, letters, extra hard tack, and so forth. What's more, the convenient carryalls often doubled as makeshift pillows.

Holly Springs, December 20, 1862

After carefully reading Texas Colonel John S. Griffith's proposal, CS General Pemberton had no doubt that he could put an end to Grant's Central Mississippi campaign. Griffith's concept was to deny Grant his supply base at Holly Springs, thereby neutralizing him. The clincher for Pemberton was that a relatively small force was all that was needed to get the job done. It was a brilliant plan. Pemberton ordered Griffith to assist CS General Earl Van Dorn in executing it.

Griffith and Van Dorn reigned in their horses near Holly Springs on the morning of December 20, ending the last leg of their covert approach to the city. Under better conditions it would have been hard to keep secret the arrival of 3,500 cavalrymen on the eastern edge of town. But on this moonless, frigidly cold and drizzly Saturday morning, it was easy. The annual Christmas festival had ended just hours ago. Ample stores of wine and whisky had dulled the senses of most of the Union officers and enlisted men.

The predominantly female citizenry of Holly Springs had not yet awakened when Van Dorn signaled the final advance on the city with the tip of his saber. The Rebel yell and the pounding clatter of hoofs brought the ladies to their windows and into the streets, some wearing only their robes. All cheered and waved as the cavalrymen galloped into town on Depot Street. North of the city, the piercing howls of the dismounted cavalry provoked a scene of frenzied Union soldiers scrambling from their tents, fumbling for their rifles and boots. All were quickly subdued and forced to surrender. By good fortune, the 2nd Illinois Cavalry had camped beyond the depot on the northern end of the fairgrounds, away from the invaders, the only unit that would fight its way to freedom.

Lieutenant Colonel Quincy McNeil, the commander of the 2nd Illinois Cavalry, was an exception, having camped closer to town in the officer's area. He awoke in his tent to two Confederate cavalrymen placing him under arrest, their pistols aimed squarely at his head through the parted flaps of his tent. His six company commanders fared better, having risen earlier to prepare the day's orders, their tents adjacent to the enlisted men they commanded. Distant gunshots and explosions brought them from their tents where they would quickly scratch out a plan in the Colonel's absence. Within minutes, all six companies converged upon the rolling hill north of the fairgrounds, the high ground advantageous for their defense. With carbines, pistols, ammunition and sabers ready, they formed a protective square, four of the six companies forming the sides and two forming in the middle to fill in where needed. Within less than an hour, the 500 men of the 2nd Illinois Cavalry fought their way out and fled 26 miles southwest to Coldwater, an intermediate outpost between Oxford and Memphis.

Those that remained, some 2,000 Union men and officers, were quickly captured and herded to the eastern side of town, while 1,000 Confederate prisoners were released. The ladies flooded the streets, wildly cheering, as pillaging of the city began. Confederate cavalrymen, the worst equipped outfit to be found anywhere in the West only hours before, took all that they could carry: the uniforms, blankets, boots, revolvers, and carbines that they had miserably lacked. Meanwhile, the citizens, mostly women and elderly men, scrambled to grab the things that would help sustain them in the coming months—food, tools, saws, hardware, light farm equipment and, of course, whiskey. Then the fires came, climaxing the pandemonium.

Grant's enormous supply had been accumulating for weeks, trainload upon trainload of food and goods required to support his massive army—too much for the Confederates to carry away quickly. There simply wasn't enough time to remove the prodigious stores before the Union would return in great force. To render the remaining supplies useless to the returning Union troops, the Confederates torched what couldn't be handily carried away: newly constructed wagons packed with poles and tents; train cars loaded with bacon; countless barrels of dried fruit, tons of flour and bagged potatoes, and thousands of bags of coffee. Even the hundreds of bales of Southern-grown cotton had to be destroyed, incinerated to ashes so that the North could not sell it to help finance the war. Whatever whiskey remained was dumped into the streets. All buildings containing war munitions were torched, their huge explosions shattering windows throughout the city. Grant's loss was monumental: over 5,000 rifles, 2,000 pistols, 100,000 suits of clothes, 5,000 barrels of foodstuffs, and nearly two million dollars worth of medical and miscellaneous supplies. The city of Holly Springs was all but destroyed by Van Dorn's raid, a complete success from a military point of view, its impact upon Grant beyond calculation. In less than five hours, Van Dorn had brought Grant's magnificent army to a standstill, eliminating his ability to attack Vicksburg from the east, and with the telegraph lines cut, there was no way to warn Sherman.[30]

Diary - December 20, 1862
We marched through town to the boats. Our regiment boarded the Edward Walsh. We took 7 days' rations when we boarded. I visited Mr. Orton on an adjacent boat while it was moored.

Albert Orton, a private in Company "I" of the 1st U.S. Light Artillery, was a 20-year-old farmer who enlisted in Kankakee Township in 1862. His tour eventually took him to Scottsboro, Alabama, where he reenlisted in March of 1864. He transferred to the Veteran Recruitment Corps in late October of 1864. Disabled for unknown reasons, Orton was later determined to be unfit for battle and was discharged on May 17, 1865.

On the evening of December 20, 1862—the same day that Holly Springs fell—the entire Memphis harbor was bustling with warships and transports when Adjutant Parker wrote, "We were up early this morning and have been loading all day....We are loaded in good Shape, and have a first-rate boat with only our regiment on board. There are some 50 or 60 large boats leaving for Vicksburg, and the men all feel well."[31]

Diary - December 21, 1862
I awoke in Helena, Arkansas, 80 miles below Memphis.

US Major General Frederick Steele's division joined the flotilla at Helena, Arkansas, and all boats assembled a few miles farther down river at Friar's Point, Mississippi. Informed that General Forrest had cut up the Mississippi Central rails to Grant's rear, and having received last minute word of the Holly Springs disaster, Sherman knew that Grant might be forced to alter his plans in some way yet to be communicated. With no word from Grant, Sherman continued to operate on the plan that they had formulated, detailing the strategy to his commanding officers on the morning of December 22. Sherman distributed identical maps to minimize interpretive errors and explained that Grant could be expected to advance down the ridge between the Big Black and the Yazoo Rivers. He indicated where he and Grant would meet and, together, take Vicksburg.

Diary - December 23, 1862
We passed, after daylight, a small town named Napoleon.

Diary - December 24, 1862
We arrived at Buckhorn Plantation, a little below Milliken's Bend [Louisiana] about 1:30 a.m. We were 25 miles from Vicksburg. It was cloudy all day today.

Contradicting what Sherman later wrote in his memoirs, Chatfield twice penned that there were two brigades, not one, that shared the honor of turning the rails that particular night.* Sherman wrote:

> We reached Milliken's Bend on Christmas-day, when I detached one brigade (Burbridge's), of A.J. Smith's Division, to the southwest, to break up the railroad leading from Vicksburg toward Shreveport, Louisiana. Leaving A.J. Smith's Division there to await the return of Burbridge, the remaining three divisions proceeded, on the Yazoo...—W.T. Sherman [32]

Diary - December 25, 1862
Christmas morning at Buckhorn. We burned several buildings this morning, including a large cotton gin. We drove the Rebel pickets away, and at 3:00 p.m. we marched off toward the railroad between Vicksburg and the interior of Louisiana. We pushed back the Rebel defenders there and reached the railroad at dusk with General Smith.† We all lay hold of the ties of our own accord, and with one tremendous boost, the whole track for over a mile went over amidst tremendous cheers. We tore up all the ties, piled them up, laid the whole, and set it all on fire.

---

*   Diary entry – December 25, 1862 and Letter – December 31, 1862

†   Chatfield wrote, "General Smith," but he meant Colonel Smith, his brigade commander. Many brigade commanders were generals, but not all of them. Chatfield had a lot of Smiths to keep track of back then.

Apparently, after Colonel Stephen Burbridge's brigade had disembarked to cut the rails, General Morgan L. Smith sent out a second brigade at the next stop—that of his brother, Colonel Giles A. Smith, Chatfield's brigade commander. Unlike Burbridge, who would rejoin Sherman's division in the afternoon of December 26, Colonel Smith was ordered to return to the boats that same evening.

At dawn on December 26, the boats continued down river, passing Pawpaw Island, before departing the Mississippi and steaming 2.5 miles up the Yazoo to the point where the river turned directly east. A mile beyond the turn, on the south side of the Yazoo, the transports passed a wide bayou, known as *Old Bed River*. Just beyond that, to the east, stood *Black's Sawmill*. From that point to the *Chickasaw Bayou*, a distance of roughly two miles, Sherman had determined to establish his lines. Sherman recognized that the swampy delta wasn't the best place to land; nonetheless, when Admiral Porter explained that the Yazoo contained far too many deadly torpedoes ten miles up river near Haines' Bluff and that a powerful Rebel force was forming up there, Sherman chose to settle on the delta for his initial attack. Roughly three miles of marshy land separated him at the Yazoo from the *Walnut Hills* to the south—Vicksburg's high bluffs.

> There was a road from Johnson's plantation directly to Vicksburg, but it crossed numerous bayous and deep swamps by bridges, which had been destroyed; and this road debauched on level ground at the foot of the Vicksburg bluff, opposite strong forts, well prepared and defended by heavy artillery. — W.T. Sherman[33]

With the exceptions of Johnson's Plantation, a mile east of the Black's Sawmill, and a series of old cotton-fields, most of the delta was densely wooded. Sherman knew it would be a difficult fight. Chatfield's regiment camped with General Morgan L. Smith's division on the east side of the road near the charred remains of the Johnson Plantation house. Once in camp, Chatfield, still a bit of a kid, did what kids do.

Diary - December 26, 1862
I climbed a tree and made a bed of Spanish moss.

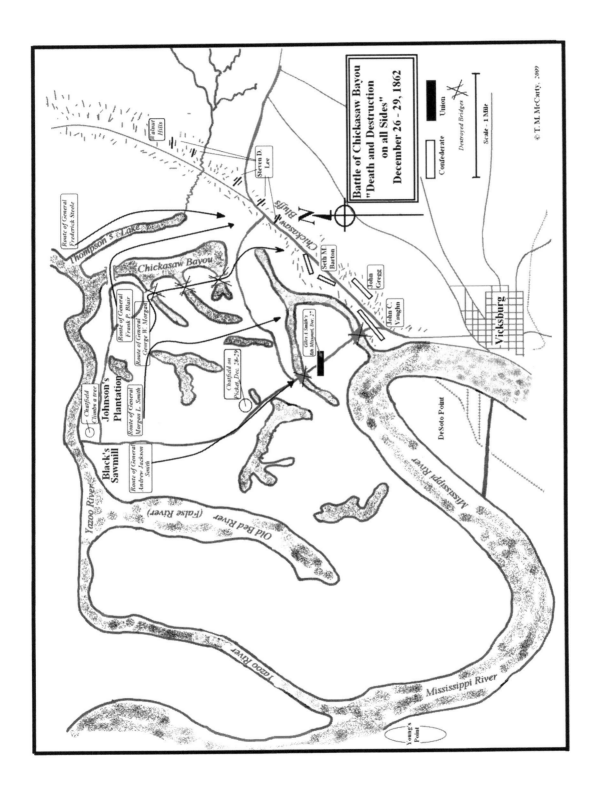

Battle of Chickasaw Bayou
"Death and Destruction
on all Sides"
December 26 - 29, 1862

Union

Confederate

Destroyed Bridges

Scale - 1 Mile

© T. M. McCarty. 2009

N

Tabut
Hills

Steven D.
Lee

Chickasaw Bluffs

Seth M.
Barton

John
Gregg

John C.
Vaughn

Route of General
Frederick Steele

Thompson's Lake

Chickasaw Bayou

Route of General
Frank P. Blair

Route of General
George W. Morgan

Chatfield on
Picket, Dec. 26-29

Giles A. Smith's
8th Missouri, Dec. 2?

Vicksburg

Route of General
Morgan L. Smith

Chatfield
climbs a tree

Johnson's
Plantation

Black's
Sawmill

Route of General
Andrew Jackson
Smith

DeSoto Point

Yazoo River

Old Bed River
(False River)

Mississippi River

Yazoo River

Mississippi River

Young's
Point

CHAPTER 6: BATTLE OF CHICKASAW BAYOU

"Of all the horible things, war is the worst that can be thought of."

Pemberton, prompted by Grant's retreat north following the loss of Holly Springs, hastily summoned his eastern forces to deploy and strengthen the bluffs overlooking Vicksburg. Sherman, uncertain as to how Grant would respond to the Holly Springs losses, prepared to test Pemberton's lines. The battle of Chickasaw Bayou erupted with skirmishing actions on December 27. The 8th Missouri, in Colonel Giles Smith's brigade, was among the first regiments sent toward the bluffs along the main road to test the Confederate positions. Scores of Union soldiers fell while taking heavy fire from the rifles and artillery directly above them, while Chatfield and his companions looked on, trembling with an equal mix of anticipation and terror.

Diary - December 27, 1862
We camped beside the Yazoo and trained quite hard this morning. There was heavy cannonading all afternoon. The 8th Missouri charged and fired on the enemy and took fire as well. The action could be plainly seen from this camp. The battlefield is about 5 miles from here.

Diary - December 28, 1862

The ball opened as it has a number of times with heavy firing commencing before daylight. I was placed on picket a short distance from the field. The place where we are posted is in an open field with timber on two sides—east and west. The Yazoo River is on the north and our forces are on the south. There are a great many ambulances passing by us with wounded soldiers, and heavy volleys of musketry bring death and destruction on all sides.

Chatfield was unaware, when he wrote this, that General Morgan L. Smith, his division commander, had been disabled by a hip wound so severe that he was removed from the field of battle. General Sherman transferred the command of the 2nd Division to Brigadier General David Stuart.

By the evening of December 28, Sherman had concluded that Grant had not been able to divide Pemberton's forces. Even so, Sherman would choose not to withdraw; he had concluded that he could take the bluffs by means of a frontal assault. There were two locations along the bluffs that he believed to be vulnerable: one was directly south of the Chickasaw Bayou, in front of General George Morgan's line; the other was one mile to Morgan's right, in front of what had been General Morgan L. Smith's line. Sherman resolved that he would initiate his attack after sunrise.

The assault began on Monday morning, December 29. Naval guns pounded a heavy diversion toward Haines' Bluff, some 4.5 miles north of Sherman's location, while Sherman rushed his outside forces in an effort to draw attention away from the two center focal points. Sharpshooters from his 13th Illinois Regulars held down the enemy on the right extreme flank, as infantrymen rushed the two center positions. A hail of bullets and cannon-fire rained down, eventually devastating all of Sherman's forces, scattering bodies across the entire southern quarter-mile strip of the delta. Those who actually reached the bluffs took bullets from muskets directly above them. Pointing their rifles vertically downward from outside their hillside parapets,[*] the Rebels blindly peppered the Union boys clinging to the cliffs beneath them. Some of the Federals survived by digging caves into the banks and waiting until nightfall to withdraw. By his own count, Sherman had incurred 1,848 casualties, his December 29 charge having failed severely.[34]

---

[*]   Parapets were merely low walls or banks used for protection. Often they were no more than shallow mounds.

Diary - December 29, 1862

The cannonading started again at 5:00 a.m. and became increasingly heavy. We stayed on picket another full day. All of our men were throwing up entrenchments, so we could not be relieved. The heaviest of battles is raging, and the wounded are coming in very fast this forenoon. Our soldiers were all cut to pieces. It was the worst sight I ever have seen. Our boys are being slaughtered by the hundreds. It started raining at dark. I went on post at 10:00 p.m. to stand another 4 hours.

Diary - December 30, 1862

The firing gradually ceased last evening, until I could hear only one gun every half-hour. It rained all night. There has been no firing since 8:00 a.m. today. A few wounded men were carried in this forenoon. I have not been relieved yet and must stay on picket for another day.

Aboard the *Edward Walsh*, on the evening of December 30, Adjutant Parker penned another update to his wife:

> ....I can only write a few lines. Col. Hoge is in command of the Reserve Detachment – 4 regiments – and I am A.A.A. General [Acting Assistant Adjutant General] and have just all I want to attend to. The army has been hard at fighting for two days and are at it again this morning. I have been out to the front to see the contest twice – Sunday and yesterday. – Our men fight well and have driven the enemy two miles to a high bluff which they still hold. The 1st brigade of Steel [sic] division made a charge up the bluff yesterday and were repelled with some loss. The 16th Ohio were in the charge and were cut up considerably.... —Adjutant D.S. Parker[35]

Most of the fighting had ended by nightfall. Sherman had planned one more attack for the morning of December 31. General Steele's division was to strike upriver just below Haines' Bluff, with cover afforded by Admiral David Dixon Porter's gunboats. But Porter's boats never got underway, their path hidden by thick fog, soon followed by heavy rain. In Sherman's words, "...it was simply impossible to move, so the attempt had to be abandoned."[36]

Diary - December 31, 1862

I was relieved from picket last night and came back to camp this morning. We were mustered for pay this forenoon. I was detailed for fatigue duty this afternoon, and there was no fighting. It has been quiet all along the lines. The weather has been pleasant all day. I wrote a letter tonight.*

Letter - December 31, 1862
Camp near Delti, on the Yazoo Dec 31st 1862

Dear folks at home,

Here I am away down in the state of Mississippi, encamp about 10 miles from Vicksburg & about 3 miles from the Battle field. When I wrote my last letter we were just ready to leave Memphis. The next day we went on board a transport named the Edward Walsh. That night we started down the river. The next morning we found ourselves at Helena 80 miles below Vicksburg. [Chatfield must have meant 80 miles below Memphis.] We went a short distance diste below Helena & landed & stayed all day & night awaiting the arrival of the remainder of the fleet of which there was 130 boats of all kinds, that is, gun boats transport & provision boats. Our boat carried, besides our Reg't and all of the Quartermaster stores, 206 of beef cattle, 100 head of horses & mules, 12 wagons, and then there was about 100 chords of wood for fuel. Christmas Dec 25th found us at Buckhorn Plantation where a large cotton gin and all of the buildings were burned. One brigade landed here. This place is 25 miles above Vicksburg. After the Brigade had landed we started down the river & landed, that is our Brigade, about ____ miles below where the first Brigade landed on the Louisiana side of the river. The Brigade was formed with our Reg't at the head. When, we marched 6 miles to a RR called the Vicksburg & Marshal RR. Our whole Brigade was drawn up in line beside the track. When, the order came every man lay hold. When, with one tremendous boost, over went the whole track bottom side up for about 1 mile. In this way we tore up 2 miles of track. We then pulled off the ties, laid them in piles with the rails on top. When, we set fire to the whole, which entirely spoiled the rails, some of them being bent double. The first Brigade that went out, destroyed 5 miles of the track which cut of [off] communication with the interior of Texas. We got back to the boats at 10 PM.

---

*   "Fatigue duty," was considered to be any kind of labor other than drill, instruction, or the use of arms.

Thus ended our Christmas excursion. The 26th, we again started down stream. We went a few miles. When we came to the mouth of Yazoo river, which is about as large as the Kankakee we came up stream river, we ascended about 10 miles when we landed at our present encampment. Dec 27, the first cannonadeing was heard this P.M. when a Rebel battery* was taken. I have picked up some of the pieces of shells that were fired at this time. The firing was plainly heard from our camp. On Sunday 28th, we were put on picket 1½ miles from the battlefield (for the battle commenced yesterday) to stop all stragglers that might have left their Reg'ts and to see if that enemy did not surprise and take our boats. Cannonadeing & musket firing was very heavy all day. Our post was but 40 rods from the road where all of the wounded was brought in. Oh what a painful sight it was to see our brave soldiers come in, some with a shot in the head. Well, in fact, wounded in every part of the body you can think of. Of all the horible things, war is the worst that can be thought of. On Monday, the battle was at its hight. There was a continual roar of cannon & musketry. We could plainly see the smoke rising from the battle & hear the several our boys yell as they charged on the Rebel batteries. But our poor boys were slaughtered in vain. The Rebel fortifications are on a high hill which was covered with heavy timber, but which has since been cut down, and it forms an almost impregnable Abattis. We have lost, as near as I can make out, between 700 & 800 killed wounded & missing & some of our men got hold of a Vicksburg paper which stated their loss was about the same as ours. My health is first rate except that I had the dia diareah a short time, coming down the Mississippi, caused I think by drinking the river water which is very riley. Last night we were drawn up in line of battle expecting that the enemy was but a short distance from us & we did not know but that we might be attacked. But this morning we were allowed to go to our tents. Oh, I had quite forgotten, I wish you all a happy new year.

Give Mary a kiss for me. I expect that the battle will be renewed today or tomorrow. We are bound to conquer or be conquered. Thus far our Reg't has not been called upon to fight, but I cannot tell how soon we may be. Thus far I have been kept & preserved from all harm, and I hope and pray that you will pray for me that I may return safe & sound, if it be the will of god that it shall be so. Well, it is almost time for the mail to close & I must stop. There is boats going North tonight which I expect will carry the mail. Please do write every week, at any rate. For the come [is] so uncertain that it is a long time between sometimes. Direct the same as usual via Cairo.

From your affectionate son
Edward L. Chatfield

---

*   Chatfield is referring to an emplacement or fortification of heavy guns.

By the end of New Year's Day, 1863, President Lincoln had delivered his *Emancipation Proclamation*. On the same day, General Sherman had concluded that the time had come to withdraw from the Chickasaw battlefield. After nightfall, Sherman ordered all of his troops to return to their boats. Chatfield's casualty estimate of "between 700 & 800" paralleled Adjutant Parker's estimates. "Our loss at the battle at the Heights or Chickasaw Bluffs was about three hundred killed and some four or five hundred wounded."[37] Contemporary sources place the Chickasaw Bayou casualty count at 1,176 U.S. and 187 CS.[38]

Diary - January 1, 1863

New Year's morning broke fine and clear. What a change this was since last New Year.[*] *I did some washing. Our whole company got sent out on patrol duty this afternoon. We went 5 miles and arrested 12 men for being absent from their respective regiments. We just got back to camp when orders came to move at 9:00 p.m. We went aboard the Edward Walsh and lay down for the night.*

It was Admiral Porter who met with Sherman on the morning of January 2, bearing bad news. General McClernand waited on the *Tigress* at the mouth of the Yazoo with orders to supersede Sherman. And it was from McClernand that Sherman first heard the specifics of what had happened to General Grant: that, following the staggering losses at Holly Springs, Grant hadn't engaged Pemberton near Grenada and that he had retreated to Grand Junction, Tennessee, in search of supplies. Sherman was incensed over losing his command to McClernand. He needed a plan that would enable him to maintain command while appearing to give it up.

Diary - January 2, 1863

One man of our regiment was buried this morning, then our retreat down the Yazoo commenced. The Edward Walsh started downstream at 3:00 p.m. It rained all afternoon and evening.

---

[*] Chatfield, not yet at war, had celebrated New Year's Day, 1862, at home with his family.

Private George W. Gable, of Company "D", a 25-year-old married farmer from Onarga, Illinois, had died of disease and was buried near Johnson's Plantation on the Yazoo River. Disease, above all else, was the war's supreme threat and the greatest cause of casualties, its shadow haunting every man, including Chatfield.

Diary - January 3, 1863
It rained hard all night. We stayed on board the boat all day. The boat did not move today, and it has rained continuously for the last 30 hours.

The January 3 letter from Adjutant Parker to his wife, written while aboard the *Edward Walsh*, provides additional information about the regiment's circumstances:

....We were unsuccessful in our attacks upon Vicksburg and were compelled to retreat, or rather fall back and await reinforcements. We left our position on the Yazoo yesterday and are now landing at Milliken's Bend on the Louisiana side of the Mississippi. Gen. McClernand is here with his army corps and assumes command. Our Brigade and Division are transferred to McC's army corps at least so I hear. We have but just formed the junction with McC or rather have just landed so as to communicate with him and so do not know all the news or arrangements. Our loss at the battle at the Hights or Chickasaw Bluffs was about three hundred killed and some four or five hundred wounded. We will organize [illegible.] We can make another attack which I hope will be successful. There is undoubtedly a large force at V. [Vicksburg.] Our men are in good spirits and feel like fighting it out and winning. We have no news from the outer world since the 1ˢᵗ and of course many events of importance have occurred since that time. We have some 30 or 35 on the sick list; we buried two men on the banks of the Yazoo. It was a Sad Sight to see them interred in a strange land with no coffin, or ceremony only a grave dug and the bodies laid in and then covered by a few barel staves and a little board placed at the head to mark the place....We will probably lay here a few days, perhaps weeks. I do not know how long. Just the minute comes in an order for our Col [Paddock] to act as Provost Marshal which will give us plenty of work. My health is Still good. I have not yet lost a day of duty. There are several of our officers on the sick list. Lieut Cowgill [Lieutenant Aquilla Cowgill] is sick, but none of our officers are dangerously so....It has been raining hard for a day or so here, but it is clearing up here. The grain looks green and the buds are starting as if it was Spring....

Faithfully thine — D.S. Parker[39]

Second Lieutenant Aquilla Cowgill had enlisted in Kankakee City on August 9, 1862, two days after his 20-year-old brother, Wilder, had enlisted. Lieutenant Cowgill was 39 years old and had not yet married. He would resign from the army within seven months and return to his Kankakee farm. His younger brother, not having officer's privileges, would not muster out until he had fulfilled his 3-year commitment, incurring a reduction in rank along the way.

CHAPTER 7: AN IMPORTANT SECRET MISSION

"The fleet . . . landed just opposite the mouth of the White River after dark."

Within two days, Sherman had his plan. A Rebel boat, out of Fort Hindman at the *Arkansas Post*, had recently captured a small Union steamboat, the *Blue Wing*, loaded with mail, coal, and ammunition. A successful attack of Fort Hindman would restore the troop's confidence, free upriver traffic from further attack, and require leadership beyond that of McClernand. Sherman had hoped to direct the entire operation; the only task was to convince McClernand that the strike was necessary. From Sherman's point of view, McClernand wouldn't even have to go. With Admiral Porter supporting him, Sherman presented the idea to McClernand. To Sherman's chagrin, not only did McClernand give his blessing, he decided to command the operation.

Union morale had already dropped considerably and for several reasons. The major loss at Chickasaw Bayou was indeed discouraging. Added to that was the transfer of control from Sherman to McClernand. And now the troops found themselves aboard their boats traveling upstream on an undisclosed but "important expedition" of which the details had been kept secret, not just from the troops, but from most of the officers as well. In a veiled account of the dismal situation, Adjutant Parker summed up his impressions.

> January 4, 1863: We are now moving up the river to what point it is not yet definitely decided, or if so, not to my knowledge. We shall probably go as far north as Napoleon, at the mouth of White River. Gen. McClernand is in command now, the army is in good condition for duty, or at least tolerably so; but there is some

discouragement in view of the appearance of matters in Grant's army and on the Potomac. From the various reports we have which I doubt not and pray are much distorted – things do look a little blue. But I have faith in an overruling Providence that He will not permit the triumph of so wicked and justice-destroying an Oligarchy as the Southern Slave confederacy. I believe God reigns in justice and that he will Secure success to the Right….Gen. Morgan L. Smith, our Division commander…was severely wounded at the late engagement on the Chickasaw Bluffs. He is badly wounded but will probably recover. Brig Genl. David Stuart is in command of his (the 2d Division.)

The rain of yesterday has subsided, and today is as fine a day as we often see. Our boats glide along up the river as lively and gaily as if we had Severely whipped the "rebs" and were feeling good over the event…. Adjutant D.S. Parker[40]

Parker had it right. The boats would stop briefly at Gaines Landing to take on wood then would continue on to Montgomery Point at the mouth of the White River. The entire journey, roughly 140 miles, would be accomplished in no more than 60 hours.[41]

Diary - January 4, 1863
Our brigade was ordered back to Memphis at 8:00 a.m. We were all ordered aboard at 11:00 a.m. and the Edward Walsh started with the rest upstream. There were no quiet Sunday scenes. The weather was fine today.

Returning north from Young's Point, Louisiana, on Sunday, the sizable flotilla hadn't cleared Milliken's Bend until Monday, a startlingly massive scene when viewed from the river banks, hundreds of boats forming a lengthy tail at least five miles long. The *Edward Walsh,* carrying the 113th, steamed along somewhere in the middle of the procession. The gunboats took the lead, a scarcity of coal requiring that they tow the three ironclads, the *Baron DeKalb,* the *Louisville,* and the *Cincinnati,* with engines silent. Aboard the *Edward Walsh,* Chatfield's back pained in protest of the cold weather, repeated lifting, and cramped quarters.

Diary - January 5, 1863

I have a hard pain in my back that is very distressing this morning. Otherwise, nothing else happened worthy of note. The boat stopped a few minutes, and a lot of boys piled off. Our mess got a turkey, honey, and a few other articles.

The fleet tied up at Gaines Landing on January 6, a stopping point near the railroad just south of what is today Arkansas City, Arkansas.

Diary - January 6, 1863

The boat ran all night and tied up in the morning to take on wood. I did a lot of cooking, then got detailed with the Company to unload a lot of commissary stores from the White Cloud onto the Edward Walsh; we were relieved at dark.

The *Edward Walsh* sat moored on the Mississippi banks as Chatfield helped transfer supplies, the heavy lifting only exacerbating his back pain. In great discomfort, Chatfield likely concluded that he was better off than a particular soldier in Company "K".

Diary - January 7, 1863

My back pains me greatly this morning, and I do not feel like stirring. The boat did not stir all the forenoon. A man in Company K is dying. His last name is Blood.

Private Carlos Blood, of Company "K", was from the township of Yellowhead, near Pilot in Kankakee County. He died that night and was buried off the shores of Gaines Landing, about 120 miles up the Mississippi from Milliken's Bend.

Diary - January 8, 1863

The man named Blood died at 8:00 last evening. We buried him this morning. The fleet moved again up the river at 2:00 p.m. and landed just opposite the mouth of the White River after dark. We had some rain today.

McClernand, on the advice of Sherman and Porter, had deliberately ordered the fleet to sail past the Arkansas River, a pageantry of northbound ships designed to convince observers that the fleet was on its way back to Memphis. But the maneuver taking the fleet north of the Arkansas River was merely a ruse, a feint that ended at Montgomery Point, the fleet's second stopping place, a small peninsula poking into the Mississippi on the north side of the White River.

Evidently, the rest of the fleet had already heavily crowded the peninsula's shores by the time that the *Edward Walsh* arrived on the night of January 8. According to Chatfield's diary entry, the *Walsh* dropped anchor on the east side of the Mississippi River, opposite the White River's mouth. The fleet's departure from the Mississippi the next morning signaled a destination other than Memphis, a clue to Chatfield that they weren't heading any farther north. Having reached the White River, the fleet would enter it on the morning of January 9 and travel back to the Arkansas by way of the "bayou," a cutoff that the commanders hoped would be less closely watched and monitored.

Diary - January 9, 1863

The fleet moved up the White River a few miles, then across to the Arkansas by what is called a bayou. We anchored for the night. It rained some again today.

The ruse failed to produce any surprises. Confederate lookouts stationed along the cutoff sped notice of the Union fleet's presence back to Fort Hindman. Under the command of CS Brigadier General Thomas J. Churchill, five thousand troops from Arkansas, Louisiana and Texas prepared themselves for battle. Their dozen guns included three 9-inch Columbiads, three hard-hitting 8-inch rifle cannon, and six pieces of field artillery. Four hundred feet to a side, the concave, four-sided, year-old Confederate earthwork rested on high ground at the head of a horseshoe bend in the river, the site of an old French trading post known as the Arkansas Post. Impressive as it was from the river banks, Fort Hindman was vulnerable from the rear.

The east side of Fort Hindman faced the river, cannon threatening passers-by from their parapets. In bitter cold rain, Confederate soldiers scurried to man the 1.5-mile-line of rifle pits that stretched southwest from the fort to a swamp. Other gray uniformed soldiers took positions along the rifle pits east of the fort, just a short distance up river from where their Union enemy was expected to land.

Ascending the Arkansas River, the Federal fleet landed at Nortrib's Farm, two miles south of Fort Hindman. By 9:30 on the morning of January 10, Chatfield was one of nearly thirty thousand troops that had already disembarked. The transports sat nearly empty as the brigades took their respective positions below Fort Hindman. The 113th marched upriver along the levee in General Stuart's 2nd Division as the miserable, stinging rain continued to fall.

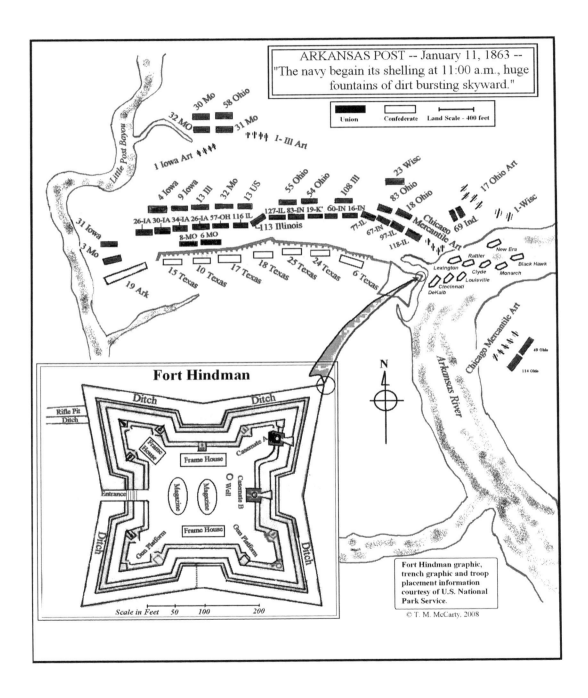

ARKANSAS POST -- January 11, 1863 --
"The navy begain its shelling at 11:00 a.m., huge
fountains of dirt bursting skyward."

Union   Confederate   Land Scale - 400 feet

Fort Hindman

Fort Hindman graphic,
trench graphic and troop
placement information
courtesy of U.S. National
Park Service.

© T. M. McCarty, 2008

CHAPTER 8: THE BATTLE OF ARKANSAS POST

"The ground fairly seemed to tremble."

Diary - January 10, 1863

We heard some firing from our gunboats this morning as the troops were disembarking. Our regiment was ordered ashore at 9:00 a.m. to form up and march against the Rebels. At 12:00 noon, our brigade of the 113th and 116th Illinois, and the 6th and 8th Missouri, started for the battlefield. After we got a mile from the boats, we came to the first line of their entrenchment. We had passed them a short distance when a couple of shells whizzed over our heads to let us know that there was somebody around. We moved forward to another line of fortification that had just been evacuated. They left blankets and other things in their haste and retired to another fortification called the Arkansas Post. We advanced to a position three-fourths of a mile from the fort. Our brigade was on the extreme left of the line. The Rebels sent several shells over our heads, several striking within a few feet of me. At 5:00 p.m. our gunboats moved upstream and fired upon the Rebels, giving the Rebels perfect fits. They replied quite spiritedly for some time and sent occasional shells right over our heads that were so close that they made us think of hugging the earth. The fiercest lightning and loudest peals of thunder are no comparison. The ground fairly seemed to tremble. The cannonading lasted an hour; then there was silence. The weather was fine and pleasant during the day.

The pleasant daytime weather soon deteriorated into a miserably cold night. No fires or tents were allowed. Thirty thousand soldiers passed the night secluded within the trees on the north side of Fort Hindman—the side considered most pregnable. All were fully dressed with belts, cartridge boxes, and guns at hand, protected only by the blankets that they had found or carried with them. Throughout the night the Confederates axed and sawed trees in a desperate effort to obstruct and tangle the field, and while General McClernand enjoyed a comfortable sleep on his transport, the *Tigress*, General Sherman and his Union scouts reconnoitered behind trees and stumps, men and teams wheeling heavy cannon into potent firing positions.

By 10:30 A.M. on January 11, Union commanders had deployed their formations in an umbrella line curving around the north side of the fort. The 113th took the very center of the line, at the far left of Giles Smith's brigade. The 116th Illinois and the 6th and 8th Missouri stood to the right of the 113th, and the 127th Illinois, in Kirby Smith's brigade, to its left. General Sherman took a position near the forward lines while General McClernand safely located himself to the rear of the vast assemblage with an observer reporting down to him from a tree.

Off the shores of the Arkansas River, the Union navy began its shelling at 11:00 A.M., pounding its targets and causing fountains of dirt and debris to burst skyward. Inside the walls of Fort Hindman, war's brutality wreaked its havoc. Screaming horses collided with the ground, their eyes huge and nostrils puffing heavy sprays of red. Exploding shells hurled flailing soldiers from their trenches, their limbs torn away like paper. At 12:30 P.M., the violent chaos was given respite by a lull in the firing.

The lull wouldn't last long. At 1:00 P.M., the army artillery, about 100 yards to Chatfield's right rear, opened fire, bursting the air, shaking the ground and sending flocks of ring-billed gulls skyward. The roaring fury continued until 1:30 P.M., then trailed off, its silence a cue that the time to advance was near. Only the ominous clanking, shuffling and coughing of the Union soldiers conveyed the immensity of what was about to occur.

Bugles sounded the charge, and a stunning pageantry unfolded across the half-mile-wide battlefield. A field of 10,000 Union infantrymen moved off as one, battle swords stabbing the sky, a carpet of dark blue slowly unrolling down the sloping terrain. With the synchronous rhythm of crunching boots, thousands upon thousands of soldiers advanced toward the 2,800-foot line of trenches that stretched westward from the fort—banners unfurled, drums beating, fifes sounding, and muskets glistening in the afternoon sun. After the first wave of blue coats had marched 100 yards closer to the fort, the offshore Federal gunboats resumed fire.

Union troops rushing forward on Chatfield's right were quickly met with heavy resistance from the Texas and Arkansas defenders, blasting from their rifle pits.

Chatfield, with his regiment in the center of the line, raced headlong toward the Texans directly in front of him, a blazing firefight that resulted in major Union losses. Midway to the fort, Chatfield was among the more fortunate who managed to find shelter behind a log, firing from that position for two hours and from behind a tree for another hour, where he was wounded two separate times.

At roughly 4:30 P.M., just as McClernand was preparing to order a climactic frontal assault, a number of bayoneted white flags waved the air from behind Rebel parapets, causing confusion from within the fortress and disagreement as to whether an order to surrender had been given. Nonetheless, the firing gradually trickled to an end, allowing the Union boys to march forward and force the Confederates at gunpoint to stack arms. CS General Churchill protested that he had not surrendered, condemning the ill-guided soldiers who had done so. But his protests were of no avail. His soldiers had no guns, and Colonel Giles Smith, Admiral Porter, and General Sherman were already standing in front of him. McClernand had already returned to his transport, the *Tigress*, stating that he was hungry.[42] Union casualties were reported as 134 killed, 898 wounded, and 29 missing; incomplete Confederate reports showed 60 killed and 80 wounded, with 4,791 of the garrison captured.[43] The battle was over, and history would herald General John McClernand as the victor.

Diary - January 11, 1863

We had a very disagreeable time last night. We slept on our arms and were ordered to fall in at daylight. Our brigade was then ordered to the right and formed in the very center of the line. We waited there while several of the batteries got into position. At 1:00 p.m. the ball opened with our batteries firing on the Rebels. After shelling them for about a half-hour, they ceased firing, and we were ordered to advance. We were about a half-mile from the Rebel entrenchment when we started. When we had advanced about halfway, the Rebs commenced pouring in volleys of musketry upon us. As for my part, I felt like getting out of the way of their bullets as soon as possible, and so I threw myself behind a big log and commenced loading and firing. About 2 hours after the fight commenced, as I was firing from behind a tree, I was struck by a rifle shot in the side, a slight wound. I had another scratch from a ball that hit my right leg. The fight continued about 3 hours, then the Rebels raised the white flag. We took about 8000 prisoners. They were formed in line and stacked their arms after which they were put on board some of our transports. We got our Enfield rifles tonight, taken from the Rebels. We slept on the battlefield in pleasant weather.

The English-made Enfield rifle was considered to be a better weapon than the 1861 Springfield; it was more reliable and less likely to malfunction or, even worse, explode when fired. The most popular was the .577 caliber Enfield, Model 1853. It was fifty-four inches long (with a 39-inch barrel) and weighed 8.7 pounds (9.2 with the bayonet). Its rear sight could be graduated to a range of 800 yards. Both long and short-barreled models were available. Although Chatfield doesn't specify which model he had been issued, the long barrel would have been preferable due to its greater accuracy.

Diary - January 12, 1863

We slept on the battlefield last night. The Rebels call this place Camp Hope, and the fort is called the Arkansas Post. I feel pretty sore this morning. My side pains me considerably. But for all that, I went over to where the Rebel camp was and found me a blanket, a shirt, two pairs of drawers, and several other little articles that I could use. All of the dead men and horses lying around showed me that our ammunition was not spent in vain. I got no mail tonight.

Chatfield's wounds were of sufficient concern to his superiors to have him sent ahead to the boats, a place of better shelter. Chatfield, opposed to malingering, explained the separation from his regiment in different words.

Diary - January 13, 1863

I was not sleepy this morning at about 3:00 o'clock and got up and wrote a letter home by firelight. I enclosed a Secesh letter and cartridge with it. There are a lot of men at work today leveling and tearing down the fort and entrenchments while burying the Rebel dead at the same time. All the Rebel prisoners were put on board 3 of our transports: the John J. Roe, the Nebraska, and another one. We were ordered to march down to the river this evening after dark. They had detailed me to go to the boat with our things. The night was cloudy, and it looked like rain.*

---

*   Chatfield's January 13 letter was not among the letters of the collection. Perhaps it never found its way home. How very interesting it and the accompanying "Secesh letter" and cartridge would have been!

Diary - January 14, 1863

It was raining quite hard this morning. The boat moved down the river one mile to where our boys had camped all night, and they came aboard feeling ill and very uncomfortable. Five companies of our regiment [Companies "C", "D", "F", "I", and "K"] were sent up the river to guard the Rebels to Cairo. It is still raining tonight, and my side is sore, but is slowly getting better.

Diary - January 15, 1863

The rain turned to snow at midnight, and we had 3 inches by this morning. It is quite cold—colder than ever before this season. A lot of sanitary stores and other things arrived here today c/o Mr. Hoyt from the Chicago Sanitary Commission. The boat moved downstream a little this afternoon, and it was not as cold as it was this morning. We stopped at dark to take on wood.

Diary - January 16, 1863

It was cold and snowing this Friday morning when we started down the river at 8:00 a.m. We got to Napoleon at the mouth of the Arkansas at 10:00 a.m. and stayed all day. We saw an accident while here. A small skiff tipped over and drowned a man before help could arrive. It is very cold and freezing hard tonight.

The boys passed the night of January 16 aboard the *Edward Walsh* tied to the dock at Napoleon, Arkansas, as more and more Federal ships arrived throughout the night, General Grant's transport among them. The next morning, General Grant met with his commanders, receiving word from General Sherman and Admiral Porter that they distrusted General McClernand's skills to command. Their assessments of McClernand's battlefield deportment came as no surprise to Grant, who had received their earlier messages urging him ..."to take command in person..."[44] Grant summed up the events of January 17 in two paragraphs:

> On the 17th I visited McClernand and his command at Napoleon. It was here made evident to me that both the army and navy were so distrustful of McClernand's fitness to command that, while they would do all they could to insure success, this distrust was an element of weakness. It would have been criminal to send troops under these circumstances into such danger. By this time I had received authority

to relieve McClernand, or to assign any person else to the command of the river expedition, or to assume command in person.

I felt great embarrassment about McClernand. He was the senior major-general after myself within the department. It would not do, with his rank and ambition, to assign a junior over him. Nothing was left, therefore, but to assume the command myself. I would have been glad to put Sherman in command, to give him an opportunity to accomplish what he had failed in the December before; but there seemed no other way out of the difficulty, for he was junior to McClernand. Sherman's failure needs no apology. – Ulysses S. Grant[45]

Having placed McClernand under his own command, Grant dispatched his forces back to Milliken's Bend and Young's Point. Yielding to pressure from Washington, he had agreed to resume General Thomas Williams' earlier efforts to nullify the guns above Vicksburg by pursuing an incredible strategy. To end the war, a massive experiment with nature would receive renewed attention, a military construction project that would heavily involve Chatfield and the boys of the 113th. There were many doubters, including Grant, but if a canal could actually change the course of the mighty Mississippi, the accomplishment would be his. Could he, by digging a ditch, eliminate Vicksburg as an obstacle without firing a shot?[46]

As the day came to an end, Chatfield discovered that he had more than just his wounds vexing him.

Diary - January 17, 1863

A lot of transports came down the river last night all loaded with soldiers. It is very cold this morning and more pleasant in the afternoon. I found an empty room for our mess this morning that provides us very pleasant and warm quarters. The sutler [an authorized non-military vendor] has a store in the front part of the boat. I found out tonight that I have the mumps coming on. My mouth feels pretty sore.

Wounded in his side and leg and tormented by throbbing pain in his throat, on January 18 Chatfield nonetheless elected to go shopping in Napoleon with a large group of friends. He had enough money with him to buy a velvet mantilla, a type of shawl with decorative beads, to adorn the shoulders of his little sister Mary. But when he and his companions returned to the dock, they discovered that the *Edward Walsh* had already departed. Hoping that they could catch up, they scrambled aboard another transport.

Diary - January 18, 1863
Our boat left behind eleven of us, but we got on later when it stopped for supplies. We caught a stray hog for our meals. My mumps are getting worse, and my throat feels pretty sore.

Diary - January 19, 1863
The cold disagreeable night passed, and we got back to the boat this morning. We stopped near a Rebel plantation this morning and got a lot of chickens, molasses, and sugar. We started down the river again at 11:00 a.m., then stopped a second time at 3:00. I feel very unwell today. My head and teeth ache with pain in my jaws. The wind blew hard all day.

Diary - January 20, 1863
It's been one month since we left Memphis, and the weather is pleasant.

It would take four days for Chatfield to meet up with the troops back at Milliken's Bend. From there his regiment would move farther south—to Young's Point—where they would soon view man's attempt to harness nature.

CHAPTER 9: CHANGING THE COURSE OF A RIVER— AND POSSIBLY A WAR

"Lincoln championed the strategy…"

According to an 1853 survey sponsored by the townspeople of Vicksburg, DeSoto Point—the Louisiana peninsula across the river from the city—was vulnerable to the river's erosion and might someday be cut through in time of flood. Worried that such a flood might spell disaster for their city, Vicksburg's leaders and townspeople did all that they could to keep the peninsula from washing away, including encouraging Louisiana to construct levies and maintain heavy forestation across the Point.

Upon learning of the survey, Union war planners, deeply concerned about the Rebel blockade of Mississippi River traffic at Vicksburg, reasoned that by cutting a canal across the DeSoto Peninsula, they might help nature run her course and achieve a military triumph in the process. The river's new path would relegate Vicksburg to a backwater region, a city with no river coursing past it, and conceivably, a city with no port whatsoever. By thus altering the course of the Mississippi River, the Union could achieve a safe route that would completely bypass Vicksburg, making the guns on the bluffs of Vicksburg irrelevant. Union vessels would be free to travel up and down the Mississippi at will. The story of the canal dates back to 1853.[47]

- **1853** — Charles Ellet, Jr., a nationally prominent civil engineer, reported that DeSoto Point was vulnerable to flooding. He said that it was a place along the river that might someday wash away and isolate Vicksburg as a back bay.[48] Concerned over Ellet's report and the possible economic consequences of such a disaster, the state of

Mississippi outlawed any human activity along the water that might trigger such a flood.

- **April 28, 1862** — Vicksburg began fortification of its bluffs when New Orleans fell to the West Gulf Blockading Squadron, commanded by Union Flag Officer David G. Farragut.* Farragut soon received orders to challenge Vicksburg.

- **May 18, 1862** — Farragut's advance fleet arrived south of Vicksburg and demanded that the city surrender. Seven hastily constructed batteries confronted him from atop the bluff. The mayor of Vicksburg refused to surrender. Lacking the troops to enforce his demand, Farragut returned to New Orleans and conferred with Major General Benjamin Butler. They agreed on a two-phase plan to take Vicksburg. First, they would attack the city from the water. If the attack failed, they would try to isolate Vicksburg by cutting a canal across DeSoto Point—a massive effort to reroute the Mississippi River.

- **June 25, 1862** — Farragut arrived south of Vicksburg again, this time with all the power he thought he needed to take the city. Under his command, he had all of Commodore David Porter's mortar-schooners and 3,200 troops under the command of Brigadier General Thomas Williams. By that time, Vicksburg had 29 guns positioned on the bluffs. While Farragut prepared to attack the city, Williams began his preliminary survey work for the canal while rounding up all of the "contrabands" ("freed" slaves) that he could find in the area for clearing the trees and digging the canal. In June of 1862, Union Brigadier General Thomas Williams cleared off the trees, an act eliciting horror from the citizens across the river.

- **June 27, 1862** — Porter pounded Vicksburg with mortar shells but was unable to set the city afire.

- **June 28, 1862** — In a tremendous battle, Farragut assailed Vicksburg with his fleet of gunboats and sloops. His boats took 30 hits, but none were sunk; 16 of his sailors died, and 28 were wounded. It was a standoff with neither side claiming a victory. Farragut concluded that a naval force, alone, could not take Vicksburg. The decision was made to isolate the city with a canal.

- **July 4, 1862** — The rainy season was ending, and the river was falling. Twelve thousand black workers labored on the ditch in the summer's miserable 90-degree temperatures and high humidity. Rations were inadequate, water was impure, and mosquitoes were merciless. Hunger, dysentery and death soon followed. Flag Officer

---

* Following his successful routing of New Orleans, Farragut was promoted to the rank of Rear Admiral, the first admiral in United States history.

Charles Davis, Commander of U.S. Naval Forces of the Mississippi, arrived to supervise the project.

- **July 11, 1862** — The river continued to fall. General Thomas Williams, still expecting a big rise in the river within 10 days, asked Commodore Davis to assist in an experiment to open the cut-off. Sternwheelers were backed into the canal's upriver opening in an attempt to force water across the Point, but the water wouldn't run up hill.

- **July 21, 1862** — Malaria was widespread. Seventy-eight percent of the original 3,200 troops were so sickened that only 700 remained healthy enough to muster. The loss of black workers was even higher—only 500 of the original 12,000 remained, with many running off and even more dying from disease. DeSoto Point was littered with over 600 graves.[49] Williams was recalled to Baton Rouge, Louisiana, and work on the unfinished canal was terminated.

- **January 17, 1863** — With the return of the cooler winter months and the river at flood stage, the pressure was on Grant to revisit the construction of the canal. Lincoln championed the strategy and Grant complied, commanding his troops to resume digging with the prospect of quick success.

CHAPTER 10: BUTLER'S DITCH

"I saw the mighty wonder, Butler's Ditch, for the first time today.
I think it will not amount to much."

A northwest view of Grant's Canal as it appeared in late February, 1863. A steamer turns its wheel at the canal entrance in an effort to churn water into the canal. The canal entrance was strategically located on the Tuscumbia Bend where the Mississippi curved to the northeast. (Sketch by H. Lovie, in Frank Leslie's *The Soldier in Our Civil War, Vol. II.*)

Diary - January 21, 1863

We reached Milliken's Bend this afternoon where the boat stopped for a couple of hours near a fine mansion before moving down to the mouth of the Yazoo where we tied up for the night. There is quite a large fleet here with a large number of gunboats.

Chatfield had moved down river on the Mississippi from Milliken's Bend to Young's Point, a plantation located across from the mouth of the Yazoo, just north of the unfinished canal on DeSoto Point. Chatfield's wounds had not yet healed, and his mumps still raged. Although he was again detailed for lighter duty, his responsibility as a regimental soldier was about to change.

Diary - January 22, 1863

Our boat moved a short distance down the river, then landed, and we went ashore. We formed our regiment and marched down the river, following the levee all the way, but several others and I were detailed to come back to the boat to take care of our things. I stood guard tonight. The weather is warm like a summer day.

Diary - January 24, 1863

There was much rain last night as I wrote to Father.* Today is also very rainy and disagreeable.

Diary - January 25, 1863

I stood guard 2 hours this morning. We have been here for 3 days, and I am still on guard duty. The mud is so deep that the stores cannot be passed out. I visited the sick boys at the hospital; 3 of them are getting sent to Memphis: George Van Valkenberg, Rick [John] Bickle, and Allen Smith. Old Mr. Rice died today.

---

*   Chatfield's January 23 letter to his father was not among the letters in the collection.

Private Oliver Rice, a 58-year-old married farmer from Kankakee Township, had been a wagoner for Company "H" before succumbing to disease. The *Illinois Roster** places Rice's death on January 24. Private Rick Bickle enlisted in Ashkum, Illinois. He was discharged on April 22, 1863, due to disability. Private Allen M. Smith, from Norton, was discharged May 8, 1863, also due to disability. Van Valkenberg, Bickle and Smith were all in Company "B".

Diary - January 26, 1863
I helped load provisions on mules to pack out to the regiment, 5 miles from here. The wagons can't go there; it's too muddy. Our guns disabled a Reb transport today; she floats downstream. We also captured a Rebel ferryboat. It's still cloudy and raining.

Diary - January 27, 1863
Today was windy and rainy. Jack Jeffcoat has been sick all day. I received another letter from Twinsburg, [Ohio].†

Diary - January 28, 1863
I had routine duties today. The weather was warm and pleasant. Captain M. Sutherland [Mason Sutherland] died last night.

Captain Mason Sutherland was 44 years old and married when he enlisted, the commander of Company "E" of the 113th Illinois. Highly admired by his men and by his commander, Colonel Hoge,[50] Sutherland grew ill while at the Arkansas Post and his condition steadily plummeted while hospitalized at Young's Point. Desperate, Dr. Mack tried to get Sutherland sent up to Memphis.

> This is to certify that Capt. M. Sutherland has been ill over two weeks with a depraved state of the secretions, a torpid condition of the liver and general debility. We request the privilege of being sent to the hospital at Memphis. It is my opinion that he will not live one week if he remains here. — J.M. Mack, Regimental Surgeon[51]

---

*   The title *Illinois Roster* refers to the Illinois Civil War Muster and Descriptive Rolls Data Base at: http://www.ilsos.gov/genealogy/index.jsp
†   The letter from Twinsburg would have been from one of the Herricks, Edward's mother's family.

Although approved for transfer to the Memphis Hospital, Sutherland died before the boat could move him.[52]

Diary - January 29, 1863

It froze 14 inches of water last night, but it was fine and warm today. No mail came, but we got soft bread today, the first soft bread in 6 weeks. General Grant arrived with his army and will cooperate with Sherman and Mr. McClernand's corps. Our troops rode aboard a flatboat loaded with ammunition. I began writing a letter to David this evening.

Not so subtly, Chatfield prefaced McClernand with "Mr." Perhaps he did not consider him to be a "real" general, reflecting the well-known opinion of his top commanders, Generals Sherman and Grant. Then again, maybe Chatfield was just used to calling him "Mr. McClernand"—an Illinois politician who would historically have been referred to as "Mr." Whatever his title, McClernand had been Lincoln's choice, and Grant couldn't fire him—or at least, not yet.

Grant reorganized his Army of Tennessee, dividing his 45,000 troops into three corps: the Thirteenth Corps under McClernand, the Fifteenth Corps under Sherman, and the Seventeenth under Major General James B. McPherson.* With these preliminaries completed, Grant directed his attention to the canal, summarizing his understanding of the project and its significance on January 29:

> It was Williams' expectation that when the river rose it would cut a navigable channel through; but the canal started in an eddy from both ends, and, of course, it only filled up with water on the rise without doing any execution in the way of cutting. Mr. Lincoln had navigated the Mississippi in his younger days and understood well its tendency to change its channel, in places, from time to time. He set much store accordingly by this canal…After my arrival the work was diligently pushed with about 4,000 men—as many as could be used to advantage… – Ulysses S. Grant[53]

---

* Eventually, Grant would add two more corps when the siege began, bringing his total strength to 75,000.

Diary - January 30, 1863
Only monotony today; camp is dreary. We had a bright moon tonight.

Diary - January 31, 1863
I got up early and came out to the regiment with the teams and found the boys. I saw the mighty wonder, Butler's Ditch, for the first time today. I think it will not amount to much. I went down to a cotton gin a short distance from camp and got a lot of cotton. I'm going to have a fine bed. It was fine and pleasant today.

The "mighty wonder" had several nicknames back then, including "Butler's Ditch," and "Williams' Canal," honoring the originators. By early April a second canal, later referred to as the Duckport Canal, would be started below Duckport, the southern extreme of Milliken's Bend. Some of the soldiers would call it "Pride's Canal," honoring Colonel George G. Pride, the commander overseeing the project. Only later did the various canals dug in the area become collectively known as "Grant's Canals."

<u>Letter</u> - January 31, 1863
Before Vicksburg Jan. 31st 1863

Dear Father and Mother,

    I thought that I would write a few lines and put it in Davids letter. My health is first rate and I enjoy myself as well as could be expected.

    I have today for the first time viewed the far famed and Celebrated Ditch or Canal as you may choose to call it. ~~since we have been here~~ Our men have been at work in it every since we first arrived here, and now its average width is about 20 feet and average depth 6 feet. But it does not wash as it was expected that it would. There is men at work at it all of the time widening it. I do not think that this whole expedition depends upon the ditch being made, but that it is merely a feint made to turn the attention of the Rebels. When, we would strike them in some place where they do not expect. Our Reg't is now within 3 miles of Vicksburg and we can plainly see the town.* You never wrote whether you had made any disposition of that county order or not. Have you got those things that I sent in the box that we sent from Memphis? What prospect is there for

---

*   Chatfield, standing at Young's Point, could see Vicksburg across the river because six months earlier, General Williams had cleared away the thick carpet of trees on the north and east sides of the peninsula.

trying to see such things? We have not received any pay yet and I cannot tell when we shall.

We have nearly 5 months pay behind and there is lots of regiments that have not had a cent for 8 & 10 months. But, you know that when it does come it will all be in a pile. We have a plenty to eat and to wear and enough duty to keep us from being lonesome or homesick. It would not be strange if a shell from the Rebels should land among us at any moment. We are in such close proximity to the [exploding shells that we] all hold our lives, as if it were in our hands. And, if I should be called to give it up at any time, I hope that I should see that better place where there is no more war or conflict. Pray for me that I may at last reach that better place where there is no more sorrow or sighing. All of the boys send their wishes and respects.

Give Mary a kiss for me.

— Edward*

Diary - February 1, 1863

It rained all night and through the forenoon today. Our company was put on guard along the levee today but was cleared off tonight.

Diary - February 2, 1863

We were relieved from guard at 9:00 a.m. by Co. A. They issued clothing to our company today, and I drew 2 pair of socks. A strong force worked on the ditch today. The weather is fair. Roll call came at 8:00 p.m. I retired for rest after that.

Diary - February 3, 1863

It was cold with frost last night. I was detailed as a permanent wagon guard this morning. My duty is to go with and take care of the team. The river is rising fast, and the water is making an impression on the ditch. The day was pleasant, but the night was chilly.

---

* After experiencing the horrors of war, Chatfield had temporarily dispensed with some of the formal pretense, signing only his first name.

Diary - February 4, 1863

It rained all last night and most of today. We were not out of our tents very much. I stayed inside and mended clothes, then went to bed early.

Diary - February 5, 1863

The rain cleared off, the weather warm and pleasant, but there was 2 feet of mud on the roads. Even so, I went with the wagons to the boats to help get provisions.

Diary - February 6, 1863

They had us move our camp this afternoon to a less flooded position, but our company went on picket this morning, so the boys had to come in and help move our things. It was a pleasant day.

Diary - February 7, 1863

They sent our teams to the boats to get sanitary stores, but we did not get them. We tried again this afternoon; I took a drink of ale to pay for it, but we still couldn't get the stores. I heard, for the first time, that Joseph Hicks was dead. He died from the wounds he took at the Battle of Arkansas Post. Joe was the first in our company to die. John Blanchet and several of the boys returned from the hospital today.

The *Illinois Roster* shows Private Joseph Chard Hicks's death to have occurred on January 21. He was on the steamer *John J. Roe* at the time. His death came only three months after he had mustered into the 113th. Corporal John Blanchet, born in Aroostook, Maine, was a 25-year-old farmer from Limestone Township when he enlisted. The grim reality of sickness and death was all around. Eventually, about one-third of all war deaths—Union and Confederate—were due to wounds: 204,000 in all. About two-thirds were due to other causes, principally disease: 416,000 in all.[54]

Diary - February 8, 1863
I got up early this morning and was again ordered to go down to the boats to get more sanitary stores. But Mr. Hoyt said he didn't work on Sundays. So we went and got some wood, instead. A man in Company K died last night; I helped dig his grave and bury him; poor fellow; his sorrows are over; he will have no more troubles in this world.*

Diary - February 9, 1863
We were up early again, and I drew a lot of forage duties today. I have a bad cold and sore throat that trouble me considerably.

Diary - February 10, 1863
Dan Durham and I went about 4 miles to the bakery for bread. We had a first rate time. I had a loaf of bread with hot butter for dinner, a treat I had not had for a long time. We returned at 2:00 p.m. when my work was over for the day. Today was a regular spring day.

Daniel Durham held the title and rank of wagoner for Company "B". A 25-year-old married farmer, Durham had enlisted in the place of his birth, Bourbonnais Township of Kankakee County.

Diary - February 11, 1863
The team started before daylight this morning, and we got back with no incident at 10:00 p.m. Our sutler was relieved of $30.00 by some of the 8th Missouri boys. Our company was placed on picket today. The Rebels fired a few shells, but no harm was done. More rain seems likely.

---

*   Although several boys from Company "K" were discharged due to disability in early February of 1863, the *Illinois Roster* listed no deaths, attesting to the chaotic realities of war.

Chatfield may have been privately amused at the sutler's loss. The boys in the 8th Missouri might have been getting even. Thirty dollars was a lot of money—over two month's pay for a Union private. Some sutlers would earn a private's pay in just one day, justifying their lofty price tags on the "risks" they had taken.

Diary - February 12, 1863

We had a heavy shower this morning, but it cleared by noon. Albert Smith got detailed on the engineer corps today. They told us at roll call this afternoon that Mr. Delamatre died today of chronic diarrhea. The weather was pleasant.

Corporal Richard V. Delamatre of Company "B" was a married 43-year-old farmer from Salina Township of Kankakee. The *Illinois Roster* correctly places his death at Young's Point, but erroneously cites the date as February 27, 1865. Albert G. Smith, often referred to as "Bert," was a loyal friend of Chatfield, a companion frequently mentioned by Chatfield in his letters and diary entries. Like Delamatre, Smith was also from Salina Township, but the 20-year-old Smith wasn't married when he enlisted, a fact that his friend Chatfield would one day help remedy.

Diary - February 13, 1863

We went down to the boats with the teams to get boards to make a coffin for Mr. Delamatre. We made a coffin for him, then buried him with honors of war. Three others died today: The orderly of Co. G, the others in Co.'s D and E, respectively. I got 3 letters this p.m. Dan [Durham] and I went down to the boats and got several blankets of rubber this evening, presented to the 113th by the Board of Trade of Chicago. Bully for the Board of Trade. Today was warm and pleasant. The mud is drying up fast.

From Chicago, Corporal Gould P. Norton, 25 years old and unmarried, had been a bookkeeper before the war. After promotion to First Sergeant of Company "G", he died at Young's Point of disease. No February 13 deaths are shown on Company "D" and "E" rosters.

Diary - February 14, 1863

The first letter from home in 2 months came today, and I wrote home answering it. We formed a mess of teamsters and guards today with 10 boys in the mess. The weather was pleasant.

Letter - February 14, 1863
Army of the Mississippi Before Vicksburg in Louisiana.
February 14th, 1863

Dear Father and Mother,

It was with much pleasure that I received and read your welcome letter dated January 18th, it being the first that I had got since leaving Memphis, which is nearly two months ago. It was with a great deal of pleasure that ma had been enjoying tolerable health and that pa and all of the boys and little mary was well, for I had feared that you were sick. My health is good and it has been all of the time. Since I wrote my last letter we have lost two of our company— Joseph Hix [Hicks] who was wounded at the battle of Arkansas Post, & Richard Delamater [Delamatre], who died here in the Hospital of Chronic Diareah. There is a great many dying here every day of various kinds of diseases. There is some cases of smallpox. There has been one in our Reg't. I was vaccinated last fall in camp Worcester* & I was vaccinated again yesterday, and my arm is begining to get sore already. The principal kinds of diseases in camp are Diareah, typhoid fever, billious fever, fever & ague† etc. etc. Dear Mother I hope that you will not worry on my account in any particular. I have aplenty to eat drink & wear. Today we all had a present made to us of a rubber blanket apiece. They were given to us by the Chicago Board of Trade. They are a nice article and will help much in keeping us dry when we have to be out in the rain. I work just enough every day to exercise myself & when night comes I lay mysel self down and roll up in my blanket and sleep soundly as ever I did at home. "Why" I have seen soldiers

---

*   Camp Worcester was located near Camp Hancock and Camp Douglas, near what is now Chicago's Grant Park. After the war, a G.A.R. Post named *Worcester* was organized at Grant Park.

†   Recurrent chills, severe shaking, and fever (symptoms of malaria) characterized "the ague." Quinine was the usual treatment.

lay right down in the water, as it were, and sleep as well as you would in your beds. In fact, I have done it myself. One thing that I miss very much is that we do not have any Sabbaths, the sab Sabbath being the same as any other day. We have no preaching nor any thing of the kind. If we had have had Mr. Hall for our chaplain we would have had one worth something. But the one that we have [Adam L. Rankin] is not worth a snap of the finger. There is a good deal of mud here, but the weather seems just about the same as it does there the latter part of April. The buds on the trees are bursting and every thing looks like Spring. The ground is in good order for ploughing. We lay in much the same position that we did when we first landed here. There is a strong force working on the Canal. The river is still rising and it is expected before long that it will be large enough for boats to run through. Last night I was awakened by hearing heavy cannonadeing. I found that one of our gunboats had run the blockade. The enemies batteries played on her with their heavy guns. It was very dark at the time. I have not learned the particulars whether they hit her or not. There has been other boats run the blockade before and the enemies never hurt any at all. Dear Father & mother I think that I did perfectly right in enlisting as I did, but and should do the same again if I had the same feelings. But for all that, I would not advise any one to enlist. I think that they would be the best of at home. I hope that you will not go beyond your strength in carrying on that awful large place. I am afraid that pa will work himself out. If I were him, I would rent a part of the place this year and not try to farm so much. By Cousin Mary Herricks* letter, I find that Grandpa [David Herrick] is failing fast. I am afraid that he will drop away before long unless he gets better by the coming Spring.

Sunday, Feb 15ᵗʰ [Chatfield continues with his letter begun on February 14.] It has been raining hard all night and it is still raining this forenoon. The mud in the roads being almost impassible for the big six mule teams that are used. The Rebels, once in a while, throw a few shells over towards our camp but they have never done any harm yet. I will send in this a few beads to Mary that I took of [off] a ladys mantilla which was of velvet.† I got them in Napoleon, Mississippi. Well, I must bring this to a close. Please write soon.

From your affectionate son,
Edward L. Chatfield
TO N S. Chatfield, Kankakee City, Ill

---

* Chatfield was referring to Cousin Mary I. Herrick, who lived in Twinsburg, Ohio. One month shy of 18, Mary was the daughter of James Oliver Herrick and Mary Jane Conant Herrick. James was Chatfield's mother's brother.

† Evidently, Chatfield did not have enough postage to send the whole mantilla.

[On Backside of letter]

Dear Brother,

Well Newton, well done for a new beginner. I was much pleased with your letter. I think that you are making good progress in writing, at any rate. That is the way. Make the best of your time. When you have a chance, I should be much pleased to see you all in your peaceful quiet home. But, I am afraid that it will be sometime before such good fortune shall be ours. Here we never know one day what the next will bring forth. Well Newton, there is smaller boys in the army than you. There is one in the Brigade Band. He is a drummer. He is not any larger than Orin Hosmer.* He is a fine little fellow to. Do you have any spelling schools this winter? I suppose that us boys are missed a great deal, but remember that we are in a good cause fighting for our country. We have been in one little fight already and I cannot tell how soon we shall be in another. I have got now a splendid Enfield Rifle, and, if we do have another fight, shall try to make it do good service. If I had a chance, I should send some more clothes home, for I have more than I can carry. I wrote a letter to David and William a few days ago and so I will not answer theirs this time. Now Newton, you must write again. And James, you must write to. Write soon.

From your Brother,

Edward L

Be sure and direct to ELC, Co. B. 113ᵗʰ Reg't. Ill. Vols. Via Cairo, To follow the Reg't Youngs point Louisiana Care Capt C Williams, and it will be Sure to go through.

Fifty-year-old Adam L. Rankin, the regimental chaplain, was a married clergyman from Salem, Illinois, when he enlisted on October 11, 1862. Chatfield's February 14 letter reveals his disappointment with Rankin.

There is a dramatic incongruence between what Chatfield communicates in his letters and what he writes in his diary. He tells his family, "My health is good and it has been all of the time." Yet, his diary entries say otherwise. Chatfield clearly wishes to avoid creating additional cause for his family's concern.

The soldier with smallpox was George Van Valkenberg. His condition was steadily worsening. Smallpox vaccinations were in high demand during the war. The best vaccine came from the pustules on cows or calves, but the scarcity of pustules prompted many to use human vaccination scabs. Infant scabs were especially valued,

---

*   Orin Hosmer was likely a neighborhood child.

because the recipient could be better assured of not contracting other serious communicable diseases such as syphilis.

Chatfield wrote that the guns above Vicksburg woke him up on the night of February 13. Indeed, they must have. The Confederate gunners had been shooting at the *Indianola*, a heavily protected 511-ton ironclad carrying provisions and over two month's worth of coal. She passed relatively unscathed beyond Vicksburg's guns. The guns awoke Chatfield at 10:48 P.M. and continued firing until 11:16 P.M. Twenty-one shots were fired, all from the bluffs above Vicksburg.[55]

The Confederates took advantage of every opportunity to seize a boat, as did the Union. The *Queen of the West* had run the Vicksburg blockade February 3, taking 12 hits in the process. She remained sufficiently seaworthy to fire on the docks and ram the Confederate steamer *City of Vicksburg* and, within two more weeks, capture four Confederate steamers. On February 14, the day Chatfield wrote his letter, the *Queen of the West* ran aground near an enemy shore-battery and was captured. The Confederates quickly repaired her and put her to work on their side.

Diary - February 15, 1863
We had hard rains last night and this morning with much thunder and lightning. I wrote a few lines and included Bert's letter. Company B got sent out on picket today.

Diary - February 16, 1863
It is still raining today. I received a letter from Hank and wrote a letter to Cousin Georgianna this evening, ending my day. We had supper at dark.

"Hank" was Henry E. Chatfield, the son of Albert Alonzo Chatfield, Lucy and Isaac Chatfield's third born and Chatfield's father's older brother. Sergeant Henry E. Chatfield fought for the 18th Michigan, in Company "I." Cousin Georgianna Robb was the daughter of Chatfield's father's younger sister, Maryetta Chatfield Robb.

Diary - February 17, 1863

I drew a new pair of shoes this morning. It's the same old story. Rain, rain, rain. I think it will flood us out if we stay here.

Diary - February 18, 1863

The rain stopped last night. The sky is thick with clouds. They are firing upon Vicksburg every 15 minutes with shells from one of our mortars, and the Rebels reply now and then.

Diary - February 19, 1863

The sun rose clear for the first time in several days. It was a warm and pleasant day. I washed in the forenoon. Our boys are still firing the mortars. Many sanitary stores arrived for the regiment today.

Diary - February 20, 1863

I had a refreshing night's rest and did duty as a cook this morning. Company B got sent on picket this morning. It was a clear and pleasant day.

Diary - February 21, 1863

It rained some during the night and hard today, all through the forenoon. Heavy cannonading came from down river and up the Yazoo. There must be something going on. Rumors have it that we are going north in a short time.

Diary - February 22, 1863

It rained some during the night, but it was pleasant today. We packed today, and our teams went out twice. The gunboats fired a salute to honor Washington's birthday. We shared two dozen figs among us for supper, a rarity.

Diary - February 23, 1863

We hitched up the team, went down to the boats, and brought up a bake-oven and other things sent by the Chicago Board of Trade. After this we shall have bread. I went with Dan [Durham] up to the hospital. On the way back, we took in a load of beets. We had pleasant weather today.

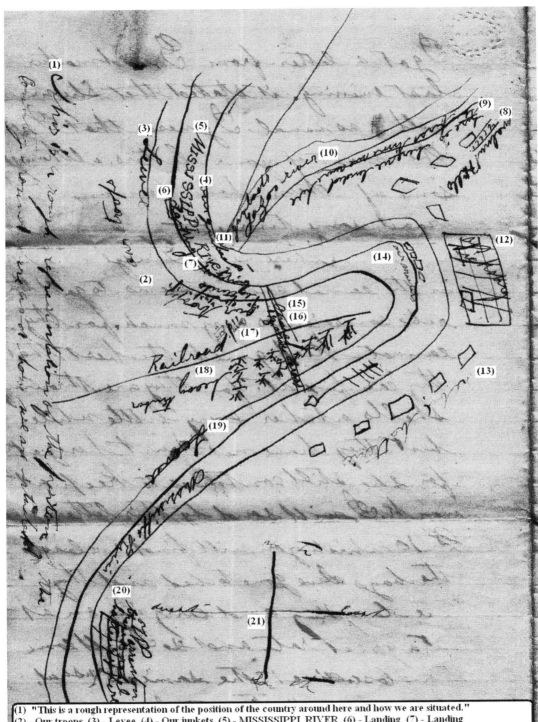

(1) "This is a rough representation of the position of the country around here and how we are situated."
(2) - Our troops (3) - Levee (4) - Our junkets (5) - MISSISSIPPI RIVER (6) - Landing (7) - Landing
(8) - Walnut Hills (9) - Here is where we landed the first time we were here   (10) - Yazoo River (11) - Gunboats
(12) –Vicksburg (13) - rebel batteries (14) - Our Mortars (15) -Canal (16) -1 1/8 miles across (17) Rgmt. 113th
(18) - Railroad Heavy Timber (19) - Levee Mississippi River (20) - Warrenton — there is a rebel battery here.
(21) - North-East-South-West

MAP SKETCH by E. L. Chatfield, March 20, 1863

CHAPTER 11: PURSUING STRATEGIC ALTERNATIVES

"Commodore Foote says that he can knock all of the batteries along the river to pieces in twelve hours, just give him a chance with his gunboats. But Grant says wait a few days, I have not got my plans quite ready."

Diary - February 24, 1863
We saw a lot of Negroes that have been sent here to work on the ditch. We drew our rations at the boats, then had some bread baked in the new oven. The bread was first rate. Charles Calkins died this evening, just at dark.

Private Charles L. Calkins in Company "B", a 28-year-old married farmer from Pilot, had died "of disease" at Young's Point.

<u>Letter</u> - February 24, 1863
Army of the Mississippi Before Vicksburg February 24th, 1863

Dear Father & Mother,

You must excuse me for writing on such poor paper, but there is some consolation that there is not much more of it. For the truth is that I confiscated a lot at Arkansas Post. I am as well and hearty as a buck. Enjoy myself first rate. Hardly ever think of home. Not a bit homesick nor having been. It is a fine Spring morning. The birds are singing and every thing looks cheering and pleasant. I got Mothers much prized letter dated Jan 27th day before yesterday (or Feb. 22nd). I also rec'd one on the 14th dated Jan 20th, which I answered. It rained almost all last week, and the roads are frightful. But, the weather has been fine for the last two days, and if it will only keep so for a few days longer the roads will be passable again. Every[thing] is now pointing towards a heavy battle in a few [days] and when they do strike I think that the blow will be felt. They have got Vicksburg almost surrounded, and they have the holes stopped up so there will be no chance for them to skedaddle. Commodore Foote* says that he can knock all of the batteries along the river to pieces in twelve (12) hours, just give him a chance with his gunboats. But Grant says wait a few days, I have not got my plans quite ready. I think that within another week some thing is agoing to be done. There is rumor in camp now that there is no more mail a going to be allowed to go up the river till after the battle comes of. So you must not feel anxious if you do not get any more letters for some time. I cannot tell for certain whether such is the case, however, so you need not give yourselves any uneasiness about me. Where I was hurt in my side is entirely well. So you need not feel uneasy about that. I was vaccinated a short time ago and it worked first rate. My arm is quite sore yet. As for my part, I would not accept of a discharge if one was given me. I have been with the teams some time now and it does me good for I exercise just enough to give me an apetite for my rations. It makes me feel sorry that you are so afflicted. Cannot you get some help for yourself some where? Do be carefull of yourself, at any rate.

You wished to know what was my opinion of this war coming to a close. I think that, the way all things are tending now, it cannot last a great while longer. The way that the Democrats are working in the North and in the army also is a going to bring about a state of things before a great while. To go through the camp and hear the soldiers talking and the cry is that they want to have the war brought to a close as soon as possible. And some would even give up all that we have gained to have it brought about. While others say, give us the union as it had ought to be or give us none at all. Well, I guess that I must bring this to a close. The Cap't says that the Paymaster is in this part of the country, and if so, we shall be paid before a great while. The boys are all as well, as usual, and send their best respects. Give my best respects to all inquiring friends.

From your affectionate son,
Edward L. Chatfield
To Mr. N.S Chatfield
Kankakee City, Ill.
Direct your letters Via Cairo, which is a plenty. Write often.

---

* Chatfield is referring to Union Commodore Andrew Hull Foote, the commander of the Mississippi River Squadron.

On February 24, while near the mouth of the Red River, the Confederates' newly captured Union vessel, *Queen of the West,* and a 665-ton side wheel steam ram, the *Webb,* rammed the *Indianola* seven times, pushing her aground. The Confederates eventually captured and tried to salvage the *Indianola.* Displeased and begrudging this loss, Union Admiral David Porter ordered that a raft, dummied to resemble an ironclad, be set adrift to move down the river toward the salvage operation. He hoped that the fearsome appearance would scatter the salvagers. Instead, the Confederates detonated the *Indianola's* magazines. She would remain submerged until after the war.

Diary - February 25, 1863
There was heavy firing down the river and up the Yazoo last night. Our captain procured a good coffin, and we buried Charlie Calkins with the honors of war. Poor fellow. The chaplain [Adam L. Rankin] made a few remarks at the grave. We heard more cannonading this evening.

Diary - February 26, 1863
It rained hard last night, and we had another terrible storm of wind and rain in the forenoon today. So, I stayed in camp most all day. Went with some of the boys down the river a ways; they say that the levee is broken.

Diary - February 27, 1863
Friday, I helped the sutler bring his things from the boat and made 25 cents for doing it. I signed for payroll this evening. Soncey [Francis Soncey] got his discharge papers today. He will start home once he gets paid. We were ordered to mount mules to draw rations at night. The whole regiment was called out to do it. They loaded the mules onto a flatboat brought to help us; we worked the mules until nearly midnight. I drew 10 days' rations.

According to the Company "B" *Illinois Roster,* Francis Soncey, a 29-year-old married farmer from Martinton, didn't get paid for another month. He was finally discharged on March 31 due to disability.

Diary - February 28, 1863

We all had to mount mules again and pack in more rations from the flatboat. We got done by noon. I went down to the boats again in the evening and packed back enough hats for the regiment, including one for myself.

Diary - March 1, 1863

My turn cooking this week. Divine service this a.m. Flag of truce came over from Rebel lines this p.m.

Both Union and Confederate forces honored the use of the white flag to signal a request for negotiation. The understanding was that the approaching negotiator was unarmed and should not be fired upon. The flag of truce was often used to arrange prisoner exchanges.

<u>Letter</u> - March 1, 1863
Butler's Canal
near Vicksburg Sunday eve March March 1st 1863

Dear Father & Mother,

Having finished the duties of the day I will try and have a little communion by means of the pen. I rec'd your welcome letter dated Feb' 22nd and was very glad to hear from you. For you know that every thing that comes from home is very welcome and much prized. My health still remains very good. I think I can praise God for his goodness towards one in his kind care of me. Let us praise him day & night for his goodness to us. I attended Divine service this forenoon. Had a very good sermon. We frequently have tracts and sunday school papers given us, and I can assure you that they are much prized & the eye of the soldier boy may be seen to sparkle as the good man comes around distributing them. I often think, Oh that I were a christian in the full sense of the word. But, I fear that I am not. Evil thoughts are continually before me and pride and vanity are to strong to be mastered. Pray for me that I may at last be brought to see the evil of my ways and turn from them & seek the path of the Lord.

Albert [Smith], John Fundy, Loyal [Blair], Ira [William], John Titcomb and James Henry are well and tough as bears and can eat their rations every time.

John Blanchet & George Shays* are sick and have been some time. George Van Velkenborg [Van Valkenberg] was sent back to Memphis about a month ago. I have not heard from him since. Joseph Hix [Hicks] died while on the Hospital Boat on her way up the river. I do not know where they buried him. Frank Houghton [Francis Huton] also died while in some of the hospitals up the river, I do not know where.† Richard Delamater [Delamatre] and Charley Corkins [Calkins] who lived over near the poor farm, died a few days ago here in the Hospital. We buried them with the honors of war on the Levee which runs along beside our camp. The Levee is the common burying place, and for miles it is just one string of graves. And they are putting them (the poor soldiers) into it every day. No one knows whose turn will come next. There was a flag of truce came over from the Rebel lines this PM. The flag was brought in a yawl up the river and was met by one of our small boats accompanied by a gunboat. The conference lasted two hours when they returned. I have not yet learned any of the particulars. There is some great event pending, I am sure. The Rebels have got the best gunboat that we have, the Indianola, and we have lost the Ram, Queen of the West. The Queen of the West was up Red river and had taken several Rebel boats. When, she ran in an ambush of Rebel batteries and, in trying to escape, she run aground. When, the Rebs captured her. A part of the men, however, escaped. We are all expecting a battle to commence every day, & I think that something must be done before a great while. The weather is quite fine, regular Spring weather, the days are quite warm already. We have had a great deal of rain, however along back, and the roads are impassable for wagons. We have to pack all of our rations and forage on mule back from the boats. The river is rising very fast. It has risen ten feet since we first landed here.

You wished to know how I rested nights. I will tell you how I manage it. When I can, I first get some hay, straw, cotton, or board, if they are to be had, and if not I do without. I then spread my blankets of which I have three and Albert [Smith] generally sleeps with me so that with his we make a pretty good bed. And, as for a pillow, I take my knapsack. We then turn in and sleep just as soundly as though we were resting on feathers and just as well (it is all in getting used to it you know.)

I recd your letter that had Grand Mothers letter in and was very glad to learn the address of my Cousins. I have not found any of my relations yet. I heard got a letter from Cousin Mary Arrene [Mary Irene Herrick.] She gave all of the particulars of uncle Samuels [Samuel Eells] death.‡ She also said that grand pa's

---

*   Private George E. Shays, in Chatfield's company, was a 19-year-old single farm boy from Limestone Township.

†   Private Francis Huton, a farmer before the war, died in Memphis on April 11, 1863, from the wounds he took at Arkansas Post. He was 34 years old.

‡   Uncle Samuel Eells was Chatfield's mother's brother-in-law, the husband of Zipporah Herrick. Eels had died in December of 1862 after serving his 47th day of military service for the state of Iowa. He was a 30-year-old private in Company "F" of the Iowa 6th Cavalry when disease took his life while he was hospitalized in Davenport, Iowa.

health was not any better. I have not rec'd any letter yet with poetry. It must have been lost or mislaid on the road. I have your letters that I have received dated thus—one dated Dec 6th rcd Feb 16th Jan 20th Re'd' Feb 14th another dated Jan 27th rec'd Feb 20th and the last that I have got which was dated Feb 22nd rec'd Mar 1st. This comprises all of the letters that I have received from home since leaving Memphis December 20th. I am glad if the blanket is handy for you. I have a coat that I wish was at home. It is only a bother to me. I shall send it if I get a chance.

We are mustered for pay every two (2) months. We were mustered yesterday being the last day of the last two (2) months from January 1st to Feb 28th. There is now six (6) months pay due us. The paymaster is down here and we expect to get some of it soon, probably about two (2) months pay. ~~We eat hard bread half of the time now.~~ We have half ration of soft bread or Bakers bread now so that we fare well. The rest is hard <u>tack,</u> as we call it, (that is hard crackers, and they are hard to, for we need a hammer to break them into.) Well, I guess that it is time for me to close. My companions are sleeping around me while I am seated on the ground penning you this. Give my best wishes and respects to all inquiring, and save my love for yourselves. Tell Mary that if Edward lives he will come to her some time.

I remain your dutiful son,
Edward

Hard tack, also known as "tooth dullers,"[56] was a military survival food, a ration made infamous by the Civil War, and the precursor of today's MRE, a "Meal Ready to Eat." Structurally, hard tack was a compact, solid food of high gluten content, three-inch square wafers about a quarter of an inch thick. A single square of hard tack would last many years if kept dry and free of worms. Nine to ten wafers constituted a single ration. The soldier would carry the wafers in his haversack and eat them while on the march. But they weren't easy to eat, soldiers often dubbing them, "sheet iron crackers." Chatfield emphasized that point by writing, "…we need a hammer to break them…." Another vivid appellation for hard tack when not kept clean and dry was "worm castles,"[57] too disgusting to eat. Hard tack became the subject of many jokes:

> Sergeant: "Boys, I was eating a piece of hard tack this morning, and I bit on something soft; what do you think it was?"
> Private: "A worm?"
> Sergeant: "No by G__d, it was a ten penny nail."[58]

A Recipe for Hard Tack

Use one part water to six parts flour. Mix and knead. Roll dough flat and score into cracker shapes. Bake 20-25 minutes, and cool off until completely dry before storing in canisters. The crackers should be hard as bricks and indestructibly unappetizing. If not consumed by hungry soldiers, the crackers might last at least until the Lord returns!

Note: The moisture content of flour varies; so more water may actually be necessary. Add tiny amounts of water at a time to reach the consistency of dough that can be rolled out.[59]

Diary - March 2, 1863

The entire regiment was ordered to work on the canal 12 hours out of every 24. I saw the dredging machine work on the canal this morning. It's quite an institution for bringing out the mud. Another flag of truce came across the river this evening.

On March 3, President Lincoln signed *The Enrollment Act of 1863*, the Union's first conscription act, requiring the enrollment of every male citizen and those immigrants who had filed for citizenship between ages twenty and forty-five. The central registry provided a national pool from which individuals could be drafted should they fail to volunteer, pay the exemption fee, or successfully hire a substitute. Unpopular and discriminatively punishing to the poor, the first induction to come would prompt bitter riots on the streets of New York within four months.

Diary - March 3, 1863

I did my washing in the forenoon and some cooking. Lieutenants Beckett and Daniels started up the river this evening. The Rebels were firing at our forces all evening. I haven't learned of the results yet, but the shells could be seen bursting, making many fires at night.

104
The Chatfield Story: Civil War Letters and Diaries of
Private Edward L. Chatfield of the 113th Illinois Volunteers

Both Lieutenant Andrew Beckett (age 32) and Lieutenant Harrison Daniels (age 47) were married men from Kankakee County. Beckett, a saddle maker from Martinton Township, would be promoted within nine months to Captain while stationed in Corinth, Mississippi. Daniels's home, in Chebanse, was 12 miles northwest of Beckett's.

Diary - March 4, 1863

Lieutenant Beckett did not start up the river yesterday after all. There was considerable cannonading going on both sides today. We have two heavy Parrott guns planted on the ditch. Our boys were trying to get the range of them this morning.

Diary - March 5, 1863

We had a fine spring morning today. The birds are singing. It was cheerful. I went to the upper landing on an errand for the quartermaster this evening and saw several heavy siege guns. The water is rising very rapidly. The clouds cleared away this evening.

Letter to Edward - March 5, 1863
[Upside down] "Recd March 19th"
North Ridgeville, Lorain, Co, O, 1863, March 5th

My Dear Edward,

Your thrice wellcome letter came to hand yesterday, Dated Feb 15th, and it allmost leads us to extucies to receive a letter from our army boys. We are constantly worrying about them by night and by day, wondering where they are, wondering if they are not sick. But all this would not do you any good. If you was sick, we could not get to you, all we can do for you is to go to the throne of grace and pleade with our Heavenly Father for you. It is there alone that we can find help in time of need. He is still holding out the golden scepter of mercy and saying unto you, come, come unto me. Enter the Mansion prepared for you from the foundation of the world.

Please write to me whether you think the soldiers get any of the good things sent to them from there friends. The soldiers Aid Societies send a great many Boxes from all parts of the country. They try to help the poor distrest soldiers all they can. But I expect it goes through a great many hands before it gets to you. But you must hold up good courrage. Think your Heavenly Father is at the Helmn and will bring it out right at last. I had a letter from your Father and Mother yesterday. They think that you do not get there letters. They are very anxious about you, affraid you will get sick. They say, Oh, poor Edward, how I wish I could hear from him. Your Mothers health is usually good. The rest all weel and going to school. Your Father has to woork a lettle, I guess, but he dont complain one word. He thinks that you all have the same protector there that you would if you was with him. Oh Edward, what a blessing that you have such good Praying Father and Mother to interscede for you at the throne of grace. I hope your life will be spared, that we shall all see you again in this life. The old must die and the young may, so it stands us all in Hand to have our lamps trimed and burning, ready to go when ever we are called for. My health is as good as I can expect to be at my age [almost 76]. I live alone. Only children come and sleep with me. The friends are all well for what I know. I have just heard that Georgianna and Charlotte Robb are have gone to Oberlain to school. I will write a line and put your letter into it and send to them. They are some, like you, away from home and gladly receive news from a friend. I sent some Geauga papers to your Father. Perhaps he will send them to you. They gave an account of Harriet Cook Chapmans Death. She and Hiram with two small children moved to Illinois, Logan, Co, last Dec. She had been there six weeks when she was flung from a horse and killed. He took the remains and the two children back to Burton.* It overcame Marcellus very much, not being very well. It brought on conjestion of the Brain which terminated his life in a few days. She died the 21st of December, and he the 21st of Jan, so you see, there is something to carry us out of this world beside warfare. Remember Edward, and prepare to meet your God.

    This from your loving Grandmother

    Lucy Chatfield

    [P.S.] If you ever get this letter dont forget to write soon. For we are so glad to hear how you get along and how you live and where you live and how the country looks and whether ther is any Sabbath in the army.

    Your Uncle Alberts son, Henry Chatfield, is in the 18, Regt, Michigan, Infantry, Vol, Sergt, Henry Chatfield, Company I, Lexington, Kenty, Care of Capt Move [On side of letter] 18 Michigan Infantry

Harriet Cook Chapman, thrown and killed by the horse, was one of Lucy and Isaac's many grandchildren, the second child born to Lucy Almira Chatfield and her husband, Joseph Cook. Harriet was married to Hiram Chapman, and the couple had two children when Harriet was flung to her death. Marcellus, who succumbed to

---

*   Burton is in Geauga County, Ohio, near Middlefield, where Edward was born.

"congestion of the brain," was Harriet's older brother. Not mentioned by Grandmother Lucy was Harriet's younger brother, Thomas Corwin Cook. Uncle Albert was Isaac and Lucy's third child. Henry Chatfield was the second of Albert's two children. Henry's brother's name was Sterling. Both were Lucy and Isaac's grandchildren.

Diary - March 6, 1863

The Colonel was out exercising today, playing ball. He made his long legs get around pretty fast. I tended my cooking today and wrote a letter.

On the night of March 6, the north dam blocking the canal entrance broke, sending rushing water down the canal. Instead of washing out the dam at the south end, the water tore through a side outlet and flooded the southeast side of DeSoto Point, leaving some places five feet deep under water. Everything of value at Young's Point was readied to move onto the main levee at a moment's warning. Two huge steam-driven dipper-dredges, the *Hercules* and the *Sampson*, were put to work clearing the flooded channel. Two additional dredges were eventually added, but their names are no longer known.[60]

Diary - March 7, 1863

We had pleasant weather today.

Diary - March 8, 1863

There is considerable excitement, our fearing the levee will break. A large force is at work to strengthen it. All of the sick have been removed from the hospital and taken to the boats in case of a flood.

Letter - March 8, 1863
Butler's Canal Near Vicksburg
Sunday afternoon, March 9th, 1863 [sic] [Sunday, March 8]

Dear Father & Mother.

Having a few moments leisure (as we have very [little] of that when there is not something to be done) I will try and pen you a few lines. I attended Divine service this forenoon at 10. The text was Malachi – C9 – V8. The Chaplain [Rankin] preached a very good sermon showing how that we had revolted from God and went astray. Oh how I wish I was at home so that we all could go to meeting together and join in the worch worship of God. My health still remains good. Together with what work we have to do, and to cook, and one thing and another, we have enough to keep us stirring most of the time. They have been digging in the canal every since we came here, and now it (that is the water) threatens to break over the Levee and drown us all out. For you know that in time of high water the water is several feet above the surface above the ground. The water is now about 5 feet above the level of the country. We have now got every thing ready to move onto the Levee at a moments warning. The talk is now that we are to be paid tomorrow. The Paymaster has paid several reg'ts already. There is considerable talk that we are going North to Chicago or Springfield to guard prisoners. But there is no certainty yet what will be done. You know that part of our Reg't is at Springfield. I wish that you would write what you hear about it. I suppose that you are now enjoying very pleasant weather. We are having regular May weather. It is getting quite warm. The grass is begining to start and the trees are leaving out.

Monday afternoon, Mar 10th [sic] [Monday, March 9]

Before I could finish my letter yesterday afternoon we were ordered to hitch up a team and go to the boats with some clothing. So you see that we cannot tell one moment what order will come next. As I am writing now the cannon are booming away. They are on the gunboats. I have not learned what they are firing at. Just a few steps from my tent they are playing ball. The Captains units, surgeons and even the Colonel are all out. They all seem to take as much interest in the game as little boys would. I have not found any of my relatives yet. Did you see McLane* when he was home? He is [in] the 20-M. He got back yesterday. Well I do not know as I have any more news to write at present. Give my respects to all inquiring friends. My love to you all.

I remain as ever your Obedient son,
Edward

Direct to E — Company B 113th Reg't Ill Vols 1st Brigade 2nd Division, 15th Army Corps. Vicksburg. Via Cairo, Care of Capt Williams

---

*   Information not found on McLane from "20-M."

The Chatfield Story: Civil War Letters and Diaries of
Private Edward L. Chatfield of the 113th Illinois Volunteers
108

P.S. I will send in this letter a stem of the Mistletoe, a parasite that grows on any kind of tree. Now please write and tell me all of the news, and tell me what you are doing, and I will do the same. There has not any mail come for our Regt for the last ten days. We are expecting a mail every day.

Edward L. Chat

To N.S. Chatfield

Diary - March 9, 1863

I cleaned myself up and attended Divine service. Then I hitched up the team and moved the commissary stores onto the levee. I went down to the canal this afternoon. It was washing away very fast. While there, several soldiers attempted to cross the water, and one of them nearly drowned. Once back, I took some clothing to the boats. It rained hard on the way back.

Diary - March 10, 1863

We heard heavy firing at about 3:00 in the morning. Our boys fixed up a couple of barges and sent them down the river all alone, and the Rebs just pitched into them. I didn't get my expected pay today. There was a footrace this afternoon. The stakes were $5.00. John McDearmon of Company A won the money.

Corporal John Demster McDearmon (age 23) was from Northfield, Illinois, as was his brother Merrill (age 20), a private. Evidently, John could outrun his younger brother, but the race in rank was another thing. John mustered in as a corporal but mustered out as a private. Merrill mustered in as a private and mustered out as a sergeant.

Diary - March 11, 1863

We all went down to the boats this morning and packed back a lot of grain on the mules. The dredge in the canal is making very good progress. I received a letter from Cousin Clark [Samuel] Chatfield.

Clark Samuel Chatfield, a Corporal from Bath, Mason County, Illinois, was the second-born son of Chatfield's father's older brother, Levi Tomlinson Chatfield. Clark enlisted in August 1861, at the age of 22, and was assigned to Company "C" of the 2nd Illinois Cavalry.[*]

Diary - March 12, 1863

We fixed up the harnesses and did other little chores today. It was quite warm. I wrote to Cousin Clark Chatfield and Father.

<u>Letter</u> - March 12, 1863
Head Quarters 113th, Youngs point, near Vicksburg.
March 13th 1863

To my Dear Father & Mother.

I had been down to the boats all day yesterday helping to get rations & the first words on returning to camp was that there was a letter for me. You cannot imagine with what feelings of pleasure I received & read it. It brings tears of gladness to my eyes, and new courage to my heart as I read your courage inspiring letters. They make me feel more like battling for the Union which those detestable Copperheads ate at the North are trying to destroy. Just give us soldiers a chance and we would gladly sweep them from existence. Had it not been for our Northern traitors the war would have been ended long ago without the great sacrifice of human life that we have had. It is my wish, and it is the wish of all the soldiers, that we had all of the Northern traitors where we could get our hands on them, and we would make short work of them all. I think that the Conscription act is just right. It will make every man walk up and do his part. And when that is done, the war will be ~~shortly ended~~ ended in a short time.

---

[*] Edward, whose parents had many siblings, had many cousins. Levi Tomlinson Chatfield and his wife, Lovina Mastick, had three sons and one daughter: Isaac Willard, Clark Samuel, Charles Henry, and Ellen Charlotte. Isaac Willard Chatfield, the first-born, enlisted in August of 1861. Assigned to Company "E" of the 27th Illinois, he moved up from 1st Sergeant to 2nd Lieutenant before resigning on February 19, 1863, just three weeks before Edward received Clark's letter. Charles Henry Chatfield, the youngest brother, was the first to go to war, having enlisted in May of 1861 at the age of twenty. A private in Company "K" of the 17th Illinois, he was soon promoted to Corporal. Wounded at the February 13, 1862, battle of Fort Donelson, Tennessee, he was discharged in June of 1862 and returned to his home in Bath, Illinois. The wounds failed to discourage him, and he mustered in again two months later, this time as a 2nd lieutenant. He was assigned to Company "D" of the 85th Illinois and was eventually promoted to Captain, a proud officer who would die in a place he may never have heard of. On June 27, 1864, Charles Henry Chatfield would be cut down in brutal battle at Kennesaw Mountain, Georgia.

My health still remains good, and I can give the great giver of all good the praise that he has given me [for] such good health so far. I got a letter from Clark Chatfield last evening. He is at Memphis acting as orderly to General [James C.] Veach. He says that his health is quite good. His address is Co C. 2nd Ill Cavalry Memphis Tenn. He said that his brother Willard [Isaac Willard Chatfield] had resigned and gone home. Charles [Willard's younger brother] was at Nashville Tenn.

The weather is quite warm & pleasant but the roads are in an impassable condition. We have so much rain that it has almost flooded every thing. The river is on the rampage. It is rising very fast and threatens to flood every thing. The work on the Canal is progressing favorably. There is three dredging machines at work widening & depening it. There is a good many sick but I think that the health of the boys is on the gain. There was a man by the name of Frank Harter, of Bliss Sutherlands Company, that died very suddenly. He was well at night and before morning he was dead. The boys from our neighborhood are usually well and send their best wishes & respects. Well, I must close. Direct the same as usual and write soon.

From your affectionate son,

Edward

To N.S. Chatfield

[On side of letter]

I will send by this letter a piece of what is called Spanish moss that grows on any tree. Hangs from the limbs. It is not like plants. It receives its nourishment from the air.

Captain Bliss Sutherland was a 38-year-old married farmer from Kankakee Township when he enlisted. He survived the war. Private Frances Harter, an unmarried farmer in Sutherland's Company "H", died at Young's Point on March 12. The sudden cause was listed as "disease."

The Yazoo Pass Alternative

Even though the canal was "progressing favorably," as Chatfield had written, there was always the chance that it might not work as planned, leaving no change in the river's path and all navigation still vulnerable to the guns on Vicksburg's bluffs. If Vicksburg could not be bypassed, then it had to be taken by force. To do this, Grant needed a place of entry.

As early as January, Grant knew that Vicksburg was well protected along its westward facing bluffs—a Confederate line of heavy fortification extending northward from the city to Haines' Bluff. But the region to the north of Haines' Bluff was thought to be vulnerable, offering entry into the city if need be. The problem facing the Union was to find a means of transporting troops and supplies into that position. A joint Army-Navy expedition to establish a lodgment to the north of the city had been underway since late February—the Yazoo Pass Expedition.

A network of narrow streams and shallow river ways led to the Yazoo River from a point on the Mississippi River, several miles south of Helena, Arkansas—about 300 miles north of Vicksburg. Union Brigadier General Leonard F. Ross, with his division of foot soldiers aboard transports, trailed two ironclads through the vine-entangled passageways to the Yazoo where they were blocked on March 11 by a sunken ship and a hastily assembled Confederate earthwork called Fort Pemberton.*[61] Learning about this, General Grant sent Brigadier General Isaac F. Quinby's 7th Division south along the same water route, to meet up with Ross and subdue the Confederate forces blocking Union passage. Responsible for the ironclads preceding Ross and Quinby, Admiral Porter had meanwhile learned of another route that might provide direct support to Ross and Quinby from the south—an alternative passageway to Yazoo City by way of Steele's Bayou.[62]

The Steele's Bayou Support Route
Porter's support route would enter the Yazoo at its mouth—directly across from Young's Point. Upon reaching Steele's Bayou, he would ascend to Black Bayou, where he would cross eastward to Deer Creek. There he would steam north some 30 miles to Rolling Fork and continue on to the Big Sunflower, a river way that would return him to the Yazoo, well north of Haines' Bluff. It was a clandestine route that might evade Confederate eyes. If all went correctly, both Porter and Grant hoped to be able to "hem in" the Confederates who had been blocking Ross and Quinby from the south.[63] Once done, they would have their foothold on Mississippi soil, the Yazoo River and the road from Yazoo City affording a convenient supply line.[64] With this mission in mind, Admiral Porter departed Young's Point on March 14 with a fleet of five Cairo-class ironclads, four mortar boats and four tugs.

Diary - March 15, 1863
The dredges are steady at work and have reached the railroad across from the Point.

---

*   Fort Pemberton sat at what is today Greenwood, Mississippi—some 53 miles north of Yazoo City.

Letter - March 15, 1863
Youngs point oposite Vicksburg, Sunday March, 15ᵗʰ 1863

Dear folks at home.

The Holy Sabbath has again rolled around and finds me enjoying good health and the blessings of life. It has been raining all the forenoon but it has cleared up now and it is quite warm and pleasant. We finally got a little pay yesterday. We were settled up with until the first of Nov. I got $24.25 cts. I shall not send any this time. Beckett is going home and I may send some by him. The Paymaster said that we must get two months more pay in about 10 days. I suppose that you get all of the news before we do by the papers. So I cannot tell you much. The canal is progressing finely. The sick are all being sent to up the river to Memphis, St Louis, and other Hospitals. Well, as I have not any more to write at present, I will close. The boys all send their best respects. Please write often.

I remain as ever your son,

Edward —

Diary - March 16, 1863

At 3:00 p.m. the Rebels were vigorously shelling the Point, trying to hit the dredges. Some of their shells have been falling pretty close to our camp. Our batteries at the mouth of the canal are replying.

On March 16, Admiral Porter's expedition had reached Hill's Plantation—located at the junction of Black Bayou and Deer Creek, northeast of Young's Point.[65] Before dawn on the morning of March 17, the 113ᵗʰ (in Colonel Giles Smith's 1ˢᵗ Brigade of Stuart's division) was dispatched to help support General Porter's fleet, then steaming up Steele's Bayou. Because Chatfield's responsibility was to guard the wagons and to tend the teams, he was left behind. By daylight, Chatfield's friends in the 113ᵗʰ had boarded transports and steamed away.

Diary - March 17, 1863

We were awakened at 3:00 a.m. by the drums beating reveille. There has been heavy cannonading all night. Our regiment fell in at 6:00 a.m. and was told to take

6 days' rations with them. The teams were not going so I was left behind along with the teamsters.

By the evening of March 17, Porter's fleet was in trouble. Slaves in the area had been sent out by the Confederates to obstruct Porter's movement. At that point, Porter was approaching Rolling Fork, more than 15 miles north of Black Bayou. Conditions worsened for the fleet throughout the night. By the morning of March 18, Porter's warships had become targets to six pieces of artillery and roughly 800 Confederate infantrymen and some 40 cavalrymen, a situation that would steadily escalate over the next two days. Chatfield would not get the facts about much of this until after his regiment returned to camp.

Diary - March 18, 1863

There was some cannonading this morning. They made the dredge get out of the way. Some of the shots were getting very close. News came that our whole brigade had been taken as prisoners. This was rumor I guess.

Letter - March 18, 1863
Youngs point near Vicksburg March 18th, 1863.

Dear Father & Mother,

Having a little leisure I will try and write you a few lines to let you know what we are doing way down in this southern country. As for my own part I have been acting as a wagon guard for sometime. There has been hard fighting around Vicksburg for several days. But our Reg't had not been called into action until yesterday. When, they marched at daylight to the boats on which our whole Brigade embarked. When, they went up the Yazoo. My being with the teams exempted me as they did not go. No horses being allowed to go, not even the Colonel's. The Rebels have batteries planted so that they could shell us with ease if they were so disposed. For yesterday & today they have thrown shells and solid shot within 80 rods [1,280 feet] of us. There was news came this PM that our whole Brigade was taken prisoners, but there is no certainty in what we hear, at any rate. It is fine weather. The days are quite ~~short~~ warm, so as to make the sweat run freely, while the nights are quite cool.

March 20th - -

I find that the Reg't went up the river about 30 miles. They are going to build a bridge over or across a bayou. Commodore [David] Farragut has Finally got up here. There is two of his gunboats laying about 4 miles below here and some of the Officers have been up here. It is pretty sure that operations are to commence shortly. The most of the ~~men~~ soldiers that were [at] this point have all been removed to some other place. I got a letter from Grandmother [Lucy] last evening. It stated that she was well & as usual. I guess that I get the most of your letters, although some of them have been on the road some time. ―――― There is a Dredge at work in the canal and it seems to gall the Reb's consciences very much. For they cannot keep quiet [and are doing] the best that they can [to] fix it. For they are throwing shells at her every little while. But they have not hurt her yet for she still continues to keep at work. I will send by this letter $10 which you will find enclosed. The boys have gone to bed and they are laughing and carrying on at a great rate, and so I will come to a close. Direct the same as usual.

From your affectionate son,

Edward. ――――

On the backside of this letter, Chatfield sketched the map shown at the beginning of this chapter. His drawing shows the Louisiana and Mississippi locations of his regiment, the railroad, the canal, landings, gunboats, levees, mortar batteries on DeSoto Point, batteries on Warrenton, and his December position on the Chickasaw Bayou delta below Walnut Hills. Although drawn without the benefit of surveyor's equipment or formal cartographer's training, Chatfield's sketch is remarkably similar to strategic military maps of the time. As he put it humbly, "This is a rough representation of the positions of the country around here and how we are situated."

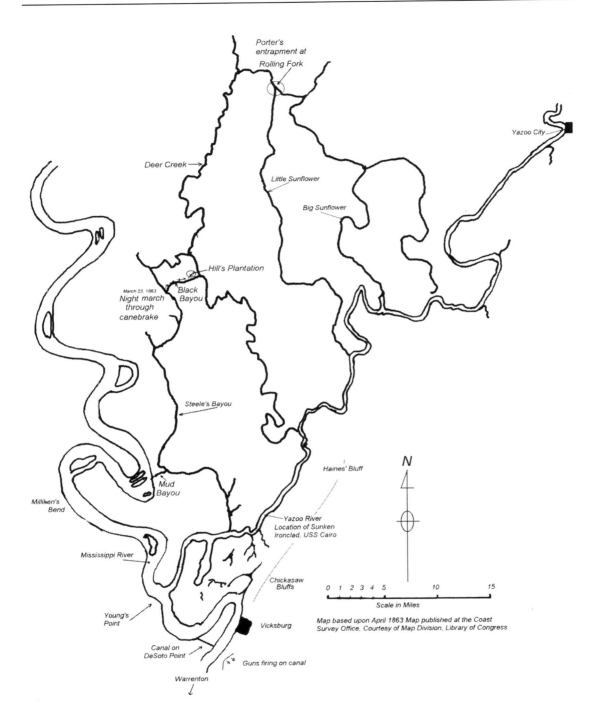

Rescue at Black Bayou

CHAPTER 12: RESCUE AT BLACK BAYOU AND RUNNING THE GAUNTLET

*"I am afraid that before Vicksburg is taken
... there will be a good many lives lost."*

Early on March 19, entrapped by the Rebel's felled trees to the rear of his warships at Rolling Fork and helplessly unable to defend against the surrounding Confederates, Admiral Porter dispatched his secretary, Mr. Guild, with an urgent message calling for General Sherman's help. Sherman received Porter's plea at midnight.

> I beg that you will shove up troops to us at once. I am holding the mouth of Rolling Fork against Adams' [CS General Wirt Adams] troops, which have attacked our 200 men. We have only two pieces of artillery; they have six, and 200 men. We should take possession here at once with the army. There is everything here the heart of a soldier could desire; everything in abundance. Please send; it takes all my men to defend the position I have taken. I think the distance is only 14 miles by land. I shall look for these reinforcements. . . . Please send on troops. I think a large force will be used to block us up here. We must have every soldier to hold the country, or they will do it. Our difficulties increase. — David D. Porter.[66]

Porter was about fifty miles due north of Young's Point at the time, much too far away for the relatively light gunfire to be heard. But closer to camp there was still a lot going on that occupied Chatfield's attention.

Diary - March 19, 1863

There was heavy cannonading all night. The Rebels were shooting at the dredge, but they haven't hit her yet. At 7:00 this morning we heard heavy firing down by the river, 10 or 15 miles. Our regiment has gone up the Yazoo River about 30 miles. They are going to build a corduroy road* through a swamp and a bridge over a bayou.

The overnight firing had come from Confederate guns placed across the mighty river, four miles south of Chatfield's campsite at Young's Point. The distant 7:00 A.M. cannon blasts that Chatfield heard had drifted up from Grand Gulf, 15 miles to the south. Rear Admiral Farragut's ships, the *Hartford* and the *Albatross*, had been steaming northward that morning. When they passed the bluffs at Grand Gulf at 6:40 A.M., the Confederate guns there fired down upon them and continued to do so for the next 28 minutes, an event where two sailors were mortally wounded.[67]

By March 20, Porter's fleet remained desperately trapped, his sailors battling for their lives at Rolling Fork. The situation had become so desperate that Porter distributed instructions on how to scuttle his vessels:

> In case the order is given to destroy the ship, every precaution must be made to build a fire that will certainly ignite, using all the incendiary stuff, turpentine, oil, camphene, coal oil, etc. The magazine must be left open, with powder open and spread about, so that an explosion will be certain. The machinery must be broken, guns loaded with shell, run in, pointed through the deck, and primed. Every arrangement must be on hand to fire the ships, tugs, and mortar boats, and the commanders will themselves apply the match, having removed the sick and wounded back to the edge of the woods. The signal for firing the ships will be a number of rockets or blue lights or Coston [Coxswain] signals, and orders will also be sent to avoid mistakes. Before the men leave the ship they must arm themselves with muskets, pistols, or pikes, and form together back in the edge of the woods, where we will try and retreat to the place we started from. The tugs must be kept close to the steamers. Have the men supplied with one day's provisions, cut up into pieces, so they can carry it. — David D. Porter [68]

---

*   Corduroy roads were built with logs laid side-by-side; such roads were among the earliest form of wooden roads constructed for wagon use.

Back at Young's Point, the incoming cannon fire had become a constant worry, Chatfield writing about it for the next two days.

Diary - March 20, 1863
The Rebels fired a shot or shell about every half-hour all night and several more this morning.

Diary - March 21, 1863
The Secesh must feel bad about the dredge, for they keep firing at her. There was very heavy firing at sundown. Our gunboats have come as far north as Warrenton and are shelling there, setting the town on fire. We could see it from here.

Throughout the day of March 21, transport after transport carrying Union infantrymen found their way to Black Bayou.* It wasn't until nightfall that the final complement of Colonel Giles Smith's 1st Brigade—three steamboats carrying the 113th and other regiments—docked. By then, the earlier arrivals had already marched away, intent on defending Porter's fleet. But a much larger force would be needed to provide Porter with an adequate defense. Aware of this and with little time to spare, General Sherman took direct command of the final arrivals and personally guided them through the dense canebrake and swampland, candles affixed in each of his soldiers' gun barrels to light the way.[69]

By the morning of March 22, Sherman's efforts had successfully moved the 13th Regulars and the 113th Volunteers to the main road above Hill's Plantation at Deer Creek, Mississippi. Chatfield, tending his teams back at Young's Point, alternated his focus between the guns firing on the canal and the news from the Yazoo.

At about 3:00 P.M., on March 22, the advance guard of the 13th Regulars came under fire near the northern head of Deer Creek, three miles below Rolling Fork. Colonel George B. Hoge of the 113th Volunteers detailed Company "B" to deploy as skirmishers. They rapidly drove back all Confederate resistance.[70] Over the next several days, Porter's warships would back their way down Deer Creek in the direction of

---

*   On this day, having not yet received reinforcements from Porter and Sherman, Generals Quinby and Ross, running low on ammunition and still blocked at Fort Pemberton on the Yazoo far to the north, had no choice but to withdraw up river—bringing the Yazoo Pass Expedition to an end. (*Official Records*, Series 1, Volume 24, Part 1, 398)

120
The Chatfield Story: Civil War Letters and Diaries of
Private Edward L. Chatfield of the 113th Illinois Volunteers

Black Bayou, the infantry defending Porter's gunboats until all had finally returned to camp by March 27.[*] By late evening of March 22, however, bits of information about the battle on Deer Creek had already reached Chatfield's ears.

Diary - March 22, 1863

Company B skirmished with the Rebels today, firing for some time from Deer Creek. Our regiment has driven the Rebels back for some distance, killing several.

Chatfield was clearly proud of his regiment's accomplishments. The boys had nobly done the job asked of them and took no casualties while doing it. Nevertheless, General Sherman, having traversed much of the heavily-vined, tree-entangled swampland, concluded that the Black Bayou and Deer Creek areas were not places suitable for an infantry and pronounced them useless as military channels.[71]

From the south side of DeSoto Point on March 22, Admiral Farragut advised General Grant that the Confederates in Warrenton were building "a very formidable case-mated work"—a heavily fortified, armored fortress wall. The day prior, Farragut had fired on the Confederate guns there with negligible effects. With Admiral Porter having been ensnared at Rolling Fork, Grant and Farragut had been communicating directly and had decided to cooperate in taking Warrenton.[72]

Diary - March 23, 1863

A couple of shots were fired over this way this evening. Steele's Division went down the levee this evening, bound for Warrenton. A wharf boat was burned at Warrenton on the 21st by Farragut's gunboats.

---

[*] In his official report dated March 29, 1863, General Sherman cited two deaths, relying on his subordinates to tally the other casualties of which there were few. Colonel Hoge reported no casualties for the 113th Illinois. (*Official Records*, Series 1, Vol. 24, Part 1, 436 and 441) Admiral Porter reported two sailors wounded and the death of one officer. (*ORN*, Series 1, Vol. 24, 478)

Rapidly losing faith in the canal's usefulness,[73] Grant hoped that he might be able to extract some value from the colossal project by sending troops to help silence the guns menacing the canal. Grant directed General Frederick Steele to send two of his regiments to the east side of the DeSoto peninsula to help Farragut take out the guns at Warrenton. The challenge Grant then faced was to arrange transportation to taxi Steele's troops across the Mississippi River. He would request assistance from his commander of the U.S. Army Ram Fleet, Brigadier General Alfred W. Ellet.

Diary - March 24, 1863
Rumors came this evening that Vicksburg has been evacuated.

By March 24, General Alfred Ellet had firmed up his plans. Within 24 hours, two rams would speed past the Vicksburg batteries, an adventure referred to as "running the gauntlet." A successful run would carry the warships past the wall of heavy guns atop the city's bluffs. Once beyond, they could assist in transporting Steele's two regiments across the river to Warrenton. After neutralizing Warrenton, the rams would steam south with Admiral Farragut to cut off Confederate supply lines at the Red River. Although General Ellet would orchestrate the expedition, family members would carry out the risky mission. The senior officer, Colonel Charles Rivers Ellet, not yet 20 years old, would lead the mission aboard the *USS Switzerland*. His cousin, Lieutenant John A. Ellet, would skipper the *USS Lancaster*. Although John was General Ellet's son, the general made it clear to his nephew that Charles could not stop to assist John if, for any reason, John's ram were to become disabled.[74] There was one more Ellet involved in the mission: Lieutenant Edward C. Ellet, the son of John's oldest brother. Edward would accompany Charles aboard the *Switzerland*.

The operation began at 4:30 A.M., March 25, the night sky still dark and clear with morning stars shining. The two rams quietly cast anchor from the docks at Young's Point, the *Switzerland* taking a lead position 200 yards ahead of the *Lancaster*, all lights aboard both vessels extinguished to avoid detection. Were it not for a gentle western breeze carrying the boiler sounds across the water, the Confederates might not have detected the two stealthy ships. But as the low rumbles drifted across the wide Mississippi waters, lantern signals flashed all along Vicksburg's formidable bluffs.

When the two ships came into view, the heavy Confederate guns burst alive. The determined warships managed to proceed to the immediate front of the batteries before balls ripped through both vessels. The first strike smashed through the *Switzerland's* boiler, its explosion stopping her engine and rendering her helplessly adrift. Moments later, a huge explosion erupted on the *Lancaster*. A shell had pierced her steam drum, enveloping her entirely in a fiery hot cloud. Men rushed from below to escape the blistering gasses as a second shell plunged through the hull, directly in the center near the bow, sinking the *Lancaster* almost instantly. With both ships devastated, the mission was abandoned. The guns at Warrenton continued to be a major threat—one that would prompt General Grant to reformulate his plans for taking Vicksburg.

Surprisingly, most of the lives of those onboard the ships were spared, despite the morning's violence. Three black workers who had been tending the boilers aboard the *Switzerland* died from severe scalding; one crew member, Orderly Sergeant William McDonald, on the *Switzerland,* had drowned; T.W.L. Kitson, the *Lancaster's* steersman, lost a foot, and about a half dozen other crew members had been badly scalded.[75]

Although word often traveled fast in the army, by the evening of March 25, Chatfield had received only scanty details about the calamity.

Diary - March 25, 1863
Two gunboats ran the blockade last night. One received a shot that sunk her.

Letter - March 25, 1863
Camp 113th Youngs point near Vicksburg. March 25th, 1863

Dear Father & Mother,

I have been reading over your old letters and I just thought that I would write you a few, although I have not received a letter for the last two weeks. My health still remains good as I could wish for, thanks to the protecting hand of the great giver of all good.

Our Reg't has been gone now 10 days & I do not know exactly where it is, although I think that they are quite a ways up the Yazoo. — We still remain in our old camp (that is we teamsters and wagon-guard and a few sick.)

Commodore Farraguts fleet has got up the river past fort Hudson, and they are ready to cooperate with our fleet and with Grants Army. There has been cannonadeing every day for the last two weeks, and sometimes it is very heavy. Some of the shells have been pitched right over this way. You cannot imagine what a dismal sensation a shell conveys to a person as one comes shrieking & screaming through the air. To one who has never been in such a place it is not very pleasant at any rate. Two of our gunboats ran the blockade last night, and there is rumors that one of them was sunk, but the news is not confirmed.

I will send you 10 dollars in this and I sent the same amount in a letter a week ago. As soon as you receive this please write and let me know. It is fine Spring weather. The grass is starting finely. The trees are all leaved out as much as they are in the middle of May up North. There has been a good deal of rain along back and the mud has been horible. But, the weather is getting more settled now. All of the boys were well when they went away. All of the sick have been sent up the river to Memphis, St. Louis, Mound City, Paducah and other Hospitals. Cap't Williams & Lieu't Jeffcoat are well. Lieut Becket is in command of the camp and what is left, now that the Reg't is gone. He is a real good and fine man. Is quite accommodating to the boys, moreso than the Cap't. We have got a new Major. Cap't [George R.] Clark of Co A has been promoted to that position. How I should like to just step in and surprise you some of these evenings, but that is impossible just now. To see your dear faces would give new courage and inspire new feelings. Oh, I hope that this terrible war will soon come to a close. How is the Conscription Act liked by the neighbors around there? I suppose that it makes the Copperheads howl and try to stir a disturbance, but it will do no good. The government is strong yet, and able to put down all of its enemies. Well, I must close. Give my respects to all inquiring friends reserving my love to yourselves. Kiss Mary and tell her and Charley that I will come home sometime. Direct the same as usual,

From your absent son Edward ———
Mr. N.S. Chatfield

According to the *Illinois Roster*, Captain Clark of Company "A" had listed his occupation as "Real Estate" when he volunteered in August 1862, at the age of 36. He was married and had children. Upon his March 1863 promotion to Major, while at Milliken's Bend, his occupation-listing had changed from "Real Estate" to "Lawyer." Within six months, Major Clark would be promoted to Lieutenant Colonel. In his letters and diary entries, Chatfield provides ongoing updates of George R. Clark's activities.

Diary - March 26, 1863
William Wurts died today on the hospital boat Nashville at Milliken's Bend.

The *Illinois Roster* lists Private William Wurts as having died on March 31, but Chatfield had recorded Wurts's death on March 26.

Diary - March 27, 1863
The boys got back this evening from their trip up the Yazoo.

Diary - March 28, 1863
There was more heavy cannonading down by Warrenton this morning.

Diary - March 29, 1863
A very hard storm came up tonight. The wind sounded like a perfect tornado. It blew almost all of our tents down.

Letter - March 29, 1863
Youngs point, La Sunday, March 29th / '63

Dear Father & Mother,

Although I have not received [a letter] for some time, the last one that got here on the 12th, I have written three or four letters since. So, I think that you will get some of them. I wrote one on the 21st & another on the 25th. In each of which I put in ten dollars ($10.) which, if you receive, you can make the best use of that you think best. My health keeps first rate, so, that I can eat my rations with a good apetite. [Loyal Blair] has been sick about 3 weeks. He had the brain fever but I think that he will get along now.* James Henry is rather unwell but not serious. John Blanchet is on one of the Hospitel Boats. I have not seen him for 3 weeks.

---

*   Chatfield remained hopeful about Corporal Loyal S. Blair, his 28-year-old friend from Limestone, an optimism he would maintain until early May.

Our boys have got back from their trip. They went up the Yazoo to relieve some gunboats, 5 in number, which had got up a small bayou and could not back out on account of the Rebels who had surrounded them. They had ~~that is scr~~ a skirmish with the Rebels and drove them back. Our company was in the skirmish. None of them were hit, however, although the balls whistled pretty lively. When they came back they brought a lot of cotton mules & Negroes. They said that the corn was about 4 inches high. There was one whole plantation of 600 acres planted to corn. They destroyed every thing they came to. Every thing is about the same that it has been for some time. I am afraid that before Vicksburg is taken that it will be a good while, and that there will be a good many lives lost. The Rebels are strongly fortified and have a large force. They have every avenue of approach strongly fortified, but I think that our Generals will overpower them in the end. I will send by this a dollar ($1.00) and I wish that you would get some stamps and send them to me. They are very scarce here. Some of the boys have given 10 cts for one. There is plenty of postage Currency for change but no stamps. Send 50 cts in each letter. I will write a few lines to David. Give my respects to (all the gals) I remain as ever your son. Edward.

Dear Brother David, Well old long legs, what is the matter with you? Are not sick I hope? For unless you are really sick I shall think that you are lazy. What are you a doing nowadays and what are the news? I suppose that you have fine times going to see the (Old maid) if no one else. Mrs. Lerne writes that there is only one young gentleman in the Neighborhood, John Bragan. I suppose that she forgot you. Now David, I remind you that you owe me a letter that you have not written yet.

I remain as ever your loving Brother
Edward

Diary - March 30, 1863

William Scoon got back to the company today. He had been in the Mound City hospital. I got a letter from Cousin Isaac W. Chatfield today.

William Scoon, age 21, had two brothers: James (also age 21 and likely a twin), and John (age 18). James was a sergeant. William and John were privates. Unmarried farm boys from Martinton Township of Iroquois County, all three siblings survived the war.

During his 18-month stint with the 27th Illinois, Chatfield's cousin, Isaac Willard Chatfield, developed recurrent kidney and bladder infections, a chronic debilitating condition that forced him to resign following the battle of Stones River, a three-day fight in Rutherford County, Tennessee. Stones River was one of the bloodiest battles of the war, with 23,000 casualties, 13,000 of whom were Yankees. Isaac Willard Chatfield mustered out as a First Lieutenant on February 19, 1863.

Diary - March 31, 1863
Flooding prevented me from getting to the boats. Another man in the company died today.

Although no March 31 deaths in the 113th are listed in the *Illinois Roster*, two men in the regiment are listed as having died on March 30: Private Maurice Higgins, 24, of Company "H" and Private John Runyon, 26, of Company "E". Both were farmers. Runyon was from Cuba, Lake County, Illinois. Higgins was from Kankakee Township, near Chatfield's home.

Diary - April 1, 1863
Today is April Fools' Day. Company B went on picket this morning while the 127th and several other regiments moved farther up the levee to a better camp.

Diary - April 2, 1863
I cleaned up my gun and other accoutrements this morning. We underwent Grand Reviewing this afternoon by General Stuart. Two brigades were on the ground. I received a letter from Twinsburg.

On April 4, General David Stuart, a man highly regarded by Sherman, was relieved from command of the Second Division. The Senate, after reviewing some "old affair at Chicago," had declined Stuart's nomination for brigadier-general. Having resigned his commission as colonel, Stuart was out of the service. General Grant replaced Stuart with Major-General Frank P. Blair.[76]

Diary - April 3, 1863
A very strong battery is being built down on the Point aiming towards Vicksburg. It is being bomb proofed. George T. Van Valkenberg died today of the small pox.

CHAPTER 13: DISAPPOINTMENTS AT DESOTO POINT

"Well, the water has washed the levee nearly away..."

Diary - April 4, 1863
Our regiment was ordered to move this evening to the top of the levee.

Diary - April 5, 1863
I finished hauling all of the tents and stores up from the old camp this afternoon. The officers are more scared than hurt about the levee breaking.

<u>Letter</u> - April 5, 1863
Youngs point, La. Sunday April 5th / 63

Dear Parents,

It being the holly Sabbath and I have a little time, I will try and write a few lines to lett you know how we get along, and what we are doing. In the first place, I am enjoying good health as I ever did and can eat my allowance without any trouble. I weigh the most now that I ever did, my weight being 150. We have plenty to do to keep us out of mischeif, hauling rations and wood and moving about from one place to another. (You doubtless remember that I am detailed to go with the wagons now, and have been with them for the last two months.) You know that we have been digging a ditch or canal. We had to build a levee on the land side about ten feet high in order to keep the water in its place. Well, the water has washed the levee nearly away for a short distance and threatened to break through. So we were all ordered on to the old main Levee, out of reach of the water. We had just got our camp in tolerable order again. I was at work all the forenoon. You know that we have no Sunday in the army. There was a flag of truce came up the river from Vicksburg yesterday afternoon, and one of our transports went down and met them. And there was another one this forenoon. I have not learned what either of them were for, although it is said the one yesterday wanted to exchange one of Gen. Smiths Orderlies (which is a prisoner) for one of their officers. It has been nearly a month since got a letter from you, during which time I have written 4 or 5; in two of which I put $10 each, and in another, $1.00 which I sent for some stamps. I wish that as soon as you receive them you would let me know, as for the money if you do not need it. I think that it be a good plan to get some young stock yeerling calves. It may be. Every thing is very high here. Flower is worth $10.00 per Bbl., apples $15, potatoes $8, & onions 5 dollars per bbl, Cheese 35 cts, butter 50, eggs 50 cts per doz. and every thing else in proportion. Mother, you felt so bad because I had no vest. I will send you a piece of one that I wore out this winter. The boys are as well as usual, that is, what remain of them. Loyal has been sent up the river. John Blanchet is at Memphis. Milton Rounsavell has gone up the river to. They said that he was poisoned but I think that he had the Dropsy.* Well, my sheet is full and I must close.

I remain as ever, Edward ———

Wednesday April 8th — By mistake my letter is not sent. There was a flag of truce went down this forenoon. In fact there is one almost every day.

[Continuing on the side of letter] Now dear parents, I want to establish a regular mail line to run every week. Our Regt. is at work on the canal at Milliken's bend today. They go up on the boat in the morning and come back at night. Distance 8 miles.

Diary - April 6, 1863

The levee broke last night at 9:00 o'clock. The water rushed through the break so fast that in 4 hours it was up to our camp 1½ miles away. I, with the teamsters, had

---

* Fluid retention, probably causing the legs to swell

my tent on the flat. We all had to turn out at 3:00 a.m. and move up onto the levee. We've been busy today pitching our tents and arranging things. Our regiment and brigade went up to Milliken's to work on the canal. They just returned at dark.

Diary - April 7, 1863

Another brigade went to work on the canal today. The levee is lined with peddlers of all kinds.

Diary - April 8, 1863

Our brigade and regiment went up to Milliken's, again this morning. A flag of truce came down this afternoon, and the boys got back at 5:00.

Diary - April 9, 1863

We commenced moving again this morning. They drained the hay and grain first, and I stayed and guarded it all day.

Diary - April 10, 1863

It took all day to finish moving. Riley Beach got back this morning.

Diary - April 11, 1863

We've been busy all day drawing water and wood, etc.

Letter - April 12, 1863
Youngs point, La Sunday, April 12ᵗʰ / 63

To the Dear Ones at home,

I was much pleased by the arrival of your long looked for letter which I rec'd Friday of the 31ˢᵗ Ult.* I had been looking for a letter for some time. Riley Beach & Richard McGraggory [McGreggor] came down on the same boat. They said that they left Chicago friday and they reached here just one week after. We have been pretty busy for the last two weeks. We have moved twice. First, onto the levee out of the reach of the water, and the last time to a nice camp where we are now situated where we are pleasantly situated with plenty room to drill and other purposes. The weather has been quite warm and pleasant for some time. There was quite a hard shower last night. It has cleared up again today and it is quite warm and every thing looks green while by far of nature looks very cheerful to one who looks upon it in the light of a Christian.

---

* Chatfield uses the abbreviation "Ult" multiple times, the Latin abbreviation for "ultimo" meaning "last month." On one occasion he wrote, "Ul-time," meaning, "last time."

Dear mother — you mentioned about sending me some things. If you could send me some paper envelopes & stamps. I would like by some one that is coming through direct. It might do. But I do not think it would be best to send any other way. As for Hand kerchiefs, I have a good supply. You know that we are in an enemies country and any thing that we can get our hands on very naturally finds its way into our possession. There is nothing that you can send me that I need. I have a plenty of every thing, more, in fact, than I can carry. So, dear parents, do not be uneasy on my part. I think that the health of the boys is gaining. We have, as it were, gone through the fire and have come out purified. For all that is left now will stand it. Our coming down here last fall was the best thing that has been done. We have become acclimated to the climate. While in bringing the new troops into the field, a great many will be swept away, like chaff by the many diseases to which this part of the country is inherent. They have been mustering the troops of this division within the last two days to find out the number of men we have preparatory to filling up our reg'ts with conscripts. I think that every[thing] has been for the best [including] my coming, as I did, in enlisting last fall. If I had not enlisted last fall there would have been no chance to have enlisted since, and I surely should have been drafted. I did not get William's letter yet. I sent some letters with money in them. I do not know whether you have rec'd them or not. Two letters with $10 each and one with $1.00. The Paymaster is paying the Reg'ts around us up to the 1st of March. We expect to be paid shortly. Dear Mother, we have been in no danger of being drowned at all, and there has been no soldiers drowned that I know of. The levee has broken, I know, but the water is not over 3 feet in any place.

Well, my sheet is full and I must close. I will send a flock of Grandpa's hair [David Herrick, Chatfield's mother's father] which he sent me, which I wish you to keep. Direct the same as before.

I remain as ever your loving son,

Edward

Riley Beach (misspelled "Beech" in the *Illinois Roster*) was not with the regiment when it left Camp Hancock on its way to Cairo, and later, Memphis. Seriously ill with the bilious fever, he remained up north, hospitalized near home and under the close watch of his father. Two years younger than Chatfield, Beach was only 18 when he enlisted from Limestone Township. Although five months had passed, Beach was still recovering when he arrived at Young's Point to join his company. His frail appearance led the boys to josh that they would have to plant him "… in the levee before a month passed."[77] Private Richard McGreggor of Company "H", also recovering from illness, was a 19-year-old farm boy from Limestone when he enlisted. Failing to regain his health, McGreggor's life would end in Corinth, Mississippi, on August 9, 1863, at the age of twenty, a victim of disease.

Diary - April 14, 1863
We had some very hard rain last night. The tent leaked very badly. I went 1½ miles and got a load of wood. The roads were very bad.

Three Union gunboats attacked the *Queen of the West* on April 14, 1863, while in the open waters of Grand Lake, near what is today Morgan City, Louisiana.[78] The object of the attack was to recapture her, but one of the shells set her ablaze and totally destroyed her. The noble *Queen of the West* was no more.

Diary - April 15, 1863
We went on a march today; the roads are drying. We saw some transports and gunboats being fixed up with hay. They are going to run the blockade.

Diary - April 16, 1863
The paymaster came today, and I got $52.00 and $1.50 more for my work done last fall. All was received of Captain Williams.

After more than two months of backbreaking effort to alter the course of a great river, Grant felt convinced that the canal experiment was futile:

> Even if the canal had proven a success, so far as to be navigable for steamers, it could not have been of much advantage to us. It runs in a direction almost perpendicular to the line of bluffs on the opposite side, or east bank, of the river. As soon as the enemy discovered what we were doing he established a battery commanding the canal throughout its length. This battery soon drove out our dredges, two in number, which were doing the work of thousands of men. Had

the canal been completed it might have proven of some use in running transports through, under the cover of night, to use below; but
they would yet have to run batteries, though for a much shorter
distance.

— Ulysses S. Grant[79]

Grant sought a new plan for taking Vicksburg. All of his previous attempts to take the
city had been fruitless: the Central Mississippi Expedition, the battle of Chickasaw
Bayou, the canal experiment, and most recently, the Black Bayou Expedition. He
needed a foothold on the land and simply hadn't been able to achieve one from the
west side of the city. He concluded that he must approach the city, once again, from
the east side. He realized, however, that if he were to return his forces north to
Memphis to reach the east side of Vicksburg, Washington would view his actions as
a retreat. He therefore determined that he would move toward Vicksburg by marching south, although the risk would be great. His gunboats and transports would be
required on the south side of Vicksburg in support of the troops. There seemed to
be no way to avoid the inevitable: a sizable fleet of warships and transports would
have to attempt to run the gauntlet.

Per Grant's orders, sailors had been toiling all week to ready three transports, the
Silver Wave, the *Forest Queen*, and the *Henry Clay*. They filled barges full of coal and
covered their decks and sides with bales of hay. They then lashed the barges to
the sides of the *Lafayette*, *Louisville*, *Mound City*, *Pittsburgh*, *Carondelet* and *Tuscumbia*.
In lieu of a lashed barge, the *Benton*, Admiral Porter's boat, was flanked by a tug.
There was no moon at all to light the river, darkness a friend at 11:16 on the night
of April 16. With Porter on the *Benton* leading his procession of five barge-strapped
gunboats, three transports, and the *Tuscumbia* at the rear, the encumbered flotilla
entered the majestic river bend faced by the city, exposing the fleet's presence to
the mighty guns across the river.[80] The Confederate batteries quickly opened, the
concussions so powerful that they were said to have extinguished lighted candles in
Union tents on the Point.[81] Sherman recalled the night's events.

> As soon as the Rebel gunners detected the *Benton*, which was in
> the lead, they opened on her, and on the others in succession, with
> shot and shell; houses on the Vicksburg side and on the opposite
> shore were set on fire, which lighted up the whole river; and the
> roar of cannon, the bursting of shells, and finally the burning of the
> *Henry Clay*, drifting with the current, made up a picture of the terrible
> not often seen. Each gunboat returned the fire as she passed the
> town, while the transports hugged the opposite shore. — General
> Tecumseh Sherman[82]

Diary - April 17, 1863

A fleet of transports and gunboats ran the blockade last night. One gunboat was sunk. I went to the supply boats twice today and got some hay. I had my likeness taken today and sent it home along with a letter via the chaplain [Rankin] who starts north tomorrow.

To keep Pemberton occupied and to divert his resources, Grant had arranged for a series of raids to begin on April 17. Exiting La Grange (49 miles east of Memphis) that day, Colonel Benjamin Grierson led a 1,700-man cavalry on a mission to raid the state of Mississippi, tear up its railroads, free its slaves, burn its buildings, and inflict casualties wherever possible, forcing Pemberton at Vicksburg to come after him. The plan worked. Pemberton sent out an entire division.[83]

Letter - April 17, 1863
Youngs point, La Friday, April 17th / 63.

Dear parents —

As I write this to you, the sound of the Booming Cannon jar's on my ear, and tells me that this is no childs play that we are engaged in. For several days past there have been preparations making to send some gunboats and transports down the river. They put bales of hay all around the transports and other ways fixed them so as to secure the boilers. Last night they were all ready. 4 transports & 9 gunboats. At Midnight they started in solemn procession one after the other. As they neared the Rebel batteries the Rebs opened upon them with shot and shell. It was a terriffic sight to behold, but they kept underway. The Rebs, however, knocked a hole in one of the transports, the *Henry Clay*, and sunk her. All of her crew got of [off] safe. There was 9 men killed and few wounded in the affair. Today there is heavy cannonadeing which we can plainly hear. The Paymaster gave us a call yesterday and the fecuniary result of it was that my pocket is $52.00 heavier than it was before. We are now paid up to the first of march. Our chaplain [Rankin] is going North, and I think that I will send my money, that is fifty dollars $50.00 of it, by him. He will leave it at Parkers or Perry the County Clerk. He has gone today to see if he can get a permit of [off] Gen Grant. There has been some change of Officers in our Brigade Division. Gen David Stuart has been relieved by Gen Frank Blair. Blair is quite an energetic looking man. There is some talk that Blair's Division was ordered

136
The Chatfield Story: Civil War Letters and Diaries of
Private Edward L. Chatfield of the 113th Illinois Volunteers

to Texas. If that is so, why, we will be sure to go. Mother! I thought that I could please you a little & so I went this PM and had my likeness taken. The boys all say that it looks very natural! And I think that it does to, if I am any judge. My health still remains good, so, that I have no reason to complain at any rate. The boys are all usually well. We are getting acclimated to the Climate so that what is left of us stand at first rate. Oh, how I long for the time when we can all see each other face to face and speak with the natural voice instead of the silent pen. Oh, pray that we all may be spared to see each [other] in this visible world. But, if we are not permitted to meet on the shores of time, I hope and pray that we may all meet on that blessed shore where parting will be no more.

The Chaplain has been up to Millikens bend today and has got permission from Gen Grant to go up north. He will carry the mail and our Money. Now, as soon as you get the money, please write. My love to all the children and a good share for Father and Mother.

From your dutiful son,
E L. Chatfield.

Diary - April 18, 1863
The chaplain started home this morning. Two more batteries are being planted on the levee and two more in front of General Blair's headquarters. There has been some cannonading from below today.

Diary - April 19, 1863
We had a hard rain last night. Even though today is the Sabbath, there has been plenty of gambling in camp. They pay no regard to the Sabbath. I helped draw two loads of water for the regiment and sent a letter home via Lieut. Col. Paddock.

Letter - April 19, 1863
Youngs point. La. Sabbath Eve, April 19th / 63.

Dear Mother.
Although I wrote you a letter last friday, I thought must write a few additional lines which I will send by Lieut Colonel Paddock who starts North tomorrow,

if I am rightly informed. O how I long for the peaceful quiet Sabbaths which we used to spend when we were all at home. When, we would get up in the morning and prepare ourselves for Church or Sabbath school as it might be. But now we are separated, and no one knows but the great giver of all good whether we shall ever be permitted to see each other again in this world. Oh let us pray that every thing may be for the best. The way that the Sabbath is spent in the Army is shocking in the extreme. Here is a group gambling, worse than throwing away their money, cursing and swearing. There is another around drinking and carousing. It is enough to make ones heart sick. But enough of this. Let us turn to something else. Our boys are kept busy most of the time on guard, fatigue duty or drill. The Officers are perfecting their Regts in drill as fast as possible. For we expect shortly to have work to do and they want to be ready for it. There is some more boats going to run the blockade tonight, it is said. I sent $50.00 to father by the Chaplain [Rankin] which he will leave with Parker (that is, if he should go through safe.) Loyal, John Blanchet & Milton Rounsaville are 8 miles above here at Millikens Bend in the Hospital. They are all getting better.

The Captain [Cephas Williams] was up to see them yesterday. Our Major [George R. Clark] is making himself very officious. He is not all liked by any of the boys. Our Colonel [John W. Paddock] is liked better & better all of the time. He is showing himself the man. He is provost Marshal and is president of the Court Martial that is progressing now. Well Mother, I do not know as I can think of anything more to write at present. The drums are beating for roll call and it is almost bedtime, and I must close. From your affectionate son,

Edward ———-

To Mrs Margaret Chatfield

P.S, Tell David that he must not forget to write occasionally. He will have time enough Sundays if he cant get any other time. My love to Mary and all the boys. E.L.C. ——

For reasons unexplained, the boys referred to Corporal Milton Rounsavell as "Uncle Fuller."[84] Rounsavell was a 24-year-old unmarried farm boy from Limestone Township when he enlisted as a corporal. Milton would become one of Edward's life-long friends. The correct way to spell Milton's last name was a puzzle back then. Chatfield sometimes spelled it "Rounsaville" and the Illinois Roster spelled it "Ronnsaville." Milton finally settled the issue when he spelled his name "Rounsavell" on the penny post card that he sent Chatfield many years later.

By April 20, Grant had made his plan explicit. He would march his divisions south of Vicksburg, cross the river, advance north, and return to Vicksburg from the east. The divisions would cross the Mississippi River at or below New Carthage.

138
The Chatfield Story: Civil War Letters and Diaries of
Private Edward L. Chatfield of the 113th Illinois Volunteers

HEADQUARTERS DEPARTMENT OF THE
TENNESSEE, MILLIKEN'S BEND, LOUISIANA
April 20, 1863 Special Order No. 110

The following orders are published for the information and guidance of the "Army in the Field," in its present movement to obtain a foot-hold on the east bank of the Mississippi River, from which Vicksburg can be approached by practicable roads.

1. The Thirteenth army corps, Major-General John A. McClernand commanding, will constitute the right wing.
2. The Fifteenth army corps, Major-General W.T. Sherman commanding, will constitute the left wing.
3. The Seventeenth army corps, Major-General James B. McPherson commanding, will constitute the centre.
4. The order of march to New Carthage will be from right to left.

....

MAJOR-GENERAL U.S. GRANT.[85]

Diary - April 20, 1863

Dan and I drew more water for the regiment today. Then I did some washing. Milton Rounsaville came back from the hospital today. The river has fallen several inches at the landing. The battery down on the Point is vigorously at work shelling Vicksburg. Colonel Paddock started up the river for home today.

The previous July, Congress had given President Lincoln the authority to use black troops. To help assure cooperation from white soldiers, the generals at Milliken's Bend announced that black regiments would soon be operating within the area.

Diary - April 21, 1863

We went for more water, but our wagon broke down. Then the whole of the 2nd Division was formed in a hollow square in front of the 6th and 8th Missouri and was addressed by Generals Thomas, Sherman, and Blair on the subject of forming the Negroes into regiments. Their speeches were unanimously received.

Diary - April 22, 1863

We went to the landing this morning and were given 10 days' rations. I got a letter from Aunt Zipporah this evening. Illinois Governor Yates is visiting us at Milliken's Bend.

Twenty-nine-year-old Aunt Zipporah Herrick Eells was Chatfield's mother's youngest sister. She lived in Waukon, Iowa. She had been widowed on December 5, 1862, when her husband, Samuel Eells, died after serving his 47th day of military service for the state of Iowa. He was a 30-year-old private in Company "F" of the Iowa 6th Cavalry when disease took his life while he was hospitalized in Davenport, Iowa. Zipporah would marry again but would never bear children.

Diary - April 23, 1863

Six more transports ran the blockade last night. There was very heavy firing. The Tigress was sunk. We went to the boats twice this morning, first for hay, then for the sutler's goats. I wrote a letter to Grandmother Lucy this evening, then packed a box of clothing.

Porter had run a large supply flotilla past the batteries on the night of April 22. The sunken *Tigress* was the side-wheel steamer that had served as quarters for General McClernand in January. Reports and updates of Grant's progress clicked their way by telegraph to Washington:

OFFICIAL CORRESPONDENCE

Young's Point, La., April 23, 1863

Edwin M. Stanton, Secretary of íWar

SIR: Last night 6 steamers and 12 barges attempted to run the batteries at Vicksburg, about 11 p.m., when the moon went down. The first two steamers came within range, when heavy firing commenced. The *Tigress* received 15 shots, one in the stern, carrying off two planks. She rounded to at Johnson's plantation, 3.5 miles below Vicksburg, grounded, and sank, breaking amidships. She is a total loss. Crew all safe. ... The *Anglo-Saxon* passed comparatively safe.

The *Moderator* was badly cut up and had several wounded. She drifted by Warrenton batteries about 3:00 a.m. The *Horizon* passed Warrenton at daylight. The *Empire City* was totally disabled at Vicksburg, and was lashed at Johnson's plantation to the *Cheesman*, both of which were seen to pass Warrenton, where the fire was heavy, shortly after daylight. The barges designed to carry troops are supposed to have all passed. One pilot was mortally wounded in the abdomen and another person in the thigh, both of whom must have died shortly thereafter. ...

    Respectfully, L. Thomas, Adjutant-General

    [Brigadier General Lorenzo Thomas][86]

Having reconnoitered the sizable and rapidly growing Rebel forces at Grand Gulf for the past two days, Admiral Porter wrote to General Grant, subtly suggesting that landing farther south might be a good idea.

Flagship Benton,

Off New Carthage, April 23, 1863

    ... They are throwing in troops from Vicksburg as fast as they can by land, and bringing down guns, etc., as fast as they can by water. There are four forts in all, well placed, and mounting 12 large guns. They have been preparing this place six weeks, and have known all about this move; expected it sooner.

    ...They may have 12,000 troops at Grand Gulf, and still increasing the number.

    ... If the troops can get by we can land them below...on a road leading up to the fort. As you know your own plan, I won't pretend to offer any suggestions. ...

    Very respectfully, David D. Porter[87]

Diary - April 25, 1863

I secured a load of wood from 5 miles off; I actually had to swim for it. I started a letter to Father this evening.

Letter - April 25, 1863
Youngs point, La. Saturday Eve, April 25th, 1863

To my Parents,

I have been busy most all day and I thought I would [write] you a few lines to let you know what we are doing and how we get along. I recd your last welcome letter dated March 11th (but I guess that you meant April instead of march) in due time. I also recd yours of the 1st April all right. The boys all look first rate and are in fine spirit as well as myself. We are expecting to start on a trip in a day or two down the river, I think, to make some kind of demonstration in the rear of Vicksburg. So I can't tell where you will hear from me next. But, you may direct the same as before at any rate.

Us boys had put up some boxes to send home, but there was an order read on Dress parade this evening that all clothing that was not needed should be boxed up and left with the Quartermaster at Millikens Bend. So now, whether they will be sent home I can't tell. But if the box should be sent home, you will find it at Mr. Smiths. I will enclose a list of articles which I put up. If the box should go, you will find a package of my old letters which I wish Mother to take care of and not show them to every body.

Since I wrote my last there has been some more boats running the blockade, 9 transports in all. One was sunk & I somewhat disabled. The others were not materially injured. On the whole it was quite a successful adventure, there being a perfect storm of shot & shell rained down upon them. The firing was incessant for over four hours.

The weather is very pleasant and warm. The grass is 6 inches high. The trees are in full leaf. Corn a foot high. Flowers of all kinds (and there are very many very beautiful kinds) are in full bloom, and every thing in full proportion. There is number of Negro Reg'ts being got up in this part of the Country, and they [are] appointing white officers over them. Jeffcoat, I suppose, will be Lieut Col & Kellog & Titcomb will be Captains. They are to be mustered in as regulars for 5 years. Well, it is getting dark and I must close. I remain as ever your loving son, Edward Chatfield, To Mr NS Chatfield, Grand Prairie, Ill.

Diary - April 26, 1863

My turn to cook began this morning. Teamsters drew harnesses for their teams today; I have been busy today. We had pleasant weather today.

Diary - April 27, 1863

We had a heavy shower last night, and it rained almost all day today. There was heavy cannonading down at Vicksburg last night. I received a letter from Cousin Clark and finished a letter to Father.

On this day, Grant invited Sherman to conduct a "demonstration" at Haines' Bluff—a show of force with the object of deception—to draw Pemberton's troops north, away from Grant's river-crossing below Vicksburg. Grant was clearly mindful of the political harm that such an action could bring his friend, and suggested a way to counter it.

OFFICIAL CORRESPONDENCE

SMITH'S PLANTATION, La., April 27, 1863

Major General WILLIAM T. SHERMAN, Comdg. Fifteenth Army Corps:

If you think it advisable, you may make a reconnaissance of Haines' Bluff, taking as much force and as many steamers as you like. Admiral Porter told me that he would instruct Captain Breese [Flag Captain, K. Randolph Breese] to do as you asked him with his fleet. The effect of a heavy demonstration in that direction would be good so far as the enemy are concerned, but I am loth to order it, because it would be so hard to make our own troops understand that only a demonstration was intended, and our people at home would characterize it as a repulse. I therefore leave it to you whether to make such a demonstration. If made at all, I advise that you publish your order beforehand, stating that a reconnaissance in force was to be made for the purpose of calling off the enemy's attention from our movements south of Vicksburg, and not with any expectation of attacking. I shall probably move on Grand Gulf to-morrow.

U.S. GRANT[88]

Diary - April 28, 1863

Some of the troops in this division have now been ordered to Milliken's Bend.

Diary - April 29, 1863

The entire 1st Brigade moved onto the boats, except the 113th. We were left behind to do guard duty. They are going up the Yazoo. Four of our teams were ordered away this evening, carrying rations for the division. The boys feel pretty well.

Sherman had done as Grant suggested, his explanation of the exercise circulated among his officers before they moved off on the boats. The 113th remained in camp on picket to witness the departure of McClernand's corps marching south to construct a road to New Carthage. Meanwhile, on the Mississippi, Porter bombarded the Grand Gulf batteries for five hours in an unsuccessful attempt to silence them. By nightfall, Grant concluded that a crossing at Grand Gulf would invite catastrophe, and he ordered the troops to march farther south, crossing over to Bruinsburg. By April 30, only Sherman's corps remained to defend DeSoto Point.

Diary - April 30, 1863

Our regiment was placed on picket this morning, and we had a great scare in camp today. The rumor was that a large force of Rebels had landed on this side of the river, but it was a false rumor. Heavy cannonading came from the direction of Old River.

From well over five miles away, Chatfield had heard Sherman's demonstration. Positioning his brigade along the delta between the Old River and the Chickasaw Bayou—as he had done with his division on Christmas Day—Sherman commenced firing on Walnut Hills, the thunder of cannon clearly audible from the canal at DeSoto Point.

Diary - May 1, 1863

News came that our forces have taken Haines' Bluffs and Walnut Hills. Our company was ordered to fall in at 6:00 p.m. upon word of Rebels crossing to this side.

Chatfield would soon learn that the activity at Haines' Bluff was merely a demonstration, and that May 1 was actually the first day that Union forces fought after crossing the Mississippi south of Vicksburg. The action erupted on the road to Port Gibson, about eight miles above Bruinsburg. Generals McPherson and John A. Logan gained a field advantage, driving the Rebels back. General Grant summarized the Union victory at Port Gibson:

> The enemy was here repulsed with a heavy loss in killed, wounded, and prisoners. The repulse of the enemy on our left took place late in the afternoon. He was pursued toward Port Gibson, but night closing in, and the enemy making the appearance of another stand, the troops slept upon their arms until daylight. In the morning it was found that the enemy had retreated across Bayou Pierre.
> — Gen. U.S. Grant[89]

CHAPTER 14: THE LONG MARCH BEGINS

*"Our brigades, the 1ˢᵗ and the 2ⁿᵈ, were ordered to fall in
without knapsacks to go to Grand Gulf."*

Diary - May 2, 1863
We were awakened before daylight and received orders to move up to Milliken's
Bend. We spent the night on a boat named the Harry Bullitt.

Diary - May 3, 1863
We moved up the river 3 miles and pitched our tents. Loyal Blair died today of
brain fever on board the hospital boat. We were mustered for pay, then marched
to the boats at 10:00 p.m. and steamed down to the levee and landed. The Rebs
had destroyed two barges and a tug. They knocked a hole in the boiler and blew
her up.

Only two months earlier, Chatfield's close friend Loyal Blair was "well and tough
as a bear." Blair had grown ill after March 1, but having received word of Blair's
improvement in mid-April, Chatfield had been anticipating the return of his chum
within days. The May 3 news of Blair's death was totally unexpected. Chatfield
could barely write about the loss, preferring to move on to the calamitous events
that occurred off DeSoto Point that evening—the two barges and steam tug that

were destroyed while attempting to run past Vicksburg's mighty guns. The barges had been loaded with supplies needed by the troops that had marched south from Milliken's Bend to Hard Times, Louisiana. Hard Times—a plantation almost directly across from Grand Gulf, Mississippi—would be used by the Union as a staging area and forward supply depot. Aboard one of the barges rode four influential news correspondents who were captured by the Rebels during the episode. The disaster that occurred on the night of May 3 initiated a nasty behind the scenes tug-of-war that wouldn't be settled until shortly before the war's end. CS General Pemberton was the first to write about the four correspondents.

OFFICIAL CORRESPONDENCE
Vicksburg, May 4, 1863
General S. COOPER, Richmond:

> Last night two large barges, laden with hospital and commissary stores, with [a] small tug between them, attempted to pass here; were burned to the water's edge, and 24 prisoners taken from them, among whom were one correspondent from the *New York World,* two [from the] *New York Tribune*, and one from the *Cincinnati Times*.
> — J.C. PEMBERTON [90]

Richard T. Colburn of the *New York World* was released within a few days, his paper's editorials occasionally critical of Lincoln. It's not known what became of the *Cincinnati Times* correspondent. He may have been injured and eventually released as well. But the two correspondents from the *New York Tribune*, A.D. Richardson and Janius H. Browne, were transferred to the Libby Prison in Richmond, Virginia.[91] *The New York Tribune* was a friend of Lincoln, and anyone who was a friend of Lincoln was a foe of Jefferson Davis.[92]

Diary - May 4, 1863
We got back from our trip at 6:00 in the morning without seeing any Rebs. Company A Wagoner, Jim Martin, was ordered to go with the division teams to New Carthage with provisions.

Jim Martin, a blue-eyed, unmarried farmer, was a 22-year-old French Canadian who had resided in Chicago when he volunteered for service. Wagoners were essential to an effective army, responsible for the ammunition, cooking utensils, food, and supplies that would travel with the troops. Martin was responsible for moving the supplies of Company "A". He was also tasked with maintaining the wagons and caring for the horses and mules used to pull the wagons.

Letter #1 - May 4, 1863
Millikens Bend, May 4th 1863.

Dear Father & Mother,

Your very welcome letter of the 26th Apr was duly rec'd yesterday, and its contents speedily consumed. I was glad to learn that although Mother had had so many sick ones to take care of she did not get sick herself, which I was afraid would be the case. The weather is getting pretty warm, being equal to any of the hottest days in July, which is almost enough to swelter any one that has to be out on duty. Since I wrote you my last, which was I week ago yesterday (which was Sunday) there has been a considerable stir among us here. In the first place, a very heavy force has been sent down to New Carthage, which is on the Red River oposite the Mississippi shore, and have commenced operations against Vicksburg in that direction. While, there has been a strong force sent up the Yazoo to attack Haines Bluffs and so draw the attention of the Rebs from the real main point of attack. In taking away so many troops as they have for these expeditions, it left a pretty small force at Youngs point and there was danger of the secesh crossing over from Vicksburg and bagging us. So it they ordered us to move to Millikens Bend where we are now encamped in a very nice field with a hedge fince all around it, while a short distance from the camp, is the Mansion of the Estate which is used as a hospital. We were busy all day yesterday (which was Sabbath) in moving to our camp from the boats and pitching our tents. At nine oclock in the evening we were mustered for pay. They always muster on the last day of every other month, but the last few days had been so busy that we did not have time. At 10 oclock last night, the drums beat to fall in. And so, of course, I fell in with the rest. We marched down to the boats and went aboard. We went down the river to the canal across youngs point, which is a little below where we used to be encamped, and landed, when we found out, for the first time, that they were a going to run the Blockade. And it was supposed that the Rebels had sent over a force on to this side, and they had sent us to drive them back. For it was feared that unless we had a force down there that if any of the boats were disabled they would fall into the hands of the Rebels. And so we started down the Levee at the same time the boats started that were to run the gauntlet, which were two coal barges loaded with provisions and army stores towed by a little tug covered with cotton & hay. As they came within range of their guns they pitched in. Our boats kept on quite gallantly on till at last a shot struck the boilers of the tug and she blowed up and set the barges on fire, which were entirely consumed. The crew were all scalded, drowned, and taken prisoners except one who swam to shore. We returned to camp, which we reached about one hour after sunrise after having a hard nights work marching through mud knee deep and expecting to meet the enemy at every step. — I am all right, getting along first rate, hearty as a buck, and tough as a horse. Why, I have got so you would not recognize me.

I suppose that poor Loyal is no more. News came to camp that he was dead. He has been sick since the first of March and had apretty hard time of it. He was on the Hospital which lies here at the bend. He had the Inflamation on the Brain with the Diareah. I hear also that Frank Houghton [Huton] is dead. He was wounded at the battle of the Post & was sent up the river. I have not heard what caused his death.

I suppose that you have heard of the Death of George Vanvalkinburgh [Van Valkenberg]. He died in St Louis. I hope that the children may all recover. It is a mother's care that alone can cheer the sick and do all the little things that if they are not attended to end fatally. If you could go through some of our Hospitals you could see enough to last for a long time. But to go through where our soldiers are buried, thousands upon thousands, it is heart rending to think what misery this war entails.

There is no use of sending papers for we get the papers later than we could by the mail. O that box that we were going to send home cannot go, so you need not look for it. I sent you my picture and $50.00 by the Chaplain [Rankin] which I suppose you have rec'd ere this. The picture the boys say is very natural. The Boys are all well and hearty and send you their best wishes and respects. Give my respects to all the people generally reserving my love to yourselves. Kiss Mary for me.

I remain as ever your loving son,

Edward Chatfield

Mr. N S Chatfield

Direct to Millikens Bend, La.

Letter #2 - May 4, 1863
Millikens Bend May 4th / 63.
Mr. Newton Chatfield

Dear Brother,

As you have taken the pains to write me a few lines, I will gladly answer your note. I thank you very much for thinking enough to write to me once in a while. You know, a soldier has pretty rough times, sometimes, and the greatest pleasure that I have is to get a letter from home. It is a real pretty place (or I should say a very nice country) about here (that is Millikens Bend.) There is some very nice houses and plantations with hedges, fruit and ornamental trees set out on them, and some of the prettiest flowers that you can find. There is straw berries and blackberries in abundance while the figs on the trees are about as large as hickory nuts. But, it is hard to think of the desolation of war. For whenever we leave a part of the country we burn every thing that will burn. Some of the finest houses I have seen committed to the flames. We have enough to eat, such as it is, but if we had more vegetables I would like it better.

I wish that this war was over. And what good times we will have. There is a man in our Reg't that is a spy. He has been all through the Rebel stronghold, and he think that we will all go home in the next six months. Well, I must close. Remember me.

From your Brother who loves you,
Edward L Chatfield

Clearly, soldiers' Civil War letters were not censored, as demonstrated by the above letters. They reveal in considerable detail Grant's intentions and strategies. The practice of mail censorship was not formally established until World War I.

Diary - May 5, 1863
George Sheldon was ordered to go to Carthage with provisions. Other teams got back this forenoon, but they have to go back again.

George W. Sheldon was a private from Chicago in Company "A". Like Chatfield, he tended teams. Sheldon would be disabled in less than a year and discharged on June 9, 1864, just two days before Chatfield would face his own challenging fate.

In an earlier letter, Chatfield bitterly complained about the Copperheads, Northerners who opposed the war, espousing his desire to "...make short work of them all." He wanted them silenced. On May 5, 1863, he got his wish, or at least part of it. Clement L. Vallandigham, an influential Copperhead and prior Ohio congressman, was arrested. He had violated General Ambrose E. Burnside's *General Order Number 38*, prohibiting non-combatants from declaring sympathies for the enemy. In a major speech on May 1, 1863, Vallandigham said that the war was being fought, "...not to save the Union but to free blacks and enslave whites." Union soldiers arrested him on May 5, and a *writ of habeas corpus* was denied.[*] A military trial commenced the following day, May 6; on May 7, the tribunal found Vallandigham guilty of voicing disloyal sentiments, sentencing him to 2 years' confinement in a military prison. Out of concern that Vallandigham would be martyred, President Lincoln eventually ordered him banished through the lines to Tennessee.[93]

Diary - May 6, 1863
Four hundred-fifty prisoners were brought in this afternoon. We put them on the D.G. Taylor.

The Union forces sent south were already taking Rebel prisoners along the way and sending them to the rear, a signal to Chatfield that he would soon be experiencing some major action.

Major General Frank P. Blair's 2nd Division, the last to leave Milliken's Bend, had three brigades: 1st Brigade, under Colonel Giles A. Smith, 2nd Brigade, under General Thomas Kilby Smith, and 3rd Brigade, under Brigadier General Hugh Ewing. Ewing and his brigade remained behind to garrison Milliken's Bend and to complete the construction of the road from Young's Point to a point below Warrenton. Ewing's challenge would be to catch up with the other two brigades by the time that they had reached Vicksburg.[94]

Diary - May 7, 1863
Our brigades, the 1st and the 2nd, were ordered to fall in without knapsacks to go to Grand Gulf. We took 10 days' rations and marched out at 9 a.m. Most of the way the country was very fine. We passed Richmond at 4:00 p.m. where about 150 Rebel prisoners were brought through on the way back to Milliken's Bend.

---

[*]   *Habeas Corpus* was the privilege specified in Article 1, Section 9 of the *U.S. Constitution* endorsing the English Common Law principle that a person could not be imprisoned without showing the courts just cause.

Governor Yates passed us at Richmond, addressed all the Illinois boys and was heartily cheered. We camped at sundown.

If the boys were told anything at all as to why they were to leave their knapsacks behind, they were likely advised that they would be making a very long march. There was no sense in carrying the extra weight. Perhaps they were even told that the knapsacks would eventually be brought forward to them. The commanders probably did not disclose the reason for marching to Grand Gulf.

Orderly Kellogg of Company "B" recalled the march, the sights, and the bedding: "That day we marched 14 miles and at night camped on a beautiful plantation and procured raw cotton from a nearby gin to sleep on."[95]

Riley Beach, who was still sick at the time of the march, remembered Kellogg's response to his request to join the march.

> The Orderly came to the tent. I told him that I wanted to go on the march. He said that the Captain said I couldn't go unless the Surgeon said I could. I went on sick call and told the Surgeon I wanted to go. He smiled broadly and said that a gust of wind would blow me away.
> — Private Riley Beach[96]

Chatfield rode as wagon guard. On May 8, the 113th halted for a meal on the banks of Brushy Bayou, Louisiana, then marched to a plantation belonging to a Confederate general, helping themselves to one of his steers. They covered 19 miles that day.[97]

Diary - May 8, 1863
We moved out a little after sunrise and passed many fine plantations and buildings. We passed the 72nd Illinois (or First Board of Trade) this evening. Dan Freeman and Jim Martin joined us this evening.

Dan Freeman and Jim Martin, like Chatfield, were wagoners—Freeman from Company "E" and Martin from Company "A". Freeman was a 34-year-old married farmer from Barrington, Illinois, and a native of Clay, New York. Martin, the 22-year-old French Canadian, would be carried away by disease within six months. The 72nd was the first regiment to be organized by the Chicago Board of Trade, hence the name of distinction. In eight days, the 72nd would fight its first battle at Champion Hill, Mississippi.

Diary - May 9, 1863
We pushed our wagons across very rough roads today and reached the Mississippi River at Perkin's Landing at 1:00 p.m. After dinner, we marched another 4 miles, then camped for the night.

While the healthier boys made their way south, the less healthy still had duties to perform at Young's Point, on the DeSoto peninsula, including efforts to convince observers on the bluffs that a strong force still remained.

There were 240 of us ordered down to the bend on the levee to watch and keep the Rebs from crossing the river. From there we could look over into Vicksburg, so near, yet so far. We were there on top of the levee for 24 hours, spread over our blankets, but not to sleep. The mortar boats were throwing 13-inch shells into the town every 15 minutes. — Private Riley Beach[98]

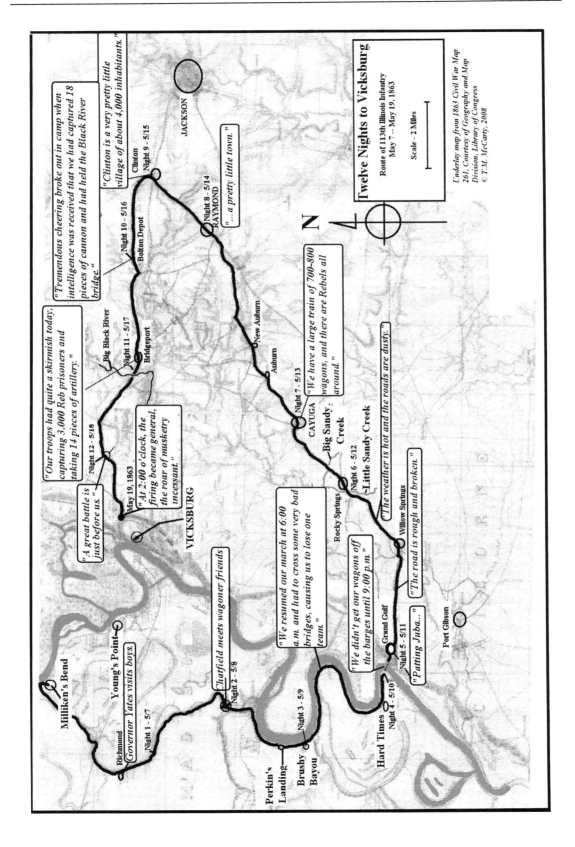

Twelve Nights to Vicksburg

Route of 113th Illinois Infantry
May 7 – May 19, 1863

Scale - 2 Miles

Underlay map from 1863 Civil War Map 261, Courtesy of Geography and Map Division, Library of Congress
© T.M. McCarty, 2008

JACKSON

"Tremendous cheering broke out in camp when intelligence was received that we had captured 18 pieces of cannon and had held the Black River bridge."

"Clinton is a very pretty little village of about 4,000 inhabitants."

Clinton
Night 9 - 5/15

Night 8 - 5/14
RAYMOND

"...a pretty little town."

Night 10 - 5/16
Bolton Depot

New Auburn

Auburn

Night 7 - 5/13
CAYUGA

"We have a large train of 700-800 wagons, and there are Rebels all around."

"Our troops had quite a skirmish today; capturing 3,000 Reb prisoners and taking 14 pieces of artillery."

Big Black River
Night 11 - 5/17
Bridgeport

Big Sandy Creek

Night 12 - 5/18

Little Sandy Creek

Night 6 - 5/12

"The weather is hot and the roads are dusty."

"At 2:00 o'clock, the firing became general, the roar of musketry incessant."

May 19, 1863

Rocky Springs

Willow Springs

"A great battle is just before us."

VICKSBURG

"The road is rough and broken."

N

"We resumed our march at 6:00 a.m. and had to cross some very bad bridges, causing us to lose one team."

Chatfield meets wagoner friends

Night 2 - 5/8

"We didn't get our wagons off the barges until 9:00 p.m."

Grand Gulf
Night 5 - 5/11

Port Gibson

"Patting Juba..."

Milliken's Bend

Richmond

Young's Point

Governor Yates visits boys.

Night 1 - 5/7

Perkin's Landing

Brushy Bayou

Night 3 - 5/9

Hard Times
Night 4 - 5/10

CHAPTER 15: FROM GRAND GULF TO VICKSBURG

*"We have a large train of 700 – 800 wagons,
and there are Rebels all around ..."*

Diary - May 10, 1863

We resumed our march at 6:00 a.m. and had to cross some very bad bridges, causing us to lose one team. We reached the river this evening below Perkin's Landing at what is called Grand Gulf. We camped for the night with a fine view of the river and Grand Gulf.

Chatfield and his regiment had reached Hard Times. To their east, across the Mississippi River, the Rebel forts on the bluffs above Grand Gulf had been abandoned. The Confederate soldiers there had been needed to defend at Port Gibson, Mississippi, where on May 1, Generals McPherson and McClernand had attacked—the first battle of resistance. On May 10, the two Union corps were heading north toward Raymond. The boys spent the night anticipating their ride across the river the following day.[99]

Diary - May 11, 1863

Four transports are busy here carrying troops across the river to the village of Grand Gulf. We went over this evening. The bluffs are 50 -100 feet above the river and give a very imposing appearance. We didn't get our wagons off the barge until 9:00 p.m. After that, we drew our wages for 15 days. I did not lie down to rest until midnight.

The regiment crossed from Hard Times to Grand Gulf on the gunboat *Louisville* at 4:00 P.M. The wagons were shipped across in the evening by barge. Once there, the local performers in the area provided entertainment for the newly arrived Union troops.

> The camp was full of happy contrabands who *patted juba* and danced nearly all night to the music of a cane instrument unlike any other musical instrument I ever saw.
> — Orderly Kellogg [100]

"Patting juba" was indeed an art form, but one that only marginally concealed black protest. The music and spirited dance helped preserve black culture, but the words themselves revealed anguish. Juba (jibba, jiba) was a stew containing a week's leftovers from the plantation-owner's house, discarded food either fed to the animals or given to the slaves.

> Juba this and Juba that
> Juba killed a yella' cat
> Get over double trouble, Juba . . .
> Juba up, Juba down,
> Juba all around the town,
> Juba for Ma, Juba for Pa,
> Juba for your brother-in-law. [101]

Diary - May 12, 1863

We were awakened at 3:00 a.m. to prepare to move. We started out at sunrise. The country is very rough and broken, but I feel first rate. I saw lots of Negroes all bound for Grand Gulf or Milliken's Bend, all presenting a very motley appearance. Water is scarce, the roads are very dusty, and the weather is very hot. All the land has been planted to corn. As we moved along the road, an occasional Reb showed himself in the distance.

Battle of Raymond

Leaving Grand Gulf, Chatfield's wagon train was 40 miles southeast of Raymond, where the second episode of Confederate resistance to Grant's presence on Mississippi soil was about to take place. The battle of Raymond erupted at about 10:00 A.M. Major General John A. Logan of General McPherson's 17th Corps faced off with Captain Hiram Bledsoe's Missouri battery and with the battle-hardened Confederate brigade of Brigadier General John Gregg. The battle ended around 4:00 P.M., with Gregg finally withdrawing.[102]

The tenacious battle at Raymond convinced Grant that he must attack Jackson before proceeding to Vicksburg.[103] Jackson, the capitol of Mississippi, was an important rail and communication center, a hub through which passed all manner of troops, machinery, and supplies—war-making capabilities that Grant wanted neutralized before he descended upon Vicksburg.

Major General Frank Blair's train, with Chatfield's wagon in it, would follow the road north from Grand Gulf to Willow Springs, on to Rocky Springs, from there to Cayuga, and then to Auburn where it would join up with McClernand's 4th Division, doubling the train to more than 200 wagons before moving on to Raymond.[104] Orderly Kellogg described the evening of May 12.

> At the end of 18 miles we went into camp for the night in a beautiful grove on a hill close to a spring of pure, cold water. We killed some sheep and chickens for supper, but where they came from only the Lord and some of our boys knew. — Orderly John J. Kellogg[105]

Diary - May 13, 1863

The country presents the same appearance as yesterday. The weather is hot, and the roads are dusty. Occasional whites can be seen staying on their farms. We are getting to the rear of Vicksburg. I heard some cannonading this morning.

[On] the 13th we continued our march through Rocky Springs, across Big and Little Sandy Creeks, and through a vastly finer country than yesterday. We arrived at the town of Cayuga that night and made our quarters in a church, and when the church bell rang furiously about midnight, we were told that [the non-combatant ringing it] wanted the Corporal of the guard. — Orderly John J. Kellogg[106]

On May 13, 1863, CS General Joe Johnston, reaching Jackson, saw a chance to defeat Sherman and McPherson at Clinton and quickly issued an order to General Pemberton to help make it happen.

OFFICIAL CORRESPONDENCE

I have lately arrived, and learn that Major-General Sherman is between us, with four DIVISIONS, at Clinton. It is important to re-establish communications, that you may be re-enforced. If practicable, come up on his rear at once. To beat such a detachment, would be of immense value. The troops here could co-operate. All the strength you can quickly assemble should be brought. Time is all-important. — J.E. Johnston[107]

Diary - May 14, 1863

We started at sunrise. The sky was cloudy, and we had a little rain. When we reached Cayuga, the Colonel took strict measures to guard against surprise. We have a large train of 700 - 800 wagons, and there are Rebels all around us within 3 miles. It rained hard in the afternoon, making the roads very muddy.

Believing his forces to be too small to challenge an entrenched enemy, Pemberton refused to honor Johnston's order to move to the rear of Sherman's forces, then en route toward Jackson. Pemberton offered, instead, to move southwest of Raymond.[108] Johnston countered by ordering Pemberton to Clinton, but Pemberton never got farther east than Edward's Depot, about 17 miles short of reaching Clinton.[109]

Battle of Jackson

Shortly after Sherman and McPherson's forces had arrived at Jackson on May 14, the battle of Jackson began. This was the third battle of the march—one that began at 9 A.M. in heavy sheets of rain. Interrupting the fight until about 11:00 A.M., the downpour was so thick that it threatened to wet the Union's gunpowder. When the rain tapered off, McPherson's soldiers, with bayonets fixed, rushed their opponents in a savage free-for-all that ultimately forced Confederate troops into their fortifications. Conceivably, General Johnston could have withstood a siege, but with only 8,000 men to defend the city, he concluded that continuing the battle would be futile and ordered evacuation.[*] By 3:00 P.M., the Union flag waved above the capitol building, and McPherson's and Sherman's troops had set about crushing the city's war capabilities. Before departing, the Federal troops destroyed the rails, machine shops, factories, telegraph lines and part of the town. With the capitol's war capacities nullified, Union forces exited the demolished city—an action allowing reoccupation by Johnston's forces. Jackson's loss as an industrial base posed an imminent threat to the city of Vicksburg, prompting its people to brace for a crisis.[110]

Diary - May 15, 1863

When they told us the news this morning that Jackson, Mississippi, and Richmond, Virginia, had been taken, there was a great cheer from all of us. The roads here are bad, very much cut up. We passed through the pretty little town named Raymond today. A lot of our wounded soldiers and Rebels were in the hospital there. After passing through, we camped at dark.

Although the report that Jackson, Mississippi, had been taken was true, the news about Richmond, Virginia, was not. The final Union assault at Petersburg, and hence, Richmond, would not occur for another two years—April 1865. Nevertheless, Richmond in mid-May 1863 faced multiple problems, inflation and food scarcities among them, fomenting uncontrollable bread riots.[111]

The 113th halted at Raymond at 2:00 P.M. and visited friends from the 20th Illinois, boys that had been wounded three days earlier in the fierce battle there, southwest of the town. General Blair divided his troops and wagon train in Raymond, sending all to Bolton, but by parallel roads. The larger portion of Colonel Giles Smith's

---

[*]   Johnston's assessment has ever since raised controversy. Would Vicksburg have been saved had he held on?

brigade took the short route, the heavily encumbered northwest road, where they would soon see some action.[112] The train of wagons with the 113th took the long route along the northeast road through Clinton, where they camped comfortably on the pleasant grounds of Mississippi College.[113]

Diary - May 16, 1863

Clinton is a very pretty little village of about 4,000 inhabitants. General Grant is encamped here now. We waited for General Sherman to return with his army corps. Tuttle's and Steele's Divisions passed on their return from Jackson between 12:00 and 1:00 p.m.* We left camp at 1:00 o'clock but marched only one mile before halting at dark to allow troops and trains to move ahead of us. Then we marched another 10 miles and camped near a small stream. We ate supper after midnight. Tremendous cheering broke out in camp when intelligence was received that we had captured 18 pieces of cannon and had held the Black River Bridge.

Battles at Champion Hill and the Big Black River

The excitement concerned what has since become known as the battle of Champion Hill. The larger part of Giles Smith's brigade participated in it, driving the Confederate skirmishers through the thick forest and over very broken and difficult ground.[114]

Diary - May 17, 1863

We were up at daybreak and moved out on the road to Vicksburg, full of trains and troops for miles. We marched about 15 miles today, then camped on the Black River. Our troops had quite a skirmish today, capturing 3,000 Reb prisoners and taking 14 pieces of artillery. We rejoined Blair's Division and crossed the river this evening on a pontoon bridge, then camped about 2 miles from the river. I stood guard this evening over some of the prisoners we took. The country here is very rough and hilly.

---

*   Union Generals, James M. Tuttle and Frederick Steele had both distinguished themselves in the battle of Jackson, their divisions a part of Sherman's Corps.

Eighteen guns were captured and 1,751 prisoners. Our loss was 39 killed, 237 wounded and 3 missing. The enemy probably lost but few men except those captured and drowned. But for the successful and complete destruction of the bridge, I have but little doubt that we should have followed the enemy so closely as to prevent his occupying his defenses around Vicksburg. — Ulysses S. Grant[115]

The Confederates had suffered some losses, but their destruction of the Black River Bridge had succeeded in delaying Grant, while earning Pemberton the valuable time he needed to return to the heavy fortifications guarding Vicksburg. The Union troops could not yet enter the city. Chatfield, among others, had heard otherwise.

Diary - May 18, 1863

In the morning, our trains all crossed a very narrow and deep river. At the time, rumors freely circulated that Vicksburg had been evacuated and was occupied by General [Nathaniel P.] Banks, who had come up from Port Hudson, and General [Stephen A.] Hurlbut, who had come down from Memphis. The country along the way was very rough and much broken, but the roads were good. Most of the land was planted to corn with occasional wheat and rye. We made about 20 miles today and camped 5 miles from Vicksburg in the rear. Company A had a skirmish. One man was wounded. We learned when we got here that Vicksburg was neither taken nor evacuated. A great battle is just before us.

Chatfield's wagon trailed the procession, pausing on the Jackson Road at the intersection running northeast to Benton. Once General Sherman drew close from behind, the train resumed its trek toward Graveyard Road, heavy skirmishing ahead of them.[116] Blair's 3rd Brigade arrived close to midnight, but the night was too noisy and action-filled for anyone to go to sleep.

And what a noisy night was that, my countrymen! The pickets on both sides kept up a steady fusillade throughout the night. — Orderly Kellogg" [117]

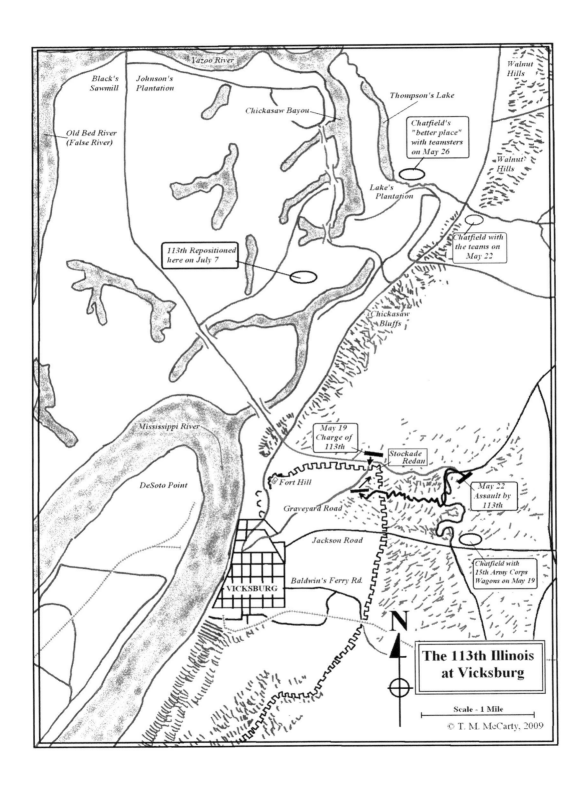

The 113th Illinois at Vicksburg

© T. M. McCarty, 2009

CHAPTER 16: STORMING VICKSBURG

"Our regiment was badly cut up yesterday."

Convinced that the Rebels manning the fortresses of Vicksburg lacked both the will and the strength to withstand a heavy assault, Grant directed Blair's division of Sherman's corps to rush the Stockade Redan,[*] a heavily fortified earthwork protecting the northeastern approach to the city along Graveyard Road.

Diary - May 19, 1863

We camped our 15ᵗʰ Army Corps wagons about 1 mile in the rear of our troops. At 8:00 a.m. some of the troops were ordered to retire back out of range. Eight teams from our brigade were ordered back to the Big Black to bring back the captured guns. Firing was light this morning. At 2:00 o'clock, the firing became general, the roar of musketry incessant. I heard this evening that Frank Ponto was killed. Frank Fender, Enos Shreffler, and Levi Walters were wounded, and someone said that Colonel Smith had been wounded in the head.

Private Francis Ponto of Company "B" was killed during the May 19 storming. The injuries suffered by 30-year-old Corporal Benjamin F. Fender, from Pilot, led to his

---

[*]   The name "redan" refers to a V-shaped fortification with an open back, its forward angle projecting toward the enemy.

discharge on April 11, 1864. Private Enos Shreffler, from Salina, was discharged in July 1865, 11 months after his brother, Private Peter Shreffler, died of disease while in Corinth. Private Levi Walters, 27, a single farmer from Pilot, incurred minor wounds, as did Colonel Giles Smith. Contrary to what Chatfield had heard, Smith's wound was in the hip—not in the head.

On the morning of May 19, from the cover of ravines and fallen logs, Union and Confederate infantrymen engaged *tit for tat* fire, the repeated cracking of rifles a hint of what was to come. By 1:00 P.M., Colonel Giles A. Smith's 1st Brigade (including the 113th) and Brigadier General Hugh Ewing's 3rd Brigade were positioned on Graveyard Road directly in front of the Stockade Redan. To their left was Colonel Kilby Smith's 2nd Brigade, and to their right was General Frederick Steele's 1st Division, Fifteenth Army Corps. Breathlessly, each man awaited the signal to charge. The signal came at 2:00 P.M.[118]

Orderly Kellogg described the charge:

> When the signal for the general assault came, my regiment ... was among the first to make a determined attack. ... The leaden hail from the enemy was absolutely blinding. The very sticks and chips scattered over the ground were jumping under the hot shower of Rebel bullets. As I recall that experience I can but wonder that any of us survived that charge. The rough and brush-strewn ground over which we had to charge broke up our alignment badly, and every soldier of our command had to pick his own way forward as best he could.... When I again stood up, I could see a fragment of our line only, to my left, with which I recognized our colonel and regimental colors. I started towards our flag, but I had gone only a few steps when one of the enemy's shells exploded in front of me, and when the smoke had lifted a little I saw that our regimental flag and the colonel had gone down. ... [In] a shallow gully where the freshets had some time worn a little ditch, I found a squad of seventeen of my regiment hugging the ground and keeping up a steady fire on the Rebel works. ... [There,] lying flat on our backs and loading our pieces in that position, with the merciless sun blistering our faces, we passed that day of dreadful fighting. ... [We] lost one of our number killed, shot in the center of the forehead, and five others wounded. Often that day the bullets from front and rear passed so closely above our prostrate bodies that the short cane stalks forming a part of our cover, were cut off by them and lopped gently over upon us. But we fared better than other regiments of our brigade. — Orderly Kellogg[119]

Referring to Colonel Giles Smith's wound, General Frank Blair wrote:

> In the affair of the 19th, Col. Giles A. Smith received a slight wound
> in the hip from a musket-ball.[*] He remained, however, at his post at
> the head of his brigade throughout that day and the ensuing days of
> combat up to this time, leading his brigade to the assault, and attend-
> ing to every detail of duty under circumstances which you know to
> have been most trying. — Frank P. Blair Jr.[120]

Diary - May 20, 1863
*The fighting continued all through the night. Our regiment was badly cut up
yesterday. They got within a few rods of the enemy's breastworks but were not
able to get any farther, and they could not retreat without losing a great many.
They fell back a short distance last night and are in the same position today. The
musketry is not as heavy as yesterday. I went out to the battlefield this evening with
ammunition. I received three letters.*

Pemberton's army had been far from the weakened state that Grant had hoped
for. For the next two days, Grant reconnoitered the ground, regrouped his forces,
placed his artillery, and prepared for an all-out attack. His grand army would challenge Vicksburg from her northern, eastern and southern sides while Admiral
Porter's naval fleet would pound the city from the west. Meanwhile, the troops on
both sides exchanged warnings and retaliatory volleys as if to atone for the deaths
of their fallen friends.

> The smoke that filled the heavens during [yesterday's] conflict had
> rolled together into one great windrow[†] and hung away out on the
> rim of the horizon. The light breath of wind wafted from over the
> battlefield, it seemed to me, savored of blood. At the rear of the field
> hospital a score of legs and arms were stacked up awaiting burial and

---

[*] General Sherman would later praise Smith's dedication to his troops, writing: "… In making special
mention of Col. Giles A. Smith, commanding First Brigade, I but repeat former expressions of praise. An
officer who is always present with his command, who carries a severe wound without a flinch or the loss
of a minute's duty, and who takes a pride in studying his chosen profession, deserves the special notice
of his commanders, without a just cause for the envy of any other. Being in command of a brigade, and
worthy of it, he should have the rank." (*Official Records,* Series 1, Volume 24, Part 2, 259)

[†] Windrows, rows of hay raked together to dry, were familiar sights to the farmers of the time.

some blood stained stretchers laid where the tired stretcher bearers had carelessly abandoned them. The faithful surgeons had plied the knife, and worked on, ever since the assault began, and now at the dawn of another day were not nearly done. — Orderly Kellogg[121]

Diary - May 21, 1863

Heavy cannonading thundered throughout the night. I went out with Dan [Durham] in the morning and got a load of bedding for the sick and wounded — of which there are a great many. The teams have all gone to Haines' Bluff to draw provisions and ammunition. A little shower fell today, just enough to settle the bad dust. Our teams all went back this evening for more ammunition.

While Chatfield's teams pulled large quantities of ammunition forward, Company "B" had been assembled in a ravine, about one-third mile east of the Stockade Redan, to receive orders and instructions on what was about to come.

On the night of May 21st we were informed that tomorrow morning we would again assault the works by the engagement of the whole line. It was arranged for the assault to take place at precisely 10 o'clock on the morning of the 22nd. So determined was Grant to have the attack by the various corps simultaneous that he had all of the corps commanders' watches set by his own. — Orderly Kellogg[122]

An officer from Sherman's staff approached Captain Williams and requested three men (5% of the company) to volunteer for the initial 150-man storming party. The volunteers were to rush the ditch in front of the Stockade Redan and bridge it with logs and boards. Followers would cross. Parties of this sort were traditionally known in the army as the *Forlorn Hope.**

We looked into each others faces for some seconds. We were speechless and felt a dread of what might develop. We knew that as a general thing the man who volunteers and goes into the storming party "leaves all hope behind." It means nearly sure death. Like the Irishman, I didn't want to go "and leave my father an orphan." Finally

---

* "*Forlorn Hope*" is derived from the Dutch phrase, "verloren hoop," literally meaning, "lost heap." To the soldier, however, the term suggested that all hope was lost.

there was a movement. Old Joe Smith, white headed, rough visaged and grizzled by the storms of a half century, stepped to the front and calling back to his bunkmate said, "Come on, Lish," and Elisha Johns filled out by his side. Then, after a brief interval, Sergt. James Henry volunteered for the third place. Company B's quota was now complete, and those brave fellows hurried away to take their places in the ranks of the storming party. — Orderly Kellogg[123]

"Old Joe Smith," even though gray-haired, was actually only 41. He was a private from Chebanse, eight miles south of Kankakee. Elisha Johns was a 26-year-old private from Martinton, southeast of Chebanse. Sergeant James Henry was a 29-year-old carpenter from Kankakee. All three were married men. They were among the bravest of men, and all in the company assumed that they would soon be dead.

Diary - May 22, 1863
A general charge was made today clear along the lines, and there has been very heavy firing all day long. I heard this evening that the Captain had been wounded. Here with the teams, we killed a calf and cooked it this evening for dinner.

The news about the Captain being wounded may have been rumor. If not, the wounds he took were minor. Captain Williams remained in command for many months to come. Chatfield would soon learn additional details about the May 22 assaults.

The plan was for Porter to hammer the city throughout the night and into the morning. He would silence his guns at 10:00 A.M., signaling Sherman's *Forlorn Hope* to rush in by way of Graveyard Road, with the regiments behind in close support. McPherson would storm from the east at the line's center via the Jackson Road, and McClernand would strike from the south through the entrances marked by the *Vicksburg and Jackson Railroad* and the road from Baldwin's Ferry.

The distinct rumble of Admiral Porter's mortars could be easily heard from as far west as Chatfield's wagons. Before sunrise, the *Benton, Carondelet, Mound City,* and *Tuscumbia* churned up the Mississippi River, north of Warrenton, announcing to the Confederates that May 22 would be no ordinary day.[124] Joining Porter at 6:00 A.M. that Friday morning, the heavy guns of the army pummeled the city of Vicksburg while Grant's entire army from Fort Hill to South Fort prepared for the 10:00 A.M. charge.

The *Forlorn Hope* assembled itself at the Graveyard Road entrance to the city, and the 113th stood ready in a ravine that afforded a glimpse of the action. At 10:00 A.M., the guns fell silent, the void that all had been waiting for. Thunder's absence was the signal to charge.

> This storming party ... led the advance or attacking column.... I watched that little force of 150 men rush forward towards the battlements of the enemy. How they scurried forward, leaping over the logs and brush lying in their pathway as they pushed on through that leaden and iron hail of death! A scattering few seemed to reach the salient of the bastion and laid down against their works in time to preserve their lives, but as it appeared to me through the clouds of sulphurous smoke a greater part of the blue forms were scattered along their line of advance stretched upon the earth motionless in death. — Orderly Kellogg[125]

Regiments from Ewing's brigade directly followed the *Forlorn Hope;* behind them stormed the 30th Ohio; they, in turn, were followed by the 37th Ohio. By the time the 47th Ohio and the 4th West Virginia were to charge, the road was so clogged with grisly carnage and panicking soldiers that it was impassable. Seeing this, General Blair ordered the two regiments forward by way of the densely forested, abatis-strewn hillside on the south side of the road, an obstacle course of felled trees that he described as "another route, to the left of the road."[126] He then ordered Colonel Giles Smith's entire brigade, with the 113th, to take the same alternative route. After double-timing his brigade due south about three-fourths of a mile, Smith commanded his regiments to ascend the heavily obstructed hill. It took four hours for Smith to move his brigade up the hill—by no means a charge.

When he reached the crest of the hill, Colonel Smith met up with General McPherson's Seventeenth Army Corps, including Thomas E.G. Ransom and his 2nd Brigade. The two brigade commanders, Smith and Ransom, agreed to work together. It was afternoon, and the initial charge had ended. Soldiers had taken secure positions, the 113th about 300 yards south of the ominous Stockade Redan at the crest of the hill on the east side of the road. The rim of the hill was their only protection as they peppered away at the distant Confederates. Beyond their cover, to their right and stretching north, ran Graveyard Road and a field strewn with hundreds of bodies. If a new order came to charge the bastion, only the hands of random fate—not speed or agility—would determine who would be the next to die. The order came at 3:00 P.M.

During that run and rush I had frequently to either step upon or jump over the bodies of our dead and wounded, which were scattered along the track. The nearer the enemy we got, the more enthusiastic we became, and the more confidence we had in scaling their works, but as we neared their parapet we encountered the reserved fire of the Rebels which swept us back to temporary cover of a ridge, two-thirds of the way across the field, from which position we operated the rest of the day. ... We lay there on our backs and looked back into the throats of the artillery as it shelled the enemy's works over our heads. We could see the balls distinctly as they were discharged from the cannons, and they looked like bumblebees flying over us, only somewhat larger. While we were thus watching the flight of the balls, one of them struck and cut off the top of a tall sapling standing between us and the cannon; the ball by that means was depressed, and instead of going over us came directly for us and into our midst. ... I heard the dull thud of its striking and a scream of agony, and I stood up and looked. That ball had struck and carried away the life of Morris Bird a private of Company H, and the only son of a widowed mother. — Orderly Kellogg[127]

Morris Bird was actually a corporal. He enlisted in the township of Kankakee, as did many boys in Company "H". He died at the age of twenty.

One close call of an exploding shell knocked me senseless and took off the right arm of Louis Cazean a private in my company. They told me afterwards that poor Cazean, when he lifted up the fragments of his shattered right arm dangling from the white cords and tendons, said, "Boys, I'd give five hundred dollars if that was my left arm instead of my right." When I regained my senses, I found Sergeant Whitcomb (sic) [Titcomb] of my company bathing my head with water and trying to force some commissary whisky down my throat. He didn't have near as much trouble getting the whiskey down me after I came to and found out what it was. — Orderly Kellogg[128]

Seriously wounded, Private Lewis Cazean (19) from Kankakee was discharged on November 18, 1863.

Sherman later considered the afternoon charge to have been a mistake. He would not have ordered it had General Grant not received a written note from General McClernand, in which McClernand claimed the successful capture of the Rebel parapet to his front, roughly two miles south of Graveyard Road. McClernand requested Grant "to give renewed orders to McPherson and Sherman to press their attacks on their respective fronts, lest the enemy should concentrate on him."[129] Grant felt compelled to honor the request, although he doubted the veracity of McClernand's claim, there being very little chance that he had truly broken the Rebel lines.

The 3:00 P.M. charge ended in disaster. When it was later determined that McClernand had only taken two small outlying lunettes,[*] leaving their men at the mercy of the main parapet, Sherman, McPherson and Grant were furious. The afternoon assault had resulted in the unnecessary loss of many good soldiers and officers. It would be one of the reasons that Grant would soon seek Lincoln's approval to have McClernand dismissed.[130]

> We had failed to take Vicksburg by assault, notwithstanding the bravery of our men [and] notwithstanding that many stands of colors [that] were planted on the enemy's works.... We not only failed to take it, but we failed to break their lines of defense and make permanent lodgment anywhere along our front, General McClernand to the contrary notwithstanding. ... We lost 3,000 men while the sheltered confederates within their formidable works lost only 1,000.
> — Orderly Kellogg[131]

With two failed attempts to take Vicksburg by storm, Grant concluded that he would take it by siege—an operation of constant armed harassment coupled with deprivation of all food, medicine, and supplies for as long as necessary to force the Confederates to surrender. Chatfield, still camping behind the lines with the teams, helped load and move whatever was needed forward—the food, water, medical supplies, ammunition, and other weapons of war. On the morning of May 23, Chatfield awoke to the news that although the attempt to take Vicksburg had failed, his company's three volunteers for the *Forlorn Hope* had miraculously survived.

---

[*] A lunette was a small, two or three-sided earthwork, having the rear side open. Sometimes crescent-shaped, it was given the French name meaning "little moon." Lunettes differed from redans in that they stood alone, were usually smaller, and were not connected by adjoining walls.

CHAPTER 17: THE SIEGE ON VICKSBURG

"We have got the Rebels pretty closely hemmed in now."

Diary - May 23, 1863
We went out to the regiment this morning. Many of our troops were still firing and rattling away.

Diary - May 24, 1863
We wen2t out to the regiment again this morning with rations, then went out foraging this afternoon and brought in two barrels of molasses and some corn. It felt quite pleasant running around seeing what we could find. We got back to camp at 11:00 p.m. and were told that our generals have abandoned the plan of taking Vicksburg by assault or storm and have adopted the slower but surer one of taking it by siege.

On the 24th, my company was detailed for picket duty, and we occupied the advance rifle pits already dug, and industriously dug others in advance of those, under cover of night. That night myself and [a] comrade went without orders onto the battle field, armed only with spades, and buried three of our dead comrades who were killed in the assault of the 19th. It was a dangerous business, and only the

intense darkness protected us from the enemy. We could only bury them by throwing dirt upon the bodies just as they lay upon the ground. Five days of exposure to the heat and sun had produced in those bodies a fearful state of decomposition, and the stench was dreadful, but we accomplished our task after a fashion.
— Orderly Kellogg [132]

A Confederate soldier later described the city on the morning of May 24:

Sunday dawned clear and beautiful, yet its holy quiet was disturbed by the fierce storm of war, which swept over the city of hills, and thundered in angry surges around its whole circumference.... The houses of worship were deserted, and women and children sought shelter from the exploding shells in their underground habituations.
— Sgt. William H. Tunnard, 3rd Louisiana Infantry [133]

Diary - May 25, 1863

Before retiring last night, I visited some of the boys of the 76th Illinois Volunteers. This morning, we went down to the Yazoo River to get rations for the regiment. The boats lay right where the battleground was last January [battle of Chickasaw Bayou, Dec. 27—Jan. 1]. Later, we passed where the fighting was along Walnut Hills. We returned to camp at 11:00 p.m.

Diary - May 26, 1863

This morning we moved our camp to a better place on the Chickasaw Bayou at the foot of Walnut Hills. We found good spring water within 60 rods of where we are camped. Our knapsacks were sent over from Young's Point today. Ed Swortfiger and I went to the Yazoo looking for forage this evening. After that, I went out to the regiment at the front lines and got my things that were supposed to be sent home.

Private Edward H. Swortfiger, a 20-year-old farmer, enlisted in Company "K" in August of 1862. He was discharged November 17, 1863, due to disability. Sufficiently healed and attracted by a substantial state bounty, Swortfiger re-enlisted in February 1865.*

---

* Bounties served as the primary Union stimulus for enlistment, over $750,000,000 paid out by federal, state, and local authorities during the war. Boatner, *Civil War Dictionary*.

Prior to May 26, the main body of the 113th had been camped above the Chickasaw Bluffs. To strengthen supply lines and enforce the siege, a decision was made to consolidate the regiment. In preparation, the supply base and the sick, left behind at Milliken's Bend in early May, had been relocated to Young's Point, across from the mouth of the Yazoo. On May 25, Sergeant James Henry was sent over to Young's Point to orchestrate the final move. Of significance to the commanders, the May 26 mobilization to Chickasaw Bayou was strategically important. The location would serve as a superb aperture through which supplies could be funneled to the front lines, immobilizing the city of Vicksburg while helping to quell any attack from CS General Johnston, rumored to be amassing an immense force near the Big Black.[134] Of significance to the sick at Young's Point, including Private Riley Beach, they would rejoin their regiment. Of significance to the boys in the main regiment, they would finally get their knapsacks back.

Chatfield wrote in his diary that "…we moved to a better place," yet tragically, the Chickasaw Bayou would be remembered instead as the most lethal location near Vicksburg. The May 26 move had unwittingly unleashed a massive assault by disease that would eventually kill or disable the entire regiment.

Diary - May 27, 1863
We heard very heavy firing all last night, and today, they're still pitching in. Two letters were waiting for me at the front when I delivered rations today. I had just returned to camp this evening when they brought me a third letter.

Letter - May 27, 1863
Headquarters 113th Regt, 1st Brigade 2nd Division 15th Army Corps of the right wing in the rear of Vicksburg, May 27th, 1863

Ever dear & loved Parents,

It was with the pleasure imagineable that I rec'd your last welcome letter of the 7th Ult, the box which you sent to us has been received and distributed. ~~Were~~ We are all very thankful for the thoughtfulness of our dear friends at home. The things all came very acceptable. Our box was distributed right on the battlefield. There is hard fighting going on today, if the roar of cannon tells anything. We have been fighting here now 9 days, and there is no telling how much longer the fight will last. We now have our teams kraaled [corralled] and our camp where the Officers stay when not in the fight, on the very battle-ground where our troops under Gen Sherman fought so hard last January and were forced to retire at last.

We have got the Rebels pretty closely hemmed in now. We [are] a very strong force, I presume from 150 to 200,000 strong. And our lines extend from Warrenton on the river on the south oft of town to the river on the north side, while our gunboats are playing on to them [from] the river side. There has been no more of our company hurt since I wrote my last of the 23rd. Most likely you will hear some great stories relative to our doings, but do not believe every thing that you hear until it is confirmed. For there is many rumors that go like the wind that has not the least particle of truth in them. In your last of the 7th, David stated that you were just beginning to plant corn.

While down here at the tho same time in Louisiana, the Corn was waist high. Winter wheat is ripe. Also rye. Oats will be ripe in a couple of weeks. Plums are ripe while peaches are two thirds grown. There is any amount of blackberries, while strawberries are gone. The weather is quite warm, about the same that it is in July up North. We are now encamped on what is called Chickasaw bayou, and the misquitoes are very troublesome in the night especially. Ever since we left Millikens bend, we have had plenty of marching and hard work. But I stand it first rate. In a letter that I got from Sarah T. [Sarah Titcomb], she said that you thought that I must be getting sick of the war, of which I really am, but not in the sense that you meant. For in that part, I like it as well as I did in the first start.

Well, I have a chance to send this and so I will close. I rec'd four stamps in your last. Give my respects to all the neighbors reserving my love to yourselves.

I remain your loving son & brother,

E.L Chatfield.

Much of the "roar of cannon" this day came from the Confederate river-batteries atop the bluffs. Their precision firing drove off four ironclads and seven mortar batteries and sank the 512-ton Cairo Class Ironclad, *Cincinnati*. This was the second time that the *Cincinnati* had been sunk. She would soon be raised again, repaired and returned to Union service. According to Chatfield, in his letter dated June 1, 1863, the projectile that sank the *Cincinnati* was determined to be a section of railroad iron.

Diary - May 28, 1863

I went to the landing on forage with Dan's team this morning. A large number of boats had brought in food for the troops. We took a large load of hogs up to the regiments in the afternoon, then sat in the afternoon shade. There was leisurely firing all day.

Diary - May 29, 1863

My knapsack was lost, missing from the ones they brought over. I feel very dirty and have no change of clothes to put on. The cannonading has been heavy today. It's cloudy, and we're having light showers. The regiment came over here to the pontoon bridge and helped us move heavy siege guns across for firing this evening.

> On the morning of the 29th my regiment was sent out to the Chickasaw Bayou to get some big cannon. We found on arriving at the bayou four 32-pound Parrotts on the opposite side, which we proceeded by means of ropes to pull across on temporary pontoon bridges. Although we supplemented the strength of the bridges with thick plank laid lengthwise, and pulled the guns across on the run, still their immense weight broke almost every plank in the bridges as we snaked them across. Had we allowed one of them to stop a second midway on the bridge it would have crushed through and gone to the bottom of the bayou. — Orderly Kellogg[135]

By afternoon, the heavy Parrotts roared away, propelling into the skies over Vicksburg an iron storm of grapeshot, canisters, and 32-pound balls.

> Federal gunners stepped up their rate of shelling. For four hours the cannonade from land and river pummeled the city without interruption, ruining and setting fire to a large number of buildings and causing casualties among both civilians and soldiers. — CS Sgt. William H. Tunnard, 3rd Louisiana Infantry[136]

Diary - May 30, 1863

I wrote a letter in the morning, then went out to the regiment in the afternoon where there was very heavy firing from our side and rare replies from Rebels.

As part of the siege, the heavy Parrotts continued their harassment of Vicksburg, their deafening roar camouflaging the routine popping of muskets up and down the line. Only the mortars on the barges sounded louder, their concussions so overwhelming that men boasted that such blasts could shred their overcoats. As powerful as the weapons were, they failed to destroy the several principal earthworks guarding the city. The skills of experienced coal miners were tapped to get that job done.

First, the men dug "saps," trenches paralleling the earthwork. They then extended approach saps toward the earthwork, concealing themselves in the process behind bullet stoppers called "sap rollers." A simple sap roller could be made with two empty barrels lashed together, one on top of the other, then wrapped round and round with willow cuttings and filled with earth. At a safe distance, the digging would go underground and proceed below the earthwork. The final step involved the setting and detonation of powder kegs.

> Each tier of rifle pits brought the contending forces closer together, so they could easily converse with each other...The soldiers of the blue often met the gray between the lines and swapped knives, buttons, papers and tobacco in a most cordial and friendly way...One night a voice said, "Is any of the boys of the 6th Missouri in the rifle pits over there?" "There's lots of 'em," was the answer. "Is Tom Jones there?" "He is," said our man, "Is that you Jim?" "Yes," came the answer, "and say Tom, can't you meet me between the lines? I've got a roll of greenbacks and I want to send them to the old folks in Missouri." And so Yank Tom went out and met Rebel Jim, his brother, got the greenbacks, and after a brief visit returned safely to our picket quarters. — Orderly Kellogg[137]

Diary - May 31, 1863
We went out foraging today and got some sheep. We have a very warm thermometer today; it's 95 degrees in the shade.

Diary - June 1, 1863
This was a lazy day for me. I picked some blackberries, then went out to the regiment. It's still very warm, and the siege continues with brisk firing from our side.

Letter - June 1, 1863
Walnut Hills June 1st 1863

Loved ones at home,

As I have a few leisure moments I will devote them to writing a few to you who I suppose must be very anxious to hear from me. The blessings of heaven still continue to be showered down upon me in the shape of Good health apetite & spirits. We have a plenty to do, so, that I would not have time to be home-sick even if I would. It is getting to be quite warm. Yesterday it was 93 Deg in the shade, and it is quite as warm today. It just makes sweat pour of [off] a fellow in streams.

The fight here at Vicksburg is still progressing. It has now turned into a regular seige. We are bringing heavy seige guns (which take 6 & 8 teams to draw) every day and we are getting so close to their entrenchments that is we are within 10 or 12 rods, [so close] that a man dares not show his head. If he did, he is a dead man. We lost one of our gunboats, the Cincinati, the other day. They shot her through the stern with peices of rail-road iron. But we did them equally as much harm if not more. For, about the same time, we captured [a] large ammunition train that belonged to Sydney Johnson [sic] [Joe Johnston.] He was trying to make a connection with Vicksburg. But our forces drove him back.

A soldiers [life] is a curious one. He cant tell [from one] minute what is to happen the next. I thought, when I commenced this, that I surely would have time t to finish it, but I was mistaken. I have just got back from the Reg't. The boys all seem to be in first rate spirits. They have been laying still for severl days. They are down in a deep ravine about 80 rods [1/4 mile] from the enemies breastworks. The ridges run parallell with their works, so that they are in a sheltered position. There has been none hurt since the first days fight and they have been at it two weeks today.

Vegetation is a little farther advanced here than it is up north. I guess corn is as high as my head. Wheat & rye was ripe two weeks ago, and there is any amount of plums blackberries etc. Poor William has rather of a hard sick of it. I hope that he may soon recover. But Will, you may be comforted that you are at home where you can have a mothers care. There is many a poor soldier, no older than you, that lies f suffering in some hospital with no one to look with a pitying eye upon him. They are sending the sick & wounded from the Hospitals near the f battle-field to the Hospital boats and are sent up the river as fast as possible. But it is so warm that it is very bad for the wounded ones, for their wounds become inflamed a great deal more in warm than in cold weather. I thank you very much, my dear mother, for those things which you sent me. They all came very acceptable.

If you have any chance to send me a pair of good heavy Calf Boots (Nr 8) I would like it. Our army shoes don't pay well. I have written you all the news

I can think of. I had a letter from Grandma the other day which I immediately answered. It stated that she was well.

My love to you all from your loving son,

Edward L Chatfield (Private!) Co B 113th Reg't Ill. Vols. Inft,

1st Brigade, 2nd Division, 15th Army Corps

NS Chatfield Esq.

B Grand Prairie PO, KKK [Kankakee], Illinois

Meanwhile, from the Executive Mansion:

OFFICIAL CORRESPONDENCE

Executive Mansion, Washington, June 1, 1863

Colonel Ludlow, Fort Monroe

Richardson and Browne, correspondents of the *Tribune* captured at Vicksburg, are detained at Richmond. Please ascertain why they are detained and get them off if you can. — A. Lincoln [138]

And Colonel Ludlow dutifully complies with his president's order...

OFFICIAL CORRESPONDENCE

HDQRS. DEPT. OF VIRGINIA, SEVENTH ARMY CORPS, Fort Monroe, June 2, 1863

Honorable ROBERT OULD, Agent for Exchange of Prisoners:

SIR: A.D. Richardson and Janius H. Browne, correspondents of the *New York Tribune*, captured about the 4th of May last, near Vicksburg, are said to be confined in the Libby Prison. Mr. Colburn, the correspondent of the *New York World*, who was captured with them, has been released. It has been the practice to treat attaches of the press as non-combatants and not to retain them. The release of Mr. Colburn is a partial recognition of this practice. Will you please inform me if you will release Richardson and Browne; and if not, why not?

I am, very respectfully, your obedient servant,

WM. H. LUDLOW,

Lieutenant-Colonel and Agent for Exchange of Prisoners. [139]

Diary - June 2, 1863

I received a pass from Colonel John Paddock, the Provost Marshal of the 15th Corps, to go after my knapsack at Young's Point. I came down here to the Point on the

Ben Franklin. My knapsack was all right. There are plenty of sick men here.

Diary - June 3, 1863

After taking several glasses of beer, we, that is, Edward Wainwright and I, started back for Walnut Hills. We secured a passage on the Diligent and arrived at Yazoo Landing in due time. I found a letter waiting for me there, then drew new clothing: a blouse, pants, shirts, and shoes.

Edward Wainwright was a married 31-year-old private from Chicago in Company "A" and in the prime of health. He could not have known at the time that the swamp's pathogens at Chickasaw Bayou would prove to be his most formidable enemy. He was dead of disease seven months later, January 31, 1864.

Letter - June 3, 1863
Walnut Hills In the rear of Vicksburg June 3rd 1863.

Beloved Brother David,

You thought that I had been rather neglectfull of you in not answering your oft repeated letters, which I will own was rather negligent in me. I received your very welcome letter of the 23rd Ult, and was very glad to hear from you all. I was rejoiced to hear that William was getting so much better. Well, David, I suppose that you have to work pretty hard this Summer. But remember that you will have your reward in the end. Are you working all of the farm this Summer or do you have to let some of it lay idle? I do really hope that this unholy war will soon end so that we can all remain home in peace. The way that affairs are situated here at Vicksburg, I think that we will soon and whip them out and lay the whole of them. It is said that we [will be] with-drawn from the Brigade and as soon as Vicksburg is taken you may expect to hear from us from Springfield or somewhere there-abouts. For we have been promised by the Colonel that as soon as we get this place that we should go North so as to get the Regt together. And our Reg't needs recruiting very bad. For, of our five Companies, we can only muster for duty about 100 men. John Fundy & Al Smith send you their best respects & compliments. There is a fellow of Company E, he is Sergt Major now, and has a furlough. And I send this by him. His name is Malcomb Smith.

Well David, I hope that you will never get the fever to go to war. It is no childs play at any rate. Well, I must close for this time. My health still remains first rate, thanks to the great being of all good. I will write often as I can.

I remain as ever your loving brother,

Edward —

The Chatfield Story: Civil War Letters and Diaries of
Private Edward L. Chatfield of the 113th Illinois Volunteers
180

Recruited by Captain Sutherland in Cook County, Sgt. Major Malcomb F. Smith was a married 26-year-old dentist when he enlisted. He was Acting Sgt. Major when this letter was written. Smith's promotion didn't actually come until September 7, 1863.

Diary - June 4, 1863

I went out this morning and had a splendid shower bath. When I came back I found Frank Wickens of the 20th Regiment waiting to see me. We had a good visit. I also saw George Palmer and Tom Welch of the 76th. It was still raining this evening.

Private Frank Wickens, in Company "G" of the 20th Illinois, enlisted in Kankakee on January 5, 1862, and mustered in at Bird's Point, Missouri. Private George Palmer of the 76th had immigrated to Kankakee with his parents from Ingersoll, Canada. He was a 20-year-old farmer in Pilot Township when he enlisted. Twenty-five-year-old Corporal Tom Welch, in Company "F" of the 76th, a native of Ireland, enlisted in Limestone Township. Welch was promoted to Sergeant before mustering out in Galveston, Texas.

Diary - June 5, 1863

There was considerable firing in the morning. I went out with rations for the regiment in the forenoon. The boys were all in good spirits. I got a box of caps for a revolver which I found the other day. Dan [Durham] went to the landing last night and today brought up a load of Board of Trade sanitary supplies of which we got a good share. The siege still progresses.

The citizens inside the city found refuge in hand-dug caves. Mrs. Mary Loughborough, the wife of a Confederate officer stationed in Vicksburg, was one of them.

One thing I had learned quite lately in my cave was to make good bread. One of my cave neighbors had given me yeast and instructions. I, in turn, had instructed a servant, so that when we used the flour it would be presented in a more inviting form.

. . . after breakfast, the shells began falling so thickly around us that they seemed aimed at the particular spot on which our cave was located. Two or three fell immediately in the rear of it, exploding a few moments before reaching the ground, and the fragments went singing over the top of our habitation. I . . . became so much alarmed . . . that I determined, rather than be buried alive, to stand out from under the earth; so, taking my child in my arms, and calling the servants, we ran to a refuge near the roots of a large fig tree. . . . [Soon] a shell that seemed to be of enormous size fell, screaming and hissing, immediately before the mouth of our cave, within a few feet of the entrance, sending up a huge column of smoke and earth, and jarring the ground most sensibly where we stood. . . . . I found on my return that the walls were seamed here and there with cracks, but the earth had remained firm above us. I took possession again, with resignation. . . . — Mary Loughborough[140]

Diary - June 6, 1863
I went with Dan's team to the landing, and we brought back assorted cargo. William Mitchell, of the 76th, rode out with us.

William P. Mitchell, a redheaded 30-year-old native of Scotland and a Kankakee butcher before the war, was a 1st Lieutenant in Company "F" of the 76th Illinois when he accompanied Dan Durham and Chatfield. Within the next 17 months, something went seriously wrong in Mitchell's life as an officer. The *Illinois Roster* records do not provide the details. Mitchell was dishonorably discharged on January 25, 1865.

Diary - June 7, 1863
The musketry was quite sharp and heavy this morning. The day was very warm.

Letter - June 7, 1863
Walnut Hills in the rear of Vicksburg June 7th, 1863

Dear Parents,

The holy Sabbath has again rolled around and brings in its [presence] to me no such calm and soothing influences that it does to the peaceful ones at home. But, we must hope that soon we may all be permitted to meet around our own fireside in peace and harmony and not have to go forth to battle for our country. For then all will be peace and harmony throughout the land.

This is a very fine Summer day. The sun is shimmering brightly. The birds are singing cheerfully and all nature seems redolent with the praise our maker. But for all this, the distant sound of booming cannon jars upon my ear and reminds me that this is a time of war instead of peace. Oh, what reflections it brings to a persons mind as he looks back on the future past and then look's forward to the future and thinks what is in store for him. But, oh, let us pray that we may all be brought of conquerers, yea more than conquerers, and that we may ever remain in peace with all parts of the land. I shall continue to write to you every week if not oftener, as unless something occurs that I cannot write. So do not worry, for the letters will get around after a while.

While we were on the march I missed one week, for I did not have time to write, and if I had I could not have sent it. So you must excuse me for that time. I wish that it was so that I could be permitted to be at home to assist you this Spring to get in the crops but that cannot be. I saw several boys of the 76th the other day. George Palmer looks fine. He has been sick in Memphis for some time but he is well now. Lieut. William Mitchell and Tom Welch that need to live with widow Halshouser were here to. They look first rate. I saw Frank Wickens the other day. He has grown long large and strong. Says he to me, tell your mother that she must go and see my mother and that together they can cheer up each other. Now mother, you say that you have not been out to the neighbors or any where away from home. Now you must not confine yourself to much, for it will hurt your health. I am getting along as well as you could wish, have nothing to trouble me, and so I wish that you would [not] worry or trouble yourself about me in the least. For I am confidant that if it is the will of God that I shall return home, that it will be so. And if it is not, there is no use of repining or finding fault with what we cannot change or alter in any shape. So we must bide the fate of time.

My dear mother, you must may rest assured that as sure as I went away from you pure and with-out spot or blemish, so sure shall I return the same, although there is many in the army, yes even in our reg't, that have acted shamefully. Yet, in the army, it seems as though constraint was thrown of, and men that were said steay [steady] & sober men are here seen in their true light. – (but we will let this subject pass) —

Loyal is gone. You wish to know why he was not sent home. I will tell you it. He died just before we started on the march around to this [place] and we had no time. He was at the Hospital some 3 miles from our camp and he was dead and buried before we knew it. And the weather was so warm that it was impossible to keep his body.

We made an march of 175 miles to get 10, but we won great victories. We whipped the enemy at every point that we met them, and I trust that Vicksburg will soon fall. And as soon as it falls, it is expected that our regt will go north so as to get our reg't together again. Well, I have written a pretty long letter this time and I must close. I will write Some to William & Newton.

Direct the same as usual. I remain as ever your loving son,

Edward L. Chatfield (Private) – Co B 113th Reg't Ill Vols Inft

(N S Chatfield, Esq)

Brother William,

As you have written me several letters which I have not answered, I feel in duty bound to write once in a while. I seem be more favorably prospered than you in regard to to health, for since I have been in the army I have not had a single real sick day thanks to the great giver of all good. but I am glad to hair hear that you are getting better. our camp is situated at the foot of Walnut Hills right on the ground where that terrible battle was fought last January while right before me within 3 miles is the town of Vicksburg over & in which shell are continually bursting, while at my back or towards the North is Haines bluffs. So you can see by looking at the map of Vicksburg and the surrounding Country. I think that you & Jimmy have got a pretty good job this summer & it pays pretty well to from your account. you & David & what few boys are at home are having your time now and you had better improve it. for when we soldiers go home you will have a pretty slim chance (with the girls I mean) (for the soldiers are the boys.) Well, no more till the next time. Write as often as you can, and I will try and answer them. From your loving brother,

Edward Chatfield

William S Chatfield

Dear Brothers Newton & James,

Well New't, as you have been very kind and have tried to cheer me a little by writing occasionally I will answer your letters, for I think a great deal of every letter that comes from home. It seems that you have plenty of work to do this Spring, but I hope that William & James will not be sick any more. I suppose that help is pretty scarce up that way since so many have gone to war. John Blanchet has got about well again. He has joined the reg't again. It was 10 months yesterday since I enlisted and there has not been a single day that I regretted it since I have been in the army. I have always had enough to eat drink wear. Soldiering seems to agree with me very well. In fact, I rather like it. I never have hurt myself at work yet. I will own that we have had some pretty hard marching but that dont last long. I presume that you and James have to work pretty hard. There is but very few white people left in the Country. These men are most all in the army and what there is left of the inhabitants are strong secesh. It is very warm nowadays in this part of the country.

Well I guess that I have written all of the news and so will close. Write often and remember your Absent brother,

Edward Chatfield

To Messers Isaac Newton & James Herrick Chatfield

Battle of Milliken's Bend

While writing his two June 7 letters, Chatfield had not yet learned about the vicious battle of Milliken's Bend, a fight that occurred across the Mississippi River early that morning. Milliken's Bend, some four miles above Young's Point on Louisiana soil, remained Grant's main supply base. If the Rebels could destroy Union forces there, they might succeed in breaking Grant's siege. To test that possibility, forces from CS Major General John G. Walker's Texas Division had moved toward Milliken's Bend before dawn on June 7. Flanking the Union soldiers in a heavy crossfire, the Confederates quickly closed, engaging in furious hand-to-hand combat, forcing the 9th Louisiana Colored Infantry and the 23rd Iowa Infantry to retreat behind the levee. At that moment, Admiral David D. Porter's gunboat, the *Choctaw*, opened fire on the Confederates, interrupting what may have otherwise resulted in a Confederate victory. When the gunboat *Lexington* arrived, the Confederates withdrew. Although the Confederates concluded that their test had failed, it actually had nearly succeeded. By the end of the day, the US had incurred 652 casualties, while the Confederates had lost 185. Yet for the people of Vicksburg, the Confederate retreat crushed the hope that the siege could be broken from the west, leaving one final hope still in place: assistance by CS General Joe Johnston from the east.[141]

Diary - June 10, 1863

It rained quite hard this forenoon and into the evening. I went down to the landing and got forage, but the roads were very bad.

Diary - June 11, 1863

They made me the Acting Corporal this morning. My first action was to take 3 men and get the Colonel the mare that the Signal Corps had refused to give him. After that, I went out to the regiment this forenoon with rations and did the same again this evening. The roads are still badly cut up but are getting dry.

One good turn deserved another. Colonel Paddock, the Provost Marshal, was the officer that had issued Chatfield a pass to Young's Point on June 2. Chatfield made a point of returning the favor on June 11; as a wagon guard and acting corporal, he had the opportunity to fetch a fine mare for his colonel.

Diary - June 12, 1863

I went down to the landing in the morning and brought back two loads of supply. Then I went out to the regiment in the afternoon. While out there, John Fundy and I went over to the 20th Illinois and saw Frank Chester, Frank Wickens, and Morris Lamb. All were in fine spirits. Charley Rodgers of Company E died in the hospital of wounds this evening. I feel quite unwell this evening with bad diarrhea.

Private Frank Chester, from Kankakee, was 24 years old and still a private when Chatfield saw him in 1863. Through a succession of enlistments, Chester moved up the ranks to become the Company "G" adjutant by May of 1865. Private Morris Lamb, 23, from DuPage, Illinois, would re-enlist in 1864, still a private. According to the *Illinois Roster*, Corporal Charles Rodgers, a married 27-year-old from Cook County, died in Vicksburg on June 1. Chatfield's record of his death was probably more accurate.

Diary - June 13, 1863

I feel somewhat better this morning. We had to move our quarters this forenoon because we were too close to the Colonel, and our noise disturbed him. I've been busy this afternoon cleaning my gun and revolver. The day is very warm and sultry.

Without Grant's approval, General McClernand's *Congratulatory Order No. 72* was printed on June 13 in the *Memphis Bulletin*. The final sentence especially enraged Grant and the other corps commanders. McClernand, a clever writer, imputed in an obscure dance of words that his failure to hold his position on May 22 was the fault of other commanders.

> If, while the enemy was massing to crush it, assistance was asked for by a diversion at other points, or by re-enforcement, it only asked what in one case Major-General Grant had specifically and peremptorily ordered, namely, simultaneous and persistent attack all along our lines until the enemy's outer works should be carried, and what, in the other, by massing a strong force in time upon a weakened point, would have probably insured success. — Major General John A. McClernand [142]

Stripping McClernand's tangled verbiage to its core, the translation becomes, "If the diversion or reinforcements we had requested had been ordered, our success would probably have been insured." With President Lincoln's approval, McClernand would soon receive orders that clarified Grant's level of dissatisfaction.[143]

Diary - June 14, 1863

I lay still all day.

Letter - June 14, 1863
Walnut Hills, Miss. Sunday Rear of Vicksburg, June 14th 1863

Dear Parents,

Another week has rolled around & brings with it the same old story that Vicksburg is not yet taken although closely beleaguered. My health is tolerable good excepting a bad diareah, which is a very general Complaint among the soldiers. The weather is very warm, so, that it is quite uncomfortable. We are laying right beside the hills and there is lots of nice springs where we have a plenty of good water which is a great advantage to us. Mr. Hoyt of the Chicago Sanitary Commission is down here. He brought down a lot of sanitary stores. He ate dinner with us today. He is a very good sort of a man. Has the right sort of principle about him. Mrs. Hoge [Colonel George B. Hoge's wife] is here, also, taking [care] of the Colonel who is very sick. The last letter that I had from you was dated the 23rd. We have not had any preaching in our Reg't since the fore part of March. Sundays are passed just about the same as any other day. Why, in fact, we have no Sunday in the army. We are kept on duty pretty steady going every day & standing guard nights. But we are in hopes that this state of things will not last much longer.

We have been looking for the Rebels to surrender every day for the last 3 weeks. But, they are holding out to the last extremity. Deserters say that they do not have half enough to eat. The first word almost that they say when they come to our lines is (give me us something to eat, we are almost starved.) We are being heavily reinforced every day. Some 30,000 or 40,000 are here and on the road, and it is said that the Rebel General Johnson [Johnston] is receiving heavy reinforcements back near Jackson somewhere, and that he is going to try and raise the seige. But, I think that before he gets into Vicksburg that he will find some obstacles in the way. For we have to strong a hold to be driven out very easy. The boys are all getting along firstrate, and are in good spirits, and feel confidant that they can whip the Rebs out yet —

Well, I have not got much to write this time, and, so, will close, thinking that I will do better next time. My love to you all.

I remain as ever your dutiful son,

Edward L. Chatfield

To Mr. N S Chatfield

Diary - June 15, 1863
I went out to the regiment this morning with rations.

The threat of being hit by a stray bullet remained a constant concern to every soldier, stories of injuries and deaths a part of everyday gossip. If stray bullets were a worry, then the ones sent by sharpshooters must have been of even greater concern.

> June 15, today walking with my comrade, John Gubtail, over the crest of a hill, suddenly fell prostrate at my feet. I thought he was trying to act funny, but he got up in a few minutes and showed me a bullet hole through his cap and a shallow furrow across his scalp where the bullet had ploughed. The Rebel sharpshooter had just missed his target partially. We went down to lower ground then. — Orderly Kellogg[144]

Lieutenant A.W. Beckett had recruited both John Gubtail, 21, and his younger brother, Lucius, 19, in Ashkum, Iroquois County. John, fortunately, recovered from the head wound and eventually became a corporal. Lucius, who within ten months would have an unpleasant legal "run in" with his company commander Captain Bliss Sutherland, remained a private.

Diary - June 16, 1863
Dan Durham and I went to the landing for the sutler this morning and brought up a load of goods. Then, we went out to the regiment this afternoon. The Paymaster paid the boys in the regiment today, but I was not present, so I didn't get paid.

Diary - June 17, 1863
The Paymaster failed to pay me this morning, because he did not have the registers with him.

Diary - June 18, 1863
I was gone from camp and out at the landing all day.

OFFICIAL CORRESPONDENCE
SPECIAL ORDERS HDQRS DEPARTMENT OF THE TENNESSEE,
No. 164. Near Vicksburg, MISS., June 18, 1863.

* * * * * * *

IV. Major General John A. McClernand is hereby relieved from the command of the Thirteenth Army Corps. He will proceed to any point he may select in the State of Illinois, and report by letter to Headquarters of the Army for orders. Major General E.O.C. Ord is hereby appointed to the command of the Thirteenth Army Corps, subject to the approval of the President, and will immediately assume charge of the same.

By order of Major General U.S. Grant:

JNO. A. RAWLINS,

Assistant Adjutant-General.[145]

OFFICIAL CORRESPONDENCE-
BATTLE-FIELD, near Vicksburg, MISS., June 18, 1863.

Major General U.S. GRANT, Commanding Department of the Tennessee:

Your order, relieving me and assigning Major-General Ord to the command of the Thirteenth Army Corps, is received. Having been appointed by the President to the command of that corps, under a definite act of Congress, I might justly challenge your authority in the premises, but forbear to do so at present. I am quite willing that any statement of fact in my congratulatory [order] to the Thirteenth Army Corps, to which you think just exception may be taken, should be made the subject of investigation, not doubting the result.

Your obedient servant,

JOHN A. McClernand, Major-General.[146]

Charles A. Dana, appointed as special commissioner to the War Department by Lincoln's officials, rendered his opinion on McClernand's firing:

Though the congratulatory address in question is the occasion of McClernand's removal, it is not its cause, as McClernand intimates when he says incorrectly that General Grant has taken exceptions to this address. That cause, as I understand it, is his repeated disobedience of important orders, his general insubordinate disposition, and his palpable incompetence for the duties of the position. As I learned by private conversation, it was, in General Grant's judgment, also necessary that he should be removed, for the reason, above all, that

190
The Chatfield Story: Civil War Letters and Diaries of
Private Edward L. Chatfield of the 113th Illinois Volunteers

his relations with other corps commanders rendered it impossible that the chief command of this army should devolve upon him, as it would have done were General Grant disabled, without most pernicious consequences to the cause. ....

C.A. Dana

Hon. E.M. Stanton. *Secretary of War*[147]

CHAPTER 18: FINAL DAYS BEFORE VICKSBURG

"If all accounts prove true, Vicksburg must shortly fall."

Diary - June 19, 1863
We moved our teamster camp from the bottom to the top of the hill where the water is splendid.

Twenty-three days had passed before the teamsters received permission to move back up the hill to a position atop the bluffs where the water was said to be "splendid"—away from the swampy delta where many had taken sick. But within hours of relocating themselves, the teamsters received orders to move the rest of the regiment down the hill—to the place on the Chickasaw Bayou from whence the teamsters had just come. Chatfield was already sick.

Diary - June 20, 1863
We were ordered to go up to the regiment and move the baggage. Our regiment has been relieved of its position and ordered to take the place of the 127th as provost guards. Colonel Paddock is the Provost Marshal. We moved the regiment

down the bluff to its new position beside the Chickasaw Bayou, about 1 ½mile away from the landing. I was taken sick this evening. I have a considerable fever and am going to bed early. I hope to feel better in the morning.

After stopping for water and food from the sutlers at the Chickasaw Creek atop the bluffs, the regiment reached the Chickasaw Bayou at 3:00 P.M. They received tents brought across from DeSoto Point, their first protection from heavy summer rains in over 40 days. As welcome as the tents were, they gave no protection to the soldiers from the deadliest enemy:

> On June 20th my regiment was changed in the line to ... the banks of the Chickasaw Bayou. We established our new camp at that point, little thinking at the time what an unfortunate move it was for us. ...
>
> Though I had built [my bunk] high enough to escape the prowling alligators I had not built high enough to get above the deadly malaria distilled by that cantankerous bayou. We soon learned what a loss we had sustained in exchanging the pure cold springs of the Walnut hills for the poisonous waters of our new vicinity. At first the blue waters of the Yazoo fooled us. It was as blue and clear as lake water, and we drank copiously of it, but felt badly afterwards. We didn't know we were drinking poisoned water until an old colored citizen, one day, warned us. Then we looked the matter up, and found that the interpretation of the word Yazoo was "The River of Death," ... We learned too late, however, ... and lost in the next few weeks nearly half of our regiment from malarial or swamp fever. — Orderly Kellogg[148]

Two days after having moved up the hill above the swamps, Chatfield and the teamsters received unsettling orders from the regiment encamped below on the Chickasaw Bayou.

Diary - June 21, 1863

I felt considerably better this morning. I had a good night's rest. The quartermaster promised us this morning that we should have a day of rest, but orders came before noon to pack up our camps up here on the hill and join the regiment below. My strength was pretty small when trying to load the wagons, so I couldn't do much, in fact. We camped with the regiment this evening. Some pioneer*corps of blacks are camped right beside us. There was some preaching this afternoon, and a meeting was held this evening. It was a good service. The weather is still very warm.

Things were quieter down on the bayou. There were no more singing bullets; the roar of the artillery was more distant; and the tents with their woven-bark bunks felt comforting. The surprise attack would come silently, however, as the swampland of toxic water and malarial-infested mosquitoes would gradually wreak havoc on the regiment.

Diary - June 22, 1863

I felt pretty well in the morning and went down to the landing with the teams after tents and other camp equipage, but I was taken with quite a high fever before I got back to camp. I got some medicine off the doctor which helped me some.† I feel a little better this evening.

Diary - June 23, 1863

I went with the wagon this morning. Today was a well day for me.

---

*   Military road construction engineers

†   The doctor probably gave Chatfield some quinine pills. Quinine was well known and abundantly used to alleviate the symptoms of malaria during the war. Significantly, neither in his diary entries nor in his letters does Chatfield ever use the term "malaria" to name his or others' illnesses. Invariably, he uses the more general and less threatening term, "ague." But, at this time, it is evident that Chatfield and his friends were suffering from bouts of malarial fever.

Letter - June 23, 1863
Lake's Plantation
Rear of Vicksburg June 23rd 1863

Dear Parents,

I was very hapily yesterday by receiving your very welcome letter which was very gladly perused as are all your Cheerfull letters. My health is tolerably good though for the last 3 or 4 days I have been a little unwell but which I do not think will result in any thing serious. Since I wrote my last dated the 14th our Regt has been relieved from fighting and digging of ditches & have been detailed for provost guard duty, Col. Paddock, being Provost Marshal of the 15th Army Corps. So that the boys are not engaged in standing guard on picket duty and as patrol guard which keep them busy the or rather on duty the most of the time. On account of our Reg't being so small, only about 100 men being fit for duty, that it keeps the boys right at their posts the most of the time.

If all accounts prove true, Vicksburg must shortly fall. A deserter came over to our line yesterday and he said that all the men had to eat was a little bean soup with less corn meal each day. And he said that Pemberton made them a speech the day before, which was Sunday, and told them that if they would stay in their places in the entrenchments and rifle pits, that they should all have 100 $ bounty extra and should all have 60 days furlough as soon as they should drive the Yankeys from thiss place (Vicksburg.) For they calculate that Johnson [Johnston] will raise the seige and so deliver them. But he said that if they did not get relief by that time, that they would be obliged to surrender for they had nothing to eat.

It is calculated that they have about 20,000 men in Vicksburg. But put them and all Johnsons [Joe Johnston] force together and they cant help themselves. On Sunday, Grants army met Johnsons [Johnston's] at black river and had a terrible battle killing & wounding some 8,000 & taking 2,000 prisoners. Fever & ague is getting pretty thick in this part of the army. There is also a considerable typhoid & billious fever to.

Adjutant D.S. Parker got back to the old 113 yesterday. He was heartily unclean and looks rather slim and bony, though he brought quite a number of packages & letters for the boys, & I was in hopes that there was a letter for me if nothing more. But, I was disappointed. Al Smith has not [got] very tough yet, although he is around the most of the time. The rest of the boys of our neighborhood are all well & hearty. The Reg't was paid for two months last week, but I did not happen to be around to sign the payroll and so did not get mine. But, nothing lost without some small gain. I shall have the bigger pile the next time. My letter's full. My love to you all, and I will close.

Your loving son,
Edward L Chatfield

Diary - June 24, 1863

This is one of my sick days. I have chills, fever, and pain in my limbs, my back and my head. I can't eat much.

For some time now, the men of General McPherson's division had been digging a mineshaft beneath the Jackson Road redan in front of them. A fortification guarding the Jackson Road entrance to Vicksburg, the redan was a separate earthwork about ½ mile south of the Stockade Redan at Graveyard Road. McPherson's objective was to place a few tons of black powder beneath the Jackson Road redan and detonate it, opening a path to the city.

Diary - June 25, 1863

I feel considerably better after lying still all day. There is poor water here. We are in an unhealthy place. There has been very heavy bombarding of Vicksburg for the last four days. They're still firing away very hard this evening. At 4:00 they blew up one of the enemy's forts on the main road to Vicksburg, causing an immense slaughter among them. Our men now hold the position.

The huge explosion at the Jackson Road redan occurred Thursday morning, June 25. The blast instantly killed six Rebels who were digging a "countershaft" through which they hoped to waylay the approaching Union shaft diggers. Chatfield had received incorrect news regarding the "immense slaughter," as no other Confederates were harmed, the countershaft having vented the upward force, sparing the redan.[149] Expecting little resistance, McPherson's infantrymen rushed forward but were quickly repulsed, their casualty counts high, "… 60 to 100 killed and wounded, including 2 lieutenant-colonels and 1 major."[150]

Diary - June 26, 1863

I feel about the same as I did yesterday. I'm just able to crawl around. I did sign my clothing list; it showed that I drew $49.14 worth of clothes on June 3rd. The weather today is very warm.

Diary - June 28, 1863

I felt a little better this morning and got permission to go out and visit the 76th. Most of the boys were in good spirits and enjoying good health. I took supper with William Warden, the orderly of Company F this evening. After that, we went out into the breastworks and rifle pits where there was considerable firing on both sides. It was very warm today.

This was the first reference to William "Billy" Warden, one of Chatfield's 20-year-old friends from Kankakee Township, and a railroader before the war. Warden's destiny was grim. Chatfield would write about Billy three more times.

Diary - June 29, 1863

I visited with the boys in the 76th through the forenoon. After dinner, I bid the boys goodbye and returned to the 113th and found camp in its usual quiet state.

And far away, officials continued to wring their hands...

OFFICIAL CORRESPONDENCE
WAR DEPARTMENT, Washington, June 29, 1863.

Colonel LUDLOW, Commissioner of Exchange, Fortress Monroe:

You will exert yourself to procure the release of Richardson and Browne, *Tribune* reporters, captured at Vicksburg. Browne's health is said to be failing. If they are held as hostages or for any special reason, ascertain and report it.

EDWIN M. STANTON

HEADQUARTERS DEPARTMENT OF VIRGINIA,
Fort Monroe, June 29, 1863.
Honorable E.M. STANTON, Secretary of War, Washington, D.C.:
    I am making every effort for release of Richardson and Browne. My first application was refused peremptorily. I have made another, the result of which I shall know and report to you on the return of the flag-of-truce boat from City Point on Thursday. They are held in retaliation for citizens arrested and held by us. This is the assigned reason. The real reason I believe to be that they are connected with the Tribune and are held to annoy.
    WM. H. LUDLOW, Lieutenant-Colonel and Agent[151]

Conditions in Vicksburg were beyond desperate. Disaster, starvation and death reigned. Family dogs and even baby kittens were skinned, boiled and eaten. Henry Ginder, a civilian construction engineer inside the city, wrote a letter home describing the chaos.

    This morning a man walking in town had his arm shot off. Major Reed's wife had her arm taken off by a piece of shell; and two ladies, day before yesterday, were struck by balls from a shrapnel shell and so severely wounded as not expected to live. The Yankees have placed sharpshooters on the opposite bank of the river to annoy our men as they go there to fill their casks with water.
    Flour is selling at $600 a barrel, biscuits $8 dozen, pies $4 apiece. Our cornmeal has given out; the men now get ¼ lb. bacon, ½ lb. flour or rice flour, sugar 1/8 lb., peas 1/12 qt., 1/50 gal. molasses.[152]

Diary - June 30, 1863
I went out with one of the teams and helped to get a load of brush [for kindling fires] this morning. Today was our day to muster for pay, but pay was not given for some reason. So I gathered blackberries.

Diary - July 1, 1863
I went down to the landing and drew back some rations, then returned to my company in the forenoon and did some washing.

South of Sherman's division, McPherson had not given up on his attempts to destroy the main redan off Jackson Road, stuffing it again with explosives. The detonation occurred at 1:30 P.M. This time no countershaft vented the violent outburst.

> The entire left face, part of the right, and the entire terra-plain of the redan were blown up, leaving an immense deep chasm. Our interior works were materially injured. One sapper and 8 Negroes, of the engineer department, occupied at countermining, were buried and lost, and the Third Louisiana lost 1 killed and 21 wounded and the Appeal Battery 4 wounded by the explosion. The loss of the Sixth Missouri by the mine I cannot state. It must have been serious. ….
> Respectfully submitted.
> LOUIS HEBERT, Brigadier-General, CSA.[153]

While the harassment with explosives raged on in Vicksburg, the harassment with words raged on from the Confederate Agent of Exchange at Hampton, Virginia …

OFFICIAL CORRESPONDENCE
FORT MONROE, July 2, 1863
Honorable E.M. STANTON:
> …. The release of Richardson and Browne is again refused on the ground of retaliation. ….
> WM. H. LUDLOW, Lieutenant-Colonel and Agent for the Exchange.[154]

Diary - July 2, 1863
I went on guard at the Provost Marshal's office, and that kept me pretty busy all day. It was another very warm day.

Diary - July 3, 1863
I returned from guard duty at 10:00 a.m., then went blackberrying with Bert Smith this afternoon. By evening, it looked like rain.

A flag of truce appeared between the lines this day, and discussions began between Grant and Pemberton as to the surrender of the city and all fortifications. Grant demanded an unconditional surrender, and Pemberton refused. Late in the evening, Grant offered more acceptable terms, and Pemberton accepted them. A cease-fire went into effect, and all guns went silent. Many later wrote colorful retrospective accounts of the day, including Orderly Kellogg:

> An old grizzly Reb straightened up out of a nearby pit. He sported long, gray Billy goat whiskers and his shaggy eyebrows looked like patches of hedge rows. Just opposite him on our side another old graybeard stood up in his pit and the two old warriors surveyed each other for several minutes; then old Johnnie said, "Hello, you over thar!" "Hello yourself," said old Yank. "Is that your hole your stan'nen in over thar?" said Johnnie. "I reckon," said Yank. "Wal, don't you know Mister, I've had some tarned good shots at you?" "I reckon," said Yank, "but s'pose ye hain't noticed no lead slung over thar nor nothin'?" "Yes," said Johnnie, "you spattered some dirt in my eyes now 'n' then." "So'd you mine," said Yank. And in that strain those two old veterans talked aand [sic] laughed from their respective roosts as though trying to shoot each other was the funniest thing in the world. About 3:00 o'clock that afternoon we saw some Union officers go out of our lines and part way over to the rebel works sit down under a tree on the grass. We afterwards learned those men were Grant, Rowlins [J.A. Rawlins, Grant's Assistant Adjutant General], Logan, McPherson and A.J. Smith. A short time afterwards some men in gray uniform came out of the rebel works and met our men under the tree. Those men were Pemberton, Bowen and a staff officer... — Orderly Kellogg [155]

Diary - July 4, 1863

Hurrah for our flag and the Union! Three cheers! Vicksburg is ours! The Rebels surrendered at 2:00 a.m. last night. I went on fatigue duty loading wagons and worked until 3:00 p.m. Colonel Paddock gave a dinner to all of the officers and some of the privates. I received a letter this evening and wrote one home. We have marching orders. We are to march at 3:00 a.m. tomorrow morning.

Letter - July 4, 1863
Vicksburg Miss.
July 4th 1863

Dear Parents,

Three Cheers for the Army & navy forever – Vicksburg is Ours. The Flag of this glorious Country doth wave in triumph over the Rebel stronghold. Oh let us rejoice in our victory. Last night at two oclock the Rebels surrendered. Gen. [John Alexander] Logans Division went into the city today & the General watered his horse at the Miss river the first thing. This was a very appropriate day for the surrender of the Rebs. ——

As for my part, I spent the day as follows. Was detailed on fatigue this morning. Went down and worked as hard as I could pitch in, loading wagons with Commissary stores until 3 this PM., when I returned to camp & had a dinner which was given by Col Paddock. ——

And now, the next thing in the programe is that we have marching orders. Shermans Corps is back of here to the black river to catch Old Jo Johnson [Johnston] who has quite a force wh with him. We are going to clear the western part of Rebeldom of all Rebels this time.

Shermans forces are composed of Steeles, Blairs & Tuttles Divisions. —— Smiths Brigade of Blairs Division is Composed of 6th & 8th Mo., 113th & 116th Ill. & 13th Regulars. We start tomorrow morning at 3 oclock & cannot tell what will be the events of the next few days. We may have some fighting, there is no telling. Every thing is excitement, and I cant tell you any news at this time. The boys are all usually well. They are all able for duty, except Bert. My health is good & we are all in first rate spirits. Excuse this hastily written letter & hope for the best. Direct the same as usual. My love to all. ——-

From your loving son,
Edward L. Chatfield
N S Chatfield

The surrender brought with it many celebrations. Chatfield's Mess # 2 welcomed the occasion with regimentally supplied foods not seen for the past eight months: fresh fish, potatoes, tea, freshly baked bread, butter, molasses, canned pineapples and tomatoes, and a liberal amount of wine supplied by the regimental adjutant, Daniel Parker, a friend of the Chatfield and Beach families back home. Every soldier in Mess #2 slept soundly that night, awakened too early the next morning to perform heavy duty at the docks. Once there, they witnessed a severely ill Colonel Paddock being assisted off one of the boats, an officer on either side of him. The sight of his officer friend, so ill, troubled Chatfield. No one at the time knew how truly grave Paddock's condition was.

CHAPTER 19: THE CHICKASAW BAYOU

"The most disagreeable nasty & sickly place that well could be found"

Diary - July 5, 1863
All who were able for duty were ordered out to load wagons at the landing at daylight. We worked very hard all day through 12:00 midnight.

Chatfield and all of the other privates in the regiment labored from before daylight—17 hours total—fully expecting to march away with General Sherman on the morning of July 6. But when morning came, only four men from Company "B" marched away: Corporal Alfred G. States, Private Wallace Beebe, Private Charles E. Boswell, and Private Ira William. All others in the company were judged too sick to march and remained behind, their duties unclear for another two days.

Diary - July 6, 1863
We all remained in camp today. I had a good rest. A nice shower fell this evening.

Letter - July 6, 1863
Chickasaw Bayou, July 6th, 1863

Dear Parents,

I will endeavor to address you a few lines. I wrote a letter the 4th and I stated then that we expected to march the next morning. But the next morning, instead of starting on the march, we were all detailed on fatigue loading wagons with provisions to be sent out to the army that goes to black river. We worked hard all day, it being Sunday to. But, then, you know that we have no Sabbath in the army. Now that which we have been contending for so long is in our hands, all is quiet.

It seems quite strange to hear no more cannonadeing or the rattle of musketry after having been kept up steady for six and half weeks or 46 days with out any intermission. The town of Vicksburg looks as though it had been pretty badly used. There is not a house in the town but that shows the effects of shot & shell, and the ground is all ploughed up in every direction. We have taken from 25 to 30,000 prisoners & some 4,000 stand of arms. When the Rebs [surrendered] they did not spike any of the cannon or render them useless in any way. Although there is a good many dis abled mantled by our own shot. It is said that the prisoners are all to be paroled and marched out of our lines. I have not been in the town, myself, but I have my news by our boys that have been in and seen it.

Our reg't got is very small. We have only about 80 effective men for duty, a great many being sick and detailed on other service. We have only 16 men for duty in our company at the present. I will send you by this, a list of the names of the [boys] that remain. Cap't Williams is quite sick. He has the Billious Fever. James Henry, Elisha Johns & Joseph Smith [forlorn hope] have furloughs, and they are going home, to be gone two months, for bravery displayed on the memorable 22nd of May when they volunteered to charge on the enemies works. It is said that James H & J Smith particularly distinguished themselves.

My health is quite good. I expect that we have to move tonight about 2 miles from here on to the hills where it will be healthier & we will have better water. As I have been making out this list several of the boys have requested to ask you to show it to their folks. It will please them much. Well, I must close.

My love to you all (from your loving son,)

Edward L. Chatfield

Mr. N S Chatfield

Diary - July 7, 1863

We moved our camp to a nice place on the top of the hills within 1½miles of Vicksburg. We have good water. Our new camp is ¼ mile from the Mississippi River.

With nearly everyone in the regiment sick, the decision was made to move back up the hill again, where Chatfield and his company finally received word of their new duties. They would serve as provost guards—the keepers of peace and good discipline, and the enforcers of martial law. They were to deter marauders, raiders, looters, and stragglers. They would do searches, seizures and arrests. They would hear citizen's complaints and take custody of enemy deserters and prisoners of war. They would issue passes to soldiers and civilians. Chatfield's duty as wagon guard had come to an end.

Diary - July 8, 1863

All able for duty in Companies A, B and H were detailed to the corps hospital for fatigue and guard duty. When we got there, I was just tired out. The boys buried three soldiers that died yesterday. Three more died this evening.

The *Illinois Roster* shows no deaths within that interval. The corps hospital was located back down at the Chickasaw Bayou, four miles from camp. Only sixteen men were able to make the walk, but not with ease, six succumbing to their sicknesses before reaching the hospital, arriving as patients instead of as duty soldiers, adding to the 400 sick men already there. The bayou was close to the Yazoo, available to boats, but beset with mosquitoes and disease. The area was simply no place for a hospital. Yet, there it was.

Diary - July 9, 1863

I helped cook today, and that kept me on my feet all day. I am very tired this evening. Another man died tonight.

The specific date of death of one man had not been recorded in the *Illinois Roster*: Private Joel Moffatt, 19, of Company "K", from Newton County, Indiana. Perhaps it was he who died that night. Private Moffatt would be one of many men who would die of disease during the summer of 1863.

At the cost of 17,500 Union and Confederate lives, Port Hudson, 200 miles south of Vicksburg, fell on July 9, ending Major General Nathaniel P. Banks's 43-day siege and marking the time after which the Union had full control of the Mississippi. With the Anaconda stranglehold tightening, Sherman and his Expeditionary Army prepared to close in on the city of Jackson for the second time.

Diary - July 10, 1863

I helped get breakfast ready and then felt very bad after breakfast. We were relieved of duty at 10:00 a.m. but [due to illness] had a hard job getting back to camp. It took us 8 hours to go four miles.

After two days of fatigue and guard duty at the hospital, the boys of Company "B" had grown so sick that, by today's standards, they could have just as easily been patients, themselves. But at Vicksburg in the summer of 1863, a soldier had to be dying to be hospitalized. Failing that test, Chatfield and his nine companions were told to return to camp—a four-mile walk from the swamp to above the bluffs. Had they been well, the boys could have walked the distance in about an hour. Instead, it took them eight hours to ascend the hill to return to camp. They took their longest rest at what they called the "Big Springs," a favorite place beyond the crest of the hill where the cool, clear Chickasaw Creek cascaded in a natural waterfall. In his recollections, Private Beach vividly recalled what took place there.

I had gone but a short distance when I was taken with a chill. I went a little farther and had to stop. I had just sat down on a log when the chance came along for me to get a ride up the hill. When we reached the Big Springs, two of the boys were lying there on their rubber blankets while some of their chums were pouring cold water on them. My chum carried my gun and canteen, so I finally got to camp. — Private Riley Beach [156]

Diary - July 11, 1863
I am very sick today with considerable fever and feeling very weak. I have pain in my legs, back, arms and head.

Diary - July 12, 1863
I am still quite sick today. I had a chill and fever. The doctor gave me a prescription. I have no appetite.

In response to the first Union draft, violence erupted in New York on July 12. The New York Provost Marshal's office was burned to the ground. Railroads were torn up, and telegraph lines were cut. Mobs consisting principally of Irish immigrants targeted the powerful rich and the free blacks—the rich, an elite class able to buy its way out, and the blacks, a willing source of cheap labor. The city raged in riot for nearly a week. When it was all over, more than one hundred people were dead, thousands were wounded, and an untold number of blacks had fled the city.

Letter - July 13, 1863
Vicksburg, July 13th 1863

Dear Parents,
    Feeling a considerable better than I have for the last 3 or 4 days, I will try and answer and ans your very welcome letters of the 28th June & 4th July. I also wrote you a letter on the 4th and one on the 6th. We are now encamped just outside of the enemies line of entrenchments on one of the highest hills. We have plenty of good spring water & fresh air. The Rebels are being paroled as fast as it can be done. A good many have got out and gone home on their paroles already. There is to be a paroled camp to be somewhere down here where all of the most rabid secesh will be sent. A good share of the men from Mis, Ark, Kentucky & other parts say that they will never take up arms again to fight against the only true government that

ever was. The way that every thing looks now I think that this wicked war will be brought to a close soon. Vicksburg & Port Hudson have fallen. Johnson [Johnston] out here near Jackson is as good as whiped, while Lee, [who] is trying to overrun the North, has his communication cut of [off] with a good many prisoners captured & likely to be entirely bagged. I think that, to put every thing together, that every thing together looks as though the war could not last much longer. The most of the Army down here are in good health and in the best of spirits. Our Reg't, though, are about all sick, hardly enough well ones to take care of the sick. While we were on Provost Guard, we were encamped down on what is called the Chickasaw bayou, the most disagreeable nasty & sickly place that well could be found. Well, the consequences was we were all very billious and had the fever and Ague.

I am glad to hear that Mothers health is so much better. It will bring a great deal of happiness to our home to not have to be bothered by lazy hired girls. But, I am afraid that you will be to ambitious and do to much and bring yourself down again.

The prospect of our going North has grown beautifully small since Vicksburg has fallen. Now we have got to stay here and stick it out. But, if we have got the fever & ague, we will soon be all right again & then let them do what they please with us. Here in my tent is five sick — Albert [Smith], Thomas [Carrow], Riley Beach, John Blanchet & myself. All of us have the fever & ague. John Fundy is doing his very best that he can for us & he will be amply repaid. I have not have a chance to go into Vicksburg yet. They are very strict.

Father wished to know what office or business I was in. I will tell you. I am High Private in the front rank of the Glorious comp B. I was detailed last Feb to go with the wagons, which they call wagon guard, and help load and unload them, which I have been doing every since, until about 2 weeks ago, when I was returned to my Comp. Mother, you need not look for me at home. When the time comes, we or I, or what is left of us, will go home and then rejoice all together. But, you may put all your expectations at rest. There is no getting furloughs here, so there is no use of thinking of that. There has not been a single [soldier] of our Comp. under arrest or in any trouble, but Capt. Southerland [Bliss Sutherland] is the same man that he was at home — a mean, sneaking, pufing [man] picking a fuss with his Comp. Only yesterday he sold Thomas Darly, one of his own Comp., whiskey. And he got drunk and fell. Well, when, the Capt. Commenced abusing him, which led on to one thing to another, he finally tied him up & bucked & gaged [gagged] him, which was perfectly scandalous. Well, my sheet is full.

My love to you all.

From your loving son,

Edward L. Chatfield

N S Chatfield

Captain Bliss Sutherland was evidently well known for his blustery and stormy ways. To buck and gag Private Darly, Sutherland sat him on the ground with his knees drawn up, then placed Darly's hands and arms under the knees and tied them. Next he ran a stick over the arms and under Darly's knees, leaving him "bucked," immovable. Darly was then gagged with a strip of cloth forced into his mouth and tied at the back of his head, preventing him from speaking or crying out. Thomas Darly was a tall, single, 25-year-old, Irish-born farmer from Aroma Township.

Tom Carrow (spelled "Carroll" in the *Illinois Roster*), like John Fundy, was one of Chatfield's good friends and another messmate. Like Fundy, Carrow was from Canada and had lived and farmed with his family in Limestone Township before enlisting at the age of 21.

Diary - July 13, 1863

I feel some better this morning. No fever. I wrote home today. The weather is cloudy and cool.

Diary - July 16, 1863

I borrowed $4.00 from John Blanchet yesterday and spent $1.25 of it for fruit. Then my pants were stolen by some thief or other from under my head while I slept last night.

Diary - July 17, 1863

I feel some better again. I think that my disease has turned. Fred Glass died yesterday morning.

Private Frederick A. Glass, 28 years old, died of disease. His farm home was in Norton Township, but he was born in London, England. Captain Williams had recruited Glass just as he had Chatfield. Beach later wrote, "We buried him on a high mound near the Mississippi River."[157]

Letter - July 18, 1863
Vicksburg Miss July
18th 1863

Dear Parents.

Having been silent some time, I will write you a few lines. I wrote you last the 6th.* The 7th we moved to where we are now on the top of one of the highest hills 1¾ miles from Vicksburg, ½ mile from the river of which we have a pleasant view. On the 8th, all that were fit for duty of our Comp. & Co H were sent down it to the Corp Hospital. We staid there two days and it was there that I was taken sick. It was just as much as I ~~can~~ could [do] to get back. And since then, I have had a pull down of the fever. But now the fever is ~~eff~~ broken, and I am gaining slowly. I am very weak, but hope that, if nothing happens, that I will get along. I am glad to hear that Mother is so good. She has been afflicted so long.

If we were at home to attend Sunday School occasionally, it would [be] one of the best of treats. For Sunday is so seldom [observed] that it seems as though we had none at all. Who did you sell fanny to & did you raise any colts this Summer? We have some fun occasionally & sometimes we play tricks on one another. The other [night] some light fingered — he was not very light fingered, for I saw him, — stole my pants from under my head while we were all asleep. But, the loss was not much. I had a little over 3.00 $ in the pocket, with a few stamps. So, that's the way the world goes.

One of our best men died night before last, Corporal Frederick A. Glass. He had the fever & ague in the first, and it then turned into sinking chills or congestive chills. He was decently buried in a good coffin. Lieut. Charles Squires of Co K died day before yesterday. They procured a metallic coffin and sent him home today. Well, I will not write any more at present, not feeling very stout, You hear all the news of the army sooner than we do. My best respects to all inquiring friends.

My love to you all.

From your loving son,

Edward Chatfield

N S. Chatfield

Lieutenant Charles Squires, of Company "F", was 21 when he enlisted from Yellowhead Township in Kankakee. The cause of death wasn't listed, so the odds would have it that his death was due to disease.

---

*   Edward's latest letter was actually written on July 13.

Diary - July 19, 1863

I went down to the spring after breakfast and had a nice wash. The water falls 20 feet to the ground. I stayed in our tent most of day and read some good books. I'm gaining more strength every day. It's very hot in the daytime and very cool at night. The mosquitoes are very troublesome at night. I wrote several letters today.

Diary - July 20, 1863

I felt pretty smart this morning. The boys are getting along finely. One of the boys in Company A died this morning, Bowers, by name. This was a very sultry day. I went down to the spring again and had another fine wash this evening.

Private James A. Bowers was a 34-year-old married man from Cook County, Illinois, a mason born in Canada before enlisting. He died of disease.

Letter - July 20, 1863
Vicksburg Miss July 20th, 1863

Dear Brother,

Well David, as it is Monday I presume that you are very busy about harvest. How do you get along? How is the wheat? Is it a good quality? And, what do you think that it will yield to the acre? I should like it very much [if it] was so that I could be with you and help to gather the grain. But, I think that we did about as well here harvesting as we did about 30,000 Rebs, which I think will amount to a Considerable. What harvesting there was done here in the grain line was about two months ago. I had the Billious fever, but that has left me now and I am slowly gaining my strength again. Al & John Blanchet is about like myself, not worth much yet. John Fundy has the ague & fever. There is none of us dangerous. We manage to take pretty good care of ourselves.

Well, I shant write any news this time. You may expect a longer letter next time. Write often. I remain as ever your loving Brother, Edward Chatfield

Co B 113th — Ill Vols. Vicksburg Miss — Care Capt. Williams

D A Chatfield

Diary - July 21, 1863

I was up this morning before light after a very refreshing rest. I went down to the spring and took another nice bath. Frank Wickens and John Rohrer of the 20th Illinois were here and took dinner with us. The weather was not quite as warm as yesterday.

John Rohrer was a 20-year-old sergeant from Chatfield's neighborhood, a farmer who had mustered into service in 1861. Within less than a year he would be discharged, having satisfied his three-years of service.

Diary - July 22, 1863

I felt pretty smart in the morning, so Bert Smith and I got a horse and mule and went out to see if it would not be good for our health. We went about 3 miles and found some blackberries and ripe peaches to eat. Then we went to one of the houses and got a nice glass of buttermilk and had quite a chat with the old lady who is Secesh to the backbone. We returned to camp at 4:00 p.m. feeling pretty tired but well repaid for our trouble. It was quite warm all day. Tom Carrow felt worse today. Frank Showbar returned to the company today and is sick again tonight.

That evening Chatfield and Bert stewed the blackberries for supper, sharing their pickings with the sick boys in Mess #2, an effort to hasten the return of good health to all. Frank Showbar, from Iroquois County, continued to suffer. Not yet 21, he was eventually discharged in Memphis on February 7, 1865.

Diary - July 23, 1863

We had a little sprinkle last night cooling the air considerably. It's not as warm today. A corporal in Company A by the name of Walker died today. I washed my clothes this afternoon, and the work tired me out. I'm not very strong yet. Frank Showbar is still pretty sick today. Frank Chester of the 20th made a call this evening. He looks as hearty as a buck. I received no mail today.

Private Martin Walker was a married blacksmith from Cook County. He was 40 years old when he died of disease. By July 23, the entire company was seriously ill. Everyone was hoping for a move. One delightful rumor held that Colonel Hoge and Major George R. Clark had been in contact with Illinois Governor Yates, urging that the regiment be transferred to General Burnside's Department, then operating out of Cincinnati, Ohio.[158] Cincinnati was close enough to Chatfield's relatives in Twinsburg, North Ridgeville, and Middlefield that they might have been able to visit him at camp, the rail connections south having been well established by this time. The conditions in Ohio would have also been far healthier than those at Mississippi's Chickasaw Bayou. But the hoped-for move to Ohio wouldn't happen.

Diary - July 24, 1863

I was not as well this morning, common for the last few days, so I went to the doctor and got some medicine. I had some fever and a hard headache. Albert Smith got a pass and went into town and got us some catfish.

Diary - July 25, 1863

I went to the doctor again this morning. The mosquitoes were not much trouble last night. I cleaned my revolver, but that was all I did today. Most of boys are getting better now.

Diary - July 26, 1863

I had a good night's rest, then got more medicine from the hospital after breakfast. About noon today, we received orders to report to General Hurlbut at Memphis. Three cheers. Hurrah, hurrah! We will receive our pay before we leave. We got the sad news this evening that Wallace Beebe had been killed and Ira William and Charles Boswell were taken as prisoners. We had a big shower and a blow of wind that leveled a good many of our tents.

Beebe, William, and Boswell were three of the four soldiers in Company "B" who had been selected to accompany General Sherman's troops on the day following Vicksburg's surrender—an expedition to Jackson, Mississippi, to pursue CS General Joe Johnston, who had reoccupied the city following Sherman's May departure. Wallace Beebe (Beeby in the *Illinois Roster*), born in Michigan, was a 22-year-old farmer from the Essex Township, Kankakee County. Ira William, a native of Kane County, Pennsylvania, was a 22-year-old farmer who had enlisted in Salina Township. Charles Boswell, born in Leicester, England, was by far the oldest of the three, a 34-year-old married farmer from Essex Township. The news of the three men's fate was sketchy, mostly rumor—a mystery that would remain unresolved for many months to come.

Chatfield had not yet heard that on July 26, Adjutant D.S. Parker had resigned, after having served but ten months of his three-year commitment, his reasons for resignation unknown. Circumstances that occurred in the months and weeks prior to July 26 may have given him cause to resign, however. Charley Frith, the man who had competently served Parker as clerk, had deserted the army on April 1, 1863, likely staining Parker's reputation. Three days later, General David Stuart, under whom Parker had been serving, had been removed from command, altering Parker's chances for further promotion. Finally, Colonel Paddock, Parker's close messmate, the friend whom Parker had faithfully served, had become desperately ill in early July and had been shipped north to the Memphis hospital. Aware of his lack of support from the ranks above him, Parker may have chosen to resign, returning to his family and his responsibilities as editor of the *Kankakee Gazette*.

Letter - July 26, 1863
Vicksburg Sunday July 26th 1863

Dear Parents & Brothers

You see this paper is of a different kind. It is sesesh paper. Some that was Captured at Vicksburg. The last letter that I received from you was dated the 5th of this month. Although there has been a mail every day or every other day for the last two weeks. But, there was not a letter for me since that time. My health is not very good yet. The Climate seems to be very debilitating. It is very hot through [the] day, while the nights are very cool with a nice breeze stirring. The boys of our Company are unwell and Complaining. There is but one man reported for duty in our [company] and he is Riley Beach. We have plenty to eat, such as it is. But a sick fellow needs some of the little niceties that we cannot get without paying a very high price. And then [I] had the good fortune to have my pants stolen from under my head. I had about $3.50 that I had just borrowed from one of the boys. So my purse is pretty low. But, I will manage it some way. It is very dry here. There has not been any rain of any account for the last two months. Peaches are just getting ripe about here, but I have not had but I have not had any of any account yet. Our Division has just returned to this place from Jackson, I hear, and I suppose that some new expectation [will go] somewhere, for there is a plenty [work to be done] in different parts of the [country] to crush the Rebellion yet. But, it seems to me the way things look now that they (the Rebels) could not hold out a great while. Johnsons [Johnston's] army is just about annihilated, while Bragg is retreating southward & Rosecrans is following him up. Lee is badly used. I hear, since I commenced this, that we have orders to go to Memphis within two or three days. Well, I am tired and I must rest awhile.

(3 oclock P.M.) Since I commenced this letter we have received sad news, although it is not fully confirmed. I will give the particulars in full. These 4 men detailed from our [company] to stay with the Brigade teams (You will understand by that, there are what is called Brigade & Division teams, as well as Reg't teams.) Their names were Corp. States, Private Beebe, [Charles] Boswell, & Ira Williams. Well, in this last expedition to Jackson, they went with the Brigade. And, while they were out there, the teams went out Foraging — Beebe, Boswell & Ira Williams with [them.] And, while they were out, they were attacked by Guerillas and all taken prisoners or killed. Wallace Beebe was killed & Boswell & Williams were taken prisoners. This is as full news as we have received &, as I said before, that it had not been fully confirmed.

We have just received orders to go to Memphis and to report to General Hurlbut, and we are to be paid soon. Our Officers had orders today to make out their Payrolls immediately & have them signed by their Companies. There has [been] quite a number [who have] died since we have been in this camp. We have been in this camp about 3 weeks & have had 9 men die in that time. There are some pretty bad cases yet, but the most of the sick are getting better.

Well, my sheet is about full & I must close. My love to you all.

I remain as ever your loving son & Brother,

Edward L. Chatfield

Direct the same as usual until further orders.

N S Chatfield

Diary - July 27, 1863

I felt some better today but saw the doctor anyway. He thought that some bitters* would help me, but I refused them. My strength is improving every day. Another man in the regiment passed away today. His name is Private Elias S. Jones, in Company E. News is that we will be paid tomorrow morning. Camp is very quiet. The boys are lying around smoking their pipes and taking it coolly. Thomas Carrow is still not well, as usual. He thinks he has the symptoms of typhoid fever.

Elias Jones, a married farmer from Palatine Township of Cook County, enlisted at the age of 24. He died of disease.

Diary - July 28, 1863

The paymaster came and paid our regiment two months' pay. I received four months' pay equal to $52.00. A heavy rainstorm came in the afternoon and blew our tent flat. It thoroughly soaked us. We took shelter in mess number 3's tent for the night. Other than Thomas Carrow, who is quite sick tonight, the rest of us are gaining slowly.

---

*   Bitters, in the 1860's, were medicines—alcoholic drinks that were said to improve digestion. Common ingredients included aromatics such as angostura, cascarilla, and orange peel; bitter tasting quinine; cassia as a laxative, and gentian as a digestive tonic.

CHAPTER 20: NORTH TO MEMPHIS, EAST TO CORINTH

"We have had another death in our Company."

Diary - July 29, 1863

We commenced to move this morning. We moved ½mile to the river about 3:00 p.m. and waited until after dark before the boat Silver Wave came. We loaded everything on the boat, then lay there until morning.

Diary - July 30, 1863

Our boat went up to the city, and I went ashore and looked around a little. I was so weak that I did not go very far. But, I got a cup of tea that refreshed me considerably. John Fundy and I went up town and bought a box of strawberries. We got it for $20.00 per 2 dozen and made $6.00 by selling them again. George Shays died just after we got to Young's Point. We got a coffin for him at Milliken's Bend and had him buried. I went and saw Loyal Blair's grave, then I returned to the boat, and we started on our trip again. The diarrhea is pretty hard on me today. It ran me very bad last night.

Private George Shays, from Limestone, had been sick for nearly five months, Chatfield first mentioning Shays's sickness in his March 1, 1863, letter. Shays died while aboard the steamer, *Silver Wave*.

Diary - July 31, 1863
Our boat kept on her way all night. It's not very fast, only making 6 miles per hour. There's nothing of interest along the way, just the same monotony all along the shore.

Diary - August 1, 1863
Rain threatened last night, but none fell. We had several little showers today. We passed Napoleon in the morning. It looks very much worse for wear. There were only 3 or 4 persons visible. Our boat tied up a little after dark. It's dangerous to navigate after dark.

Diary - August 2, 1863
We started up river at daylight and reached Helena, Arkansas, by 10:00 a.m. I went ashore and bought some edibles. A man of Company E died this morning, Private Henry Jackson. They left him at Helena.

Private Henry Jackson was born in New York but lived in Barrington, Illinois, when the war started. He was a 25-year-old farmer when he enlisted, another married man who died of disease. The slow steamer continued its up-river push, laden with sickened men. Riley Beach had taken ill again.

Diary - August 3, 1863
We lifted anchor at daylight and reached Memphis at 10:00 a.m. Our officers reported to General Hurlbut, and we were ordered to Corinth. Fruit and confectionery peddlers were plenty, but I was put on guard when we landed and did not go ashore.

Diary - August 4, 1863

It's my 21st birthday, so, I suppose that now I am my own man. But I cannot see any difference in my prospects. There seems to be a good deal of business going on here. The streets and wharves are lined with people. I went uptown this forenoon and made a few purchases. I expressed $35.00 home by the Adams Express Company and $57.00 for Bert Smith and Tom Carrow. When I got back to the boat, I found them unloading. They moved the baggage to the depot. We won't be going until tomorrow morning, so I found Cousin Clark and stayed with him all night. We had a pleasant visit.

Letter – [August 4, 1863 – undated]

[Chatfield included this hastily written and undated addendum in the express package.]

Dear Parents,

Since this letter was commenced I have concluded to Express my money home. Three of us put together — Bert Smith, Tom Carrow and myself.

Albert sends $35.00 $22.00. Thomas, $35.00, and myself, $35.00, in all 92.00 $. If you have a chance to see Toms folks, or Als, let them know.

Yours truly, Edward Chatfield

Letter - August 4, 1863
Memphis Tenn. August 4th, 1863

Dear Parents,

You will see by this that we are somewhat Northward to what we were when I wrote my last. We started from Vicksburg the 30th July and got here yesterday. The health of some of the men is improving, but there is a great many sick now. My own health is gaining slowly, but I have not got very stout yet. What we are to do next, or where we shall go, still remains a mystery. We are still on board the boat that we came up on, the Silver Wave, and our Officers and, in fact, all of us want to go to Cairo or St Louis on her, but I hear that we are ordered from [here] to Corinth. I cannot tell what will be done. We got our Pay the day before we started, and I will Express $40.00 from here to you. We have had another death in our Company. George Shays is no more. He died the 30th, the day that we started from Vicksburg. He was buried at Millikens Bend. He lies in the same graveyard that Loyal does.

The Cap't just Came along, and he says that we go to Corinth. Albert does not seem to gain at all. He keeps about the same, just able to be around. Thomas Carrow & Riley Beach are a little better. John Fundy is well. It keeps him pretty busy waiting on the sick. Orderly Kellogg is quite debilitated. He looks pretty slim. Lieut. Jeffcoat is quite sick also. We are in hopes that we will get into a healthy part of the Country, somewhere, so that we can regain our strength again. Well, I will close. Write often, and direct to the Regt Via Cairo.

My love to you all.

I remain as ever,

Edward Chatfield

N.S. Chatfield

[On back side of letter] The Fourth of August, my Birth Day. Good wishes to you all, hoping that by the time the next 4th [comes] that this nation may be at peace and we all once more rejoined. When I look back on the past year, it seems as but a short time. Yet, it has been a year since I enlisted. Remember me in your prayers is the wish of your son, Edward

In early August, the 113th was assigned to the U.S. Army Post of Corinth, Mississippi, part of the 3rd Brigade (and in December the 2nd Brigade) of the 2nd Division of General Hurlbut's 16th Army Corps. Chatfield would remain in Corinth until January 1864.

While the regiment slept on the boarding platform in Memphis, Chatfield enjoyed a nice evening and rested in a fine hotel with his cousin, Clark Chatfield, an orderly from Company "C" of the 2nd Illinois Cavalry who had been assigned to assist General J.C. Veach. Perhaps they had spent the night at the Gayoso, said to have been the best hotel in Memphis. The noble building featured over 100 luxury guest rooms decorated in hardwood and exquisitely furnished. Adorned by six tall columns, the Gayoso's towering front of heavy stone overlooked the bluffs. Scores of famous guests had slept in the Gayoso, including Generals Grant and Sherman. No better birthday celebration could have been arranged, except, of course, a nice long furlough home.

Diary - August 5, 1863 (A.M. entry)
We had a good breakfast at the hotel, then I bid goodbye to Cousin Clark. We boarded the cars at 7:00 a.m. and started out. It was an unpleasant and tiresome ride.

Before departing, the surgeon arrived and passed out two quinine powders to every man sickened by malaria, instructing them to take the first one immediately and the second in two hours. The *Memphis and Charleston* tracks stretched southeast from Memphis and turned east into the sizzling sun near the McKee Station. The rails were safe for any speed up to twelve miles per hour, requiring nine hours on average to travel from Memphis to Corinth. The sickened bodies of exhausted soldiers lay exposed to the searing sun, jolting the distance in open gondolas past heavily guarded stations. Given no disturbance of the rails, the schedule was predictable.

Train Stations from Memphis to Corinth
- Start: 7:00 A.M.   Memphis
- Mile 2:   7:12 A.M.   McKee Station
- Mile 4:   7:24 A.M.   Bunton Station
- Mile 8:   7:48 A.M.   White's Station
- Mile 15:   8:30 A.M.   Germantown
- Mile 25:   9:30 A.M.   Collierville
- Mile 33:   10:18 A.M.   La Fayette (Today's Rossville Junction)
- Mile 40:   11:00 A.M.   Moscow Station, with its northbound branch to Somerville
- Mile 49:   11:54 A.M.   La Grange
- Mile 51:   12:06 P.M.   Grand Junction (Linking the *Mississippi Central*)
- Mile 56:   12:36 P.M.   Saulsbury
- Mile 66:   1:36 P.M.   Middleton
- Mile 72:   2:12 P.M.   Pocahontas
- Mile 82:   3:12 P.M.   Chewalla
- Mile 90:   4:00 P.M.   Corinth hospital tents west of town
- Mile 91:   5:00 P.M.   Battery Robinette and Battery Williams, ¼ mile from the Corinth Station

Chatfield and others were well enough to survey the rolling hills rich with lakes, small streams, ponds, and trees, not yet displaying the advance of fall. At roughly 4:00 P.M., the train slowed to a stop one mile out of Corinth, where a large array of hospital tents stood pitched in front of four farm buildings. A score of ambulances stood by as stretcher-bearers mounted the cars, removing Albert Smith, Riley Beach and 110 other severely sick soldiers before sending the train on to Battery Williams, a U-shaped earthwork on the south side of the tracks. Behind Battery Williams, an empty barracks awaited the 113th Regiment. Four hundred yards northwest of Battery Williams, on the opposite side of the tracks, the left flank of Battery Robinette wedged upward from the horizon. Together, the two earthworks defended the western entrance to Corinth along the *Memphis and Charleston Railroad.*

Diary - August 5, 1863 (P.M. entry)

We reached Corinth at 5:00 p.m., and we are now pleasantly situated in the barracks of Battery Williams, ¼ mile from town. It's quite cool and pleasant today. I feel pretty tired and lame, but I am stronger than when we left Memphis.

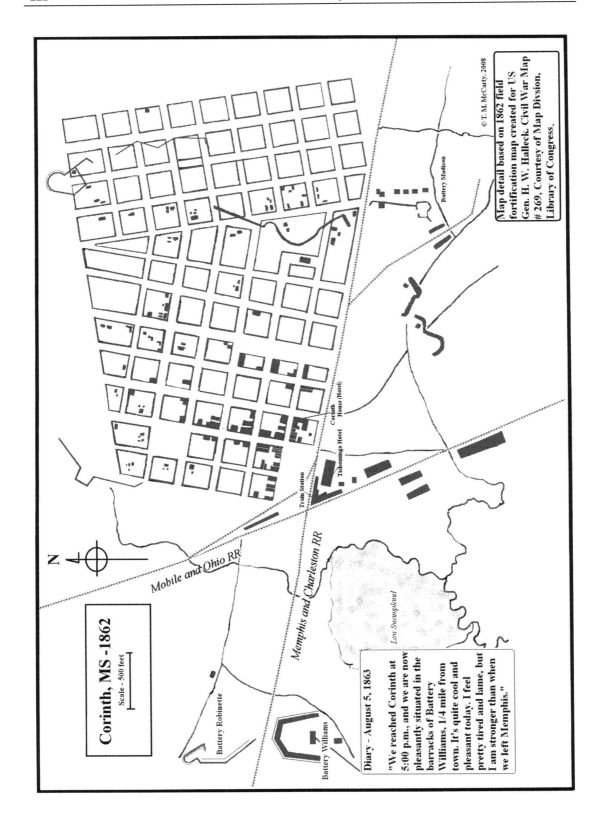

Corinth, MS - 1862

Scale - 500 feet

N

Mobile and Ohio RR

Memphis and Charleston RR

Low Swampland

Train Station

Tishomingo Hotel

Corinth (Hotel) House (Hotel)

Battery Madison

Battery Robinette

Battery Williams

© T. M. McCarty, 2008

Map detail based on 1862 field fortification map created for US Gen. H. W. Halleck. Civil War Map # 269, Courtesy of Map Division, Library of Congress.

Diary – August 5, 1863

"We reached Corinth at 5:00 p.m., and we are now pleasantly situated in the barracks of Battery Williams, 1/4 mile from town. It's quite cool and pleasant today. I feel pretty tired and lame, but I am stronger than when we left Memphis."

CHAPTER 21: DEATH'S CHALLENGE IN CORINTH

"There is a considerable fever and ague among the boys."

Diary - August 6, 1863
I took a good rest this morning but still feel real tired and sore. The Kansas J-Hawkers came in today from a 17-day scout.

The Kansas Jayhawkers—the 7th Kansas Cavalry—had been searching for Nathan Bedford Forrest, dubbed by Sherman as "the devil cavalryman," who had been systematically tearing up all of the rails. The 7th was the same cavalry that cleared CS General Price out of Holly Springs and forced him south to the Tallahatchie in November, and the 7th was the cavalry that Price later trapped down in Coffeeville.

In the meantime, the stalemate over the fate of two correspondents continued...

OFFICIAL CORRESPONDENCE
Washington, D.C. August 6, 1863.
Colonel Hoffman, Commissary-General of Prisoners:

Sir: On the evening of the 3d of May, 1863, three newspaper correspondents, Messrs. A.D. Richardson, and Janius H. Browne of the *New York Tribune*, and Richard T. Colburn of the *New York World*, were taken prisoners at Vicksburg while attempting to run the blockade on a small tug-boat to join our forces below. They were taken to Richmond and thrown into Libby Prison. In a few days, Mr. Colburn was released, while Messrs. Richardson and Browne were retained and have ever since been kept confined notwithstanding all efforts to secure their release or exchange. Late letters represent Mr. Browne (whose health has always been precarious) as being very ill and not likely to survive a much longer confinement. Both the gentlemen were formerly citizens of Cincinnati (and Mr. Browne still is) and a special interest is therefore felt in having every means possible exhausted to procure their release. Cannot some specific retaliatory measure be adopted under the President's recent proclamation to secure the exchange or release of these gentlemen, or if that be deemed inexpedient is there not some further step in their behalf the Government can take?

I have the honor, colonel, to remain, very respectfully, your obedient servant, Whitelaw Reid.....

Endorsements.....

I respectfully recommend that two rebel prisoners of war of the rank of captain be placed in solitary confinement and so kept until the two (Richardson and Browne) shall be released by the rebel authorities, notice of the fact being sent through Mr. Ould. If this does not effect the purpose, more severe measures may be resorted to.

E.A. HITCHCOCK, Major General[159]

Diary - August 7, 1863

I stood guard for 2 hours last night and had no breakfast until quite late this forenoon. I got some apples and potatoes today. The weather has been cool and quite pleasant.

Diary - August 8, 1863

I feel considerably better today. I was able to draw some vegetables and think now that I will fare first rate.

Corinth had the shape of an irregular square, the distance around it easily walked within 15 minutes. Within the small city stood three large hotels, five churches, and a number of fine homes. The Corona College for Women sat southwest of town. Of strategic importance, two railroads bisected the southwest corner: the *Memphis and Charleston*, west to east, and the *Ohio and Mobile*, north to south. Near the rails, workers toiled in government shops repairing engines, cannon, and other heavy equipment of war.

As a consequence of the war, Corinth's resident population had dwindled from 1,500 in 1861 to close to 1,000 by the time that the 113th arrived to garrison the city. The townspeople had endured almost a full year of war and all its ugliness, including occupation by both the Confederate and Federal armies. Ten months earlier, October 3 – 4, 1862, the battle of Corinth had been waged in the city, a battle of unmatched ferocity, leaving a legacy of agony, horror and lasting bitterness among the Confederate townspeople.* At the battle's end, scores of bodies lay unburied about the city, a carnage scene forever imprinted on the citizens' memories.

With the city's courts rendered inoperable by the war, martial law provided all governance, questions of right and wrong and civil justice decided by the military commander in charge, then Brigadier General John D. Stevenson. The privilege of *habeas corpus*, the principle that a person could not be held by the government without a valid reason for being held, was greatly restricted, if not virtually ignored during this time period. Even so, the citizens of Corinth, predominantly female, maintained what they could of their social life, attending lunch socials, band concerts, and church on Sunday. It may have been the devout women of Corinth who helped inspire Riley Beach, recovering from illness, to seriously consider religion as his calling.

> I took no medicine but a glass of ale three times a day while on a low diet. The bread and beef that I got in Memphis came in handy. A low diet would starve a church mouse. The hospital [one mile west of Corinth] was made up of large tents. Each tent formed a ward that would accommodate about 100 patients. A large white house served as headquarters and surgical department. It was once used to be General Grant's headquarters. We were ravenously hungry. But here at the hospital I got something more. I was converted here. I was under conviction for three days and miserable. Just after I lay down on my cot one evening God's peace came upon me mightily. I remember it as well as if it was only yesterday. — Private Riley Beach[160]

---

*   The battle of Corinth pitted 22,000 Confederate soldiers under CS General Earl Van Dorn against 23,000 Union soldiers under US General William S. Rosecrans, then occupying the city. After two days of fighting, the Confederates withdrew. Casualties were high: 4,800 CS, 2,350, US. (Kennedy, 129-132)

Letter - August 9, 1863
Corinth Miss Sabbath Eve
August 9th, 1863

Dear Parents,

I will endeavor and keeping up the practice of writing to you every Sabbath, although I have failed in receiving any mail for some time. I think that our mail must have gone on to Vicksburg, but it will get around in time. We have now been in our present camp 4 days, and from what [I've] seen and felt, think that this is about as good a place as they (the Officers) could have sent us. The climate is very fine. We have not had any very warm days, and the cool weather and fire fine air is very invigorating. The soldiers here are healthy and look as though they never knew what sickness was. Our boys that were sent to [the] hospital are doing finely, and many will soon be able to return to the Regt. John Fundy, Tom Carrow and myself are all that are left of our mess. Tom has just had a fine shake, and he has a high fever now. There is a considerable fever and ague among the boys. I am getting along finely although I am not very stout yet. We have plenty of vegetables, which is much better than the regular rations. You may think that the money which I expressed home (if it ever gets there) is rather small, $35.00 only, but I have used a considerable for eatables not having much of an apetite for our rations. Please use it as you think best, and it will be all right, I only wish it was more. We do not have any duty to do but to take care of ourselves.

Captain has been quite sick for the last 3 days, but is better today. Jeffcoat has had a pretty sick time. He is gaining slowly. I have not heard from Bert since we got here. He was sent to the Hospital, but I think that he is getting along fine. Well, I have no more news to write at present and so will close.

From your loving son, Edward L. Chatfield —
Co B 113th Ill Vols — Corinth Miss

Diary - August 9, 1863
It's quiet in camp today. They held Divine service, but I did not attend. Tom Carrow had a hard shake and fever this afternoon.

Letter - August 10, 1863
Monday Aug 10th

Just after I finished my letter yesterday, the mail came, and, with a letter for me from my dear parents dated August 3rd, which I can assure was very gladly received, and read. I think that father and David have had binding enough for once and I only wish that I could have been at home to help you. But, I do not know but what I am [doing] — my duty here in the army fighting for my country — [helps] as much, if not more, than if I was at home helping my dear Parents and enjoying myself. But, I cannot say that I do not enjoy myself as it is. I never trouble myself about any thing. Let the world may as it will. Mother knows that, well enough, because I always used to say there is no use of fretting. The loosing of so much stock is quite a loss. Was their running mad caused by being bitten bya a mad dog or what? What was the cause? Father, when you get me those boots have them of heavy Calf and lined. (size small 8s.) I do not need them now, but would like them for winter use.

Mother, I hope that you will put all anxious fears out of your mind. You must consider that we have been in the service a year now, and we have learned pretty well how to take care of ourselves. Why, we are not bad nurses, and then we have got tolerable cooks. So, that we manage it first rate. And here is another another thing, it is very seldom that we are all sick at the same time. So, we always have some one to wait on us. And here is another thing, we have learned to put up with a good many things that we could not have thought of at home. I do not know but what we have done our part, but there is a great deal more to be done yet. I think that It would only be an aggravation to be at home a few days and then have to return again.

Mary must be a nice little girl by this time. She must be a good girl and learn fast, and be a nice lady when Edward comes homes. David, kiss her good for me. David, I will write and answer your letter shortly. The boys all send their best respects and wishes. From your loving son, Edward L Chatfield

Diary - August 12, 1863
William Forman died in the hospital this afternoon.

Private William Forman was 34 years old when he died of disease, his death leaving a wife behind in the township of Salina. *Illinois Roster* records show his date of death as August 13.

Diary - August 13, 1863

Peter Shreffler died in the hospital this afternoon.

The *Illinois Roster* cites Shreffler's date of death as August 14, 1863. He was from Salina, married, and 34 years old when he died of disease.

Letter - August 16, 1863
Corinth Miss Aug 16th, 1863

> Dear Parents,
>
> Another week has rolled around, and the Holy Sabbath, the day of rest and the day of all others that we should respect, has come again. My health is not very good. I have the Diareah and it makes me pretty weak. John Fundy went out this morning and got me some blackberry root of which I have made a tea, and I think that it will be apt to help me. There is nothing of importance to write. Capt. [Bliss] Sutherland started home this morning. Albert [Smith] is in the Hospital. He is pretty weak. The Chronic Diareah has about run him out. Tom [Carrow] & John [Fundy] are gaining. They are a getting better. I have two deaths to record. William Foreman [Forman] died Aug 12th, & Peter Shreffler died Aug 13th. Well, I am tired and will close.
>
> You must excuse my short letter. I will try and do better next time.
>
> From your loving son,
> Edward Chatfield
> N S Chatfield

By Saturday, August 22, Albert Smith and Riley Beach had grown weary of hospital life. Both felt well enough to push for release. Noting that the surgeon in charge, then away to town, would likely refuse to release them, they saw their opportunity when the substituting physician walked in the door. It was Dr. Mack, the company physician and their neighborhood doctor. Smith and Beach coaxed and begged, and

Dr. Mack finally agreed to discharge them from the hospital. The two soldiers quickly packed their belongings and set out along the road into town, only to discover that they were so weak that they had to rest every "ten to fifteen rods" (55 to 83 yards.) Returning from town, the primary physician happened upon them while resting. "Why boys, have you got your discharges?" "Yes sir," they answered. "Well," said the primary physician, "You have stole a march on me, but you will soon be back."[161] The boys may have been foolish, but to their credit, they never returned.

Letter - August 23, 1863
Corinth Miss Aug 23rd

> Dear Parents,
>   I have been very sick during the past week and I can't write much now. I am some better and gaining a little strength every day. I have grown vary fair, so, that you would hardly know me. Jack Fundy & John Carrow take good care of me. If you get this before James Henry [of the *Forlorn Hope* charge on Vicksburg] starts back please send some canned fruit by him.
>   Well, I must close.
>   I remain as ever your loving son, Edward Chatfield

Fundy's nickname may have been "Jack," but Carrow's first name was not John; it was Tom. Chatfield's thoughts were confused, and he had to keep his letters brief.

Diary - August 25, 1863
It was very cool last night. I'm getting better. I walked around some today. We have squad drill in the mornings and evenings. Albert Smith started home on a furlough this morning.

Diary - August 26, 1863
The weather was cloudy and quite cool today.

Chatfield would eventually learn that his friend Colonel John W. Paddock had died this day of disease while in the officer's hospital in Memphis. Paddock had been a lawyer in Kankakee Township and a friend to many, including D.S. Parker and the Chatfield family.

Diary - August 27, 1863
I am some better, gaining slowly, but feeling pretty weak.

After four futile months, the Northern Agent of Exchange had not yet given up ...

OFFICIAL CORRESPONDENCE-
HEADQUARTERS DEPARTMENT OF VIRGINIA,
Fort Monroe, August 27, 1863.
Hon. ROBERT OULD, Agent of Exchange, Richmond, Va.:

SIR: I would again earnestly call your attention to the case of Messrs. Richardson and Browne, correspondents of the *New York Tribune*. In yours of August 20 you state "that there is no fair and reciprocal rule which may be proposed for mitigating the horrors of this war that will not be cheerfully adopted by the Confederate authorities." Now, sir, I think that the Confederate authorities could not have a better opportunity for reciprocating than in the case of the two gentlemen above named, for when Vicksburg was captured the editors of the *Whig* and *Citizen* fell into our hands and were immediately paroled and sent away. If you are sincere, then, in your offers, I call upon you to give me evidence thereof by immediately releasing Messrs. Richardson and Browne.

Respectfully, your obedient servant,
S.A. MEREDITH,
Brigadier-General and Commissioner for Exchange[162]

Nor had the Southern Agent of Exchange given up...

OFFICIAL CORRESPONDENCE
RICHMOND, August 28, 1863
Brigadier General S.A. MEREDITH, Agent of Exchange:

SIR: I still adhere to my declaration of the 20th instant in respect to the release of non-combatants. To that and almost every other communication involving a principle you have not replied. Fairness requires that you should answer it in some form before you criticize it. Will you agree to the unconditional release of all non-combatants?

Your reference to the parole of the editors of the *Whig* and *Citizen* at Vicksburg has no sort of force. They were paroled by the terms of surrender and not by any special grace of your authorities. You could not have retained them without a breach of the terms of capitulation. Their cases are in no respect analogous to those of Richardson and Browne, except in their avocation of driving the quill. Richardson and Brown will be released just as soon as you agree to discharge non-combatants.

I still say there is no fair and reciprocal rule which may be proposed for mitigating the horrors of this war that will not be cheerfully adopted by the Confederate authorities.

Respectfully, your obedient servant,
RO. OULD, Agent of Exchange.[163]

Diary - August 28, 1863
We have cool nights now. It rained all forenoon. My legs and body are very weak, but in other ways I feel well. Alfred G. States died today. He had the flux. Thus, another of our number has fallen.

Illinois Roster records cite the date of death as August 20, 1863. Corporal Alfred G. States was from the township of Norton. The "flux" was a mercilessly severe form of bloody diarrhea. He was a single 27-year-old when he died.

Diary - August 29, 1863
It was cold and chilly last night. I had to get up early to warm myself by the fire, but it was warm and pleasant in the daytime. My health is gaining slowly.

232
The Chatfield Story: Civil War Letters and Diaries of
Private Edward L. Chatfield of the 113th Illinois Volunteers

Diary - August 30, 1863

I'm taking tincture of iron now and think that I am gaining slowly. I, or we, were happily surprised at 3:00 p.m. by seeing Mrs. Hall in our midst. She brought me dried fruit and cheese from Mother, for which I was very thankful. Lieutenant Aquilla Cowgill of Company H also returned.

Mrs. Hall was the wife of Private Moses W. Hall, a 40-year-old farmer from Limestone in Company "H", then hospitalized and gravely ill.

<u>Letter</u> - August 30, 1863
Corinth Miss. Aug. 30th, 1863

Dear Parents,

Again another week has rolled around, and the holy Sabbath day, that day of rest, has come again. Now I can imagine where you all are just at the time that I am writing this letter. II AM, that you are all seated in the Williams School House listening to a good sermon or having Sabbath school. Oh, how I should like to be among you to enjoy the Sabbath as we used to do. We have no Chaplain with us now. He was taken sick down at Vicksburg, and when we came to Memphis, he stopped there and did not come any farther. It has been a long time since I have heard any preaching. The last sermon that I heard was in March. All that our Chaplain [Rankin] ever seemed to care about was to be the first one at any new place to get the first chicken and to get his pay. So you can imagine that he was not a very so much of a soul cheering minister of the cross as he might have been.

My health has not got to be very good yet. I do not think that there is any particular disease about me now. But, you know that after the disease is broken, or has left the system, that a person is often left very weak and in an emaciated condition. And that is just my fix. Now, let me walk a little distance and I am entirely tired out. And, besides, my blood is weak and thin, so, that I have to put on extra clothing to keep warm. But, for all this, I can see that I am gaining a little every day. ——

I suppose that Albert [Smith] must be at home, by this time, and he will give you all the particulars of things in general. I am glad that he got a chance to go home. He had been sick so long that it needed a mothers care to fetch him up. If he had been like some, [who] had given up and had no courage, he would have been in his grave long ago. Albert is a good boy, and we have been like brothers to each other. He was my bedfellow and messmate, and if he was here, now, I would like it, for I sleep very cold. —— other of our brave boys has fallen, Corp. Alfred G States died in the Hospital the 28th. The flux carried him off. Our numbers are being gradually reduced. We have lost four within a month, all carried of [off] by disease. If we had have stayed in Vicksburg much longer, I am afraid that we all would have gone. I do not think that there is any more dangerous cases in our Company at present. We have not heard any thing of Ira Williams or Boswell. It is supposed that they are prisoners somewhere, and it is supposed that Wallace Beebe was killed. But, there is no certainty about this. He may have been only wounded and may be alive yet.

The weather for a week past has been very pleasant through the day. But, the nights have been very cool, which makes it first rate weather for ague, of which there is quite a number of cases in camp. But, we expect warmer weather shortly. There has been several showers lately, but the roads are in good condition. Corn is about the same that it is there at this time of the year. John Fundy has been trying to have the ague yesterday and today.

Tom Carrow is rather unwell to. Riley Beach & John Titcomb are pretty smart. John Blanchet is about the same as myself. They all send their best wishes and respects, hoping that you will continue to write often. I will close. My love to you all. I remain your loving son,

   Edward L Chatfield
   direct to Corinth, Miss.

[On side of letter] Father, have you received that money that I sent you from Memphis? If you have, please write, as I am anxious to hear. Do not forget to mention in your next. Your last letter that I have received was dated Aug 3rd.

[On back of letter] Dear Mother, you wished to know whether it it would be best for you to come down here and, if so, what it would cost. In the first place, I do not think that it would be best for you to come down here (not because I would not like to see your dear face) but because I think that it would be to much for you, and they need you more at home. And, second, it would cost you $50.00, at any rate. I hope that you will not overwork your self and get down again, for I think that you have had about sickness enough to last for a while. And Father, to, must not do to much. If he does not have much help, it will be better to let the work go than to kill yourself trying to do it all. You can do as I do when I am well (that is play old soldier.) The meaning, of which, is not to hurt yourself when your are at work or on duty. What is the matter of Newton & James? They have not written to me for a long time. I hope that they have not forgotten me. When James Henry and those other two get back it may be possible for me to get a furlough. So, do not despair of never seeing. Ed.

234
The Chatfield Story: Civil War Letters and Diaries of
Private Edward L. Chatfield of the 113th Illinois Volunteers

Diary - August 31, 1863

I feel tolerable smart today. Have light diarrhea. Mustered for pay at 10:00. With so few men in the company, we are all working all of the time. Lieutenant Jeffcoat received a furlough to go home tonight.

Although weak, Chatfield pulled constant duty, one of only 15 men in the company able to muster at the time. This was his last entry in his first diary, postponing any further journaling until the first of the new year. Picket post duty, the task of checking passes and inspecting wagons for authorized content in and out of town, occupied his days. Soldiers performing such duty discovered that it was helpful to confiscate the contents of a wagon to satisfy personal needs. Items not on a permit could be confiscated, and this power was often abused, an unchecked hazard of martial law that resulted in a black market of confiscated vegetables, milk, butter, chickens, corn pone,* chestnuts, coffee, bacon, flour and salt.

Letter - September 6, 1863
Fort Williams, Corinth, Miss
Sabbath Morn Sept. 6th, 1863

Dear Parents,

I will try and write you a few lines to let you know that I am still in the land of the living and getting tolerable smart. My disease has, to all appearances, left me, and I am regaining my strength slowly, but am not fit for duty yet. But, I am doing as well as I could ask for. John Titcomb is quite sick. Has slight chills with high fever. John Fundy, John Blanchet & Tom Carrow are getting all right again. We have only Officers in company fit for duty. Capt. Williams, Orderly Kellogg & Corp Milton Rounsavell. So, you see, our roll of Officers Commissioned and non-Commissioned is pretty small, and what men that we have for duty have to be on duty every day or every other day at most.

Here it is the 6 of September, 13 months from the time I first became one of Uncle Sams boys. How swift the time has sped by, and can we all say that our time has been well spent both in the service of our Country and our Creator? To the former, I think that we can answer that we have done our best. Myself, here

---

*   Flatbread made of corn meal

trying to defend the Constitution and our country from one common ruin, and you, at home, are doing your part in raising the necessaries of life etc. But, as to the second part I fear that some of us will fall short, that it will be found that we have not done our whole duty. I am afraid that will be found to be the case with myself, that it will be found that I have come far short of doing my whole duty. But, we must keep on and never give up entirely. If we only have faith, and believe, we will come out all right in the end. I try to do my best, but there are so many temptations that it seems almost impossible for a man to keep in the straight and narrow path in which he should go. —

I have not seen Mrs. Hall since the first day that she got here. She has been at the Hospital, where her husband is, taking care of him all [of the] time. The boys say that he is getting a little better. They say, also, that he would not have lived a month longer if she had not have come as she did. He was failing fast and soon would have been under the sod. The general health of the boys in Company is some better than it was when we came here, but there is a good many sick yet. The loss of Old Charley and so many cattle must be pretty heavy on you is it not father. I don't see how you will hardly get along without Charley. He was always such a good faithful heart. How many head of cattle and hogs are you keeping this Summer? Please write in your next. I was sorry to hear that Grand-mothers health was so poor, I am in hopes that she will be better shortly. James Henry's furlough runs out today, but he has not returned yet. But, I expect that he will be along in a day or two. Do you think that the change of Climate has been of any benefit to Alberts health? We get our mail now very regular every day. Your last letter by mail was dated Aug 15. Some of the boys have got mail in 4 days from home. Well, I have written all that I can think of. The boys all send their best respects. My love to you all.

From an absent soldier boy, (from home),

Edward. ————

[On side of letter] If you have a plenty of Stamps, please Send along a few. You know that my corespondence is So large that it takes a few. — Ed

Despite what the boys said, Private Moses Hall wasn't getting any better; his wife's tenacious efforts couldn't save him. He died the very day that Chatfield wrote this letter. Private Henry August Miner, an 18-year-old farm boy from Chebanse, was another man in Company "H" that died in Corinth on September 6. The cause of death for both Hall and Miner was listed as "disease."

Letter - September 8, 1863
Fort Williams. Corinth Miss
Tues. morn before breakfast Sept 8th 1863

Dear Parents,

I thought that I would improve the oportunity that I had of sending a letter right through, direct, as Mrs. Hall intends to start for home tomorrow. Mr. Hall, poor fellow, has fallen a victim of disease. But, so it is. They are falling on every side. Mrs. Hall did her best to revive [his] exhausted nature, but he was too far gone. It seemed so good to see the familliar face of one of our neighbors. I am sorry that she returns so soon. ———

James Henry returned, or got back to the Company, yesterday afternoon, and we welcomed him back with hearty good will. He looks as though the Northern climate was good for soldiers (that is he looks as rugged and tough as a bear). He brought back with him Elisha Johns and Harrison Ash both of Iroquois Co. Ash has never been with the Company since we left Chicago, and I think that he has been reported as a deserter. If so, it he will be apt to have to go through a course of sprouts (which may not be so very light either.)*

I think that you must be enjoying yourselves highly having so many picnics, celebrations, meetings etc. etc., and it seems to me that David is getting into pretty big business monopolizing all the Young ladies in town, and all that sort of thing. But, let him go it while he has a chance, for when the soldiers get back again, I am afraid that "that" sort of business will play out. ———

I will now speak a few words about my health. I am now getting so that I feel pretty smart, am gaining strength little by little every day, but after all, my body feels rather weak espec my legs. I guess that all that you have heard about my getting [a furlough] will not amount to much. Well, I must go to breakfast.

II A.M. — Well, I will now try and finish this letter. I was speaking about getting a furlough. I am getting better every day although I will own that I am not strong enough to do much yet. But, there are others here that are in a worse condition than what I am. So, I have no thoughts of going home at present. And, as for your looking for me [at] home, that is useless. When you see me, it will be time enough to look and expect me then. And, as for your not writing until you see me, if you wait until that time, I am afraid that I shall have to wait a long time.

I am glad, dear Mother, to hear that you are so much better. And, I hope that you will be spared from having any more of those bad spells. — I think that if Father has got through Haying & Harvesting that he does better than when I am

---

*   No soldier by the name of "Harrison Ash" appears in the *Illinois Roster;* two soldiers, John and William Ash are listed for Company "B". A "course of sprouts" translates to rugged repetitive drill and punitive harassment.

there to help him. James says that all the corn is killed all through the Country. Do I suppose that your crop will not be worth much?

I will send by Mrs. Hall my diary and a lot of old letters that I have which you will oblige me much by taking care of and put them away and not show them. If you can send me some stamps, my money has about run out, or I would get them here. But, I believe that I spoke about it in my last letter.

Now mother, do not get discouraged because I do not come home. You must think that our country needs men, and that we must all do our best, and not think on the enjoyments of home until the last armed Rebel is put down. Now, I hope that you will write often.

From your affectionate son, Edward Chatfield

Mr. N S. Chatfield

Direct to Corinth Miss not Tennessee

P S. If you have a chance to send me those Boots, please send them along.

Letter - September 11, 1863
Fort Williams. Corinth, Miss.
Friday, Sept. 11th 1863

To my dear Parents,

We were all much pleased yesterday afternoon by the arrival of Capt. [Bliss] Sutherland and Mrs. Williams. But, I was most pleased by what I got from home, a letter and a can of strawberries for which I thank you very much. But, your letters are what I prize the most. You wished me to write immediately and let you know all about myself. And, I will do the best that I know how. My health is about the same as when I wrote you last with the exception that the Diarrhea has got a hold of me and it is running me pretty hard. Am not very stout yet, just able to be around, and that is about all. I think, myself, that if I could go north that I should recover my health than sooner I will here. Yet, I do not know as there will be any chance for me [to come home] for a good while to come.

(after dinner) Well, I will try and finish this. The boys keep just about the same. They all send their best respects. I have just been talking with the Captain about getting a furlough. There is an order from the War Department that there can only [be] 5 perct of a Regt or Company can be furloughed at a time. We have only about 40 men here, in all, so you see by that, that only two can have a furlough at a time. And, you know that there is two that have furloughs now, Albert [Smith] and [Enos] Shreffler. So, there is no chance in that direction until they return. But, the Capt. says that there is hope from another direction. Gen.

238
The Chatfield Story: Civil War Letters and Diaries of
Private Edward L. Chatfield of the 113th Illinois Volunteers

Grant has issued an order that only the sick shall have furloughs, that all that will not be able to [report for] duty for thirty days shall have a furlough immediately. And we are expecting that this order will come now every day. I do not believe that you could get me a furlough any sooner than they would give me one. So now, I wish that you would give up all expectation of seeing [me] until you see the real (bona fide Ed Chat.) I have very good care taken of me, for I am able to take care of myself.

My love to you all, from your affectionate son,
Edward L Chatfield
To Mr. N.S. Chatfield
PS. Please Send me a few stamps in your next, and oblige, yours truly

Letter - September 14, 1863
Corinth, Miss.
Monday Sept. 14th / 63

Dear Parents,

I generally make it a rule to write every Sunday, but I did not feel well enough to write yesterday and then I wrote you a letter last friday.

I was getting along first rate until last week. By imprudence on my part in eating, the Diareah got hold of me and it, as a natural consequence, just pulled me right down. Since it got hold of me the worst, I just put myself on allowance eating nothing but a piece of toast and a cup of tea.

There was preaching in camp yesterday but I did not feel well enough to attend. I received a letter from Grand-mother yesterday. She said that she was some better than she had been.

Mother, in one of your letters you said that you had two little girls with you. I suppose that with their help you get along finely. But you did not tell me their names. The Capt. seems to enjoy himself first rate since his wife came. He think that his boy is just about right. The baby has been sick ever since she got here.

John Fundy has the Ague about every 4th or 5th day. The rest of the boys are right including myself. I have not much to write at present and so will close.

From your loving son,
Edward —

On September 17, 1863, Secretary of War Edwin M. Stanton made Lincoln's March 3, 1863, proclamation official on this day. Lincoln also declared that rebellion had compelled him to revoke one of the most sacred of civilian legal safeguards – the privilege of *habeas corpus*.[164] Non-combatants in occupied areas were at the mercy of provost enforcers, an unchecked power that was already out of hand.

Letter - September 20, 1863
Corinth, Miss.
Sept. 20th, 1863

To my Parents,

Another week has rolled around and I will try and improve a few moments in writing to you, although I hardly know what to write that will be of interest to you. Although, I suppose that there are many things which we see and which are continually occurring around us which would be of interest to a stranger to such scenes.

My health is gaining every day. I am now getting so that I am tolerably smart, so, that I can say this much, that I g do not have to take any more medicine and am out from under the Dr's care. I can see that health of the Regt is gaining perceptibly. We have 23 in company now, and when we first came to this place we had only ten (10). But, since I wrote my last to you, two more have been called from this sphere of action toil and trouble. Their names were John Bartholemew [Bartholomew] and Noah Buck. And so, our numbers are continually being lessened. We do not have any preaching on the Sabbath, or I would have not, had until last Sunday. A gentleman from down town came out and addressed a few words to a small audience. Our Chaplain [Rankin] you know, is never with [us] when he can help it. He is now at Chicago on sick leave, and he might just as well stay there. For, any good that he ever did is of but [a] small amount. But, it is not all the Chaplains that can do everything. If a man is only true to the trust that is given him, [if] he keep on his guard, and be at all times ready to meet whatever may come, life or death, sorrow or pain, sickness or trouble, and I hope that such may be my course, that I may at last be enabled to say — well I cannot express my thoughts. You can better imagine them than I can write them.

The weather is fine and has been for some time in the past. We had a pretty hard frost last night and it was real cold but it is quite warm and pleasant today. You must tell Bert that he must hurry up and get well, for I miss my bedfellow badly these cold nights. The boys are all about the same as usual. John Fundy has the ague regular every 4th or 5th day. They all send their best respects. Kellogg sends his best wishes. He is just giving us a little music on the violin as I am writing. Mrs. Williams still stays she does not go out much. She is well, I believe. We have heard within the last few days that Capt. [Cephas] Williams has been promoted to Major, and [George R.] Clark to Lieut. Col. So we have lost our Capt., which I do not like very well.

Well, I must close for the want of something to write. Write often and let me know how the corn and potatoes will be this year. This from your loving son, Edward Chatfield

Private John Bartholomew, from Martinton Township, succumbed to disease in Corinth on September 15, 1863, only 19. Private Noah Buck, 24 and married, a carpenter from Middleport, Illinois, died two days later, September 17.

George R. Clark, who had been promoted to Lieutenant Colonel, was not present in Corinth when Chatfield wrote the above letter. Clark had been dispatched earlier to Springfield, Illinois, to take command of the five companies sent there while guarding prisoners following the battle of Arkansas Post—Companies "C", "D", "F", "I" and "K". With sickness having stripped the regiment down to the size of a company, the return of the detached companies had become an urgent priority. Clark's role was to ensure that the troops were battle ready and to return them to the field.

CHAPTER 22: DARK DAYS FOR SHERMAN

"Little Willie closed his eyes for the final time."

<u>Letter</u> - September 28, 1863
Corinth, Miss.
Sept, 28th, 1863

Ever Dear Parents

I again seat myself to try and let you know how I get along and what I am doing etc, etc. In the first place my health is slowly improveing considerably, and I am getting quite smart, and I hope to be able to do duty in a short time. All that now remains is for me to fully regain my strength before I shall do much at any thing. I received your very welcome letter of the 15th Ult on the 24th. Was glad to hear that all well. I found that you all have as much to do as ever. It does seem as though you would never get so that you could take life any easier than you have had to for a good many years past. Just to see how we lazy fellows are, idleing away our time here, it seems as though it was not hardly right when our help is needed so badly at home. We are having a very pleasant time here now. The weather is very fine and pleasant, quite warm through the day, while the nights are quite chilly and cold. There have been two frosts which has destroyed every [thing] susceptible to its freezing influences.

We are going to have a new lot of arms. We are to turn over all the arms which we have (they are the Enfield and Springfield) and to have new Springfields of the best pattern. The Springfield is calculated to be the best arm in the service. The Boys are all getting along finely. They send their best respects.

I hear that Albert has been to the surgeon and reported not fit for duty yet. And I hear also that the certificate is no no good, for the reason that it did not state the length of time that it was extended. His furlough ran out on the 25th. Well, I have no more to write, at present, and it is about mail time, and I will close by bidding you good bye. Yours as ever, Edward L

While Chatfield wrote his September 28 letter, a tragic story concerning one of General Sherman's children had begun playing out, one that began in Bovina, Mississippi—six miles east of Vicksburg at the Big Black River.[165] For the past several weeks, Sherman's family had been visiting from Ohio, a visit strongly encouraged by Sherman, one that Sherman had assured his wife, Ellen, would be safe. He hadn't seen her or his children for many months. At the time, Sherman and his wife had two daughters and two sons: Minnie (12), Elizabeth (11), Willie (9), and Tom (7). During the visit, the children slept in white tents just like those of the soldiers in the 13th Regulars, and they accompanied their father during inspections. They were still in camp on September 28 when Sherman met with General Grant to discuss the unsettling conditions in Chattanooga, Tennessee. Just ten days earlier, US General William S. Rosecrans had suffered a major defeat in his September 18–20 battle with CS General Braxton Bragg in the northwest corner of Georgia, 425 miles northeast of Vicksburg at Chickamauga Creek. After inflicting more than 18,000 casualties and suffering more than 16,000, Rosecrans retreated north to Chattanooga, where heavy troop reinforcements would be vital for maintaining the Union occupation of the city. Grant's intentions were clear: Sherman's entire corps was needed to block Confederates from retaking Chattanooga. Sherman knew that it was time to send his wife and children home.

On September 29, while boarding his family on the steamer to move north, Sherman noticed that Willie seemed ill. The child was quiet, his cheeks felt warm, and he wouldn't eat. Concerned, Sherman accompanied his family to Memphis to locate the best doctor he could find. It would take two days to reach their destination.

Willie's condition had deteriorated by the time the family arrived at Memphis on October 1. He had a high fever, chills, a headache, severe diarrhea, and he couldn't hold down the smallest cup of water. Summoning an ambulance to the boat, Sherman had his son taken to the Gayoso Hotel and sent his aides in search of the best doctors. He and his family would remain in Memphis to care for Willie while sending the corps east. Sherman intended to catch up with his corps as soon as he was certain that Willie was on the mend.

On October 3, in an effort to delay Sherman's column, the Rebels attacked the rails near the La Grange Depot, roughly midway between Memphis and Corinth, an action that led to the Union capture of a number of Rebels and a new form of guard duty for the boys in the 113th. Lacking prison facilities in Corinth, those healthy enough in Company "B" received rotating orders to guard the prisoners who were hauled west by boxcar to the Irving Block Prison in Memphis, not far from the Gayoso Hotel, where a distressing battle was about to be lost.

Little Willie had been drifting in and out of consciousness for the past 24 hours. The doctors said that he had contracted typhoid fever, an illness understood at the time as a non-communicable disease caused by the ingestion of contaminated food or water.* Observing that Willie was slipping away, a Catholic chaplain administered the Last Rights. Whispering that he did not want to leave his mother and father behind, little Willie closed his eyes for the final time at 5:00 P.M. on October 3, 1863, a tragic and mournful day for Sherman and his wife in Memphis.

Back in Washington, that same day, President Lincoln had no way of knowing about the Sherman family's grievous loss. Nevertheless, it is likely that he shared their mood. Deeply troubled about the war, he presented what might be considered his prescription for a grieving nation: his *October 3, 1863, Proclamation* establishing the national custom of celebrating the last Thursday of November as "... a day of Thanksgiving and Praise to our beneficent Father who dwelleth in the Heavens."[166]

Three days passed, and on October 6, still grieving, Sherman returned to the Gayoso Hotel, after having placed his family on the boat to return home. The bitterness of his loss and the guilt he felt for encouraging his family to stay with him in camp would forever haunt him. Some historians today speculate that Willie's death may have served as Sherman's incentive to severely punish the South.[167]

Riley Beach may have caught a glimpse of the Gayoso on October 6. He had arrived in Memphis that day by train, among the first in the company to serve as a train guard. At the Memphis station, Beach and four other soldiers unloaded 32 Rebel prisoners from Corinth and discharged them at the "Irving Block"—a large commercial building that had been converted into a prison. The badly deteriorated place of confinement sat on the east side of Second Street across from Court Square—a filthy and foul-smelling four-story confine with a sickening cellar below, a structure generally unfit for anyone. But Private Beach had no choice as to where he took his prisoners. The building's condition was well beyond his purview.[168]

---

* Although Willie's doctors did not yet understand that the disease was caused by a specific bacteria (Salmonella typhosa, a bacillus) the diagnosis was basically correct. Typhoid fever, often referred to as "typhoid" today, is now treated with antibiotics.

Before returning to Corinth, Beach had time to tour the city and visit friends who had been hospitalized there. He slept at the Soldiers' Home* and then returned to Corinth by train on October 7, when the tracks were literally lined with Union soldiers on the march for the full 91-mile distance. Four more days would pass before Sherman would follow along the same heavily fortified rails, not anticipating the furious assault that he would soon face.

Sherman left Memphis on Sunday, October 11, boarding his train's rear car at 9:30 A.M., his attendants accompanying him. His 13th Regular battalion and several horses were in the forward cars, including his favorite horse, Dolly. After passing White Station and Germantown, Sherman's train rumbled through Collierville at noon. A half mile beyond that station, Sherman's train clanged and lurched to an abrupt stop, voices shrieking of an impending attack. Sending orders to the forward cars for his Regulars to disembark, Sherman dispatched one of his men to the station to telegraph for help. Minutes later, a Confederate messenger came forward bearing a flag of truce, demanding the surrender of all persons aboard the train. Refusing, while delaying the messenger, Sherman ordered the train to be reversed to the depot, affording him shelter in a small earth redoubt. There, Sherman parceled his Regulars to places of cover—the nearby fortress and the shallow man-made dugouts flanking the tracks. He had little time to spare. To Sherman's south was an uncut cornfield, and to his north was the town of Collierville, with several houses close enough to the train that the enemy might decide to occupy them. Ordering the houses set afire, Sherman focused his attention on the cornfield where he spotted the approach of a long line of Confederate soldiers. Along the tracks from the west came a second line, and similarly, from the east a third, all with bayonets fixed. Within moments, the battle of Collierville erupted in full fury. The force from the west eventually boarded the train and confiscated its contents, including Sherman's sword and his prized horse. For the next three hours, Sherman's 13th Regulars and the 76th Indiana managed to fend off successive waves of CS General James R. Chalmers' Cavalrymen, a force of close to 3,000 men.

Having received word of the telegraphed plea for help, elements from the division of U.S. Brigadier General John Murray Corse rode in from Germantown between 2:30 and 3:00 P.M., a force that Chalmers estimated to outnumber his own. The battle slowed, and Chalmers withdrew, ending the fight. Had Sherman not issued a call for help just before the Confederates cut the telegraph wires, Corse would not have arrived when he did, and Sherman summarily may have lost more than his sword and horse. As it was, the three-hour battle yielded 158 casualties: 108 US, 50 CS.[169]

---

*   Ironically, in 1851, it had been Jefferson Davis, then a U.S. senator from Mississippi, who had introduced legislation establishing Soldiers' Homes, asylums for old and disabled veterans. During the war, the Union used the Soldiers' Home in Memphis as a military hotel.

After replacing his train's destroyed engine, Sherman moved east on October 12, arriving in Corinth that day. Two days later, Chatfield took a train from Corinth to Memphis with 56 Rebel prisoners in custody.

Letter - October 14, 1863
[Soldiers' Home Stationery with printed Heading]
Soldiers' Home,
Memphis, Tenn., Oct 14th 1863

Dear Brother David,

As I have a few minutes before bedtime I will write you a few words. You see by this that I am at Memphis. This morn Tom C— [Carrow] & I was detailed with some dozen others to come here with prisoners. There was 56 of them, pretty rough looking fellows. This eve — Tom & I have been running around town. The other boys have gone to the theater and other places of amusement.

My health is getting pretty good. You must try and make ma cheer up. Tell her that she has got boys enough without me and, so there is no use of worrying. A soldiers life is very pleasant (when the sun shines). There has been several skirmishes along the R.R. between the guerillas & Rebs and our troops, which places I saw today. I suppose that you will begin going to school soon. I hope that you will, but the Army is a very good school of its kind. There is a great deal to be seen & learned. Now David, you must write to me soon, and write all the partie-news.

My love to Father & Mother with a good share for yourself,
From your Brother, Edward L Chatfield

By this point in time, the boys in the 113th had been told that they were now permanently assigned to the post at Corinth. Colonel Hoge, until then their regimental commander, would be commanding the post, and Major Cephas Williams, who had been commanding the company, would command the regiment—a regiment so small due to many deaths that it was the size of a company. With Hoge commanding the post and Williams commanding the regiment, only the leadership titles had changed. For all practical purposes, day-to-day orders would come from the same two men. By the second week of October, Corinth had become a place of heavy traffic, troops constantly arriving and departing in support of Sherman's corps.

Social opportunities remained important to the troops throughout the war, "normal" events that helped offset the unbalancing chaos of the time. Riley Beach became a member of the Corinthians, a debating society in Corinth that met every Thursday, an activity he immensely enjoyed until the regiment was ordered to move to Chewalla—the first station nine miles west of Corinth. The regiment's new duty was to man the Chewalla Stockade in the hills there, defending the rails below. The order came on October 24.

Letter - October 28, 1863
Chewalla Tenn. Oct 28ᵗʰ / 63

Brother Newton,

Well Newton, as you was so kind as to think of a poor, miserable, forsaken & forlorn, chap like me, once in a while, and to think for enough to [write a letter to] me ocasionally to, why you can't tell the pleasure I had in reading it. Well New't, I expect that you would like to know what sort of a looking place this [is] around here. In the first place, you know that we moved to this place which is 10 miles west of Corinth last saturday (the 24). Chewalla was once once composed of half a dozen houses and the station house. But they have all been burned, and you would not see anything in sight at the stopping place. Our camp is nearly half a mile from the camp R. Road. On the top of quite [a] hill, right in the woods, is the camp & stockade, incloseing about 4 acres.

I do not know as you will know what a stockade is. Well, I will tell you. In the first place, they dig a ditch 4 or 5 feet deep, then cut trees from six inches to two feet through and set [them] close together in ditch. This will form the stockade which will [be] about 10 feet high. There is small loop holes about as high as a mans head so that we can shoot through.

(Nov 1ˢᵗ)

I will try to finish this. I was telling you how things are situated here. Well, inside the stockade all around the outside are built the barracks, which are built of logs. Just back of the barracks are the cook houses where we cook & eat at. And It will be one year, day after tomorrow, since I was at home from Chicago to attend the Election, How quick a year has passed away, and what changes we have passed through [and] seen. As for myself, the Battles of Arkansas Post, Chickasaw Bluff & Vicksburg have been enacted before my vision, while you have had the most peaceful and quiet scenes of the farm and home. There is not much of anything that I can think of to write. My thoughts are badly scattered, and so, you must excuse this short and badly written letter.

Now Newton, you must write soon, for I prize your letters very much because you write all the news. Direct to Chewalla Tenn.

From your loving Brother, Edward L. Chatfield

Everywhere that the army went, throughout the war, a horde of traders and hucksters followed, vending medical cures, foodstuffs, gold watches, marching boots, and anything else that might bring them quick cash. Many among them were young able men from the North, capable men venturing beyond their own state lines where drafts were difficult to enforce. Their very presence in the towns along the railways, roadways, water sources and traffic centers limited troop movement. Fights would break out when the hucksters were challenged as draft dodgers. To counter their growing number, from luka, Mississippi, came General Sherman's *October 28 Order #4*, raising a bitter controversy.

General Orders, No. 4

HDQRS. Dept. AND ARMY OF THE TENN.,
luka, Miss., October 28, 1863.

I. This department being an insurrectionary district, and the execution of the laws of the United States being resisted by armed rebels, every citizen is liable to be called on for military service; and, if so called on, must render it.

II. Every commanding officer of a fixed military post, or of an organized brigade or division of the army in the field, may impress any citizen whatever, and may compel his services in any of the old organized regiments or companies. If the party so impressed be a conscript, according to the laws of Congress, his name will be properly enrolled by the provost-marshal-general, and he will be entitled to all the pay, bounty, and allowances provided by law; but if the individual is not enrolled on the proper lists his services will be compelled till such time as he is no longer needed, when he will be dismissed. During the period of such forced service the individual will be entitled to rations and clothing, but no compensation, in the nature of a posse comitatus* called out by a United States marshal.

III. Every officer making such forced levies will report the same, with lists, to the provost-marshal-general of this department, to be filed with the Provost-Marshal-General at Washington, D.C., and will assign them by Special Orders to old regiments and companies. Their names will be borne on the muster-rolls of the companies to which they are attached, with a remark explanatory of the nature of the service, its beginning and ending.
By order of Maj. Gen. W.T. Sherman:
R.M. SAWYER, Assistant Adjutant General[170]

---

*   From the Latin phrase meaning "force of the county"—a body of men armed with legal authority.

Letter - November 1, 1863
Headquarters 113th Ill Vols
Post Chewalla Tenn. Nov 1st 1863

Dear Parents,

I will try and write you a few lines to let you know how I get along. I am getting pretty well with the exception that I am troubled by my legs swelling from above my knees down to my feet. The Dr. calls it the Dropsical Debility. Other ways, I am all right. Al Smith got here yesterday afternoon. He look, Oh, what a change a short stay at home makes in a fellow. There is not one in the Co that "looks" better than he does. That box which you sent has not got along yet. But I shall look for it every day. All the women that are down here with their husbands have been ordered away from here. Mrs. Williams, I expect, will start home shortly. Well, I have not much to write at present. The boys are usually well and send their best respects. From your loving son,

Edward L. Chatfield
Direct to Chewalla Tenn

At the Collierville Station where Sherman had narrowly escaped capture or death, Confederate muskets cracked and popped again on November 3. Once again, the assailant was CS General Chalmers, and once again, Chalmers withdrew. But his activity up and down the line so threatened Sherman's communications between Memphis and Chattanooga that Union General Hurlbut ordered all train stations to be strengthened. The raid prompted Major Williams to double the watch at Chewalla. Strategically important, Chewalla's stockade offered a fine shelter for troops, and its location above the rails provided a strong platform for observation and defense. Williams may have known that Chewalla's place in history had been established thirteen months earlier, when CS General Earl Van Dorn and his troops had crossed the Tuscumbia River and camped there while en route to Corinth. At dawn on October 3, 1862, in a fiery skirmish, Van Dorn had pushed back Union troops from Chewalla toward Corinth, many men dying on both sides.*

Williams' soldiers took their duty seriously. The loss of Chewalla could be devastating to Sherman's column en route to Chattanooga. Even so, young soldiers always managed to find ways to have fun. When not on duty they might hunt for squirrels and bring back chestnuts as did Kellogg, Chatfield, Beach, and four others, out

---

* On page 19 of his recollections, Beach wrote that the body of a fallen Union soldier from the 26th Missouri had been buried following the October 1862 skirmish. A wooden marker identified the soldier's shallow grave on the banks of the Tuscumbia River. The fallen boy's father arrived to Chewalla on November 4, 1863, and Beach helped him disinter the body, a job made hideous by the severe state of decomposition.

on passes on November 5, an off-duty day that had been set aside for camarade-rie, diversion, and merriment. They explored the hills and forests and splashed through the Tuscumbia before returning to the stockade, picking burrs from their clothes and retiring wearily after sundown. Barely asleep, all were awakened by the only emergency of their two-week stay in Chewalla. An 8:30 P.M. "long roll" sent them, with muskets ready, rushing down the northern slope to the charred station platform.* Although they feared the worst, they encountered nothing more than the shadows of the night and the distant barking of one or two stray dogs. All was well.

From his cluster of Corinth and Chewalla memories, Chatfield probably recalled November 7 and 8 as two of his more miserable "hurry up and wait days." Shortly before lunch on November 7, Major Williams received orders to move the regiment back to Corinth on the 3:00 P.M. train that day. The time crunch left Williams with less than four hours to move his entire regiment, with its tons of gear and supplies, down the steep half-mile road to the tracks north of the stockade. He would have known that the trains rarely stayed on sched-ule, but if a train did come and he wasn't ready, he would be the one blamed. In what must have been a furious common effort, Williams managed to have his entire regiment with all its gear and provisions standing by the platform by 4:00 P.M.—an hour late. But fortunately for Williams, the train had not yet come.[171]

The hurry had ended, and the wait had begun. Night's approach brought with it an unusually bitter cold. Soldiers donned blankets while complaining of hunger, having had nothing to eat since breakfast. By seven o'clock they had kindled several fires, some with kettles stocked with sweet potatoes suspended above them, an imagin-able scene of orange faces, frosty breath, flickering shadows and sparkling rails. The train of boxcars didn't arrive until 9:00 P.M.[172]

Through icy winds, the cinder-spewing locomotive gasped its way back to the Corinth Station, reaching the frozen platform by 11:00 P.M. After unloading the cars, word arrived that the regiment could not return to its barracks at Battery Williams, a quarter mile west, due to the fact that transient soldiers were spending the night there. As a result, the waiting game began once again. The 113th was forced to remain on the icy platform until the transients moved out, a stay that would not end until noon the next day, November 8. But for those who were anticipating a meal, the wait would not end until suppertime.[173]

---

* Both the village and the station at Chewalla had been destroyed by fire during the October 1862 battle of Corinth.

Letter - November 10, 1863
Headquarters, 113th, Ill, Vols,
Corinth, Miss.
Nov, 10th, 1863,

Dear Parents,

I will now try and write you a few lines. It has been ten days since I have had a letter from you. I should have written to you on Sunday, but just as I had got ready, instead of sitting down and taking my pen, we got orders to pack up and move. This was about eleven oclock, and by 1 oclock at night we were back to Corinth again. And, you had better [know] that we were all pretty tired, having to be on the move all the time until we got on to the cars. That is we, that is, the whole company, had to ride in the same car that we had our baggage in. And you can imagine that we did not have a very pleasant ride it being so cold that a fellow would almost freeze. I slept that night on the Depot platform.

(over)

We have quite a pleasant camp just outside of the town limits. Our barracks are nice and comfortable. I am getting so that I feel first rate. For the last two days I have been cooking and it just keeps me on my feet all the time. Two of us does the cooking. The boys have plenty of duty to do, standing guard and patroling the town.

The box that you sent us has finally got here. — It is still at the Express office. I shall get it tomorrow. — I will send 50 cts and I wish that you would send me some stamps. We cannot get any here at this time. I suppose that they have not got any at the post-office is the reason. We are expecting to be paid again in a few days when I shall be enabled to send some money home.

Bert told me something about some matches. If matches are scarce up your way I might send you half a dozen or so. Please let me know. I received your letter dated the 25th on the 1st of this month relating to the box. the I had just sent my letter to the office when I got yours. I generally get your letters 7 or 8 days after they start. We do occasionally get mail in 4 days. How much did you get? Or, I would say, do you think "that" that Ditch has paid come to count all the costs. How much did you get for what you did this fall?

I got a letter from Grand-mother Sunday. She was well. She was very kind and thoughtfull. She sent me $2.00, for which I thank her very much. Well, I believe that I have written all the news & so I will close. It is getting about bedtime and I am pretty tired. The boys have all gone to bed except John Blanchet and myself. The weather is quite pleasant. It was quite cold last night. Froze, ice ¼ inch thick on water in a dish. The boys all send their best respects. My love to you all. - - - from your son

Edward L. Chatfield

N S Chatfield Esq.

Direct to Corinth, Miss.

[On back] I will send you in this a rose that I picked at Millikens Bend when we came up the river. It was at the same time that we stoped to bury George Shays.

Northerners suffered far fewer scarcities during the war than did Southerners. But one of the scarcities on both sides was the stick match. Extremely useful to soldiers and civilians alike, stick matches became a scarce commodity during the war, demand far exceeding supply.[*]

<u>Letter</u> - November 13, 1863
Corinth Miss Nov 13th 1863[†]

My Dear Parents,

I will improve the moments this evening in writing to you. Mrs. Hercher intends to start to home tomorrow and she say that she will carry a letter for me. Jacob Hercher Died the 7th of Nov., just the day after she got here, I believe. He was a faithful, brave, and ever to do his duty, but he has fallen, another victim to the fell destroyer disease.[‡] He died of congestion of the lungs. Mrs. Ward goes North with Mrs. Hercher. My bodily feelings are on the improve every day. I have been cooking since we came back to this place. It keeps us on our feet from morning till night (there is two of us.) We have 33 to cook for. The swelling in my legs has entirely gone and I am getting so that I look kil like my natural self. I am alone here this evening with no one to disturb me. John Blanchet, with two others of our Co, have gone to Cairo to guard refugees. (over)

John Fundy, Tom & Bert are all on guard down to town. They have to come on guard every other day. (They cannot put them oftener than that.) We got our box on the 11th. My things came through all right, and John's also, but Tom lost his molasses. The can got jammed and every bit of the molasses was wasted. It got broke after it got to Corinth, I think, by their knocking the box around. The Boots fitted me first-rate. They are a tiptop pair. Tell David, if he did get the first wear of them, that they made, did not make, as [much] of an impression on the young ladies as they would on their present owner. David and the William must make the best of their time, now, for when us soldiers get home, they may

---

[*] Interestingly, the compounds of the stick match remained fairly poisonous throughout the war. It wasn't until 1910 that the Diamond Match Company came up with a non-poisonous match.

[†] Some of Chatfield's stationery had been embossed in the upper left corner. Stamped into this one was a locomotive billowing smoke from its stack and the words "Holyoke, Co" [Colorado.]

[‡] The "fell destroyer disease" named a variety of severe ailments of the lungs, including what is known today as pneumonia and tuberculosis.

stand a poor chance. There was quite a large sized paper in the box and it was not marked to any particular. I wish that you would let me know whose it is. Say Mother, you did not say how that Laudanum [a preparation of opium*] was to be taken in the case of Diarrhaea. We are expecting Cap't Becket here tomorrow. Lieut. Jeffcoat is getting some better but has the ague occasionally. The Orderly [Sgt. Kellogg] is looking fine and well. He sends his best respects. The weather is very fine and pleasant. If you are only having as good, you yo will have a splendid time to get your falls work done. I suppose that you have got the corn almost all husked by this. Albert says that it seems as though the folks at home get along better than they used to do when we were all at home. If that is so we had better stay away I guess. Money is so plenty I hear that every little boy has his pockets full of [greenbacks.]

Well, I have not anything to write at present and so will draw to a close. The Drums of the various Reg'ts around are beating roll call and time to go to bed, and so I will follow suit. My love to you all & a kiss for Mary.

I remain your affectionate son, Edward L Chatfield
N S. Chatfield Esq.

Mrs. Hercher carried Chatfield's November 13 letter home, her husband Jacob having died in Corinth on November 7, according to what Chatfield had written. The *Illinois Roster* cited Jacob's death as November 9. Private Hercher was 28 when he died, a farmer from the Kankakee township of Otto.

Mrs. Ward was Hospital Steward Caleb Ward's wife. Born in New York, Corporal Caleb D. Ward was 30 years old when he enlisted in Kankakee in 1862, recording his occupation as "physician." Chatfield called Caleb "Dick."

Letter - November 17, 1863
Corinth, Miss.
Nov 17th 1863

Dear Brother David,
     It has been some time since I have written you a line of any kind & now I will try & make up for lost time. I suppose that you are going to the Academy by this time and so I will address this to K.K.K. [Kankakee]
     I got fathers letter dated the 7th on Saturday night. I had that morning just sent a letter by Mrs. Jacob Hercher. She was just returning home. Well, how do

---

* Laudanum, at the time, could be purchased without a prescription. Its heavy use became associated with the "soldier's sickness" — what is understood today as drug addiction.

you like the school? Does Proffessor Hair keep as good a school as Woodruff? Does he keep you strict or let you do as you please? Al says that he has not near as many scholars as Woodruff. What are you studying? ~~Do~~ Have you tried Algebra? Is it not nice?

Now, I will tell you what it is. I want to establish a regular corespondence with you, that is, write every week, regular, and I will engage to answer all letters. I want to hear what is going on in town. I am all alone here. The boys are all on guard or out at work. We have a plenty to do every day. I have got all right again and am doing my part of the duty right along. Bert is as hearty and rugged as a bear. John Fundy wrote you a letter a long time ago and he has been wondering why you did not think of him and answer it.

Now, you must write to, for he thinks that you are slighting him. We are g doing Provost guard duty around town now. Our barracks are just in the City limits. Well, I will close by wishing you success in your studies. Write soon.

Yours as ever, Edward L. Chatfield

By November 18, Sherman's October 28 *Order #4* had erupted in broad controversy, complaints that the Union had gone too far. Some interpreted Sherman's order to mean that all citizens must take up muskets and enter into the ranks or be considered fugitives. The Memphis Provost Marshal targeted Jewish merchants, triggering a dramatic increase in their enlistment numbers. Not one of them was assigned to the 113th, however. Referring to the lot as "conscripts," Beach noted that eight merchants who had refused to sign up were arrested on November 19 and were assigned to the 1st Alabama Cavalry.[174]

If civilian life was chaotic under martial law, life under military regulations was equally exasperating. All irregularities triggered reviews. Lieutenants Beckett and Jeffcoat, both furloughed earlier due to sickness, failed to return from the hospital on time, and both men were barred from pay until a board in Memphis reviewed their cases. Daily fights erupted among disgruntled soldiers, including some at the supper table, triggering more arrests and reviews. There was little that any soldier could trust, including the "greenbacks" that they received for their pay—1862 paper money that called to mind the worthless currency issued by the Continental Congress when the colonies broke away from England.[*] Rather than trust the Union money, the boys preferred to trade the paper for watches and pens plated in gold or for photographs that they could mail home to their loved ones. Despite the difficulty of their circumstances, the soldiers of the 113th managed to celebrate their first Thanksgiving that year—the day which had been set aside by President Lincoln to reflect upon

---

[*]   This led to the phrase, "Not worth a Continental."

life's blessings—a historical milestone and a handsome feast that Chatfield would longingly recall a year later.

That first Thanksgiving—Thursday, November 26—not only brought with it a leisurely day and ample food for the boys in the 113th, it brought news that the Confederates had withdrawn from Lookout Mountain, Tennessee, abandoning their high-point controls overlooking Chattanooga. Their retreat to Georgia under cover of night made Chattanooga the pivotal hub for moving Union forces and supplies, leaving the Deep South wide open to Federal invasion.

The turn-of-events so delighted Major Williams that he extended the Thanksgiving celebration through the night and into the morning of November 27, issuing double rations of whiskey, promising more "...if the boys did not get too drunk."[175] Colonel Hoge, the Post Commander, chipped in with a barrel of beer, leaving all of the participants with hangovers on November 28. As the boys recovered from too much celebrating, heavy rain transformed the barracks into a pigpen of mud and water. Such were the circumstances when the boys helped Riley Beach celebrate his 21st birthday on Sunday, November 29.[176]

At dress parade on December 4, the boys were informed that the acting postmaster, Corporal Wilder J. Cowgill of Company "H", had been pilfering the mail, appropriating the contents of packages and letters. Of all of the things that were important to the common soldier, the mail was among the most sacred. Cowgill's acts of mail theft so enraged the boys that they were pleased by his reduction in rank and by the order that he sweep the streets for the next 30 days. Not only had Cowgill brought shame to himself, he had also shamed his older brother, Lieutenant Aquilla Cowgill, of the same company.

Offsetting Cowgill's betrayal, the good news heralded that day was that General Sherman's 25,000-man relief column had broken CS General James Longstreet's 17-day siege on Knoxville, Tennessee. Sherman had liberated US General Ambrose E. Burnside's Army of the Ohio—removing Confederate control over northeastern Tennessee. This called for another celebration in Corinth, one quickly arranged by Colonel Hoge, who ordered a banner parade and more whiskey for all. Union merchants joined the celebrating soldiers in the streets of Corinth, and by day's end, even the regiment's musical marching band was "...nearly all drunk."[177]

<u>Letter</u> - December 16, 1863
Corinth Miss. Dec. 16th, 1863

Dear Brothers David & William,

I received your very welcome letter of the first Ult last Thursday night and I should have answered sooner but I have been so busy that I have not had time. — It has been raining hard all day and it is hard at it now, I am glad that I do not have to stand guard such a night as this for it is very disagreeable indeed. It is bad enough to have to be out when it is pleasant.

I went to Memphis last Friday and came back on Sunday. We took down 35 prisoners. While there, saw Cousin Clark Chatfield. He is in the Second Ill. Cavalry. He is orderly for Col. Hinsdell on Gen. Hurlbut's staff. Had a good visit with him. Stayed all night and went to the theater. Had a good time. The play was splendid. One part of the Play called (Dot) or the Cricket on the Hearth and was well acted out.*

I just received a letter this evening from George Palmer. He is with his [76th] Reg't down at Vicksburg. He is well and so are most of the Boys. He says that their Orderly, (his name) is William Warden, has a furlough at home. If you see him give him my best respects that I should be very glad to hear from him.

You wished to know candidly and heartily, how I liked the soldiers life, and I will tell you. If I can only have my health, I like it first rate. In fact, better than Farming. Take it all in all, it is not very hard. Why, if we had to work only half as hard as we do at home, we would think that we had dreadful hard time. And I see that you cant hardly get it through your head that we ever had to sleep on the ground. But, I tell you that it is so. We slept on the ground all the time from the time that we got to Memphis a year ago last November till we came here to Corinth (over)

this last August. And, I can tell you that I slept just as well and sweet as ever I did at home on Mothers best Feather Bed. But it was not very pleasant, sometimes, when the [tent] was blown down in some terible storm or other and we would get all wet through. Beckett has got his Commission and is Capt. now. We all like him first rate.

Orderly Kellogg got a furlough and started home last Monday. He is [looking] pretty poorly. Levi Walters was wounded at Vicksburg last may and has been in St Louis Hospitals ever since. He got back yesterday. His wound is just healed up. I had nearly forgotten to tell you whether I was or am sick or well, and I do not know as it would make much difference. I am quite well and can eat my rations as well as any of them. The Boys are all well well as usual, except Tom. He has

---

*   Chatfield is referring to Charles Dickens' 1845 tale, *Cricket on the Hearth*, a story centering on John and Dot Perrybingle's struggle to preserve their marriage, which was threatened by their wide differences in age. Told by Dot that the chirping cricket is good luck, John consults it and receives assurances that all will be well. In this same story, the tough-minded toy maker, Tackleton, is transformed in a "Scrooge-like" conversion.

the ague and keeps him down a good deal. Well, I will close. the Boys all send their best respects.

My love to you from your loving Brother, Edward Chatfield
David A Chatfield & WM S. Chatfield Esquires

Letter - December 20, 1863
Corinth Miss. Dec.—20th 1863

Sunday, 1 oclock, P.M.

Ever Dear Parents,

I have just eaten my dinner and now find myself at the table before the fireplace with writing before me to write you a few lines. It is a fine pleasant day. The sun shines brightly and it is quite Comfortable out of doors. But the weather has been quite cold for the last three days. Ice froze an inch thick which reminded me of what weather you must be having up North. The boys in the next room are having a great time carrying on at the greatest rate. Sunday is but very little respected here among the soldiers. There is no meetings and, less, thoughts of anything religious.

I have not had a line from you since I got those few lines that Mother sent in David's letter dated the 26th Nov, and I have been looking very anxiously for several days past, but none (over)

has come. — My health is pretty good. Am not troubled with any particular disease, except lazyness, which troubles me badly. I believe that the Boys are mostly well. Tom Carrow, however, still has the ague and his legs trouble him the same that mine did some time ago. John Fundy, too, occasionally has a shake so as to keep in practice. Burt [Albert Smith] is as fat as a pig. His going home last fall was what brought him out.

We are going to have a prize drill Christmas Day and the best appearing, and best drilled Company is to have an oyster supper to be given by Major Williams. I suppose that you know that Becket has got his commission as Capt. It is dated August 19th. Kellogg got a furlough and started home last Tuesday and I suppose that you have seen him before this time. There is a good deal of talk and excitement about enlisting in the Veteran Volunteers. Lieut. Jeffcoat has been appointed recruiting Officer for this Reg't., so prepare for hearing of my [reenlistment.]

Well, I will close. Bert will put in a little.

From your Loving son, Edward L. Chatfield

Corinth Sabbath afternoon,

Absent But not forgotten friends,

By the blessing of god & My dear Friend Eds request I will write you a few lines, alltho I expect that He has written all of the news. So I will write a few stry thoughs. Ever since my Return, my health has been a best, whitch is one the greatest blessings that the giver of all good bestows on mankind. We try to do our duty as soldiers should — Hoping to be an End to this Cruel war in the cource of 2 or 3 years longer at the least. Edward & my selfe try to injoy our selves the best we can under present surcumstances. We ar of the best of friends trying to shair each others joys & sorrowers, but, I ashure you, these ar not Frequent Accurencys. For we strivs to be Merry, Now that Ed ~~rirtay~~ regaind his health. Give my kind reguards to all of the Inquiring Friends & Please give my love to Mother & Father & Brothers & sisters.

Your Friend as Ever,

Albert G. Smith

[On backside of letter] P.S., I had my letter all finished and Sealed up when the mail came bringing a welcome letter from home. It was dated Dec 12th. I hear a drum beating and I must go and See what is up — The 47th Ill. & 11th Missouri and the Water-House Battery have just come in on the cars and passed by here on their way to Camp. You Say that Father has just gone to Ohio. I hope that he will have a good time. Well, I believe that this is all for this time. Good bye until next time.

As Ever Yours Truly Edward Chatfield

Letter - December 27, 1863
Corinth Miss.
Dec, 27th, 1863

Dear Mother,

Another week has rolled around and it is the Holy Sabbath again, and I will try and write you a few lines. And, you must excuse me for it will be but a few lines at most, for I feel very negligent and lazy today.

My health is pretty [good] and I hope that the few lines will find you all enjoying this greatest of blessings for which we should thank the Lord every day and for the various blessings which are bestowed upon us.

On Christmas the Prize Drill of [which] I spoke of Came off. We had a good time through the day & Oyster supper in the evening. The Prize that was contended for is a nice flag. The Decission has not been given yet, so I could not tell which is the lucky Co. Well, I have not much to write. ~~The~~ Dr. Mack and

Serg't. Ja's P. Scoon got back yesterday having been home on furlough. My love to you all from your son,

Edward L Chatfield

PS. What is David agoing to do? Is he enrolled. If his name is, will he Stand the draft or what? Please consider and write in your next. E L C —

Having purchased a second diary, Chatfield celebrated the new year by resuming daily journaling. Chatfield initially had hoped to send his first diary home by way of Mrs. Hall, but that plan somehow failed to work out. He notes in his January 21 letter that he had mailed the first diary home that week. Before mailing it, he had summed up the many deaths in his regiment, losses of his friends. The list was thorough, with one notable exception; Chatfield had overlooked the recent loss of Moses Hall. Also listed in his first diary, but not included here, were the names of all of the steamers and gunboats that Chatfield had seen up until then.

Addendum to First Diary — The Dead in Company "B"

Joseph Hicks, January 21, 1863, hospital boat bound for Memphis
J.W. Lyman, 1/27, hospital at Memphis [Illinois Roster places Jonathan W. Lyman's death at the Jefferson Barracks and the date as January 21, 1863.]
R.V. Delemeter [Richard Delamatre] *Cpl, 2/12, hospital at Young's Point*
C.L. Corkins [Charles L. Calkins] *2/24, hospital at Young's Point*
W.B. Wurtz [William B. Wurts] *3/26, onboard hospital boat Nashville at Milliken's Bend*
George T. Vanvalkingburg [George T. Van Valkenberg] *4/4, hospital in St. Louis*
Frank Houghton [Francis Huton] *4/11, in a hospital at Memphis*
L.S. Blair [Loyal S. Blair] *Cpl, 5/3, Van Buren Hospital at Milliken's Bend*
F. Ponton [Francis Ponto] *5/13, killed in rear of Vicksburg* [Chatfield had recorded the correct date of death, May 19, in his diary entry that same day.]
H.I. Brandenburg [Henry I. Brandenberg] *6/18, in division hospital, rear of Vicksburg*
F.A. Glass [Frederick A. Glass] *7/16, died in Vicksburg*

George E. Shays, *7/30, on boat near Young's Point, buried at Milliken's Bend*

William Foreman [William Forman] *8/12, in hospital at Corinth, Mississippi*

Peter Shreffler, *8/13* [in Corinth]

Alfred G. States, *8/28* [in Corinth]

John Bartholomew [Private John Bartholomew] *9/15*

Noah Buck, *9/16* [*Illinois Roster* shows date of death for Noah Buck, a 25-year-old carpenter from Middleport, as September 17, 1863.]

Ambrose Layton, [Ambrose Leighton] *9/22, at the post hospital in Mississippi* [*Illinois Roster* shows Leighton's date of death as September 27, 1863. Private Leighton was 25 years old and married when he died. He had been a farmer in the township of Middleport prior to the war.]

Jacob Hercher, *11/4, at post hospital in Mississippi* [Chatfield had previously written that Hercher died on 11/7.]

CHAPTER 23: GOODBYE CORINTH, HELLO MEMPHIS

"There is a good deal of talk that Corinth is to be Evacuated."

Diary - January 1, 1864
Today was the coldest day this winter. John Fundy and Tom Carrow went on the train. Captain [Andrew] Beckett treated the company to $2.00 worth of ale, and we drank a lot of it.

Diary - January 2, 1864
It's pretty cold today. I went on the train, on the passenger car. Lieutenant Chatfield had charge of the guards.

Lieutenant Charles A. Chatfield in Company "E" was from Cook County, Illinois, a native of Albany, New York, a distant cousin to Edward, and five years older. Charles enlisted as a corporal in October 1862. He was promoted to 2nd Lieutenant in May 1863 and to 1st Lieutenant in June 1864.

Diary - January 3, 1864

Sleet fell this morning. It's been raining and freezing all day. I stayed indoors and have been reading and writing.

<u>Letter</u> - January 3, 1864
Corinth, Miss. Jan. 3rd / 64

To My Dear Mother,

How "do you do" this Sabbath morning the first of the new year. I hardly know how to address you or what to say. The New Year opened quite cold, and this morning it is raining and freezing as far as it falls. But, I have no duty to do today but to set by the fire. So, I do not mind how cold the weather is.

Well, I suppose that you would like to know how we get along. My health is pretty good, at the present, and I am enjoying myself very well. And, I hope that you are all doing as well at home. Well, dinner is ready and I will stop until it is over.

Well, I have finished my dinner and I will ——

[upside down on the letter, Albert wrote:] "Ed is a smoking a cigar. Albert"

Well now, if here is not some of Bert's scribbling, but I guess that it is half true. [I'll] try and finish this letter but I do not know as you will find very interesting. I suppose that Father has had a very pleasant time visiting out in Ohio and will cheer up Grandmothers old age very much. And I hope that I may be permitted to visit my home ere long. But, then, you need not look for me. Only one can have a furlough from the Company at a time, for it is so much reduced. And then, there are so many that need to go home, so much worse than I do, that they will have the first chance. So, you need not expect to see me until you see me for good. I do not think of any thing that I need that Kellogg could bring. For he will not have much chance to bring anything. Of those things that were sent to us they were all made good use of and have all disappeared. The butter was of the most good of all. It costs so much here that I cant hardly afford to use much, it being worth 50 cts per lb and Cheese 55 cts. Our living does very well, so that I cannot complain. We have soft Bread with occasionally hard tack, Fresh Beef, hams & shoulders, smoked and salt pork, potatoes, beans, rice, sugar, coffee and Tea with salt, soap & Candles thrown in between. And then, we have two cooks who do the cooking for the company so that we have our meals as regular as you do at home. And, as to sleeping good and warm, "why" I have got so used to sleeping on a hard bed that I do not know but what it would spoil if I were to go home and sleep on a feather bed. Bert and me sleep together and we have four blankets and we have nice bunks so we sleep as warm as kittens. And, I have nothing to trouble my mind with nor do not get homesick. So I take it easy, "let it come as it will." Tom has been fussing around the fire, some time, and by the actions we are to have a piece of roast Pork for supper to which we will all do our parts, I guess. Pork is worth only 20 cts per lb. We are doing Train Guard duty now. We have to go every third day as far as Grand Junction and return to guard the train against guerillas who occasionally fire at the train and tear up the track. But, there is not enough of them to do much harm. Let them do their best. Does Mothers likeness look natural? Well, I guess that it does, and so does Fathers, Charley's & Mary's. And they are often gazed upon with feelings of much interest. Why, I would not take a fortune for them if I could not get any more. Well, I have written all that I can think of at the present, and so I will close.

The Boys all send their best respects. My love to you all.

From your loving son, Edward L Chatfield

To Mrs M.P. Chatfield

P.S. I received one dollars worth of Stamps from David all right, besides those that I got from you. E —

Diary - January 4, 1864
It's very cold, and it snowed a little. Fundy was sick this morning, so I went in his place on the train.

Diary - January 5, 1864
I went on the train again today and found an engine off the tracks at Grand Junction. They got it back on all right. The company has been divided off into messes, and I'm no longer cooking for all.

Diary - January 6, 1864
We went off into the woods in the forenoon and loaded wood. The weather grew pleasant in the afternoon.

Diary - January 7, 1864
I helped out loading wood again. There was a slight chill in the afternoon.

Diary - January 8, 1864

I was on the train again today. Lieutenant Harrison Daniels had command of the squad. Pretty cold day. I had another chill this afternoon. I received a letter from George Palmer in the 76th, this evening.

Diary - January 9, 1864

I had the hardest shake of the ague I've ever experienced so far. I stayed in all day with a high fever.

Diary - January 10, 1864

The Holy Sabbath. I had another shake of ague an hour earlier than yesterday. The weather has moderated considerably. I wrote a short letter home.

<u>Letter</u> - January 10, 1864
Corinth Miss.
Jan 10th, 1864

Dear Parents,

I do not feel very well this evening, having had a shake of the ague, and the fever is just beginning to leave me. And so, I shall not write much. I have been pretty well until within two or three days. Had a shake three days running. Daniel Durham, of our Comp[any], got a furlough and started home on the eighth. I have just [heard] that he is at Memphis yet waiting for a Boat to go up the River. and I recd a letter from George Palmer and hearty and well. Well, I have been making some pretty crooked lines. So much for writing in the dark. Have not had a letter from home for over a week now. I suppose it is because the mails have not come through.

Well, you will have to excuse a short letter this time. I will try and do better next. I remain as ever your loving son, Edward L Chatfield

Diary - January 11, 1864

I was detailed to go on the train; but Herman Foote took my place. I had another good shake and fever in the afternoon. A lot of cavalry came in here a couple of days ago. They have been going out on the cars for the past 24 hours. They are going after Forrest.

Chatfield appreciated the way train guard duty broke up the boring routine of camp life and no doubt wished that he were well enough to have gone instead of his friend, Private Herman Foote, a 27-year-old married farmer from the township of Salina. The clipped forcefulness of Chatfield's sentence, "They are going after Forrest." leaves little doubt that Chatfield seemed convinced that Forrest was doomed. In precisely six months, Chatfield would entertain thoughts to the contrary.

Diary - January 12, 1864

I went to the surgeon today, and he gave me some ague pills. I had another good shake again today. The train was fired into by guerillas out near Collierville, but no one was injured.

Diary - January 13, 1864

I spent a very restless night and got more medicine from the doctor this morning. I had no shake today.

Diary - January 14, 1864

I attended surgeon's call this morning and got some more medicine. I feel some better and hope that the ague has left me now. It's not very pleasant. There's a good deal of talk that our troops here will be sent off to Texas or Arkansas or somewhere else.

Diary - January 15, 1864

I saw the surgeon for more medicine in the morning and felt pretty well today.

Diary - January 16, 1864

I feel pretty well and did my first work this afternoon, bringing in wood. Dull day as can be.

Diary - January 17, 1864

I went to Grand Junction. The rain came while I was out, and it's still raining hard tonight. Word is just now that pickets are alarmed, and we must be ready to fall in at a moment's notice.

Letter - January 17, 1864
Corinth Miss Jan 17th/63 [Misdated, "63" instead of "64"]

Ever Dear Parents,

I will try and write you a few lines this evening to let you know how I get along. When I wrote my last I mentioned that I had the ague. Well, after having four shakes, I stoped it, and now feel tolerably well with the exception of a bad Cold. Since the recent changes of weather, bad colds have been very prevalent. Today has been the holy Sabbath but for all that I have been on duty. Went on the train as guard. Got back about 3 o'clock. No incidents of any account occurred. The weather has been moderating and today it was quite comfortable. It commenced to rain at 2 o'clock and has kept on, and this evening is raining quite hard. And I may be thankful that we do not have to be out in such storms as this. But, I am afraid that we are not to have such good times much longer. For, I am afraid that we shall have to move from here before long. There is a good deal of talk that Corinth is to be Evacuated, and I think that it looks much like it myself. For, all the heavy seige guns and the men that work them, and the wagons of which there is an immense lot of them that have been sent here to be repaired (for there is large government shops here,) are all being sent off. And so it is, all along the road between here and Memphis, all are on the move. So, something must be up. There is not much news, so you must not expect much. I got a letter from Char-Robb [Charlotte Robb*] a day or two since. She spoke about Fathers being there and that they enjoyed themselves first-rate.

There has been a promotion, John P. Campbell [was] promoted from Private to Corporal. Malcolm Smith [Malcomb Smith], who has been Sergeant Major

---

* Charlotte was a daughter of Maryetta Chatfield Robb, Chatfield's father's sister.

for some time, has been promoted to a First Lieutenancy in a Negro Battery. And John S Titcomb has been promoted to his place (that is Sergeant Major.) We have had an addition to our Company of a new recruit. He is a boy about as large as James. He says that he thinks that he can make a soldier. He is a smart little fellow at any rate. By the papers I see that you have been having a pretty cold time, but I hope that you did not all freeze up entirely. For, I should like to hear from you once more. As for us, we made out by keeping a good fire to roast one side while the other side froze. But, after all, we managed to live and I cannot see any bad effects as I know of unless it is bad Colds generally. I will close this by wishing you all success.

  I remain, as ever Your loving son,
  Edward L. Chatfield
N S. Chatfield

Corporal John P. Campbell, of Company "B", was one year younger than Chatfield, a farmer from Norton Township. Sergeant Malcomb Smith transferred to the 7th Colored Infantry of the 1st Alabama Heavy Artillery on January 6, promoted to the rank of 1st Lieutenant, where he served through the close of the war. The new recruit "about as large as James" (Chatfield's brother) had been likened to a 12-year-old.

Diary - January 18, 1864
We heard heavy gunfire last night. All of us expected to be called out but were not. We've had hard rain and freezing all night. Washed some today and wrote a letter to Uncle Lafayette.

"Uncle Lafayette" Chatfield was born in 1826, the tenth child of Edward's grandparents, Isaac and Lucy Tomlinson Chatfield—Chatfield's father's youngest brother. The "heavy gunfire" that Chatfield heard likely involved a small band of guerillas, possibly some of Forrest's men. On January 18, a Union scout reported having seen 250 men of Forrest's command below Collierville near Holly Springs. Some reports held that Forrest's main body had already destroyed the *Nashville and Chattanooga Railroad*.[178]

Diary - January 19, 1864

I felt pretty well in the morning and was detailed to go out and help cut ½dozen loads of wood. The weather was quite warm this afternoon.

<u>Letter</u> - January 19, 1864
Corinth Miss Jan 19th, 1864

Dear Brother David,

I will endeavor to write you a few lines this Evening in answer of your kind letter which I received in Father's night before last. Was very glad to hear that you was well and enjoying yourself so well this winter in attending school and that you are making such fine progress in your studies. I see by your writing that you are making rapid progress in Book-keeping and I will compliment you on your advancement. Well, it is getting dark and I must stop until I get a light.

—— Well! now I have a light and I will proceed with my writing.

My health is pretty good now although last week I did not feel quite so keen having a shake of the ague for four consecutive days. There has been considerable of that kind of pleasure (ague I mean) in our Reg't this fall & winter. But there has [been] nothing very serious attended it.

2. I think that my memory will have to be freshened a little or I really Cannot reccollect of what Lady you had reference, but as to going down into that part of the world and making a few calls would be exactly to my mind, and I intend, if my life is spared, to return home to make such a trip. Enlisting again for 3 years is played out with me. They would not let us enlist when we wanted, and so I think that when my present term of service expires that I shall be my own master for awhile! We finally found out that we could not enlist unless we had been in the service two years or more. If we had have had the chance, the largest share would have reenlisted. So, that point is settled.

But, you have got the wrong impression about our fighting for the Negroes. On the contrary, we are making the Negroes fight for us. There is in the field already about 35,000 and by spring there will be 60,000, and they make the best of soldiers. There is two Reg'ts of them here, and they do the picket, and they do it right up to the handle to. But, for all that, I don't want them around me. ——

3. Well, I have made a nice mistake of writing upon the wrong page. But, if you will notice, that the pages are numbered and by the reading you will come

out all right! I expect that you will find this very dry and tiresome but if you do not wish to read it just [toss] it into the fire. I expect that we shall shortly be ordered to move from here shortly. Every thing belonging to the government is being [moved] as fast as possible. All of the merchants have moved and gone to Memphis. And, in the course of a few days, I expect that we will go there to. There has been several scares within a few days such as the pickets being fired on etc. etc. —— Got a letter from George Palmer a short time ago. He was well. They were still at Vicksburg. Joseph C. Smith was discharged on Sunday and started home this morning. He was from Iroquois Co. He was discharged on account of disability. He was promoted to Corporal last Summer on account of bravery at the Charges on Vicksburg. —— Were it not for this disgraceful Rebellion we might all be at home enjoying the Comforts of life.

4. But let that this Cursed Rebellion may soon be crushed out. It seems to me that it Cannot last much longer. But, we will hope for the best and all will come out right in the end. Well, I have about run out of anything to write and so will close. Albert & John Fundy and all the rest of the boys send their best respects. My resp love to Father & Mother with a good share for yourself.

I remain your loving Brother,

Edward L. Chatfield

David A. Chatfield

P.S. When we had our box sent to us there was some large sized letter paper sent but there was no name to whom it was sent to. I wish that you would find out whose it is and let me know. Now do not forget it. Edward

Diary - January 20, 1864

Our company went on the train as guards today, and the train made very slow time. Only went as far as Saulsbury. I finished a couple of letters today, one to David.

Diary - January 21, 1864

We were detailed to Memphis with prisoners today. Nine were Rebs and 15 were Federal prisoners. We took them from the train to Irving Block, and then went to the Soldiers Home where we stayed all night. I went to bed in good season. I did not run about much.

Diary - January 22, 1864

We had an early breakfast and got to the cars at 8:30. Our train got to Grand Junction, then had to return. We transferred to a freight train and came as far as Pocahontas, where we stopped and spent the night. Another train had derailed at Chewalla and had torn up the track.

Diary - January 23, 1864

I passed a very uncomfortable night sleeping on uncushioned seats in the passenger car. By 9:30 the road was in running order, and we started for Corinth. We found that our regiment was ready to move when we arrived. I was detailed this evening to go to the post hospital and put up some headboards on the graves of our boys.

Diary - January 24, 1864

We packed our knapsacks after breakfast and were ready to move.

Letter - January 24, 1864
Corinth, Miss,
Jan, 24th, 1864,

Dear Parents,

Amid the confusion tumult and stir, incident to a move I take up my pen to write you a few lines. —

My health is pretty good with the exception of a bad cold. The ague, after giving me four good shakes, left me. Thanks to the all wise Providence that I am as well as I am. For the week past I have been on duty almost all the time. Last Sunday, had to go on the train as guard. Monday, I did a big washing. Tuesday, choped wood most all day. Wednesday, was detailed as Train guard again. Thursday, was detailed to go to Memphis with prisoners. We had 9 Rebs, (one of which was one of Gen Braggs spies) [CS General Braxton Bragg] and 15 of our men that have been put in prison for various offences. Stayed at the soldiers Home while at Memphis. Friday, we came back as far as Pocahontas when we learned that there had been a regular smash up of the Passenger train the day before. And so, we had to stay there that night. It is supposed that the accident was caused by the Bridge breaking down, it being so rotten. Others think that one of the rails was loosened and when the train came along it spread apart. The Engine and 6 freight Cars was thrown from the track. One man of Co A.

had his shoulder put out of place and another had his big toe torn off. No other accidents.

They got the track fixed Saturday morning, and we got back here about noon and found that the Reg't was ready to move, and we have been in hourly expectation of having to start ever since. Well, the ~~we have~~ drums have just beat for us to fall in and I must stop. ———

I will now again resume my pen. The mail has just come in but there was nothing for me. On Dress Parade, we had orders read to us that we should not leave Camp on no account, but should be ready to move at a moments notice, and that all the buildings and barracks should be burned by a special detail. There has been quite a number of fires already within the last three days. I recd your welcome letter of the 16th Ultimate yesterday. Was glad to hear that you was all well, and I see that you always have enough to do. When it is not one thing it is another. But I suppose that if there was not some thing to be done that you would get lonesome. Well, I suppose that by the time that I get home that I will not be good for any thing at all. Why, I am getting so Lazy that I hardly know what to do with myself. ———

We are having fine pleasant weather. It seems as though it were Spring. It is so warm and pleasant. Sam Place [from Limestone Township] was just in here and he said that he had just got a letter announcing the Death of his little boy. It makes him feel pretty bad. ———

I am glad that David is enjoying himself so well this winter and progressing so fast in his studies. I see that he has carried the mail several times. Has he taken the job of carrying it? ———

You wrote in one of your letters, some time ago, asking if I should like to have the Advocate sent to me. It had slipped my mind several times or I [would] have written about it before. I should be very glad, indeed, if you would send it every week. It seems so much like home to get that paper. We are expecting to be paid off in a few days. The Pay master has already commenced paying the 16th Army Corps. ———

Well, I guess that you will say he does not take much pains with his writing, but you must excuse this, for I am in a hurry, and (I feel rather nervous.) I expect that we will not have much rest tonight, for ~~the~~ Gen. Stevenson [Brigadier General John D. Stevenson, the commander at Corinth] says that everything must be on the Cars and away from here before morning ———

Well, I must close for the want of something to write and my page is almost full. My love to you all, from your dutiful son,

E L. Chatfield

P.S. Direct your next (via Cairo and that will be enough)

CHAPTER 24: MARTIAL LAW IN MEMPHIS

*"We are in a very nicely situated Camp on ...Vance Street
just in the outskirts or suburbs of the town."*

Diary - January 25, 1864

We did not go to bed. We stayed up all night getting ready to move. The company fell in at 5:00 a.m. and marched to the station. We boarded the cars at 11:00 and started a half-hour after. We rode on top of the cars. We got to Memphis at 8:00 p.m. and unloaded the cars. I was detailed to stand guard over the baggage and guns.

By evening, all Union troops had vacated Corinth—leaving the town open to Confederate reoccupation. But those who returned to Corinth found the rails to be of little use. The Confederates had not built a single locomotive since the start of the war, and there was no equipment or machinery in Corinth to do so. The once valued rails of Corinth had become virtually useless to the Rebels. Their only utility was limited to what could be pulled about on them by mules. As such, the city's reoccupation posed minimal threat to Union soldiers who had returned to Memphis, ninety-one miles to the west, where Chatfield's unit temporarily settled on the outskirts of the city.

Diary - January 26, 1864

We fell in at 11:00 a.m. and marched to camp about ½mile east of the station. Our camp is on a high knoll with fine shade trees scattered over it. We relieved the 117th Illinois that has been here for over a year. I was ordered to go on picket at 5:00 p.m. while the entire regiment went out about 2 miles.

Diary - January 27, 1864

I was relieved from picket at 4:00 p.m. Our camp has been moved ½mile south of where we had been and closer to the tracks at Vance Street. I felt pretty tired.

Diary - January 28, 1864

I stood guard at a large stable. I drew a small wedge tent, just large enough for four men.

Diary - January 29, 1864

I have been busy all day at our tent with Al, his partner Tom Carrow, and Fundy. I'm still pretty tired.

Diary - January 30, 1864

I felt not well all day. My limbs and bones ached all over. A shake of ague came on at 11:00 a.m. and lasted until night. I feel miserable tonight.

Diary - January 31, 1864

I got no rest last night. My body was in pain all over. I had ague again at noon, a real hard shake and fever. A hard storm of wind and rain came on at 6:00 p.m. and our dwelling leaked considerably. Most of the boys went out on picket. We have only 20 months more to serve. Hurrah!

Letter - January 31, 1864
Memphis. Tenn, Sabbath Morn, Jan 31st, 1864

Dear Parents,

    I will now try and improve a few moments in addressing a few lines to you. To inform of what we are doing and how and are getting along. ———

My health is pretty good now and has been for some time with the exception of having the ague yesterday. But I went to the Dr. this morning and got some pills and I guess that they will knock the ague end ways. ———

The boys from our neighborhood are all usually well except J. Fundy. He has the ague regular all the time. ———

There is a detail made to go to Springfield to recruit and bring down recruits. Sam Place [company musician from Limestone] & Albert Nichols are going among the rest. A Lieut [from] Co G has charge of the squad. They start on Monday, I believe. They will be apt to visit home before they return. ———

I wrote you a letter the 24th, but being so busy I did not send it until day before yesterday. We were paid off up to the first of Jan., day before yesterday. The boys of our mess made up a package of money and sent it by Express to G J Smith. A Smith to G J Smith $20.00, Tom Carrow to Peter Carrow $20.00, John Fundy to J Michael $10.00, Ed Chatfield to N S Chatfield $20.00, the freight to be paid at Kankakee. The last letter that I rec'd from home was dated the 8th. ———

Well now, I will tell you what we have been doing for the last week. When I wrote my last letter I left off at Sunday evening. Well, that night we were up all night and redy to start.

Just before daylight we fell in and marched to the Station with knapsacks on our backs and guns on our shoulders. At 11 AM we got on to the cars and started for this place. We got here about 9 PM., when we laid down on the platform and had a good nights rest.

Tuesday, we moved out to our camp ground. In the evening went on picket.

Wednesday, got back to Camp from picket this evening. We are in the same camp that the 117th Ill was in. They have been here every since they left the state and have gone down the river to take the field for the first time.

Thursday, & Friday we were busy fixing up our Quarters. We have the small Wedge tent just large enough for four to stay in. Bert, Tom, John Fundy & myself stay in one and we have things fixed up in style. If you could just step in and make us a call I should be much pleased.

We are in a very nicely situated Camp on what is called Vance Street just in the outskirts or suburbs of the town. We have had nice spring weather for some time past. Night before last, we had a fine shower and again last night, and today it is raining some. I do The folks have begun to plow and I saw one man (or rather woman) planting potatoes on last Thursday. During all this winter, I have not seen only at one place where any of the people have fed any thing at all. The cattle get their own living and they look a good deal better than the cattle generally do at the North. The grass has been green here all winter. –

The 108th, 120th, & 113th are in one Brigade and Col. Hoge is in command, [the] acting Brigadier. This morning, for the first time for over a year, I heard the church bells ringing and it brought [to] my mind former times and associations of when the Sabbath came round, of how we all used [to] repair to the house of God to hear the word of God propounded by our worthy ministers. If we stay here any length of time I shall try and attend church. Well, I must stop for the want of something to write. You must overlook my poor writing.

My love to you all. I remain as ever your loving son. Direct your letters to Memphis Tenn.

Ewd L Chatfield

N S Chatfield

P.S. As Soon as you get that money please let me know. I sent you my diary about 10 days ago. It was up to the first of Sept. I sent it by mail. Please let me know when you get it it. E.L C.

Diary - February 1, 1864

I feel pretty well this morning; I got ague pills from the surgeon. I was detailed to stand guard at the horse stable today. Mr. Bliss has been our sutler today.

Diary - February 2, 1864

I was relieved from guard at 9:00 a.m. Albert Smith was detailed to drive a brigade ambulance, so he now stays at the Colonel's headquarters. Lieutenant Jeffcoat is in command of the company. He has been for some time, Captain Beckett being sick.

By early February, General Sherman had arrived back in Vicksburg where he resumed his efforts to plunder the rails and countryside, thus tightening the Union stranglehold over the South. Sherman also hoped his havoc would attract CS General Nathan Bedford Forrest, leading to Forrest's capture. Before marching his army east from Vicksburg and keenly aware that he would need a cavalry of his own to defeat Forrest, Sherman ordered General William Sooy Smith's Memphis Cavalry to meet him in Meridian, Mississippi, no later than February 10. Sherman's route from Vicksburg to Meridian passed through what were then all-too-familiar places of destruction: the fallen bridge at the Big Black River, the devastation at Edward's Depot, the sight of burned wagons and spiked cannon at Champion Hill, the twisted rails at Bolton, the pillaged community of Clinton, and the badly beaten and heavily battered remains of Jackson.[179]

Diary - February 3, 1864

I was detailed to go to the Colonel's headquarters on fatigue. After that I went downtown to the navy yard for lumber. I took Tom's and my box to the Express Office this evening and got myself a new diary today.[*]

Diary - February 4, 1864

I felt well this morning and was detailed, again, as a guard at the stables. I did some mending while off duty. A letter from home made me feel much better.

Meanwhile, Union officials continued their efforts to address the correspondent prisoner impasse ...

OFFICIAL CORRESPONDENCE-

WASHINGTON CITY, D.C., February 5, 1864.

Major General B.F. BUTLER, Commanding, &c., Fort Monroe:

SIR: A.D. Richardson and Janius H. Browne, correspondents of the *New York Tribune*, are said to be prisoners in Richmond. I am induced to believe that we have some prisoners at Nashville available for their exchange.

Will you be so good as to inform me whether you can accomplish the release of the *Tribune* correspondents, and what you desire may be done for that object?

Very respectfully, your obedient servant,

E.A. HITCHCOCK,

Major-General, U.S. Vols., Com. for Exchange of prisoners.[180]

Sherman reached Jackson on February 4, having traversed the 45 miles from Vicksburg in two days. From there he would continue east toward Meridian, making feints in the direction of Mobile, Alabama, and encountering resistance here

---

[*]   Although Chatfield purchased his third (and final) diary on February 3, he would continue journaling in the second one through the end of the month.

and there while expecting the arrival of Sooy Smith's Cavalry no later than February 10.[181]

Diary - February 6, 1864
I was ordered with 6 others to take 6 days' rations and go with General Buckland who put us on patrol duty in the south part of the city.

Fifty-one-year-old General Ralph P. Buckland had been raised in Ravenna, Ohio, 29 miles south of Batavia (Middlefield). Like the Chatfields, his family was among the early Ohio pioneers.[182] In 1861, Buckland entered the Union army as a colonel of the 72nd Ohio Infantry. By the time Chatfield wrote about him, Buckland had risen to the rank of Brigadier General in charge of the Military District of Memphis.[183]

Diary - February 7, 1864
The 108th relieved us this morning. We will alternate days. They gave us first rate quarters in a barracks. I'm not on duty today, a Sunday. They sent us back to camp this evening.

Letter - February 7, 1864
Memphis Tenn February, 7th, 1864,

Ever Dear Parents,

  Having a few spare moments that I am not on Duty I will try and write you a few lines to answer yours of the 30th Ult., which was rec'd on Friday. Was very glad to hear that you were all well. ——

  My health, and so is that of the boys, is very good. I have, this forenoon for the first time in 17 months, attended meeting where they had meeting in a civilized form. It was at a Methodist Church in town in the same square where we are doing duty. The church was well filled and mostly by the female sex. We listened to a very good sermon. The text will be found in Deut. 35-48. And the Lord said unto Moses get the up into Mount Nebo etc. etc [Deuteronomy, 32:48-52.] To attend the church, where the word of god was preached once more, it seemed like home almost. Oh, how we soldiers will prize the privileges of home, if we are ever permitted to return home again.

We are now doing patrol Duty in town. We have to patrol the streets to keep order and see that every thing goes right. The white troops have all left here except the 113th, 108th & 120th and some batteries. The rest of the troops here are Negroes.

Tom Carrow & myself started a box of Clothing home on the 3rd. It was directed in Fathers name. You will have to pay the Charges. Mr. Carrow has to pay his share. I will tell you something how the box is packed and then you will understand it. When you open the box from the top, you will find a white blanket (or one that once was white). This is mine. Then, there is a — two quilts, quilt with a pair of pants, Rubber and some other things in it. These are Tom's. Then, you will come to a dress coat. This is mine, and all below also. I had in the box I blanket, 2 pr pants, I Dress coat with a button in the right side, this was made at Arkansas Post, 5 shirts, I believe the coarse cotton one was also Captured at the post, 2 pr Drawers, and a pillow case that once was white that was Captured at a rich plantation on the Miss, and some other little trinkets.

Well, I have not time to write much this time. I have got to go back to my Duty, down town. We do not have much idle time now, I can assure you, having so much duty to do with so small a number to do it. The weather is very fine and pleasant. I think that winter is over entirely. You spoke about my butter being gone. I guess it is. It was gone two months ago, and if we have any now we have to pay 40 cts per lb. I have got a medal that I will send, in this, as a present to Mary to remember me by. The boys all send their best respects, all being well. My love to you all.

From your loving son,
Ewd L Chatfield
N S Chatfield ———

Diary - February 8, 1864

We relieved the 108th this morning, and I was on first relief. We must patrol the streets to keep order and quiet. I wrote another letter to Cousin Clark this evening.

Diary - February 9, 1864
The 108th relieved us at 8:00 a.m.

Diary - February 10, 1864
We were on duty again today, and I was Acting Corporal of the 3rd relief. Ambrose Smith of Company G was the cook for Number 1 mess. We drew our rations.

Private Ambrose Smith, 19, of Company "G", was from Northfield in Cook County. Short in stature, the 5 ft. 4 inch private eventually became a corporal.

General W. Sooy Smith's 7,000-man Memphis Cavalry failed to meet Sherman on February 10 as ordered. Only later would Sherman learn that Smith had remained in Memphis, delaying his march until February 11, awaiting reinforcements and proper shoeing of his horses.[184] Unopposed, Smith moved toward Meridian by way of New Albany, tearing up railroads, destroying crops, and gathering several thousand former slaves.

Diary - February 11, 1864
This was a pleasant day. John Fundy, Tom Carrow, and I went uptown this afternoon. I wrote to David and William.

Letter - February 11, 1864
Headquarters Provost Guards Memphis Tenn Feb 11th, 1864

Dear Brothers David & William,

I will improve a few moments in writing a few lines to you in answer of David's welcome letter which I received in Fathers a few days since, which was dated Jan 21st. Was very glad to hear that you were well, but very sorry tho hear that Death had been in your midst and made a victim of one just entering into the bloom of womanhood. But, Death is in among us, when we least expect it, slaying our friends on the right hand and on the left. —

You say that you are progressing in your studies rapidly, of which I am glad to see. I shall be glad to have the same Chance, but I must advise you (David in particular) to look after your spelling. For a poor speller is but a poor scholar to make the most of it. David asks which I should prefer, going to school or to war. In my case I should prefer being a soldier to attending school, for the Army is a great school and there is much to be learned of some men or boys, just as you are mind to have it. Of some, I say, the Army or being a soldier makes perfect fools, and of others it makes the man of them. ——

You ask why I do not enlist again. I will tell you. It is not because I have not got the will, but because we have not the power. No one can Enlist in the Veteran Corps unless he has been in the service two (2) years. If we could have had the Chance all of us boys would have gone in again for three (3) years. ——

As to my telling you about a fellows feelings when he has the ague, I have only to say just wait until you shall be so lucky as to have it, and then you can tell better by your own feelings than I can describe it to you. ——

You want to know how I like the Negroes. I will tell you. I like them first rate, in their Places. They can stop a bullet just as well as a white soldier can. If the Negro can be used in any way to help put down the Rebellion, and if by taking the slaves from the southerners, and thus injure or weaken them and make the Federals stronger, why [we should] do it every time. And, this is the Universal voice of the soldiers wherever you may go. ——

Well, I have been writing so far and had almost forgotten myself. My health is pretty good. Have not had any ague for over a week. There is 7 of our Camp here, and we are doing Provost Duty, and we are having the easiest times that we have had for some times, having to be on duty only 6 hours out of the 48. We patrol the streets, and if any one is Caught Drunk or in any business that he had not ought to be in, we just send them to the Irving Block prison.

John Fundy & Tom Carrow are here to [too]. They send their best respects. We have good comfortable quarters with a kitchen and dining room attached. We are about 3/4 mile from our Camp. ——

Bert Smith is driving a Brigade ambulance. We have been expecting an attack from Old Forrest for some time, but we are pretty fixed. We have batteries planted all through town. Besides, Fort Pickering is well manned or garrisoned with both men and heavy guns of 8, 10, & 12 inch calibre.

Dan Durham got back last Sunday, being prompt to the time that his furlough run out. The weather is quite pleasant and does not seem much like it generally does up north at this time of the year. I will send you, in this, some pictures of several battle views before Corinth, which I wish to have you save.

Well, I guess that you will say, if he would only take a little more pains with his writing I would be glad, and so I will close. My love and best wishes to you. I remain as ever your loving Brother –

Edward L. Chatfield

Messers David A and William S

Diary - February 12, 1864

Lieut. Azariah Baird of Company A relieved Lieutenant Aquilla Cowgill of Company H today. I went on patrol at 8:00 a.m. as Acting Corporal. James Henry got a 1st lieutenant commission today, effective August 26th.

Cowgill would resign in another two months. Azariah Baird, 23, was a harness maker when he enlisted in Chicago, climbing the ranks from Sergeant to 1st Lieutenant by October of 1863. James Henry, the *Forlorn Hope* volunteer, may have received a commission, but a flurry of protests followed. The 31-year-old married carpenter from Kankakee County, a native of Sunfish Pike, Ohio, had a battle on his hands. The boys in the 113th liked him well enough but felt that the furlough was a sufficient reward. Promotion to lieutenant seemed over the top; there were others who had done more to earn that job.

Diary - February 13, 1864

I went uptown this forenoon and saw Sergeant William Warden of the 76th who was returning to his regiment. Lieutenant Baird, Joseph Call and I took a fellow to Irving Block who was suspected of being a spy and steamboat burner.

Warden had returned from his furlough, refreshed and ready to resume his duties when Chatfield mentions him again here. Private Joseph Call of Company "H" was a married man, a 39-year-old farmer from Aroma Township of Kankakee County.

Letter - February 13, 1864
Memphis Tenn. February 13ᵗʰ 1864

[Written vertically up top left side of letter] **"I have some pictures that I got at Corinth and I will give them to you."**

Dear Brother Newton,

I have just received Fathers letter, and with it, a kind letter from you with which I was much pleased. I am glad y— if I can have the assurance, occasionally, that although [I] am in a distant state that I am not entirely forgotten by those we love at home.

My health is pretty good, at present, and I am in hopes that I shall be spared having any more sickness for a short time at least. ——

I was sorry to hear that Mother was sick. Am in hopes that by the time that I hear from home again she will be better. Your loosing all your chickens was quite a loss but nothing to what the Rebs have to submit to when we come along. For, we take every thing slick and clean (I reckon).

You wish to know how I like soldiering. Why! I am falling in love with this branch of the service, and I dont know but what I shall [decide] to go into the Regular service, but as for marching on to the battlefield, I had just as like be somewhere else, if I can, consistently with my Duty. But, if you had been where we were last Summer, where the Cannon were booming continually for 46 days, and the bullets flying around sometimes as thick as hail, Why! I say, by that time, you would have got so that you would not have cared much where you were. On some, it has a very bad effect if they hear the bullets whistle. But they never made any impression [on me]. If I should ever get the chance to go home, and make a visit, I would be very much pleased, and would pay my fare and just about two ¢ sents besides. How much would you give? Now, just tell me that. But, I shall try and keep my courage up to the sticking point at any rate.

The weather is fine and pleasant. It is quite warm, and the streets are getting dusty. I was running about town all the forenoon, and this afternoon took a prisoner up to Irvin's Block, and have written several letters, and am getting tired, and my page is about full, and so I will close by sending you my love and best respects.

Ewd L Chatfield

[up right side of letter] To N Chatfield

Diary - February 14, 1864

It rained last night and today. John Fundy, Tom, and I went to the Catholic Church to meeting. I received a letter from Uncle Lafayette today. I went on patrol at 11:00 this morning. Corporal Tommy Martin kept us busy examining passes and arresting Negroes. We have sent 19 to the Block today. John Titcomb got a furlough and starts home by first boat. Lieutenant Charles A. Chatfield* of Company E relieved Lieutenant Azariah Baird of Company A today.

A year younger than Edward L. Chatfield, Corporal Thomas H. Martin was born in Canada. He enlisted in Chicago and was assigned to Company "A".

Letter - February 14, 1864
Headquarters, Provost Guards
Hernando, St Memphis, Tenn, Feb, 14th, 1864

Ever Dear Parents,

I now find myself seated to answer your very welcome letter which I rec'd yesterday afternoon of the 8th Ult, and was sorry to hear that Mother was so unwell, and I hope that it will not prove any thing very serious. ———

My health is good, at present, and the boys are all usually well, except Tommy C [Tom Carrow] ——— who has the ague occasionally. ———

We are doing Provost Duty. There is 30 of us here, and there is as many more at two other places here in town. Our Duty is not hard. We have to be on duty only about 3 hours out of the 48. Although today is Sunday, I have been on [duty] and we it just about kept us busy arresting undesirables. Why, the streets literally swarm with them. And every [man] that does not have a pass we arrest, and I had to bring up my gun and cock it on two of them before they would stop. If they had gone a few steps further there would have been a dead man sure. I think that we have got a steady job and will be apt to remain here some time. ———

Well Mother! You wish to know what we do with our old worn out dud's. Well, when they get so that they are not good for (nix) we just hoist them out of doors. Tom and me sent you a box of clothing, which I suppose you have rec'd ere this. Everything here in Memphis is at very high figures. Here is some of the

---

*   Edward's distant relative from New York.

prices at wholesale. Apples $500 & $650 pr Bbl, Butter 30 & 95 pr lb, cheese 16 & 17, Eggs 50 pr Doz, Hay $53.00 pr ton, Corn $1.80 & $1.90 pr Buch, Oats $1.35 pr Buch. These are the wholesale prices. At retail they are much higher, Butter 50 cts, cheese 25 & 30 cts, Eggs 1.00 & 1.25 pr Doz and so on. ——

You asked if I had seen Cousin Cl'k Chatfield. I have not seen him since we have been here, but I saw him about a month before. He was well then and enjoying himself first rate. His time will be out in August. I believe he has now gone down the river. He is orderly for one of the aids of Major Gen Hurlbut. He is not with his Reg't, the 2nd Ill Cav. It is now divided up and scattered in different parts of the Country. ——

But, what is the matter, Dear Mother, with the old Maid? Certainly you are not afraid that I will fall in love with her are you? Some six months, or a year ago, she very politely wrote me a letter. And for the sake of friendship, I could do nothing more than to answer it. Orderly Kellogg got back yesterday after being gone just two months. He looks very different from what he did when he went away. Sergt John S. Titcomb got his [furlough] last evening and will go up the River by the first steamer. James Henry got his Commission day before yesterday, promoteding him to the first Lieutenantcy over the heads of Jeffcoat and Kellogg. But, he is not mustered in yet, and the Company have got up a petition and sent it to Gov. Yates petitioning him to revoke Henry's Commission and to give it to Jeffcoat or Kellogg, who, by rights, had ought to have it. But, you need not tell every body what I have said here. ——

I got a letter from Uncle Lafayette[*] this A.M. He said that they were all well that he was sorry that Father could not have made him a longer visit when he was there.

The weather has been very pleasant for near a month. Last night, however, it commenced to rain and it has rained the most of the time today. But it was a warm Spring rain and the grass begins to look quite green.

Well, it is getting pretty near supper time and boys are cutting up and making so much noise that I must stop for the present. Give my ~~all and~~ respects all inquiring friends and to Jemima P. ——

My love to you all from your soldier Boy,

Ewd L Chatfield

Mr N S Chatfield

Southeast of Memphis on February 14, facing stiff resistance, General Sherman moved steadily into Meridian. CS General Leonidas Polk had removed some of the

---

[*]   Lafayette Chatfield was the tenth of Lucy and Isaac Chatfield's eleven children.

rolling stock prior to evacuating the city. For the next six days, Sherman's armies would savagely sack the city and tear up its rails.[185]

Diary - February 15, 1864
Bert Smith came out and took dinner with us. We went downtown, after, in his ambulance, then back to the Colonel's and took dinner again.

Diary - February 16, 1864
We went uptown prospecting. After that, I did some washing and cut the collar of my coat down this afternoon.

On February 16, still en route to Meridian to assist Sherman, 176 miles away, Sooy Smith's mighty 7,000-man cavalry crossed the Tallahatchie River at New Albany, Mississippi, his progress slowed by the muddy roads and the 3,000 former slaves that he had gathered along the way.[186]

Diary - February 17, 1864
This was our day to patrol. We relieved the 108th. When done, I did more clothes mending.

Diary - February 18, 1864
Lieutenant Jeffcoat relieved Lieutenant Charles Chatfield this afternoon. The 114th relieved us, and we went back to camp.

Although Edward's camp was less than a quarter mile from Memphis, security was tight, and a pass was needed to go into the city.

Diary - February 19, 1864

I was sent out to retrieve 9 men that were absent without leave.

Diary - February 20, 1864

Tommy and Seth of Co A went up to the YMCA today.

Sergeant Seth R. Cole, born in Vermont, was a 25-year-old single corn merchant from Cook County when he enlisted. He was a friend of Corporal Tommy Martin.

Having destroyed all of the rails and major buildings in Meridian, Sherman marched out of the city on February 20. Sherman, having heard nothing from Sooy Smith, had no way of knowing that Smith was then skirmishing with one of Forrest's brigades, 90 miles north of Meridian. Driving his enemy south through West Point, Mississippi, while evading entrapment in the marshes, Sooy Smith had yet to realize that the skirmish would be followed by a decisive battle.[187]

Letter - February 21, 1864
Infty Headquarters 113ᵗʰ, Ill, Vols Memphis, Tenn. February, 21ˢᵗ, 1864

My Dear Parents,

Seated to address you (I again find myself) a few lines respecting myself and Companions. —— My health is quite good, at present, and most of the boys are well. Thomas C [Tom Carrow] & John F [John Fundy] have the ague occasionally, so as to keep in practice. This forenoon some ~~fourteen~~ ten of us went up the Union Chapel to meeting. We had a very good sermon. His text was taken from Revelations C14 - V6.

We have been relieved from doing Provost Duty. (that is about half of us have) and we are doing nothing but cooking and eating which [is] the hardest work that we have to do just now.——

We have had quite an ~~accession~~ addition to this part of the Regt during the week past. I will tell you how it is. About two weeks ago, a Detachment under Capt. King numbering about 60, came down the river with prisoners and recruits. And, when they got here, they were ordered to go on down to Vicksburg with them. Well, when they got there they were ordered to report here. So, when they got here, the Colonel [George B. Hoge] just nabbed them and kept them here, which makes them awful wrathy. They think that there never was any one that had such hard times as they have.

We are having splendid weather we now. We have had, for the last three or four days, rather cool. But now it is warm enough to make it all up. I will tell you that there is no place like this part of the Country on account of the climate. We have had here, I know, warm weather for a longer period than up North, but I have seen just as warm days up there as we, even down at Vicksburg, while the winters here are nothing compared with them up there. There is lots of cattle running about here that have not had a mouthful of feed, and they look just as well as they do up there [with] hay and grain all winter. Grass is now coming, so that they will have fresh feed in a few days.

The Union sentiments of the people of Memphis are progressing satisfactorily. They are holding meetings in every part of the town. I was at one of them and the speaker just gave them the plain truth, and the houses are generally well filled. The people are beginning to see that it is best for their own interests to come back in the Old Union Under the stars and stripes again, even if they have [to] abolish slavery to do it. Tennessee will, in a short time, be back in the Union and will be a free state to. I will send you an abstract of the speech made the other evening. Well, I have run out of any thing to write and so will close. My love to you all.

From your Boy, Ewd L Chatfield

NS Chatfield Esq.

This letter provides a window into the confusion of war. The 113th had been expecting the arrival of its five detached companies from Camp Butler,[*] and Camp Butler was indeed in the process of sending troops south, apparently some with unclear orders. Captain George E. King[†] of Company "F" (one of the five detached companies) had been sent to Vicksburg with 60 troops, but all were turned away and returned to Memphis, probably to clarify their orders. This explains why Colonel Hoge felt compelled to hold on to them. After all, Company "F" was one of the five detached companies, Hoge may have reasoned. If not to the 113th, stationed in Memphis, to whom did they belong? However appropriate his decision to keep them may have been, it would backfire almost immediately.

Significantly, Chatfield comments on what he perceives as a genuine change in sentiment toward the war. The grass roots citizens of Memphis were beginning to feel disillusioned with the Confederate goal to secede, and some saw the abolishment of slavery as a necessary step for returning to the Union.

---

[*]   Camp Butler, near Springfield, Illinois, was the second largest military training camp in Illinois. (The largest was Camp Douglas, in Chicago.)

[†]   King was a single 23-year-old lawyer from Middleport, Iroquois County, before he enlisted.

Meanwhile, north of Meridian, on the morning of February 21, Sooy Smith received word that General Sherman had exited Meridian and was en route toward Memphis. Smith, anticipating that General Forrest would block his way to Meridian and concerned about the potential for Forrest to recapture the former slaves, reasoned that the wisest action would be to return to Memphis as Sherman had done. Reversing direction, Smith headed his cavalry north toward Okolona, Mississippi, unaware of the fury he would soon face. Forrest wasn't about to permit Smith to exit Mississippi unscathed.

Before dawn on the morning of February 22, Forrest's main body raced north in pursuit of Smith's cavalry, overtaking them as they approached Okolona. Following a series of skirmishes, retreats, counterattacks and galloping battles, General Forrest's youngest brother, Jeffrey, was killed, and Sooy Smith, having witnessed appalling bloodshed, retreated toward Pontotoc, 25 miles northwest, ending the battle of Okolona. The losses were nearly equal in terms of percentages. Smith lost 388 boys, 5.5% of his 7,000-man force. Forrest lost 144 boys, 5.7% of his 2,500-man force.[188] The size of Smith's force had not made a difference. Smith should have won the battle, but he didn't. Intimidated by Forrest, Smith had retreated in defeat. Forrest understood that fear mattered most in the business of war.

CHAPTER 25: UNION SOLDIER LIFE IN MEMPHIS

"… the boys coming in today say that they were badly whipped."

Diary - February 22, 1864
Mrs. Bronson did some washing for me. I saw in the papers that Colonel George R. Clark with a detachment from the 113th in Springfield has been ordered into the field.

Mrs. Bronson (Private Albert Bronson's wife) must have found housing somewhere near camp where she earned a little extra money by washing clothes.

By commenting upon what he had read in the newspaper, Chatfield clarifies the whereabouts of the five detached companies. They were still drilling at Camp Butler under the direction of Colonel Clark, who was about to accompany them south to the field. Within days, the five companies would reunite with their main regiment, the 113th, in Memphis.

Diary - February 23, 1864

I just got dinner ready when a chill came on, and I had to go to bed. I've been real miserable with ague for the next 5 hours.

Diary - February 24, 1864

The ague pills helped.

Diary - February 25, 1864

I went over to the Colonel's with Bert. Mrs. Sarah Henry got here today. I traded watches with Hank White and gave $9.00 to Bert.

Mrs. Henry was the wife of the *Forlorn Hope* volunteer, Sergeant James Henry of Company "B"—the hero whose promotion to 2nd Lieutenant was being challenged by his peers. Chatfield's mention of the watch trade was significant, the first of two made with Company "B's" Private Henry L. White, a 26-year-old married farmer from Sussex Township. At the time, Chatfield could not have envisioned how important the watch trades would become.

Diary - February 26, 1864

I was detailed on picket this morning on Pigeon Roost Road [Pidgeon Roost Road]. Another squad of the 113th came down from Camp Butler with recruits today, and the Colonel [Hoge] kept them here.

Letter #1 - February 26, 1864
Headquarters Picket Guard, on the Pigeon Roost Road,
Memphis Tenn. February 26th, 1864

Dear Brother Newton,

Here I sit all crooked up under a hovel fit only for the pigs, you would say, inditing a few lines to answer an epistle which I received in Fathers letter last night. Mrs. Jas. Henry got to our camp after dark. And as soon as I heard of it, I had to start right over to see her, and was well pleased, you can well imagine, to see one of our old neighbors. ———

It is a very lonesome place out here, and, indeed, nothing to be seen but a few cows grazing upon the grass and the birds singing. The pigs and chickens are minus so we have nothing to do but to make the best of it and try and pass off the time as well as we can. And this is the way I am doing it. We do not have any trouble at all. And you want to know if I ever fired at any body when on Picket. I never did, although I came very near it once when an ox came by and would not halt when ordered. We have to [be] very careful about shouting when out on duty for fear of causing a false alarm. With those men that came down here we have about 30 men for duty. But, this part of the Country does not seem to agree with them as well as it does with us. For they are beginning to get sick. They do not like it at all having to stay here. But, I do not think it is any worse for them than for us ———

Well Newton, you did very well, and now I shall expect that you will answer this as soon as you get time. And so, for the present, I will close and write a few lines to James on the balance of the sheet.

Good Bye until next time

——— Edward

Dear Brother James,

I will now try and write you a few lines. I am all right and O.K. John Fundy has just been to Camp and got back. He says that ~~sam~~ Sam Place and Bert Nichols had just got back. They came since we came out this morning, and John says that another squad that belong at Springfield have come down, ~~dand~~ and that the Col. is going to keep them here to. ———

I was down town to a Union meeting, night before last, at what is called the ampitheater. We had a very good speech. The speaker was a Mr. Maynard of this state.[*] There was some 2,000 persons present.

At the rate that furlough's are granted, at the present, I am thinking that it will be a long time before we all get a chance to go and see those we love best. They have stopped giving any more for the present. Don't know how long it will be before any more are given. Well, my sheet is almost full and I must close by sending you my love.

Edward

To James Chatfield

[again, but vertically on right] To James

---

[*]   It's likely that Chatfield had listened to Horace Maynard, the Attorney General of Tennessee. Maynard had remained a Unionist and refused to support Tennessee's secession.

294
The Chatfield Story: Civil War Letters and Diaries of
Private Edward L. Chatfield of the 113th Illinois Volunteers

Letter #2 - February 26, 1864
Memphis Tenn. February 26th, 1864.

Dear Brother William,

Here I am out on Picket, and having nothing else to do, I will try and answer your letter. Yes, in fact [a] letter for besides the one dated the 29th Jan., which [I] rec'd two or three days since. I got another last night that Mrs. Williams [brought] in that bag [of] dried Apples. Mrs. W. [Williams] Mrs. Sutherland and Mrs. Henry got here last night.

Well, here I am, about 2 miles out of Camp, sitting under a little hovel with my Portfolio on my knees writing to my Brother who I suppose, at this same moment, is sitting in the school room attending his studies. But [I] take every thing as it is [and] I would not change places, that is, to go home before the War is ended. My health is very good, and we are all getting along finely! Bert sends his best respects and so do all the rest of the Boys. ———

I do not blame you a bit in doing the way you did with some people. They do not know [how] it is until they have a trial themselves. As for enlisting, I should say wait. In a short time longer, the plans of the [army to be] operated upon will be known in a short time, and then, if it should be needed, there [will] be time enough yet. If I were to enlist again, I should, I think, go into the Artillery. From what I have seen, the Cav. would be the last one that I would go into. As for those Negroes, they do not trouble me in the least. I mind my business and they mind theirs. As I have said before, they can perform [their] part as well as any one, and they make good soldiers. As for telling how much longer this war is likely to last, that is more than I can tell. But you need not look for us to come home before our time is out. Last night the news came in that the great Calvary expedition that went out from here about three two weeks ago had been driven back to Germantown, which is within 15 miles [east] of here. I have not heard any of the particulars how it was really. Though, some of the boys coming in today say that they were badly whipped.* You get all the news there sooner than we do here, so it is useless for me to say any about them.

We are having beautiful Spring weather, warm and pleasant. Our post is on what is on the Pigeon Roust/oost road. There is any amount of Cotton Coming. Teams are constantly going into town loaded down with it. Well, I have not much news to write and so you must excuse me for this time and also excuse my poor writing.

From your loving Brother,

Edward L Chatfield,

Wm S Chatfield, Esq

---

*   Chatfield is referring to the returning forward units of Sooy Smith's cavalry.

Diary - February 27, 1864

We were relieved by the 120th at 8:00 o'clock this morning.

Letter - February 27, 1864
Camp 113th Ill, Infty, Vance St
Memphis, Tenn. Feb. 27th, 1864

Ever Dear Parents,

The duties and labors of the day being over, I will try and write a few lines in answer of of the letter which Mrs. Henry brought dated the 20th, and which I recd on the 25th. Was very glad to hear that you were all well and prospering finely. ———

My health is first-rate. I guess that I will get along well enough after this. Was out on Picket yesterday. Was relieved this morning, and after arranging my toilet, made a call on Mrs. Henry and Mrs. Williams. They are both enjoying first rate in the society of their husbands, if I am any judge of human nature. James Henry has got a tent here in camp that he stays in, and the Major [Cephas Williams] has a room hired in town where he lives. Quite a number of the Officers have their wives and are just going it in the best style possible. Dr. Mack is quite sick. He has had 3 congestive chills, and he told me this afternoon that he feared that he would never get well. That piece of paper in the Box was of no account. Tom's [Carrow] coat and pail of things were not in the Box. The white wollen with H's worked in corner was mine, and the pants that you spoke of also. What was the charges on the box? You did not speak of it in your last.

And now, I want to tell you, if you can make any use of that clothing I wish you would. For, it will never be of any use to me. For, when I get out of this I shall be apt to wear Citizen's dress. I am glad that you have got some calves, for I think that they will pay well. There is such a demand for Beef that cattle will, I think, necessarily be very high. How much wheat do you think you will have to sell, and did you have grain enough to keep the teams in working order? ———

When the box was packed, I was away, or I should have packed it myself. There was nothing else but what you mentioned, a brush and some little book for Mr. Michaels. Well, it is bed time, and so will stop and go to bed. So, good bye for tonight.

——— Sunday afternoon 28th.

I have been busy all the forenoon and now I have just got the dishes washed after dinner and will finish this. We have Sunday morning inspection every Sabbath morn when we have to come out with our knapsacks all packed and every part of our chatties [metal cookware] as neat and clean as possible, and with our shoes blacked so that you could see your face. And, if our arms and accoutrements are not all clean, they give us a real going over. It commenced to rain this forenoon and is raining now. Sam Place, Albert Nichols and the rest of the squad got back day before yesterday. Had quite a talk with Sam about home and friends. I have some verses that I like much. They express my feelings exactly as they were about a year ago on a certain day. Well I believe I have written enough for this time. ———

Thomas wishes me to write a few words for him. He sends his best wishes and respects and thank you for the good advice you gave in his letter. The boys all join in sending their best respects. O ! I must tell you the reason Kellogg did not call when he was in the neighborhood. When he first went up he felt so sick that he was not able to stop any where and that he did not have any oportunity to call afterwards. He sends his respects.

[on right side of letter] My love to you all, from your Soldier Boy, Edward

Diary - February 28, 1864

I visited with Mrs. Henry and Mrs. Williams today. When roll was called, four boys from Springfield were missing, making some 30 in all now missing from the regiment. It rained today.

Within six days, about half of the 60 soldiers sent south from Camp Butler to Vicksburg and returned to Memphis were already sick. Apparently four had deserted camp—a problem that would only worsen within a few days.

Diary - February 29, 1864

It rained, hailed and was freezing all day. Twenty-seven men in our company were sent out on picket, but I did not have to go, having been excused because I had to

cook. They had a dismal time. A soldier by the name of Ash of Co. F refused to go on duty this morning, and he had to chop wood all day.*

Diary - March 1, 1864
[Chatfield's first entry in his third diary]
We had rain, snow, and sleet today, enough that it broke tree limbs, probably two inches of snow. The boys out on picket last night had a severe time. We have 14 men in our mess now.

Private Beach had written that on March 3, 1864, fifteen of the sixty Camp Butler troops from Springfield, Illinois, "nabbed" by Colonel Hoge in February (see Chatfield's 2/21/64 letter) failed to make roll call. A patrol was sent out to the wharf where they were found on a steamer bound for Cairo. The men were arrested and taken to what Beach called the "military prison." Later that evening, they were brought back to camp and tied up by their thumbs for several hours, to the dismay of many onlookers. From the boys' point of view, as explained by Beach, the Camp Butler troops had been sent to Vicksburg, not Memphis, and actually were not Hoge's men to command.[189]

Diary - March 4, 1864
I felt lazy this morning. John Fundy, Tom Carrow and I formed our own mess and broke off from the other larger mess. We had a game of ball. The weather grew cold, windy and rainy in the evening.

Diary - March 5, 1864
Tom and I went to a Union meeting and listened to speeches from Mr. Smith, Mr. Morgan, Mr. Bland, and Colonel Bingham. After that, Tom, John Fundy and I went to the theater and saw Lady Audley's Secret. It was quite good.

---

*   The "Ash" from Company "F" remains obscure. The *Illinois Roster* records show no soldier by the name of "Ash" in Company "F". A soldier by the name of "Lorenzo D. Ash" is listed for Company "I." But, Company "I" had not yet arrived from Camp Butler. Two other soldiers with the surname of "Ash" were in Company "B": John and William. But Chatfield, familiar with everyone in Company "B", didn't seem to know much about the noncompliant soldier, suggesting that neither John nor William were the ones who had disobeyed orders.

Lady Audley's Secret was an adaptation of Mary Elizabeth Braddon's sensational novel written in 1862. The plot involves a Victorian woman in acts of crime, bigamy, and attempted murder. The controversial play netted huge audiences.

Diary - March 6, 1864

We had company inspection in the morning. Then Tom, John, Andrew Forman, and I went to meeting at the Methodist Church. The 25th and 52nd Indiana came up the river today on the way home from Vicksburg, having re-enlisted.

Private Andrew Forman, from Essex, was 23 and married. He would be captured on October 10, 1864, when Hoge's 113th Regiment was routed by Nathan Bedford Forrest's forces on the Tennessee River at Eastport, Mississippi. According to the *Illinois Roster,* Forman would die in a Confederate prisoner of war camp in Columbia, Alabama. In his final efforts to cheat death, Forman's sickened body would lie 105 miles southwest of five of his close comrades who were also desperately clinging to life in an infamous Georgia war prison.

Letter - March 6, 1864
Infty Camp of the 113th Ill.
Memphis, Tenn. March, 6th, 1864

Ever Dear Parents,

Your welcome letter of the first was received Yesterday and I will now try and answer it. Although I have no news of any Consequence I will try and write every week any how. I was sorry to hear of Mother's continued illness. I hope, Dear Mother, that you will be careful of yourself and not over do yourself. For your welfare and well being is one of the objects of the greatest solicitude to the minds of your Boy. My health is very good, at present. I never was as fleshy before, in my life as now, or felt better than at present. We have just enough to do to give us good exercise. —— John Fundy, Tom C [Carrow], Andrew Foreman [Forman] & myself went to the Methodist Church to meeting this forenoon. We had a very good sermon. The text was Luke 15: 18, 19.* —— O, how good it will seem if

---

* The King James Version for Luke reads: [18] "I will arise and go to my father, and will say unto him, Father, I have sinned against heaven, and before thee, [19] And am no more worthy to be called thy son: make me as one of thy hired servants." It was the kind of sermon that Chatfield believed he needed to hear.

the time ever comes that we can all attend Divine service together once more and have to go out no more to Battle. ——

Two Regts, the 25th & 52 Ind., came up the river from Vicksburg today. They have reenlisted and are on their way home. They were with Sherman in the Expedition that he made into Alabama, and they say that he is back to Vicksburg now. What he is going to do next, there is no telling. ——

We expect the Detachment of the 113th that was at Springfield here this evening. And it is the general opinion of all that we will go down the River and join Sherman within a month. ——

Both of the Quilts and the Inkstand were Tom's. I had only that one white Blanket. —— The weather is very fine and pleasant. We had a few cold disagreeable days the fore part of last week, and I believe the hardest sleet storm I ever saw. It even broke down trees. The storm lasted 48 hours and ended in a snow storm. The snow fell ~~aber~~ about 2½ inches deep — Thomas Carrow & John send their best respects. James Henry and wife are well and enjoying themselves, I guess. I will close by sending you my love. From your soldier Boy, Edward

N S Chatfield

Diary - March 7, 1864

We fell in on picket today. Lieutenant Baird is in command of our division.

Diary - March 8, 1864

Grand rounds did not come around last night, but we were relieved at 8:00 this morning. Corporal Charles Westfall returned to the ranks. A grand review of all the Negro troops in this district was held this afternoon. I visited Mrs. Henry this evening. Major Williams took sick this afternoon, so sick that an ambulance took him home.

Enlisting in Cook County, Charles Westfall, was a single 30-year-old blacksmith from Company "A" who was apparently returning to the regiment, likely having been sick for some time.

Diary - March 9, 1864

Tom went after wood with the teams. It snowed this afternoon but cleared toward the evening. I went to the theater with a party of ten, including Tom. The play's title was The Ghost.

On this day, President Lincoln appointed General Grant as General in Chief, replacing General Halleck and redefining Halleck's title as "Chief of Staff of the Army."[190] Meanwhile, in Memphis on March 9, the peripheral dramas of war played on. In the heavy morning rain, Captain Andrew Beckett, sick off and on for the past four months, steamed north on a leave of absence, his second effort to recuperate. Surgeon Mack, also sick and unable to help the troops, accompanied him. Division headquarters distributed applications to white soldiers who might be interested in becoming commissioned officers to command Negro companies. For many soldiers, the lack of much action slowed military life in Memphis to a boring pace. Within days, some of the restless soldiers would get their excitement through senseless acts of vandalism.

Diary - March 10, 1864

The officers had a great time spreeing it over at the sutler's today. Frank Showbar, who has been sleeping with me, left my bed and board today, deserting me. Lieutenant Daniels of Company H was honorably discharged. The detachment of the 115th at Springfield joined the regiment. Mrs. Sarah Henry was quite sick today.

Lieutenant Daniels thought he had been discharged on December 12—three months earlier—but that discharge was revoked on January 21, 1864. It wasn't until June 20, 1865, that Daniels actually received his final discharge papers.

---

* The *Phantom Ghost*, by Amelia Edward, was written in 1864. Perhaps this was the play enjoyed by Chatfield and his friends.

Diary - March 11, 1864

The boys went out on picket this morning, but I was detailed to go with the teams after wood. The roads were rather muddy. I came through the 25th and 52nd Indiana. They were about ready to go home. Upon return, the other five companies in our regiment had just got here 480 able-bodied men. We have 1 new recruit for Company B. After coming back, I went over to the 108th after a stove for Dr. Brown.*

Dr. Lucian B. Brown was to be the new regimental surgeon, replacing Dr. Mack, soon to resign. Dr. Brown, from Sheldon, Illinois, was 29 and unmarried when he mustered in.

Per Major General E.A. Hitchcock's February 5 request, General Butler entered the reporter-exchange fray ...

OFFICIAL CORRESPONDENCE-
HDQRS. DEPT. OF VIRGINIA AND NORTH CAROLINA,
OFFICE COMMISSIONER FOR EXCHANGE,
Fort Monroe, Va., March 11, 1864.
Hon. ROBERT OULD, Agent for Exchange, Richmond, Va.:
SIR: Will your authorities make a special exchange of Mr. A.D. Richardson, correspondent of the *New York Tribune*, for James P. Hambleton, of Atlanta, Ga., a prisoner in Fort Warren? I have the honor to be, very respectfully, your obedient servant,
BENJ. F. BUTLER,
Major-General and Commissioner for Exchange.[191]

Diary - March 12, 1864

I guarded the sutler's shop until 2:00 a.m. out of concern that other companies would try to tear it down. The boys returned from picket at 9:00 this morning.

---

* The 5 companies Chatfield referred to were C, D, F, I and K. All were under the command of Lt. Colonel George R. Clark.

Colonel Clark had a lot of the boys arrested for tearing down some fences and a barn this morning. A squad of us went to theater to see Mazeppa.

Mazeppa began as a folk tale, its fame spreading after Lord Byron wrote a poem of the same name. In 1831, the British playwright Henry M. Milner adapted the tale for the stage. The play became highly popular on both sides of the Atlantic when Adah Isaacs Menken[*] added her unique touch. At the climactic point, Menken reclined on the back of a horse, garbed so as to appear naked, her body undulating as the horse pranced about the stage. If it had been Menken who starred in the play in Memphis, no doubt Chatfield and the rest of the squad would have been truly entertained.[192]

Diary - March 13, 1864

I felt miserable this morning. Tom and I policed the camp parade ground for inspection at 10:00 a.m. Then Levi Walters and I went to church. We had dress parade this evening. Cousin Clark Chatfield just came up from Vicksburg and visited me. Lieutenant Charles Chatfield is Acting Adjutant today.

Letter - March 13, 1864
Camp of the 113th, Memphis Tenn. March. 13th, 1864

Ever Dear Parents,

This beautiful Sabbath Eve I find myself seated to pen you a few lines. My mind is all on a whirl. There is so much noise and Confusion going on around me that I hardly know what to write but I will do my best.

My health is good. Never felt better in my life,[†] and I am in hopes that this will find you enjoying the same blessing. I have not rec'd any news from you for the week past, and you may be all sick for what I know. But I rather think the reason is that you have been so busy that you have not had time to write. —

I was much surprised today by seeing Cousin Clark Chatfield in today. He came up the river from Vicksburg night before last. He seems to be in good

---

*   Adah Isaacs Menken was her stage name. Her birth name was Bertha Theodore, b. 1835, d. 1868.
†   Once again, regarding his health, Chatfield's March 13 letter home contradicts his March 13 diary entry.

health and as hearty as ever. He is Orderly for one of the Aids of Gen. Hurlbut. I attended Church at the Methodists today. Had a good sermon. —

For the last few days we have had quite stirring times in Camp. The Detachment of the 113th that have been at Springfield for the last 14 months joined us here in the field. And I can tell you that I never saw a much more homesick set of fellows than they are. They are as awkward as greenhorns well can be. The 113th now numbers about 600 effective men, and we can make about as good a show as any in these parts. And there is another thing which we are expecting, and which I hope will take place, that is, that we will be sent out to take the field. Let onward to Victory and Glory be our motto.

I see by the papers that the 16th & 17th Army Corps are likely to be sent down to the Potomac. And, if they are, we will be apt to go to. Col. Hoge is fishing for a little star, and if he can do any thing to help it he will do it.

Mrs. Sarah Henry has been quite sick for several days past but she is some better today. Mrs. Major Williams is not very well nor the Major either. The Boys are all well, except John Fundy. He has the Ague about every day. Capt. Becket and Dr. Mack started home last week. They have both been sick for some time. I expect that we will be paid off the coming week. We have one new recruit in our Company, Johnny Foreman [Forman.] I expect that the Companies will be equalized. If they do, we will have quite a respectable Company. ~~tool~~ L't Col. Clark is in Command. —

The weather is quite pleasant and the gardens about here are beginning to look nice. Well, as I have not much news, I will close hoping that I may receive a letter before long. Please excuse my poor scribbling. I remain your loving son,

Ewd L Chatfield.

N S Chatfield

"Johnny" may have been the nickname for Charles M. Forman, an 18-year-old recruit from Essex Township of Kankakee. Forman was soon transferred to the 120th Illinois.

Diary - March 14, 1864

The ague has been hanging about me for several days and got worse this morning. Ninety men from the returned companies went on picket this morning. They were not on for one hour before one company shot a Negro and broke his arm. I had a

*shake of the ague so did not go to drill or dress parade. John Blanchet was relieved
from carrying the banner. Sergeant Hamblin or Sergeant Dennison will carry it.*

Corporal Stephen Hamblin, of Company "H", was a married man, a 27-year-old
farmer from Kankakee Township. Sergeant James Dennison, of Company "K", 25
and also married, was born in eastern Canada, but enlisted in Ganeer, Kankakee
County, Illinois. Like Chatfield and many other soldiers, Dennison maintained his
own diary, one that was eventually published in 1987.[193]

Diary - March 15, 1864

*I felt a little better this morning, but my bones ache badly yet, and I have no appetite.
I cleaned my rifle and did little else. Lieutenant Jeffcoat got for the whole company
a pair of white gloves. Fundy, Carrow and some others went to the theater.*

In mid-March, General Forrest, with roughly 3,000 cavalrymen, set out from
Columbus, Mississippi, on a month-long cavalry raid into Western Tennessee and
Kentucky. His objective was to recruit soldiers, capture Union supplies, and demol-
ish the Union posts and fortifications from Memphis to Paducah.[194]

Diary - March 16, 1864

*The boys went out on picket this morning. That included four men from Company
B. Even though the ague has left me, I felt unfit for picket. I have no strength, so
I helped sweep the parade ground and got ready for inspection at 10:00. Tom
Carrow and John Fundy went to the national theater tonight.*

After Chatfield helped sweep the parade ground, general inspection was rescheduled for
March 19, and Colonel Clark personally drilled the regiment with knapsacks on. When
evening came, Chatfield, not feeling well, stayed back while his friends visited town and

recreated. In his own personal diary, Chatfield's friend, Private Riley Beach, wrote that he attended the Ladies Evening Association meeting, evidently a pleasant and informative occasion.[195] One of the many people Beach saw there that night was Union General Benjamin Henry Grierson, the famed cavalryman. It was then-Colonel Grierson who had conducted raids out of La Grange, Tennessee, drawing away a full division of Pemberton's troops, thus easing Grant's April 1863 crossing below Vicksburg.[196]

Diary - March 17, 1864

It was quite cold last night. The company drills for an hour at 10:00; it's a daily event. Major Williams moved with his family to town. I'm alone, today, wondering what is to come.

Diary - March 19, 1864

We had general inspection today, and Company B won the best drill. Our arms were in the best order ever inspected. The boys went to the picture gallery this evening. Camp seems as dull and stupid as could be imagined.

Diary - March 20, 1864

I slept well last night, then put on my Sunday best to go to meeting this morning. I went with Tom Carrow and John Fundy to the Catholic Church and witnessed the most heathenish mummery that I ever saw. Our reverend chaplain [Rankin] preached the first time in a year today. A soldier named Shufeldt died yesterday, and we buried him today with honors of war in the Elmwood Cemetery.

Barely 19 years old when he died of disease, Private Theodore Shufeldt, of Company "E", was from Lake County, Illinois. Although historical records cite Shufeldt's death as occurring on March 11, Chatfield writes that he died on the 19th and was buried on the 20th.

Letter - March 20, 1864
Camp 113th Ill. Infty Memphis Tenn. March 20th 1864

Ever Dear Parents,

I seat myself this beautiful Sabbath afternoon to write you a few lines. Every thing in nature around me is smiling and I can but thank my Creator for his great goodness and kindness towards me. ———

306
The Chatfield Story: Civil War Letters and Diaries of
Private Edward L. Chatfield of the 113th Illinois Volunteers

My health is good and I can Bless the Lord for ~~his~~ the mercies which he has bestowed upon me. By your last of the 6th & 12th Ult., which you sent at the same time, I saw that Mother's health was not very good, and the whole reason was because she would work to hard. O, when will the time come when you & Father will not work so hard? It seems to me that there is no need of it, and I am in hopes that You will both lead Easier lives and not work so hard. ——

Today, for the first time in a year, our old Chaplain preached a sermon to us. But, I and several others, instead of hearing him, went down town to Church. One of our Regt Co. E., I believe, and Shufeldt by name, died yesterday and was buried today in the Elmwood Cemetery. ——

For the last week, since Lt. Col. Clark has had command, he has kept us busy drilling the most of the time, and we are making rapid proficiency in the art of Drill. ——

Yesterday we had an Inspection and the 113th made a fine appearance, I can tell you. It made me feel proud, I can assure you. Co B. had the praise of the Inspecting Officer and of Col. Hoge of being the best Drilled and best appearing Co. of the regt. (Bully for Co B). We are having a good deal easier times since the other boys came down. It has been over a week since I have been on Duty.

My Dear Mother, you have written so much about my coming home that I am afraid that I will get homesick yet. So, I wish that you would not say any thing more about it. Every thing, I think, is for the best as it is. If I should go home, I would only spend my money and maybe make me and you feel worse at parting than to stay away entirely. Now Mother, do you not think so yourself? The time is slipping away very fast, and 16 months will soon roll round. If you were to see me and see how well the soldiers life suits me, you would then think that it ~~was~~ is not so bad after all. ——

Mrs. Henry was here, and made us a call this afternoon. She is quite well, again, and is thinking of returning North soon. —— Got a letter from George Palmer today. He say that he is well, and that they are encamped on the Big Black in the rear of Vicksburg. His Regt (the 76th Ill) was with Sherman in his late expedition into Alabama. Cousin Clark C—d [Chatfield] is well. Saw him today.

By the papers, I see that there is another call made for 200,000 more men. Now what do you think of that? There will be a Draft this time, no doubt, of which I will be very glad. For it will bring some of those Copperheads and those that have hung back so.[*]

The weather is quite pleasant, but we have quite cool nights. Well, I have about run out of anything to write, and so will close. The Boys send their best

---

[*]   President Lincoln had called for 200,000 men on March 14, 1864. The quota for Illinois was set at 18,524.

respects hoping that this may find you all well and enjoying the Blessings of life. I close by sending you my love and respect.

From your Boy, Edward——

Diary - March 21, 1864

I wrote letters to Grandmother [Lucy] and David today, then visited with Mrs. Major Williams and Mrs. Ward. Camp is so dull that I hardly know what to do with myself. I helped draw rations this afternoon.

Diary - March 22, 1864

John Fundy and Lucius Gubtail of Co. B went on picket. We had company drill at 10:00. Then I wrote a letter to William. After that, we marched 1½miles to the fairgrounds and had brigade drill under Colonel George B. Hoge. There are 3 regiments in the brigade: 110th, 113th, 120th. Ours made the best appearance. We returned much fatigued. The roads were dusty.

Letter - March 22, 1864
Camp, 113th, Ill. Infty Memphis Tenn. March 22nd, 1864,

Dear Brother Wm S. Chatfield,

I will try and write you a few lines in answer of the kind letter which I received some time ago. ——

My health is first rate and so is the health of the men generally in camp. Sore throat is quite prevalent among the boys, and, in some cases, it has almost turned into Diptheria.* There is a good deal of small Pox among the blacks mostly. There

---

* Diphtheria is typically transmitted through nasal and oral particulate, much like the common cold. Its first symptoms usually include a low-grade fever and enlarging lymph nodes in the neck. Swelling membranes in the throat clog the airways, severely obstructing breathing. Untreated cases sometimes result in paralysis, heart failure and blood disorders. Death took roughly 5 to 10 percent of the soldiers who contracted the disease during the Civil War. Haphazard "remedies" of the day attempted to open the airways by lathering the body with various oils laced with scotch snuff and administering heavy doses of calomel, a purgative. It wasn't until 1883-84, some 20 years after Chatfield had written this letter, that two German bacteriologists (Edwin Klebs and Friedrich Löffler) isolated the microorganism associated with diphtheria, and it wasn't until the early 1890's that researchers understood that the toxin given off

has been, however, two men of our Reg't taken with it lately. The city papers think that the disease is mostly caused by the putrifying carcasses of dead animals laying about in every direction. And they are being [buried] as fast as possible.

We are to have a Brigade Drill this afternoon when the whole Brigade will be out. And so, I am improving these few spare moments in writing to you. Business here, in general, seems to be pretty brisk this Spring. New buildings are going up and repairing is being done in every part of the town. Boats are arriving and departing most every hour and [the] Levee for a full half mile is just covered with cotton in bales. And, it is being brought in every day in vast quantities. I hardly know what to write that will be interesting to you. There is not much news, and so, if I do write a very stale letter you must excuse me. —

It is thought by some that all the drilling the we are having at present is for nothing else but to prepare f us for the march and the field. We think that if [we] leave here we will go east to Chattanooga or to join the Army of the Potomac. Well, if it is to be so, why all right. I am suited with any thing. I believe that I should go on the march than not, if I had my choise.

Well, the drum has beat for us to fall in for Company drill, and so I must close. So you must excuse me for this time. Hoping that this may find you all in good health and that you will write often.

From your loving Brother,
Edward L Chatfield

Letter - March 22, 1864
Headquarters 113th Ill. Infty Memphis Tenn. March 22nd, 1864

Dear Brother David,

I will now try and write you a few lines in answer of your kind letter which I received some time since. My health is very good, at present, and I try and enjoy myself to the best of my ability. ——

I suppose that you are well employed in following the plow and other equally pleasant employments. Well, I hope that we may have good harvests in return for our labor. And, as to my self, I hope that the coming Campaign will end victoriously to our Arms, and that we will come off Conquerors over those despicable villains of Rebels. And, that we may all soon be permitted to return home in peace. They are forming New Negro Reg'ts here now, and there has been applications made for Officers by several of our Company. For a number

by *Corynebacterium diphtheriae* was the causative agent. Current-day treatment for diphtheria makes use of antitoxins and antibiotics.

of days past there have been Reg'ts going up the river almost every day that have reenlisted again for three years.

Well David, does it not make you feel rather uneasy for fear of being drafted under the Call for 200,000 more men? If they should Draft, you will have to stand your Chance as well as the rest. But, I can tell you that there is nothing dishonorable or disgraceful in being a soldier. We make enough. I can tell you of these new recruits. I never thought men could be quite as simple and slothful as some of them are. Albert is still driving Ambulance for the Col. We all do just about as we please. [We] go to the Theatre nights and to other places of amusements. So, we never get very lonesome. As for myself, I have been entirely strapped for some time and we are waiting very patiently for the Paymaster to come around with some of those green backs. I see there is a good deal of talk in Congress of raising the soldiers Pay. For one, I shall not object to that part at all. For, I think that I shall be able to take Care of all the green backs that I can get hold of. Well, the Drum has just sounded for us to fall in for Battalion Drill, and so I must close. I send you my love. Hoping that you will not forget to write.

From your soldier Brother,

Edward L

D.A.C.

[Upside down at bottom of letter, in different handwriting]

E L Chatfield & D.D.

Diary - March 23, 1864

I was detailed on fatigue duty, which is nothing in reality but cleaning up camp, with a nice name. Commissary Sergeant Charley Newton's wife got here today. The officers shut down on the sutler's selling ale today, because so many of the men were constantly drunk. A man from Company F was taken to the hospital with smallpox.

Charles A. Newton, of the 113th Company "D", was a married merchant from Onarga in Iroquois County. He was 30 years old when he enlisted. He quickly advanced to manage the commissary (as the Commissary Sergeant) in October 1862.

Diary - March 24, 1864

John Fundy and I sold our extra rations to the grocery. I visited Mrs. Henry today. Captain Bliss Sutherland is living in the same house as she is. Kellogg, being our drillmaster, conducted company drill today. It rained at 5:00 p.m. I saw in the papers that Dr. Mack, who had gone home, got married.[*]

---

[*] After returning home to Kankakee and marrying, Surgeon Mack resigned from the Army on April 26, 1864.

CHAPTER 26: MEMPHIS BRACES FOR FORREST

"... Forrest's forces were coming this way and there was a general scare."

Diary - March 25, 1864

Orders were given last night that the long roll will come at 4:00 a.m. It is said that Forrest is threatening this place. Through some mistake, however, the long roll was not played. It rained most all night and this forenoon. I was sent to the commissary with Dan Freeman and got a sack of potatoes for $2.00 per sack for the mess. I sent my second diary home this afternoon. Am in hopes that this diary, or these few scattering sentences in it, may be of some little interest at some future day. John Fundy and Tom Carrow went to the theater this evening. I feel pretty well tonight. I will pray that Providence may protect me.

Forrest raided Paducah, Kentucky, on March 25 and quickly occupied the town. He took all the supplies, horses and mules that he needed and destroyed everything else of value. Federal forces began to recognize that "...Forrest, or someone like him, could strike anywhere at any time."[197]

Diary - March 26, 1864

We were called out at 4:00 a.m. We formed in line of battle and stacked our arms. Colonel Hoge even came around to see if the 113th could get out as soon as the other regiments. We had a skirmish drill in the afternoon. William Scoon sent in an application for furlough today. I was detailed this evening to go on picket tomorrow. I feel first rate. J.C. Powley returned from home to the company today, then went to the hospital.

Private Joseph C. Powley, a married 22-year-old farmer and another Canadian immigrant, had enlisted in Weygandt, Iroquois County, Illinois, 34 miles south of Chatfield's home.

Diary - March 27, 1864

We were called out at 4:00 a.m., and I was detailed on picket on Pigeon Roost Road. Today was the Sabbath, so there were only a few travelers on the road. Some very fine ladies were passing by in a fine carriage, and an accident occurred. The horse stumbled and fell, turning a complete summersault. The ladies were terribly frightened, but we shortly set things to right. Thanking us, they went on their way.

Diary - March 28, 1864

I was relieved this morning at 8:00. We had a little shower in the morning. In the evening the wind blew up a perfect hurricane, hurling dust in every direction. I traded watches with Hank White.

This was Chatfield's second watch-trade with Hank White, a trade that would prove to be an extremely important one. Also significant is the fact that White was Riley Beach's bunkmate—probably the friend to whom Beach later penned a letter describing the grim circumstances that he, Chatfield, and three others in the company were then facing.

Diary - March 29, 1864

We were awakened by the bugle at 4:00 a.m. Company B was the first on the ground. I've been busy this afternoon writing out the history of Company B. Edmund Landis is cooking for the mess. He makes hard work of it.

Private Edmund M. Landis was a 19-year-old farm boy from Kankakee Township.

Diary - March 30, 1864

The long roll was beaten at half-past three this morning. In 5 minutes we were drawn up in line of battle. Fundy went to the picture artist and had some pictures taken. Carrow and Orderly Kellogg have the ague this evening. The weather is quite warm and balmy. The leaves are bursting out, and all nature is smiling. Let us offer up thanks for the goodness of the Great Giver of All Good.

Diary - March 31, 1864

Again we were up with the bugle sound and the long roll. Rebel Colonel Falkner is in these parts, so the General has issued very strict orders for heavy camp guard around each camp. No one should go to town without a pass signed by General Ralph P. Buckland. I chopped some wood for Mrs. Bronson, her husband being sick.

Only time would tell if 41-year-old Private Albert Bronson, of Company "G", from Galesburg, Illinois, would survive with his wife's tender care.

William Clark Falkner, the Confederate Colonel, was said to have personally removed the "u" from his name. A highly gifted cavalryman, he led the famed 1st Regiment, Mississippi Partisan Rangers. Also a talented writer, he authored more than a half dozen works of fiction, inspiring his great-grandson, William Faulkner, the famous 20th century Mississippi writer and Nobel Prize-winning novelist.

314
The Chatfield Story: Civil War Letters and Diaries of
Private Edward L. Chatfield of the 113th Illinois Volunteers

Diary - April 1, 1864

Today was "All Fools' Day," and some pretty good tricks got played on some of the boys. It rained some through the night. We fell in line this morning, and we were dismissed by the Lieutenant Colonel. John Fundy and Tom Carrow went on picket, and it rained some more this afternoon. I visited Sarah Henry and chopped Mrs. Bronson some more wood. Sergeants Henry M. Williams and Asa G. Harwood of Company A got promoted to a Negro regiment and left here today. John Mandegold of Company B got back from Furlough.

Twenty-nine-year-old Private John Mandegold, a Prussian by birth, was married and worked as an office clerk when he enlisted in Essex Township. Mandegold was among the fortunate boys to be furloughed when he was sick.

Diary - April 2, 1864

We fell in again this morning, stacked our arms, then went back to bed. John and Tom came in from picket at 9:00 this morning. I came near to having ague this afternoon. My bones ached very bad, and I felt dreadful mean, so that I did not go out on drill. I did go out to dress parade, however. Mrs. Bronson washed my clothes for me, charging me 5 cents apiece. I went to the surgeon, got some pills, and feel a little better this evening.

Diary - April 3, 1864

We did not have to fall in line of battle this morning, but we did have company inspection at 9:00 a.m. Twenty-nine men were out sick. Church call was made at 10:00, and we heard the venerable chaplain [Rankin] deliver a speech. I wrote Father a letter today and sent him a history of Company B. At 12:00 o'clock, Colonel John C. Black established a strong guard around the camp, consisting of one man.*

---

*   The copy of Chatfield's history of Company "B" was not included in the collection of letters.

Colonel John C. Black of the 37th Illinois Infantry was from Danville, Illinois. He had enlisted as a major on August 15, 1861, at the age of 22. By the age of 24 he had attained the rank of colonel.

Letter - April 3, 1864
Camp. 113th. Ill, "Infty"
Memphis. Tenn. April 3rd, 1864

Ever Dear Parents,

Your welcome letter dated March 26th was received in due time on 1st Apr', and was read with much pleasure. Was glad to hear that the blessing of good health was still granted to you all. Was much pleased with that lock of hair of Mary's and if my hair was long enough I would send you a lock of it. —

My health is good, and so is that of most of the Boy's. —

We have just been to meeting, and I heard the Chaplain for the first time for over a year. I will send you by this letter a history of Co. B. It is only a general outline of what we have passed through, but I thought it would be interesting to you, and so I send it. I will also send you John Fundy's Photograph. I will send mine as soon as we get Paid off, so that I can get some. We would have been paid off last week if some of the other Companies had have had their Pay Rolls made out right.——

For some time we have had to get up every morning at 4 oclock and fall in line of Battle and stack our Arms. And now, there is orders that there shall be a strong camp guard around every camp.——

But the L't. Col.' says that 1 man makes a strong guard and so does fifty, and so he still trust to the honor of the men and put on only one man at once. I do not know why there is such strict orders, but they come from Gen. R. P. Buckland. But, the best of the orders are that but two officers can be absent from camp at one time. And then, they have to have passes signed by the Gen.' Of the five Companies that have been here, all the while, are sadly reduced. Co B. has 30 men while some of the others have not got 20. ——

John Manegold [Mandegold] who has been home on furlough for some time, got back a day or two since. We are having fine pleasant weather now. The gardens about here all look fine. The people say that the Spring is a month later than usual. ——

We do not have very hard duty now. I have not been on Duty since I was on Picket last Sabbath. There is a number of Officer's wives down here now. Several of them intend to start home as soon as we are paid off. Mrs. Henry is well.

Well, I hardly know what to write that will be interesting to you. But, will do my best. There have several of the boys got positions in Negro Reg'ts, and I expect that we will lose the Orderly yet. He [Kellogg] has been offered a Captaincy and

316
The Chatfield Story: Civil War Letters and Diaries of
Private Edward L. Chatfield of the 113th Illinois Volunteers

I think will except of it. Lieut. Cowgill has gone down the River to ~~Lack~~ Lake Providence to see about taking a certain plantation. If he gets it, he will resign and go into the business of a planter. He is in for making money and the fastest way of making it is what he is after.[*]

I expect that Lt.' Jeffcoat will go home this week. And, there is to be several of non commissioned officers to go North ~~from~~ to recruit for the five Co's that have been here all the time. I expect that the Orderly will go from our Camp. Well, I have run out for any thing to write and so will close by sending you my love.

From your soldier Boy, Edward ——
N S Chatfield

Letter - April 4, 1864
Camp, 113th Ill. "Infty"
Memphis Tenn. April 4th 1864

Dear Brothers Newton & James,

Although the Bugle has just said "put out all lights," yet I will, for all that, write you a few lines. The Boys are just pulling off their Boots to go to Bed, while the dogs are barking, and the fire bells in town are ringing, and the noise and confusion of the Camp jars on my ear, and brings me back to the reality that here I am, a soldier Boy, far away from home and loved ones and all the pleasant ties of peace. But, when I call to mind that all about me are my mates and comrades battling and for what — "to save our union"— which these miserable bloodthirsty wretches have been doing all in their power to destroy, then I feel as though I would fight them and that "to the Death," rather than to see our Union destroyed. Well, I had almost forgotten myself. Your very welcome letters, which you have sent me, I just appreciate very much. And, they are read with much pleasure. I only hope that soon this wicked Rebellion will be crushed out and that traitors will meet their just deserts. And then, we can all go home and enjoy, once more, the Comforts and pleasures of life. But, the time is fast slipping away, and soon the three years will be gone. Twenty months ago, today, I enlisted in the U.S. Service. And now, to look back over that time, it hardly seems as but yesterday. Hoping that you will both write often, I will close by wishing you good bye.

From your loving Brother,
Edward
To Newton & James Chatfield

---

[*] Lieutenant Aquilla Cowgill officially resigned his commission on April 4, 1864.

Diary - April 4, 1864

I did not rest very good. I was much disturbed by dreams. It rained most of the night. I felt better this morning. The ague has left me. Camp is quite dull today. Major Cephas Williams and Sergeant John Kellogg from Company B, and Sergeants George Woodruff of H, Seth R. Cole of A, Henry Friel of G and Richard Lintleman of E are to go to Springfield on recruiting service. George Woodruff started home today. Also an order came compelling the officers and men to attend Divine worship on the Sabbath.

Redheaded 2nd Lieutenant George Woodruff, 32 and married, of Company "H", had enlisted in Otto, Kankakee County, and had worked his way up from Sergeant. Governor Yates enlisted Sergeant Henry C. Friel, 22, an unmarried Chicago train conductor before the war. Richard F. Littleman, of Company "E", was born in Germany and had been a carpenter before enlisting in Cook County at the age of 28.

Diary - April 5, 1864

The long roll sounded at 4:00 a.m. We fell in line of battle and stacked our arms. I had Mrs. Bronson do some more washing for me. Orderly Kellogg and the others went up the river, and Mrs. Williams went with them. Lieutenant Cowgill came up the river day before yesterday and went north this afternoon. I wrote to David and sent it by Mrs. Williams. I got some new accoutrements. Now I am busy reading and writing. Beach, who is my bedfellow, now has the fever and has been quite sick today.

Letter - April 5, 1864
Camp. 113th. Ill. "Infty."
Memphis Tenn. April 5th, 1864

Ever Dear Brother David,

    Your very welcome letter of March 20th was read with much pleasure, and now I will try and answer it. Mrs. Major Williams leaves for the North today, and she has kindly offered to carry this for me. My health is quite good. Last night I was weighed and found that I was increaseing in weight, my weight being 156½ lbs. It seems that you are kept pretty busy at work, now that the season for f plowing and sowing has Come. But, I do not know as I envy you at all. For, I think a soldiers life is much easier than to be drudging on a farm. Now, this morning got up and had my breakfast, after which, instead of going out to work, have nothing to do but to set down and write or any thing else that I please. As for all the girls that there is anywhere about Kankakee, you can go in as much as you please "for all me." Last night on Dress Parade, the order was read Detailing Major Williams and five sergts, "one from each of the Companies that were here in the field," to report at Springfield immediately as recruiting Officers. Kellogg will go from Co' B. Now if there is any one that you know of tell that will enlist, just tell them that now is the time. Co' B 113th Regt has just as good a time name as any other Co or Regt in the field. And if you should want to enlist, now is the time. There is nothing dishonorable in being a soldier. Now just think of it and consider well. It seems that Smith's folks [Albert Smith's parents] do not believe but what James Henry is Lieut., for all his letters from there are directed in that way. But, he is not Lieut. and there is no sign's of his being one very soon, and he never would be one if the boys have any thing to say about it. ———

We are having very pleasant weather at present. Well, I will close this by wishing you good bye.

From your Brother,
Edward

To Mother,

My dear Mother, I will write you a few lines. I often think of you and I know that it must make you feel sad to have one of your the members of your family gone. But, Dear Mother, you must consider that we cannot always be together. We are getting grown and soon must scatter. So, I hope that you will not think so much about my being away as to worry for me as that can not do either of us any good. But, I will pray that all things may be for the best.

From your loving Son,
E.L.C.

Diary - April 6, 1864

Guard mount came at 4:00 a.m., and we went on picket. Our squad from Company B was put with the 2nd Division and went out on the Stateline, or Germantown

Road. I carried a book with me to read. The title was Les Miserables. And so, I passed the day. The 6th Tennessee Cavalry came in today, completing another scout. Strict orders cautioned us to keep a very vigilant lookout for a force of Rebels in Germantown. John Blanchet and Lieutenant Jeffcoat cut down a tree this evening.

The guard mount was a form of muster that included a brief equipment issue and inspection of the guards who were assuming duty at the beginning of a shift. *Les Miserables*, by the French writer, Victor Hugo, was among the best-known novels of the 19th century. The story involves an ex-convict who tries to redeem himself in a lengthy examination of the nature of good, evil, and the law—good fodder for a Union soldier who viewed the challenges of war through the lens of good versus evil. Hugo's work may even have been the inspiration for Chatfield to try his own hand in composition while on picket on April 18.

Diary - April 7, 1864
We were relieved at 8:00 a.m. by the 108th Illinois. The people in town are scared that Rebels may be coming. So, the stores are all closed, and the militia is out. But a bulletin this evening said there was no danger at all. The 6th Indiana Battery is now in our brigade. They moved up near our camp yesterday.

Diary - April 8, 1864
We fell in and stacked arms again at long roll. It was raining. I saw Bert at the Colonel's and got his photograph. We went to see Mrs. Henry and bid her goodbye. Lieutenant Jeffcoat left for home on a leave of absence for 12 days, and Mrs. Sutton, Mrs. Ward and Mrs. Henry went with him. The 108th got paid today, and we will be paid soon. A soldier of Company H was badly wounded this afternoon. He accidentally got shot through the arm, which he will lose. Company B was consolidated with Company A at dress parade today.

Mrs. Sutton was the wife of Sergeant Peter D. Sutton, a 28-year-old from Otto Township. Peter's younger brother, Smith Sutton, 26, was a private, but although Smith was married, he wasn't allowed to lodge with his wife away from camp—only the officers were allowed such privileges. Private William Griffin, 46 and married, was the Kankakee soldier who was accidentally wounded. Griffin was discharged on April 13, 1864, after an army surgeon amputated his arm.

Letter - April 8, 1864
113ᵗʰ, Ill. "Vol's." Infty.'
Memphis Tenn. Friday, April, 8ᵗʰ, 1864

Ever Dear Father & Mother,

    Mr. Jeffcoat, or rather, Lieut.' Jeffcoat starts for home this afternoon, and so I will write a few lines. Your welcome letter of the 1ˢᵗ was received yesterday. Was glad to hear that you were all well. —

    My health is good, and I am doing duty and all of the other various etcetiras of a soldier's life. I was on Picket day before yesterday. Came in yesterday morning. There was rumors that some of Forrest's forces were coming this way and there was a general scare. We had very strict orders, and all the troops about the city were held in readiness for any danger at any moment. at any moment, All business was stopped, and the Malitia called out, but it was found to be nothing at all. And, now they feel easier and since the danger as was suffered has passed by. ——

    Lieut. Jeffcoat goes up on a leave of Absence for 12 days. By the letter which I sent you by Mrs. C. Williams (which I suppose you have rec'd before this,) I told you of Major Williams and Orderly Kellogg's going up on recruiting service. I have not much news to write this time and I hardly know what to write. Well, here on one side of me is John Fundy with his sleeves rolled up (he is Cook for the mess this week.) [He is] smoking a cigar and talking, while on the other, is Tom [Carrow] and several others talking and chatting and making rings. So you see what lazy times. We have nothing to do but to pass of [off] the time as best as we can. Last night we had Dress Parade and there was about as large a turn out as we have had. The Reg't., in general, is very good health, there being only four or five patients in the Hospital. There has been four or five cases of small-pox in those Co's that came down from Springfield, three of which have proved fatal. There is a small-pox Hospital about half a mile from here, and there is a large number that have the disease there. It is mostly among the Negroes, and there is a good many of the Refugees that have it. The refugees are those who have been driven from their homes all through this country, and they seek refuge within our lines. They are a miserable set of people, being old men, women and children. We find them all about here. Some in houses — they have very good shelter. Others, in rude shanties and in tents, and still others who have no shelter at all, but live in the open air exposed to every thing and in all the misery and wretchedness that can be imagined. —

    We have in mess 1, which is the mess that (Ed Chatfield) stays in, 4: Tom Carrow, John Fundy, Edmund Landis, at whose fathers house you stayed one night while we were in Worcester, and the afore said Ewd. Chatfield. We live and cook together, each taking his turn in cooking a week a piece. Those dried apples that you sent me came very good as a variety. Butter costs so much that I cant hardly afford to use much. And then, such butter as we get here is of not much account. Yesterday was very pleasant and warm. Last night we had quite a shower and today it is warm again, just the kind of weather to make every thing grow. Well, the drum has beat for drill and so I must stop.

Well, it has proved that we ~~were~~ are not going to have drill, but we had some Cartridges given to us. We have to have 40 rounds in our Cartridge-boxes all the time. Tell Jemima that John Fundy sends her his best respects.

Well, ~~my brain is~~ I have not any thing more to write at present and so will close. I have a photograph of Gen. Grant, but it is a very poor one, which I will send you. My respects all the friends around. My love to you all.

From your loving soldier Boy —

Ewd L Chatfield

N S Chatfield

Although Edward received many letters from his family throughout the war, only a few survived. The James Herrick Chatfield family *Bible* contained a combination letter penned to Edward by his mother, father, and 15-year-old brother Isaac Newton. The family made remarkably efficient use of paper; all three messages were confined to a single sheet of pale blue stationery measuring 7.6 by 11.6 inches.

<u>Letter </u>- April 8, 1864
[Letter from Edward's mother, Margaret Prudentia Chatfield]
April the 8, 1864

My dear Son

I had just written to Mother [Lucy] and I will write a few lines to you — how do you get along — how is your health — do you keep up good courage — that is half the battle — dont get into the Slough of Dispondency — Look up — it needs all the Strength of a valient man to go to the field of battle — I dont beleive I should make a very good soldier — I am afraid I should get into deep water and they might overthrow me — But I remember you used to say to me keep up good courage it would all come out right — now Edward stand fast in the faith — keep firm hold of the promises — dont get discouraged — count up the weeks and months and let them swiftly fly — take care of thyself — beware of thyself as Aunt Charlotte* used to say for me — one cares for thee — I find It does no good for

---

* Chatfield's mother is referring to her husband's younger sister.

me to care so I am determined to hope on pray on – and the victory you will won – my heart rises in thankfulnes for such a son – our communion will be sweet when we each other greet – well I must stop – It rains hard and the boys are all in the house – pa is shoemaking – Willy is down on the bed – has been sick 4 days – think he will be better soon – My love to you – I shall get a letter from you to morrow – then I will bee glad – Thomas Ella and Julia and Mina was here the other evening – all well there –[up left side of letter] we had a good quarterly Meeting – the neighbors are well – my respects to all enquiring friends – My love to Edward – good by – MPC

[Letter from Edward's father, Nathan Stoddard Chatfield]

To my Dear Son -- mother sick has gone and we are all still alive but not as well as we generally are –Wm has been sick 4 days, last night he was better—we don't think that he is going to be sick long –was taken with a kind of fever and ague –Mary was taken with fever yesterday but I guess that ma will break it up – we have had a good deal of cold wind lately – wheat that was sowed the first of March is not up yet – cold and dry – good time to sow – have sowed 110 buch wheat – it is a hard time here for feed for cattle -- Prairie hay is worth ten dollars and one dollar per bush – a good many cattle are dying – they was near frozen to death in the cold storm that we had the first Jan – they live out back very well but as soon as it comes warm they soon to be very weak and when they are skinned there is a time of wroting jell all over them and but a very little blood in them – we lay it to the weather – we have lost 4 – Mr. Schoby 10 – Dort Nott 10 – Mr. Vaughn 6 & we have made up our minds to build a barn at the earliest possible moment and try to shelter our stock; you wrote that you had rather we write not expect you to come home – we hardly know how to help it – our minds affection are on you so much that we cannot but write what we think – but we will try to be reconciled to your lot – and may the Lord's will not only be done but we shall even pray for you that you may ever be found on the Lord's side – put your trust in that – Live and he will have you up – stand you up for muster—and he will keep you drum nigh to God – and he will drum nigh to – we will try to feel and may [it be] the Lord's will – and not only be done in his good time – may you return to our embrace without spot or stain – time up for the night – give my respects to all the boys – we send our love to you. [Unsigned]

April 9 – all well this morning – William and Mary is better to my [delight] [Unsigned by Nathan]

[Message from Edward's brother, Isaac Newton Chatfield]

April 9 —

Dear Brother

I will take my pen in hand to let you know that I had not forgotten you. David and I Startted out to plow this morning but it commenced to rain, So we turnd around and came back – it has raind all day and is raining now – w̄ mary is rather unwell to day – William is about the Same – we are a going to Sow about 15 acres of flax and 35 acres of oats and /plenty/ 39 acres of corn.

    [Unsigned]

[up left side of letter] Newton commenced to write, but we could not wait for him this time – you must excuse him—he felt of[f] the hook˚ [Unsigned by Nathan]

Diary - April 9, 1864

We were up again at 3½o'clock. The alarm bells rang, and a gun was fired. All of the militia had to form in line of battle along with us. Lieutenant Colonel Clark's wife arrived here today with family. We were not paid today and had no drill. Sergeant James Henry had command of the company. The wind is cold, and the bugle is just playing reveille. I hear other drums beating.

Diary - April 10, 1864

I was detailed for camp guard this morning, reporting at 7:00 a.m. When Tom and I got there, there were enough men, so we were dismissed. We passed inspection. Lieutenant Baird was in command. This afternoon some of the Negroes who live here in camp had a meeting. I went to meeting with others where quite a discourse was given with more meaning in it than correctness.

Letter - April 10, 1864
Camp. 113ᵗʰ. Ill. "Infty."
Memphis Tenn. April. 10ᵗʰ, 1864

Dear Parents,

    I again take my pen to address you a few lines. The mail will be sent away soon. So I must hurry. Today is the Holy Sabbath and it seems quite still in camp today. There was preaching at nine this morning, but I had to prepare for

---

˚ "Off the hook" was a relatively new idiom in the 1860's—a phrase alluding to the freedom of the fish that somehow extracts itself from the fisherman's hook. Here, Nathan uses the expression to describe how 15-year-old Newton's slow writing pace had circumvented his having to pen a longer message.

Inspection, and so, did not go. Now that Lieut. Jeffcoat has gone home, Lieut. Baird, of Co A, has command of the Company, and he is a first rate fellow. Lieut. Cols. Clark's wife came yesterday, bringing her family with her. I am on duty today here in Camp. Lieut. Jeffcoat said that he would bring down any little thing that we wanted, and so I was going to ask you to send me some good Butter if you had it. I suppose that you have commenced making Butter by this time. If you will send from 5 to 10 lbs. I would like it much. Mr. Smith's are going to send Albert some, and Sarah will speak to you about it. You can either pack it in a small box or put it in some close vessel, and Lieut. will bring it in his trunk. My health is good, and I hope that this may find you enjoying the same blessing. The weather is quite pleasant today, but it was quite cool yesterday. Well, I have not much to write, and so will close.

I remain as ever your dutiful soldier Boy,

Edward ————

[on backside] To my dear Home

Diary - April 11, 1864

We were up at 3:00 a.m. to the long roll. I'm cook this week. James Henry came into Mess 1 today. We sold some extra rations this evening, and we bought the potatoes we needed with the proceeds. We had a big battalion drill this evening lasting two hours.

Diary - April 12, 1864

Company B was the first in line with the long roll this morning. I spent the forenoon very foolishly, playing poker with several of the boys. Companies B and A went on drill together. We are making good progress in the use of arms under the direction of Lieutenant Baird. William H. Ash of Company B, who had been reported as a deserter for a year, was restored to duty on the 10th by order of General Buckland.

---

* The only William Ash of Company "B", according to the *Illinois Roster*, was a William W. Ash, from Iroquois County.

The Carnage at Fort Pillow

By the end of the day, on April 12, Chatfield had not yet heard of the devastation that took place at Fort Pillow, Tennessee, about 40 river-miles north of Memphis. General Nathan Bedford Forrest, with roughly 1,500 cavalrymen, attacked the fort by land from the hills to the east, the fort's most vulnerable entry point. Major Lionel F. Booth, the Union commanding officer, was killed shortly after the attack began, and Major William F. Bradford assumed command. Forrest demanded surrender, and Bradford refused, prompting the storming of the fort and a savage hand-to-hand battle. An important recruiting site at the time, Fort Pillow had nearly as many black soldiers as white. Of its 557 men, 262 were black, former slaves from Tennessee and Alabama. When the battle ended, 127 of the white Union soldiers were either dead or seriously wounded—a casualty rate of 43%. In marked contrast, 204 of the black soldiers suffered the same fate, a casualty rate of 78%.[*] The Northern papers quickly fanned news of the massacre. A detailed review by the Federal *Committee on the Conduct of the War* concluded "…the Confederates were guilty of atrocities which included murdering most of the garrison after it surrendered, burying Negro soldiers alive, and setting fire to tents containing Federal wounded."[198] The Confederate position held that the report and findings were "sheer propaganda, fabricated to stir up war hatred…"[199] Yet, after "…his men slaughtered their surrendered black prisoners at Tennessee's Fort Pillow, an enthused Nathan Bedford Forrest called it a clear demonstration that 'negro soldiers cannot cope with Southerners.'"[200] "Remember Fort Pillow" would be a familiar Union battle call from that time forward.

---

[*]   These percentages were derived from the data supplied in Mark M. Boatner's *Civil War Dictionary*, pp 295-296.

CHAPTER 27: "THAT DEVIL, FORREST"*

"… I should like to …. shoot those brutal villains
who took the garrison at Fort Pillow last week …"

Diary - April 13, 1864
Privates Thomas Scotland of Company A, William Griffin of Company H, and
Ezekiel Clark of Company I were discharged today and sent home. Scotland was
disabled. We are having two drills a day. Each company is trying to see who is
the best. A barrel of beer will go to the best company on inspection next Sunday.
Companies B and A made a good show on dress parade today.

All three of the soldiers were in their upper forties—men over twice Chatfield's age
at the time of their discharge, all disabled. Private Thomas Scotland, 46, had been
a sailor before he enlisted in Chicago. A native of Scotland, "Scotland" may have
been the name given to him when he immigrated. William Griffin, 46, was a married farmer from Kankakee. Clark, 47, born in Batavia (Middlefield), Ohio, where
Chatfield was born, was a married farmer from Iroquois County, Illinois. The *Illinois
Roster's* citing of Clark's discharge in Memphis as taking place on March 15, 1863, is
undoubtedly an error. That date corresponds to when the regiment was digging the
canal at Young's Point.

---

*   A phrase used by General Sherman in a letter penned to General Grant on November 6, 1864. *Official
Records*, Series 1, Volume 39, Part 3, p. 658.

Diary - April 14, 1864

We had a very exciting day in camp today. We got paid for the months of January and February. Usually when boys get paid, they will go to the sutler to drink beer and get as tight as bricks. But after paying off my debts, I only had about $4.00 left. I was detailed to picket for tomorrow.

Diary - April 15, 1864

I was detailed to picket this morning on Pigeon Roost Road and at the Reserve. First Lieutenant Virgil Dashill of Company K had command of our division. Much travel and many goods have been carried out on this road. We took away plenty of whiskey. Some of the boys took more than they could carry. A lot of the cavalry came in, reporting a skirmish today at Coldwater, about 20 miles south from here.

Coldwater, Mississippi, was a small rail-station community of houses and stores straddling the *Mississippi-Tennessee Railroad*, the namesake of nearby Coldwater River, and the site of numerous skirmishes during this time period. First Lieutenant Dashill was from Ganeer Township. He was a 20-year-old schoolteacher when he enlisted as a sergeant.

Diary - April 16, 1864

I stood picket for 3 hours during the night. We were relieved at 8:00 a.m. by the 120th. Lieutenant Hosmer of Company C got arrested for drunkenness and insulting his superior officer, and his sword was taken from him. All are well at home except for William and Mary. A fight broke out between Lucius Gubtail and another man. That despot of a Captain (Sutherland, by name) put Gubtail under arrest and stopped his pay.

Lieutenant Harvey P. Hosmer's arrest for drunkenness evidently had little impact on his progression up the ranks. He was promoted to Captain on August 10, 1864.

Diary - April 17, 1864

We turned out on long roll at 4:00 a.m. and stacked arms. Then we packed our knapsacks and had regiment inspection. Companies C and B were perfect. We would not take Sutherland's beer. Instead, we bought our own barrel.

Letter - April 17, 1864
Camp, 113th, Ill. "Infty"
Memphis Tenn. April 17th 1864

My Dear Parents,

Having now a few spare moments I will devote them to addressing you a few lines. Your very welcome letter of the 9th was received yesterday just after I had come in from Picket. Was glad to that hear that you were mostly well, but was sorry to hear that Wm. and Mary was unwell. But, hope that by the time this reaches you that they will be restored. My health is good, at present, as well as that of the rest of the Company. I am cook this week and I have just cleared away the things after dinner. We had preaching this morning by a minister from town. Had a very good meeting which was well attended. After meeting, there was a Regimental inspection (which comes of every Sunday morning regular) at which Company B made the best appearance of all.

My dear Mother, I am very thankful for the good advice you give. As you say, it does require a good deal of resolution to go forward at all times and never falter. So far, I never have failed to perform every duty that has been assigned to me, and I pray that I shall always have strength and Courage given me in future. So far the Lord has been very good to me, and I can not be thankful enough for the mercies that I have received. As for myself, I am in hopes that we will not have to [go] into another battle. But, if we should have to, I should try and do my part without any faltering. For, I think it is my duty to go where ever duty calls me.

There is one thing that I should like to have. That is to shoot those brutal villains who took the garrison at Fort Pillow last week and, after they had surrendered, murdered them in cold blood. I suppose that you have heard before this of the fight at the latter place and all the particulars than I could tell you. There was several there that used to be members of this Reg't who had command of the Negro Batteries. Fort Pillow is only about 40 miles up the river from here. And there was a good deal of excitement for a day or so. The fort is in our possession now, and the boats can go up and down without trouble.* The Guerillas do some mischief in firing into boats in passing up and down.

We were paid off last Thursday for two months, but owing to my financial embarrassments, should not be able to send any money home this time. Memphis is a bad place to be in, for a fellow spends so much. But, I shall try and do better next Pay Day. There has a detail just come, and I expect that I will be on picket again tomorrow. But, as long as I have my health, I go do not care for the duty. Let it come as often as it will. I am taking the daily Memphis Bulletin and will send you one occasionally. Think that you would like to read them. Well, I have not much to write this time and so will close. My love to you all with a kiss for Mary.

from your soldier Boy,
Edward ————————

In the Civil War army of volunteers, the enlisted men often took exception to the privileges afforded to the officers, typically men volunteering from the same communities who in many cases had neither superior education nor advanced training in soldiering. Some officers were competent, and some were not; they were subject to the same weaknesses and earthly temptations as all men. Nevertheless, the officers gave the orders and had special rights: the right to special housing, special meals, special medical care, furloughs, conjugal visits, and even the right to resign. In marked contrast, the enlisted men enjoyed very few rights; by military design, their rank placed them at the bottom of the hierarchy. Having observed the glaring disparity of privileges and the questionable conduct of many officers for twenty months, Chatfield lifted his pen to ridicule the military class system, calling the practice "a curse to our country all honest men."

---

* Directly following the massacre, on the same day as the attack, Forrest had evacuated Fort Pillow, taking needed horses and supplies. His exit left the fort open for immediate Union reoccupation.

Letter to Editor - April 17, 1864*
Camp. 113th, Ill. "Infty."
Memphis Tenn. April, 17th, 1864

Mr. Parker

Sir,

I have some verses and if you think best you can insert them in your paper. They are, as follows, entitled: "The Soldiers Life for two years in west Tennessee."

Come Citizens and soldiers attention give ear
While I speak of the hardships of our brave Volunteers
For two year experience in West Tennessee
Is altogether sufficient for me
God only knows how the soldiers are used
how wrongfully treated and brutally abused
for a private in the army to say at the worst
are the most abused creatures on the face of the earth

While the Officers are made wise and the governments expense
privates are mere things without reason or sence
they practice and monopolize with the principle of rouges
that soldiers without rank are no better than dogs

They do not intend to give a private one inch
while a man that wears strips can go his whole length
they think they have authority the private to ape
with that cursed abomination of blue and red tape

Our trials and hardships are many and great
more sad and painful than I can relate
and none but ~~we soldiers~~ the privates who are bound to oppression
Can realize ~~a soldiers~~ how pitiful is a soldiers condition

Who knows but the soldiers the suffering and woe
In case of much sickness he must undergo
they are treated with discouragement grief and dismay
and their life hopes and glory are just fading away

---

*   Chatfield's letter to the editor—in verse—accompanied his April 17 letter to his parents. The recipient was Daniel S. Parker, the former regimental adjutant who had resigned in July 1863, following his loss of promotion opportunities. Parker, as of April, had already resumed his editorial position at the *Kankakee Gazette*. Due to a fire, all early issues of the *Gazette* are missing. It is not known if Chatfield's verse was ever published.

The doctors do study with great treatment and skill
their poor dying patients to cure or to kill
Some quinine and jalap* will make them all right
in case they expected a march or a fight

A soldier gets wounded no matter how slight
they will cut of [off] their limbs and call it all right
they do up a wound in the same length of time
as would take a smart butcher to cut off a limb

Hundreds of Officers that belong to the line
are gambling and drinking and spending their time
like a lot of town loafers infesting broadway
and the debts there contracted not able to pay

Now a word for myself before I make any foes
there is necessity in fighting as every one knows
but unless it is conducted ~~in~~ on a far better ~~manner~~ plan
tis a curse to our country all honest men
— A.C.B.— [Anonymous, Company B]

Diary - April 18, 1864
*Company B was detailed on picket on guard call. Companies C and K came first
and second. The rumor of a Rebel cavalry near us was found untrue.*

Having tried his hand at verse, Chatfield moved on to another form of creative
expression. On April 18, or thereabouts, he made a noble effort to improve his
prose.

---

* Jalap was a powerful purgative.

Letter – [April 18, 1864 - date estimated]

– A few scattered thoughts of a sentinel on picket –

A soldier while standing through the silent watches of the night naturally has strange thoughts. Sitting by a low glimmering fire or standing as he ~~does or should dos~~ do Some distance in the gloom that surrounds all nature. It is then, if ever, he will have lonesome feelings, and he will naturally think of those pleasant times he has spent at home among his friends and kindred far away at home. But, to come back to the stern reality, here he is, with Cartridge Box belted on, and his trusty Springfield by his side, standing guard over the country's welfare which he so truly loves, that he has given up all those social joys and pleasures and gone forth to Battle for his Country's rights and to see that her Laws are not trempled upon, and for the double purpose of helping and aiding by all the strength in his power in accomplishing that end, and that Freedom may be secured to all. But, I am leaving the subject that I commenced with. ——

All nature is enshrouded in the surrounding gloom of the night, and all is silence except the howl and bark of the numerous canine species that inhabit these regions of country. And, there is nothing to relieve the loneliness of the sentinel on duty at the midnight hour but the thought that he is not entirely alone in the world. For the occasional snore that he hears tells him that, if danger is near, that he is not entirely alone to contend it. For, at a second's warning, he can awaken his companions, who do not sleep but a few paces distant, and be ready to meet it.

Hark! The booming of several Cannon in the direction of German town fall on his ear. What can that mean? Is the enemy advancing upon us? But, there is none to answer. And so, he resumes his duty again with attentive ear on the alert to make up for the want of seeing what is going on about him. And so, the mind wanders on back to the friends that he has left, and the pleasant scenes of former years ~~he is is now~~ of his boyhood days, and of the many truant acts that he has had a share in, and of a kind Father and doting Mother of how he was the idol of their hearts, and yet, how poorly he repayed all their best efforts for his welfare, (and yet cannot forget) the quiet joys of home.

And then, the mind will wander of into the future, and brilliant plans and prospects will be laid out, and of what is in store for us. But, after all, every thing of the future is as a blank. Nothing can be told of what is to happen on the morrow.

And now the mind reverts back to the experiences we have had of the soldiers life of enlisting, of parting from home, and friends for the first time, and going into the first camp, and of standing guard the first time, of afterwards going into the field, and of active operations, of marches and of battles and sieges, and camp life, and sickness pain and disease, and of moves, constant rumors, and every thing else that goes to make up a soldier's life, and of the Demoralizing influences around him when he is suddenly brought to his former thoughts by the approach of the relief. And so he goes of to bed to dream of home and friends left behind.

Diary - April 19, 1864
A band of 100 to 150 Rebels stole mules and horses from a man's nearby farm. The 120th relieved us this morning, and our whole regiment marched away at 2:00 p.m. to guard the fort [Fort Pickering] while Negro troops were on review.

Diary - April 20, 1864
I got a pass after breakfast, went to town and paid $3.57 for a barrel of potatoes. Also got some chokers [collars] and a tie. Went to town again this afternoon and got my potatoes. We had drill in the afternoon. Colonel Clark was quite unwell, so he did not come out. A gentleman is setting up a picture shop in Memphis today, so I'll have some taken soon.

Diary - April 21, 1864
The order is still in force. We had to turn out at 3½o'clock this morning and stack our arms. Then we went back to bed. A couple of deserters were brought in to camp today. They had just been brought down from Springfield. They were sent to the Irving Block. They belonged to Companies J and I. We had no drills today—a very dull day in camp.

Diary - April 22, 1864
We turned out again at 3:00 a.m. and stacked our arms. I did some washing. I can't afford to hire it done, my having so little money. My health is good. My weight is 156 pounds. I borrowed $5.00 off John Blanchet yesterday until next payday. We had dress parade this evening and a hard rain thereafter.

Diary - April 23, 1864
Lieutenant Jeffcoat returned this morning from Cairo, on the Belle of St. Louis. He said that everything looks fine and prosperous at home. He brought me a pair of shirts for $5.50 and also each of the boys in the company a hat. The cost was $2.75. The company is pretty well uniformed now. It rained all day and hard tonight. I borrowed $5.00 off Dick Ward [Caleb Ward] for which I will have to pay $6.00 on payday.

Diary - April 24, 1864

I was detailed as camp guard today. The weather is quite cool. It sprinkled some. Lieutenant Colonel Clark is afflicted with an ulcerated tooth and is not ready for duty. The whole talk now is that we will be ordered away soon, which is all they have to talk about. My health is first rate. I am getting as fat and sassy as can be.

Diary - April 25, 1864

Tom Carrow and I got a pass after breakfast and went downtown — Tom, to pick up pictures taken last week and I, to sit for some photographs. Today was the warmest day yet of the season. Battalion drill was very uncomfortable due to the heat. I visited Bert this evening.

Diary - April 26, 1864

I got a pass this morning and went to town again. Lucky that I did so, for by an accident, the negatives that I had taken were broken. So I sat for one again. I did not get back to camp until after inspection, so I saved myself so much trouble. It was very warm again, so battalion drill was postponed until after dress parade. I am troubled with a boil in the worst place it could be.

Diary - April 27, 1864

The bugle sounded again at 3:00 a.m., and we all fell out and stacked our arms. The day was warm and sultry and threatened rain this evening. We had general inspection at 10:00 a.m. I had a touch of the ague this afternoon but was detailed on fatigue duty most of the afternoon. I felt so miserable that I came for duty and let the work go for what it would fetch. I borrowed a dollar off Lieutenant Jeffcoat until payday.

Diary - April 28, 1864

Tom Carrow and John Fundy went on picket this morning. Every time that the boys go on picket there is a general race among the companies to see which can get on the grounds first. It has been so hot for several days past that we had battalion drill at 7:00 a.m. but no drill later. I went downtown and got some of my pictures. Orders came today requiring us to be ready for the march, yet no one knows where. There is much speculation on that point. It rained again today. Sent a letter to Father with my photographs.

CHAPTER 28: A FRUITLESS FIRST MARCH

"We fell in again at 7:00 a.m. and went after Forrest...."

Following the catastrophe at Fort Pillow, Washington politicians demanded that a new commanding officer of the District of West Tennessee be designated. Sherman responded by replacing General Hurlbut with General Cadwallader C. Washburn. Of urgent concern to Sherman was Washburn's ability to protect Union resources, especially Sherman's supply line. It was Washburn's duty to keep Nathan Bedford Forrest occupied in the west and involved in peripheral battles, away from the all-important *Nashville to Chattanooga Railroad* that supported the push against Chattanooga and Atlanta. And Washburn would rely upon General Samuel D. Sturgis to get the job done.

Diary - April 29, 1864

General Washburn's order came out this morning impressing all of the horses of the citizens of Memphis into the U.S. Service. The rumors are that we will be leaving here soon. We have packed up all of our surplus clothing and will leave it here if we go on the march. Tom Carrow, John Fundy, Bert and I also packed a box to send home. It was raining during the day and hard, this evening. A man named Smith was hung today in the fort for smuggling.

The April 29 Hanging in Memphis
Memphis Daily Bulletin-Saturday Morning, April 30, 1864

Yesterday being the time appointed for the execution of Thos. Martin Smith for the crime of smuggling and treason, by favor of a pass from Gen. Buckland, we were admitted within the Fort where the solemn event was consummated. In the center of the extensive works we found standing a substantial gallows put up for the purpose. ... At nearly half-past eleven o'clock the prisoner arrived, having been brought to the grounds from the Irving Block in an ambulance. He was led to the scaffold, the cap being drawn over his face.... Smith was a slight-made man of about five feet six, and twenty years of age, light and slender. His features were good, the expression of the countenance was gentle and kindly, and we should judge him to have been an amiable and affectionate disposition. He looked like one who might lack firmness, and the power of resisting temptation, but who would not be deliberately guilty of malignant or manifestly vicious actions. His teeth were good, and he had a handsome beard and moustache of light brown. His temperament was evidently of the nervous kind. His actions showed much mental suffering, but none of the shrinking of fear. As the sentence was read he continued to lift up first one leg and then the other in nervous restlessness. The influence of depressing and overwhelming emotion was startlingly manifest on drawing back the cap, for not a particle of the pupils of the eyes were visible—they were turned up, and only the white could be seen, and during the whole scene only a small portion of the pupil became visible—he never looked around or showed any consciousness of the presence of the gazing crowds before him. ... The Provost Marshal gave the fatal signal by waving his handkerchief. The executioner drew the rope, thus removing the support by which the doors forming the platform, on which Smith now stood alone, was sustained in their place. Unfortunately, the edges where the two doors touched each other had not been rounded, and the rain that had fallen in the night had so swelled the wood that they were pressed together with considerable force. This afforded a support that the slight weight of the unfortunate man could not overcome. He still remained standing where the executioner had placed him. That the effect was agonizing to the poor fellow was evidenced by his uttering a prolonged —Ah! in an accent of distress. The carpenter, by a sudden wrench, brought down the platform, and Smith was quivering in his last agony, suspended from the beam above him. In twenty minutes time, the attendant physicians pronounced pulsation to have ceased, and soon after the lifeless body was cut down and placed in the coffin which had been prepared for it.[201]

Diary - April 30, 1864

Orders came at 10:00 p.m. for us to march in the morning. I was up all night cooking and getting ready. We fell in at 4:00 a.m. and marched down to the north side of town where we waited for the rest of the force to join us, perhaps about 12,000 cavalry, our regiment, and 40 wagons. The rain made the march so hard that the whole regiment got loaded into the wagons and rode during the rain. Everybody foraged for all the horses, mules, chickens and turkeys they could find.* We marched 20 miles.

Diary - May 1, 1864

Stopped for the night at Raleigh and stayed in what was once a large store. We were called up at 4:00 a.m., got breakfast, and started on the march again at 5:00 toward Laurel Creek. Rode in wagons part of the time in the forenoon. Passed through Union Station on the Memphis and Ohio Railroad. Stopped at 2:00 for dinner. Then the wagons were sent back to Memphis with a guard of cavalry. The wagons were a part of a train for the 16th Army Corps. A Rebel spy was caught at the house where we took dinner. We marched about 20 miles and camped just at dark. Here I got a gold pencil and a quilt.

Diary - May 2, 1864

Felt good during the night. Called up at 4:00. Started at 5:00. Quite pleasant marching today and yesterday. Passed through the little town of Hopeville this forenoon. Got to the village of Somerville, a very pretty little place. Very few inhabitants. Only old men and children. Stopped 2 miles east of town for dinner, then 3 more miles before ending the day's march, about 15 miles. Rumor has it that a large force of Rebels is near and that our forces had a fight with them and took a lot of prisoners.

Alerted to General Sturgis's column, Forrest had vacated Jackson and had headed for Tupelo, in northeast Mississippi, his forces taking separate routes. Forrest, with his escort, followed a westward route that took him near Bolivar, Tennessee, on

---

*   Confederates referred to Union pillaging as "jay hawking," colloquial slang for marauding, robbery and thievery. The Union army preferred the euphemisms "foraging" and "procurement."

May 2, where Union Colonel Joseph Kargé's 700-man joint cavalry encountered him. Two hours of fighting ensued. Withstanding Forrest's classic charge, Kargé aggressively pressed Forrest back through Bolivar where Forrest crossed over the Hatchie Bridge, destroying it to prevent further pursuit. Kargé lost two soldiers, and five were wounded. Forrest lost seven, with 20 more wounded, including four officers—but he had nonetheless managed to evade capture.

Diary - May 3, 1864

We awakened at 4:00 a.m., ate and marched out at 7:00 on the road to Bolivar. It was quite warm, roads dusty, countryside hilly, soil mostly clay with a little sand, and roads and fields badly washed. A force of 500 cavalry and 2 pieces of artillery came into Bolivar and surprised the Rebs under Forrest and drove them out after a brisk little fight. We got into Bolivar about 5:00 p.m. and found it to be a real pretty place. We marched out about 18 miles and camped on the banks of the Hatchie River. A man in Company C had his arm accidentally shot off. I felt very tired tonight; we had marched about 20 miles.

The soldier in Company "C" who lost his arm was a new recruit named Henry T. Gibbs. Gibbs was from Adams County, Illinois, approximately 100 miles west of Springfield. The 19-year-old lost more than his arm that day. Records show that Private Gibbs died in Bolivar, Tennessee, on May 3, 1864. His length of service was barely five months.

Diary - May 4, 1864

After a good night's rest I felt much better. Just across the river, where our pickets stood, the Rebel forces were about 40 rods off all night, building a floating bridge across the river. Another division from Memphis got here today, on a different road. We drew 6 days' rations today, went down the river about 2 miles with a squad, and helped bring up a ferryboat. They have got the bridge just about done this evening. I have to go on guard tonight. My health has been first-rate good on this march. I learned this evening that Billy Warden, Orderly of Co. F, has crossed the river. That gives us a spy in the enemy's country.

This was the last time Chatfield wrote about his friend Billy Warden. The war would soon separate them. Within 11 months Billy would be badly wounded while in battle at Fort Blakely, Alabama. His leg would be amputated on April 9, 1865, and he would be discharged on June 27.

Without Chatfield's knowledge, on May 4, 1864, Ira William, one of the three Company "B" soldiers who had been missing for the past nine months, returned to regimental headquarters in Memphis, ending the mystery of what had happened to him—and a glimpse into what had happened to Wallace Beebe and Charles Boswell. All had been captured by General Johnston's troops during a skirmish in Jackson, Mississippi, in mid-July. After being moved from prison to prison, only William and Beebe had been transferred to a newly constructed Georgia stockade in late February. Boswell had been too sick to be transferred, and his fate was unknown by William. After remaining in the new stockade for three months, Ira had been "exchanged" and released to the Union forces. Despite its being new, William reported that the conditions at the stockade near Americus, Georgia, had been deplorable. He referred to the place as "Andersonville"—a name that would remain chillingly infamous 150 years later. Prior to his exchange, William had heard that Wallace Beebe might soon be exchanged as well. With William returning alive, fresh hopes flourished for Wallace Beebe's safe return. The fate of Charles Boswell—quite ill when last seen—was still murky; after being separated from William and Beebe, no one knew what had become of him.

Diary - May 5, 1864

We fell in again at 7:00 a.m. and went after Forrest, traveling south on the Mississippi Central Railroad. The pontoon bridge built yesterday was cut and sent down the river, just before we started. We are now in what is called "The Independent Brigade" under the command of Colonel William L. McMillen. The country is mostly hilly with much timber. We marched 23 miles and camped on the Little Hatchie, near the railroad, between Pocahontas and Middleton.

Diary - May 6, 1864

We were up at 4:00, got breakfast, and marched out at 6:00. We crossed the Memphis and Charleston Railroad and marched southwest all the forenoon, then south and southeast during the afternoon. The country is very hilly, and there is scarcely an inhabitant in the country. At 1:00 p.m. we stopped to rest and eat dinner. We were marching on the road to Ripley all day. We camped [on the Wolf River] in the woods, 3 miles out of Ripley. We marched 24 miles today. Our "Independent Brigade" has 5 regiments of infantry and 3 batteries.

342
The Chatfield Story: Civil War Letters and Diaries of
Private Edward L. Chatfield of the 113th Illinois Volunteers

Diary - May 7, 1864

We were up at 2:30, had breakfast, and started on the march back to Memphis at 5:00. Forrest has got clear out of reach. Our cavalry's horses were played out for the want of feed. So we were forced to give up the chase. We had a pretty hard march today. It was very warm, and we were foot sore. My feet hurt real bad. We passed through Salem and camped 4 miles beyond in the direction of La Grange. We ran out of meat tonight, so we made a draw on the sheep, cattle, and hogs within 3 miles of camp.

Diary - May 8, 1864

We did not move today. We just lay still and rested. We re-supplied all kinds of provisions by foraging. Two men of Company G, Orderly Walter S. Joslyn and Daniel Cole, were captured by guerillas, but they both managed to escape before midnight after losing their arms, watches, and all their money. About 5:00 p.m. reports came that Forrest was advancing upon us. The long roll was given, and we were ready for a fight in about 2 minutes. It turned out to be a false report, ending the scare. There is no doubt that there is quite a force of guerillas about to pick up stragglers.

Orderly Joslyn had been a railroad conductor in Chicago before he enlisted at age 19. Private Daniel Cole, 22, had been a farmer in Northfield, Cook County. Cole would be captured a second time within six months.[*]

By May 8, forage was low and the stock was suffering. General Sturgis felt convinced that the May 2 encounter at Bolivar had been enough to remove Forrest from Tennessee and issued orders to return to Memphis.

Diary - May 9, 1864

We were awakened at 2:30 a.m., ate breakfast, and marched out at 4:00. Our brigade took the lead, and our regiment was ahead. We crossed the Mississippi Central Railroad at a little town by the name of Lamar. We passed through two destroyed villages and stopped for dinner in a nice grove at 1:00 p.m. After that, we did some pretty fast marching today, covering about 25 miles. Then we came

---

[*]   Daniel Cole was captured again on October 10, 1864, at Eastport, Mississippi, near Iuka, while on another expedition to capture Forrest. Unlike Andrew Forman of Company "B" (also captured that day) Cole survived his imprisonment and mustered out on June 20, 1865.

upon a railroad 4 miles west of Moscow where we boarded and came to Memphis, arriving here at 10:00 p.m. I am glad to be back. My feet are sore.

Diary - May 10, 1864

My bed felt as good last night as it ever did, and a decent meal seemed good. I washed my clothes, and an ague spell fell on me at noon. I stayed in bed the rest of the day. I learned that Lex Wilson has had the smallpox. Riley Beach, who marched with us, also has the smallpox. It rained today, hard this evening.

Private Alex "Lex" Wilson was in Company "B", a 28-year-old married farmer from Kankakee Township.

Diary - May 11, 1864

It rained all night. The air was cool and pleasant. I wrote a letter to Cousin Herrick [probably Mary Irene Herrick] then went downtown with Bert in the ambulance and got the rest of my photographs, costing me $5.00 per dozen. I got fifteen. Lieutenant Jeffcoat bought a barrel of beer and treated the company all around. A good many of the boys got rather more than they could carry handily. As for myself, I kept perfectly straight.

Diary - May 12, 1864

I was busy all forenoon cleaning my gun. Tom Carrow and I were detailed to go to Alton, Illinois, at 11:00, and we had to get ready to go as soon as possible. Forty others were also detailed. Lieutenant Baird of Company A had command of our squad. We went down to the Irving Block, and at 3:00 p.m. we took 89 Secesh prisoners, 12 of whom were officers, and marched them down to the C.E. Hillman. The boat pushed out at 5:00, and we started north.

Diary - May 13, 1864

On board the steamer, Hillman, we passed Fort Pillow at 1:00 a.m. last night and New Madrid today. We passed Wolf Island at 1:00 p.m. Four guns are mounted there, but it's a very small force. We have kept steadily on our course all day. We reached Cairo at 8:30 p.m. Thomas and I went ashore for a few moments and were left behind. The steamer, Courier, was about ready to start. We boarded, and she started about 2 hours after the Hillman left.

Diary - May 14, 1864

On board the steamer, Courier, there was a corporal of Company I who was left behind with us. Having no blankets, we passed the night very uncomfortably. We had left them on the Hillman with our arms. We passed Commerce, Missouri, at 10:00 a.m., once a very pretty town but now very dilapidated. We passed Cape Girardeau at 3:00 p.m., now garrisoned by the old 20th Illinois and commanded by Major Williams. Having nothing with me to eat and being out of money, I washed dishes for food until we reached St. Louis, Missouri.

Diary - May 15, 1864

The Courier made very slow progress. She stopped at Chester, Illinois, this morning and took on coal. We passed St. Genevieve, Missouri, a little later. As we get farther north, it gets cooler, and the vegetation is not so far advanced. We reached Jefferson Barracks at 2:30 p.m. and Carondelet at 3:00 p.m. — both pretty places on the Missouri side of the river. We reached St. Louis at 4:00 and found that the guards had gone on up to Alton by way of the Chicago and St. Louis Railroad. So we went to the Soldiers' Home in St. Louis for lodging for the night.

Diary - May 16, 1864

Here we are, again, this evening, on board the Hillman, bound down the river. At the Soldiers' Home last night we found Orderly Kellogg. He told us that Major Williams was in town and at the 4th Street Hotel. We went and saw him, and he got our transportation for us. Since the boat did not leave until late, we explored the city. At 8:00 p.m. we boarded and started down the river. We stopped at 1:30 a.m. at Jefferson Barracks and took on a company of men.

Diary - May 17, 1864

We are still on the Hillman, and we have made good time. We stopped only a few times to take on passengers and coal. We passed Cape Girardeau and Commerce this morning and arrived at Cairo at 10:00 a.m. We went up to the Soldiers' Home where we found the rest of the squad of guards who had come down from Alton on the cars. We took dinner. At 5:00 a.m. we started at Bird's Point. We reached Columbus, Kentucky, just before dark.

Diary - May 18, 1864

The steamer stopped several times to take on wood. We passed Fort Pillow at 10:00 a.m. This place was the scene of a horrible massacre committed by Forrest's forces. We reached Memphis at 4:00 p.m. When we got back to camp, we learned of several promotions: Milton H. Rounsavell from Corporal to Sergeant and Privates Levi M. Walters and John Scoon were both promoted to corporals.

Diary - May 19, 1864

It seemed good to get back to our companions again and rest comfortably in our quarters. The officers and men were celebrating the charge on the enemy at Vicksburg on the 19th of May last year. Any amount of beer has been drunk. A good deal of both officers and men showed the effects of it this evening. As for myself, I kept pretty straight. Lieutenant Conway, our Acting Adjutant, was put under arrest for drunkenness and striking another officer.

First Lieutenant James J. Conway of Company "G" was a native of Ireland and a 36-year-old married bookkeeper before the war. He enlisted in Cook County and worked his way up the ranks from sergeant. He would be killed in action within 22 days at a place called Brice's Cross Roads.

Letter - May 19, 1864
Camp. 113th, Ill, "Infty."
Memphis. Tenn. May, 19th, 1864

Dear Parents,

Today is the anniversary of the first Charge on Vicksburg, and we have been having quite a spree. So you must excuse me if I do write poorly. —

Last night we got back from St. Louis & Alton where I went with those prisoners. We had a very pleasant trip, having been gone six days. My health is good, and we are enjoying ourselves first-rate. The weather is quite warm and pleasant. John S. Titcomb got back to the Company last Thursday. While we were gone up the river (that is Tom & I) John Fundy Expressed a box home. It was sent to John Michael. I had in the box some clothing. — I cap, I overcoat. — I woollen Blanket. — I Jacket, — and some other little things. Every piece has my name on it. — I have no news to write at present so I will close.

I remain as ever your loving son,
Edward L Chatfield

Diary - May 20, 1864

We were detailed on picket this morning. The division that our company's squad was in went out on the Pigeon Roost Road. The lines were closed on the 15th of this month by order of Gen. Washburn. No one is to be let out without a special permit from Brigadier General Washburn. Today's news said that Lee's army had been reinforced to 200,000 strong, but for all of that, Grant was steadily pressing on toward Richmond. His motto is to press them—that is, the Rebels—to the last. It is very dull out here on picket.

Diary - May 21, 1864

We were relieved at 8:00 a.m. by the 120th. I drew new clothing this afternoon: a blouse, a pair of drawers, and a pair of shoes. We had dress parade at 7:00 p.m., the largest turnout we ever had. General Washburn ordered the whole regiment to have caps and to wear them when on duty and on dress parade.

Diary - May 22, 1864

After performing my morning's ablutions, I went down to the Methodist Church meeting. Eight of us from Company B went. Wallace Beebe, who had been taken prisoner near Jackson, Mississippi, on July 22, 1863, returned to the company today, having been exchanged May 7th, 1864. I felt real mean this evening, having a touch of the ague. Edmund Landis was detailed away a day or so ago; now John Titcomb is my bedfellow.

As hoped for, Beebe was exchanged three days after Ira William had been released. That left only Charles Boswell to account for. That mystery would not be resolved until the war's end.

Diary - May 23, 1864

It is my week to cook, so I commenced making breakfast. Thomas and I packed a box; I went down to the Express Office and expressed it. I went down in the ambulance with Bert. Wrote a letter to Grandmother [Lucy] last evening and sent her my photograph. The boys built an arbor before our tents this forenoon. General Washburn posted a strong camp guard around the camp, on account of the men plundering the gardens in the neighborhood of the camp.

Diary - May 24, 1864

Major Cephas Williams is in command because Lieutenant Colonel Clark is sick. I had quite a shake of the ague today. I felt very bad all day. I feel some better this evening but retired to bed early.

Diary - May 25, 1864
I felt some better this morning but not as well as I could wish. I was detailed for camp guard today. There is a strong guard of 80 men around the camp. One hundred-sixty men from the regiment were detailed this afternoon to guard the Irving Block, the military prison downtown. The boys guard the prisoners, then go to the theater at nights and have a pretty good time.

Diary - May 26, 1864
John Fundy and Thomas Carrow were sent out on detail, leaving only 3 of us in the mess number 1: James Henry, John S. Titcomb, and me. We concluded that we would not mess with mess 2, as they have a cook, and we let the boys downtown have our cooking utensils. Another touch of the ague came today; not as hard as before. John Titcomb is suffering with indisposition being rather out of time every way*. Company B has now more corporals and sergeants than it does men. There being so few of us we have to come on duty very often.

Diary - May 27, 1864
Two of the men were detailed for camp guard and 2 others for picket, taking every man. I am on camp guard. There are only half as many guards as there were yesterday. There was another rumor that Forrest was advancing upon this place. Dispositions have been made so as to receive him this way, but no one really believes the rumors.

Diary - May 28, 1864
I was relieved from guard at 7:00 a.m. I read most of the time; there was nothing else to do. We had dress parade this evening with about 200 men. Lieutenant Colonel Clark started for home yesterday, and Major Cephas Williams is in command of the regiment.

Diary - May 29, 1864
We had our usual Sunday morning inspection at 9:00 a.m. and the preaching from Reverend Chaplain Rankin. I went downtown with Thomas Carrow to the Irving Block and then spent 2 or 3 hours rambling about the park. The Sabbath seems to be a day of pleasure to all classes, the rich and poor. Both soldiers and civilians devote this day to pleasure.

---

*   "Indisposition" was akin to "malaise," suggesting a mild illness.

Letter - May 29, 1864
Camp 113th Ill. "Vols." Infty.
Memphis. Tenn. May. 29th, 1864

Dear Parents,

    I again take my pen this beautiful Sabbath morning to indite you a few lines. Your very welcome letter of the 20th Ult' was received in due time and read with pleasure. Was glad to hear that you were all well. I think that you must have been disappointed after hearing, as you did, that I was coming and then to have [it] turn out as it did. You may readily believe that I was much disappointed. But, as things happened, there was no help, so there was no use of repining over it. We are still doing Picket Duty, and we have also a strong camp guard around the Camp. There has been so much thieving, pillaging of gardens, and other mean practices going on, of late, that there have been complaints entered before General Washburn. And he has issued very strict orders to see if he can't put a stop to such proceedings. There is a detail from our Reg't guard, what is called the Irving Block, (or military prison) down in town. John Fundy and Thomas Carrow are there. There is some 200 or 300 prisoners in there all the time. I expect that [you] have got those things that I sent in those boxes before this one was sent to Mr. Michael and the other to Mr. Carrow. The drum has just made the church call and I must stop and go.

    We had a very good meeting. Chaplain Rankins preached. He delivered a very good sermon. My health is good, and the boys are all well, and send you their best respects. Wallace Beebe, who was taken prisoner down at Jackson Miss. last July, returned to the company about a week ago. He is well, and does not look as though he fared very hard while in Rebel hands. It has been several months, however, since he was paroled.

    It is very warm down here now, and our tents are very uncomfortable during the day. The heat strikes through them so easy. Well, the mail will be sent off in a few minutes and I must close if I would have this go today. Tell Mary to keep up good courage, for it is only about 15 months till my three years will [have] ended. Good bye for the present. My love to you all.

    I remain your loving son,

    Edward L Chatfield

Diary - May 30, 1864

I was detailed for camp guard at 7:00 a.m. It was a very warm day. The heat of the summer has come, making the day seem very monotonous. A brigade of troops came up the river from Vicksburg and went into camp about a mile south of us.

News came that General Grant's advance on Richmond is glorious and betokens our future success.*

Diary - May 31, 1864

The nights are quite cool, so we can rest good. I gave a good cleaning to my gun in the forenoon. Sgt. James Henry and Corporal John Campbell of Company B, were detailed to go to Alton, Illinois, with more prisoners. I got a letter from George A. Palmer. The guard around the camp was taken off just before dress parade. Orders were read at parade: the first man caught pillaging gardens or stealing in any form will be severely punished.

By May 31, CS Major General Stephen D. Lee, in command of the Department of Alabama and East Louisiana, had dispatched orders to CS General Nathan Bedford Forrest to move his 2,000 man cavalry northeast from Tupelo, Mississippi, into middle Tennessee. CS Brigadier General Philip Dale Roddey, commanding 1,000 North Alabama cavalrymen and two batteries of artillery, would join Forrest. Their mission was to destroy the *Nashville and Chattanooga Railroad*, cutting off Sherman's supply lines to Northern Georgia.[202] After destroying the rails, they would head southeast to Chattanooga to help General Joe Johnston in his attempt to defeat Sherman.

---

*   Grant was approaching General Robert E. Lee at Cold Harbor, Virginia.

CHAPTER 29: A DISASTROUS SECOND MARCH

"Chatfield ended his June 2 entry in mid-sentence, his final act of journaling."

On June 1, CS General Nathan Bedford Forrest exited Tupelo, en route northeast to dismantle the rails in Nashville. That same day, Union General Washburn, in charge of Memphis operations, ordered a second march to attract Forrest and confine him within the state of Mississippi. The march would be led again by Brigadier General Samuel D. Sturgis, whose entire command would number 8,100 cavalry and infantrymen, 400 artillerists, 22 cannon and 250 wagons—a size far greater than that estimated for Forrest, thus thought to assure a Union victory. The march would be remembered as "The Expedition into Mississippi." Supporting Sturgis, Brigadier General Benjamin Henry Grierson commanded two brigades of cavalry: the 1st Brigade, under Colonel George E. Waring, Jr. (1,500 men) and the 2nd Brigade, under Colonel Edward F. Winslow (1,800 men). Also supporting Sturgis was Colonel William L. McMillen, commanding three brigades of infantry: the 1st Brigade under Colonel Alexander Wilkin (2,000 men), the 2nd Brigade, under Colonel George B. Hoge (1,600 men, including the 113th Illinois) and the 3rd Brigade, under Colonel Edward Bouton, a 1,200-man brigade composed of two black infantry regiments and one black artillery unit. Each man in Bouton's brigade sported a badge on his uniform that read, "Remember Fort Pillow."[203]

Colonel Hoge's 2nd Brigade was an amalgam of five Illinois regiments: the 113th, 120th, 108th, 95th and 81st, plus Company "B" of the Second Illinois Artillery.[204] The 113th was commanded by Major Cephas Williams. Chatfield and the boys formerly in Company "B" had been assigned to Company "A", commanded by Lieutenant Azairah Baird.[205]

Diary - June 1, 1864

The regiment received orders this morning to be ready to march at 1:00 p.m., so I had to stir and box up my stuff for we do not carry anything but a rubber blanket. We did not calculate to be gone but a few days. At 1:00 p.m., the regiment fell in (with the exception of those that were guarding the Irving Block and those who were not able to march) and marched down to the depot where we formed the remainder of the brigade. We got on the cars and went out about 10 miles between La Fayette and La Grange, where we got off the cars and camped for the night. Rain began in the afternoon; it is raining hard now.

Chatfield's estimate as to where his regiment disembarked seems to have been slightly off. His diary entry specifying that they "…went out about 10 miles between La Fayette and La Grange …" before getting off, would place them 43 miles east of Memphis. Colonel Hoge, in his official report, wrote that they disembarked "at a point about half way between Collierville and La Fayette," a position 29 miles east of Memphis.[206] Assuming that Hoge's official report is the accurate one, by nightfall, the boys in the 113th would have been sipping soup beside the railroad tracks near what is today the small community of Piperton, Tennessee.

> Reveille was sounded at 4:30 o'clock on the ensuing morning, Thursday, the 2d, and the brigade marched at 6 o'clock, by land, [eastward] toward La Fayette, where, about 11 a.m., the First and Third Brigades were found encamped. I passed on beyond La Fayette one mile and went into camp. — Colonel George B. Hoge[207]

Diary - June 2, 1864 (Final Diary Entry)

It rained hard all night. I slept dry, having had my rubber over me. Ed Landis and I bunk and eat together now. We found out this morning that there was quite an expedition going out on Forrest. The force is composed of two brigades of infantry, one of cavalry, and several batteries of artillery—in all, about 15,000 men. We marched about 4 miles south of the railroad and camped. Had plenty of fresh pork for supper and ————

Regarding the size of the Union force, Chatfield had given his best estimates, although there were actually three brigades, not two, and there were closer to 8,100 men, not 15,000.[208]

Chatfield ended this June 2 entry in mid-sentence, his final act of journaling.* The next written record from Chatfield (a letter) would not come until April 1, 1865, 10 months later. At that point, Chatfield would be writing from a location 725 miles northeast of his La Fayette campsite: the Grafton Hospital in West Virginia.†

A Narrative of the Ten-Month Void‡

Thursday evening, June 2, 1864 – The Gossip at La Fayette
La Fayette was the base position for the march, a hubbub of gossip by nightfall on Thursday. Rumors flew that General Sturgis, commanding the entire expedition, was nowhere to be found when the troops left Memphis at 1:00 P.M. the preceding day. Sturgis had finally shown up in LaFayette Thursday morning at roughly 8:30 A.M.

Word was that he had been drinking heavily Wednesday evening, enjoying himself at the Gayoso Hotel, his presence observed in front of the hotel while he and an unknown lady awaited an omnibus.[209] What's more, went the gossip, the infantry commander, Colonel William McMillen, an officer known for his heavy drinking and hot temper, was said to have been "falling-down drunk" when he arrived with Sturgis at the La Fayette Station.[210] If the rumors were true, the commanders would have been in bad shape when the entire column marched away before daybreak on Friday morning.

Friday, June 3, 1864
The march began at 3:00 A.M. General Grierson, with his two brigades of cavalry, marched ahead of the three infantry brigades. Colonel Hoge's 2nd Brigade, with the 113th, took the forward position among the three infantry brigades that morning. Following Hoge marched Colonel Wilkin's 1st Brigade, and to the rear marched

---

*   Chatfield later entered a supplementary note in this (his third) diary, possibly upon his return to Memphis. The supplemental entry could have been made on or about June 9, 1865.

†   The diary somehow found its way back to Memphis after this June 2 entry. Evidently, Chatfield decided to safeguard his diary by sending it back to Memphis some time along the march.

‡   Without letters or diary entries from Chatfield during the next ten months, the first-hand accounts of others provide the living narrative perspective of what transpired during this time period.

Colonel Bouton's 3rd Brigade, guarding the supply wagons. Heavy rains turned the march into 7½ hours of drudgery, muddying the roads and forcing a stop at Lamar, a small rail station about 18 miles southeast of La Fayette—the wagons far behind. It took the wagons another 12½ hours to close the distance to 4 miles. Grierson's cavalry continued on toward Salem, Mississippi, the town known today as Ashland.

In the meantime, Forrest had reached Russellville, Alabama, well on his way to Nashville. There would have been no way that Sturgis's army could stop him, nor even reach him, had Forrest continued north. But he didn't continue north. While in Russellville, Forrest received a message from Major General Stephen Dill Lee stating that a sizable Union force was marching toward Tupelo and that he must return to Tupelo immediately.[211]

Saturday, June 4, 1864
No one in Colonel McMillen's infantry slept dry that Friday night in Lamar, the heavy rain not tapering off until early Saturday morning. Annoyed by the rain's interference and hoping to catch up with Grierson east of Salem, McMillen tried to get something out of the day and ordered the infantry to resume the march at 11:00 A.M., the supply train still shoveling and planking its way toward Lamar. Although the rain had ceased completely by 1:00 P.M., McMillen, once again awaiting the wagons, halted the infantry after traveling only nine miles. The boys ate their suppers of hard tack and bacon near Robinson's Plantation, four miles west of Salem. Remarkably, most were still in good spirits.[212]

Sunday, June 5, 1864
McMillen's troops were up at 4:00 A.M. and marching by 6:00 A.M., the air quickly turning hot and sultry as clouds towered aloft, promising more drenching downpours by early afternoon. The sweltering teams rapidly tired in their struggle through the deeply rutted aftermath of preceding wagons and infantry. Six hours later, the march had gained only ten miles. The weary column stopped two miles east of Salem at noon, having met up with Grierson's cavalry that had been waiting there for the past 40 hours. At 4:00 P.M., Grierson broke camp and traveled 14 miles farther east, stopping at what is today Falkner, several miles short of Ruckersville.[213] There Grierson dispatched Colonel Joseph Kargé of the 2nd New Jersey Cavalry toward Rienzi, 27 miles east. The mission for Kargé and his 400 men was to keep the Confederates guessing about the purpose of the Union march.[214] Kargé would tear up the rails at Rienzi, collect whatever stores that might be available there, and seize the Tuscumbia River Bridge. In the meantime, Forrest had arrived back in Tupelo, 49 miles south of Ruckersville.

Monday, June 6, 1864
In the still-cool hours before dawn, McMillen's infantrymen broke camp. At 4:00 A.M., the march resumed from its starting point on the Ruckersville road, two miles east

of Salem.[215] Colonel Hoge had detailed the 113th to guard the supply and ammunition wagons at the rear of the column. The somewhat drier roads helped to improve the pace and made it easier to keep the wagons closer together, a formation less vulnerable in the event of an attack. And that was fortunate.

At about 9:00 A.M., when Hoge's brigade had traveled ten miles east of Salem, a small party of Confederate pickets spotted the approaching Union wagons and positioned itself within nearby groves of blackjack oak, awaiting an opportunity to strike. The band was far too small to stop the advancing army, but it was large enough to issue a stinging Mississippi welcome. Focusing on the rear of Hoge's supply and ammunition train—the wagons guarded by the 113th—the Confederates began their assault.

The foot soldiers in the 113th, their hearts pounding, pulled their Springfields around, taking aim at the small puffs of smoke appearing from the distant trees. After firing their first shots, the boys rushed for cover, relying on wagons, culverts, trees and logs for protection as they loaded and fired again and again. The 30-minute skirmish ended when the 2nd Brigade's mounted infantrymen chased the Rebels away. No one had been hurt, all stores had been protected, and Chatfield and the 113th had reason to celebrate.[216] As for the Confederates, they would soon have another day.

Hoge's column resumed its march at 10:00 A.M., about the time that Chatfield and his fellow infantrymen would have noticed the ominous southern sky—an advancing black mantle accompanied by distant rolls of thunder. In less than an hour, abrupt wind gusts convulsed tree limbs while inch-wide splash marks spotted wagons and the shoulders of men. Moments later, the canopied sky released its heavy burden—a dense curtain of rain through which lightning exposed the dance of frantic oaks. Sheltered beneath their shuddering wagons on a steep decline, the boys grasped whatever they could to avoid washing away until the howling wind slowed, the skies began to lighten, and the heated tantrum of Mississippi's summer rage finally ended. The downpour had interrupted the march for three hours, the column moving again at 2:00 P.M. and halting three hours later at the intersection of the Salem-Ruckersville and Saulsbury-Ripley roads, an area of scant forage, where the overworked and hungry wagon teams suffered through the night.

Down in Tupelo that same evening, Forrest met with General Stephen Lee, who had arrived there by train from Meridian. Lee suspected that the huge body of bluecoats invading from Memphis was en route to Corinth, or Tupelo, or perhaps even farther south—possibly on its way to Okolona, the fertile Black Prairie, the breadbasket of Mississippi. Lee wanted them stopped; he tapped Forrest as the cavalryman best suited for the job.

Tuesday, June 7

By the morning of June 7, General Sturgis, having received word from General Grierson that the enemy had moved far to the south of Corinth, notified his commanders to change course toward Ripley—directly south. After waiting four hours after sunrise for the roads to dry, McMillen's three brigades decamped at 10:00 A.M., heading south on the road to Ripley, the wagons flanked on both sides with marching infantry. Chatfield would have been one of the many soldiers whose legs and feet labored tired and sore. Twelve days had passed since his last "shake," and there was no telling when another would come. Possibly, Chatfield carried quinine pills issued by the doctor. Four hundred boys were already too sick to continue much farther.

The road had not dried. After six hours of strenuous effort, the expedition had gone only five miles, reaching Crowder's Plantation four miles north of Ripley. The 2nd and 3rd Brigades stopped there in the 4:00 P.M. heat, while General Sturgis, intent on catching up with Grierson, pushed ahead toward Ripley with Wilkin's 1st Brigade, the temperature so stifling that more rain would have seemed like a blessing. During the march, Grierson's advance cavalry encountered a small party of CS Colonel Edmund W. Rucker's horse soldiers and drove them south, through the town of Ripley and down the road toward New Albany. In support of his advanced cavalry, Grierson pushed forward mounted units from Colonel Winslow's 2nd Brigade and Colonel Waring's 1st Brigade. A full brigade of Confederate cavalrymen lay in wait for them four miles south of Ripley. A two-hour skirmish erupted, one that did not end until nightfall. Casualties were light, four for the Union and twenty-one for the Confederates,[217] but the fight marked the first bloodshed incurred by the expedition. The fact that the Rebel skirmishers numbered so few may have convinced Sturgis that the enemy was scattered and distant from Ripley on June 7. But he was mistaken. General Forrest, with his force of 2,000, was in Baldwyn, just 31 miles away.

Wednesday, June 8, 1864

Back at Crowder's Plantation, the 2nd and 3rd Brigades broke camp in the pre-dawn cool and reached Ripley shortly after sunrise, reuniting with Colonel Wilkin's 1st Brigade, General Grierson, and General Sturgis. By this point, Sturgis was deeply concerned about his army's readiness to fight. The march had been delayed day after day by the tormenting rains, the artillery and wagons all but immobilized axle-deep in mud. The livestock had been weakened by the lack of decent forage, and some had gone completely lame. Four hundred soldiers were deathly ill, and there was no reason to believe that Forrest was anywhere around. The vexing problems so concerned Sturgis that he considered heading back to Memphis.

Meeting with his officers, Sturgis reviewed the dismal situation, discussing the option of turning back. If they continued south and tore up the rails at Guntown, they might successfully attract Forrest. If not in Guntown, they would surely encounter Forrest in Tupelo. Either way, Forrest would most assuredly have much fresher horses, affording him the advantage. Sturgis opined that his weakened army could not defeat Forrest under those conditions. On the other hand, returning to Memphis empty-handed, as had happened back in early May, would leave Sherman's supply lines vulnerable to Forrest's attacks. Sturgis recognized that this would constitute his own political suicide. The expedition's mission was to attract, engage, and bring to an end Forrest's potential to interfere with Sherman's communications; there was no alternative but to move on. Ending the discussion, the commanders resolved that they would go as far as Tupelo, Mississippi, if need be, to tangle with Forrest.[218]

Fate's outcome had been sealed, forever altering the destinies of thousands of men—including Chatfield's. In the late afternoon of June 8, the tired and worn massive Union force worked its way out of Ripley. Deluged by another heavy rain on the narrow muddy road to Guntown, they stopped after four miles, where they camped for the night.[219]

Thursday, June 9, 1864
After seven days of marching, the expedition had consumed the stores of 41 wagons. Nearly 30 animals were sick, lame, or both, and badly nourished. The surgeons reported that at least four hundred sick soldiers showed no signs of getting any better. General Sturgis decided to send his problems back to Memphis.[220] Escorting the wagons and ailing animals, all ill soldiers moved north up the road toward Ripley in the early part of the day.* Soon after, the cavalry and infantry slogged their muddy way across the Hatchie River basin, ascending beyond it to camp by Stubb's Plantation "on a fine high ridge" about nine miles north of Brice's Cross Roads.[221] Having sighted no more Rebels, Chatfield may have concluded that Forrest was in Tupelo, staying clear of Union forces, as Forrest had done back in May.

Such was not the case. On the evening of June 9, Forrest had moved north from Baldwyn to Booneville, roughly 28 miles due east of Ripley. There he was joined by CS Colonel Rucker's brigade. At the same time, CS Colonel William A. Johnson's brigade reached Baldwyn twelve miles south, soon to unite with Forrest. Having received Rucker's report of Sturgis's exact position, Forrest issued orders to his 3,000 men and two artillery batteries to move out the following morning at 4:00 A.M.[222]

Friday, June 10, 1864
Upon waking well before dawn, Chatfield had no way of knowing that his next sleep would not come for 36 hours. He, and the rest of the boys in the 113th, spent the morning hours breaking camp at Stubb's Plantation—scraping boots, cleaning

---

*   If Chatfield still had his diary with him, this may have been his opportunity to send it back to Memphis.

weapons, rolling blankets and helping hitch the teams for the muddy march. General Grierson, with his cavalry, left camp at 5:30 A.M. and headed south toward Guntown. General Sturgis and Colonel McMillen were said to have downed stiff whiskey "eye-openers" that morning, possibly relieving hangovers left by the heavy flow of alcohol the night before.[223] Whatever their state of mind might have been, their military objective was clear: the expedition was to move southeast in the direction of Guntown and tear up the *Mobile and Ohio Railroad.*

Colonel McMillen, commander of the three infantry brigades, departed camp at 7:30 A.M. with a small infantry escort and a company of sturdy pioneers, Sturgis accompanying him. The two commanders rode five miles southeast before stopping at a low point crossed by the Hatchie River, a section of road so sludgy and degraded that it was all but impassable for the forthcoming wagons. The two commanders planned to wait there until the pioneers had properly repaired the road and the wagon train had arrived. It was 9:00 A.M. Neither officer was yet aware of the cavalry chase then underway some five miles beyond them. Meanwhile, back at Stubb's Plantation, waiting for the roads to dry, the three infantry brigades remained in camp until 10:00 A.M.—a delay that would prove to be exceedingly costly.

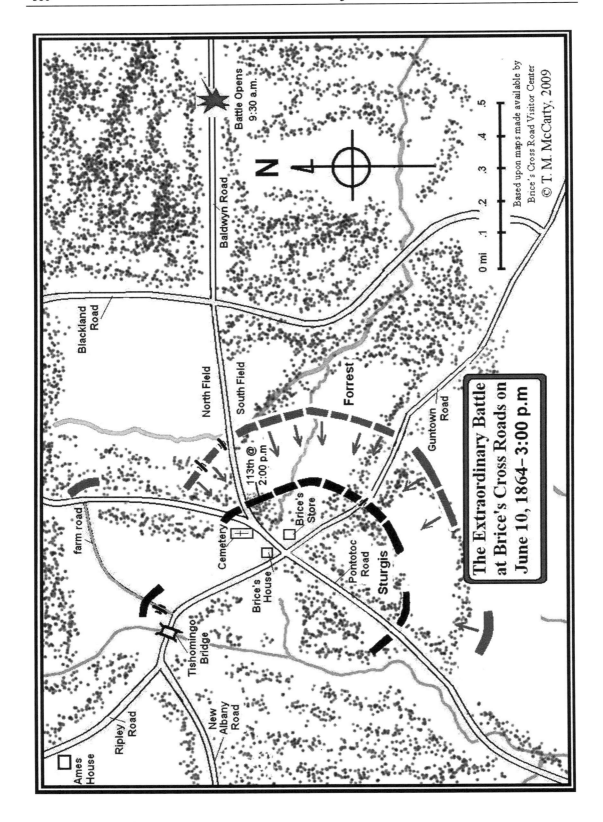

Battle Opens
9:30 a.m.

Baldwyn Road

N

0 mi .1 .2 .3 .4 .5

Based upon maps made available by
Brice's Cross Road Visitor Center

© T. M. McCarty, 2009

Blackland Road

North Field

South Field

Forrest

Guntown Road

113th @
2:00 p.m

Brice's Store

Cemetery

Pontotoc Road

Brice's House

Sturgis

farm road

The Extraordinary Battle
at Brice's Cross Roads on
June 10, 1864–3:00 p.m

Tishomingo Bridge

Ripley Road

New Albany Road

Ames House

CHAPTER 30: THE BATTLE AT BRICE'S CROSS ROADS

"… the "damn cavalry" is retreating, and Hoge's boys are needed immediately."

Forrest had planned out the day. He would rely on strategies not used by academy graduates like Sturgis and Grierson, executing a sequence of moves that would bring about the seasoned generals' undoing by day's end. He would intimidate them with bold and daring horse-mounted charges with riders firing repeating rifles and six-shot pistols. He would combine feints and flanking movements to either side and to the rear of enemy lines. He would call on his artillery to charge the enemy, fully unprotected, a tactic unheard of and not taught in the military academies. Forrest would gallop where needed, filling holes, driving the enemy back, a hand-picked escort of 100 with him. While firing his pistol at point blank range with his right hand, he would slash with his razor sharp saber—an ornamental weapon for Northerners—with his left. No textbook had advised these procedures, but Forrest hadn't bothered with "book learning." Experience had taught him that such methods worked, providing him with what he called the "bulge" (advantage) that put the "skeer" (scare) on his enemy.[224] Several hours before the battle, while riding with Colonel Rucker (who had skirmished with the 113th on June 6) Forrest summarized his plan.

Forrest's Plan for the Yankee Invaders

I know they [the Yankees] greatly out-number [us.] … but the road along which they will march is narrow and muddy, they will make slow progress. The country is densely wooded and the undergrowth so heavy that when we strike them they will not know how few men we have. Their cavalry will move out ahead of the infantry, and should reach the crossroads three hours in advance. We can whip their cavalry in that time. As soon as the fight opens they will send back to have the infantry hurried up. It is going to be as hot as hell, and coming on a run for five or six miles over such roads, their infantry will be so tired out we will ride right over them. I want everything to move up as fast as possible.—Nathan Bedford Forrest[225]

The action began at about 9:00 A.M. Colonel George Waring's 1st Brigade, the vanguard to Grierson's cavalry, sighted a Confederate patrol near the Tishomingo Creek Bridge and swiftly pursued it along the Guntown Road to where it crossed the road to Baldwyn, an intersection known as "Brice's Cross Roads"—so named because Mr. Brice's home and store stood there. The countryside in this part of Mississippi was essentially a forest cut by roads and patchworked with a few clearings.

Reaching the Cross Roads, the chase took a hard left, ascending the Baldwyn Road some 275 yards before curving right—due east—toward Baldwyn and continuing along a tree-flanked road for three-eighths of a mile. At that point, clearings opened on both sides of the road, a short 300-yard *south field*, on Waring's right, stretching east to the trees, and a *north field*, three times longer on his left, ending at Blackland Road. Waring, still on Baldwyn Road, charged for about half a mile beyond Blackland Road, trees again heavily flanking him on both sides. The Confederate patrol vanished into the woods on the south side of the road, where Forrest had just arrived.

When Waring's cavalry thundered to within pistol shot range, Forrest ordered his 7th Kentucky Mounted Infantry into a fearsome charge—one that brought Waring's cavalry to an immediate halt. The sights and sounds of the galloping horsemen racing toward him, shooting their rifles, waving their sabers, and screaming their piercing cries caused Waring to conclude that he faced a substantial force. Turning back, Waring retraced nearly the full length of the *north field* before setting his forward line behind a small stream about 250 yards from the far west end. Behind his front line, along the north-south stretch of trees, he positioned his main forces, the 7th Indiana Cavalry anchoring his right extreme on the south side of Baldwyn Road.

Grierson, arriving at the Cross Roads and noting Waring's location, directed Colonel Edward Winslow's 2nd Brigade to deploy on Waring's right, extending the line through the *south field* and terminating 300 yards south of Guntown Road. To Winslow's east, across the 300-yard-long *south field*, facing him from within the trees, stood three regiments of CS Brigadier General Hylan B. Lyon's cavalry ready to charge. Lyon, at that moment, had no support on either side of him, but he was aware that reinforcements were on their way. Until they arrived, Lyon had the job of persuading the Federals that a superior force was lurking behind the trees. Lyon made his startling charge at about 10:00 A.M.

Grierson had been warned that Forrest was extremely aggressive, but he had failed to grasp the full implication of that description. The sight of Lyon's mounted cavalry bursting through the trees with revolvers and rifles blazing resembled no bluff—at least not one that Grierson had ever witnessed before. The combination of Rebel cries, pounding hooves, cracking guns, agile riding, swinging sabers and savage maiming produced a scene of terror so stirring that it unnerved Grierson and convinced him that he faced a sizable force—one that included an infantry.[226]

Just as Forrest had predicted, Grierson sent a rider back to summon the Union infantry. Had Grierson rushed Lyon, as he could have done at that point, he may well have won the battle. But Grierson was a raider whose fame had come from destroying towns and tearing up rails; he wasn't a born fighter like Forrest. A full hour passed before Grierson's messenger found General Sturgis at the Hatchie River basin. Colonel McMillen joined Sturgis after the rider approached; both commanders were still overseeing the construction of a corduroy road through the knee-deep mud. In his hastily written note, Grierson had scribbled that he faced a force of about 600 Rebels, but his own position "...was a good one and he would hold it."[227] Grierson's note made it clear that he was in dire need of an infantry brigade to assist him. Alarmed, Sturgis ordered that the roadwork be sped up—he needed artillery and wagons rushed to the front. Turning to McMillen, Sturgis asked that a rider be sent back to summon the infantry. They must come on the run, despite the torturous sun already steaming the countryside. For Forrest, back at the battlefield at 11:00 A.M., everything was going exactly according to plan, and it was time to press Grierson to the limit.

Forrest ordered Lyon to make a second charge. This time, Grierson's cavalrymen, wizened by the first assault, held strong and thundered their 7-shot repeating rifles in deadly accuracy, repelling Lyon's furious advance. Meanwhile CS Colonel Rucker's units rode in and aligned themselves to the left of Lyon, doubling Forrest's size and completing his mile-long line through the trees to Guntown Road. It was high noon.

Although Grierson had stopped the charge, he was reeling from its unparalleled viciousness and sent another aide galloping back to plea again for reinforcements. He had 3,000 men but had concluded that he was outnumbered. Forrest had about 2,000 soldiers at that time but was rapidly growing. CS Colonel William Johnson's Alabama Brigade had arrived shortly after Rucker, extending Forrest's line across Baldwyn Road into the *north field*, facing Colonel Waring's 1st Brigade.

With Colonel Johnson's arrival, and the sun at its highpoint for the day, Forrest readied his troops to push the Federals off the field. It would be his most massive charge yet, a brutal attack that would continue for nearly an hour—one that would successfully force Colonel Waring's boys to withdraw, leaving a gap in the line that Colonel Hoge's infantry, then on its way, would have to fill.

The 113th Regiment, under command of Major Cephas Williams, was among the first infantry units to leave camp, departing Stubbs Plantation at 10:00 A.M. They were almost 9.5 miles northwest of Brice's Cross Roads, a name unknown to most of the soldiers that morning. Chatfield and the boys marched in Lieutenant Baird's Company "A"—the consolidation of Companies "A" and "B" and part of Hoge's 2nd Brigade. They knew that they faced a long hot march, and they assumed that it would take them closer to Guntown where the drudgery of marching might be interrupted by the adventure of tearing up some rails within a day or two.

Hoge's brigade was in the lead position that morning, Colonel Wilkin's 1st Brigade behind, followed by Colonel Bouton's 3rd Brigade with the supply wagons. The march was slow, the regimental and artillery wagons bogging deep in mud, so that the rate of progress was barely two miles per hour. By 1:00 P.M., when McMillen's rider reached Hoge, they were about 3½ miles above the Cross Roads. From that point forward, all notions of another mud-slogging day shifted to visions of combat and survival.

Informed that Grierson was "fighting and hotly pressed,"[228] Hoge ordered his infantrymen to move out on the double-quick, McMillen's escort setting the pace, one forcing Chatfield and his fellow soldiers into rhythmic strides. After the first mile, their mouths were forcefully venting, their tongues dry, and their lungs screaming. Due to their bodies' merciful chemistry, the second mile may have felt a bit easier. Even so, for some soldiers, the 22-minute run in the midday summer heat proved catastrophic. At least five boys in Chatfield's regiment staggered and fell out of ranks, and two reportedly died.[229] When the regiment approached Dry Creek[*], a mile from Brice's Cross Roads, Colonel Hoge signaled the pace rider to halt. Lieutenant Baird of Company "A" ordered the boys to fill their canteens, and then he fell to the ground overcome by the heat.[230] The beleaguered soldiers managed to fill their canteens, swallow some water, and soak their heads and bodies before Colonel Hoge ordered them to form up again and move out on a slightly more moderate pace.

Meanwhile, at the Cross Roads, General Sturgis had met up with General Grierson, but somehow Sturgis failed to understand how severe the situation had become. Forrest's massive charge had all but entirely disabled Grierson, exhausting his cavalrymen, depleting his ammunition, battering his lines, and sending Waring's 2nd Brigade fleeing across the Tishomingo Bridge. Sturgis had trouble understanding

---

[*]   Dry Creek may have been dry most of the time, but after so much rainfall, there was ample water for the boys' canteens.

how Grierson could have used up so much ammunition in the four hours that he had been fighting.[231] Only by facing Forrest himself would Sturgis grasp Grierson's reality.

Crossing the Tishomingo in the Final Mile

Hoge's boys double-timed over the ridge, past the Ames House, and down the hill. It was not quite 1:30 P.M. when Chatfield gained sight of the Tishomingo Bridge with scores of ambulances nearby and battle-weary Union cavalrymen milling about in disarray. At that moment Chatfield would have seen that he was rushing into something much larger than a mere skirmish. He could see that some of Waring's cavalrymen had been badly torn up—firm evidence that the enemy was far more powerful than an isolated detachment. This may have been the moment that Chatfield realized that he was about to fight the Rebel general he regarded as responsible for destroying Sooy Smith's cavalry, for brutalizing Fort Pillow, and for evading all Union efforts to subdue him thus far. He may have even reflected upon having once wished for this day—even though it might end up being the day he would die.

Approaching the bridge, Chatfield may have witnessed Colonel McMillen shouting Hoge forward, hearing him bellow that the fight had become desperate, "the 'damn cavalry' was retreating,"[232] and the infantry must plug a gap near the *north field*. Hoge quickened the already grueling pace and maintained it while crossing the heavily clogged bridge. Once beyond it, with shells bursting overhead, Hoge barked his men into a full run, propelling them through the Cross Roads and up to Baldwyn Road. The punishing run in the oppressive heat left only 70 percent of Hoge's brigade able to stand.[233] Chatfield was one of them. The moment that Chatfield had been anticipating had finally arrived.

Hoge placed the 113th at the far left of his line, anchoring the regiment to the south side of Baldwyn Road—about 30 yards east of the "Y" junction to Pontotoc Road where a roadside grove of trees afforded natural camouflage. Hoge's voice sounded like a trumpet as he hollered, "Come on boys, we have got them where we want them now."[234] Hoge fanned his remaining regiments across the field, south of the road: the 120th to the right of the 113th, followed by the 108th, the 95th, and the 81st at the far right—beside one of Winslow's cavalry regiments that was soon replaced by the 114th Illinois Infantry Regiment from Wilkin's 1st Brigade. All of Hoge's regiments, including the 113th, were firing away at the Rebels by 2:00 P.M.

The foliage allowed the 113th a degree of protection, the leaves, branches and vines obstructing precise enemy fire. Fallen trees and vine-tangled logs provided additional safety. The Alabama Cavalry, challenging from the north within the same shrouded cover, enjoyed the same benefits. Both sides blindly exchanged fire for 15 minutes before the Alabamians pulled back and readied themselves for their next charge.

At that point in time, Chatfield happened to notice the fallen body of a soldier a few yards away, his face buried in the leaves, his rifle suspended in the brush above him. It was Beach.[235]

Crawling to Beach's side, Chatfield saw no blood or other signs of injury, and the same was true when he rolled Beach over on his back. Beach was still breathing. Hoping for the best, Chatfield doused Beach's head and chest with water. Sputtering back to consciousness, Beach opened his eyes and saw his friend kneeling over him, saying, "Drink some water, Riley, we've got a battle to fight." Beach hadn't been shot. He had fainted from the heat and the heavy run. Within minutes, he was on his feet again with his gun readied for the next assault.[236]

An Extraordinary Military Event

The heavy firing eased up just enough by 4:00 P.M. to allow the boys to detect veiled movements and snapping branches in the groves on their north and east sides. Sensing another rush was on its way, the Union boys resumed rapid firing, their enemy obscured within the trees. One or two minutes later, amidst great confusion, someone yelled out to stop shooting.

> "You are firing on your own men." "But," says one of the boys, on the right, "they are Johnnys, I can see their gray jackets." Someone says, "They are prisoners our boys have captured and are marching to the rear." We soon found out. I got sight of them marching along a rail fence. Trail arms four ranks deep. Sooner than I can write it, bullets came from the front and right. We knew then that we were flanked, at that time. If the Rebs pushed their advantage they could have captured the whole regiment. — Private Riley Beach [237]

The boys of the 113th were stunned by the unexpected turn-of-events. They hadn't been firing on their own men—in truth, they were nearly surrounded by Rebel forces. Beach was only one of many who concluded that the entire 113th could have been easily captured at that moment.

Forrest had never attended an academy; it didn't matter to him that his procedures violated sanctioned rules for the use of weaponry. What mattered was that his paralyzing methods worked. The glaring muzzles of two 3-inch rifled Rodman cannon emerged from the trees, unprotected, facing the Union line from a distance of 60 yards. To the right of the Rodmans, the soot-blackened barrels of two Rebel 6-pounders and four 12-pounders rolled forward on Baldwyn Road, their angles of fire set horizontally.[238] It all had happened too suddenly to allow for careful scrutiny. The sight of the Rebel troops and blazing guns pressing forward proved overwhelming when, in an unprecedented tactic, Forrest ordered his artillerymen to charge their unprotected cannon on Hoge's line. Four of the Rebel guns had been double-shotted with canister* when fired.[239]

The cataclysmic close-range volley dissolved the left side of the 113th—the boys scattering in retreat across the Pontotoc-Baldwyn junction, trumpets sounding. Beach and Chatfield repositioned themselves in a small ravine just north of the cemetery. It was probably little more than a ditch, but it was deep enough to duck the bullets. From there, they managed to fire away at successive waves of charging Rebels, each successive rush announced by a fearsome and distinct yell—a blend of whooping Indians and howling wolves.[240] Prone to the ground, the overwrought warriors waited for the sight of pumping Rebel kneecaps, then fired. Some of the Rebels would drop; others would fall back. After the fourth charge, the junction was awash with blood and littered with dead and moaning soldiers from both sides.[241] But the Rebels were not about to relinquish their "bulge," regrouping once more for their next onslaught. Expecting the worst, Chatfield, Beach, and others from Hoge's once-proud line fell back again—this time, to the cemetery where the battle could not have seemed more macabre.[242]

Battle in the Cross Roads Cemetery

Death's markers became life's protection. Bullets whizzed and buzzed, splintering the rail fences and sparking chips from tombstones—soldiers pressing the ground behind obelisks of marble, slate, and granite. Beach's rifle grew so hot and soot-fouled that it would no longer accept a cartridge—his forceful tamping failing to ram one down. Desperate, Beach thrust his ramrod into a tree, chest high, but the cartridge, as if welded inside, withstood the blow and transferred the force to the tree's piney trunk, leaving Beach with no gun and a tree holding one by the barrel.[243]

It was about 4:15 P.M., and the Rebels were firing from the woods directly across Pontotoc Road, while Forrest, with his escort, was pushing toward the Cross Roads from the south. Beach quickly found a gun that had been dropped by a fallen comrade, but like the other defenders in the graveyard, his supply of ammunition was running low. Sheltered behind tombstones, the graveyard force survived the next rush. When that blitz finally ceased, the boys knew that they could not survive another attack.

> Finally, only the road was between us. The right had melted away, so they massed their troops on our left. This could not long continue, so confusion—worse confounded—reigned.... The near-wheel horse on a caisson had been shot in the hip. When the bugle sounded

---

*   To "double shot" a cannon, artillerymen forced two shells down the muzzle, instead of one. Canister shells, cylinders of thin sheet iron packed with smaller shot, would disintegrate when fired, hurling the deadly fragments outward like buckshot.

retreat, the horse fell and the caisson turned over. The other horses were cut loose and mounted by the fleeing soldiers. It was now about 4:30 P.M. All organization was demoralized; hardly 5 men of the company were together. — Private Riley Beach[244]

The overturned caisson had blocked the Tishomingo Bridge, the fleeing soldiers' only escape route, converting the bridge into a scene of stampeding chaos. Running for their lives, the infantrymen collided and fell, trampling over one another in desperate retreat—ramming and jamming themselves in competition for the narrow passage between the wagon and the bridge siding. With only one or two men able to slip through the passageway at a time, the pressured mass spread to either side of the bridge where panicked soldiers careened off the cliffs, their boots crushing the bones of others who had fallen in the river brush below. All the while, the Rebel cannon continued their relentless shelling.

Beyond the bridge, a semblance of order returned. Passing Bouton's 3rd Brigade of black infantrymen north of the bridge at about 5:00 P.M., Chatfield and his comrades fell into the long line of war-torn soldiers who would trudge their way back to Ripley throughout the night. Their retreat would not have been possible had it not been for the protection provided by Bouton's brigade of brave soldiers. Bouton's boys engaged in heavy skirmishing and hand-to-hand fighting that kept the pursuing Rebels from overtaking the disheveled column of Union soldiers, wagons, and ambulances that worked its way back to the muddy Hatchie River basin in the gloom of night.[245]

Yet the tragic losses for the Union had not ended. When the wagons and ambulances reached the Hatchie Bottom, nearly all of them became so thoroughly mired in axle-deep mud that they could roll no farther. Panic-stricken teamsters cut their horses loose and abandoned their wagons loaded with weapons, ammunition and rations. Ambulances laden with wounded and dying men were left behind, the incapacitated begging for water and succor from the soldiers slogging past. For the Union troops, the night of June 10 had deteriorated into a ghoulish nightmare.[246] But for Forrest and his men, it was a night of triumph—Forrest's finest moment in history. He wasn't about to let up. He would rest his boys after midnight only briefly and then resume his pursuit of the Federals.[247] The only sleep that Chatfield obtained on the night of June 10 was the sleep that might have come while still afoot.

An Unforgettable Saturday Morning, June 11
The greater portion of Sturgis's battle-weary and disheveled column had reached Ripley at close to 7:00 A.M., elements of the two cavalry and three infantry brigades fragmented and intermingled up and down the line—a happenstance blend of horsemen and foot soldiers, including scatterings from Colonel Hoge's 2nd Brigade.

Chatfield, upon arrival, probably searched around for his close friends—Bert Smith, Tom Carrow, John Fundy, John Blanchet, and Ed Landis. It's unknown if he ever found them, but the four companions he did find included Riley Beach, Wallace Beebe, Levi Walters and Calvin Maggee—all from his original company. They were exhausted, and their feet were badly blistered; their throats were parched, and their stomachs groaned hollow with hunger; yet all felt grateful that they had survived. Their sense of good fortune was short-lived, however. Forrest's troops were close behind—intent on more attacks.

Most of the Union forces' ammunition, heavy guns, and rations had been abandoned in the mud-mired road at the Hatchie Bottom. The best that Hoge could do was to give the appearance of protection. Those who still had guns would shoulder them. Aware that the enemy was close behind, Sturgis ordered his battered army out of Ripley at 7:30 A.M. Sturgis, McMillen, and Grierson would lead the beleaguered column along the La Grange and Ripley Road, a hilly, pine-shrouded route that would take them northwest in the direction of Salem. Hoge would march near the front of the procession of broken regiments and companies, the whereabouts of his regimental and company officers undetermined.

Forrest, having lived in the Ripley area for most of his life, took advantage of his familiarity with the local roads. He ordered his cavalry to pursue the retreating Federals using a bypass road farther south.[248] It didn't take long for Forrest's horse soldiers to catch up with Sturgis's column. At 8:30 A.M., the forward part of the Union column was three miles beyond Ripley when Colonel Hoge received word that the infantry at the rear of the column was under attack.

> At a distance of about three miles northwest of Ripley the enemy's cavalry flanked the infantry which were marching in the rear of the cavalry, except one regiment of cavalry which was acting as a rear guard. My command, such as had guns, formed for defense with fixed bayonets, but many of them were captured, owing to their exhausted condition and lack of ammunition; many to escape capture and to hasten their retreat toward the main column, abandoned their guns and cartridge-boxes. — Colonel George B. Hoge [249]

Pandemonium ensued at the rear of Sturgis's column. Union forces scattered in all directions as Forrest's cavalry advanced to flank the entire rear section of the retreating army, a blend of Hoge's, Wilkin's and Bouton's foot soldiers. Sturgis had no choice but to order his nearly defenseless army to continue its retreat toward Salem, with McMillan, Grierson, Hoge, Wilkin, Bouton, and the entire front section of the column evading the direct impact of Forrest's attack. The rear section of the column, including Chatfield and his companions, did not fare so well, however.

Although a handful of fleeing soldiers managed to escape, many were killed, and those remaining were quickly captured by Forrest's advancing troops. Beach recounted that fateful and unforgettable moment on the morning of June 11:

> About two miles this side of Ripley, at a sharp bend in the road, I heard the Rebel yell. I supposed it was some of our cavalry behind me, but I was soon undeceived. I was soon looking into the muzzles of several Reb guns with the unwelcome demand "Surrender." I dropped my gun, tore off my cartridge box, threw it with it. "You want me to go to the rear?" "I certainly do," was the reply. Forrest was a few rods behind the head of the column.
> — Private Riley Beach [250]

Surviving the attack and among the captured that day were all five friends: Riley V. Beach, Wallace W. Beebe, Calvin Maggee, Levi M. Walters and Edward L. Chatfield.

At this point, Forrest wasted no time. He spurred his way forward toward Salem, intending to form a roadblock. His large force included CS Colonel Tyree Bell's Tennessee Brigade, of CS Brigadier General Abraham Buford's division—the strength he would need to halt Sturgis. The rest of Buford's division would follow Sturgis's column along the Ridge Road, trapping them from behind. If all went according to plan—and it had up until that point—Sturgis's entire army would be captured before the day's end.

Yet fate would determine otherwise. Had Forrest's horse not stumbled and fallen, pitching Forrest hard to the ground and knocking him unconscious, history may have recorded that only a small handful of Sturgis's army had survived the battle of Brice's Cross Roads. But the fateful fall, which temporarily disabled Forrest, allowed Sturgis's defeated army to pass unobstructed through Salem and struggle back to Collierville, Buford pushing them hard from the rear for much of the distance.

Beach later described that even after the attack was over, the scene following their capture continued to be a sordid one. Black soldiers were systematically targeted, the roads strewn with their bodies in a horrifying carnage.[251] Beach wrote of having watched a Rebel soldier remove three black soldiers from the march and guide them into the timber, and after that, he "...never saw them again."[252] Although he never witnessed the shooting himself, he said that his "...messmate saw the Rebs call six Negroes just out of the road, put their revolvers to their heads and shoot them."[253] Beach seemed convinced that many of the captured blacks were outright murdered.

Beach later wrote that 85 boys in the 113th had been captured that day.[254] Sergeant Dennison of Company "K" had placed the count at 87.[255] By either count, what is certain is that by the time that the captured soldiers reached the prison pen known as Andersonville, all of them were white.* Historian David Williams explains:

> ...Rebel commanders usually wanted their men to kill as many black troops as possible, at times including those who could have been taken prisoner. Despite the government's official policy that captured blacks were to be enslaved, the unofficial policy of many Confederate officers was that blacks in uniform should be shot on sight—even those trying to surrender.[256]

The battle of Brice's Cross Roads had ended, and the accounting of losses (killed, wounded and missing) told the tale well. General Forrest, with a force of 3,500, had soundly defeated General Sturgis, commanding 8,100, over twice the size. Forrest lost 493 men, 14 percent of his command. Sturgis lost 2,612 men, over 32 percent of his force.[257] According to Forrest's records, Sturgis had also lost: [258]

- 161 horses and 23 mules
- 168 six-horse wagons, 7 four-horse wagons, 1 two-horse wagon, 16 ambulances
- 16 of his 18 cannon, 28 limbers, 15 caissons, and hundreds of rounds of artillery ammunition
- 1,500 stands of small-arms and 300,000 rounds of small-arm ammunition
- Hundreds of accoutrements and multiple sets of artillery harnesses.

The follow-up investigation of the disaster filled 73 pages of the *Official Records*† but arrived at no conclusive findings. Even so, Sturgis would finish the war sitting idle, "awaiting orders."[259]

Although the Mississippi Expedition resulted in a solid Union defeat and Forrest had been neither killed nor captured, Sherman's larger purpose had been accomplished. Forrest had effectively been kept occupied in Northeast Mississippi, thereby protecting vital Union supply lines into Chattanooga. But the cost to the Union was great. The combination of illness and battle casualties left over 3,000 of Sturgis's 8,100 men dead. According to Colonel Hoge, of the 293 men in the 113th that marched out of Memphis on June 2, 106 were missing as of June 14—a full 36 percent of the regiment.[260] Of those, 85-87 would end up in Andersonville Prison, and one was Edward L. Chatfield.[261]

---

* Volunteer Civil War historian, Kevin Frye, notes on his website, however, that 22 Andersonville graves bear the initials "U.S.C.T." identifying "United States Colored Troops," all having been captured elsewhere, primarily at the February 20, 1864, battle of Olustee, Florida.
See: www.angelfire.com/ga2/Andersonvilleprison

† *The War of the Rebellion: a Compilation of the Official Records of the Union and Confederate Armies.* See bibliography.

CHAPTER 31: THE EXPEDITION TO HELL

"Although searched, Chatfield still had a tangible asset in his pocket."

Prisoner Intake

Chatfield may have thought about escape, but he would have been too "used up" (as he was apt to say) to try it. He had been on his feet for the past 30 hours: running and fighting all day on June 10 in the relentless heat, completing a grueling, battle-driven 23-mile overnight retreat back to Ripley, then marching nearly three miles north of Ripley (where the skirmish and his capture occurred) and finally, marching back to the city as a prisoner. Even if he could have somehow summoned the strength to run, Chatfield had guarded prisoners himself and knew the risk was too high. His best chances for survival would come by doing what his captors told him to do.

The guards marched the prisoners to the Ripley Courthouse, a noble place made filthy by war.[262] A Union surgeon, himself a prisoner, toiled in the center room on the first floor, no ambient odor of chloroform detectable as pitiful shrieks and moans echoed through the corridors from the nearby jury room. Six lean, grim-faced Confederate guards worked the line, their eyes tired and uniforms tattered. A coal-scraped line marked the halting point where the first guard stood, pistol in hand. Beyond him a marred but once handsome dining table had been pulled into place, two guards standing on the nearside, one armed with a pistol. Two more guards seated at the table glared disdainfully, paper and pens in front of them, and one more stood on the far side with a bayoneted Enfield in his hands. Chatfield would have been familiar with the intake process; it was about the same for both armies.

When it was Chatfield's turn, the first guard motioned him to move beyond the black line and stop where the next armed guard stood. Once there, the second guard directed Chatfield to empty his pockets on the table while the third guard briefly patted Chatfield down. The fourth guard, seated at the table, sorted the take, pushing back the hard tack but keeping the $2.50 in currency and coin that Chatfield had given up. The fifth guard recorded Chatfield's name, rank, regiment and company, and with a brief swing of his bayonet, the sixth guard gestured Chatfield out the back door, completing the intake process. Though Chatfield's money was gone when he exited the room, his gold-plated watch remained in his pocket, the third guard having somehow missed it.

Chatfield, Beach, Beebe, Maggee, and Walters slept outside with the other prisoners in a well-guarded field. Beach had been allowed to keep his rubber blanket, and he shared it with his four companions, whose blankets were either left behind or confiscated. There was no food provided for the prisoners that day. If the boys ate anything at all, it was the hard tack returned to them when they were searched at the courthouse.

Pain was the Sabbath's Sermon for June 12

Chatfield awoke from his first sleep in 40 hours, still captive. The nightmare was real. The Sabbath of June 12 hosted a discordant soldier choir beset with ill health, ripped tissues, fractured bones, torn muscles and savage hunger.[263] The early morning sun soon worked the air hot and sticky, adding to the misery. Rebel guards distributed buckets of water, but no food. The day's only blessing, an unexpected reminder of Southern civility, came when the Ripley ladies appeared at the sentry point carrying baskets filled with cornbread. Parceled out, there was not much for any one soldier, just a small wedge, but it was food—the first real food in 48 hours.

After simmering in the courthouse field for much of the day, the order came at 5:00 P.M. to fall out on the road. Above the courthouse, a welcomed wind gently stirred the Confederate banner, distant rumbles of thunder promising relief from the day's miserable heat. There was a train to catch in Guntown, 32 miles south of Ripley; a light rain might help ease the march. But as it turned out, it wasn't a light rain. Instead, a torrent ended their march within four miles of the courthouse. All were soaked by the night-long downpour, and no one slept.

The March to Guntown

The drenched prisoners resumed their arduous march at 8:00 A.M., despite their lack of sleep. It was Monday morning, June 13, and they had been given water but no food. The horrid sights, sounds and odors of the country's most savage war were inescapable: bodies of blue-uniformed black soldiers on the roadsides; moldering horse carcasses entangled in overturned wagons—harsh barking stray dogs and rustling turkey vultures picking over them; a heavy, gag-inducing stench of death interrupting every breath.

Sickened and demoralized by the devastation, the column of prisoners reached the Tishomingo Bridge at 4:00 P.M. More burnt wagons and corpses lay about, beset with vultures. Cannon, rendered useless by spiked touchholes, sat in disarray. Taking water from the creek, the procession continued south, through the crimson-stained Cross Roads, where a scramble of bodies dressed in blue and gray lay stacked on wagons awaiting burial.

The dismal march continued southeast another 6 miles before arriving in Guntown near sunset. Forrest's men sat about baking johnnycakes* in cast iron Dutch ovens. A Confederate private came around with a pencil and paper, again recording the prisoners' names, ranks, companies and regiments. Once done, rations of johnny-cakes were served all around, and the prisoners were herded into boxcars on the *Mobile and Charleston* at about 8:00 P.M.[264]

Meridian, Mississippi: Wise Prisoners Don't Complain

To keep the air sufferable, the boys moved the sick to the rear of the car for the 14-hour boxcar ride to Meridian—the railroad town torn up by Sherman in mid-February. The prisoner-train did not arrive in Meridian, 160 miles south of Guntown, until 10:00 A.M. on June 14.

Moving their captives off the cars, the guards herded their charges to a nearby vacant lot, securing them there by roping off the exits and posting sentries with warnings that if any Yankee touched the rope he would be shot. With their prisoners in place, the Rebel guards invited the Union boys to write home, explaining that their letters would be carried back to Vicksburg under a flag of truce.[265] Chatfield may have writ-ten a letter; it is likely that he would have if given the opportunity. But if he did write while in Meridian, the letter's whereabouts are unknown today. Beach later told how he wrote to a former messmate, although he did not specify the person's name. The recipient might have been Hank White, a soldier in Company "B" who had been known to have bunked with Beach—the person with whom Chatfield had twice traded watches. Significantly, the letter was received in Vicksburg and forwarded to Beach's father, informing him of the capture and the circumstances.[266] Beach's father, in turn, would have shared the important news with the other Kankakee parents. It is likely that by early July, Chatfield's family would have received word

---

*   Cornmeal flatbread had many regional names, recipes and cooking methods then and now, including: ashcake, battercake, corn cake, corn dodgers, cornpone, hoe cake, johnnycake, mush bread, and pone. The origin of the name, **johnnycake**, is in dispute. Some historians hold that the word is a corruption of **Shawnee cake** (made by the Shawnee Indians) **journey cake** (because of its resistance to spoiling and ease of preparation by travelers) and the Indian word for corn cake, **jonikin**.

that their son was still alive—but that he had been captured and imprisoned by the Confederates.

Poorly baked cornbread distributed at nightfall gave every prisoner diarrhea in less than four hours, severely impacting the morning of June 15. An altogether different event made the afternoon hours no less memorable. One of the guards patrolling the captives carried an old 1841 .58 caliber Mississippi percussion rifle, its barrel pointed off to one side as he strode about, his finger near the trigger—"not on it," he later claimed—when the gun went off. [267] An Ohio youth fell dead with a bullet deep in his chest.* Uncertain if the soldier had been an annoyance to the guard, the boys resolved to refrain from any complaining after that.

"Prisoner" was a disturbing title. As a group, the boys were expected to replace combativeness with resignation. To do otherwise would mean certain death from a guard's ready rifle. Yet, the choice to uphold the prisoner role was not an easy one; the immediate consequence of resignation was simply more pain.

Planning their Survival: The Ride to Selma

By Thursday morning, June 16, the boys were back on the train again, this time to Selma, Alabama, an eleven-hour ride that afforded them ample time to discuss prison survival. Wallace Beebe was the "old hand" of the group; this was the second time for him to make this trip. He had spent three months in Andersonville and had some conclusions about what it took to survive there. The ride to Selma may have been when the tall, blue-eyed, blond-haired Beebe offered his best advice on how to survive the infamous prison. His companions would have listened intently to the tips he likely shared that day:

- Without good blankets we'll die. We need blankets for shelter; the only shelter we'll have is what we carry in.
- We'd best camp in groups of four. That's all one blanket will cover. It's the "blanket rule." One of us needs to find another three boys to camp with. We should move about camp in groups of two or three and never leave the shebang† unmanned; otherwise we'll be stolen blind.
- We need plenty of matches and something to cook on; even an old shovel blade will do. We could use paper money if we can get some; it works in prison.
- We need to hide everything we don't wear; there are thieves every-where.

---

*   Both Beach and Dennison wrote of the event, but neither named the Ohio soldier.

†   Makeshift tent, lean-to, or hovel

- Only drink boiled water; the water from the *Branch*[*] is foul.
- We should camp as high above the *sinks*[†] as possible; the west side is better than the east when the wind blows to avoid the worst of the stench. The only way to survive is to get extra rations. We need to work together on this.
- Make friends with the guards; some can make good allies.

Of the 824 prisoners arriving at Selma on June 16,[268] most had been captured following the Union collapse at Brice's Cross Roads. Post-battle tallies revealed that 1,623 soldiers had been taken in all.[269] Upon unloading their captives from the train that Thursday evening, the guards immediately marched them at gunpoint to the gangplank of a waiting steamer that would carry them up the Alabama River to Montgomery, Alabama. There was no opportunity to escape.

The Riverboat to Montgomery

The only food aboard the old steamer was parched corn, hard kernels that had to be sucked to make soft.[270] This was a slow riverboat that moved no faster than three miles per hour, a boat so sluggish that it would take 25 hours to reach Montgomery, Alabama, 75 miles away by water. When the old sternwheeler churned up to the dock on Friday evening, June 17, some of those aboard were too weak to step off. Chatfield and his four companions, although filthy, exhausted and sorely hungry, recognized the important work that they needed to accomplish. Chatfield remembered the watch that remained secure in his pocket. His challenge would be to make wise use of it before being shipped out again the following morning.

Chatfield does Business in Montgomery

Imagine the Montgomery guards' Saturday morning excitement when word circulated that so many prisoners had arrived from Northern Mississippi, nearly 250 miles away. Their hero, General Nathan Bedford Forrest, had prevailed. Who among the prison duty guards wouldn't want to hear the details of the battle? How did the battle start? Which units fought? Did the CSA lose many men? What is the condition of Memphis, Corinth, and Vicksburg? What are the values of gold, Union "greenbacks" and Confederate "bluebacks" in those cities?

Chatfield awoke Saturday morning with a plan to take full advantage of the guards' curiosity. Following Beebe's advice, he knew that he had to find a way to trade off the gold-plated watch that he held in his pocket. Chatfield recognized that although the watch had initially cost only $15.00, he would need to parlay it into something worth much more—his survival. He had some important trading to do and less

---

[*]   The soldiers' name for the small stream passing through the Andersonville stockade
[†]   The soldiers' name for the privy area located where the *Branch* passed under the east prison wall

than two hours to get it done before the next ride would carry him to Columbus, Georgia and Andersonville beyond.

The trade began with a conversation, and this particular conversation began with a question. Hoping for a friendly dialogue, Chatfield selected one of the guards who showed the right countenance; then he waited to be questioned about the battle. When the inevitable happened, Chatfield presented the news as best as he could, including what went wrong: the heat, the long run to the battlefield, the confusion and apparent lack of leadership. He may have even faulted his commanders for drinking so heavily the night before. At some point he branched over to a discussion on the conditions in Montgomery, the war's impact on the South, and the scarcity of food. When he sensed the guard's good will, he may have taken a deep breath before offering to trade his watch for paper currency. "After all," Chatfield may have explained, "I won't be needing such a fine watch in prison; it's worth a lot of money, well over $200.00 Confederate.[*] I could use the money more, now. I need blankets; without them I could end up dead." It was a big risk—the guard could have decided to confiscate the watch by force—but the risk of dying as a prisoner was real, and the guard knew it. Fortunately for Chatfield that morning, the guard elected to bargain and trade; in exchange for the watch, he handed Chatfield $80.00 in Confederate money and allowed him to purchase two woolen blankets and two loaves of bread from the local street vendors.[271] Minutes later, the prisoners were herded to the train.

The 82-mile ride from Montgomery, Alabama, to Columbus, Georgia, normally would have taken eight hours, but heavy rains slowed the train measurably, and the boys didn't reach Columbus until sunset.[272] No one was comfortable in the boxcars that day, but all five boys from Company "B" celebrated their small but significant victory. Calvin Maggee had a blanket and arranged to share it with three boys from another company. Chatfield, Walters, Beebe and Beach had some food, two woolen blankets, and Beach's haversack and rubber blanket. The rubber blanket would prove especially necessary. By the time the prisoners disembarked, the sky had turned black, and the wind was howling.[273]

Columbus to Andersonville on Sunday, June 19, 1864
Sheltering themselves from the rain on the bare, sandy ground, Chatfield, Beach, Beebe and Walters sandwiched themselves between the new woolen blankets, with Beach's rubber cover over the top and their legs protruding below the blankets from the shins down. For the next six hours, the heavy rain pelted down, thoroughly soaking but not flooding the porous ground. No one got much sleep, but all were dry to their knees; from the knees down, the boys were wet and numb.[274] Up at

---

[*]   By June 1864, it took 15 Confederate dollars to buy a dollar's worth of gold, making Chatfield's $15.00 watch worth about $225.00 Confederate. In financial terms, the guard ended up with the better deal.

3:00 A.M., and on the train at dawn, the final ride to prison began. This time the ride was on unfenced flatcars with guards poised to shoot if someone jumped—an easy shot from a slow train. It was while they were aboard the train that Beach acquired a new hat that would serve him in multiple ways for the long months of imprisonment that would follow.

> A Reb riding beside me pulled my hat off and dropped his on my head saying, "Trade hats." The hat I got was gray steeple-crowned, nearly one half inch thick. It served me for a pillow and was still good when I got to Annapolis. That Reb was woefully cheated, for those [Union] hats were shoddy. — Private Riley Beach[275]

The train moved no faster than a hardy walk, the captives enduring 12 hours of exposure in the Georgia summer rain. The end of the ride marked the beginning of their new lives as penned prisoners—and the putrid stench of Hell greeted them at the door.

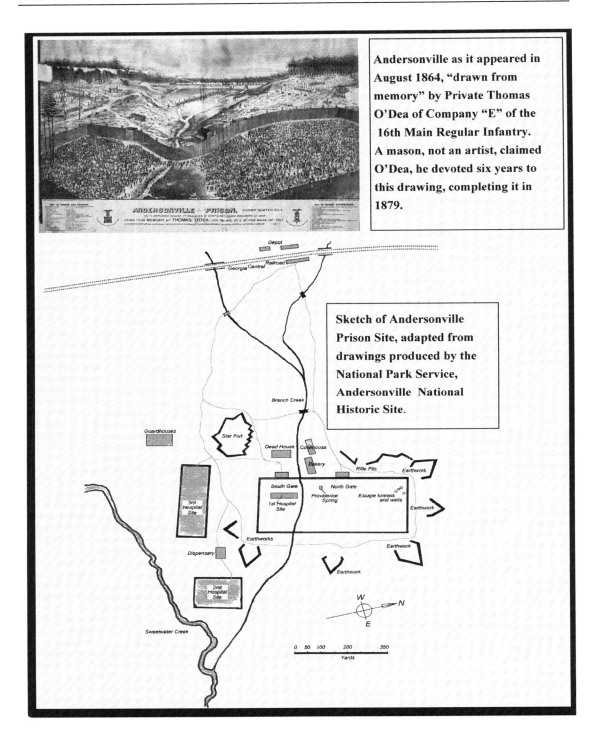

Andersonville as it appeared in August 1864, "drawn from memory" by Private Thomas O'Dea of Company "E" of the 16th Main Regular Infantry. A mason, not an artist, claimed O'Dea, he devoted six years to this drawing, completing it in 1879.

Sketch of Andersonville Prison Site, adapted from drawings produced by the National Park Service, Andersonville National Historic Site.

CHAPTER 32: ANDERSONVILLE

"… a smell worse than a hog pen."

The trainload of prisoners reached Andersonville on Sunday afternoon, June 19, 1864. A mix of unseasoned guards strode boldly toward the cars. All were shabbily clothed and water-drenched, their nostrils covered with cloth and their guns ready. Some were gray-haired, but most were baby-faced. A crackling voiced 15-year-old with his finger tight on the trigger greeted the captives, "This here's Andersonville, boys, your last stop." After conducting a quick platform count, the assembly of maladroit guards impatiently prodded the prisoners down a heavily trod path toward the rain-obscured stockade, a fortress capped by a thick layer of brown-tinged pitch pine smoke and a smell worse than a hog pen.

With the guards goading them from behind, Chatfield and his companions crossed the log bridge spanning Branch Creek* and trudged up a short slope before seeing the full configuration of the stockade for the first time. The daunting stockade offered little hope of escape, its acreage sealed by rough hewn pine timbers tightly spaced and too high to climb without ropes or ladders. From the crest of the small hill on the south side of the creek, Chatfield may have noticed that the east wall of the stockade contained two gates, and he may have wrongly concluded that he would be passing through the gate nearest to him on the south side of the creek. Instead, the guards marched the procession in the direction of the north gate, crossing the creek again and passing the cookhouse and bakery before finally halting. Only later would Chatfield learn that the north gate had been dedicated to ingress and the south gate to egress. He would also learn that the north gate was often referred to as the "gate of death."[276] Both gates made use of outer and inner gates with a small

---

*   It was so named because it was a *branch* that led to Sweetwater Creek.

382
The Chatfield Story: Civil War Letters and Diaries of
Private Edward L. Chatfield of the 113th Illinois Volunteers

containment area in between them—a system designed to prevent mass escape when the doors swung open. All people and equipment entering and exiting the prison were required to pass through two gates. If a wagon were to enter the prison at the north gate, it would pull up to the outer gate and wait for the sentry to open it. The wagon would then pass into the containment area. Once the outer gate was securely closed again, the inner gate would be unlatched and swung open, allowing the wagon to pass into the stockade—on the narrow road that the inmates called "Main Street" or "Broadway."[277] Chatfield and his friends were about to experience the procedure for the first time.

One of the escorting guards lifted the heavy timber latch barring the outer gate and with a grunt pushed the doors inward, revealing the containment area and the inner gate on the far side. It took several minutes for the new arrivals to crowd into the restrictive enclosure. Once inside, the outer gate was closed again, the sound of the heavy latch echoing its finality—leaving four walls towering on all sides. At that moment, the inner gate groaned open, exposing the gruesome panorama within the stockade itself. A crowded mass of humanity filled the landscape, forming a cinereous sea of gray. Men partially clad lay about within and around shebangs of all varieties, the din of voices and an odor of decay filling the air. Exiting the containment area, the grounds sloping downward toward the creek to his right, Chatfield beheld the spectacle in disbelief. The men before him, once brave soldiers, had been reduced to living skeletons, some walking around shirtless, their bodies and whatever rags they wore heavily stained gray-brown by pitch pine smoke. It was at that moment that Chatfield may have heard the sardonic cries announcing the arrival of new prisoners: "Fresh Fish!"[278]

Chatfield entered Andersonville on its 116th day of operation, the stockade having taken in its first prisoners on February 25.* Since that day, 2,214 men had died there.[279] On June 19 when Chatfield arrived, the prison population exceeded 23,000, and death was in the air. By sundown that day, another 49 prisoners would die. The hospital southeast of the prison was so overburdened with inmates that only those certain to die were admitted. The pattern was fairly predictable—at least one life would seep away every thirty minutes, around the clock. Andersonville had become a savage sump of sickness, elevating all conditions to the extreme: intestines evacuated by dysentery; legs rotted by gangrene and teeming with maggots; gums putrefied from scurvy, teeth falling out; faces pimpled by smallpox; and once nimble and strong bodies reduced to skeletons by lack of food. Beach later

---

* According to Andersonville's volunteer historian, Kevin Frye, "…a couple thousand names are missing from the rolls." The Andersonville POW database does not contain the names of Edward L. Chatfield, Riley V. Beach, and Calvin Maggee of Company B. The names of Ira A. Williams (Ira A. William) and Wallace W. "Beeby" (roster spelling) are in the database, entries that appear to correspond with the February 1864 imprisonment following their capture in July 1863. Beebe's second "tour" of Andersonville is not in the database.

wrote of a fellow prisoner who had no shoes and whose feet had blistered and had become infected. Lamenting that he had no kerosene, the man tried to use scalding water to kill the maggots infesting his feet.[280] There was no medicine available, and to many, death had become the final relief. Prisoners came to think of dying as "being exchanged"—God's merciful parole.[281] There could have been no greater place of suffering than Andersonville. Even so, there were five fewer prisoners in Andersonville than there should have been on June 19, a source of hope. Five boys had somehow managed to escape.[282]

The proper name for Andersonville was "Camp Sumter," built on land bordering Sumter County, Georgia. Both the construction and the operation of the prison were associated with three men from the Winder family: CS Brigadier General John H. Winder; his son, CS Captain W. Sidney Winder; and his nephew, CS Captain Richard B. Winder. The parole actions set forth in the *Dix-Hill* agreement had broken down, creating a need for large prisons; but the Winders hadn't anticipated the vast number of prisoners that would eventually be sent to Andersonville. Originally, the stockade contained only 16 acres, having been constructed for 10,000 prisoners. By the time Chatfield arrived, ten more acres of land outside the north wall of the prison had been cleared, and that area was in the process of being enclosed. Once done, the old north wall would be removed, expanding the stockade to a 1,620 by 779-foot rectangle, enclosing nearly 29 acres of land, 26 of them usable. Nonetheless, the prison proved to be far too small for its many inmates. Two acres had been given up to the Branch Creek and swamp. Another acre was lost to the land behind the *Dead Line,* marked by a short fence tracing the interior of the stockade at a distance of 22 feet from the towering walls. The land between the *Dead Line* and the walls was off limits for use. If a prisoner passed beyond the *Dead Line*, the guards in the stockade's 32 sentry boxes[283] had orders to shoot him. One Confederate official later described how he had notified General Winder "…that the prison was worked beyond its capacity, that it was a vast, unwieldy thing, and to send no more prisoners; but they kept coming."[284] Camp Sumter had become an overfilled prisoner dump site, a trough of filth, misery and despair.

The Branch Creek provided the only water in the stockade, yet it was unfit to drink. The creek drained from west to east, mired by a swamp thickly fouled by human excrement. The "cleanest" part of the creek was located at the *Dead Line* by the west wall, but even it—usually thick with grease from the bake-house outside the wall—was hardly clean. Nevertheless, other than the rain that the prisoners trapped in their blankets or tinware, there was nothing else to drink in Andersonville.

As Beebe had forewarned, there was no shelter inside the stockade. The prisoners had to devise their own makeshift lean-tos known as shebangs—blankets patched together with rag strips and suspended on sticks over pits dug by hand in the hard red Georgia clay. The shebangs would provide the prisoners' only protection against summer's heat and winter's cold.

Prisons weren't in the War Plans

When the war began, very little consideration was given to the need to construct prisons. Planners, both in the North and in the South, opined that the war would end within a matter of months. They argued that what few prisoners would be taken could be held in field camps for their return to the opponent by means of a prisoner-exchange agreement. The original *Dix-Hill Cartel*, agreed upon in February of 1862, required that all prisoners were to be released by means of exchange or parole within ten days of capture. Prisoners who could not be exchanged were to be released on parole with the understanding that they could not serve in the military until they had been officially "exchanged."

Major problems with the agreement developed during the summer of 1863, when the Union began using black soldiers to help fight the war. The Confederates refused to recognize blacks as prisoners of war and threatened to execute the Union officers commanding them.[285] The Union countered with retaliatory threats, suspending the exchange agreement. Prison camp populations swelled on both sides. The exchange system had been flawed from the very beginning; not only was it based upon an assumption of trust between combatant enemies, it assumed that exchange would work to the mutual advantage of both sides.

By mid-August 1864, General Grant had serious reservations about the system's advantages for the Union. Sherman would be launching his massive assault on Atlanta within two weeks, and Grant reasoned that the Confederates in Georgia had more to gain by the return of 33,000 of their soldiers than did the Union by the return of 33,000 of its own. Confederate appeals to exchange the Andersonville prisoners would have been difficult for Grant to refuse. Many of the soldiers imprisoned there had served under him, and his refusal to exchange them could easily be seen as an act of betrayal and abandonment. But Grant was convinced that the war would end sooner if he blocked the exchange. On August 18, 1864, despite pleas to exchange the prisoners at Andersonville, its horrid conditions well known, Grant resolutely refused.[286]

Andersonville's Construction, Operation and Management

In November of 1863, following the urging of General John Winder, CS Secretary of War James A. Seddon had authorized Winder's son, Captain Sidney Winder, to select a location near Americus or Fort Valley, Georgia, and to construct a prison that would hold up to 10,000 Union prisoners.[287] Boasting that he had absolute discretion in determining the appropriate location, Captain Winder selected land near the small community of Americus. He would oversee the building of the prison

in an area purposefully stripped bare of trees. The location, from the very beginning, offered only a meager amount of water—considerably less, in fact, than what
was available only three miles away.[288] According to Ambrose Spencer, a citizen of
Sumter County who resided near Americus, Captain Winder had described the
type of prison he planned to build.

> Between the 1st and 15th of December, 1863, I went up to Andersonville
> with him [Captain Winder] and four or five other gentlemen, out of
> curiosity to see how the prison was to be laid out. …. I asked him
> if he was going to erect barracks or shelter of any kind. He replied
> that he was not; that the damned Yankees who would be put in there
> would have no need of them. I asked him why he was cutting down
> all of the trees, and suggested that they would prove a shelter to the
> prisoners from the heat of the sun at least. He made this reply, or
> something similar to it: "That is just what I am going to do; I am going
> to build a pen here that will kill more damned Yankees than can be
> destroyed in the front." — Ambrose Spencer [289]

Spencer also had more than a passing experience with General Winder, the Captain's
father. General Winder commanded the Confederate prison system, including Camp
Sumter, when Chatfield arrived in mid-June 1864. After having met with the general
on "many" occasions, Spencer had arrived at the opinion that he was a "brutal
man …utterly devoid of all kindly feeling and sentiment."[290] Spencer was not alone
in his opinion.

> Brigadier General Winder who was long in charge of prisoners in
> Richmond, Virginia, had so many complaints by the southerners of
> his cruelty, the Reb government placed him in charge of all of the
> prisons in the South. I have seen him many times at Andersonville,
> Savannah and Millen, Georgia & Florence, South Carolina. He was
> noted for one thing: unrelenting cruelty. A Richmond paper (Reb, of
> course) says, "Thank God, we are at last rid of old Winder, but God
> pity the people to whom he is sent." — Private Riley Beach[291]

There were three separate commands at Andersonville:[292]

- **The officer commanding the prison,** Captain Henry Wirz, was
  described by Private Robert Sneden, from New York—among those
  longest held in Andersonville. Captain Wirz was "… the Rebel jailor
  and commandant of the prison. He wore an old slouch hat, his beard
  and hair were black, mixed with gray, and he had a villainous look of

authority."[293] General Winder assigned Wirz to this position in late March of 1864.

- **The officer commanding the post**, the Post Quartermaster, was Captain Richard B. Winder, assigned to the position by his uncle, General Winder, in late December of 1863. His initial task was to obtain the supplies that would help his cousin Sidney build the prison. He would later be in charge of camp supplies, the bakeshop, and other operations, including fuel and transportation. Richard Winder served as Post Quartermaster through early October of 1864.

- **The officer commanding the troops**, CS Lieutenant-Colonel Alexander W. Persons, had been with the 55th Georgia Volunteers before being assigned to this position by General Winder in mid-February of 1864. His duties were to direct troops stationed at the prison. According to Persons, the Winders worked "in concert" to aggravate the prisoners' plight. When Persons tried to improve prison conditions, General Winder took over his responsibilities.

While there I took steps to erect shelter for the prisoners inside the stockade.... Every time I could get a train, I would have that train loaded with lumber and brought through. During my stay, I had concentrated there, I suppose, about five or six train-loads of lumber. I suppose there were six, eight, or ten cars in a train. There were altogether about fifty carloads. I was in the act of erecting shelter, was just carrying the lumber, when I was relieved by General Winder. He arrived there about the same day I was relieved.[*] I went into the stockade several times after I was relieved from duty, and I saw no shelter there. I saw forty or fifty houses springing up outside of the grounds. The lumber disappeared in that way. — CS Colonel Alexander W. Persons [294]

James K. Davidson, of the 4th Iowa Cavalry and imprisoned in March of 1864, later testified, "I have heard Captain Wirz say that he was killing more damn Yankees there than Lee was at Richmond."[295] Horatio B. Terrell, of the 72nd Ohio Infantry, entered Andersonville on the same day as Chatfield. Terrell later testified, "I remember that he [Wirz] came into the stockade one day during the winter and one of the men showed him his rations of corn bread, and asked him politely if he could not give us a little more. Captain Wirz turned around, drew his pistol and said "G - d damn you, I will give you bullets for bread."[296]

Wirz was indeed hated by the prisoners, but according to Norton P. Chipman—the Judge Advocate who prosecuted Captain Henry Wirz in Military Court in July

---

*   Persons testified at the Wirz trial that he was relieved from his position "...about the last of May." (Chipman, *Tragedy of Andersonville*, 52)

of 1865—it was General John H. Winder who was the "moving spirit of evil."[297] Nevertheless, Wirz's vicious impact on the captive soldiers would never be forgotten. Indeed, 41 years later, on office stationery, Chatfield would sketch a caricature of Captain Wirz, rendering a detailed close-up of the commandant's wicked eye, a drawing that he stored behind the back cover page of his copy of N.P. Chipman's book, *The Tragedy of Andersonville*.

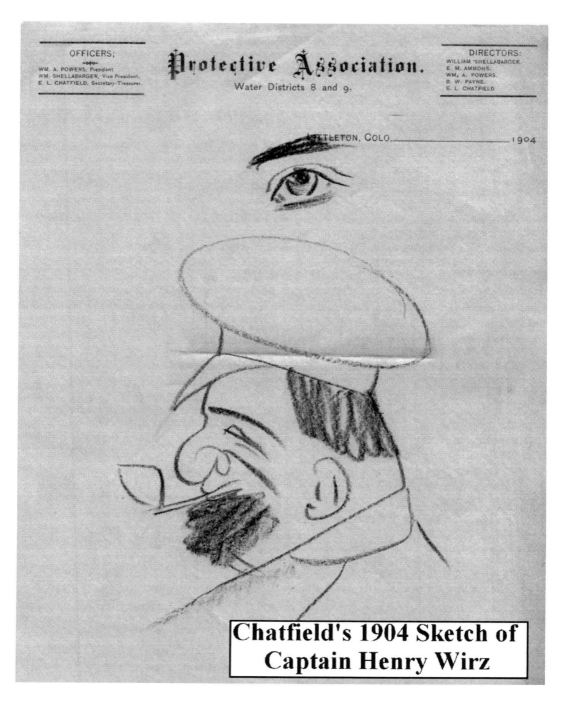

Chatfield's 1904 Sketch of Captain Henry Wirz

Ticketing

When a soldier became severely ill, onlookers would mutter that he would soon be "ticketed," the bearer of death's data card with his name, company, regiment and date of death written on it. Sixty to 100 new tickets were issued each day; in total, *12,912 men* were ticketed between February 25, 1864 and May 4, 1865.[298] Inmates tending the dead would tie the body's hands and feet together, place a ticket on the breast, and cart the corpse off to the dead house—a large hut built of pine boughs forming a screen. Bodies were placed in two rows with aisles between them, their feet next to the aisles.[299] Chatfield would have been one of many to help stack the dead on wagons for carting away to the dead house. Following this, the deceased were buried in mass graves without coffins.[300]

For the living, daily activity centered on life's basic necessities: shelter, water, food, protection from disease, and humor now and then for morale. Chatfield, Beach, Walters and Beebe maintained their shelter, an in-ground pit for four, using sticks to brace one of the blankets above them to shield them from the scorching sun and to capture the rain. Nearly every prisoner dwelled in something similar to theirs, and some did more than that—some continued to dig, hoping to find water; others dug toward the stockade walls, hoping to escape.

Prison Families

Most of the soldiers grouped themselves in "families," small groups like the one formed by Chatfield, Beach, Walters and Beebe. Striving for survival, "family" members watched out for one another, pooled their resources, tended their sick, shared stories and common memories, prayed together, helped spot vermin and tended wounds. The rubber and woolen blankets that Beach and Chatfield had brought in undoubtedly saved their lives. With some exceptions, all four in Chatfield's "family" had reasonably stable health, and when sickness developed, the foursome worked as a team in efforts to help each other. When Beach developed the bloody flux, the others tended to him, boiling the water he drank and softening the foods that he ate. When he came down with the mumps, they kept him still in the cool of their dug shelter and brought him his rations. When Chatfield suffered from a bout of "cholera morbus,"* Beach browned him some cornmeal and served him boiled coffee root. By the next day, Chatfield could whisper again.[301]

The Prison Marketplace

Marketplace activities emerged as a means for efficiently distributing goods and services. James Selman, a Southerner who worked in the prison, set up the first sutler's store.[302] His enterprise provided such items as soap, tobacco, candy and fresh vegetables for sale or trade to the prisoners. At least 200 inmate businesses quickly

---

* The broad term used during the 19th century naming non-epidemic, epidemic and other gastrointestinal diseases.

followed. Andersonville functioned like a small city and soon had its own "Market Street" that even included barbershops.[303] Not surprisingly, inmate-brewed beer became very popular. At almost any hour voices sang out, "Who will have a glass of beer? Good for the diarrhea and scurvy."[304] To create the brew, inmates mixed sorghum molasses and cornmeal in barrels filled with water. After a few days of sitting, it was ready to drink. If kept long enough, it smelled a little like whiskey.[305]

Chatfield and his companions tried their own hand at business. On one occasion, they bought 12 biscuits from another prisoner for $2.50 and tried to sell them for 25 cents each. They sold 10 of the biscuits, breaking even, but couldn't sell the final two. Their only profit was half of a biscuit each. When they somehow got hold of a shovel blade, they fried corn dodgers* on it and sold them to amass $6.00 before going broke again.[306]

Others tried their own businesses. Some sold chews of tobacco for brass buttons, which could later be sold to the Rebel guards for a good price. Others carried pails of water around, bartering for a spoonful of meal. The Andersonville market functioned according to the laws of supply and demand, and goods and services would range in price accordingly:

Beach's Summary of Market Prices in Andersonville[307]

Biscuits very small: 25 cents
Onions: 75 cents to $1.00 a piece
Potatoes: 15 cents, or 2 for 25 cents
Spider [skillet]: $6.00 to $10.00
Small apples: 5 cents a piece

4 quart pail: $4.00
Badly worn axe: $10.00
Eggs: 35 cents a piece
Tobacco: Large plug for $1.00

Not all of Andersonville's prisoners relied on the marketplace to meet their needs. A sizeable number found thuggery to be easier and more efficient. Since the prison guards did little to discourage them, it wasn't long before the bullies teamed up.

The Raiders

Like wolves in packs, the antisocial element prowled the stockade, robbing from the sick, beating those who resisted, and taking whatever they wanted: money, food, tobacco, blankets for warmth, pails for water and cooking, shovels for digging, and anything else of interest. This body of men became known as the "Raiders." By early June, shortly before Chatfield and his friends were captured, Andersonville's prisoners had organized a prison police force. Beach called it a "Vigilance Committee." The group soon became known as the "Regulators."[308]

---

*   Small round corn-cakes; a variety of johnnycake

The Regulators

On June 29, 10 days after Chatfield and the boys arrived, the Regulators rounded up the most ruthless Raiders, including six of the principal ringleaders.[309] On July 10, a formal trial was conducted inside the stockade with General Winder's approval. A prisoner court of 24 Union sergeants judged all six of the ringleaders guilty and sentenced them to death by a public hanging, which would take place the day after the trial. The court sentenced the remaining 119 gang members to lesser punishments. Eighty-six were forced to run through a gauntlet while being beaten by prisoners' swinging clubs; three were killed. Twelve of the 86 had been whipped 20 times each with the cat-o'-nine-tails* before being sent through the gauntlet. Fifteen of the convicted men were attached to 32-pound balls and ox chains and taken out to the stocks† for 30 days. Those remaining were bucked and gagged.[310] One of the jurymen, John McElroy, later became the Editor of the *National Tribune*, published in Washington D.C.[311] Having endured fourteen months of imprisonment in Andersonville, McElroy wrote a comprehensive, four-volume discourse on Andersonville and other Confederate prisons in 1879.[312]

The Hanging at Andersonville on July 11, 1864

The six ringleaders of the Raiders were to be hung, and Captain Henry Wirz, the prison commandant, supplied the gallows. After the condemned inmates were positioned, their necks in nooses, Father Peter Whelan, an Irish-born Catholic priest from Savannah, administered the *last rites*. Sergeant-Major Robert H. Kellogg, of the 16th Connecticut Volunteers, later gave his vivid account of the hanging that took place in Andersonville that day:

> As they were about mounting the scaffold, one of them broke from the men who were holding him, and ran through the crowd, across the swamp, to the opposite hill-side, as if by one desperate effort he would escape his fearful doom, that began to take on the semblance of reality. He was captured, however, and led back; and as he was securely placed with the other five, such *forlorn wretchedness*, such *miserable hopelessness*, was visible in his countenance as is impossible to describe. Opportunity was given them to speak, if they had any thing they wished to say. They said a few words, bidding their comrades take warning by their fate. One, mindful of his relatives in this last hour, wished a friend to call upon them in New York City, if he should live to get home. These words ended, meal-sacks were drawn over their heads, the fatal ropes were adjusted, and, as the drop fell, the rope around the neck of the leader of the gang broke,

---

*　This was a special form of whip, consisting of nine braided cords. Its strikes left marks resembling cat scratches

†　These were timber frames fitted with holes that bound the prisoners' ankles and wrists.

thus setting him free. He was at once taken up, had it re-adjusted, and was pushed off; the whole six were thus suddenly launched into the eternal world. — Sgt Robert H. Kellogg [313]

By prisoner request, all six of the Raiders were buried dishonorably in a separate part of the cemetery.[314] With the constant struggle for life, the high incidence of death, the market place, the prison police, prison trials, and hangings, one might be tempted to conclude that prison life provided more than enough excitement to vanquish boredom, but just the opposite was true. Andersonville was a place of unending monotony. To counter the prison's dismal pace of life, the soldiers relied on age-old remedies.

Prison Games, Gossip and Fights

Chuck-a-luck became one of the favorite games in Andersonville. Beach called the game, "Chuckle up."[315] Boards ran constantly throughout the prison. The gambling game was played with three dice, with nine betting positions marked out on make-shift boards (or on the bare ground when no boards could be obtained). When all bets were down, the dice were thrown. If one die showed the value bet, the player won even money. If two dice showed the number bet, the player won double his bet. There were two ways to win three times the bet: if the number bet appeared on all three dice or if the dice sum equaled the "field bet"—any of 16 dice sums from 3 to 18. If the player bet "under 11" or "over 10" and the sum came up in his favor, he would win even money. Bets not won would go to the house. Because some players would leave the games with more money than when they arrived, Chuck-a-luck sometimes proved to be a very useful pastime.

Gossip flourished in three varieties: within-group gossip, between-groups gossip, and gossip about what was going on outside the prison. The audience fed on the gossiper's prattle, thus assuring a steady supply. Inmates took turns as gossipers and audience, skillfully improvising when necessary. If there were no news to report, it was time to start a good rumor. When the prisoners tired of gossip, there were always the fist fights to stir things up a bit. Many fights erupted as a result of accusations, and the accusations usually resulted from false rumors. Each fight brought with it an audience, and after the fight ended, there was always more to gossip about.

A Soldier Gives Birth to a Baby

On July 14, W.J. Kerr, an Andersonville surgeon, reported to the *Sumter Republican* that a baby had been born within the stockade. The mother, Mrs. H. Hunt, was the wife of a prisoner. Dressed as a man, she concealed her identity and pregnancy until she actually gave birth. Once discovered, Mrs. Hunt and her baby were removed from the stockade and sheltered by a local family.[316]

Unbearable Crowding and Scarcity

On July 25, General Winder wrote CS Adjutant General Samuel Cooper in Richmond, informing him of the mounting need for food; 29,400 prisoners, 2,650 troops, and 500 laborers were present at the post, and there was barely anything to feed them. Worried that he might have a riot on his hands, Winder opined, "There is great danger in this state of things."[317] But Winder's request netted little more than a reply that there simply wasn't enough food to go around. Food problems in Andersonville steadily worsened after that.

The distribution of each day's meager ration had its own formality. Ninety men constituted a mess, and there were three messes to a detachment. Each 90-man mess was divided into several minor messes. The food was hauled into the prison on a wagon in a bare box and unloaded on the ground. A Union sergeant for the detachment would divide it into three piles and issue it to the sergeants of the three messes. The mess sergeants separated the food into individual rations. To prevent first-comers from having an unfair advantage, each soldier had to take his ration with his back turned.[318]

When Chatfield and his companions arrived in mid-June, the daily ration was usually no more than six ounces of corn bread or three ounces of meat. On the days that there was no bread or meat, the rations would be a taste of cow pea soup, some mush, and a little sorghum. In calories, the daily intake was barely 500. The only way to survive was to somehow obtain extra rations. Extra food could sometimes be purchased with money and sometimes secured by carrying out the dead. Food was an ever-present concern demanding considerable ingenuity. Some of the prisoners ate everything as soon as it was given to them, but Chatfield and his buddies made two meals of their rations—breakfast and supper.[319] Chatfield, who had weighed 156 pounds in late April, would have lost more than 20 pounds by mid-July. By August 1, Chatfield's weight would have dropped another 10 pounds—down to 126. The plight was much the same for everyone.

> When I attempted to arise from a sitting posture I would find myself dizzy and *blind* for a few moments, and I could attribute it to nothing but our exceedingly meagre diet. It was poor in *quantity* and miserable in *quality*. At this time we had but just wood enough to cook a little rice for breakfast, and we could have nothing more the remainder of the day. Let the intensity of our *cravings* be ever so great, there was no remedy. — Sergeant Robert H. Kellogg [320]

Despite CS Secretary of War Seddon's July 28 order that no more prisoners were to be sent to Andersonville, additional prisoners continued to come in.[321] And despite the fact that a dense forest surrounded the stockade, there wasn't enough wood to go around to fuel the fires that were necessary for cooking. A piece of wood the size of one small fence post would be divided among 60 men each day. A handful of splinters would sell for 25 cents. Rations came cooked one day and raw the next.[322] Given the desperate situation caused by the scarcity of food and other necessities, the prisoners talked incessantly of ways to escape, and they dreamed vividly of favorite meals, home, and hearth, while praying nightly to be rescued.

Buried Hopes

Rumors of impending rescue made their way through camp like common colds. Convinced that a Union raid was imminent, General Winder ordered the construction of earthwork fortifications and placed cannon above the prison to be fired into the stockade if an attack were to come, ensuring that no prisoner within would survive.[323] When the crushing news arrived on July 30 that two Union cavalrymen had unsuccessfully attempted to reach Andersonville, a sense of gloom permeated the prison. Part of Sherman's advancing forces, Major General George T. Stoneman and Colonel Edward M. McCook had advanced as close as Macon, 58 miles northeast of the prison, but the local militia, commanded by CS Major General Howell Cobb, confronted them there. McCook and his men managed to escape, but Stoneman and most of his men were captured and taken to Andersonville. Stoneman became the highest-ranking Union prisoner in the stockade.[324] By then, the prison population was just 322 shy of 32,000.[325]

The starving prisoners, their hopes of rescue thwarted, viewed escape as their only way out of Andersonville alive. But in many cases, it would be fellow prisoners, tempted by rewards of extra food, who would betray potential escapees who were attempting to tunnel their way out. Eighty-three escape tunnels were "discovered" by early August. Captain Wirz ordered the prisoners to fill in all of the tunnels, withholding rations until they had done so, thus burying the prisoners' hopes in red earth and pushing hunger beyond its previous limits.[326]

Summer Storm Followed by Spring

The morning of August 11 seemed just like any other summer morning in Georgia, reaching a temperature of 83 or so by 10:00 A.M., the usual large, dark, lumpy cloud masses billowing up in the southern skies. By 1:00 P.M., a menacing wall of clouds towered in the distance—a heavy summer rain was on its way. Captive soldiers, at least the ones marginally well, would have welcomed the storm, viewing its advent as an opportunity to bathe and collect drinking water. The sick would have dreaded the storm, knowing that they would soon suffer its fury, too weak to move or stand and helplessly vulnerable to the mud and filth that would cascade into their dugouts. The intense downpour began in the mid-afternoon, a deluge that quickly transformed the Branch Creek into a forceful river that soon undermined the section of the west wall that straddled the creek.[327] Within minutes, the earth supporting the mid-section of the west wall washed away, and the timbers fell, inviting escape. But flight was too risky—the gap was beyond the *Dead Line,* with nearby guards poised with ready muskets and the furious waters rushing far too swiftly to challenge.[328]

> The large timbers which had composed the stockade, came floating down the stream and as wood was an almost priceless treasure to the men, many of them plunged into the angry waters, at the risk of their lives, to secure, if possible, the much coveted article. Many were successful, but even then, after all their risk and their labor, they were not allowed to cut it up, under penalty of the whole camp losing their rations for five days. We could ill afford to dispense with our ordinary fare, if we thought of remaining in the terrestrial sphere, although that day it was nothing more than a few boiled beans cooked without salt, and full of dirt. — Sergeant Robert H. Kellogg[329]

The day after the storm, Friday, August 12, would always be remembered. A spring had erupted about 90 yards north of the creek on the west side of the prison. Never before had water been seen trickling from that location. The spring flowed clean and pure and provided what seemed to be an unlimited supply. When someone called it *Providence Spring,* the name stuck. Some of the soldiers said that lightning had released the water from beneath the earth, a miracle of nature. Others, including Riley Beach, believed that the spring came forth through Divine Intervention.[330]

Boston Corbett

Thomas P. "Boston" Corbett, the man who would shoot and kill John Wilkes Booth[*] within nine months, had been serving in the 16th New York Cavalry when captured by the Confederates. Corbett passed through Andersonville's gates shortly after Chatfield had arrived. According to Riley Beach, Corbett set up his lean-to close to where the spring eventually surfaced.[331] When the water bubbled up, Corbett—an evangelical Christian—was among the many who proclaimed the flow to have been God's Work. Prior to the war, Corbett had worked as a hatter in Boston, an occupation made hazardous by the use of mercury. The hat maker, like most young men, found himself distracted by the female gender; yet he believed that his attraction was inappropriate for a proper Christian. Finding that he could not wish away his sexual urges, Corbett eventually castrated himself with a pair of scissors. People claimed that Corbett was insane, blaming the poisonous metal of his early occupation.[†] Had Corbett not been so volatile a person, John Wilkes Booth might have remained alive long enough to face prosecution for assassinating the president.[332]

---

[*]   Lincoln's assassin

[†]   The association between the 19th century hat maker's exposure to mercury vapors and his subsequent behavioral changes led to the expression "mad as a hatter." The diagnosis of *mad hatter's disease* continues to be used in medical circles today.

Fatalities Spiral Upward

By August of 1864, the Confederacy was coming apart. The South was suffering a 300 percent inflation rate, wages were low, the cost of living was high, manpower was limited, and the Union blockade was taking its toll. Unscrupulous speculators preyed on Confederate soldiers' families. Food and medicine were scarce for everyone in the South.[333] Given this context, the soaring end-of-month tallies of Andersonville fatalities—nearly 3,000—probably came as no shock to the Confederate authorities. The conditions in Andersonville had become so torturous that the number of inmates who attempted to escape during the month climbed to 30. Ignoring the atrocious prison conditions, Captain Wirz blamed the increase in escape attempts on the ineptness of the guards.

> Of the thirty prisoners eleven escaped while on parole of honor not to escape as long as they would be employed to work outside. The balance of nineteen escaped, some on bribing the sentinel with greenbacks, some simply walking off from the guard while returning from the place where the tools are deposited at night that are used in the stockade in daytime. Perhaps twenty-five more escaped during the month, but were taken up by the dogs before the daily return was made out, and for that reason they are not on the list of escaped nor recaptured. That only four were recaptured is owing to the fact that the guard nor the officers of the guard reported a man escaped. The rolls-call in the morning showed the man missing, but he was too far gone to be tracked. As we have no general court-martial here all such offenses go unpunished, or nearly so. The worthlessness of the guard forces is on the increase day by day.—H. WIRZ, Captain, Commanding Prison[334]

Despite being well-informed of the tragic circumstances at Andersonville, the Federal leadership continued to decline Confederate offers to exchange Union troops. The Union leadership did pursue the release of the elite, however—men such as Daniel Gerhart of Miami County, Ohio, a 60-year-old wealthy businessman. Gerhart was taken into Confederate custody while attempting to visit his ailing son, who was a Union soldier imprisoned in Winchester, Virginia. The Union's practice of ignoring the plight of the majority of its imprisoned soldiers seemed deplorable to CS Agent of Exchange Judge Robert Ould:

OFFICIAL CORRESPONDENCE
James A. Seddon, Secretary of War
September 3, 1864

The Yankees have made several strenuous efforts to secure the release of this man [Daniel Gerhart.] He is represented as being a 'wealthy citizen of Ohio.' He and Richardson and Browne of the *Tribune* seem to be the only citizens for whom the enemy show any solicitude. I most earnestly recommend that Gerhart be held until the last Confederate non-combat is released from prison.

I suppose he can have his money.

RO. OULD [335]

Sherman's Threat to Andersonville

Following Sherman's September 2, 1864, capture of Atlanta, Andersonville was no longer secure. The thousands of Union captives amounted to a sizeable army. Every effort would have to be made to ensure that Sherman did not reach and release them. Accordingly, CS General Winder ordered that all healthy Andersonville prisoners be transferred to more remote prison sites. Posing no military threat to the Confederacy, the sick would be left behind. Prisoner optimism rekindled when the guards spread word that the inmates were being paroled as part of an exchange—an untruth fashioned to discourage escape. Trains began emptying Andersonville on September 5, a daunting task. Every arrival and departure ran the risk of derailing, the tracks in dire need of repair. On September 14, the feared mishap occurred some ten miles north of Andersonville, ending the lives of seven prisoners.[336] Several days passed before the tracks were made operable again.

Throughout the month of September, in the event that the prison might not be emptied before Sherman arrived, Winder tried to strengthen his fortress of misery. Outside the stockade walls, his commandeered slaves struggled to erect a second wall, a defense that quickly proved to have been unnecessary. By October, Winder had successfully removed 86% of the prisoners, reducing the inmate population from over 33,000 to fewer than 5,000.[337] The falsehood that the prisoners were to be exchanged played a big part in achieving the successful move.

A Mournful Death 823 Miles from Andersonville

A cruel irony took place during the time of optimism when Chatfield believed that he was going to be paroled and possibly returned to his family. Some time on Sunday, September 18, 1864, Chatfield's dearly loved brother, the witty and irreverent next-eldest son David, died. The cause of David's death at the age of 18 will probably remain unknown, as no records explaining the reason for his death can be found. It is likely that David died as a result of disease, possibly cholera or typhoid fever, both rampant at the time. His death probably occurred at home, leaving his parents and five younger siblings mourning. In Andersonville, Edward had no way of hearing about the death of his brother—and this may have been a blessing, his grief delayed until he was stronger. A full six months would pass before Edward would learn that the brother to whom he was closest was dead.*

---

* A boy named "David Chatfield" (likely a distant relative) enlisted in the Union Army on May 14, 1864. The enlistment occurred in Morris, Illinois, 40 miles west of Kankakee. That youth, David, had given his

The Long Awaited Exchange

By mid-September, the trains had hauled many prisoners away from Andersonville, but Chatfield and his companions remained. The decrease in the number of inmates had brought relief from the overcrowding and a modest increase in ration size.[338] Even so, the death rate remained high, the chilly autumn weather impacting the frail soldiers. With the night temperatures dipping into the 50's, the cold extinguished more lives.[339] Averaging 80 deaths per day, 561 captives died from September 19 through September 25.[340] With the promise of exchange as their incentive, Chatfield and his friends somehow managed the burden, each successive sunrise greeted as possibly *their day* for release. But the days continued to come and go. Having watched the prison population dwindle to 4,000 of the sickest men by the first of October, Chatfield and his buddies figured that their luck had run out.

And then it happened. On Sunday morning, October 2, 1864, a guard approached Chatfield's shebang and gave notice that he and his companions must be ready to depart by 10:00 A.M.[341] Whooping and hollering, the boys piled out of their hovel, hugged the guard, hugged one-another, and hugged the guard again, wide grins on their faces and tears on their cheeks. One hundred six days had passed since they had entered Andersonville, a nightmare they would never forget. After enduring the most deadly 15 weeks of Andersonville's sordid history, they were still breathing—and amazed that they were still alive.

Andersonville opened its gates for the first time on February 25, 1864, and closed them for the final time on May 4, 1865, having operated for a total of 436 days, during which its 12,912 deaths were recorded.[342] Chatfield and his friends, there for 106 days, were present while 8,091 of those deaths occurred—marking the interval from Sunday, June 19, 1864, through Sunday, October 2, 1864, as particularly lethal.[343] Chatfield would not have overlooked the remarkable coincidence of the morbid journey: he had marched into Hell on the Sabbath and marched out on the Sabbath as well.

---

age as 16 and his place of birth as Fleming, New York. He had black hair, black eyes, a dark complexion, and stood 5 feet 3 inches tall when he died of disease while at Fort Leavenworth, Kansas, on August 10, 1864. But unlike the 16-year-old David from Fleming, New York, David Avery Chatfield was two months short of 19 years old when he died on September 18, 1864. David Avery had light hair and complexion, was born in Ohio, and was buried at the Mound Grove Cemetery in Kankakee.

CHAPTER 33: A GAME OF PRISONER KEEP AWAY

"… Georgia's farms went untended, food was scarce, and Confederate money had become useless…"

The train pulled away from the Andersonville platform at noon, on its way north to Macon, Georgia, a seven-hour ride at eight miles per hour, again on flatcars. Macon was Georgia's transportation hub, the crossroads for 1,400 miles of track, the official arsenal of the Confederacy, and the site of Camp Oglethorpe—a prison camp for Union officers. Eighty-six miles southeast of Atlanta, Macon was a likely target for Sherman, and conditions there were harsh. Most of the city's white males were away to battle, with only the women, children, old men and slaves remaining to accomplish any hard labor. With the shortage of manpower and the threat of invasion, efforts were underway to conscript the community's slaves to help defend the city.

Sherman's Plans for Macon, Augusta and Milledgeville

Sherman had considered attacking Macon and Augusta, two major cities along the *Georgia Central* railway. But he soon realized that he could paralyze both locations by destroying their supply lines. Instead of attacking the two cities, he would make feints in their direction but slip in between, concentrating on the state capital, Milledgeville, where there was an abundance of corn and wheat. From there he would move on to Savannah.[344] But Sherman's assault on Milledgeville wouldn't take place until November 23—fifty-two days after Chatfield had left Andersonville. Meanwhile, Georgia's farms went untended, food was scarce, and Confederate money had become useless, replaced by bartering. Georgia newspapers told the story.

Macon Telegraph —

NOTICE TO THE CITIZENS OF TWIGGS COUNTY

Having received orders to impress one fourth of all the male slaves of the county, between the ages of 18 and 50 (whether able-bodied or not) for the completion of the fortifications around the city of Macon, you are hereby requested to meet me either at Bullard's Station on the 5th of October next, in the morning, or at Macon in the evening of that day, with your quotas. It is hoped that each one will be prompt, as I shall be obliged to impress your slaves if you do not come upon that day.

> L.A. Nash
> Enroller of slaves of Twiggs Co.
> Sep. 29, 1864 [345]

Albany Patriot —

TRADES OFFERED

Salt, Cotton Cards, Calico, 4-4 Sheeting, Osnaburgs and Cotton Yarns, in exchange for Country Produce.

We will give one pair of Whittemore Cotton Cards for 12½ bushels corn; one bushel Salt for 10 lbs bacon, 6 bushels corn for 2½ gallons good syrup; one bunch cotton yarn for 15 lbs bacon, 20 lbs lard for 9 bushels corn; one yd Osnaburgs or 4-4 Sheeting for 1¼ lbs bacon, 1¾ lbs lard for ¾ bushels corn; one yd Calico for 3 lbs bacon, 4 lbs lard, for 1¾ bushels corn; one pair ladies' gaiters for 3¼ lbs bacon, 44 lbs lard for 20 bushels corn; one lb good Tobacco for 1 bushel corn; 125 yds Osnaburgs for 1 bale good middling cotton of 500 lbs weight. [346]

Liberty Street Prison in Savannah

Macon was the end of the line for the train ride from Andersonville. From Macon, the *Georgia Central* line would carry the prisoners to Savannah in boxcars—the first sturdy shelter over their heads in four months.[347] Only the guards had to endure the outside weather, riding atop the cars on four-hour rotations. The distance from Macon to Savannah was a little over 160 miles, a twenty-hour ride. An ink black sky swallowed dusk's haze as the prisoners slept above the drumming clatter of rolling steel.

The train pulled into the Savannah Station in the late afternoon of the following day, Monday, October 3. Disembarking near the harbor, the boys expected that they were about to be shipped north on a boat and were greatly disappointed when they were told that they would have to wait another week or two until all of the details of the exchange could be arranged. Until then, their captors prevaricated, they would be held at the "prison pen" on Liberty Street, a short march from the train. In truth, the hastily converted facility would house the boys until the Camp Lawton stockade, above Millen, Georgia, could be completed—information the Confederate guards purposefully withheld. Savannah had been transformed into a prison town. Many other prisoners were being held there at Camp Davidson, the location of the U.S. Marine Hospital before the war. Union officers were imprisoned in a separate facility near the Savannah city jail. Altogether, the city held more than 10,000 prisoners. It was a drastic change for a city that had long been a prosperous port town, regarded as one of the most affluent and charming areas of the South. But for the boys, their new accommodations felt luxurious compared to the squalor of Andersonville. Savannah still had sufficient resources to provide superb rations, and the boys rejoiced that they had returned to "civilization." Beach wrote that one of the servings from a quarter of beef looked "as good as might be found on a fine ranch back home."[348] He described his new whereabouts as "the beautiful quaint old city of Savannah, Georgia, where some of the buildings were built when Georgia was a colony of Great Britain."[349]

As if a pattern had been set, the two-week stay in Savannah ended on a Sunday—in this case, October 16. Confederate guards spread the word that the agreements for exchange had been settled, and a train was on its way to carry the bluecoats north. The layover on Liberty Street had been relatively pleasant, but the boys were thrilled with the prospect of heading north—behind Union lines once and for all. Of course, none of this would materialize. The stockade at Camp Lawton had been completed, allowing Savannah to rid itself of the burden of quartering the prisoners, and beginning another round of "Prisoner Keep Away."

Millen's Camp Lawton

Anticipating that they would soon be home, Chatfield and the rest of the prisoners excitedly boarded the boxcars in the forenoon. The guards had informed them that they would be paroled in Charleston, South Carolina, by way of Augusta, Georgia—that being "the nearest and quickest route."[350] When the train began to slow after an 8-hour ride, the guards revealed that the train would stop for the night a few miles north of the small town of Millen, 85 miles northwest of Savannah. At that point, the boys began to suspect that something was going afoul. But all were hungry, and meals had been promised. Detraining reticently, the captives had no choice but to cooperate when the guards greeted them with bayonets fixed.

It was 6:00 P.M. and not yet dark as the scene turned nightmarishly familiar. Beyond the guards and visible from the tracks towered a stockade eerily similar to Andersonville's Camp Sumter. But it was even larger, over 1½ times the size, its very sight revealing to all that they had been betrayed. Viewing the stockade became the moment of common discovery for all of the prisoners that the assurances made back in Savannah, and at Andersonville before, had been outright lies designed to avoid an uprising. It was a staining moment, never to be forgotten—promises of exchange would never be trusted again.

Realizing that they had been duped, stifled rage replaced all vestiges of hope and joy. Adding insult to mounting despair, General Winder and his nephew, Captain Winder, incarnations of wickedness to the boys, stood at the gate as the prisoners passed through.[351] The very sight of those two men pummeled Sunday into a day of gloom.

The guards called the place "Millen." The official name was Camp Lawton, a 42.7-acre log stockade with plenty of wood, clean water, and no swamp. It was capable of holding 32,000 prisoners, and like Andersonville, it had ominous guard towers. Unlike Andersonville, a ditch separated the *Dead Line* from the walls.* Earthworks set in the hills above the stockade supported heavy cannon readied for attack. Although by first appearances, Camp Lawton looked like an improved version of Andersonville, Chatfield and the boys soon discovered that the conditions would be nearly as harsh:

> We had plenty of wood, but the rations were very deficient. A fellow caught an eel in the creek and sold it for a dollar. It was the only eel I ever saw. Axes were in demand, costing 25 cents per hour. A man in our mess had a half-worn axe. He said he paid $10.00 in greenbacks for it. We got some logs, rove some clap-boards, and built a shanty that was 10 feet wide, 18 feet long, 4 feet high at the eaves, and 6 feet high in the center. We called it the Big Shanty. In one respect, it was like Solomon's Temple. It had no nails in it. We had 12 in our mess here, lost two, one died while we were building the house. The other went out at 3:00 A.M., and we never saw him again. I looked the prison over thoroughly and found his hat at the gate where they carried out the dead. A number of mornings we would go down to the creek to get water and see one to three dead bodies covered with frost. Yams (sweet potatoes) were issued here, a great help to those afflicted with scurvy. — Private Riley Beach [352]

Finding themselves stuck, once again, in a Confederate prison, the captives expressed considerable discontent, much of it directed at the Rebels and some of it toward the ongoing Union policy that barred parole and exchange. With the Union elections only weeks away, the Confederates viewed the occasion as a rich source of potentially useful propaganda. If the prisoners were given the opportunity to vote in

---

*   The layout plan for Camp Lawton can be viewed in the *Official Records*, Series 2, Volume 7, p. 882.

the election, the Rebel bet was that they would endorse the Democratic candidate, George B. McClellan, over Lincoln. After all, the Confederates reasoned, Lincoln and Grant had been responsible for refusing to abide by the terms of the *Dix-Hill Cartel*. What's more, McClellan favored an easy peace and was the overwhelming favorite in the South. When the request came from the prisoners to hold a straw vote on Election Day, November 8, the prison authorities gave their wholehearted approval. But to their chagrin, the resulting tallies showed resounding support for President Lincoln.

> We held presidential elections in the prison. I sat and wrote Lincoln tickets for three hours during the day. Lincoln received 2 votes to one for McClellan. One or two men were crucified or tied to a board cross for illegal voting. — Private Riley Beach [353]

Elections were held at other Confederate prisons as well. Sergeant Major Robert H. Kellogg recounted what happened at the Florence prison in South Carolina.

> [The vote] was conducted fairly and quietly, but the result was not particularly gratifying to those who commenced it. I have not the exact figures, but I think the proportion was two and a half for Lincoln to one for McClellan. This was an expression of feeling and opinion among men who were ragged and half famishing with hunger, yet were not in favor of any peace gained by disgraceful compromise. In about a week after this, the result of the great contest at the North was known, and the rebels were blue indeed. Such a set of sour gloomy-looking fellows is rarely met with anywhere.... They knew with sorrow they could not yet lay their armor off, and that their favorite hobby of "independence from Yankee rule" was far from being realized. — Sergeant Robert H. Kellogg [354]

Almost all of the news in the South reeked of pending disaster. With the capture of Atlanta, the desertion rate for Confederate soldiers grew steadily, the commanders desperate for fighting men. Under pressure to convert as many Union prisoners as he could, Camp Lawton's prison commandant, Captain D.W. Vowles, did what he could to enlist willing "volunteers."

> They went around asking about our nationality....They counted us off into hundreds and sent us to the gate, where they offered release for enlisting as Rebs. When we got to the gate, the first two thousand were running back into the prison, preferring starvation and death to being traitors. Seems to me that that was patriotism put to a supreme test. Even so, the Rebs got a few. — Private Riley Beach [355]

Vowles actually signed up more than just a few. By November 8 he had "convinced" 349 of his 10,229 prisoners to switch their allegiance and fight for the South.[356] Most of the boys who signed had plans of their own, having witnessed the steady flow of Confederate deserters. Once out, given the opportunity, they would flee.

By mid-November, General Winder's Georgia prisons faced mounting problems. Among them, haunting stories of the sick and dying at Andersonville had reached the general public. Additionally, it was anyone's guess as to where General Sherman would head when he left Atlanta. The Georgia prisons would most certainly lie in his path at some point, and it wouldn't be long before he would reach Camp Lawton. To cope with both of these urgencies, General Winder elected to move the prisoners once again.[357] The sickest would leave first. That way, their deaths wouldn't become a part of the prison record.

Before long, "getting sick" became attractive to everyone. Summarily, prisoners having a little money in their pockets eagerly surrendered their cash to be judged ill. Captain Vowles was later accused of selling releases to healthy prisoners, substituting their names for the sick to be paroled.

> "thay took out the sick   ten hundred for exchange   thare was a great meney bought thaareself out for $5.00"—Sgt. James H. Dennison [358]

But there was insufficient evidence to prove the case. Even so, General Winder was said to have declared that Vowles "...should have no such command in the future."[359]

Flight from Camp Lawton

One week after the presidential election had been decided, Sherman set out from Atlanta on his "March to the Sea," having received lukewarm approval from General Grant back in September.[360] He would follow through with his plan to feint toward Augusta and Macon, tying up forces in both cities, while actually advancing between them to take Milledgeville.[361] The plan worked. Augusta and Macon braced themselves for attack, allowing Milledgeville to fall on November 24 with but minor fighting. Even before reaching Milledgeville, Sherman's threat to Camp Lawton was too great. On November 15, the trains began to remove the prisoners.

Again the pretext of an "exchange" was used, but no one believed the guards this time. Four prisoner divisions moved out Monday morning, November 21.[362] Chatfield and his buddies marched out early Tuesday morning, and by Friday, November 25, Camp Lawton had been emptied.[363] About 17 prisoners had died each day there, for a total of 700 during the prison's 41 days of operation.* Compared to Andersonville's death rate of 60 to 100 per day, Camp Lawton appeared to have been far less deadly. But the numbers failed to tell the true story of Camp Lawton, as most of the sick had been shipped away before they died. Camp Lawton, like Andersonville, was a malevolent place. Chatfield and his friends had been fortunate while there, their "Big Shanty" providing them with the shelter they needed to have fared marginally well. But there was no such structure to protect the boys at their next stop in Savannah, where the trains disgorged them once again on Tuesday, November 22.

> It was a cold day. At dusk we arrived at Savannah. They placed us on the ground, guarded of course. It was a tough time. We got wood about midnight, and it was a little better after that. Eight corpses were found the next morning, all chilled to death. We stayed in Savannah for three days this time, before being ordered to entrain again.
> — Private Riley Beach[364]

Winter's shadow gripped Savannah, northern winds freezing solid all standing water on Tuesday and Wednesday nights.[365] At this point, Savannah was no longer a place of plenty for the prisoners. Unlike those of their October visit to the historical city, the boys' rations on this second rendezvous were minimal—scanty servings of hard tack and molasses. While the prisoners shivered through Savannah's frigid nights, Sherman's army did the same 170 miles northwest, approaching Milledgeville on Tuesday and Wednesday. On Thursday, some of Sherman's officers would enjoy Thanksgiving Day's bounty in the governor's mansion, having taken the capitol of Georgia without a struggle.

Thanksgiving in Savannah, Thursday, November 24

No Southerners in Savannah honored Lincoln's Thanksgiving, but Chatfield and his companions may have tried, recalling year-old memories of the holiday's first celebration back in Corinth. Their only meal on this cold dismal day was a slice of cornbread brought to them by some kind women of the city. When word arrived again that the prisoners would be "exchanged" on Friday, no one believed that the story was anything more than a Confederate ruse to promote passivity.

To Charleston and then Florence, Friday, November 25

Black smoke belched from the funneled stack as the engine lugged its cargo out of Savannah, the boys imprisoned in boxcars with floors thick in manure. The train followed a half-circle route to Charleston, South Carolina, crossing pilings set in the swampy marshlands and skirting Port Royal and St. Helena Sounds. It was a 125-mile ride that did not end until Saturday morning. The cars came to a rest at

---

* The daily per capita death rate was 1.7 deaths per thousand, slightly lower than Andersonville's daily per capita death rate in June of 1864.

the Charleston Station, a masterpiece of red brick that had welcomed thousands of visitors to the majestic South prior to the war. A short walk from the station, a visitor could still view Fort Sumter to the southeast, a silent reminder of where the war had begun 43 months and so many lives ago. But Chatfield and the boys would never see the distant island. They remained locked in their fetid boxcars for three hours while the cars were switched and connected for the second part of the ride, one that would take them to South Carolina's Camp Florence, about 100 miles due north of Charleston, a location thought to be out of the reach of the advancing Union army.

History of Camp Florence
Due to the spread of smallpox and yellow fever in Charleston, South Carolina, five to six thousand sick prisoners were removed from the city in mid-September and sent to a vacant field outside of the yet-to-be completed Florence Stockade. Young, inexperienced boys—militia reserves unfit and untrained for military duty— attempted in vain to maintain order. Almost immediately upon arrival, close to 1,500 of the prisoners escaped, threatening the security of the nearby railroad city of Florence. In an effort to restore control, the commandant, Major Frederick F. Warley of the 2nd South Carolina Artillery, gathered up as many of the local townspeople and slaves as he could to rush the completion of the stockade. On September 18, when Chatfield was still suffering in Andersonville—also the day of his brother's death— Warley ordered the prisoners into the partially completed Florence prison. Two days later, his war wounds plaguing him, Warley resigned, and the command was passed on to Colonel George P. Harrison, Jr., of the 32nd Georgia Infantry. It was Harrison who was first confronted by the public criticism that soon flared in the South Carolina newspapers. A news correspondent had visited the prison and had described the horrors he observed there:

> *Sumter Watchman* — The camp we found full of what were once human beings, but who would scarcely now be recognized as such. In an old field, with no inclosure but the living wall of sentinels who guard them night and day, are several thousand filthy, diseased, famished men, with no hope of relief except by death. A few dirty rags stretched on poles give some of them a poor protection from the hot sun and heavy dews. All were in rags and barefoot and crawling with vermin. As we passed around the line of guards I saw one of them brought out from his miserable booth, by two of his companions, and laid upon the ground to die. He was nearly naked. His companions pulled his cap over his face and straightened out his limbs. Before they turned to leave him he was dead. A slight movement of the limbs and all was over. The captive was free! …. From the camp of the living we passed to the camp of the dead - the hospital; a transition which reminded me of Satan's soliloquy:

Which way I fly is hell; myself am hell;
And in the lowest deep, a lower deep,
Still threat'ning to devour me, opens wide.

A few tents, covered with pine tops, were crowded with the dying and the dead, in every stage of corruption. Some lay in prostrate helplessness; some had crowded under the shelter of the bushes; some were rubbing their skeleton limbs. Twenty or thirty of them die daily, most of these, as I was informed, of the scurvy. The corpses lay by the roadside waiting for the dead cart, their glassy eyes turned to heaven, the flies swarming in their mouths, their big toes tied together with a cotton string, and their skeleton arms folded on their breasts. You would hardly know them to be men, so sadly do hunger, disease, and wretchedness change "the human face divine." Presently came the carts. They were carried a little distance to trenches dug for the purpose, and tumbled in like so many dogs; a few pine tops were thrown upon the bodies, a few shovelsful of dirt, and then haste was made to open a new ditch for other victims. The burying party were Yankees, detailed for the work; an appointment which, as the sergeant told me, they consider as a favor, for they get a little more to eat, and enjoy fresh air.
Thus we saw, at one glance, the three great scourges of mankind—war, famine, and pestilence; and we turn from the spectacle sick at heart, as we remember that some of our loved ones may be undergoing a similar misery.

'Man's inhumanity to man makes countless millions mourn.'

Soon 8,000 more will be added to their number, and where the provisions are to come from to feed this multitude is a difficult problem. Five thousand pounds of bacon or 10,000 pounds of beef daily seems, in addition to more urgent drafts upon her, far beyond the ability of South Carolina.
The question is: Are we not doing serious injury to our cause in keeping these prisoners to divide with us our scanty rations? Would it not be better at once to release them on parole?
HOWARD [Correspondent, *Sumter Watchman*][366]

On October 12, 1864, Mrs. Sabina Dismukes, a citizen from Statesburg, Sumter County, South Carolina—56 miles southwest of Florence—forwarded the article to her president, Jefferson Davis, complaining:

In the name of all that is holy, is there nothing that can be done to relieve such dreadful suffering? If such things are allowed to continue they will most surely draw down some awful judgment upon our country. It is a most horrible national sin that cannot go unpunished. If we cannot give them food and shelter, for God's sake parole them and send them back to Yankee land, but don't starve the miserable creatures to death.[367]

If the threat of God's judgment had been acceptable, public scrutiny of such horrors was not. Even in matters of war, the appearance of civility was important. By October 23, President Davis had read the *Sumter Watchman* exposé.[368] Davis sent Mrs. Sabina Dismukes' letter back down the line to General John Winder, who at the time (November 14) had no responsibility whatsoever for the prisons in South Carolina.[369] After that, Mrs. Dismuke's message was trapped in bureaucratic shuffling. Her plea failed to reach the Florence commandant, Colonel George P. Harrison, Jr. of the 32nd Georgia Infantry before he was transferred back to his field unit. On November 21, General Winder was ordered to take command of all of the prisons and prisoners east of the Mississippi, thereby giving him the responsibility for the South Carolina prisons as well.[370]

The Camp Florence Stockade

The train arrived at the Florence Stockade on November 27—amazingly, another Sabbath. More than two months had passed since the first prisoners had been herded into the incomplete stockade back on September 18—coincidentally again, on a Sunday. Smaller than Camp Lawton, Florence was more like Andersonville in size, a rectangle measuring roughly 1,400 by 725 feet, with walls averaging 14 feet high—about 24 acres of cleared land in total, with six acres of swamp. The stream running through the center was cleaner than the one at Andersonville, but the flow was insufficient to provide for the 13,000 inmates. A shallow ditch with occasional railings marked the *Dead Line*. Like Andersonville, the stockade was barren of shelter, leaving the prisoners with no protection from the coming winter. Unlike Andersonville, the tree stumps had not been removed, providing a major source of firewood for the prisoners who had arrived in September, a fuel source that was quickly consumed. To discourage tunneling, a deep trench had been dug around the outside of the stockade, the dirt heaped against the outer walls forming an 11-foot-high earthen platform for the sentry guards to walk upon.

Colonel Harrison, still in command of the post when the boys arrived, was about to depart to resume his field command. Lieutenant Colonel John F. Iverson of the 5th Georgia served as the commandant of the prison and was also in charge of the guards, several officers assisting him. Lieutenant James B. Barrett, of the 5th Georgia, was one of Iverson's "inspectors" whose duties were to enforce prison regulations and oversee the daily counting of prisoners.[371] Barrett's enforcement duties paralleled those performed by Captain Wirz at Andersonville. In fact, most of the prisoners regarded Barrett as the de facto commandant, which he was not; he was merely an assistant to Commandant Iverson. Nevertheless, Barrett had a reputation worse than Wirz; he was well known for ordering undeserved punishments and issuing lengthy confinements for trivial offenses. Sergeant-Major Robert H. Kellogg who, like Chatfield, had been imprisoned in both Andersonville and Florence, later described Barrett:

> It seemed that a greater wretch never lived. Captain Wirz surpassed him in cruel inventions to enhance our misery, but he did not equal him in coarse brutality.—Sergeant-Major Robert H. Kellogg[372]

Fifty-three years later, Riley Beach vividly recalled a sampling of the lieutenant's brutality:

> Rations were very scant, a pint of meal a day, and never a bit of meat. There was much sickness, mostly malarial fever. Wood was very scanty, from a cord and a half for a thousand men. Some would ask the Reb lieutenant for a stick of wood. The lieutenant would tell him to go into the dead line. Then he would let some other fellow go in. Whoever licked the other would get a stick of wood. There would be several fights. Every time wood was issued. Generally each fellow got a stick. — Private Riley Beach[373]

Following the departure of Colonel Harrison, one of General Winder's first actions as the newly-appointed CS Commissary General of Prisoners was to promote Lieutenant Colonel John F. Iverson to the position of prison commander, responsible for all prison operations at Camp Florence.[374] Iverson assumed his top leadership responsibilities on December 6—nine days after Chatfield and the boys entered the gates. Lacking resources to do much about the sordid conditions at Camp Florence, General Winder shared his strategies with Iverson on how appearances could be improved. By moving out the sickest before they died, their deaths would not be counted, and the overall death rate would improve. Accordingly, Iverson made sure that successive groups of nearly dead prisoners were sent off under separate flags of truce.[375] For Chatfield and his friends, the odious conditions of prison life did not change. Clothing and other supplies, sent to the prison by Union sources, were undelivered, undistributed, or stolen. The winter nights were desperately cold and the food scant. And, as was the case at Millen's Camp Lawton, the imprisoned soldiers hoped that they would be deemed sick enough to be exchanged.

Monday, November 28 — this is a fine day — thay are sending the sick of [off] from hear for exchange — thare is ten thousand prisnors hear

Wednesday, December 7 — thay have commenced taking the sick out again for exchange — I feel dredful hungrey — rained

Thursday, December 8 — I was eximaned by the Dockter but did not pass [not sick enough for exchange] so I had to go back to my hut a gain and wait till sum other time

Wednesday, December 14 — thay have commenced taking out the sick   I was exemened but did not pas   thare was one hundred went out   it is warmer than it was —Sgt. James H. Dennison[376]

The sick prisoners who were sent out of Florence often carried letters with them—messages to the families of the soldiers remaining behind. Edward Glennon, a 23-year-old corporal from Company "F" of the 42nd Illinois infantry became one of the message carriers. Glennon and Chatfield had met at Andersonville and had become friends there. When Glennon was carried out of the Florence stockade in mid-December, he harbored a note written by Chatfield to his parents. Glennon survived his illness, and by early January, Chatfield's parents, in Kankakee, had read the missive of hope. Despite the dismal prison's conditions, their son was still alive.

In response to mounting public furor over the inhumane treatment of the Northern prisoners and aware that the war would soon end, General Winder wrote several requests calling for prison reform. On December 13, he wrote a report arguing strongly for more humane prisons to be built near Columbia, South Carolina, away from Sherman's path.[377] Skeptics might argue that his calls for reform were empty words designed solely for self protection from post-war recrimination. In any case, by that time it was far too late for Winder's suggestions to be taken seriously. And from the point of view of appearances, Colonel Iverson had the data he needed to demonstrate that the conditions at Florence had remarkably improved:

Saturday, December 17, 1864

Mrs. Dismukes may rest easy and quiet in reference to the treatment of prisoners at this prison, for since I assumed command (the 10th of October 1864)* the deaths have decreased from thirty-five to forty per day to one single demise, which my hospital and sexton's report shows for the last twenty-four hours. I call attention to the fact that the prisoners were all brought here from other prisons and solicit inquiry as to their improvement or still further degradation, and challenge any prison in the Confederacy, taking everything in

---

*   Iverson had been serving unofficially as prison commander before Harrison had actually departed; it wasn't until December 6 that Iverson received his official orders to assume the top duties.

consideration, for health, cleanliness, neat-looking prisoners, neat burial grounds, etc. They are given everything the Government issues to them. — JNO. F. Iverson, Lieutenant-Colonel, Commanding[378]

Despite Iverson's assertions, the harsh reality remained: the already miserable conditions of the Florence Stockade—and all of the southern prisons—steadily worsened. The prisoners' only hope was that Grant and Sherman would somehow free them, yet Grant stood his ground, insisting that a fair exchange for such a large number of prisoners would only extend the war. In December of 1864 when so many Union prisoners languished unparoled in Southern prisons, Grant nonetheless determined it a priority to address the 19 months of futile negotiations regarding the exchange of the two captured correspondents:

OFFICIAL CORRESPONDENCE
CITY POINT, VA. December 2, 1864
Major-General BUTLER:

I understand that Pollard, the Southern historian, is at Fortress Monroe, paroled and going about the wharf and elsewhere with freedom. The imprudence of many of our officers in telling all they know to every one makes this objectionable, particularly if he is to be exchanged. I would suggest close confinement for him until the time comes for exchanging. I would also suggest that if he is exchanged, Richardson and Browne, two correspondents that were captured running the Vicksburg blockade, be demanded for him.

U.S. GRANT, Lieutenant-General

HEADQUARTERS ARMY OF THE JAMES,
December 2, 1864 - 9.20 p. m.
Lieutenant-General GRANT:

I will attend to the matter of Mr. Pollard. I did not know that he was at large. He is not to be exchanged, unless Richardson and Browne are given up.

BENJ. F. BUTLER, Major-General.[379]

Sherman Reaches Camp Lawton

Rather than pursuing an exchange of the thousands of remaining prisoners, Grant's plan called for Sherman to attempt to free the Union men during his march through the Carolinas. When Sherman's forces arrived at Camp Lawton on Saturday, December 3, however, there were no prisoners left there to liberate. Brigadier General Judson Kilpatrick, of Sherman's Left Wing, found evidence of 650 dead in the shallow graves there.[380] Incensed, Kilpatrick had Camp Lawton burned to the ground, and Sherman ordered the destruction of Millen's rail depot and hotel.

Once done, Sherman moved his columns south, in the direction of Savannah.[381] After capturing Georgia's Fort McAllister on December 13, opening a supply line from the north, it was only a matter of time before Savannah would fall. Instead of attacking the city, defended by CS General William J. Hardee, Sherman demanded that it be surrendered, to avoid unnecessary bloodshed. Hardee refused. After Sherman had positioned himself to attack, Hardee's force slipped out of the city to South Carolina overnight on December 20, allowing the Union to occupy the city without a fight.[382] Savannah became Sherman's "Christmas gift" to President Lincoln.

Christmas and the New Year in the Florence Prison
Sunday, December 25, 1864 — One hundred ninety days had elapsed since the boys had been captured north of Ripley. On Christmas Day, Chatfield would have been difficult to recognize, his frame supporting barely 65% of the flesh once on it. He would have weighed about 100 pounds, his once proud body gnarled by the lack of food, the ravages of disease and the gnashing of the icy winter. Heavy rain fell the day after Christmas, flooding the stockade with freezing mudflows that collapsed shebangs and buried dugouts.[383]

Chatfield and the boys may have had a miserable Christmas, but the same was not true for the two correspondents who had been housed 125 miles north of Camp Florence in the wretched squalor of North Carolina's Salisbury prison. After 19 months of captivity, they had finally regained their freedom.

> **New York Times**
> ALBERT D. RICHARDSON, of the *New-York Tribune*, with Wm. E. Davis, correspondent of the *Cincinnati Gazette* and Clerk of the Ohio Senate, arrived here [Nashville, Tennessee] today. They escaped from the Rebel penitentiary at Salisbury N.C. on the night of December 18, in company with JANIUS H. BROWNE, also of the *New-York Tribune*.[384]

The miserably cold weather, the lack of shelter and firewood, and the scarcity of food served as instruments of death at the Florence Prison. Stream water froze nearly every night and would barely melt before the coming sunset. More than an inch of frigid rain fell each week, every downpour punctuating the prisoner's ongoing struggle for survival. Along with the cold and rain, hunger besieged the entire South, starving its prisoners, citizens, and soldiers—in that order. Having remained in Savannah until January 22, 1865, Sherman compounded the wretched conditions that the southeast coast faced, determined to wreak special vengeance on the leading agitator for secession, South Carolina.[385] What the war's toll had not consumed in nearly four years, Sherman would take or destroy, stripping the South bare from

Savannah through the Carolinas. During that cruel, desperate winter of 1864-1865, there simply was not enough food anywhere in the South.

By late January it was evident that Union General Winfield Scott's long-term *Anaconda Plan* was working, squeezing the life out of the South—including the lives of the very prisoners the South had taken.[386] Union forces controlled the Mississippi River; the overland rails had been cut, eliminating supply from the west; and all of the ports from Savannah south and west to Brownsville, Texas, had been successfully blockaded. Sherman's army had a firm and steady supply line, whereas the South was quickly running out of the resources it needed to maintain the fight. Colonel Iverson summarized the grim reality at the prisons:

> **HEADQUARTERS FLORENCE MILITARY PRISON,**
> Near Florence, S.C., January 26, 1865.
> Colonel H. FORNO, Inspector Prisons, South Carolina:
>   COLONEL: I have the honor to state that the post commissary is issuing the following rations to the prisoners at this prison: One pound of meal, one-third pound of peas, three pounds of salt per 100 rations per day. No soap, tobacco, or meat is issued, except one-half pound of beef per day to men who do duty as laborers on Government work. These rations are, in my judgment, totally insufficient for the sustenance of the prisoners, and I respectfully urge that, if possible, the rations be increased.
>   I am, very respectfully, your obedient servant,
>   JNO F. IVERSON,
>   Lieutenant - Colonel, Commanding.[387]

> **HEADQUARTERS FLORENCE MILITARY PRISON,**
> Near Florence, S.C., January 31, 1865.
> Captain W.S. WINDER, Assistant Adjutant-General:
>   CAPTAIN: I have the honor to state that the ration now being issued to the prisoners at this prison is totally insufficient for their sustenance, as large numbers are dying daily, and I am satisfied it is from not being properly fed. The post commissary informs me that he is not furnished with sufficient stores to warrant him in increasing the ration....Taking into consideration that these prisoners are not able to get anything but what is issued to them by the Government, for it is almost impossible for the sutler to procure supplies, coupled with the fact that they are very destitute of clothing, I feel it my duty to call the attention of the brigadier-general commanding to these facts, and I respectfully request that if it is out of his power to remedy the evil that this communication be forwarded to the War Department

for the action for the Secretary of War....If the Government is really not able to give these prisoners more to eat then no blame can be attached to any one; but if they are then I must think that the fault lies at the door of the Subsistence Department.....

If a change in the ration can be made I will have the satisfaction of knowing that the prisoners under my charge are well housed, plenty of fuel, good hospital accommodations, and in as good a condition as they could reasonably expect.

I am, very respectfully, your obedient servant,

JNO F. IVERSON,

Lieutenant- Colonel, Commanding Prison. [388]

U.S. Congress Prepares for Transition

With the defeat of the South nearly assured, Union legislators scrambled to prepare fundamental laws that would help undo the nightmare unleashed by the practice of slavery. On Tuesday, January 31, 1865—while Iverson prepared his second letter—the *13th Amendment to the Constitution* was proposed. Its sponsors had hoped that its passage, in conjunction with Lincoln's earlier *Emancipation Proclamation*, would rapidly end the brutal impact of slavery.

> **Section 1:** Neither slavery nor involuntary servitude, except as a punishment for crime whereof the party shall have been duly convicted, shall exist within the United States, or any place subject to their jurisdiction.
>
> **Section 2:** Congress shall have the power to enforce this article by appropriate legislation.[389]

It was a noble beginning, yet the *13th Amendment* would soon be challenged by clever men skilled in legal circumvention. Those who relied on slavery as a way of life would soon find ways to turn freed slaves into criminals, perpetuating the "free" labor that the Southern economy had always depended upon.[390]

CHAPTER 34: A DECISION MADE IN GOLDSBORO

"Chatfield said farewell to his friends..."

By the beginning of 1865, it had become clear to nearly all participants that the end of the war was near. The South's resources had been cut off; Atlanta, Fort McAllister and Savannah had fallen; Sherman was on the march to "wreak vengeance"[391] on South Carolina; and Union and Confederate authorities understood that the South would soon fall. Chatfield would have heard through prison gossip that the South was all but defeated. The war would soon end—but for the prisoners struggling for their very survival, would the end come soon enough?

With the fate of the South within view, Union pressure to avoid the exchange process eased. On January 18, 1865, US Secretary of War, Edwin M. Stanton, citing a communication from CS Exchange Agent Robert Ould, ordered that all Confederate prisoners of war be released.[392] Six days later, CS Adjutant General Samuel Cooper authorized his prisons to reciprocate.[393] Although the news quickly spread among the prisoners, they had no means to verify the authenticity of the story. Experience had taught the prisoners that parole promises were empty.

The Fall of General Winder

By February 3, as Sherman captured River's Bridge, South Carolina, the conditions at the Florence Stockade had steadily deteriorated. Prisoners had been found frozen dead by the creek in the mornings. The water supply was contaminated, and the captives were literally starving, having been fed little more than one pint of meal and six spoons of molasses daily for the past month.[394] Alerted to these deficiencies, General Winder had also received complaints of mistreatment—cruel and undeserved punishment, indecent searches, and theft by the officers and guards.[395]

The pressure on Winder to correct the uncorrectable could not have been more intense. Arriving at Florence on February 6 to investigate the charges and remove the offending guards, Winder surveyed the area, the fouled stream, the almost empty store of rations, and the multitude of nearly naked, bone-thin, frail prisoners—conditions even more horrid than he had imagined. Standing with his staff in front of his detective officer's tent as he convened his investigation, General John H. Winder suddenly fell dead to the ground, the victim of a severe heart attack.[396]

The Exodus from Florence Prison

Following Winder's death, CS Colonel Henry Forno, the senior officer of military prisons below General Winder, assumed responsibility for the prisons in Columbia and Florence.[397] Forno's chain of command was complicated by the fact that CS General Gideon J. Pillow had actually been assigned the job.[398] But Pillow had found ways to sidestep the politically risky assignment, resulting in confusion regarding who would ultimately be responsible.[399] Forno, from his headquarters in Columbia, South Carolina, shouldered the bulk of the work. On February 12, 1865, he received orders to evacuate both the Florence and Columbia prisons due to the proximity of Sherman's army. Having not yet received any information regarding the Confederate-US exchange agreement, Forno initially planned to move the prisoners back to Southwest Georgia. He ordered Lieutenant Colonel Iverson, still at Florence, to arrange for the immediate removal of the prisoners from the Florence Stockade. But on February 15, Forno received a telegram from Colonel Iverson stating that trains could no longer pass through Kingsville, South Carolina. This prompted Forno to order Iverson to redirect the waiting prisoner train to Raleigh, North Carolina, by way of Wilmington—the all-important Confederate port city.[*][400]

The southern outskirts of Wilmington had come under Union attack on February 11, making the rails and roadways to the north of the city essential for moving Confederate troops and supplies. By mid-February, war's brutality had descended upon Wilmington, gripping the entire city in terror. The booming of distant cannon and the sight and smell of smoke spreading gray ash over the countryside prompted a panic-driven evacuation of the area, with wagons colliding at intersections and residents rushing out with only the belongings that they could carry.

Though much of North Carolina boiled in chaos, Iverson acted on Forno's orders, loading his first trainload of prisoners to be transported via Wilmington to Raleigh on February 15. Florence prisoner Sergeant James H. Dennison, in his final diary entry, wrote that he was part of the initial group sent out of Florence on February 15.[401]

---

[*] The Confederacy's formidable Fort Fisher, guarding the harbor south of Wilmington, had fallen on January 15, a month earlier—removing the South's last port of entry for outside supplies and thereby sealing the fate of the South's inability to wage war.

Dennison's group passed through Wilmington, reaching Goldsboro on February 16 and continuing on to Raleigh with no problems. From there, the group was transported to Richmond, Virginia, arriving there on February 21, where they began to recognize that this may indeed be a true prisoner exchange. To their surprise and great joy, the first group of prisoners realized then that they would soon finally be free. On February 24, 1865, all in the first group of Florence prisoners were paroled at Aikin's Landing on the James River in Richmond, Virginia.[402]

Additional trains departed from Camp Florence on February 16 and 17, emptying all of the stockade's "able-bodied prisoners."* Chatfield, Beebe and Walters were sent out on February 16, and Beach, among the least well, was sent out on February 17. Their journeys would become far more entangled and troublesome than the one enjoyed by the first group.

> A Reb surgeon came in and examined the men; the well were to go out first. Ed Chatfield sat up and baked my meal. The three went out at daylight the next morning [February 16.] I wondered at the boys being so particular to bid me good-bye; they told me afterwards they never expected to see me again. — Private Riley Beach[403]

Coincidentally, February 17 was the day that Richmond authorities released news about the parole agreement.[404] Chatfield may have learned sometime during his train ride that this time, the promise of exchange was likely true. Emaciated and exhausted, Chatfield would have found great inspiration in the hope of being released to the North—and ultimately to his family. With so much confusion yielding unanticipated delays along the tracks, however, Chatfield's train would not have arrived in Goldsboro—a 200 mile journey from Florence by way of Wilmington—until February 18, a day when that rail hub had become so thoroughly overwhelmed with traffic and civilian refugees that it was simply impossible to manage the incoming prisoners of war. Not only was Goldsboro beset with refugees fleeing north from Wilmington, the roads from the southwest were packed with a steady flow of citizens fleeing Sherman's wrath at Columbia, South Carolina—the state's capitol. Goldsboro floundered in turmoil, its rails and roads clogged with retreating Confederate troops, equipment, and frightened refugees. So impacted was the city that February 18 marked the day that Colonel Forno received word that all able-bodied prisoners must be sent back down to Wilmington—from whence they had just come.[405]

As a temporary measure, the Goldsboro authorities herded the Union prisoners into containment areas—an action that convinced Chatfield and many others that

---

* Seven hundred extremely sick prisoners—those judged incapable of being transported—were left behind. (*Official Records*, Series II, Volume 8, p. 449)

perhaps the Rebels had no intention of paroling them, after all. It was at that point that Chatfield made a bold decision to take his chances to find his way to freedom independently. Amidst the chaos, Chatfield said farewell to his friends and separated from Beebe and Walters.

Meanwhile Beach, en route with the third group sent out from Florence on the morning of February 17, had spent the night miserably sick near Wilmington, where he encountered refugees camped north of the city.

> The train stopped and they had us get off. They strung a guard around us in the pine woods. I built up a little fire of pine cones and litter and lay down, but soon had to get up again to replenish the fire. In the morning I went up to a fire occupied by an elderly man and two young men who stared at me and asked if I was sick. 'Yes.' 'Have you had anything to eat?' 'No.' Then they began to curse the Rebels. One says, 'take this cup and get some water and I will make you some coffee.' I went to a little pond thickly covered with green scum, walked out on a log, shoved the scum aside, and got the can full of water. Then one foot slipped off and I went down, sinking above my knee. I was in quicksand. After that I got my coffee and a little to eat.—Private Riley Beach[406]

Although the orders stood that the Union prisoners were to be sent to Wilmington for exchange, US Major General John M. Schofield was too hotly engaged in battle to receive the prisoners;[407] as a result, on the morning of February 19, after spending a second night near Wilmington, Beach's group was commanded to retrain and head north to Goldsboro.[408]

Beach, extremely ill, arrived in Goldsboro late in the afternoon of February 19 and would soon learn that his friends Beebe and Walters were there as well. He would also hear startling news:

> I got off the cars and ambled along aimlessly. I heard my name called. It was a fellow who had messed with us. He told me that Beebe and Walters were there, and Chatfield had escaped.— Private Riley Beach[409]

Chatfield had escaped. But how? As weak as he was, where would he have gone to flee his Confederate captors? Chatfield has written very little on the subject. Only one letter, written by Chatfield to his brother William on April 29, 1865, offers a few, but not many, details:

I escaped from the Rebs the 21st Feb — down near Wilmington N.C. which was captured by the Union forces on the 22nd. Left there on the 28th. Got to Annapolis M.D. the 4th. ...*

With little more to go on than the few details that Chatfield included here, the full story of Chatfield's escape would require some piecing together.

Chatfield's Escape

On February 19, the Confederate War Department had set apart 2,500 prisoners to be sent into the vicinity of Wilmington on February 20 for eventual exchange.[410] Beach, Beebe, and Walters were among them, Beach explaining:

> [On February 19] I was with two of my chums again, both taken out of Florence the day before I was. — I was in bad shape. My limbs were swollen to my knees. I had a roaring in my head, and I was almost blind. One would have to speak loudly and sharp to attract my attention. The next day [February 20] we were ordered to Headquarters to sign the parole. I signed it mechanically as I could not see. I was put on the cars to go somewhere.—Private Riley Beach[411]

But where was Chatfield? Having separated from his friends, he worked his way through long lines to receive hardly more than a swallow of thin cowpea soup and a chip of hardtack, signing parole papers he did not trust, and all the while anticipating his opportunity to escape. He was among the 2,500 prisoners who boarded the freight cars to be hauled south again to Wilmington on the late afternoon of February 20. The car carrying Chatfield may have been only one or two cars away from the one carrying Beach, Walters and Beebe when the train stopped at midnight at what was probably the Burgaw Station, sixty-two miles south of Goldsboro. As Chatfield had hoped, the train was poorly guarded.

> We ran until midnight. The train was put on the siding. While there, two prisoners got outside the guard and got a turkey. They came back and cooked the bird and had a feast. About daylight [February 21] the train started again. .... Soon, a special train whizzed by us. All of the cars were covered with white flags. That was when I was sure that we would be delivered to U.S. forces. At about 12:00 noon, the train stopped.... I saw Old Glory and the Blue and Gray together. I almost had a nervous chill for fear they would stop counting before I got through.... The surgeon ordered me into an ambulance. All, who could, had to march to Wilmington, 10 miles away. — Private Riley Beach[412]

---

* See the April 29, 1865, letter that Chatfield wrote to his brother, William.

Burgaw, 22 miles north of Wilmington, was 12 miles above the Northeast Cape Fear River crossing where Beach, Walters, and Beebe disembarked at noon on February 21.[*] But when the train reached Northeast Cape Fear, Chatfield was no longer on it.

Chatfield and several others had made their getaway at the Burgaw siding during the predawn hours of February 21, their escape underway as the two prisoners in Beach's car jumped off to fetch a turkey. Almost immediately after clearing the train, Chatfield and those with him discovered that they were among a large body of runaway prisoners. All would hide and forage on the outskirts of Wilmington, awaiting its fall to Union troops—an event that would occur the following day.[413] Two days would pass before they were rescued.

On February 23, the day after the fall of Wilmington, Union troops in pursuit of re-treating Confederates came upon Chatfield and the other escapees who had found shelter somewhere in rural Burgaw. In spite of the chilling rain, the sight of the arriving Union soldiers brought cheers. The soldiers took the escapees into protec-tive custody—freeing them once and for all from Confederate hands. Chatfield's condition was far worse than the "hard looking set" that he had described at Camp Douglas back in 1862. His uniform was tattered, his body was beset with vermin, his hair and beard were tangled and filthy, and his skin was pitch-black from pine smoke. He was so gaunt and frail that he would have been difficult to recognize—even by his own mother. But he was alive.

The rescuing soldiers fed Chatfield small amounts of soup, hardtack, and freshly brewed coffee before providing him with blankets for the night. On Friday morn-ing, February 24, they transported him by wagon to the Northeast Cape Fear River crossing, where he boarded a small steamer for the final leg of travel into Wilmington. Once there, Chatfield was seen by the surgeon who administered the two medical essentials of the war—quinine and a gill[†] of whiskey. For the next three days, Chatfield ate, slept, and ate again, soothing his emaciated state. On Tuesday morning, February 28, he boarded a small steamer that taxied him south past Fort Fisher, entering the Atlantic for transfer to an ocean vessel destined to carry him and eight hundred others to Annapolis, Maryland.

The four-day voyage from Wilmington Harbor to Annapolis, Maryland, was not an easy sail, the choppy seas pitching and rolling the transport so severely that nearly all of the liberated prisoners became severely seasick, their fragile systems having had little time to adjust to normal food, let alone the taxing sea conditions. Chatfield

---

[*]   Beach wrote that a pontoon bridge afforded passage across the 400-foot-wide river. After the crossing, a small steamer carried him south into Wilmington.

[†]   One gill is the equivalent of 4 fluid ounces, ¼ pint of liquid.

was among those faring miserably. He nonetheless would have heard his ship's hail and the response it received as the ship approached Camp Parole on Chesapeake Bay: "Ship ahoy! Where bound?" "Annapolis, Maryland!" "What are you loaded with?" "Paroled prisoners!" These were words that he would forever remember.[414]

Press members stood on the Annapolis docks, recording the March 4 arrival and later reporting the news of the 3,000 liberated prisoners in the evening edition of the *New York Times* on Tuesday, March 7:

> *— NEW YORK TIMES—*
> **Names of Enlisted Men Exchanged** — *Baltimore, Tuesday, March 7, 1865 — As they came from the ship, they presented a singularly tattered and piebald appearance, bordering very closely on the ridiculous, if we could forget that their rags and scanty clothing are badges of their long and grievous sufferings in the Southern prisons. They have generally been furnished with shoes at Wilmington, but are in all other respects just as they came from the prison pens of the South. ... Below I give you the names of the enlisted men by Sunday's* transports.... [including] Edward L. Chatfield, 113th Ill. — New York Times.*[415]

Chatfield was coming home. But how difficult would the road to recovery be for a soldier who had suffered so much?

---

* Sunday fell on March 5. If, as the article indicated, Chatfield had arrived on a Sunday, that fact would have been another remarkable coincidence. But Chatfield wrote in his April 29, 1865, letter that he arrived on March 4, a Saturday.

CHAPTER 35: THE LONG WAY HOME

"You did not mention any thing about David in your letter."

Once at Camp Parole, Chatfield bathed for the first time, ridding his body of the vermin that had been infesting him for the past nine months. He received a haircut, a shave, and a new clothing issue before receiving orders to entrain to Benton Barracks in Saint Louis, Missouri, for relocation to his regiment. His 3-year hitch with the army was still not over.

Chatfield was far from well when he left Annapolis on March 6. By the time he had reached Wilmington, he had lost over one third of his body weight. He had suffered from recurrent bouts of malaria long before being captured—the feverish "shakes" that he had described in his diary entries and letters—and the eight months of imprisonment had weakened him to the point that his very life was in the balance. On the train to Benton Barracks after a two-day ride, Chatfield became so deathly ill with diarrhea and dehydration that he had to be removed and taken by ambulance to the Grafton Hospital in West Virginia on March 8.

Fortunately, as close to death as he was, his story did not end there. Chatfield couldn't walk, couldn't talk, couldn't hear, and the food he ate went right through him. Yet, he found the strength to cling to life. Within two weeks, as soon as his hand could manage a pen, still partially deaf and skeleton-thin, he scratched out a brief letter telling his parents of his whereabouts—and he followed that one with three more. On the evening of Friday, March 31, Chatfield received his parents' response. Savoring his first contact from home in ten months, yet too drained to respond, he postponed writing back until the following morning.

Letter - April I, 1865
April I, /65

Dear Parents,

Your very welcome letter of the 26th was rec'd last evening and you cannot imagine with what feelings of it was read & reread. ———

I will now tell you something about myself. I am gaining my strength fast and am in hopes that in the course of a week or ten days I shall be able to start for the west and for home. There is no disease a hold of me that I know of. It was from my being kept so long on such poor food, and having to go through so much in traveling as we did, and then, coming from Wilmington in a crowded transport on the salt Water. Altogether was more than my strength would bear up under, and so, I had to give in. But, I am getting along finely now, and you need not feel anxious about me. You say that William has enlisted. Bully for him. He will learn something that he did not know before, that he cannot have all the comforts of [life] while in the field. I wish that you would give me his address. I would write to him. You did not mention any thing about David in your letter. What is he doing? I cannot write you any news. We must wait [until] we meet, when we will compare notes. This is the fourth letter I have written you.* Please answer this as soon as you receive this. My love to you all. As ever your affectionate son, Edward

Direct US Hosp'l., Grafton W. Va.

Barely able to travel, Chatfield left the hospital on April 3, and rode the train to North Ridgeville, Ohio. One can only imagine the anticipation that he must have felt as he approached the train station, located just minutes from his Grandmother Lucy's house. Arriving on April 7, Chatfield would remain with Lucy for ten days. It was Grandmother Lucy who cared for him as he recovered during those first few days, waiting until she was sure that he was strong enough before she broke to him the terrible news of his brother David's death.

While Chatfield convalesced in Lucy's home, Confederate General Robert E. Lee surrendered his ragged army to Union General Ulysses S. Grant on Sunday, April 9, 1865. Lee accepted Grant's generous terms of surrender while seated in the parlor of the Wilmer McLean house located in the little village of Appomattox Court House, Virginia. For many, this was the end of the Civil War, but for Chatfield's brother, William, it was another day of illness as a hospitalized soldier in Nashville, Tennessee.† Back in Washington, it was time for President Lincoln to celebrate.

---

*　His previous three letters, presumably written from the hospital at Grafton, were missing from the collection.

†　William had enlisted on the very day that Edward departed Wilmington—February 28, 1865. He was assigned to Company "F" of the 156th Illinois and served provost duty in Memphis, where Edward had formerly camped.

Perhaps he and his wife and some friends could take in a play on Good Friday, April 14.

It wouldn't have been until Saturday afternoon, on April 15, that the telegraphed news of Abraham Lincoln's 7:22 A.M. death would have reached North Ridgeville, Ohio. The shocking headlines would have caused Chatfield and his relatives to reflect on the fact that they had just returned home from Good Friday's worship services, the evening before, and had been in the process of settling in for the night at the fateful time of 10:13 P.M.

That was the moment that an openly contemptuous, disgruntled advocate of slavery squeezed the trigger of his .44 caliber derringer, blasting a .41 caliber bullet into the back left side of the President's skull. The President and Mrs. Lincoln were seated in the rear of the presidential box at Ford's Theater, enjoying the third act of the play, *Our American Cousin,* when the lead slug lodged itself behind Lincoln's right eye. By Saturday morning, the assassin's identity was known. John Wilkes Booth was a strikingly handsome, raven-haired, 26-year-old Shakespearian actor who stood five feet eight inches tall—more than a half foot shorter than the man he murdered. Two conspirators were already under arrest, and others were in the process of being seized. But Booth, the assassin, and one other conspirator had somehow vanished from Washington, prompting Edwin M. Stanton, Lincoln's Secretary of War, to order the nation's largest manhunt ever on Easter Sunday, April 16.[416]

On Monday morning, April 17, Chatfield and Grandmother Lucy departed North Ridgeville—the nation's dispirited flags drooping at half-mast at all train stations through which they passed. The 350-mile route carried them to Chatfield's home in Kankakee. Nathan and Margaret greeted their boy at the Kankakee Station during the evening hours of April 18, Grandmother Lucy beside him. For the next three weeks, Chatfield would recuperate at home—his grandmother, his parents and his siblings with him. It was a time of great joy mixed with deep sadness. Chatfield had reunited with his family. They were together again. The long, horrid war was over. Yet, the nation had lost its President. And the family's reunion was poignantly dampened by the fact that William was still away, and David would never be coming back.

Letter #1 - April 26, 1865
Pilot April 26ᵗʰ /. 65

Dear Brother Willie,
    Father went to town today, and on his return we were made thrice glad by having 3 letters from my Dear soldier Brother. Was very glad to hear that your health was improving so fast. Your last letter that we rec'd was dated the 18ᵗʰ.

I wrote to you yesterday. We are all well. Grand mother, Mother, Mary & myself went over to Louisa's a visiting this afternoon. Had a very good visit. Besides Smiths and Notemans, Lucy Smith and her husband and his brother were there. Newton and James were getting out manure and plowing.

[On left side of front of letter Ed writes] Willy, I advise you to stay in the Hospital by all means, and take care of yourself.

[On back side of letter] My health has gained very fast since I have been at home. I was sick in the Hospital about a month after I came into our lines. And when I left the Hosp. — I was was not any better than skin and bones. But, am beginning to look more like myself. —— Today we rec'd the news of the surrender of Johnson [General Joe Johnston] and all of the Confederate armies. (Three Cheers for the yankee Boys, Hip Hurrah!) We may well rejoice to think that one of the most cruel wars that ever was is over. The day has been very pleasant. Mother is busy this Evening, or she would write. Newton is writing, and we will send our letter tomorrow morning. My page is full and I must close.

We all send you our love,

E.L.C.

Letter #2 - April 26, 1865
April 26th 1865

Dear Brother,

It is with much pleasure that I take my pen to write you A few lines. Pa went to town to day and got three letters from you and one was for me dated the 12th. Grandma and Edward got here last week, and I can tell you that we was glad. We had a thankes giving last Saterday. We had a first rate time. Grandma & mother, Edward and Mary went over to mr Lowesy Smiths, to day, and made them A visit. Well, William, if you were only here we would have A good time. But, that is not to be. And so, we must hope for the best.

Well, I supose that you would like to know what we have doing this Spring. I will tell you. We sowd about 17 acres of wheat. It is up about 5 inches high. And then, we sowed about 40 buchels of oats. And then, we have got about 10 acres plowd for corn. We have not thrashed one flax yet but expect to in a few days. We sold old Dell to Edward Alberts for $121. And then, we sold the three year old colt to Mr. Osbern for $100. Mr. Scoby is just going home from town. It is very dark. I have been holling out manure this forenoon, and, this afternoon, I planted potatoes.

Well, well, William, how do you like to be a soldier? And how do like to stay in the hospitle, and grunt grunt grunt? Edward is having his ears washed out with a siring [syringe], and Pa is writing $50 note for Mr. Scoby. He has bought a bull. And Jimmy sits hear a laughing. Emley Hawkins is going to keep our school this summer for $20 a month. And Marge Youngs is going to school in Mr. Lane's district. Eldy Smith has got a school in the Barber district. Sinthy Davis is keeping school on the Parmer Ridge. She makes a great schoolmarm don't she? Well, it is time to go to bed, and so I will close by sending my best respects.

This from your loving Brother,

Newton Chatfield

[On Backside, Edward wrote]

I will tell you what I think the reason was that you have not got our letters. We directed them to you like this — Wm. S. Chatfield, Co F. 156 Ill Vols Inft, U S Hospital No 1 Ward L. Nashville Tenn.—While we had only ought to have left the Co & Regt out. Now, if you will just write to the Captain of your Company you will be apt to get your letters.

Your Brother,

Edward

It wasn't until April 27 that the news regarding the apprehension of the last co-conspirator at large and the demise of Lincoln's murderer reached the Chatfields. The 16th New York Cavalry, under the command of Lieutenant Edward Doherty, had traced David Herold and John Wilkes Booth to a tobacco farmer's barn near Bowling Green, Virginia, and it was there that Booth's life came to an end during the predawn hours of Wednesday, April 26. Having surrounded the barn, Lieutenant Doherty ordered the fugitives to surrender. Refusals followed, and the barn was set afire, prompting Herold to rush out the door, proclaiming his innocence. Booth obstinately refused to exit, leveling his pistol in Doherty's direction. Observing the threatening gesture through a large crack in the side of the barn, Sergeant Boston Corbett—one of Chatfield's fellow Andersonville survivors—fired his colt revolver at Booth. The bullet struck Booth in the base of his skull, severing his spinal cord. From that day forward, Corbett would forever be remembered as the man who killed the man who killed Lincoln.

Letter - April 29, 1865
Pilot April 29. /. 65

Dear Brother Willie,

I expect that you have been looking very anxiously for a letter from us, and I know how to sympathise with it, having been ten months and a half that I never received a word from home and friends. And, Oh, what a teribly lonely time it did did seem sometimes. But, for all that, I never gave up or got discouraged.

I thought that the time would come some time, if I was only permitted to live, that I would see home and friends. And, the time has at last arrived.

Father was in town Wed — and brought home three letters from dear Brother Wm. Well, I sat right down and wrote an answer the same night, and intended to send it the next morning. But no one went by and [we] have been obliged to wait. I will send that one with this in today's mail.

I will tell you, Willie, that I saw some pretty tough times down in those horrid prisons. But thank God I am free from them now and hope that myself nor Brother may never be incarcerated in the like of them again. I escaped from the Rebs the 21st Feb — down near Wilmington N.C. which was captured by the Union forces on the 22nd. Left there on the 28th. Got to Annapolis M.D. the 4th April [sic] [4th of March] where I drew my clothes and Commutation money which amounted to $64.25. On the 6th, started for Benton Barracks St Louis, Mo. We had got about 250 or 300 miles this side of there when I became so sick that I was obliged to stop at a place called Grafton and go into the Hospital, which I entered the 8th of April. [sic] [8th of March] I had a very sick time.

By the third of April I had so far recovered that I was able to start on my journey again. As I came west I came through Cleveland and stoped and made Grandmother, Uncle Jackson,° and the folks in Twinsburg† a visit stoping 10 days. And when I came home, I brought Grandmother with me. I got home on the 18th. And, O such a time of rejoiceing as we had. You had ought to have been here.

But our number is broken, and O, how, how I wish that I had only been permitted to have seen our dear brother [David.] But, all is for the best I presume, and I will not murmur, but will say thy will O Lord be done.

Mother sent you a box of things some time ago. I hope that you have received them ere this. It seems that you have been very unfortunate in not receiving your letters and I think there must have been a mistake in directing them. If you will direct write to your captain I think that you will get them. Mother is not very well. all the rest She suffers from the Asthma so that she cannot hardly breathe nights. All the rest are usually well. Grandmother is well, and [sends] you her love. My health is improving very fast and I am getting quite fleshy again having been very poor from having been starved so long. We all join in sending you our love.

Your Brother,
Edward

---

*   "Uncle Jackson" (Jackson Robb) was Georgianna Robb's father. See Georgianna's 5/26/1860 letter to Edward.

†   Chatfield was referring to the Herricks, his mother's family, who lived in Twinsburg, Ohio.

Letter from William - May 5, 1865

[Stationary Inscription]
The United States Christian Commission
Sends this sheet as the Soldier's messenger to his home.
Let it hasten to those who wait for tidings.

U.S. General Hospital No. _____
Nashville. Tenn. May 5 1865.
Post No 5 Dalton Georgia

> Dear Parents,
>
> It is with much pleasure that I write you. I am well and hope that these few lines will find you all the same to. John Bray is quite sick. I think that he has got the Dyptheria. He had an awfull fever all night. I got up and heated some water and soaked his feet and rubbed him up and he slept better the rest of the night. I have just come of [off] guard. We only have to stand 6 hours out of 48, and the rest of the time we can fish or hunt or any thing else. The train has just gone through. It haul on a lot of Rebs. They look, on full, shabby. I have not received any mail for most two weeks. It is got a kind of lonesome having nothing to read or to do. I would rather be with the Regt. where there was something to do. Here is a silk Hdkfe [handkerchief] that I will give to Pa hoping that you will receive this. I will close by wishing you all good bye.
>
> This from your loving son,
> Wm. Chatfield
> — Co F — 156 Regt. Ill Vols. — Dalton Georgia — Wm Chatfield

John G. Bray, a 38-year-old farmer from Kankakee, was a private in Company "F" of the 156 Illinois. He enlisted the same day that William did. Bray recovered from his illness and later mustered out of service on September 20, 1865.

Chatfield's return home had been a great comfort to his grieving family. Yet as he regained his strength, he recognized that he would soon have to leave his family once again to fulfill the last few weeks of his commitment to Union service. Another reunion would lie ahead of him, and this time it would be with his fellow soldiers of Company "B."

CHAPTER 36 – REUNION AND THE FINAL MUSTER

"…a reunion, predecessor and model for the Grand Army of the Republic."

On May 10, 1865, Confederate President Jefferson Davis was captured by Colonel Benjamin D. Pritchard's 4th Michigan cavalry at Irwinsville, Georgia,[417] ending most discussion as to whether the war was really over. That same day, Chatfield, impatient to put the war behind him, felt well enough to pursue his return to service and his proper release from the army. Grandmother Lucy accompanied him from the Chatfield home in Kankakee as far as Calumet, Illinois, where they had breakfast. She would return to North Ridgeville, Ohio, and he would continue north to Chicago.

Letter - May 10, 1865
Chicago, May 10, /, 65

> Dear Parents,
>
> Grandmother and me left K.K.K. [Kankakee] at 5:10 this A M. and arrived here at 8 all right. We got breakfast at Calumet. Grandmother leaves at 5:30 P.M. I have been to the Provost Martial and Examining surgeons and find that I will have to go to St. Louis. Shall leave at 7:30 this P.M. I have got my transportation so it will not cost me any thing. I have been running about a good deal today but feel first rate. Grandmother did not get very tired Coming up. She was pretty tired yesterday, but rested good last night. She sends her best respects. You need not write until I let you know where to direct.
>
> Your son & Brother,
> Edward

<u>Letter</u> - May 11, 1865

[Stationary inscription]
For the soldiers from the Western Sanitary Commission, St. Louis, Mo.

May 11th /. 65,

Dear Parents Brothers & Sister,

I wrote you a few lines yesterday and will write again today to let you know that I am still well and that I got here safe. ——

I saw Grandmother off all right at 6:30 PM. I then went to the St. L. A & C R.R. [*St. Louis, Alton & Chicago Railroad*] Depot and got my ticket, and at 7:30 PM we started. Just after I had got on to the cars, who should I see but a soldier that was a prisoner at Andersonville with me. He was the one that you heard from me by in the winter. Edward Glennon is his name.

I slept the most of the time during the night but did not feel much refreshed this A.M. We arrived at Springfield just at day light. Springfield is a very pretty place, it being a fine rolling country about there, and then, it is well shaded by fine shade trees. We arrived at this place at 10:15 A.M. I then came here to the soldiers Home, where I now am, got dinner and then went out to see what I could find out with regard to myself.

Went to the Military Commander's of the Dep't of Mo. and of the District of St Louis and they both told me that I could not get a furlough on the account that I was an escaped prisoner. Nor, my discharge, because I did not have my descriptive List.*

So, they ordered me to report to the commander of Schofield Barracks. Well! I went there, and he said that I would have to go to my Reg't. He told me to report there tomorrow morn at 10 A.M. and he would have my transportation ready for me.

So, if nothing happens, I shall start for Nashville Tennessee tomorrow morning by the first Boat that leaves. We have very good fare here and plenty of it. I feel first rate and am getting along all right. Now, I want you to be sure and not worry about me. For, I shall take care of myself the best that I know how. And, providence permitting, I shall regain my health before long. St. Louis seems very dull, although there is a good many on the streets. Now, I want that you should write as soon as you get this and direct (thus.) E L Chatfield Nashville, Tenn. Nothing more. And write all the news & about how you got home that night. Kiss Mary for me.

From your son & Brother,

Edward Chatfield

---

* The Army considered Chatfield to have been a "detached soldier" while away. Regulations required that men who were "detached" from their companies be provided with "descriptive lists" showing the pay due to them, the status of their clothing allowances, and everything else that might be needed to settle their accounts before being discharged.

Edward Glennon, a resident of Cook County, was the severely ill soldier who had carried a brief note to Chatfield's parents when removed from the Florence Prison in mid-December, 1864. Glennon eventually regained his health and was reunited with his company. Highly regarded for his soldiering experience, he was promoted to 1st Sergeant before mustering out on August 8, 1865.

<u>Letter</u> - May 20, 1865
Nashville Tenn. ———
May 20th 1865

My Dear Parents,

When I wrote you last I was aboard [a] Boat and just about to start. Well, we left that evening, which was Tuesday. My ticket only called for deck passage, and so I had to sleep below among the freight, while the passengers, they paid their way, had a cabin and their meals. Well, we got to Cairo the next morning, Wednesday, and reached Paducah Ky. at 4 P.M. We did not get to Fort Donelson until 10 A.M. Thursday, and reached here Friday morn (which was yesterday) at 2 A.M. I reported to the Commander of the Post and he sent me to the Exchange Barracks. I had previously learned that Williams Reg't, the 1st, was not here, but at Chattanooga still. I will tell you now why I stopped here instead of going to Chattanooga. You know that in those last letters that we had from Wm. [he] stated that they expected to leave there soon and come to this place. Well, when I got my transportation at St. Louis, I got it to come here thinking that if Wm. was not here, that I could get transportation and go on to C ——— [Chattanooga] but I found I was mistaken in my calculations. And now I have to go to my Reg't without seeing him. I have got my transportation and this morning we started for Louisville Ky. We had got out about 20 miles from here and found that a bridge had been swept away by a flood of water. And so, we had to come back and wait till they could build another, which they will probably have done by tomorrow morning. It rained terible hard here last night and the Cumberland river is full. While, where there were no streams or but very small ones, there is rushing torrents.

Nashville is a very pretty place, and it is a splendid country about here. It is not exactly hilly but very rolling. The crops look fine. As I was coming up the river the other day I saw some fields of grain that was all headed out and beginning to look yellow. Corn does not seem to be much larger than it was in Illinois a week or 10 days ago. And they are still plowing for corn here yet. All of the hills, ridges & bluffs about town are crowned and covered with frowning guns, forts, earthworks, etc.

My health is good, and I feel as well as ever I did in my life. But I have not got to be quite as stout as I used to be yet. I hope that you are all well at home. Well Mother, I have not come across a girl yet, but I hope that if your health is not any better that you have got one. For you need one, since you do not have me there to pick up the dishes and help you in other ways. I shall be glad when the time comes that I can return home and settle down to some sort of business. For this way of running about is getting to be very distastefull to me. I almost feel ashamed of myself that I did not assist you more when I was there, but I felt so languid and stupid that I did not feel like doing much. If I had have known what I do now I should not have been in such a hurry to leave as I was. I have just been to supper. We had bread, boiled pork, and coffee. For dinner, we had bread, boiled pork, and bean soup. It is getting dark, and I must close for the present. Good night to all. May god protect and bless you is the prayer of your unwerthy son. Pray for me that my hard and stubborn heart may be taken away.

[Letter not signed]

The war, combined with the loss of his brother David, had changed Chatfield. His references to his "hard and stubborn heart" and to the "distastefull" nature of his "running about" with the army stand in marked contrast to the good-natured, optimistic outlook that he had expressed in his earlier letters and diary entries prior to his imprisonment and to his knowledge of his brother's death.

Letter - May 26, 1865
Louisville Ky. May. 26th. 1865

Dear Parents, Brothers & Sister,

Feeling as though I had ought to let you know where I am and how I am, I take the present oportunity to write you a few lines. I am quite well, and have been since I wrote you last. Although, for the last two days I have been troubled with wind in the stomach, which makes me feel rather uncomfortable, nothing more. Well, I finally got away from Nashville after waiting very impatiently a week. Yesterday morning, however, they have got the road fixed so that we started. The bridge across the river [Barren River] at Bowling Green is gone yet, and so, we had to leave the train and cross the river on foot, and take another train on this side, and come on through.

We left N———— [Nashville] at 6:30 and yesterday morning, and got here at 12 last night. We went, or rather, came to the soldiers Rest and got our supper at 2 in the morning, and then we had breakfast at half past 4. The Rest is capable of accommodating 3,000. And, 1,000 can sit down at the table at once. There is also a Commodious Hospital building connected with it. The most of the way between here and Nashville is a fine rolling farming country, well adapted to raising all kinds of grains as well as cotton, of which I saw but little planted. This is a very pretty place from what I have seen of it. having not much news to write I will close hoping that you are all well.

My love to you all,

Edward. ──

[Chatfield rotated the paper a quarter turn and continued in larger cursive] We are expecting that we will leave here every minute though we may not go till Monday. Direct to Memphis Tenn.

From your loving son,

Edward L Chatfield

On June 2, 1865, CS General Edmund Kirby Smith, the commander of Confederate forces west of the Mississippi, formally surrendered to Union negotiators. His was the last Confederate army still in existence. A formal end to the bloodiest four years in U.S. history had been achieved.

Chatfield's travel from Louisville, Kentucky, to Memphis, Tennessee, was at least a four-day boat ride via the Ohio and Mississippi Rivers. If he departed as he had expected on Monday, May 29, the earliest date that he could have arrived in Memphis would have been on Thursday, June 1. The long-awaited reunion with his fellow soldiers from Company "B" would follow, and Chatfield would have understood that his mustering out of the army was close at hand. Yet, the camaraderie and cause for celebration in Memphis could not extinguish the self-doubts that Chatfield was then experiencing as he contemplated the evil of war and the painful life of a soldier.

Letter - June 9, 1865
[Written in Memphis]
Friday Eve. June 9ᵗʰ 9 P.M.

My Dear Parents,

I am afraid that you have begun to think that I have not done right in being so foolish as to be in such a hurry. But, it is hard to always decide what is for the best. May the lord help us in our time of need. I feel so sorry for you, my Dear Mother, to think how much you do have to suffer. But, let us praise God. For whom he loveth, he chasteneth. His works are mysterious and wonderous in all their ways. He goeth about sending affliction there, to smite the stubborn and wayward, and peace here, to bind up the broken hearted. Oh, how I do wish that I were a true Christian, that I could have faith in the Holy Cross of Christ. But, my heart is so stubborn and hard that it seems almost impossible to do and act right. Oh, I shall be so glad when I get home away from all the evil influences that surround me here. When I shall try and act a new life and to be a better man. ———

I had a letter from Brother William a few days since. He was then at Cleveland Tenn., about 30 miles northeast of Chattanooga, and was well and getting along all right. I am glad to hear he thinks of going into business down in that part of the Country, for I think that he would do well and make money. There is an excellent chance for a person to make money down in this part of the Country now. Wages are high, and help is scarce, and there is good chances for speculators in almost any kind of business, and every thing looks fair and prosperous. There is a large amount of business done here in Memphis. Large amounts of Cotton are being brought in and merchandise carried out in return in large quantities.

John Fundy sits here, oposite me writing here, while the most of the other Boys have retired. The weather has been uncommonly warm for some time, but the nights are cool and pleasant. Far more so than they are up north during very warm weather. Well, it is getting to be about bed time and so I will close. My love to you all. You need not write again if you get this before I get home, for I think that we will be home in a few days.

Yours truly as ever, Edward L Chatfield
Mrs. M P. Chatfield

It is not known when Chatfield wrote the next diary entry. It is possible that his friends had sent the diary home to Chatfield's parents along with his other belongings after his June 11, 1864, capture. If so, he could have made the entry upon his first return home on April 18, 1865, or following his final return home after mustering out of the army. It is also possible that when he arrived in Memphis on June 1, his diary may have been waiting for him there, securely stored at the camp, in which case he may have added the notation sometime during his stay in Memphis. If so, he would have penned it almost one year from the day that he had been captured.

Diary – [June 9, 1865 - date estimated]
To my readers—
[Referring back to his June 11, 1864 capture] At this time the writer of this journal was taken prisoner by the Rebels and having unfortunately left his diary in camp was debarred from continuing this journal. So, the reader will have to be content with a few scattering remarks on his prison life as may come into his mind and which he

has jotted as they might occur. With this apology for not having kept a continuous journal, I will try and do better in the future. By the writer, Edward L. Chatfield.

<u>Letter</u> - June 15, 1865
Memphis Tenn.
June 15th, 1865.

Dear Brother,

When I wrote you last I had expected to have been at home ere this. But every thing connected with Military seems to move so slow. We should have been mustered out the fore part of this week, but there was a lot of Cavalry here which had to be mustered out before we could be. The remainder of the Cavalry have been consolidated and formed into a n Brigade, and now getting onto Boats, and are going down the river to join in the Expedition under Gen'l [Philip] Sheridan and go into Texas.* My health is excellent. Never was better in my life. ———

How does the times go with you? I hope that you are still in good health. And how long before you expect to get out of the service? And is your Duty very hard? And how do you like the country about Chattanooga and Cleveland? And what is your prospects for the future? ———

I went on Minute Duty yesterday for the first time and went to the Theatre last night. The play was excellent. It was entitled Leah the Forsaken. The Boys, that is, Bert Smith, John Fundy, and Tom Carrow, are well and send you their best respects. We will be mustered out the fore part of next week, and will go up the river immediately after. All of the Recruits are to be left here. Jesse Hawkins has just come in. He goes down the river with the rest. The Boys have a good deal of duty to do. They have to be on every other day. I have had but one letter from home since I left. They were all well, except Mother, who had had a severe spell of sickness since I had left. Hoping that you are all right, I will close by sending you my love. Write soon and direct to Grand Prairie.

E L Chatfield

P.S. John Blanchet will write a few lines. Yours truly, ELC

Friend William,

As Ed have left little Room on this sheet of paper, I thought I would try and write you A few line to let you now that I am well at present, and doing well,

---

*   Although CS General Kirby Smith had surrendered on June 2, 1865, there was worry that the emperor of Mexico, Maximillian I, was planning to recapture Texas. US General Philip Sheridan's army would occupy Texas as a defense force.

and hoping when you received these few line that it will find you Injoying the
same state of health. Well William, we ar still here at Memphis, and I Expect
that we shel stay here an antil nex thusday. Then I think that we will very ap to
go up the River for good. Ed is here and is looking forstrate, and I tel yuu, we it
was hapy to see him again. Fur we had most given up of Ever seeing him again.
And I tel yuu, Ed had been such a good soldier. It would have been very hard for
us to here of any injury be falling him, which, we know he had to suffer all the
time he was prisoner. But, at last, he got back safe. And we ar tagather and we ar
a having hight time. And I wish yuu was with us so yuu Could Go home with us.
But never mind there is good time coming when you come home. We wont forget
our soldiers life be for yuu git back. And then, what I think, that we will be very
ap to have a dance some where, where we can Rejuys our self like we usto befor
this Cruel war Camance. As I have nt knuw importance news to write, I will have
to Close. So good By.

From yuur soldier Friend,

Sergt J R Blanchet

Leah the Forsaken was written by Augustin Daly (1838-1899) when he was 22 years
old—perhaps his most famous play. It was an adaptation of a translation of Solomon
Hermann Von Mosenthal's _Deborah_. Reviews during the war drew parallels between the persecution of Jews in the play and the persecution of the blacks in the
Confederacy.

Private Jesse Hawkins, 20, enlisted in Company "I" of the 12th Illinois Cavalry on
December 26, 1863, later transferring to Company "E." He remained with Sheridan's
Cavalry until March 17, 1866, when he deserted in Jasper, Texas.

Chatfield's animosity toward the bureaucratic run-around he had just endured quickly
mellowed upon his return to Memphis, once again among his closest friends—the
boys with whom he had enlisted, drilled, camped and fought beside. For Chatfield,
reuniting with Bert Smith, John Fundy, Tom Carrow, and John Blanchet carried
with it the emotion of a reunion with family. He had not anticipated the profound
impact that his return to the unit would have upon him. He was startled by the fact
that even the sight of a single familiar soldier would set loose an avalanche of vivid
memories.

A glance at Dan Durham—his old wagoner friend—kindled full recall of the day that
their wagon had gotten stuck axle-deep in the thick mud on the road from Young's
Point to the canal. It had taken the two of them three hours to unload the wagon

and dig it free, a flash of memory that was so detailed that Chatfield could even smell the rain and taste the salt that washed down from his forehead that day.

When he saw Edmund Landis, one of his former bunkmates, he couldn't suppress a chuckle over his memory of young Ed tripping over the flour barrel while struggling to maintain the fire that was heating coffee and a pot of stew. Not only had Ed somersaulted over the flour barrel, the coffee pot and the stew ended up in the fire. It wasn't funny when it actually happened, but it somehow seemed ridiculously comical when Chatfield and Landis recollected the spectacle 15 months later.

Upon the approach of James Henry and "Lish" Johns, Chatfield was cast back to the time when Kellogg acted out his comic pantomime portraying the long silence that gripped the boys in the company—the rolling eyes, the downward-turned faces and nervous shuffling of feet that gave way to embarrassingly audible sighs after "old" Joe Smith, Henry and Johns had stepped forward volunteering for the *Forlorn Hope*. Chatfield wasn't present when they volunteered—he was with the teams—but Kellogg's account of the event had firmly cinched a strong sense of his having been there. Under the duress of imprisonment, Chatfield hadn't thought about Kellogg for many months, but now that he did, how he missed his violin-playing friend! Chatfield had last seen Kellogg while in Saint Louis, back in May of 1864—over a full year ago, when Kellogg had accompanied Major Williams to Springfield to do some recruiting. Chatfield and his companions had missed the return boat, and Williams had helped them catch another one. Although Chatfield and the others had sailed back down to Memphis, Kellogg never returned to the regiment, as he instead accepted a promotion as captain in command of a regiment of black soldiers. Chatfield hadn't seen Kellogg ever since. Time seemed to be collapsing, the past and present colliding.

The war's end seemed to have made it all possible; with no more war to fight, there was time to examine the past. A plethora of memories flooded Chatfield's consciousness, hundreds—perhaps thousands of them—far more than there were men in his company. It was a remarkable experience. Each spontaneous sharing triggered recall of related events which, when divulged, unleashed the flow of even more anecdotes—a chain reaction with seemingly no end. Significantly, Chatfield soon noticed that every soldier present seemed to be savoring the same process, some smiling and others teary-eyed. The final muster was more than a mere assembly; it was a reunion, a predecessor and model for the *Grand Army of the Republic*.[*]

---

[*]   The G.A.R was a post-war national fraternity of Union soldiers having the purpose of cultivating brotherhood, camaraderie, and patriotism among Union veterans. The brotherhood held post meetings, district meetings, and national encampments, all of which were organized for the benefit of the veterans and their families.

Of course, not all of the boys from the company were present. Chatfield and the others would remember with sadness their fellow soldiers who had given their lives during the war. And only one of the four soldiers that had been captured alongside Chatfield had made his way back to Memphis for the final muster: Calvin Maggee. In Memphis, Chatfield and Maggee would have had ample time to share stories with each other, describing everything that had happened to them from the time that they had each left the Florence Stockade in separate groups. Chatfield would check for new arrivals each day in hopes that Beach, Beebe, and Walters would also show up, but they never did; Chatfield would not see them until he returned to Kankakee.*

Nevertheless, Chatfield relished his visits with all of the boys who were present: Albert Nichols, the company musician who always played from his heart; Henry White, with whom Chatfield made the watch trade that would later play a role in saving his life; and Milton Rounsavell, the sergeant affectionately referred to as "Uncle Fuller." Perhaps Chatfield even spoke briefly with Chaplain Rankin, absent on so many Sundays but present for this heartening occasion. He was among the officers and field staff present at the regiment's last gathering—men who would muster out on the same day, including Lieutenant John Jeffcoat, Major Cephas Williams, and Colonel George B. Hoge.†

Perhaps the most frequently used phrase at the reunion was "What happened...?" as there was a great deal of catching up to do. When Chatfield was doing the questioning, a bystander would hear, "What happened after you left Ripley? How long did it take to get back to Memphis?" "What happened to Sturgis when he got back? Did he lose his command?" "What happened to Grierson and the other officers?" "What happened to Forrest? Was he ever captured?"‡ "How's Lieutenant Baird? What happened to him?" "Who got killed? Who's missing?" When he wasn't the one doing the asking, Chatfield would have been answering—as best as he could. "How were you captured? What happened after that?" "Was Andersonville as bad as they say it was? What happened there?" "I hear you escaped? How did you do it? What happened?"

But if Chatfield shared the painful details of prison life with anyone, it would have been with his closest friends Bert Smith, John Fundy, Tom Carrow, and John Blanchet. Chatfield's prison stories were the most difficult to tell, experiences so extreme

---

*   Having not mustered out with their regiment in June, the army arranged for Beach, Beebe and Walters to muster out elsewhere in July.

†   For a complete list of all of the men who mustered out that day, see Appendix III.

‡   Forrest was never captured, but he did surrender. The event occurred on May 9, 1865 in Gainesville, Alabama, following a lengthy battle with Major General James H. Wilson's 13,500-man cavalry at the Confederate ordnance center near Selma, Alabama; Forrest had been forced to concede the city of Selma on April 1.

that he knew that only those who had been there could fully comprehend. Even so, he may have tried to tell what he could, his conversation interrupted by moments of silence and his voice fading at times to a strained whisper. The friends who were like brothers were there to listen.

It was far easier to talk about the earlier battles—those that occurred at Chickasaw Bayou and Arkansas Post. Chatfield and his friends enjoyed reminiscing about the lengthy rugged stay on DeSoto Point, the back-breaking work on the canal, the frightful shellings from the guns above Warrenton, the bold midnight march through the swamps of Black Bayou to Deer Creek, the perilous levee breaks that flooded the Point, and the fiery nights when the Union ships ran the gauntlet as they challenged Vicksburg's mighty guns. They discussed the forbidding march to Vicksburg, with its many battles along the way and the heroism and tragedy of the events at Brice's Cross Roads. The final muster provided Chatfield and the boys with a chance to discuss, to debate, and to summarize all that they had experienced as brothers in arms. It also brought Chatfield a great deal of laughter—the first that he had had in a long time. The crescendo of his voice rose as he and the others relived good times such as the raucous, unbridled celebrations that had taken place when Sherman or Grant had achieved their various battle victories. Even the story of the night that Chatfield's pants were stolen was fair game. With the vicious war's end, it seemed understandable, yet strange, to have so much to laugh about.

The mustering-out process on Tuesday, June 20, 1865, must have seemed anti-climatic to Chatfield and the others after all that they had been through. The regiment was called into formation. A few brief speeches were delivered by the various company officers, including Lieutenant Jeffcoat, Major Williams, and Colonel Hoge. The rest of the out-processing involved mostly the signing of paperwork and the receiving of pay. The next day, Chatfield would board a transport to return home along the reverse route he had followed 31 months earlier, disembarking in Cairo and entraining to Kankakee, where he would have probably arrived in the late afternoon of Saturday, June 24. Although it is not known what Chatfield's final pay amounted to, family lore holds that he received part of his pay in the form of silver dollars. He kept six of these as mementos, their symbolic worth to Chatfield far greater than their face value. The coins would remain with him for years until he would later have them melted down to create a set of six silver spoons as a wedding gift for his wife.

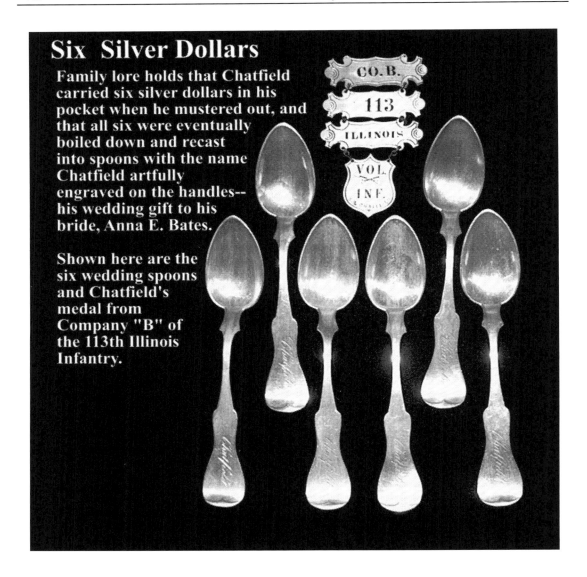

Six Silver Dollars

Family lore holds that Chatfield carried six silver dollars in his pocket when he mustered out, and that all six were eventually boiled down and recast into spoons with the name Chatfield artfully engraved on the handles-- his wedding gift to his bride, Anna E. Bates.

Shown here are the six wedding spoons and Chatfield's medal from Company "B" of the 113th Illinois Infantry.

CHAPTER 37: THE MENDING BEGINS

"… tattoos on his very soul."

Chatfield's arrival back in Kankakee coincided with the early summer season and its busy demands—a fact that may have been a blessing. The strenuous harvest activity, accomplished side-by-side with his father and brothers, would allow Chatfield distraction from his thoughts of the war and his imprisonment. The rye grass—the forage for the farm animals—had surpassed hip level. The corn was four feet high and about to tassel; it would be ready for harvest in late July. The flax, a field of blue, promised a fine harvest within 25 days. The oats and wheat had fared well thus far, their heads in the final stages of inflorescence. Early garden cabbage and lettuce stood ready for cutting and several tomato plants supported inch-sized fruit promising color for summer salads and canning for the winter months. Onion stems were eight inches high, beet leaves were four inches wide, and young green potato tops waved in the wind. Surveying the farm, Chatfield welcomed the challenges of the summer harvest—respite from the war memories that had become tattoos on his very soul.

Chatfield would never escape the intrusive burden of his memory—it had become a part of him. For Chatfield, the war would always seem to have ended less than an hour ago. Nonetheless, over time, Chatfield gradually found ways to manage the nightmares that robbed him of sleep, the fleeting images that came to him while threshing or picking, and the war scenes that shot through his consciousness while slaughtering a farm animal. Of great help was his regular participation in the *Grand Army of the Republic*, the fraternity of Union soldiers, men who truly understood the toll of *The War*. The G.A.R. Post in Kankakee was organized in 1866 with Chatfield's help.

On Saturday evening, July 22, 1865, in a geographical transposition, it was Edward who sat at the Kankakee home's kitchen table and his brother William who sat in the Memphis tent. The war may have ended for the Union with Lee's surrender in early April, but for the Chatfields, it wouldn't be over until William returned.

Letter - July 22, 1865
Pilot

Dear Brother William,

We have so much to do that I can hardly get time to write to you or any body else. I should have written to you last week but I could not get time to write before the mail came, and So I delayed, and I had almost Said that I would not write to you again till you had written to me, for I have not had a letter from you Since the 15th June. ——

Our health's are all very good. Mother is regaining her health again and has been busy all the week sewing etc. ——

We have been busy all the week harvesting, that is, when it did not rain so that we could not, for it has rained every day and every other day for the last ten days, so that it has put us back a good deal. But we will get through after a while if we only keep at it. Well, I Suppose that you are enjoying yourself at Memphis first-rate. All that I have to say is to be careful and not get into any of those dens of infamy where robbing murder & riot is the chief business of those who frequent them. I have enjoyed myself pretty well since I came home. [I] have been to see several of the neighbors & so on etc. Well, I have taken these few moments to write to you, and now I must close and go to work, so good bye for the present.

My love to you as ever,
Edward
William S Chatfield

[On the left border] We rec'd two of your pictures in your last letter for which we were much pleased,"
[On the back was a message from Mother.]

My Dear Son William,

I once more take my pen to write you a few lines. I am getting pretty well again and I am worrying about you all the time. I do wish you would stay out of the citty as much as you can. I fear you will get bulled yet by those base Rebels. Yet no dout but they lay in wate for the death of any of our brave boys. Do take car of yourself. I feel very bad about you. I want to see your face again. It seems a long time since you went away. I think of you often. It seems good to have Edward home again. He is a smart man to work. He makes it go right along. Do you think you will have to stay your year out? Do they give any furlous? I made you a pare of shorts [and] sent them ovr to Mr Hawks yesterday, but they had just sent them. I will send them by the mail. I dont know whether they will suit Edward though. Now do take care of yourself. We all think of you ofen. And I be glad to go and see you but suppose I can not. I thank you for writing often. I miss your letters when they dont come. Then I fear for my Willy boy. Great is my anxiety for you. May the Lord Bless and keep you from all evil. I hope to see Willy come home as pure as spotless as when he went away. Do not do any thing that you cannot ask the blessings of God upon it. In that way you will be left from the evil mind. I think a great deal of your likeness. Your old letters all come safe. I hope you will not have to go to Texas. Which of the boys are your nearest friends? Good By this time.

This from Ma.

Margaret Chatfield

In early August, the family received word that William had been hospitalized again, sickened by foul water. Protecting his family much like Edward had done, William softened the blow with claims of improved health.

Letter - August 5, 1865
Pilot

Dear Brother Willie

We were made very glad today by the receipt of Several letters from you and also one for myself, for which I thank you very much. For, I had not heard from you before since I had been home. But, we were very sorry to hear that you was in the Hospital. But [I] was glad to hear that you was getting Some better. I hope that you will be well by the time that you get this, for it is pretty [difficult] I know, to be Sick. But I guess that I will have to give you a little advice, and I hope that you will not slight it either, and that is not to think and worry about home any more than you can possibly help. For, I have seen too many poor fellows that have lost their lives from no other cause than getting homesick and letting their mind run on about getting home. I wish to ask you if your Regt has not been paid yet since it started out, and whether you have been mustered in yet. If you have not, you had better be as soon as possible. If it was me, I should at any rate. The young folks about here are all right, I believe. As for ourselves, we are all usually well. Mother is troubled a considerable with the asthma, but she gets along as well as she can. We have our harvesting done with the exception of stacking the oats. It has rained so much for a long time past that it will put us back a great deal. If nothing happens, we shall commence thrashing the week coming. [The] wheat is not very good, badly hurt by the bugs, oats [are] good, corn looks fine now, [and the] potatoes are nice also. Sugar cane rather backward but I think that it will come out yet. Rye [is] first-rate. We had a letter from Grandmother today. She is well & all right. We are to have a party at Mr Lanes the evening of the 10th, principally for the Soldiers. I wish that you was here so that you could be there, for I expect that we will have a good time. We helped Mr Currews to stack his wheat and have helped Mr Natern some. So, you see that we have plenty to do. Well, there is not much news & so I will close. I thank you very much for those pictures very much. I have not been to town yet since I got home so that I could [have] mine taken. I will send you $2.00. It is all that I have by me. We are very glad to read all that you can write but you we can have so much to do that we do not have much time to write. Now, Will, if you are out of money let us know, and if you want any thing, you had better buy it there, for you can get it just about as cheap as we can send them to you. You can get butter, cheese, eggs or any thing else at the market on Vance Street, and get them fresh. Well, I must close. Father has gone to town today with a load of wheat, what is worth $1.10.

From your loving Brother, as ever yours truly,

Edward L Chatfield

Wm S Chatfield

Mother sends you fifty cents. I also send you 36 cents in Stamps.

yours truly, Edward

Letter - August 19, 1865

My Dear Son Willie,

How do you do this month? I am feeble just able to ride out. [I] hope in due time to be beter. You do not seem to bring about yet. I hope your health is improving by this time. I hope they will see fit to discharge you if you do not gain your health. They thresh near 900 bushels for Meriteth two days [ago.] Pa, Ed and Newt are threshing for Mr Noatman. I suppose his threshing will come near 100 dols. He has got to build a granery before we can thrash them. He has got to finish the barn. We have not thrashed our Pas yet, so you see it goes. If there was not so many ways to turn, I would insist upon pas going down to see what he could do for you. And, as it is, if you think that if any time it will be the means of saving your life he shall start any time. But, you seemed to think you was on the gain. I hope and trust you are. May you be kept in the strait an narrow way that leadeth to life. I don't know as I have any news to write. Emily's school closes today. Mr Place has a little girl. I am sorry there is not some one to take out my paper, but most draw to a close. [I] will try to write more next time. I want my letter to [go] out with the male very much. If it does not, it gets hindered two or three days. I hope you will take good care of yourself and hold up good courage.

Your hope is about half expired and I hope when you get home again. You will belive what has been so often told you, that home is the best place. And I feel happly rejoiced when I look at Edward. To think how near he was starved to death when he got home, there was such a vacancy in his looks that It did not seem like him. And so deaf, [it] was a great trouble to talk with him. Now, when you get home, I don't know as I shall have any more trouble. I cant feel satisfied without my boys. They are my life and my delight.

Well, if I don't be careful, I shall write my hopes ovr all for nothing, I guess you will say. Now, be a good boy, be of good cheer, the Lord is on your side, is the wishes of Mother.

Good by Willie

Mr William S Chatfield

By late August, William was well enough to be discharged from the hospital, and before Christmas of 1865, William was released from the army and reunited with his family on the farm in Kankakee. The war, for the Chatfields, was finally over.

Just 19 days before Christmas, on Tuesday, December 6, 1865, the state of Georgia made history. With its approval of the proposed *13th Amendment* to the *United States Constitution*, Georgia provided the three-fourths majority that was necessary to bring the amendment into constitutional law.* But within months, all of the states that had seceded from the Union had formulated their own "Black Codes,"† enabling, in reality, the continuation of slavery—but under a different name.[418] Grandmother Lucy, lucid as ever at the age of 79, made no mention of any of this when she wrote to Edward in mid-January. Of importance to her was the overwhelming fact that both Edward, and now William, had survived the deadliest war in the country's history.

---

*   There were holdouts. Delaware did not ratify the amendment until 1901; Kentucky delayed ratification until 1976, and Mississippi held out until 1995 — 130 years after the *13th* had become national law.

†   Differing from state to state, the Black Codes regulated the newly-freed African-American's civil and legal rights, including marriage, free speech, mobility, choice of occupation, and the right to own and sell property. The Black Codes ensured that those who had once been slaves would continue to serve as agricultural laborers or domestic servants.

Letter - January 18, 1866
North Ridgeville, Lorainn Co, Ohio

My Dear Edward

I was very much pleased in receiving a letter from you yesterday. I return you thanks for remembering that you had an aged grandmother living and that she rejoices at the wellfare of her children and Grandchildren. What a mercy shown us from our Heavenly Father, that you are all living and in good health, and can gather arround the family often and sing Praises to God the and the Lamb forever and ever. I think you have great reason to cry out, Bless the Lord. Oh, my soals and all that is within me, Bless his Holy name for such preservation as we all have. But, especially you and William, for you both have been brought to see that it was but no more a step between you and death. Your Mother wrote me that your Uncle William* was there and was well. I would like to know what she ment, for it was thought [it was] imposible for him to get well. I would like to know whether your Uncle David† thinks of coming out there to live, [and] whether they went to Uncle Jameses,‡ and whether you have heard from there family. For, I expect Mr. Marthens family is there. I expect you will think Grandma is very inquisitive, but you must remember that it does me good to hear all about you all. Please write about your Father and Mother. I hope they will get time to write to me, if they live, and [tell me about] William and the Boys. Now [that] they go to school they can have time [to write.] Write whether your P.O. is changed, for you have not got letters from Margrettes family, and I think not mine neather. Remember my love to all and write soon.

This from your Grandmother.

Lucy Chatfield

Edward C and all the family

This was the final letter of the collection.

The importance of written correspondence in preserving and understanding history is underscored by the 116 letters written by Chatfield and his family, letters that would tell the story of one man's experience in the Civil War to readers of the future. More than mere descriptions of the events of the war, the letters convey a sense of what was most important to Chatfield and his family at that point in history. Given the finite number of letters in this collection, questions remain about the specific path that Chatfield would take in the years following the war. He had

---

* William Avery Herrick was Chatfield's mother's oldest sibling. She had eight more, younger than she.

† David Herrick Jr. was another sibling of Chatfield's mother, the 7th born of ten children.

‡ James O. Herrick was the third-born of the ten Herrick children. In 1866 he became Albert "Bert" Smith's father-in-law.

returned to work on the farm—back to the life that he had known well before his enlistment—but what sort of plans would the 23-year-old Chatfield make for his future? What kind of life would he lead, given that his life had been inexorably altered by his wartime experience? As the letters told in words bare and poignant, God and family were paramount in the Chatfield home. Chatfield's future endeavors and accomplishments, continuing in Illinois and across state borders in Littleton, Colorado, would follow a path of Chatfield's own design based on the values that he held dear. To Chatfield, it was a matter of priorities.

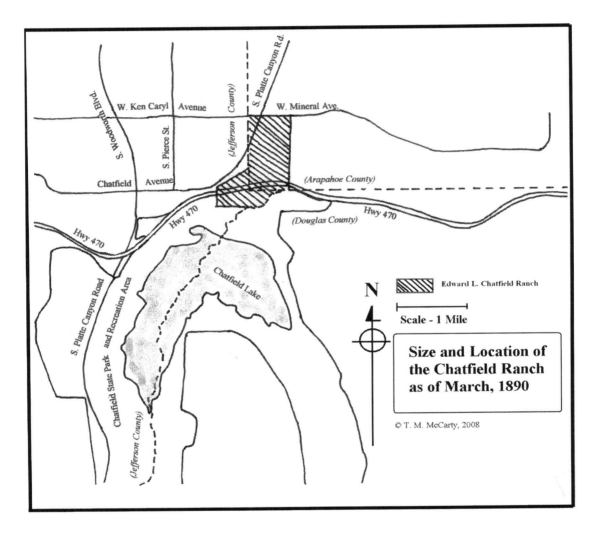

The Chatfield Ranch grew and diminished over the years. The layout of the ranch looked much like a boot in March of 1890. The southern section of the ranch crossed what is today Highway 470 at the spillway of the Chatfield Dam.

EPILOGUE: PIONEERING EARLY COLORADO

"…a section that now serves as the spillway to the Chatfield Reservoir."

With the war's end, the badly broken nation entered its first bitter year of healing. It would be a long and difficult process, one made even more arduous by the fact that thousands of families in the American South would be faced with the challenge of rebuilding their lives from the ground up. In sharp contrast to the plight of countless Southern soldiers, Edward still had a home. The sturdy stone house on the Chatfield farm had never been threatened, its unblemished serenity bolstering a reassuring sense of stability and normalcy for Edward upon his return. The home's familiar sights, sounds, and the very smell and taste of the air hastened Edward's recovery and his re-emergence as a civilian. Replacing his rifle with a plow, he picked up his life where he left off before the war, working the farm and helping to support his family. The family farm prospered, and each passing year netted higher and higher land values.

As was the tradition set by their own parents, the goal established by Nathan and Margaret Chatfield in 1869 was to provide not only for themselves but for the future of all six of their children. Having parceled out 90 acres to William, who had married Laura Dole that year, they still had five children to consider. It wasn't until affordable land south of Denver, Colorado, could be reached by rail in the early 1870's that Nathan and Margaret determined a workable strategy. They would parcel out a portion of their Kankakee land to four of their children and sell the rest for reinvestment, splitting the proceeds with their eldest son, Edward. James would receive 126 acres of land, not far from the family stone house. Newton would continue to reside in the stone house and would receive the 128 acres on which it was sitting. Charles and Mary would each inherit 120-acre parcels of nearby land upon coming of age. Mary's land would be located a mile south of the stone house, and Charles's would be directly across the road from the house. In the interim, Charles and Mary would remain with their parents, who would move to Colorado with Edward. It was up to Edward to locate a suitable and affordable ranch property for the family in Colorado.

Edward, by then 32 years old and still unmarried, rode the train to Denver in the early spring of 1874. From Denver he took the rail car to Littleton, staying in the home of his cousin, Isaac Willard Chatfield, who had moved from Florence, Fremont County, Colorado, to Littleton in November of 1871. The two cousins identified a fertile 42-acre parcel located at the junction of Arapahoe and Jefferson Counties that would suit Edward and his family's needs.[*] Nestled against Isaac's land in Douglas County on the south, the 2,700-foot by 675-foot rectangle was bordered on the east by what is today South Platte Park. The slice of land included a 1,400-foot strip of the South Platte River, a section that now serves as the spillway to the Chatfield Reservoir. With its purchase by contract through the Colorado Mortgage and Investment Company on April 12, 1874, Edward had assured himself and his family a new foothold. Before returning to Kankakee, Edward contracted with his cousin Isaac to purchase additional land over time.[†]

Having arranged his initial purchases, Edward returned to Kankakee to resume his farm duties as eldest son. It was at this point—when Edward felt that his future prosperity was better assured—that he allowed himself to seriously consider marriage. He had grown fond of a young lady whom he had met while visiting relatives in Ohio, and it wasn't long before Edward proposed. Edward and Anna E. Bates, of Hartford, Trumbull County, Ohio, married on February 8, 1877, in Anna's hometown. Six handsome spoons, inscribed with the name *Chatfield*, had been cast from Edward's six memorable silver dollars as a priceless wedding gift to his bride. The young couple returned to Kankakee to live on the family farm until the spring of 1879, when all arrangements had been completed for the enormous move to Littleton. Their one and only child, a daughter named Edaline, would be born four years later in 1883.

Not only would six Chatfields from Kankakee relocate (Edward, Anna, Nathan, Margaret, Mary and Charles), two of Margaret's family from Twinsburg, Ohio, would join them: Margaret's older brother, William Avery Herrick, and his wife, Jeanette Nichol. Once in Littleton, the families would find temporary housing until suitable dwellings could be erected on their respective properties, located directly west of

---

[*]   Specifically, the land constituted the southern fourth of the southwest quarter of section 31, township 5, range 68 west. State Highway 470 now bisects the 42-acre parcel lengthwise. This land was located in Arapahoe and Jefferson Counties. It is likely that Edward purchased adjacent land in Douglas County as well, but the records are not available, having been destroyed by fire long ago.

[†]   The details of Edward's various land purchases are noted in Appendix II.

Edward's property, near what is now the intersection of West Chatfield Avenue and South Platte Canyon Road. On April 22, 1879, following the family's arrival in Littleton, Edward made his second purchase from the southwest quarter of section 31-5-68, one of several more that would follow in the coming years.

Although Edward arrived in Colorado with the intention of continuing his work as a farmer, he would ultimately provide Littleton with far more than an additional farm.

Having obtained the water rights to his farm in April, 1879, Edward quickly became a principal water distributor in the area. By October, 1891, not only had he received the city franchise to lay, maintain, and operate all of Littleton's water pipes, he also served his neighbors and community by drilling water wells. He was made a member of the Littleton Board of Trade in May, 1892, and was elevated to a director nine months later. A respected rancher and farmer in the community, people turned to Edward when in need of fine cows or information about the worthiness of the latest Durham wheat. He was also a capable businessman. As a wheat farmer, he bagged his best seeds and sold them on the open market. As a trader of beef, he helped underwrite and oversee the operation of the Littleton Canning Company, facilitating wide distribution of canned meat throughout the west. He also leased portions of his ranch to breeders of Percherons—exceptionally strong horses that were bred specifically to pull heavy loads. The breeders, in turn, charged substantial fees for the valued, registered animals to usher mares. As he expanded his water business, Edward became a principal stockholder and eventually, the treasurer of Littleton's profitable—and wryly named—"Last Chance Ditch Company, Number 2." In addition, for many years Edward served the Platte area as one of its prominent election judges.

Not all of the Chatfields remained in Littleton. In 1882, Edward's youngest brother Charles, then 27, had gained enough experience to manage his own farm. With the Kankakee property set aside for him, Charles received his family's blessings to return home to Kankakee, where older brothers William, Newton, and James still lived. Within a year, Charles would marry.

Perhaps the most difficult adjustments Edward and his siblings would face during the 1880's and 1890's were the deaths of their parents and later, of their brother, Charles. Nathan passed away following a farm accident in 1885; Margaret died following a prolonged illness in 1887; and Charles died in Kankakee from a horrible fall in December of 1891.

Yet most of Edward's siblings would join him in the Littleton area, flourishing there. Health issues prompted James and his wife Annie to sell their Kankakee farm and move to Littleton in 1888, their two young children accompanying them. Two years later—a year before Charles died—Newton and his wife, Lizzie, with their three children, sold their Kankakee farm and moved to Littleton as well. They were hoping to establish a grocery business there. And, like Edward, both James and Newton quickly became prominent Littleton citizens. James prospered as a successful realtor, a financial consultant, a notary public, and the community's first justice of the peace, a position he maintained for many years. Newton established his grocery store on Main Street. William purchased property in Littleton and made regular visits there, but he remained a resident of Kankakee for the rest of his life. In 1895, Edward's sister Mary married Noah Shepardson, the son of a Union surgeon from Ohio, and by 1899 the couple had three children. Their first child, Charles N. Shepardson, would grow up to become the dean of the College of Agriculture at Texas A&M, and in 1955 he would be appointed by President Dwight D. Eisenhower to represent agricultural interests on the Federal Reserve Board.

All the while, Edward never left his past behind him, forever active in the G.A.R. In December of 1895, Edward was elected to the position of Post Commander of Littleton's John C. Fremont Post 83, officiating over its many functions. Edward's service to his community continued in the Littleton area for 37 years before his decline in health that quickly followed the 1916 death of his wife, Anna. In 1917, suffering from a series of mini-strokes, Edward moved to Long Beach, California, to live with his daughter and son-in-law, Edaline and Bernie Rhea. In 1920, the year that he sold his ranch, Edward was one of ten living members of his G.A.R. Post. And on December 3, 1924, at age 82, Edward L. Chatfield, *crowned by the length of days*, passed away.

There is much more to tell about the Chatfield pioneers of early Colorado—hard working, community-minded people who helped establish the roots of Littleton, Fort Collins, and Hot Sulphur Springs, Colorado. Additional details of the family constellation are presented in Appendix I: Edward L. Chatfield's Family. The Colorado story, itself, is presented as a journey through time based upon archived news clippings in Appendix II: The Chatfields of Historic Colorado.

Finally, *The Chatfield Story* would be incomplete if it didn't provide additional information regarding "the boys" whom Chatfield marched with and fought beside. What happened to them—where did they go, what sort of lives would they eventually lead? Some of the answers to these questions may be found in Appendix III: About the Boys.

Grandfather ISSAC   Grandmother LUCY   Father NATHAN   Mother MARGARET

NEWTON

EDWARD Livingston Chatfield

JAMES

WILLIAM   DAVID   CHARLES   MARY

APPENDIX I: EDWARD LIVINGSTON CHATFIELD'S FAMILY

Paternal Grandfather: Isaac Chatfield   (Jan. 15, 1787 — Aug. 1, 1861)
Paternal Grandmother: Lucy Tomlinson   (Mar 20, 1787 — Aug. 20, 1872)
Maternal Grandfather: David Herrick   (Jul. 7, 1790 — Jan. 6, 1867)
Maternal Grandmother: Zipporah Avery   (Aug. 28, 1793 — Sep. 30, 1848)
Father: Nathan Stoddard Chatfield   (Oct. 8, 1816 — August 8, 1885)
Mother: Margaret Prudentia Herrick Chatfield   (May 19, 1818 — October 10, 1887)

Edward and his Siblings:

- Edward Livingston Chatfield   (Aug. 4, 1842 — Dec. 3, 1924)
- David Avery Chatfield   (Nov. 13, 1845 — Sept. 18, 1864)
- William Stoddard Chatfield   (July 28, 1847 — Jan. 26, 1925)
- Isaac Newton Chatfield   (July 13,1849 — May 25, 1926)
- James Herrick Chatfield   (Aug. 16, 1851 — April 20, 1919)
- Charles H. (Henry) Chatfield   (Aug. 25, 1855 — Dec. 22, 1891)
- Mary Margaret Chatfield   (Feb. 14, 1859 — Feb. 15, 1925)

THE GRANDPARENTS

Isaac Chatfield, the son of Joel Chatfield and Ruth Stoddard, was born in Derby, New Haven, Connecticut, on January 15, 1787. Isaac's father, Joel, had served in the War of 1812 under Colonel Sill. Isaac's birth came just three months after the Continental Congress had adopted the dollar and decimal coinage. The infant who would become his wife was born that same year—a half year before the *U.S.*

458
The Chatfield Story: Civil War Letters and Diaries of
Private Edward L. Chatfield of the 113th Illinois Volunteers

Constitution was adopted. When George Washington took office in 1789, Isaac and his future wife were just two years old.

In 1806, at the age of 19, while still in Derby, New Haven, Connecticut, Isaac married **Lucy Tomlinson**, of Woodbridge, Connecticut. Born on March 20, 1787, Lucy Tomlinson was the fifth of twelve children of Levi Tomlinson and Amelia Beard. The 1806 wedding occurred during Thomas Jefferson's second term of office, around the time of the return of Lewis and Clark following their exploration of the Louisiana Territory—an eventful time in American history. The couple settled in Seymour, Connecticut, barely six miles away from Lucy's birthplace, where Isaac farmed while taking college coursework. After nine years of marriage, Isaac and Lucy had five children:

- Lucius Napoleon Chatfield   (b. 1807 – d. 1884)
- Lucy Almira Chatfield   (b. 1809 – d. 1850)
- Albert Alonzo Chatfield   (b. 1811 – d. 1851)
- Levi Tomlinson Chatfield   (b. 1813 – d. 1848)
- Nathan Stoddard Chatfield   (b. 1816 – d. 1885) – Edward's father.

After Nathan's birth, the family of seven moved to Batavia in Geauga County, Ohio, in 1816. One of the Connecticut Land Company's fledgling townships, Batavia was eventually renamed Middlefield. Their move came during James Madison's second term of office, when Indiana joined the Union as the 19th state. Isaac was an adventurous 27-year-old with advanced training, a man who would quickly establish a reputation as a capable farmer and knowledgeable businessman. After having settled in Middlefield, Lucy, a sturdy and resourceful frontier woman, gave birth to six more children, bringing the child count to a total of eleven:

- Ruth Ann Chatfield   (b. 1817 – d. 1904)
- Charles Henry Chatfield   (b. 1819 – d. after 1900)
- Marie Antoinette "Maryetta" Chatfield   (b. 1824 – d. 1909)
- Gilbert Lafayette Chatfield   (b. 1826 – d. 1909)
- Charlotte Ann Chatfield   (b. 1828 – d. 1844)
- Georgianna Chatfield   (b. 1829 – d. 1855)

In 1821, between the births of Charles Henry and Marie Antoinette, Isaac was elected as Geauga County's "Land Lister," his popularity well established.[*] Isaac volunteered to read passages to the growing congregation of the Episcopal Church, contributing to Middlefield's first religious edifice constructed in 1829.[419] Isaac and Lucy Chatfield remained in Middlefield for 44 years before deciding it was time to resettle on smaller and less demanding acreage in a community that afforded

---

[*]   His duties included the recording of all land sale transactions within the county.

convenient travel. North Ridgeville, 55 miles west, with its train station, seemed ideal. After dividing among their children what land they had not sold off to others, Isaac and Lucy moved to North Ridgeville in 1860, both 73 years old. Their dreams of travel and leisure time together were short lived, however. Isaac died on August 1, 1861, and was buried in the North Ridgeville Cemetery. By then, Lucy had already lost five of her 11 children, and the country was at war. Isaac's death came just four months after the firing on Fort Sumter and ten days after the Confederates had won the first battle of Bull Run, a battle that occurred one year before young Edward enlisted.

A widowed woman who had become bitterly experienced with death, Lucy's letters from North Ridgeville read like sermons—firm, God-fearing instruction from an experienced probationer of life. She was dearly loved. Even Margaret called Lucy "Mother," having lost her own mother early in her marriage to Nathan, in 1848. The dominant matriarch of the Chatfield family, she was referred to by Edward and his siblings as "Grandmother Lucy." Seventy-five years old when Edward enlisted, Lucy regularly corresponded with him throughout the war and was his first source of support after he left the hospital in Grafton, West Virginia, in April 1865.

After Edward's return, and nine years after Isaac's 1861 death, Lucy remarried at the age of 81. Her second husband, James W. Herrick—Margaret Prudentia Herrick Chatfield's paternal uncle—had been the husband of Lucy's older sister, Deborah Tomlinson. Deborah had died on March 20, 1868, and Lucy married James on October 1, 1868. The newlyweds lived in North Ridgeville until Lucy's death at age 85 on August 20, 1872. She was buried beside her first husband, Isaac, in the Chatfield-Robb plot in the North Ridgeville Cemetery. James W. Herrick died five months later (January 10, 1873) and was buried in the Herrick plot at the Locust Grove Cemetery in Twinsburg, Ohio.

David Herrick: The third of eleven children born to Isaac Herrick and Prudence Avery became Edward's maternal grandfather. David Herrick was born in Worthington, Hampshire County, Massachusetts, on July 7, 1790—thirty-two days after Rhode Island became the 13th Colony to ratify the *U.S. Constitution*. Midway between his 21st and 22nd birthday—while in Preston, New London County, Connecticut—David married **Zipporah Avery**, who was then 18 years old. Their January 5, 1812, wedding preceded the War of 1812 by five months—the period when Missouri was being organized as a territory. The daughter of William and Margaret Avery, Zipporah was born on August 28, 1793, in Stonington, New London County, Connecticut. Her birth year corresponded to that of Stephen F. Austin and Sam Houston—two time-honored historic Texas politicians. David and Zipporah's first five children were born in Worthington, Massachusetts. Following the 1826 death of their fifth child, Esther Herrick, the family moved to Twinsburg, Summit

County, Ohio. Among the young state's early pioneers, the Herricks were farmers who maintained their living through crop sales for 19 years before Zipporah passed away. Their known children, by birth order, included:

- William Avery Herrick   (b. 1814 – d. 1897)
- Margaret Prudentia Herrick   (b.5/19/1818 – d.10/10/1887) Edward's mother
- James Oliver Herrick   (b. 1820 – d. 1849)
- Mary Hewitt Herrick   (b. 1823 – d. 1885)
- Esther Herrick   (b. 1825 – d. 1826)
- Esther Brewster Herrick   (b. 1827 – d. 1915)
- David Herrick, Jr.   (b. 1829 – d. 1895)
- A son   (b. 1831 – d. at birth)
- Zipporah Herrick   (b. 1833 – d. 1903)

Zipporah (Margaret's mother) died on September 30, 1848, and was buried in the Herrick plot at the Locust Grove Cemetery in Twinsburg, Ohio. David remarried in 1851 at the age of 61. His second wife, Julia Austin, came from Connecticut, as had Zipporah. Their marriage resulted in the birth of Austin O. Herrick, born in Twinsburg on September 22, 1852. David Herrick died on January 26, 1867. He was buried in the Herrick plot in Twinsburg alongside his first wife. His death occurred at the time that both the Senate and the House were considering impeachment of President Andrew Johnson.

Johnson had ascended to the Presidency when Lincoln was assassinated—a "War Democrat" from Tennessee who supported the North throughout the war. His conciliatory attitude toward the secessionist states, and his eagerness to return them to the Union had netted him considerable opposition from the "Radical Republicans" in Congress, particularly after his veto of the *Civil Rights Act of 1866.** Led by Representative Thaddeus Stevens and Senator Charles Sumner, the Radical Republicans demanded evidence of genuine social change in the South. They wanted strong protection for the Freedmen and sound evidence that Confederate nationalism had ended before granting a seceding state re-admittance. They viewed Johnson as an obstacle to all of this and did all that they could to remove him. But it wasn't until 1868 that they could come up with a potentially substantive charge: violation of the *Tenure of Office Act* which Congress had passed in 1867 to specifically prevent Johnson from removing the Secretary of War. When the impeachment proceedings moved forward in 1868, the effort to remove Johnson from office failed by a single vote in the Senate.

---

*   This act, passed over Johnson's veto, provided sweeping civil rights reform and anti-discrimination housing and employment safeguards for all people regardless of race, including the rights to make and enforce contracts, sue and be sued, testify in court, inherit, purchase, lease, sell, hold, and convey real property.

THE PARENTS

Edward's father, **Nathan Stoddard Chatfield**, was born in Derby, New Haven County, Connecticut, on October 8, 1816, when James Madison was president. Madison was sometimes referred to as the "Father of the American Constitution," his many essays in the *Federalist* heavily influencing its ratification. The fifth of Isaac and Lucy's 11 children, Nathan was barely one year old when his parents moved to Middlefield, Ohio. Nathan would mature into a capable and hard working farmer—a disciplined and a genuinely "gentle man." Almost 26 years old and residing in Geauga County, Nathan met and married **Margaret Prudentia Herrick** on August 19, 1841, the second child of David and Zipporah Herrick. Margaret had become an astute and capable 23-year-old by then. She would be a loving and dependable companion to Nathan for many years. Nathan and Margaret had seven children—all born in Middlefield. Edward Livingston Chatfield was their first child. Margaret loved all of her children dearly and worried deeply about them in times of danger. Following the 1848 loss of her own mother, Margaret turned to Lucy, Nathan's mother, for maternal counsel.

Nathan purchased land in Pilot Township, Kankakee County, Illinois, moving his family there in the latter months of 1859. James Buchanan, still in office, seemed helplessly unable to mend the rapidly dividing nation. From their stone farmhouse eight miles west of Kankakee on what is now Highway 17, the family raised horses, cattle, pigs and chickens and grew corn, wheat, flax, rye, oats, fruit, berries and garden vegetables. After settling in Kankakee, Margaret made the family clothing using an invention that had been adapted for home use in 1854—the sewing machine—a device that afforded her more time for the endless household chores of cooking, canning, milking, churning, maintaining table-food gardens, and child care. Rarely idle, she somehow found time to foster evening sing-alongs to the accompaniment of the family melodeon.

Nathan was 46 and Margaret was 44 years old when Edward enlisted, Margaret's health problems with asthma and a diagnosis of breast cancer were ongoing concerns to Edward throughout the war. Although the Chatfields were members of the Episcopal Church while in Middlefield and Kankakee, they opted for the Presbyterian faith following their 1879 move to Littleton, Colorado. Nathan's death, in Littleton, preceded Margaret's by two years. Nathan died on August 22, 1885, and Margaret, on October 10, 1887. Both were buried in the Littleton Cemetery.

THE CHILDREN

Edward Livingston Chatfield

Edward was born on August 4, 1842, a time when John Tyler, Jr. was President. Tyler was a Southern sectionalist who ascended to the Presidency after William Henry Harrison died on April 4, 1841. Harrison had been in office barely four months before

462
The Chatfield Story: Civil War Letters and Diaries of
Private Edward L. Chatfield of the 113th Illinois Volunteers

dying of pneumonia. Tyler's emphasis on states' rights helped kindle the flames that eventually exploded into the Civil War. Edward grew up to be one of the soldiers who would fight, a young man of virtue and good conscience whose life fulfilled the wishes outlined in his encomium, one "...crowned with length of days." After three of his younger brothers had married and twelve years after the war, Edward married **Anna E. Bates** in Hartford, Trumbull County, Ohio, on February 8, 1877. Their union followed the marriage of Brother Newton and Lizzie by one week. Not many years after their marriage, the newlyweds relocated to Littleton, Colorado. Six years later, on July 27, 1883, Edward and Anna welcomed their first and only child, **Edaline Anesta Chatfield**. Edaline eventually married Bernard "Bernie" Landon Rhea, the son of the elected Jefferson County tax assessor, **K. Shelby Rhea.** The couple had no children. Upon her May 7, 1964, death, Edaline passed on her father's Civil War letters and artifacts to her cousin—the co-author of this book, Margaret Chatfield McCarty. Edward died in Long Beach, California, on December 3, 1924, and his body was returned to Littleton for burial in the family plot. Edaline, Bernie and her parents-in-law were also buried in the Littleton Cemetery.

David Avery Chatfield

Nathan and Margaret's second child, David, was born in Middlefield, Ohio, on November 13, 1845, shortly before Texas was admitted as the 28th state under James Polk's administration. David was almost 17 years old when Edward departed for war. It was David who had to shoulder his older brother's farm responsibilities, the "new right arm" to his father. Funny, impulsive, and adored by his family, David died in September of 1864 while Edward was being held captive in a Confederate prison. The details of his death have remained obscured by the absence of records. Both cholera and typhoid fever were rampant at the time. If not taken by disease, David may have died in a farm accident, another common cause. Although Edward encouraged David to enlist at the age of 18, there is no record of David's having done so, and there is no military marker at his grave site in Kankakee's Mound Grove Cemetery. Unless an obituary or other record turns up, the cause of David's death will remain a mystery.

William Stoddard Chatfield

William, the third child, was born in Middlefield, Ohio, on September 28, 1847. His birth coincided with the Mexican-American War; American forces had taken Mexico City two weeks earlier. Often sick as a child, "Willie," as Edward called him, was 15 years old when Edward enlisted. At the age of 18, on February 28, 1865, William enlisted in the army and was mustered into Company "F" of the 156th Illinois infantry. His company was soon stationed in Memphis, where Edward had been stationed earlier. By the middle of July, William had grown desperately ill, remaining in the hospital until discharged. On June 24, 1869, William married **Laura Emily Dole**, the daughter of Abijah Dole and Sibyl Packard. Born in Shelburne, Franklin

County, Massachusetts, Laura had been living in Manteno, Illinois, 12 miles north of Kankakee. After living briefly in Littleton, William continued to hold property there while visiting from Kankakee. William and Laura had five children:

- Frank Stoddard Chatfield   (b. 1872 – d. 1886)
- Bertha Laura Chatfield   (b. 1875 – d. 1931)
- William Nathan Chatfield   (b. 1879 – d. 1969)
- Royal Edward "Roy" Chatfield   (b. 1882 – d. 1950)
- Raymond Alfred Chatfield   (b. 1887 – d. 1902)

Having purchased a small house in Littleton, Colorado, William had a place to stay while visiting family there, but his heart and home remained in Kankakee, where he farmed and served as a community leader and active participant in the G.A.R. until his death on January 26, 1925. Both he and his wife were buried in the family plot in Kankakee's Mound Grove Cemetery. Frank, Bertha, Royal and Raymond are interred alongside their parents in the Mound Grove Cemetery.

Isaac Newton Chatfield

Born on July 13, 1849, Isaac's birth came during Zachary Taylor's presidency, a man who was attractive to the South (he owned 100 slaves) and equally attractive to the North (an avid nationalist). The fourth-born child, "Newton," as he was called by his family (and occasionally, "Newt," by Edward) was 13 years old when Edward enlisted. Edward made a point of encouraging Newton to write more letters, dispensing enticing tidbits of exciting war news. Twelve years after the war ended—exactly one week before Edward would marry—Newton married **Elizabeth "Lizzie" Mead** on February 1, 1877, in Bonfield, Illinois. The couple resided in the family stone house for 13 years, managing their farm and together having three children.

- Eunice Prudentia Chatfield   (b. 1879 – d. 1914)
- Newton Leslie Chatfield   (b. 1882 – d. 1971)
- Laura Avery Chatfield   (b. 1884 – d. 1962)

Newton and his family moved to Littleton, Colorado, in 1890, where Newton purchased a grocery store downtown shortly after their arrival. Operating his grocery store for 10 years, Newton became a community leader and a trustee of the Littleton Presbyterian Church before moving north with his wife to Fort Collins at the turn of the century. There he served as Colorado Agricultural College's caretaker of the Chemistry Department for the next 21 years. Lizzie died in Fort Collins on May 25, 1918. In 1921, Newton, then 72 years old, fell and broke his hip while attempting to board a trolley. Two years later, he left Fort Collins to live with his daughter Laura in California. Laura had earned her Master's Degree and was teaching school in Woodland, California. Newton died in Bakersfield, California on May 25, 1926.

James Herrick Chatfield

James was born on August 16, 1851, eleven months after the passage of the *Compromise of 1850*—a bundle of legislation that included the *Fugitive Slave Act*—a law requiring citizens to assist in the recovery of runaway slaves. Nine years younger than Edward, "Jimmy" was days away from turning 11 when Edward left home, his informative letters frequently referred to by Edward in return. Seven years after the war ended, James exchanged vows with **Annie Mary Brazier** in a Kankakee wedding held on December 22, 1872. Annie was the daughter of John S. Brazier and Mary Jane Hay of Saratoga, New York, born there on January 11, 1856. James and Annie lived on the 120-acre Kankakee plot deeded over to them by Nathan and Margaret in 1874. The couple had three children:

- Ruth Ann Chatfield   (b.1874 - d.1883)
- Edward Livingston Chatfield, Jr.   (b.1876 – d.1957)
- Nellie "Nelly" Margaret Chatfield   (b.1885 – d.1962)

Following the birth of Nellie Margaret, Annie contracted *phthisis*—the feared lung disease for which there was no known cure.[*] Proper climate was said to help. At that time, doctors gave anecdotal accounts of patients who had improved in climates with clean air, low humidity, and plentiful sunshine. The high altitudes of Colorado were considered ideal. Desperate, the family put their Kankakee farm up for sale and moved to Littleton in 1888, the sale netting enough money to afford the transition to Colorado. Once there, James established himself as a realtor and financial consultant, locating his place of business at the foot of Main Street. Annie's condition only worsened, however, and she died of "consumption" on February 27, 1889, at age 33.

James turned to his sister, Mary Margaret, for help in tending his two children (ages 13 and 3), a request that she warmly fulfilled. Active in his community, James soon was elected to the position of Littleton's first Justice of the Peace. He also became the secretary of the Littleton Cemetery Association and a trustee of the Littleton Presbyterian Church. Well-liked by the townspeople of Littleton, his friends gave him the nickname, "Sugar Jim." James is co-author Margaret Chatfield McCarty's great-grandfather.

James waited seven years before remarrying, and when he did, he married his sixth cousin, **Mary Elmina Dickinson**, the daughter of Walter Dickinson and Emma

---

[*]   The common name for Annie's breathing ailment was "consumption." The term "tuberculosis" was not in vogue until the early 1900's. Although Robert Koch, the German bacteriologist, had discovered the infectious bacterial cause in 1882, there was no real cure until the age of antibiotics following World War II.

"Elmina/Almira" Chatfield. The couple exchanged vows on September 5, 1892. The second marriage brought the couple a child.

- Elmina D. Chatfield was born in 1898, a half-sister to Edward Livingston Jr. and Nellie Margaret.

In December of 1918, James's wife, Mary Elmina, died of heart trouble. James survived her by four months, suffering from dropsy[*] and passing away in his daughter Nellie's home in Hoquiam, Washington on April 20, 1919.

Charles H. (Henry) Chatfield

Nathan and Margaret's sixth child, Charles H. (Henry) Chatfield, was born in Middlefield, Ohio, on August 25, 1855. Franklin Pierce was president, a Northerner with Southern sympathies; he favored the *Kansas-Nebraska Act* that helped to repeal the effectiveness of the *Missouri Compromise*, thus deepening the North-South divide. Almost a seven-year-old when Edward enlisted, "Charley," as he was called, was a grade school student during the time of the war. In 1879, at the age of 24, Charles and his younger sister, Mary Margaret, accompanied their parents to Littleton, Colorado, helping them settle there with their oldest brother, Edward. A few years later, Charles moved back to Kankakee where he worked the 126-acre Bonfield farm deeded over to him by his father. A Kankakee wedding soon followed. Charles and **Salina "Lina" Elmira Taylor** married on August 30, 1883, enjoying eight years together before Charles's life would come to a tragic end. As Christmas of 1891 grew near, the family's turkeys had acquired the habit of leaving home and roosting upon their neighbor's windmill. Attempting to remove them after dark on Sunday evening, December 20, Charles fell, struck his head, and never regained consciousness. His December 22, 1891, death widowed Lina and left two children without a father:

- Nathan Stuart Chatfield   (b. 1885)
- Austin Charles Chatfield   (b. 1888)

Charles was buried in the Mound Grove Cemetery. Lina eventually married William Barber, and the family moved to Spencer, Iowa. Although Charles and Lina's son Nathan never married, their son Austin did eventually marry, continuing the Chatfield lineage.

Mary Margaret Chatfield

Mary was Nathan and Margaret's last child. Her February 14, 1859, birth in Middlefield, Ohio, occurred during the middle of President James Buchanan's term

---

[*]   "Dropsy" was the name given to problems caused by fluid retention, an illness reminiscent of Edward's "dropisical debility"—the swelling of his legs while he was garrisoned in Chewalla, Tennessee. Penned in the James Herrick Chatfield family *Bible,* the cause of James's death was listed as "Heart troubles and Bright's Disease." This suggests that he had died from a combination of congestive heart failure and kidney failure.

of office, when the *Compromise of 1850* could no longer quell the nation's mood, clouds of discontent looming on all horizons. In his letters, Edward called Mary Margaret "Little Mary." She was 3½ years old when her big brother volunteered for military service—a ray of sunshine, charming, and capable. Edward mentioned her in more than a dozen of his letters. A dutiful daughter, as a young adult she cared for her parents, Nathan and Margaret, from 1879 to 1887. A caring sister and aunt, she mothered James's two children for three years following the 1889 death of his first wife, Annie Mary. With James's guidance, she bought and sold property, accumulating her own independent financial means. In Arapahoe County, on March 19, 1895, 36-year-old Mary wed 24-year-old **Noah Shepardson**, the son of a Union Civil War surgeon—and the younger brother of Otis Shepardson, who was listed as a ranch hand for Edward and Anna in the 1880 Federal Census. Mary and Noah had three children:

- Charles N. Shepardson (b. 1896 – d. 1975)
  Their first child, Charles became a dean at Texas A & M University in adulthood. President Eisenhower subsequently appointed him to the Federal Reserve Board on March 17, 1955.
- Margaret Shepardson (b. 1897 – d. 1965)
- Marcia L. Shepardson (b. 1899)

In March of 1901, Noah died of injuries from an accident that occurred as he was returning home from the nearby hills after having loaded two red spruce poles in his wagon. Along the narrow road there were many fallen trees. Noah was attempting to steer clear of one of them when the rear wheel of his wagon slipped, allowing the brake assembly to strike the tree. The impact dislodged the brake lever, throwing it forward. The lever struck Noah on the crown of his head causing a large skull fracture that ended his life within hours. Six months after Noah's death, Mary and her children moved to Fort Collins, Colorado, and settled near her brother, Isaac Newton and his family. Mary Margaret passed away February 15, 1925 in Fort Collins and was buried next to her husband in the Littleton Cemetery.

SEVEN CHATFIELD COUSINS

Edward stayed in touch with many cousins during the war. He mentions seven of his first cousins in his letters and diary entries:

1. **Cousin Henry (Hank) E. Chatfield,** the son of Alberto Alonzo Chatfield (Nathan Chatfield's older brother) and Elizabeth Kirtland, became a sergeant in Company "I" of the 18th Michigan Volunteers.
2. **Cousin Georgianna "Georgia" Robb**, the daughter of "Maryetta" Chatfield Robb, one of Nathan's younger sisters. Georgia wrote a

letter to the Chatfields in Kankakee, in May 1860, shortly before the war.

3. **Cousin Charlotte Robb**, the younger daughter of "Maryetta" Chatfield Robb and Jackson Robb.

4. **Cousin Mary Irene Herrick** ("Mary Arrene" in Edward's March 1, 1863, letter) the daughter of James O. Herrick, one of Margaret's younger brothers, and Mary Jane Conant.

Edward maintained regular contact with three other cousins, sons of Edward's Uncle Levi Tomlinson Chatfield and his wife, Lovina Mastick. All were born in Middlefield, Geauga County, Ohio, and moved with their parents to Bath, Mason County, Illinois, in 1844. Their lives have been carefully chronicled by their descendents.[*]

5. **Cousin Isaac Willard Chatfield** (b. 1836 – d. 1921) Isaac, the first-born, was six years old when Edward was born and eight years old when his family moved to Illinois. Reaching maturity, he met and married **Elizabeth Ann "Eliza" Herrington.** In 1859, the family headed west by covered wagon in search of investment property in Colorado. When the war broke out, they returned east to Mason County, Illinois, where Isaac enlisted on August 12, 1861, at the age of 25. Initially the 1st Sergeant, after a week of service, Isaac was promoted to 2nd lieutenant in Company "E" of the 27th Illinois Infantry. Within three months of service, while camped with Grant's forces in Cairo, he developed recurrent kidney and bladder infections that forced him to retire after the Tennessee battle of Stones River, among the deadliest battles of the war. Submitting his resignation in February of 1863, he returned to his family in Illinois. When spring arrived, his health on the mend, Isaac and family returned to Colorado. There, in late November of 1865, Isaac purchased land in Florence (Fremont County) and settled. Six years later, in 1871, he extended his land holdings into the Littleton, Colorado, area. His land-trading and mining interests in Leadville, 100 miles west of Littleton, likely led him to sell some of his Littleton land to his cousin Edward L. Chatfield, on May 17, 1874.[†]

6. **Cousin Clark Samuel Chatfield** (b. 1839 – d. 1906) Clark Samuel, the second son, married **Louisa Tankersley** in 1858. They had three children. When war came, Clark's August 1861 enlistment resulted in

---

[*]   Special thanks are given to Catherine Sevenau, the great-granddaughter of Isaac Willard Chatfield and the co-author's fourth cousin. The research and writings by Catherine and her brother, Gordon Clemens, provided much of the information on the three Chatfield cousins: Isaac Willard, Clark Samuel, and Charles Henry.

[†]   See Appendix II, Edward Livingston Chatfield (Littleton land purchases.)

his being assigned to Company "C" of the 2nd Illinois Cavalry. Edward regularly corresponded with "Cousin Clark" throughout the war. It was with Clark that Edward spent the night in Memphis when en route to Corinth on August 4, 1863. While in Memphis, Clark served as an orderly for a colonel on General Hurlbut's staff. Two years after his discharge from the army, Clark and his family moved to Colorado and settled near Clark's brother in Florence, Fremont County. Following his wife Louisa's 1868 death, Clark took the train back to Nebraska to bury her. Within a year he remarried and returned to Colorado with his second wife, **Mary Elizabeth Morrow**, who brought him nine more children. Clark Samuel Chatfield died in Princeton, Colusa County, California, on March 6, 1906.

7. **Cousin Charles Henry Chatfield** (b. 1840 – d. 1864) Charles Henry was the first of Edward's three cousins to go to war. Enlisting in May of 1861, Charles became a private in Company "K" of the 17th Illinois and was soon promoted to corporal. Wounded in battle, he was discharged in June of 1862. He volunteered again two months later and mustered back in as a 2nd lieutenant. He was assigned to Company "D" of the 85th Illinois. Subsequently promoted to captain, Charles Henry Chatfield died in the battle of Kennesaw Mountain, Georgia, in June of 1864.

APPENDIX II: THE CHATFIELDS OF HISTORIC COLORADO

Chatfield is a familiar name in the Littleton and Denver areas of Colorado. Various streets and a public high school bear the name *Chatfield,* and a huge recreation area is named *Chatfield State Park.* Area residents enjoy sailing on the *Chatfield Reservoir* (sometimes called *Chatfield Lake*), and a well-known landmark of the area is the *Chatfield Dam.* This appendix provides a summary of the Chatfield family in historic Colorado, a story made possible through the hard work and research of many, including:

- The Colorado Historical Society, the Colorado State Library, the Collaborative Digitization Program, and the Colorado Historic Newspaper Collection (CHNC)[*] –the source of most of the news clippings.
- The Genealogy and History Department of the Kankakee Public Library—an assortment of old records, microfilm and copies of the *Kankakee Gazette.*
- The James Herrick Chatfield family *Bible,* in which several obituaries had been placed for safekeeping.
- The Recorder offices in Arapahoe, Douglas, and Jefferson counties.
- The archives of the *Yuma Daily Sun,* which provided clippings on the death of Edward L. Chatfield's daughter, Edaline.

---

[*] Visit: www.coloradohistoricnewspapers.org. The cooperative efforts of the Colorado State Library, the Collaborative Digitization Program, and the Colorado Historic Newspaper Collection (CHNC) are commendable.

1871 — 1874 Isaac Willard Chatfield (Early Land Purchases)

- **1871 — 1874:** In 1871, **I.W. Chatfield** purchases 160 acres of land from Mr. J.B. Hendy at what was the junction of the South Platte River and Plum Creek.[*420] After purchasing 720 more acres from Dan Witter that same year—and additional land after that—Isaac controlled close to 2,000 acres by May of 1874. His influence with the *Colorado and Southern Railroad* assured that the "Chatfield Station" would be placed on his land at Milepost 14.07.[421] **I.W. Chatfield** introduced the growing of potatoes to the area.
- **December 13, 1872:** Real estate transfer from Horatis Jacobs to **I.W. Chatfield** by quitclaim deed for $1.00.[422]
- **January 22, 1874: I.W. Chatfield** buys North ½ of Section 25, Township 4, Range 69W, near Littleton.[423]
- **May 17, 1874: I.W. Chatfield** transfers quitclaim deed to H.B. Bond for South ½ of SW Sect 8, Township 1, Range 68W. In a separate transaction, **Edward L. Chatfield** purchases same land from H.B. Bond on this date.[424]

1874 — 1891 Edward Livingston Chatfield (Littleton Land Purchases)

- **April 12, 1874: E.L. Chatfield** conveys Trust Deed to Colorado Mortgage and Investment Company for part of SW ¼ of Section 31-5-68.[425]
- **May 17, 1874:** Following I.W. Chatfield's transfer of quitclaim deed to H.B. Bond for South ½ of SW Section 8, Twp 3, R 70W. **Edward purchases this land** from H.B. Bond in a separate transaction.[426]
- **August 12, 1874: I.W. Chatfield** grants Warranty Deed to **Edward L. Chatfield** for $2,092.50.[427]
- **April 1, 1875:** Grant Deed — **Edward L. Chatfield** conveys in trust property to secure three notes for $697.50 each due in 1, 2, 3 years with interest of 10% per annum, 30 days to **I.W. Chatfield** and successors.[428]
- **January 26, 1878:** Warranty Deed — **I.W. Chatfield** issues Warranty Deed to **Edward L. Chatfield** for 1,200 acres.[429]
- **February 6, 1878: I.W. Chatfield** is named successor in trust to **Edward Chatfield**, Arapahoe County, Colorado.[430]
- **April 22, 1879: E.L. Chatfield** conveys Trust Deed to Colorado Mortgage and Investment Company for part of SW ¼ of Section 31-5-68, including water rights.[431]

---

[*] The Platte River, running north and south, separates Jefferson County on the west from Douglas County on the east. The Platte River met the Plum River at what is now a point at the base of today's Chatfield Dam, 175 yards east of the observation tower.

- **February 16, 1880: E.L. Chatfield** conveys Trust Deed to Colorado Mortgage and Investment Company for part of SW ¼ of Section 31-5-68.[432]
- **May 10, 1883: E.L. Chatfield** conveys Trust Deed to Colorado Mortgage and Investment Company for part of SW ¼ of Section 31-5-68, including water rights.[433]
- **January 12, 1887: E.L. Chatfield** conveys Trust Deed to Colorado Mortgage and Investment Company for part of SW ¼ of Section 31-5-68, including water rights.[434]
- **April 10, 1891: E.L. Chatfield** has purchased a lot from David Linhart on Curtis Street. *(Littleton Independent)*

1880 — 1887 Nathan and Margaret Chatfield

- **April 7, 1880: County Affairs** — The bond of **E.L. Chatfield** as road overseer of Platte district, with **N.S. Chatfield** and Shellabarger as sureties, was approved. *(Littleton Independent)*
- **August 23, 1883:** *Society news about Pilot, Illinois* —**Mr. And Mrs. Nathan Chatfield,** former residents of this town, but for three or four years having lived in, or near Denver, Colorado, are here now on a visit with their children and many friends. *(Kankakee Gazette, p. 8)*
- **[Obituary] August 8, 1885: Nathan Stoddard Chatfield,** Edward's father, passed away this day, nearly 70 years old. He was first in the family, and among the first citizens of Littleton, to be buried in what would become the family plot in the Littleton Cemetery. His gravestone sits beside those of I.W. Chatfield's children, Wert, Myrtle and Grace, facing the rugged Colorado Mountains and **Chatfield Ranch** three miles west of the city on Platte Canyon Road. *(Littleton Independent)*
- **[Obituary] [August 17, 1885 – date estimated]** *Kankakee, Illinois*

    N.S. Chatfield, whose sudden death we noticed in last week's TIMES, was born in Derby, Conn., and with his parents moved to Wooster, Wayne County, Ohio, [sic*] when he was eight years old. In 1848 [sic†] he moved to Illinois, and settled in the western part of this county. He was the father of seven children, six boys and one

---

*   Although William Chatfield was the probable source of this information, no records have been found showing that Isaac and Lucy Chatfield (Nathan's parents) ever lived in Wooster, Wayne County, Ohio. The 1820 Federal Census records show that Isaac and Lucy and seven of their children, including five-year-old Nathan, were living in Batavia, Geauga County, Ohio.

†   This too appears to be in error. All of Nathan's children, including Mary Margaret, were born in Ohio. Mary, the last born, was born in 1859; shortly after her birth that year, her family moved to the family farm in Pilot (Cagwin/Hersher/Bonfield/Salina area), Kankakee County, Illinois.

girl. **Ed,** with his mother and sister were living with their father in Colorado. **James, Newton and Charles** are on the old homestead near Cagwin, and **William** is in business in this city. On account of the distance, the boys here have had but scant details thus far, of their sad loss, but we give here a few extracts from a letter received by **Will** from his sister.

"My Dear Brother and Sister —

Long ere this, you have heard the sad, sad news that our dear father is gone. O, how we miss him! I can't turn around but I see something to remind me of him. Dear Pa, how I loved him! It seems we can hardly live without him now. Ma is very sick. I am sitting by her; shall watch her to-night. I wrote you Friday morning how he got hurt. All day Friday it was very hard for him to breathe, but he did not complain; not a murmur escaped his lips. He was so thirsty all the time, and wanted just a spoonful of water, and every time he drank he would vomit dark green stuff, and it hurt him so. If the doctor had been here he would have known that inflammation had set it, but we did not. Doctor told us if could keep inflammation down he would get along; and we kept hot cloths wrung out of wormwood or onions on him all the time. Friday night I watched with him, he was very restless, and so thirsty. About 8 o'clock Saturday morning he seemed to grow worse and commenced to hiccough; then ma was frightened and began to think he would not live, as that was a bad sign. But Edward said it was wind on his stomach, as he had not eaten anything since he was hurt. Edward and I worked over him all the time; he said he was in no pain, only he could not breathe. About 10 o'clock he began to be delirious. He could not talk any more after that. At nearly 11 he seemed to want to raise up, and Annie told him if he knew us, to press her hand, and he did; and then, Oh, then came over his face the terrible death agony, and he soon passed away. ** At 1 o'clock the hearse came with coffin, and after he was fixed, we took our last look at that dear loving face. Then they sang "My Jesus, I Love Thee," and Dr. Bliss made a prayer and we started. We went right to the grave, as the coffin could not be opened. The services were to be held in the hall of the School House where we go to church. There they sang "Sweet Bye and Bye;" you know that was one of Pa's favorites, and the burial service read. People came from far and near; everybody loved him; scoffers respected him because he had lived up to the profession he had made. His daily walk and conversation showed he was with Jesus, and learned of him the text was in Rev. 17 chap. 13 verse: "And I heard a voice from heaven saying unto me, Right blessed are the dead which die in the Lord from hence forth. Yea, saith the Spirit, that they may rest from their labors, and their works do follow them."

Pa set such an example here as will never be forgotten. Oh, may we all live as he did! May we be worthy of such a father, and above all, may we be worthy as he was, so when our last shall come, God will say, as to Pa, "tis enough; come up higher." At the church they sang "I know not the hour when my Lord will come" and "I am going home, to die no more." That was the last piece Pa ever sang. At prayers Wednesday morning, we sang all the verses and then he repeated the chorus. How little we thought that was the last time we should ever sing together those dear old hymns from the Gospel Songs."* *(Unidentified Kankakee news clipping found in James Herrick Chatfield family Bible)*

- **October 10, 1887:** Two years after **Nathan's** death, his wife **Margaret Prudentia Herrick Chatfield**, passed away at the age of 69. She was buried in the Littleton Cemetery, beside her husband. Lacking water, the cemetery's appearance would suffer until Margaret's sons, Edward and James, laid the water pipes that ultimately helped beautify their parents' final resting places. *(Terry and Margaret Chatfield McCarty)*
- **[Obituary, 1887] Mrs. Margaret P. Chatfield was born May 19ᵗʰ, 1818** at Worthington, Mass. Hers was a christian [sic] home and the scenes of the family altar were familiar from the earliest years. Like so many others the family left the old New England hive in her childhood and located in what was then known as the "West." At the age of 18 years she was brought under deep religious convictions with which she wrestled for something like a year. At length in a state bordering on despair she yielded full submission to the terms of Divine Mercy and salvation and gave her heart to God. From that time her christian life was ever steadfast and onward. In August 1841 she was married to Nathan G. [sic] Chatfield who died about two years since. In her husband, Mrs. Chatfield found a reliable and earnest follower of Christ with whom she could fully sympathize and together they reared a family of seven children, six of

---

*   According to the dictates of culture, Nathan had died a proper death—a "Good Death"—the event having been carefully witnessed in his home by family members and scrutinized, interpreted and narrated by a loved one, in this case, by his daughter. Mary identified several signs indicative of a favorable afterlife. Nathan had lived a giving life; his "daily walk and conversation showed he was with Jesus"; he had set a positive example for all in his family to follow; and the moment of his death was honorable: although unable to breathe, he did not complain—not even a murmur. Note how the narratives of other 19ᵗʰ century family deaths contain the same elements. (See: D.G. Faust, *This Republic of Suffering, Death and the American Civil War*, p.p. 8-9.)

whom survive them. For the improvement of her health, the family moved to Colorado and located on a farm a few miles from Littleton. Here they made many friends by their kindness of heart and their exemplary walk and life. And here, after a long illness attended with much suffering, Mrs. Margaret P. Chatfield departed this life Oct. 10th, 1887, in the 70th year of her age. At her funeral her pastor, Rev Dr. Bliss preached from the text "Blessed are the dead who die in the Lord." The selection of such a text was fully justified by her long and faithful christian life. Those who were best acquainted with Mrs. Chatfield observed many marked qualities of christian character. She was a devoted wife, a faithful mother, and an earnest christian. We need say no more for "of such are the kingdom of heaven." It is such who train up their children in the nurture and admonition of the Lord. When they are gone, as in this instance, their children rise up and call them blessed. Her last words were "farewell all of you, I am going home to my rest." *(Unidentified newspaper clipping found in James Herrick Chatfield family Bible)*

1883 — 1924 Edward Livingston Chatfield

- **July 27, 1883: Edward L. Chatfield** and his wife **Anna** welcomed into the world their first and only child, **Edaline Chatfield.** *(Terry and Margaret Chatfield McCarty)*

- **October 10, 1891: Messrs. Chatfield** [Edward and James] are placing their machinery on the Littleton heights, for the purpose of perfecting the well on Mr. Lilleys property, in order to supply their artesian system with water. *(Littleton Independent)*

- **October 17, 1891: Mr. E.L. Chatfield** was suddenly taken sick last week, and for a time was in a very precarious condition. He is now improving, and it is hoped is out of danger. His disease is inflammation of the bowels and heart difficulty. **J.H. Chatfield** has also been suffering with ulceration of the throat, but is now improving. *(Littleton Independent)*

- **October 17, 1891: Ordinance No. 36** — AN ORDINANCE GRANTING TO **EDWARD L. CHATFIELD** A FRANCHISE TO LAY WATER PIPES IN THE STREETS OF LITTLETON, AND FOR THE CONSTRUCTION AND OPERATION OF WATER WORKS IN SAID TOWN. Be it ordained by the Board of Trustees of the Town of Littleton. Section 1. The right and privilege of maintaining and operating water works within the Town of Littleton, and all extensions thereof, and of laying down, continuing and maintaining water pipes, valves, hydrants and other apparatus for the conveyance and distribution of water in, upon, along, and through any and all of the streets, alleys, lanes and public places within the Town of Littleton ...is hereby granted to **Edward L. Chatfield**, his executors, administrators and assigns, for a period of twenty-five (25) years to such extent as the Town may lawfully grant the same. *(Littleton Independent)*

- **October 17, 1891: Littleton Water Works** — The Knight system for artesian water is now being pushed, and pipes are being distributed through the streets. **The Chatfield system** is being put in operation, engine in place, and tank for storage is being completed. The Citizen Water Co. have their surveys made, and when the big reservoir is completed they can furnish 300 feet pressure covering all Littleton, including Windermere and Orchard addition to Littleton. The Meyers system will be merged into the Knight system, leaving only three water supplies for the town. *(Littleton Independent)*

- **March 18, 1892: Denver, Colo.** —We the undersigned hereby jointly and severely guarantee the payment of at least ($4000) four thousand dollars of the subscription to stock of the canning company at Littleton, exclusive of subscriptions on site. Said guarantee is made to comply with conditions of proposition made to the Littleton Board of Trade by R.C. Lundy Feb. 24, 1802 — John G. Lilley, R.H. Nelson, S.W. Sprague, Mary E. O'Brien, F. Comstock, **E.L. Chatfield**. *(Littleton Independent)*

- **May 14, 1892: Mr. Ed. Chatfield** is doing considerable work on **W.A. Herrick's** ranch, putting in fruit trees and fixing up generally. *(Littleton Independent)*

- **May 14, 1892:** Duly registered in the *Percheron Stud Book of America* and his recorded No is 6902. Services fee will be $20.00 to usher for single mares. A reduced rate will be made where there are several. Headquarters will be at **E.L. Chatfield's Ranch**, but will call where desired. — Peter Longress, P.O. Littleton, Colorado. *(Littleton Independent)*

- **May 14, 1892: Littleton Board of Trade** — A special meeting of the Littleton Board of Trade will be held at the Town Hall Thursday, May 19th, 7:30 P.M. [Notice lists a membership of 50 townspeople, including **J.H. Chatfield, E.L. Chatfield, and I.N. Chatfield**] *(Littleton Independent)*

- **June 4, 1892: E.L. Chatfield** received notice from Washington that his pension had been granted. This includes back pay. The matter has been running for a number of years.* *(Littleton Independent)*

---

*   It was a common problem for Civil War pensions to be delayed. The award of Chatfield's pension had been delayed by the government for 27 years.

- **July 2, 1892:** The undersigned take this opportunity of expressing their thanks to all that so cheerfully responded in making their ice cream and strawberry festival a success. **Mrs. E.L. Chatfield, Miss Mary Chatfield.** *(Littleton Independent)*
- **September 17, 1892: Mr. Ed. Chatfield** had a severe attack of heart trouble last Thursday night which came near laying him out. We are glad to say he is better again and able to be around. *(Littleton Independent)*
- **February 22, 1893:** The Littleton board of trade, composed of citizens of Arapahoe and Jefferson counties, at their annual meeting Thursday, February 16th, elected the following board of directors: R.J. Spottwood, R.H. Nelson, **E.L. Chatfield**, J.G. Lilley, J.J. Murphy, J.W. Bowles, J.A. Hamer, J.B. Mayes, E. Jull, J.C. Mitchell, G.M. Benedict, J.C. Mathers and F.T. Caley. *(Littleton Independent)*
- **January 12, 1894: Fresh Cows For Sale** — Enquire of **E.L. Chatfield,** Littleton, Colo. *(Littleton Independent)*
- **August 17, 1894:** During the storm last Saturday afternoon, lightning killed four colts for **E.L. Chatfield.** *(Littleton Independent)*
- **November 23, 1894: E.L. Chatfield** left a large bunch of fine celery on our desk last week, for which we tender thanks. *(Littleton Independent)*
- **December 3, 1895:** John C. Fremont Post 83, G.A.R. held its annual election Wednesday and elected the following officers: **E.L. Chatfield,** P.C. [Post Commander]; A.W. Browning, S.V.C.; W.A. Powers, J.V.C; J.J. Stewart, Chaplain; Wm Stewart, Quartermaster; J.B. Markle, Officer of the Day; R.S. Moore, Surgeon; Wm. Stocks, Guard. *(Littleton Independent)*
- **August 12, 1896:** The following judges of elections have been selected to serve for the ensuing year: Platte — **E.L. Chatfield, Robert D. Herrick,**[*] Wm. Shellabarger. School House. *(Colorado Transcript, Golden, Jefferson County)*
- **October 13, 1899: For Sale** — Seed wheat for fall seeding of the Red Cross and Clawson varieties. Price given at the ranch. **E.L. CHATFIELD** *(Littleton Independent)*
- **September 12, 1901: E.L. Chatfield** took the household goods of **Mrs. Shepardson** to Fort Collins yesterday. **Mrs. Shepardson** and children will go up today and will make Fort Collins their future home. *(Littleton Independent)*
- **July 14, 1904:** Election judges appointed: Platte — **E.L. Chatfield, R.D. Herrick,** F.J. Hildebrand. *(Colorado Transcript, Golden, Jefferson County)*

---

[*]   Edward's cousin; Robert was the son of William A. Herrick.

- **June 26, 1906: Mrs. E.L. Chatfield** left for Cheyenne Tuesday to attend the meeting of the W.R.C. [Women's Relief Corps], Department of Colorado and Wyoming, to be held this week in connection with the Encampment of the Grand Army of the Republic. *(Castle Rock, Douglas County)*
- **December 1906:** Interesting Talk on Animal and Plant Breeding. — Short course Class Treated to Lectures and Discussions on Topics Too Little Understood by Many — ... **E.L. Chatfield** of Littleton, a member of the class, stated that in five years Durum Wheat will be a leading crop, because of its yield. He said that in his investigations he finds the color of this wheat against it in the market. *(Fort Collins Weekly Courier)*
- **June 24, 1907: <u>Penny Post Card from Riley Beach to Edward L. Chatfield</u>**—To: Edward L. Chatfield, Littleton, Colo; From: RV. Beach, Post Master, Big Spring, Nebraska...This picture is supposed to represent P.O. & Residence. It has [been] built a little more than a year. I don't think that I like living in town as well as on the farm. I hope the Spirit will move you to write as soon as you get this. Fraternally yours, Riley V. Beach [Photo: Riley Beach holds the left hand of one of his grandchildren as they stand in front of the Big Spring, Nebraska, Post Office as it appeared in 1907.]
- **January 6, 1910:** By 1910, **Edward** was 67 years old, and his financial circumstances were evidently sound enough to assist his cousin, **Isaac Willard Chatfield**, 73, then facing funding difficulties. In a letter to his son-in-law, Fred Adams, **Isaac Willard** commented upon **Edward's** generosity.

<u>Letter</u> — January 6, 1910

Dear Fred,

I should of wrote you before now but have neglected to do so as I had not much to write about. I was pleased to here from you and thank you very much for the 5 plenks* which helped me very much as I am short on ready money. I went down town and bought myself a pair of overshoes and gloves which I needed very much. I have met many of our old friends and all was glad to see and here from us. I was up to Littleton yesterday and saw my cousin E.L. Chatfield he was very kind. He profered to help me and Ma in any way. Said call on him for money at any time for money. Did not want me to hesitate in any matter which was good news for me—as I was quite blue. Most all my neighbors on the Platt from the Canon to Denver has passed on over the divide. I am going over to Aspen about the 20th of the month to get my mining stock all in shape. I shall stop off at

---

* The word is almost illegible. Could it be slang for the sound made by silver dollars?

Leadville and Glenwood Springs and will see Fessler and other friends while gone. I think Ma is some better. She is able to set up in the rocking chair a part of the time but most of the time is in bed and I am in hopes that she will get well soon and Ma says she will get well soon. We was all pleased to receive the Xmas presents.

Ma and Cally both send love to all.

Write often. Your Father I.W. Chatfield[*]

- **September 9, 1910: <u>Penny Post Card from fellow soldier Milton Rounsavell</u>**—To: Edward Chatfield, Littleton, Colo; From: Milton H. Rounsavell, Walsenburg, Colo …Here we are at 72 and 55 years. –M.H.R. [Photo: Milton sits on the front steps of his wood-framed house, his black hat beside him. His hair is pure white, his beard extends to his chest, and spectacles sit on the bridge of his nose. Milton's unnamed 55-year-old wife sits behind him on the porch in one of two rocking chairs.]
- **January 24, 1913: Stockholders Meeting**— The regular annual meeting of the stockholders of the Last Chance Ditch Co., No 2, will be held February 5, 1913, in the offices of Wm. H. Caley in Littleton, at 10 o'clock a.m. for the purpose of electing officers of said company for the ensuing year, and transact any business that may properly come before the stockholders. Done this 5th day of January, A.D. 1913 — Wm Hugins, Pres. F.T. Caley, Secy., **E.L. Chatfield, Treas**. Last Chance Ditch Co. No. 2. (*Littleton Independent*)
- **July 6, 1916** Mrs. F.T. Durand and daughter attended the **funeral of Mrs. E.L. Chatfield at Littleton. Mrs. Chatfield** was a pioneer woman of Southern Jefferson County, having lived there about thirty years. (*Colorado Transcript, Jefferson County*)
- **August 4, 1916: Mr. Ed Chatfield Sr.** was a visitor in this neighborhood one day recently. He seems in very ill health. (*Record Journal of Douglas County*)
- **September 7, 1916: E.L. Chatfield** is recovering from the injuries and shock received in a runaway accident recently. (*Colorado Transcript, Jefferson County*)
- **July 19, 1917: In the County Court** — Adjustment day for the estates of A.S. Juckett, J.A. Schraeder, Albert Selter and E.B.B.

Traxexor, deceased and **Edward L. Chatfield,** mental incompetent, was held. *(Colorado Transcript, Jefferson County)*[*]

- **February 27, 1920: Chatfield Ranch Sold to Charlie Newby** — The Chatfield Ranch three miles south of Littleton on the Platte Cañon road has been sold to Charlie Newby of Arvada. This ranch is one of the oldest on the river. Mr. Chatfield having moved there about 45 years ago. It consists of nearly 200 acres of very fertile soil and is considered one of the best on the river. Mr. Newby, who purchased the place, is a brother-in-law of E.E. Oviatte of Littleton. **Mr. Chatfield and Bernie Rhea** who are on the ranch at present will hold an auction sale on Friday, March 5, and Mr. Newby will take possession by the 15th. *(Littleton Independent)*

- **February 27, 1920:** CLOSING-OUT SALE! — at the **E.L. CHATFIELD RANCH** — I Mile West and 3 Miles South of Littleton on the Platte Cañon Road — on — FRIDAY, MARCH 5 — At 10 A.M. Sharp — 90 HEAD OF STOCK — 17 Head Horses — Farm Machinery — 59 Head Cattle — 16 Head Hogs — Household Furniture including Stoves, Chairs, Tables, Beds — TERMS OF SALE — Cash. The Ranch Has Been Sold and This is Absolutely a Clean-Out. <u>Free Lunch at Noon</u> **Chatfield & Rhea, <u>Owners</u>** — C.T. Boroughs, Auctioneer; D.M. Decamp, Clerk *(Littleton Independent)*

- **December 24, 1920:** TEN MEMBERS LEFT OF THE LOCAL GRAND ARMY POST — Organized December 25, 1890 With Membership of Ten — There are today nine [sic] members living of local G.A.R., Post, John C. Fremont No. 83. December 26, 1890, a meeting was held, an organization affected and officers elected and sworn in….There has been a total of 76 members mustered in since its organization, of which ten remain. They are D.M. Decamp…R.D. Haight, J.W. Montgomery, J.B. Markle, W.L. Edgerton, J.H. Goddard, John Hofferberth, **Ed Chatfield**, John M. Fritz, and Daniel Eichling. *(Littleton Independent)*

- **June 2, 1922: Edward Chatfield and daughter, Mrs. Bernie Rhea** of Long Beach, California were guests at the Hockaday home on Decoration Day.[†] *(Littleton Independent)*

- **June 30, 1922: Ed Chatfield and daughter Mrs. Bernie Rhea** will leave next Wednesday for their home at Long Beach after having spent several weeks her visiting relatives and friends. *(Littleton Independent)*

---

[*]   Chatfield was suffering from failure in memory and attention as a result of multiple mini-strokes.

[†]   Decoration Day dates back to 1868, originally only honoring the Civil War dead. Today, the holiday is known as Memorial Day, celebrating all who have died serving our country. Memorial Day is currently celebrated on the last Monday of May.

- **[Obituary] December 3, 1924: Edward Livingston Chatfield**, 82, passed away this day in his daughter's Long Beach, California home, following a sharp decline in health while at the Soldiers' Home in Sawtelle. Chatfield had been suffering from the effects of multiple mini-strokes for several years. The final cause of death was listed as "paralytic stroke" in notes found in the James Herrick Chatfield family *Bible*. Immediate family members surviving Edward included his daughter, **Edaline Rhea**, of Long Beach, California; his younger brother **William Chatfield,** of Kankakee, Illinois; and his sister, **Mary Margaret Shepardson**, of Fort Collins, Colorado. *(Terry and Margaret Chatfield McCarty)*

- **[Obituary] December 11, 1924: Former Resident Dies —** Edward L. Chatfield, former resident of this county and active in Republican circles, died at the home of his daughter at Long Beach, Calif., last Thursday. The body was taken to the home of K.S. Rhea at Littleton, where the funeral was held at the Presbyterian church Wednesday afternoon. Mr. Chatfield, who was one of the old veterans of '61, made his home in the southern end of the county for many years. He was a prosperous farmer and an ardent Republican. He was well known all over the county and his many friends will regret the news of his death. Mr. And Mrs. Bernie Rhea, at whose home Mr. Chatfield died, accompanied the body to Littleton. *(Jefferson County Republican Dec 11, 1924, p. 8)*

1880 — 1925 William Stoddard Chatfield, Laura Dole and their Children

- **July 11, 1880:** The residence of **W.S. Chatfield** is undergoing a coat of paint which adds considerable to its appearance. *(Littleton Independent)*

- *Note:* **William** and **Laura** did not remain in Littleton for very long. By 1883 they had relocated back in Kankakee where they raised their family. Occasionally, as noted below, they came out west by train for family visits.

- **August 23, 1883 — Chatfield's Agency — W.S. Chatfield** has opened an attractive place for the sale of the "Domestic" sewing machine, the Cooley creamer, Dr. Filkins' family medicines, etc., in the room until lately occupied by E.B. Warriner, on Court street, opposite Hanna's. He has an ad. In this week's *Gazette*, on the eighth page which our readers are invited to peruse. Everybody knows W.S. in this part of Illinois and in establishing headquarters at Kankakee he will be within easy reach of his many friends and customers. Give him a call. *(Kankakee Gazette, p. 1)*

- **[Obituary] September 27, 1886:** Kankakee, Illinois —**Frank Stoddard Chatfield** (b. circa May 26, 1872; d. Sept. 26, 1886) *"His sun has gone down while yet it is day."* A large and sympathizing circle of relatives and friends met on Monday afternoon to attend the funeral services of **Frank S. eldest child of Wm. S. and Laura Chatfield** who passed away from earth Sabbath noon after a sickness of 10 hours aged 14 years and four months. This beloved, departed one, was a youth of unusual intelligence and promise, gifted with a mind of uncommon ability, talents of a literary order, an extensive and diligent reader, he had already made a thorough and critical acquaintance with the works of many of the most popular authors of the day. A few articles published in the Truth Journal on "Dickens and Thackeray, Modern Fiction," "Victor Hugo," etc., with many unpublished manuscripts show a discriminating, and apprecia-tive mind, mature beyond his years. In point of moral character he was affectionate and truthful, honest and upright, and chose only such characters for companions. He was reserved and unsocial with strangers, and a somewhat intimate acquaintance was necessary to draw out his amiable qualities. He invariably read from the *Bible* before retiring for the night. The only time, for more than five years, when it was omitted, was when he lay upon the bed of death, the last night of his life. The resolutions and testimonials of his fellow students in the Commercial College read by the pastor, Rev. Mr. Upson at the funeral showed their appreciation of him, as did also their "token of love," an anchor of beautiful and fragrant flowers. Miss Shaw a former teacher, showed her esteem by a beautiful floral offering as did numerous other friends, all of which are gratefully appreciated by the bereaved parents. His last sickness, endured with patience, was short and distressing. During its continuance, he frequently said "Papa I love you" or "Mamma I love you." Shortly before his death, he said "Mamma I am going to leave you, I am going to die, kiss me for good bye." Being asked, "Are you afraid to die?" He replied "No." "Are you willing?" "Yes," he answered. Retaining his consciousness to the last minute, he kissed all the family, bade them good bye, laid his hands on his breast, closed his eyes, breathed quietly a few times, and all was over. His spirit has passed into the unseen world. Consecrated to God by baptism in infancy, he was the child of many prayers and ardent hopes. *(Unidentified newspaper clipping found in James Herrick Chatfield family Bible)*
- **June 20, 1890:** Mr. Abott of Cañon City will occupy the **W.S. Chatfield** residence on Main Street. *(Littleton Independent)*

- **August 13, 1892: Mr. and Mrs. W.S. Chatfield** and children of Kankakee, Illinois are spending a delightful time with their kinfolks here. Mr. Chatfield is a brother of **E.L., I.N., and James Chatfield**. *(Littleton Independent)*
- **May 11, 1898:** J.C. Mitchell has moved into the **Chatfield house** at the foot of Main Street. *(Littleton Independent)*
- **March 15, 1901: W.S. Chatfield** of Kankakee, Ill., is visiting his brothers in Littleton. He will remain ten days. *(Littleton Independent)*
- **August 15, 1902: Messrs. William** [Nathan] **Chatfield** [3rd born of Wm. and Laura], Mr. Steward and Mr. Hubbard, of Denver, visited **Miss Nellie Chatfield** Saturday. *(Littleton Independent)*
- **July 29, 1911: Laura E. Dole,** William's wife, was buried today in the Chatfield plot in the Mound Grove Cemetery in Kankakee, Illinois. The cause of death was listed as "spinal disease." *(Mound Grove Cemetery Records)*
- **June 13, 1913: William S. Chatfield** of Kankakee, Ill., came Sunday to visit his sister, **Mrs. Mary M. Shepardson.** He was accompanied by **Mrs. Shepardson's daughter, Marcia,** who has spent a year in the east. **Mr. Chatfield** left today for home. *(Fort Collins Weekly Courier, Larimer County)*
- **Calendar years 1913-1917:** Kankakee City Directories place **William S. Chatfield's Kankakee** real estate office in the City National Bank, Unit 30. William's home address was given as 262 S. Greenwood Avenue. *(Kankakee City Directories, 1913-1918)*
- **June 30, 1916: W.S. Chatfield**, of Kankakee, Ill., visited this week with his brothers, **Jas. H. and Ed Chatfield.** *(Littleton Independent)*
- **January 26, 1925:** 13 months following the death of his eldest brother, Edward, **William Stoddard Chatfield** passed away, and was buried beside his wife, Laura, in Kankakee's Mound Grove Cemetery. *(Mound Grove Cemetery Records)*

1891 — 1923 Isaac Newton Chatfield, "Lizzie" Mead and their Children

Newton and Lizzie Chatfield had three children: **Eunice, Newton Leslie, and Laura Avery.**

- **October 10, 1891: Mr. I.N. Chatfield** having assumed the full management of the grocery in Culp block and Mr. Mead's interest therein, the business will be continued in the name of **I.N. Chatfield** exclusively. *(Littleton Independent)*
- **October 17, 1891: "The Best Grocery"** — Is the place to buy groceries Cheap for Cash. Potatoes, Apples, Dried Fruit, Pickles, and fine Canned Goods. A fresh line of Goods will be kept in stock. Goods

delivered to all parts of the city. Give us a call. **I.N. Chatfield**, No. 2, Culp Block, Main Street. *(Littleton Independent)*

- **December 17, 1892:** Leave your order with [I.N.] **Chatfield** & Gill for Cañon lump or nut coal. — Order your coal of **Chatfield** & Gill. They keep the best quality of Cañon nut and lump coal. — **Chatfield** & Gill handle the celebrated Cañon coal and can deliver it to you in any quantity desired. — The best quality of Cañon nut and lump coal is handled by **Chatfield** & Gill. Leave orders at [I.N.] **Chatfield's grocery store on Main Street.** *(Littleton Independent)*

- **December 24, 1892:** **Chatfield's Grocery** Is the place to go to get nice, fresh Groceries. New goods arriving daily. Give him a call. *(Littleton Independent)*

- **December 24, 1892:** The Cobweb social at **Mrs. I.N. Chatfield's** last Tuesday evening was a success in every particular. About fifty young people were there, all intent on knowing their fate. Ends of the cobweb were found all over the room and it was fun to see how eagerly the young men followed the clues all around the room and around the banisters. Tall upstairs there she stood, their laughing blushing fate. Electricity and the grab bag also furnished much amusement. Quite a sum was realized for the Christmas tree. *(Littleton Independent)*

- **January 12, 1894:** **I.N. Chatfield** this week moved his grocery store into the room formerly occupied by O.M. Hurst as a furniture store, and Mr. Hurst moved his stock of furniture into the room vacated by **Chatfield. Mr. Chatfield** now has a large, well-lighted storeroom, and is better prepared than ever to meet the wants of his customers. *(Littleton Independent)*

- **August 3, 1894:** **I.N. CHATFIELD** — Dealer in Staple and Fancy Groceries — Also — Lumber and Wood. *(Littleton Independent)*

- **August 10, 1894:** Mr. Foster of Watseka, Illinois, was visiting the family of **I.N. Chatfield** last Friday and Saturday. For being the most popular teacher in his county, Mr. Foster is enjoying a trip through the West at the expense of one of the newspapers. *(Littleton Independent)*

- **September 19, 1894:** The Ladies Aid Society of the Presbyterian will meet with **Mrs. I.N. Chatfield** on next Thursday afternoon. — Judge Ames, who took in Peach Days at Grand Junction, brought home with him an immense apple and placed it on exhibition at **Chatfield's** store. It is the Alexander variety and weighs 19½ ounces. *(Littleton Independent)*

- **January 18, 1895:** **I.N. Chatfield** will soon commence construction of a new store building. *(Littleton Independent)*

- **January 23, 1895: I.N. Chatfield** has commenced work on his new grocery building. It will be a two story brick and joins the Rogers block on the west. *(Littleton Independent)*
- **November 11, 1895: Mrs. I.N. Chatfield** is rapidly recovering from her recent illness. *(Littleton Independent)*
- **December 20, 1895: I.N. Chatfield** has just received a new load of flour from the Crescent Mill which always meets with popular favor. *(Littleton Independent)*
- **December 31, 1895:** Littleton Lodge No. 44 A.O.U.W. [Ancient Order of United Workmen] held an election of officers Tuesday night, the following being selected to serve the following year, Master Workman - C.D. Abbott; Foreman - **I.N. Chatfield;** Overseer - J.J. Murphy; Recorder - J.P. Curtis; Financier - Harry Nutting; Receiver - **J.H. Chatfield;** Guide- R.F. Gill. *(Littleton Independent)*
- **January 3, 1896:** Officers Elected — Littleton lodge No. 44, A.O.U.W. held an election of officers Tuesday night, the following being elected to serve the ensuing term: Master Workman, C.D. Abbot; Foreman, **I.N. Chatfield;** Overseer, J.J. Murphy; Recorder, J.P. Curtis; Financier, Harry Nutting; Receiver, **J.H. Chatfield;** Guide, R. Gill. *(Littleton Independent)*
- **January 14, 1896:** — J.A. Robinson has purchased the [**I.N.**] **Chatfield** stock of groceries. Mr. Robinson is well known to the residents of this community and will no doubt get a part of their patronage. *(Littleton Independent)*
- **March 27, 1896: J.H. and I.N. Chatfield,** who went prospecting up Deer Creek last week, have returned. They each staked a claim. *(Littleton Independent)*
- **December 16, 1896: I.N. Chatfield** will soon open a feed store in the building which he recently moved to on Main street. *(Littleton Independent)*
- **Fall, 1898: I.N. Chatfield** leaves Littleton to accept the position as caretaker of the Chemistry Building at the Colorado Agricultural College in Fort Collins, Colorado. *(Terry and Margaret Chatfield McCarty)*
- **May 20, 1898: J.H. Chatfield** received a letter last Monday from his brother, **I.N. Chatfield,** who resides at Fort Collins, giving an account of an accident which befell **Miss Eunice Chatfield**. On last Saturday, **Miss Chatfield** and three lady friends went to the foothills for a day's outing. On their return in the afternoon and while coming down a steep grade, the horse became unmanageable and ran away. The young ladies were thrown out and all more or less severely

injured. **Miss Chatfield's** injuries consisted of a broken arm and several bruises about the head. *(Littleton Independent)*

- **January 4, 1900: Mrs. I.N. Chatfiel**d and daughter, **Laura**, came down from Fort Collins last Friday and spent Christmas with **Edward and James Chatfield** and their families. *(Littleton Independent)*

- **February 21, 1906: I.N. Chatfield** and others requested a light at Myrtle and Mason streets, the request being laid on the table. *(Fort Collins Weekly Courier, Larimer County)*

- **December 23, 1910: Mrs. I.N. Chatfield Returns Home —** **Mrs. I.N. Chatfield**, who sustained serious injuries in Denver about two months ago while visiting the capital city, has fully recovered and will leave for her home in Fort Collins today. **Mrs. Chatfield** was removed to Littleton at the time of the accident and was at the home of **Mr. and Mrs. J.H. Chatfield** [Mary Elmina Dickinson], under the care of her daughter, **Miss Eunice** who accompanied her mother today. *(Littleton Independent)*

- **September 17, 1915: J.L. Chatfield** [3rd born child of Lucius N. Chatfield, Isaac and Lucy Chatfield's first child] formerly a member of the state board of agriculture and well known in this city, is here for a visit with his cousin, **I.N. Chatfield** of 128 West Myrtle Street. **Mr.** [J.L.] **Chatfield** now resides in Del Ray, Fla. He is renewing many former acquaintanceships. *(Fort Collins Weekly Courier, Larimer County)*

- **May 25, 1918**: **Mrs. Lizzie Chatfield**, age 68 years, died. *(Littleton Independent)*

- **November 7, 1921: Pioneer of City is Injured when getting on Denver Street Car — I.N. Chatfield**, 72 years old, of 128 West Myrtle Street, is confined to his bed at his home as the result of injuries received when he was knocked to the pavement by a streetcar or fell while boarding the car, in Denver Saturday night, but is not so seriously injured as was at first reported. He is suffering from bad bruises about the shoulder and hip. **Mr. Chatfield** accompanied his daughter, **Mrs. Laura C. Graves** and her 6-year-old son, **Leonard,** to Denver Saturday by automobile, and he planned to go on to Littleton for a visit. **Mrs. Graves** expected to return home after visiting friends. While about to board an Englewood car he fell or was struck by the car and thrown to the pavement. He was taken to the hospital by Police surgeon R.M. Campbell, but **Mrs. Graves** was not informed until Sunday morning. Sunday afternoon **Mr. Chatfield** was able to leave the hospital and **Mrs. Graves** brought him back to Fort Collins in the automobile. *(Fort Collins Courier)*

- **November 11, 1921:** AGED MAN INJURES HIP ATTEMPTING
  TO BOARD CAR — **I.N. Chatfield,** 72 years old, of Fort Collins,
  is in the county hospital, and doctors fear he may be suffering from a
  fracture of the hip sustained in a fall while attempting to board an in-
  bound streetcar at South Broadway and Evans Street last Friday night.
  The Tramway crew carried him to the Broadway loop, where Police
  Surgeon Campbell was summoned. The surgeon found Chatfield's
  injuries to be serious, largely because of his age. *(Denver News)*
- **November 11, 1921: I.N. Chatfield** was formerly a resident of
  Littleton having been in the grocery business her about 25 years ago.
  He is an uncle of Miss **Elmina Chatfield,** teacher in the Littleton
  High School. *(Littleton Independent)*
- **December 22, 1921: Chemistry Building at College Destroyed
  by Fire Early this Morning; Origin Unknown.** Fire that broke
  out shortly after 2 o'clock gutted the old Chemistry building on the
  [Colorado Agricultural] college campus Thursday morning, leaving it
  a mash of smoldering ruins….Chemicals stored in the building caught
  fire and burned with celerity; combustibles cracked and popped, the
  brilliant scene holding the attention of more than 100 spectators
  who gathered within a few minutes. Flames of every color were dis-
  cernible…. Uncle **I.N. Chatfield,** who has been caretaker of the
  Chemistry building at the college since it was built 23 years ago,
  is mourning the burning of the building and the loss of all the valuable things contained therein, like unto a father mourning for his
  firstborn. In the basement where many cans of samples of different
  things, all numbered, so that the professors could say, "Uncle, get a
  sample of number so and so," and Uncle **Chatfield** could locate the
  required sample from his orderly rows and cans without a moment's
  hesitation. Valuable papers and priceless data, the result of years of
  research were also burned. *(Fort Collins Courier)*
- **May 2, 1922: I.N. Chatfield** of 128 West Myrtle Street was struck
  by an automobile said to have been driven by Mrs. Clemmo, while
  crossing College Avenue at Laurel Street Monday evening about five
  o'clock. The accident occurred in front of the College grocery. **Mr.
  Chatfield,** who is seventy-three years old, was knocked down and
  badly bruised, but other than a long gash on the hand and bruises, he
  seems to be uninjured. He is at his home and was sitting up a little
  Tuesday morning. Just a short time ago, Mr. Chatfield was struck by
  a streetcar and injured considerably while in Denver…. It is said that
  Mr. Chatfield was jaywalking diagonally across the street from the
  college towards the grocery when he was hit. *(Fort Collins Courier)*
- **August 20, 1923:** Ed A. Shenk, the barber, has purchased the **I.N.
  Chatfield** home at 128 west Myrtle Street for $3,500.00. This will

make Mr. and Shenk a splendid home. ... **Mr. Chatfield** will leave
Monday for Woodland [California] to join his daughter, **Mrs. Laura
Graves**, who will teach there the coming year. Fort Collins people
regret very much to lose the Chatfields as citizens. *(Fort Collins
Courier)*

- **August 26, 1923: Mrs. Laura Graves**, who was granted a leave of
absence last year to take graduate work at the University of California,
where she received her Master of Science degree has resigned, and
will teach in California. *(Fort Collins Courier)*

1883 — 1919 James Herrick Chatfield and Family

- **Circa June 20, 1883: Post Funeral Card of Thanks:** Kankakee,
Illinois — To the many friends who were so kind in assisting us
during our deep bereavement in the last sickness, and death of our
beloved and only daughter, Ruthie, we return our sincere thanks.
*(Unidentified news clipping from Kankakee, Illinois, found in J. H. Chatfield
family Bible)*
- **November 8, 1883:** *Society news from Bonfield, Illinois —* **Mr. And
Mrs. N.S. Chatfield and Mrs. J.H. Chatfield** [Annie Mary Brazier]
left here for Colorado on Wednesday last. *(Kankakee Gazette, p. 8)*
- **[Obituary] CHATFIELD — At Littleton. February 27, 1889,
at 1:30 a.m. Mrs. Anna** [sic] **M., wife of Mr. James Chatfield.
Aged 33 years, one month and sixteen days.** Funeral services
to be held tomorrow morning (Saturday) at 10:30 o'clock. The
sermon will be preached by Rev. C.B. Allen of Deselms, Ills. All are
invited to attend the services. *"O, not in cruelty not in wrath, The reaper
came that day, Twas an angel visited the green earth, And took the flowers away."* **Mrs. Annie Mary Chatfield** [Annie Mary Brazier] was
born in Coville, Saratoga county, N.Y., and was the eldest daughter
of a family of nine, (five daughters and four sons) by **Mr. and Mrs.
John Brazier,** seven of which are now living. Her parents came to
Illinois in 1868, where she grew to womanhood and was married to
James H. Chatfield just three weeks before she was seventeen.
She was the mother of three children, **Ruth, Eddie, and Nellie.**
A sad bereavement from which she never fully recovered happened
a few years back in the death of her eldest daughter at the age of
nine years. She was a faithful and loving mother and enjoyed a happy
life, until the past two years when she was sorely afflicted with the
dreaded lung trouble,[*] and her husband, wishing to try the curative
effects of higher altitudes, persuaded her to come to Littleton, arriving here about the first of last October, and here they have since

---

[*]   Notes found in the James Herrick Chatfield family *Bible* cite the cause of death as "consumption," meaning pulmonary tuberculosis.

resided. The lady has been a true and loyal member of the church ever since she was twelve years of age, and, although it seemed so hard to depart and leave behind a kind and loving husband and her beloved little ones, yet she became quite resigned; through her great faith, to submit to the Great and All Wise Father who had summoned her to enter the golden gate. *"She knew she would find them all again, In the fields of light above."* The sympathies of the entire community are with the bereaved husband and many a tear-drop given for the little ones who are yet too young to realize the depth of a mother's great and boundless love. "Angels of Life and Death alike are His; Without his leave they pass no threshold o'er. Who, then, would wish or dare, believing this, Against his messenger to shut the door?" *(Unidentified news clipping from Kankakee, Illinois, found in the James Herrick Chatfield family Bible)*

- **October 18, 1889**: A Denver lady has closed a lease with **J.H. Chatfield** for a lot in the State addition, and will begin the erection of a fine residence at once. The sad news of the death of Mr. Stark, the gentleman who spent a portion of the summer with **J.H. Chatfield** has been received from his home in Missouri. *(Littleton Independent)*

- **December 27, 1889**: The sidewalk movement has been started on Main Street. **Messer's Chatfield and Morse** have laid walks in front of their residences, and it is intended by the property owners to extend it to the depot on the north side of the street. *(Littleton Independent)*

- **June 6, 1890**: **Acre Properties —** Properties from 1 acre to 325 acres. Large or small farms, highly proved, near the town and good locations. Loans Negotiated. **J.H. Chatfield**, Real Estate Agent, Office at Foot of Main Street, Littleton, Colorado. *(Littleton Independent*

- **June 20, 1890: J.H. Chatfield**, is having his residence painted by Howland & Davis. These gentlemen are first class workmen for which their work speaks for itself. *(Littleton Independent)*

- **June 27, 1890: J.H. Chatfield's** residence presents a neat appearance since painted. *(Littleton Independent)*

- **July 11, 1890**: **J.H. Chatfield** while out driving on east Broadway one evening this week had a run-away which might have been a serious affair. The horse which he was driving became frightened at a dog, making a short turn, upsetting the buggy and throwing the occupants to the ground; a badly frightened crowd and broken axle is all that happened very fortunately. *(Littleton Independent)*

- **September 5, 1890: Bargains in Real Estate**: Two hundred dollars to loan at 10 per cent interest. New 5-room cottage and lot in central part of town. Price: $1,500. 220 acres lake stocked with fish. $50.00 an acre; will take lots in Denver as part payment: two miles from Littleton. 160 acres under ditch. Artesian well and trout pond. Fine ranch. $100 per acre. A new two story house with seven rooms and nice cellar. Five lots set out in orchard and small fruits. Also several five acre blocks at $250 per acre. Fine garden trucks; free water rights. 15 lots in the business part of town from $500 to $1200. Seven new cottages for rent. 160 acres on Broadway, 3 miles from Littleton. $25 an acre. 125 acres at $20 per acre – mile and a half from Littleton. A nice 5 room cottage and 320 acres of fine pasture to rent. Stock taken to pasture 1 mile from Littleton. Acre Properties: Properties from 1 acre to 325 acres. Large or small farms highly improved, near the town and good locations. Loans Negotiated. **J.H. Chatfield,** Real Estate Agent, Office at Foot of Main Street. Littleton, Colorado. *(Littleton Independent)*

- **August 2, 1891: "Squire" [J.H.] Chatfield** performed his first marriage ceremony this week, since going into office. The contracting parties were P.S. Scott and Mary Snediker, both of this place. *(Littleton Independent)*
- **July 7, 1892:** Milo Collins a refractory boy of about 10 years old was sent to the reform school at Golden, by **Judge Chatfield** for three years, yesterday. Guy Sutton, the Marshal, took him to Golden. *(Littleton Independent)*

August 26, 1892: J.H. Chatfield writes to Mary Elmina Dickinson, his 6th cousin, in Rico, Colorado:
Littleton, Colo., Aug 26th, 1892.

My dear Mary, Your good letter received this morning. It seems like a month since I left you on the car platform. I will not have time to write you only a few lines this time. I've had several callers this a.m. Sister [Mary Margaret Chatfield] has driven out to Mrs. Curtises so I'm alone for a few moments. Here they come, afternoon had two ladies for dinner. Have been to a funeral. Got home. Wiped the dishes. Mrs. Reb Scott is here for a drive out with sister. So I will be alone for a few moments. I can't say just how soon I can come to you, but keep your ticket. And I will have to get my ticket before the 31st but can't say for sure whether I can come next week or the week after. Will tell you in my next. I don't see how I can leave at all. I've had two suits this week and two for next Monday and Tuesday and 3 funerals every week. And no one knows any thing about any of that work. So I will say as the old Parson used to say The Lord be in Providence, Penitence and all be well. I'll see you and claim you inside of two weeks. You see I've been waiting for you to set the day. As you thought I was in such a hurry. I heard a lady say she'd not get married for anything this hot weather. It's as hot as dutch love in Aug here now during the day. And cool at eve. Have you got that silk dress all finished — ha ha. I expect (interrupted. I will have to stop and put this in the office. Here is a man keeps sitting.) I am yours, J.H. Chatfield *(Letter found in the James Herrick Chatfield family Bible)*

- **September 5, 1892: J.H. Chatfield** and **Mary Elmina Dickinson** are wed. This is James's 2nd marriage. *(Terry and Margaret Chatfield McCarty)*
- **September 17, 1892:** The newly wedded men came in for a goodly share of public attention. Mr. Charles Strong and **Mr. James H. Chatfield** never realized how popular they were …*(Littleton Independent)*
- **December 24, 1892: J.H. Chatfield** — Real Estate, Loans and Insurance. Bargains in 5-Acre Garden Tracts - Soldiers' Pension Papers Executed - Littleton, Colorado *(Littleton Independent)*
- **January 12, 1894:** At the annual meeting of the Littleton Cemetery association held last Saturday, it was voted that the old board of directors hold over another year. The most important of the business transacted was the appointing of Peter Magnes, S.T. Culp and **J.H. Chatfield** as a committee to confer with the water company relative to constructing a pipe line to the cemetery. It is to be hoped the committee will be able to make arrangements for conveying water to the cemetery so the burial place of our dead could be made very attractive. *(Littleton Independent)*
- **April 13, 1894:** City Council Proceedings — Resolution fixing the salaries of the appointed officers and amount of bonds to be given by each, were read and adopted. The salary of the town attorney was placed at $100 for the ensuing year, bond $500; treasurer's salary $25, bond $2000; clerk's salary $75, bond $500; police magistrate's **[J.H. Chatfield]** bond is $500 and his salary being what he can get as fees out of the cases tried before him. *(Littleton Independent)*
- **July 6, 1894:** An amusing and interesting race occurred Tuesday evening between **Police Magistrate [J.H.] Chatfield** and a soldier from the fort. The soldier had been imbibing quite freely and had gotten into an altercation with an old soldier who lives in the mountains, which resulted in the two coming to blows. The police magistrate had arrested the soldier from the fort and was leading him to the calaboose when he broke and ran, with the officer in pursuit. Being much the smaller of the two the soldier soon out-distanced the portly police magistrate and thus gained his freedom. *(Littleton Independent)*

- **July 13, 1894**: **J.H. Chatfield** and family spent Tuesday at the red rocks above Platte canon [canyon], and Thursday and Friday in Turkey creek canon [canyon], camping out. *(Littleton Independent)*
- **July 13, 1894:** The Ladies' Aid society of the Presbyterian Church will meet with Mrs. W.A. Reynolds on Thursday afternoon of next week. — **Mrs. J.H. Chatfield** [Mary Elmina Dickinson], Pres't. *(Littleton Independent)*
- **August 10, 1894:** The Mission board of the Presbyterian Sunday school was given a very pleasant picnic by **Mrs. J.H. Chatfield** [Mary Elmina Dickinson] on the church lawn last Friday afternoon. The little folks enjoyed themselves hugely. *(Littleton Independent)*
- **November 16, 1894: Officer Chatfield** informs us that the Humane society last week caused the arrest of Joe Means of Fort Logan for unmercifully whipping and otherwise cruelly treating a team of government mules. He was tried before Justice Stewart, found guilty and fined $5 and costs. *(Littleton Independent)*
- **January 23, 1895:** The Ladies Aid Society will meet with Mrs. C.M. Curtis Thursday afternoon, January 31. **Mrs. J.H. Chatfield** [Mary Elmina Dickinson], Sec. *(Littleton Independent)*
- **December 20, 1895:** A 9-year-old girl giving the name of Flossie Lucas, applied to Mrs. Montgomery of this place, last Saturday for shelter. She had run away from her home in Denver, because of a severe beating she had received with a broomstick in the hands of her mother. Mrs. Montgomery turned the girl over to Marshal White, who placed her in the care of Mrs. Casort, who provided comfortable clothing for the child, as she was thinly clad. On Monday afternoon the girl was taken back to Denver by **Humane Officer [James] Chatfield** and placed in care of the Humane society....Mrs. Patrick Lamb of Platte Cañon was at **Judge [James] Chatfield's** this week making affidavit on personal appraised property in the settlement of the estate of Patrick Lamb. The papers go to Golden where final settlement will be had. *(Littleton Independent)*
- **January 3, 1896: J.H. Chatfield**, superintendent of the cemetery at this place, furnishes us the following report: Number of persons buried in the cemetery who have died in Littleton, 18; number buried from the surrounding country, 10; number buried from Denver, 5. *(Littleton Independent)*
- **January 14, 1896:** The Cemetery Association held its annual meeting last Friday afternoon and elected J.W. Bowles, President, Peter Magnes, treasurer and **J.H. Chatfield**, Secretary and superintendent. *(Littleton Independent)*

- **March 27, 1896: J.H. and I.N. Chatfield,** who went prospecting up Deer Creek last week, have returned. They each staked a claim. *(Littleton Independent)*

- **June 10, 1898: Jim Chatfield** returned last Friday from a trip to Fort Collins. *(Littleton Independent)*

- **January 13, 1899:** City Official Listing for Police Magistrate — **J.H. Chatfield** *(Littleton Independent)*

- **November 22, 1899: J.H. Chatfield** sold lots 1 and 2, block 33 Windemere, to Peter Longsen for $250.00 *(Littleton Independent)*

- **November 6, 1903:** Notice — Five head of calves, Jersey and Holstein, have been taken and are cared for by the Humane Society agent, **J.H. Chatfield**. The owners can have stock by claiming property and paying charges. *(Littleton Independent)*

- **March 4, 1904:** Mr. Chas. Huggins had an accident by his horse running away and breaking his buggy to pieces and came in collision with **Mr. Chatfield's** team, which almost ran away, shaken. However, both of them came out very lucky. *(Littleton Independent)*

- **May 27, 1904:** Bargains in Granite and Venetian Enameled Ware at the Littleton Hardware Co's store, **Chatfield Block**. *("Little Locals," Littleton Independent)*

- **July 1, 1904: — Notary Public Lic. Supt. of Cemetery: J.H. Chatfield — Insurance and Real Estate**. Town lots and 5-Acre Garden Tracts for sale - Houses for rent - All legal and Soldiers' papers executed. Littleton, Colorado. *(Littleton Independent)*

- **April 5, 1907:** The cemetery association has bought seventy-five elm trees to be placed along the driveways in the cemetery. **Supt. J.H. Chatfield** is now engaged in the work and also has several monuments to erect. *(Littleton Independent)*

- **July 14, 1916:** Merciless Beating of Burro Brings Grief to Owner — That no leniency is given by Justice of the Peace **J.H. Chatfield** for the merciless beating of a small, over loaded burro on the streets of Littleton was well exemplified at the trial held in his court last Saturday evening when J.W. Hurley, who claims his residence to be 4036 Perry Street, Denver, answered such a charge preferred against him….The burro, being small and pulling a load of 625 pounds, had a large sore on its back, and Hurley was striking it on this wound, causing the animal to fall to the ground with each slash. **Justice Chatfield**, after hearing the evidence, decided that 90 days would be about the proper amount of time for Hurley to think over his actions, and as he had no cash to pay the costs of the trial, the sheriff was authorized to seize and sell the burro and buggy and to apply the proceeds to this use. *(Littleton Independent)*

- **July 14, 1916:** E.C. Guthiel, charged with assault upon Ed Brannon, the trouble arising from a dispute over irrigation water, was arraigned before **Justice Chatfield** Saturday evening and fined five dollars and costs. *(Littleton Independent)*
- **July 15, 1916:** Republican Ticket Primary Winner: Justice, First Precinct: **J.H. Chatfield** 354 [votes]. *(Littleton Independent)*
- **June 22, 1917:** Don't Fish Without A License — A couple of cases of 'fishing without a license' were presented before Justice of the Peace **J.H. Chatfield** last Tuesday evening and the usual fine was imposed in each instance…. **Mr. Chatfield** informs us that he now has a supply of fishing licenses on hand and any one desiring to indulge in this sport and not having a permit, can secure same of him at any time. *(Littleton Independent)*
- **August 17, 1917: Mrs. J.H. Chatfield** [Mary Elmina Dickinson] returned Saturday from a five-week visit with her [step] son **[Edward L. Chatfield, Jr.]** at Hot Sulphur Springs, Colorado, and **J.H.** is again wearing that pleasant smile. *(Littleton Independent)*
- **December 21, 1917:** Perhaps the best proof of a prosperous community is a long list of enterprising and substantial business houses… herewith we will give a brief summary of our business establishments as they come in order along Main street…North Side — West to East, [first building] **J.H. Chatfield** — Real Estate, Insurance etc. … *(Littleton Independent)*
- **November 1, 1918:** Election Ballot: for the position of Justice of the Peace, Justice Precinct Number 1: **James H. Chatfield**, Republican. Place of Business, Littleton; Place of residence: Main street. Place of office: Littleton *(Littleton Independent)*
- **[Obituary] MARY ALMINA (sic) CHATFIELD — Mary Elmina Dickinson Chatfield** passed away Friday, December 13, 1918, after a long illness due to heart trouble. She was born at Randolph, Ohio, July 1, 1856, living there until she went to Oberlin. After her college days, she taught for two years in a Home Missionary school situated near Wilmington, North Carolina. In 1892 she came to Colorado where she was married on September 5th to **James Herrick Chatfield**, and resided at Littleton since then. She is survived by her husband; a son, Edward, of Hot Sulphur Springs, Colorado; two daughters, Mrs. Nellie Driver of Hoquiam, Washington, and Almina [sic]; two brothers and a sister; and as many friends as she had acquaintances. The keynote of **Mrs. Chatfield's** life was "service," service to all she ever knew. Because of her faithfulness, especially in Christian service for the Master, she will be missed by every one who has ever come into her life. Funeral services were held Sunday afternoon at 2:30 o'clock,

and was largely attended. Internment Littleton cemetery. *(Littleton Independent)*

- **[Obituary] January 17, 1919: In Memoriam** — As God has seen fit to call one of our number to the Heavenly home. We know that her life was one of service. It is with no thought that the life of **Mrs. Chatfield** [Mary Elmina Dickinson] can be forgotten that prompts us to stir again the consciousness of that loss which we, her friends, sustain in sorrow; her coming brought happiness, her voice awoke responsive cheer, we walked within her influence as we often walk thoughtlessly in a day of sunshine and gladness, nor think of the source of light until a cloud turns our faces heavenward. Since the hands so readily extended in friendship, so ready to assist are folded; now that her genial manners and busy kindness can no longer surprise us into forgetfulness of herself; now that death comes between her life and ours, we see how many are the aspirations, deepened into prayers which awakened. And may we not add glory to the bright crown of this friend in heaven. As she sees her life she thought unworthy prompting us to better living. We feel her presence with us, and she will continue to be the Queen of our friends. — Ladies Aid Society Committee *(Littleton Independent)*

- **April 20, 1919: James H. Chatfield** dies in Hoquiam, Washington, while residing with his daughter, Nellie Margaret. *(Terry and Margaret Chatfield McCarty)*

- **[Obituary] April 23, 1919: James H. Chatfield Dead**; PIONEER LITTLETON JUSTICE — **James H. Chatfield**, for many years justice of the peace in Littleton and widely known thruout [sic] this district, is dead in Hoquiam, Wash., according to information received here today. Mr. Chatfield died of dropsy. He had gone to Hoquiam last winter in a vain effort to improve his health. The body will be brought to Littleton for burial. The funeral is to be held at 3 o'clock Sunday afternoon in the Presbyterian church. LITTLETON, Colo. April 23. [hand written in cursive] "Easter 1919" *(Unidentified newspaper clipping found in the James Herrick Chatfield family Bible)*

- **[Obituary] April 25, 1919: James Herrick Chatfield** was born August 16, 1851, in Summit Ohio. He resided in Ohio and later in Illinois until 1879 [sic] when he and his family moved to Colorado, settling at once in Littleton. In 1872 he was married to **Annie Mary Brazier**; to this union were born three children. **Ruth**, who died at the age of nine years; **Edward**, of Sulphur Springs; and **Nellie, Mrs. Driver**, of Hoquiam, Washington. His wife died in 1889 at the home in Littleton. **Mr. Chatfield** married **Mary Elmina Dickinson** in 1892, and to them was born one daughter, **Elmina**.

Just last December **Mrs. Chatfield** passed away. Since then, **Mr. Chatfield** has been with his daughter in Hoquiam [Washington], being rapidly improved at first over his previous weak condition, but sinking fast during the past month. **Mr. Chatfield** has always been a staunch Christian and worker in the church. For many years he has been a trustee of the Littleton Presbyterian Church. Because of this, he will be greatly missed. The funeral services will be held at the Presbyterian Church next Sunday afternoon at three o'clock. *(Littleton Independent)*

1891 — Charles H. (Henry) Chatfield

- **December 24, 1891: Charles Chatfield**, a brother of **W.S. Chatfield,** the well-known real estate man of Harvey, died in Kankakee, Ill., Tuesday, Dec. 22d, from injuries received by a fall from a wind mill derrick on last Sunday night. *(Unidentified newspaper clipping found in James Herrick Chatfield family Bible)*

- **[Obituary] December 24, 1891** — KILLED BY A FALL: Farmer Charles Chatfield of Salina Precipitated from a Windmill. Charles Chatfield of Salina, brother of Wm. S. Chatfield of this city, was killed at his neighbor Harry Strawson's place on Sunday evening by falling from a windmill. His turkeys had acquired the habit of leaving home and roosting upon Strawson's windmill. Mr. Chatfield decided to catch them and sell them off. With this purpose in view he came to Strawson's and the latter went across the road with him to hold the lantern while he climbed the windmill ladder. Mr. Chatfield made two trips to the top and was making the third when a rung of the ladder broke and he fell a distance of 25 feet striking upon some large stones. He was picked up unconscious with a leg broken in several places and died on the following day. The Chatfield family were among the early settlers in Salina. The senior Chatfield is dead and three of the brothers have emigrated to Colorado. Charles was the only one left on the farm. The place where he was injured was the old homestead, recently sold to young Strawson, where he was raised from boyhood and the wind mill was the one he helped to build and with which he was perfectly familiar. He leaves a family. — *(Kankakee Gazette)*

1892 — 1922 Mary Margaret Chatfield-Shepardson

- **July 2, 1892:** The undersigned take this opportunity of expressing their thanks to all that so cheerfully responded in making their ice cream and strawberry festival a success. **Mrs. E.L. Chatfield, Miss Mary Chatfield.** *(Littleton Independent)*

- **August 17, 1894: Miss Mary Chatfield**, who has been visiting relatives in Illinois the past year, returned to Littleton last Sunday. *(Littleton Independent)*
- **March 19, 1895: Mary Margaret Chatfield and Noah Shepardson** wed in Arapahoe County, Colorado. *(Terry and Margaret Chatfield McCarty)*
- **February 11, 1896: Mr. and Mrs. Shepardson** moved to the Lilley ranch Thursday. They will take care of it the coming spring. *(Littleton Independent)*
- **March 19, 1901: ACCIDENT, SAYS INVESTIGATORS — How Noah Shepardson of Conifer, Colorado Lost his Life.** LITTLETON, Colo. (To The Republican.) — As to the death of **Noah Shepardson** of Conifer, Colo., we, the undersigned, wish to make the following statement and set the whole matter right in the interests of all parties and friends of **Mrs. N. Shepardson: Mr. Shepardson** drove up into the timber in the forenoon to cut two red spruce poles to make a rack to haul ties on. He had cut the poles [and] was returning home. He stopped and called to his man, Tom Shields, who was cutting ties, about 9 rods away, asking Shields if he wanted his broad-ax. Shields answered no. Shepardson then drove on a short distance on the hillside, which was quite steep, and many trees in the road kept him busy clearing them. He was about to hit a tree and was turning his team away from it when the fore wheel missed it, but the brake beam struck it, caused by the hind wheel sliding about a foot, and that threw the wooden brake-bar, which was about seven feet long, forward with great force. He stood up in the box, leaning up hill and braced himself over the right edge of the wagon box. It threw him forward onto the sideboard of the box, striking his forehead there. The bar struck the crown of his head, causing a fracture of the skull about as large as a half dollar. Mr. Shields went down at noon to his dinner, fed the stock, went in and Mrs. Shepardson asked him where **Mr. Shepardson** was. He said he started down before noon, and probably he had stopped to bring in a load of wood. They waited an hour longer and **Mrs. Shepardson** sent Shields to look for her husband. Shields soon came back, saying Shepardson was hurt badly. Mrs. Shepardson and two men ran up the road and Shields followed in a carriage and soon overtook them. When they got there Shepardson was still conscious, but could not talk. They took him to the house and sent for Dr. Baker of Evergreen. He made an examination and said there was no hope for him to live. The place on the back of Shepardson's head had a large clot of blood under the scalp. The doctor cut it open and took it out to relieve

the pain. **Mr. Shepardson** lived till 7 p.m. **Mrs. Shepardson** sent a telephone message to her brother, **J.H. Chatfield** of Littleton to come at once and early Wednesday morning he and **R.D. Herrick** drove up there and they, with Jesse Ray, Tom Shields, Mr. Kennedy and two other men, went up to the place of the accident and made a thorough examination and all six men decided that it was purely an accident and blamed no one. **J.H. CHATFIELD, R.D. HERRICK —** **Mrs. Shepardson** says her husband has never had any trouble with any of his men and was held in high esteem by all of them. The Shepardson funeral was held this afternoon at Littleton. *(Unidentified newspaper clipping found in the James Herrick Chatfield family Bible)*

- **April 24, 1901: ADMINISTRATRIX' NOTICE — Estate of Noah Shepardson, deceased.** The undersigned, having been appointed Administratrix of the Estate of **Noah Shepardson** late of the County of Jefferson and State of Colorado, deceased, hereby gives notice that she will appear before the County Court of Jefferson County, at the Court House in Golden, at the March Term, on the first day of May next at which time all persons having claims against said estate are notified and requested to attend for the purpose of having the same adjusted. All persons indebted to said estate are requested to make immediate payment to the undersigned. Dated this 2nd day of April, A.D., 1901. **MARY M. SHEPARDSON**, Administratrix. First publication April 3. Last publication April 24. *(Colorado Transcript, Golden, Jefferson County)*

- **July 5, 1901: Mrs. Shepardson** and children arrived Thursday evening from Conifer. She will visit with her brother for the present. *(Littleton Independent)*

- **September 4, 1901: ADMINISTRATRIX' SALE OF REAL ESTATE —** Public Notice is hereby given that the undersigned will offer at private sale, bids to be received up to September 30, 1901, the Conifer estate, or Hamer Ranch, situated in Jefferson County, Colorado, consisting of 560 acres, also a homestead of 160 acres, together with all buildings and contents, stock, personal property, etc., Address all communication to Littleton, Colorado. **MARY M. SHEPARDSON**, Administratrix. **J.H. Chatfield, Agent.** *(Colorado Transcript, Golden, Jefferson County)*

- **February 12, 1903: NOTICE OF FINAL SETTLEMENT —** In the matter of the estate of **Noah Shepardson**, deceased. Notice is hereby given, that on Monday, the 2nd day of March, A.D. 1903, being one of the regular days of the March term of the County Court of Jefferson County, in the State of Colorado, I, **Mary M. Shepardson**, Administratrix of said estate, will appear before the

Judge of said Court, present my final settlement as such and will then apply to be discharged as such Administratrix, at which time and place any person in interest may appear and present objections to the same, if any there be. Dated at Fort Collins Colorado, January 10, 1903. **MARY M. SHEPARDSON**, Administratrix of the Estate of **Noah Shepardson**, Deceased. First publication February 5. Last publication February 20 *(Colorado Transcript, Golden, Jefferson County)*

- **January 4, 1922: Mrs. Shepardson Suffers Seriously Broken Hip** — It was reported Thursday that Mrs. Mary Shepardson, who was injured Wednesday by a fall on the slippery sidewalks, suffered a serious fracture of the hipbone. She is at her home, 218 West Laurel Street, and resting fairly comfortably. *(Fort Collins Courier)*

- **January 16, 1922: Mrs. Shepardson** is Recovering Nicely — Mrs. Mary Shepardson of 218 West Laurel Street is getting along very well. Her hipbone was broken from a fall on the ice two weeks ago. On Saturday ten or twelve of the members of the Women's association at the college called on Mrs. Shepardson, following the meeting at Guggenheim Hall, and she is receiving many kind and pleasant attractions from all of her large circle of friends. *(Fort Collins Courier)*

1901 — 1964 Edaline Chatfield and Bernie Rhea

Edaline was **Edward and Anna's** only child. She and **Bernie Rhea** were married on February 21, 1913.

- **March 8, 1901: Miss Edaline Chatfield** was thrown from a horse last Saturday and sustained a fracture of the collar bone. She has been attending the West Denver High School and will not be able to pursue her studies for some weeks on account of the accident. *(Littleton Independent)*

- **March 11, 1904:** Clinton Payne and **Miss Edaline Chatfield** of Fort Collins had a few days' vacation and came down to visit their parents. *(Littleton Independent)*

- **February 2, 1906: Shelby Rhea** [Bernie's father] has rented the **E.L. Chatfield** ranch for a term of years. **Mr. Chatfield** will erect a residence for him on the premises. *(Littleton Independent)*

- **August 24, 1906: Misses** [Eunice] **Chatfield** and Hart of Fort Collins visited **Miss Edaline Chatfield** on Thursday....Today a party of young folks, chaperoned by Mrs. Rhea [wife of K.S. Rhea] will leave for a week's outing at Wellington Lake and Goose Creek Dam. Those in the party from here are, **Misses** [Helen] **Herrick**, [Edaline] **Chatfield**, [Bernie's sister] **Rhea, Mrs. Rhea** [wife of

K.S. Rhea] and Messrs **Herrick** and [Bernie] **Rhea** [son of **K.S. Rhea.**] *(Littleton Independent)*

- **January 4, 1907: Deer Creek Items** — Miss Laura Peas,* a popular young lady from Harris, Colorado, was the guest of **Miss Edaline Chatfield**, Sunday....**Mr. and Mrs. E.L. Chatfield** are visiting friends at Cripple Creek, Colorado....The R.R.O. Society, under the management of **Miss Edaline Chatfield, Messrs. R. Herrick**, and **S. Rhea** gave an invitation dance last Friday evening at the Woodmen Hall, Littleton, with attendance of thirty couples. Mr. and Mrs. Leo Curtis furnished the music. *(Littleton Independent)*

- **June 14, 1907: Picnic Party up Turkey Creek** — A pleasant day was enjoyed by a party picnicking up Turkey Creek Thursday. They were: Misses **Helen Herrick, Edaline Chatfield**, Edith Libby, **Laura Chatfield, Mrs. Nellie Driver**, and **Mr. R. Herrick**. *(Littleton Independent)*

- **November 3, 1910:** Candidates for County Assessor: Democrat: Charles H. Easley, Golden Colorado; Republican: Napoleon B. Hatcher, Edgewater, Colorado; Socialist: **K.S. Rhea**, Littleton Colorado. *(Colorado Transcript, Jefferson County)*

- **January 6, 1911:** Stove Blown to Pieces; Windows shattered — The kitchen water pipes in **K.S. Rhea's** residence on the **E.L. Chatfield ranch** froze last Sunday night. Fire was started in the stove as usual Monday morning and from results the water front in the range was frozen which caused an explosion, demolishing the stove and breaking the kitchen windows. Fortunately no one was in the room when the explosion occurred. *(Littleton Independent)*

- **February 21, 1913:** Pretty Home Wedding — A pretty wedding took place at the home of the bride's parents Wednesday afternoon. The contracting parties were **Miss Edaline Chatfield, daughter of Mr. and Mrs. E.L. Chatfield, and Mr. Bernie Rhea, son of Mr. and Mrs. K.S. Rhea.** Only immediate relatives of the happy couple, numbering about thirty, were present. Many handsome and useful gifts were received. After a brief honeymoon they will reside on a ranch about two miles west of Littleton. Rev. Edmondson, of the Presbyterian Church, officiated. The Independent joins their many friends in wishing them a happy and prosperous journey through life. *(Littleton Independent)*

- **February 27, 1913: Miss Edaline Chatfield,** for many months a clerk in the county assessor's office, and **Bernard Rhea**, son of [Jefferson County] Assessor **K.S. Rhea**, were married at the home

---

*   Laura married Edaline's cousin, Robert S. Herrick and remained a lifelong friend of Edaline.

of the bride last Wednesday. They will make their home on the Bowles ranch, near Littleton. *(Colorado Transcript, Jefferson County)*

- **May 23, 1918: Mr. and Mrs. Bernard Rhea** and **E.L. Chatfield**, of Littleton, were guests at the **K.S. Rhea** home Sunday. *(Colorado Transcript, Jefferson County)*

- **May 23, 1919:** Captain **Chas. N. Shepardson** [Mary Margaret and Noah's son], who recently arrived from overseas, visited **Mr. and Mrs. Bernie Rhea** on Friday last. *(Colorado Transcript, Golden, Jefferson County)*

- **July 19, 1953: Hospital News, Yuma, Arizona** — Admitted to the hospital, **Mrs. Edaline Rhea**. *(Yuma Daily Sun, July 20, 1953)*

- **March 26, 1964:** Mrs. Roy Slaten was installed as Treasurer of the Yuma Chapter of the D.A.R. to fill out the term of **Mrs. B.L. Rhea**, who resigned because of ill health. [Thyroid Cancer.] *(Yuma Daily Sun)*

- **May 8, 1964: Edaline Rhea dies at Parkview Hospital** — **Edaline Rhea**, 81, of 407 S. 21st Avenue, died at Parkview Baptist Hospital last night. She had been residing recently at the Yuma County Nursing Home. Arrangements are pending at the Johnson Mortuary. *(Yuma Daily Sun)*

- **[Obituary] May 18, 1964: Edaline Rhea Services Set** — The body of **Edaline Rhea**, 81, who died Thursday at Parkview Baptist Hospital will be cremated. The remains will be interred in Littleton Colorado Cemetery beside her husband, **Bernard L. Rhea**, who died May 8, 1959. Memorial services will be held at the First United Presbyterian Church at a time to be announced later. It is requested that in lieu of flowers contributions be made to the City of Hope, American Cancer Fund, or the Memorial Fund of the First United Presbyterian Church. Mrs. Rhea came to Yuma with her husband 29 years ago. She was a member of the First United Presbyterian Church, the Daughters of the American Revolution, and the Rebekahs, and served as Treasurer of the church Sunday School for many years. She is survived by two cousins: **Mrs. Margaret Chatfield** [Margaret Elmina Driver Chatfield] of Temple City, California and [I.N. Chatfield's youngest daughter] **Mrs. Laura G. Heyd** of El Centro. *(Yuma Daily Sun)*

1883 — 1964 The Children of James Herrick Chatfield

Ruth Ann Chatfield

- **Circa June 6, 1883:** Kankakee, Illinois — **Miss Ruthie Chatfield** is quite sick of blood poisoning from the effect of measles. It has settled in her legs below the knees. *(Unidentified news clipping from Kankakee, Illinois, found in the James Herrick Chatfield family Bible)*

- **Circa June 11, 1883:** Kankakee, Illinois — **Miss Ruthie Chatfield** is having a very sick spell with Bilious remittent fever; we are in hopes she will soon be better. *(Unidentified news clipping from Kankakee, Illinois, found in the James Herrick Chatfield family Bible)*

- **Friday, June 15, 1883:** Kankakee, Illinois — The terrible monster, death has again entered our midst. **Little Ruthie Chatfield** was called from this earth Friday, the 15th, at ten o'clock. The funeral was held at the house on the following Sabbath, Rev. Misener preaching the funeral sermon. The bereaved parents have the sympathy of many friends. She was loving, kind and true. God has called Ruthie to his own dear loving arms, where there will be no more sickness, pain or sorrow. Peaceful be thy silent slumber in the grave. Farewell. *(Unidentified news clipping from Kankakee, Illinois, found in the James Herrick Chatfield family Bible)*

- **[Obituary] Sunday, June 17, 1883:** Kankakee, Illinois — Died, **Ruth Ann Chatfield,** on June 15th, aged nine years, one month and six days, at her home, of spinal meningitis, after 18 days of terrible suffering. During intervals of two or three days she would rally, when we would have hopes of her recovery, but on the ninth day her symptoms becoming more alarming her physician, Dr. Caldwell, was summoned to her bedside. Then, after spending one night and a day, he said to her mother: "Annie, you will have to give up your little girl; I have done all that human power can do. If she lives it will be a higher power than mine. But still she lingered on. Conscious most of the time, she recognized all who came to see her until five hours before her death. When she was first taken sick she told her mother it was not very nice to live in this world, there was so much suffering. On the ninth day she said, "It is so nice to live this way." Her Sunday school superintendent asked: "Are you happy and do you love Jesus?" She answered: "Yes sir." Every little while she would call, "papa, papa, mama, mama." She had about twenty-five sinking spells. Sometimes it seemed almost impossible to bring back the breath of life which had fled, but now she is at rest—gone no more to return. We can go to her but she cannot come to us. Even the heavens seemed to weep to-day. She had so many dear friends; every one that saw her seemed to love her. She leaves a dear little brother, eighteen months younger, who mourns her loss. There were about two-hundred near and dear friends present to-day, at the funeral, coming from far and near, to pay their last tribute of love to the lamented one. Rev. Misener spoke beautifully of the departed one. His text was 2d Samuel, 12th chapter;

22d and 23d verses. A few weeks ago, while Rev. Misener was visiting here, little Ruthie came to him with two little Sabbath cards; one was: "Behold the lamb of God which taketh away the sins of the world." The other was: "God shall wipe away all tears." She asked him the meaning of them and he explained it all. She seemed to grasp his meaning and understood all about it. We miss the, thou loved one, throughout the long day. *(Unidentified news clipping from Kankakee, Illinois, found in the James Herrick Chatfield family Bible)*

Edward Livingston Chatfield, Jr.

Reminder: E.L. Chatfield, Jr. (b. 1876) was the son of **James Herrick Chatfield and Annie Brazier Chatfield.** Edward Jr. had been named after Edward Livingston Chatfield—James's older brother and a family hero—even though convention would have held that James and Annie might opt for a different name, preserving "Edward" for soldier Edward's use if, and when, he married and became the father of a son. Soldier Edward married a year after Edward Jr. was born, and *six years later* Edward and Anna (Bates) had their first (and only) child, a daughter, **Edaline.**

- **November 4, 1896:** A pleasant Halloween party was held with **E.L. Chatfield Jr.** last Saturday. The evening was spent in playing games in which apples figured conspicuously. *(Littleton Independent)*
- **July 5, 1901:** **Edward Chatfield Jr**. is home [from Hot Sulphur Springs] for a few days. *(Littleton Independent)*
- **February 25, 1909: E.L. Chatfield Jr.** received a carload of Routt County coal the first of the week, and he has been busy supplying his customers with fuel for three or four days. The Oak Creek coal is the best that has ever been shipped into Hot Sulphur Springs — *Sulphur Springs Times (Oak Creek Times, Routt County)*
- **June 9, 1909: Edward L. Chatfield, Jr**. marries **Jessie May Henry** at the Henry farm in Niwot, Colorado. *(Terry and Margaret Chatfield McCarty)*
- **June 25, 1910: Jessie** and **Edward L. Chatfield, Jr.** welcome the birth of **Edward Henry Chatfield**, at the Henry farm in Niwot, Colorado. They called him **"Ned,"** and he was their only child. *(Terry and Margaret Chatfield McCarty)*
- **August 5, 1914:** [Election Results] The Democrats chose the following… superintendent of schools, **Mrs. E.L. Chatfield** [Jessie May Henry Chatfield]. …*(Steamboat Pilot)*
- **June 18, 1915:** Mr. Frank S. Byers, whose father laid out the town of Hot Sulphur Springs in June 1874, wrote about the community's early

history. "In June, 1874, my father laid out the town of Hot Sulphur Springs, and as I was head chainman, and the grass was quite high and the mosquitoes quite plentiful, I remember the job quite well. Shortly after we left there W.H. Ganson started the first building on the new townsite, which he completed the following year. It was known as the Ganson hotel, later as the McQueary hotel, and now embodied in the **Chatfield barn**..." *(Routt County Sentinel)*

- **August 19, 1916:** — When you think Motor Car, think Buick — It will be a pleasure to demonstrate. Phone me at my expense. **E.L. Chatfield Jr.**, Hot Sulphur Springs, Colorado, Agent for Grand and Summit Counties. Can Deliver at Once. *(Summit County Journal)*

- **September 29, 1917:** The Valve-in-the Head Motor Car — Sulphur Springs Garage — For Information Call Up — **E.L. Chatfield** or C.A. Forslund, Telephone Sulphur 6 *(Summit County Journal)*

- **May 25, 1918:** A Carload Of New Buicks — The Buicks Agents, **Chatfield** and Forslund, report that they have just received a carload of new Buicks for distribution in Summit and Grand Counties. They are also expecting another shipment before July 1, after which date the factory output for Buicks will be curtailed 75 percent the plant being turned over to the government for war work. These agents are now ready to supply prospective purchasers. *(Summit County Journal)*

- **September 28, 1918:** "When Better Cars are Made Buick Will Build Them" — **E.L. Chatfield**, H.A. Forslund, Agents, Sulphur Springs, — Colorado *(Summit County Journal)*

- **December 28, 1918: E.L. Chatfield Jr.** was called to Littleton, Colo., last Friday to attend the funeral of his [step] mother, **Mrs. J.H. Chatfield** [Mary Elmina Dickinson]. He left Sulphur Springs on a freight train, the engine of which broke down in Fraser canyon. He walked to Fraser, where he secured a saddle horse and rode over the range to the foot of Berthoud Pass. There he was met by Harry Shook of St. Luke Garage, in Denver, who took him to Littleton. Travel out of Middle Park is more difficult than it has been at any time for the last twenty years. *(Summit County Journal)*

- **January 22, 1919: E.L. Chatfield Jr.** of Sulphur Springs has been appointed under-sheriff by Sheriff Robert West of Grand County. *(Steamboat Pilot, Routt County)*

- **February 25, 1920: E.L. Chatfield Jr.** will at once begin the erection of a new garage at Sulphur Springs. *(Steamboat Pilot, Routt County)*

- **April 9, 1920:** Editor Lew Wallace of the *Middle Park Times* was elected mayor at the election at Hot Sulphur Springs Tuesday, with a full board consisting of **E.L. Chatfield Jr.**, Cyrus Sundelin and L.W.

Kennedy trustees for the full term, and A.B. Rice, L.E. Harrison and
G.C. Henry [Grover C. Henry, older brother of Jessie May Henry
Chatfield] for the unexpired term. *(Routt County Sentinel)*

- **July 21, 1920: Ned Chatfield,** son of **E.L. Chatfield Jr.** of Sulphur
Springs was painfully injured last week when he was run into by an
automobile. *(Routt County Sentinel)*

- **February 22, 1922:** Robert McQueary, **Ned Chatfield**, and Jim
Harsh of Sulphur Springs Ski club are here to take part in the [ski
jump] contests. *(Steamboat Pilot, Routt County)*

- **January 2, 1936: Edward Henry Chatfield** marries his cousin
Margaret Elmina Driver [formerly Margaret Driver Hinman] in
Kremmling, Colorado. They had two children: James Niles Chatfield
and Margaret Ann "Peg" Chatfield, who eventually married her
Whittier College sweetheart, Terry M. McCarty. *(Terry and Margaret
Chatfield McCarty)*

Nellie Margaret Chatfield and Elmina Chatfield

Nellie Margaret Chatfield was the third-born child of **James Herrick Chatfield**
and **Annie Brazier Chatfield. Elmina Chatfield** was the only child of **James
Herrick Chatfield** and his second wife, **Mary Elmina Chatfield. Elmina** was a
"half sister" to **Nellie Margaret and Edward Livingston Jr.**

- **March 8, 1901: Miss Nellie Chatfield** returned to school at
Denver University on Monday, after three weeks absence on account
of sickness. *(Littleton Independent)*

- **August 15, 1902:** Messrs. **Will** [Nathan] **Chatfield** [son of William
S. and Laura], Mr. Steward, and Mr. Hubbard, of Denver, visited **Miss
Nellie Chatfield** Saturday. *(Littleton Independent)*

- **August 17, 1917: Mrs. George Driver** and daughter [**Margaret
Elmina Driver**] of Hoquiam, Washington, who have been visiting
at Fort Collins, are spending a few days with the former's parents**,
J.H. Chatfield** and wife, before returning to their home. *(Littleton
Independent)*

- **March 24, 1922: Public Trustee's Sale** — Whereas, Rudolph
A. Butz and Frans J. Butz, grantors by their Trust Deed dated
December 31, 1919 [have defaulted on payments their property will
be auctioned off] to the highest bidder on Monday the 27th day of
March 1922, at 10 o'clock in the forenoon. [Defaults include failure to
make payments for] particularly five eighths (5/8) of one share of the
capital stock of the Last Chance Ditch Company No. Two in trust
to secure one principal note of even date with said Trust Deed for
One Thousand ($1000.00) Dollars payable to **Elmina D. Chatfield**

or order, on or before three years after date, with interest thereon from date at the rate of 6 percent per annum, payable semi-annually. *(Littleton Independent)*

- **August 18, 1922: Margaret Driver**, daughter of **Mrs. Nellie Chatfield Driver** was married in Phoenix, Arizona to **Maynard Hinman** last June, according to word received here by **Miss Elmina Chatfield**. *(Littleton Independent)*
- **April 16, 1923:** In Phoenix Arizona, **Margaret Driver Hinman** gives birth to her first child, **Georgianna Ardas Hinman**. *(Terry and Margaret Chatfield McCarty)*
- **May 25, 1923: Miss Elmina Chatfield** left Monday night for California where she will attend school at Berkeley. She stopped off at the Grand Canyon and will also spend two weeks with her sister, **Mrs. George Driver**, at Phoenix. *(Littleton Independent)*

1883 — 1899 The Chatfield and Herrick Families

- **November 4, 1883:** The Presbyterian Church of Littleton was organized this day. First elders: **Nathan S. Chatfield**; Arthur D. Bailey. First trustees: **Nathan S. Chatfield**, Arthur D. Bailey, **Edward L. Chatfield, Robert D. Herrick**, and Wm A. Reynolds. [There were eighteen charter members, among them: **Nathan S. Chatfield, Margaret P. Chatfield, William A. Herrick, Jeanette Herrick, Edward L. Chatfield, Ann B. Chatfield, Mary M. Chatfield, Robert D. Herrick, and Nancy E. Herrick**.[*] *(Littleton Independent, December 1917)*
- **October 18, 1889:** A very pleasant time is reported by the ladies who gathered at the residence of **Mrs. W.A. Herrick** yesterday afternoon. *(Littleton Independent)*
- **September 3, 1892:** Mr. Chapman[†] and daughter, of Michigan, have just arrived in Littleton after an extensive trip of all the prominent resorts. Miss Chapman is a niece of **W.A. Herrick** and a cousin of the **Chatfield brothers**. They are visiting their relatives here and will stay in this section for several days. *(Littleton Independent)*
- **October 24, 1894:** Mrs. John Jones of Denver is visiting her cousins, the **Chatfield brothers** this week. *(Littleton Independent)*

---

[*] William A. Herrick was Margaret P. Chatfield's older brother. He and his wife, Jeanette, were the parents of Robert D. Herrick who subsequently married Nancy Hart. They had two children, Robert S. Herrick (who married Laura Peas) and Helen Herrick (who became Helen Herrick Dale.) The Herrick Ranch was adjacent to the Chatfield Ranch.

[†] Mr. William Alvin Chapman was the husband of Bessie Zipporah Herrick. Bessie's parents were David Herrick Jr. (the 7th born child of David Herrick and Zipporah Avery Herrick) and Betsey Shaw Herrick.

- **March 6, 1896:** The dime social given by the Ladies of the W.R.C. at **Chatfield's Hall**[*] Friday evening, proved quite a success both socially and financially. A short program consisting of music and recitations was presented. After that, light refreshments were served. Short speeches by the comrades and the singing of patriotic songs brought to a close a pleasant occasion. About six dollars was realized with which the ladies expect to do relief work. The ladies of the corps wish to thank the G.A.R. for their assistance also to others who were not members of the order, for their services. *(Littleton Independent)*

- **January 21, 1898:** A.O.U.W. [Ancient Order of United Workmen] Littleton Lodge No. 44, A.O.U.W. meets every Tuesday evening at A.O.U.W. hall, **Chatfield block**. Visiting brothers in good standing are cordially invited. J.J. Murphy, M.W.- J.P. Curtis, Recorder -*(Littleton Independent)*

- **January 13, 1899:** G.A.R. John C. Freemont Post No 83, G.A.R. meets the first and third Wednesday of each month in **Chatfield's Hall** at 2:00 p.m. W.A. Powell, Commander; Wm. Steward, Adj. *(Littleton Independent)*

1881 — 1908 The Chatfield Cousins

- **August 11, 1881: I.W. Chatfield,** the *Denver & Rio Grande* contractor who is doing the work upon the short line through the Platte Cañon, advertises for 500 rock workers who will be paid $2.50 per day and boarded for $5.00 per week. *(Fair Play Flume, Fairplay, Park County)*

- **October 4, 1888:** A special [note] from Grand Junction to the *Denver Republican* says **Elmer E. Chatfield**, a son of **I.W. Chatfield**, arrived there Monday morning after an exciting and successful chase after horse thieves. The horses were stolen on the night of September 14, and **Mr. Chatfield** started immediately from Aspen parallel and succeeded in capturing his horses and the thieves near Green River, Utah. The young man followed the thieves entirely alone, traveling day and night, and made the capture without any assistance. He was in one of the most dangerous parts of Utah Territory, where, had his mission been known, his life would have been worth but little. For perseverance and pluck the like has not been performed in Colorado. *(Fairplay Flume, Park County)*

---

[*]   Chatfield Hall, constructed by Isaac Willard Chatfield, was the site for a variety of community activities.

- **February 9, 1891: I.W. CHATFIELD & CO.,** Jobbers and Retailers of all kinds of Groceries and Produce — Office and Store, 124 Sixth St., LEADVILLE [Colo.] *(Leadville Democrat, Lake County)*
- **May 4, 1893:** The state board of agriculture convened in special session on Thursday, April 27, at the agricultural college (including) **J.L. Chatfield [James Lauren Chatfield.]** *(Fort Collins Courier)*
- **May 3, 1894:** Gov. Waite has appointed the following members of the board of stock inspection commissioners for the year ending May 2, 1895: **I.W. Chatfield**, of Emma...[a member] of the old board." *(Fort Collins Courier)*
- **December 15, 1899: Hon. James L. Chatfield** of Gypsum, Colorado, member of the State Board of Agriculture, with his wife, were the guests of their cousins, **E.L. Chatfield and family and J.H. Chatfield and family.** *(Littleton Independent)*
- **May 18, 1901:** A CONFIDENTIAL TALK! If you want something to eat, call at **Chatfield's.** He keeps the BEST MEATS in the market. FRESH VEGETABLES and FRUITS, and a fine line of GROCERIES. If you intend to build a home we can furnish you with first-class LUMBER at a reasonable price. **C.S. CHATFIELD** [Clark S. Chatfield], BASALT, COLO. *(Basalt Journal, Eagle County)*
- **July 28, 1905: I.W. Chatfield,** of Denver, visited with **J.H. Chatfield** on Tuesday. *(Littleton Independent)*
- **September 2, 1905: Mrs. C.S. Chatfield, Sr.**, is ill at the house of her son **Clark** [C.S. Chatfield, Jr.] near Emma. **Levi Chatfield** [Clark's son] is also sick, his ailment being malaria fever, contracted while in California. *(Basalt Journal)*
- **March 9, 1906:** **I.W. Chatfield**, of Denver, made a business call in Littleton on Tuesday. **Mr. Chatfield** was at one time owner of Caley Ranch and also the **E.L. Chatfield Ranch.** *(Littleton Independent)*
- **[Obituary] March 10, 1906: Death of C.S. Chatfield** [Clark S. Chatfield]— The friends of **Mr. C.S. Chatfield** were deeply saddened to learn of his death which occurred at Princeton, Calif. on Tuesday of this week. On the Monday of last week a telegram was received that he was dangerously ill and his wife and son, **Mr. Clark Chatfield**, started immediately to go to him. From the brief message received, it would appear that he was unconscious when they reached there and died without recognizing them. Mr. Chatfield's illness was doubtless the result of a fall from his horse, which happened last fall. He has been in rather feeble health ever since then, until his case finally became alarming, resulting in his death. He died at the home of his son-in-law, Mr. Jas. Mallon. The funeral was held

---

* James Lauren Chatfield was the third born child of Lucius N. Chatfield, Isaac and Lucy's first born.

on Wednesday and it is understood that Mrs. Chatfield and Clark would start for Basalt immediately afterward, probably arriving here the first of the week. Levi and Marjory, who remained here, have the sympathy of many friends. *(Basalt Journal, Eagle County)*

- **December 19, 1908:** A sad feature of the meeting of the board of control of the State Agriculture College at Fort Collins was the absence of **James L. Chatfield** of Gypsum, Colorado. Mr. Chatfield has been a member of the board sixteen years, and has never missed a regular meeting until this one, which would have been his last, his term expiring with the close of this year. Mr. Chatfield was stricken with paralysis a short time since, and was unable to make the trip. He is past seventy years old. *(Yampa Leader)*

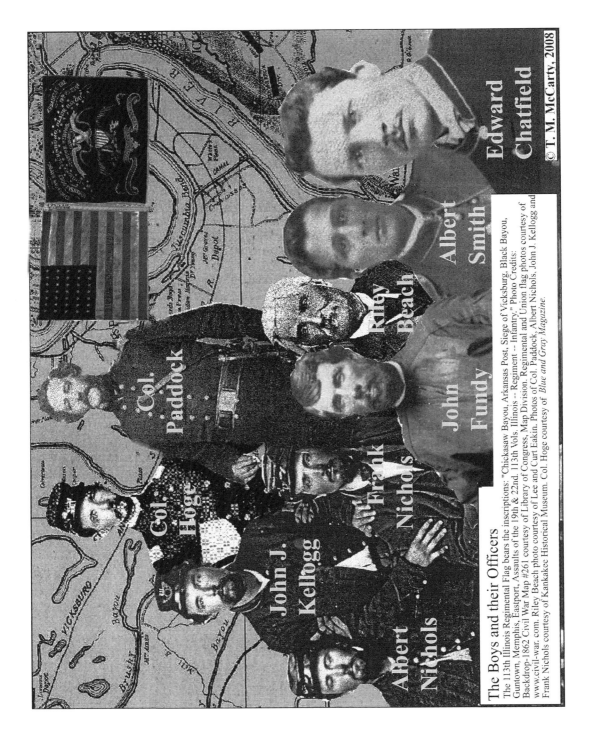

© T. M. McCarty, 2008

Edward Chatfield

Albert Smith

Riley Beach

John Fundy

Col. Paddock

Frank Nichols

Col. Hoge

John J. Kellogg

Albert Nichols

The Boys and their Officers

The 113th Illinois Regimental Flag bears the inscriptions: "Chickasaw Bayou, Arkansas Post, Siege of Vicksburg, Black Bayou, Guntown, Memphis, Eastport, Assaults of the 19th & 22nd. 113th Vols. Illinois -- Regiment -- Infantry." Photo Credits: Backdrop–1862 Civil War Map #261 courtesy of Library of Congress, Map Division. Regimental and Union flag photos courtesy of www.civil-war.com. Riley Beach photo courtesy of Lee and Curt Eakin. Photos of Col. Paddock, Albert Nichols, John J. Kellogg and Frank Nichols courtesy of Kankakee Historical Museum. Col. Hoge courtesy of Blue and Gray Magazine.

APPENDIX III: ABOUT THE BOYS

The war brought with it a second family to Chatfield. In all, he kept track of more than 120 soldiers, a number that includes nearly all of the boys in Company "B." They were mostly farm boys when they volunteered, and all would be transformed into hardened soldiers within months. To Chatfield, those "boys" were his kin—a brotherhood which would endure throughout his life.

The Boys in Company "B"

Below is the *Illinois Roster* for Company "B" of the 113th Illinois Volunteer Infantry. See the Index for corresponding page numbers.

- (*) Asterisks identify those in Company "B" <u>mentioned by Chatfield</u> in his letters and/or diary entries.
- *Italics* denote those in Company "B" who were either <u>killed or disabled</u>.
- **Boldface** marks those in Company "B" who mustered out well enough to be <u>judged free of disability.</u>

Soldier	Comments
Ash, John, Private	*Disabled. Discharged December 2, 1863, Benton Barracks, MO*
* Ash, William W., Corporal	**Mustered out June 20, 1865**
* Bartholomew, John, Private	*Died of disease while in Corinth, Mississippi, Sept. 15, 1863*
* Beach, Riley V., Private	**Mustered out July 1, 1865**
* Beckett, Andrew, Captain	**Mustered out June 20, 1865**

Beebe Orren J., Private.

Disabled. Discharged September 13, 1863, St. Louis, MO

* Beebe, Wallace W., Private

Mustered out July 1, 1865

* Bickle, John C., Private

Disabled. Discharged April 22, 1863, St. Louis, MO

* Blair, Loyal S., Corporal

Died of disease while at Milliken's Bend, LA, May 3, 1863

* Blanchet, John R., Sergeant

Mustered out June 20, 1865

* Boswell, Charles, Private*

Sick in Baltimore MD at time of dis charge, June 24, 1865

* Brandenberg, Henry, Corporal

Died of disease while at Walnut Hills, Vicksburg, June 1863

* Buck, Noah, Private

Died of disease while in Corinth, MS, September 17, 1863

* Calkins, Charles L., Private

Died of disease while at Young's Point, LA, February 24, 1863

* Campbell, John P., Corporal

Mustered out June 20, 1865

* Carrow Thomas, Corporal

Mustered out June 20, 1865

* Cazean, Lewis, Private

Disabled by wounds. Discharged Nov.18, 1863, St. Louis, MO

* Chatfield, Edward L., Private

Mustered out June 20, 1865

Clute, John, Private

Discharged by Surgeon for medical reasons, date not given

* Delamatre, Richard V., Corporal

Died of disease while at Young's Point, LA, February 27, 1863

* Durham, Daniel, Wagoner

Mustered out June 20, 1865

Earley, Daniel T., Sergeant

Deserted while at Memphis, TN, Nov.25, 1862. Reduced in rank

* Fender, Benjamin F., Corporal

Disabled by Wounds, Discharged in Quincy, Ill., April 11, 1864

* Foote, Herman J., Private

Mustered out June 20, 1865

* Forman, Andrew, Private

Died in 1864 while in a Rebel Prison in Columbia, Alabama

Forman, Charles M., Private

**Transferred to the 120 Illinois.
Mustered out June 20, 1865**

* Forman, William, Private

Died of disease while at Corinth, Mississippi, August 13, 1863

* Fundy, John, Private

Mustered out June 20, 1865

* Glass, Frederick A., Private

Died of disease while at Vicksburg, MS, July 16, 1863

---

*   Charles Boswell was captured mid-July 1863, in a skirmish with CS General Joe Johnston's forces in Jackson, Mississippi. He remained a prisoner of war until released upon the war's end.

* **Gubtail, John, Corporal**	**Mustered out June 20, 1865**
* **Gubtail, Lucius, Private**	**Mustered out June 20, 1865**
* **Henry, James, First Sgt.***	**Mustered out June 20, 1865, Medal of Honor, July 9, 1894**
* *Hercher, Jacob, Private*	*Died of disease while in Corinth, Mississippi, November 9, 1863*
* *Hicks, Joseph Chard, Private*	*Died of wounds while aboard "John J. Roe," January 21, 1863*
* **Hoge, George B., Colonel**	**Mustered out June 20, 1865**
Holloway, Martin W., Private	*Disabled. Discharged at Mound City, Illinois, February 20, 1863*
* *Huton, Frances, Private*	*Died of wounds while in Memphis, Tennessee, April 11, 1863*
* **Jeffcoat, John, 1ˢᵗ Lieutenant**	**Mustered out June 20, 1865**
* **Johns, Elisha "Lish," Sergeant**	**Mustered out June 20, 1865, Medal of Honor, July 9, 1894**
Jones, Seth, Private	**Mustered out June 20, 1865**
Jones, Stephen D., Private	**Transf. to the 120ᵗʰ Illinois. Mustered out June 20, 1865**
Keeney, John F., Private	*Disabled. Discharged in St. Louis, MO, March 31, 1863*
* **Kellogg, John J., First Sgt.**	**Discharged after prom. to Cpt., 88ᵗʰ US Colored Infantry.**
Kerns, Michael, Private	**Mustered out June 20, 1865**
* **Landis, Edmund M., Private**	**Mustered out June 20, 1865**
* *Leighton, Ambrose, Private*	*Died of disease while in Corinth, MS, September 27, 1863*
Lewis, Edward W., Private	*Disabled while in Memphis, TN, March 20, 1863*
Lyman, Andrew J., Private	*Deserted while hospitalized at St. Louis MO.*
* *Lyman, Jonathan W., Private*	*Died of disease while at Jefferson Barracks, MO, Jan. 21, 1863*
* **Maggee, Calvin, Private**	**Mustered out June 20, 1865**
Maiden, Frank E., Corporal	**Mustered out June 20, 1865**
* **Mandegold, John E., Private**	**Mustered out June 20, 1865**
* **Nichols, Albert T., Musician**	**Mustered out June 20, 1865**
Pebles, Ezra, Private	**Mustered out June 20, 1865**

---

* James Henry's promotion to 2ⁿᵈ lieutenant had been cancelled. Instead, Henry was promoted to 1ˢᵗ Sergeant. Responding to the petition submitted by the boys of Company "B", Governor Yates awarded the promotion to John Jeffcoat, increasing his rank from 2ⁿᵈ lieutenant to 1ˢᵗ lieutenant on June 28, 1864.

514
The Chatfield Story: Civil War Letters and Diaries of
Private Edward L. Chatfield of the 113th Illinois Volunteers

* Ponto, Francis, Private	Died of wounds while at Vicksburg, May 19, 1863
* Powley, Joseph C., Private	**Mustered out June 20, 1865**
Quier, Henry, Corporal	Disabled while at Young's Point, LA. Discharged April 22, 1863
* Rankin, Adam L., Chaplain	**Mustered out June 20, 1865**
* Rounsavell, Milton H., Sgt.,	**Mustered out June 20, 1865**
* Scoon, James, Sergeant	**Mustered out June 20, 1865**
* Scoon, John W., Corporal	**Mustered out June 20, 1865**
* Scoon, William W., Private	**Mustered out June 20, 1865**
Scott, Robert J., Private	Deserted while in Chicago, Illinois, November 3, 1863
* Shays, George E., Private	Died of disease while on steamer, "Silver Wave," July 30, 1863
* Showbar, Frank, Private	Disabled, by wounds. Discharged in Memphis TN on Feb.7, 1865
* Shreffler, Enos, Private	Disabled by wounds. Discharged in Chicago, Ill., July 28, 1865
* Shreffler, Peter, Jr.	Died of disease while in Corinth, MS, August 14, 1863
Shultz, Abraham, Private	**Deserted while in Chicago, October 6, 1862**
Shultz, John, Private	Deserted while hospitalized in St. Louis, MO.
* Smith, Albert G., Private[*]	**Mustered out June 20, 1865**
* Smith, Allen M., Private	Disabled. Discharged in St. Louis, MO, on May 8, 1863
* Smith, Joseph C., Private	Disabled. Discharged in Corinth on January 18, 1864
Smith, Richard Hix, Private	**Mustered out June 20, 1865**
* Soncey, Francis, Private	Disabled while at Young's Point. Discharged March 31, 1863
* States, Alfred G., Corporal	Died of disease while in Corinth, MS, August 20, 1863
Steinenger, Frederick, Private	**Transferred to the 120 Illinois. Mustered out Sept. 10, 1865**

---

[*] In December of 1866 (or early 1867) Albert (Chatfield's friend "Bert") married Mary Irene Herrick, the daughter of James Oliver Herrick and Mary Jane Conant. With this marriage, Bert truly became part of Chatfield's family. James Oliver was Chatfield's mother's brother—the 3rd child of David Herrick and Zipporah Avery. By 1880, Albert and Mary had 3 sons and a daughter: Ernest T. Smith, A. William T. Smith, Walter Earl Smith and Lucy P. Smith. All were living on their farm in Kankakee's Salina Township. They later had two more children. (1880 US Census Record for Albert G. Smith of Salina, Kankakee, Illinois; Cross, Reverend R.T., *Twinsburg, Ohio, 1817 – 1917, Part II, Genealogies*, 335)

* **Titcomb, John S., Sergeant**	**Promoted to Cpt., 88th US Colored Infantry before dischg.**
Tunks, George E., Corporal	**Mustered out June 20, 1865**
* *Van Valkenberg, George T., Pvt*	*Died of Small Pox while hospitalized in St. Louis, April 3, 1863*
* **Walters, Levi M., Corporal**	**Mustered out July 15, 1865**
* **Ward, Caleb D., Corporal**	**Hosp. Steward; Mustered out as Physician June 20, 1865**
Wheel, Alexander, Private	*Deserted while hospitalized in St. Louis, MO*
* **White, Henry, Private**	**Mustered out June 20, 1865**
* **William, Ira A., Private**	**Mustered out June 20, 1865**
* **Williams, Cephas, Major**	**Mustered out June 20, 1865**
* **Wilson, Alexander, Private**	**Mustered out June 20, 1865**
Wise, Samuel, Private	**Mustered out June 20, 1865**
Woody, Enos H., Private	*Transf. to Invalid Corps, Nov. 20, 1863. Mstrd.out June 15, 1865*
Write, John W., Musician	**Mustered out June 20, 1865**
* *Wurts, William B., Private*	*Died of disease aboard hospital boat, "Nashville," Mar. 31, 1863*

Other Soldiers Mentioned by Chatfield

Beyond the boys in his company, Chatfield mentioned the names of many others. Below is a summary listing. Those who **survived** the war are in **bold print**; those who *died* during the war are in *italics*. See the Index for corresponding page numbers.

Ash, Lorenzo D., Private, Company "I", 113th Illinois
Baird, Azariah M., Lieutenant, Company "A", 113th Illinois
Bird, Morris, Corporal, Company "H", 113th Illinois
Black, John C., Colonel, 37th Illinois Infantry
Blood, Carlos, Private, Company "K", 113th Illinois
Bowers, James A., Private, Company "A", 113th Illinois
Bray, John G., Private, Company "F", 156th Illinois
Bronson, Albert, Private, Company "G", 113th Illinois
Brown, Lucian B., Regimental Surgeon, 113th Infantry
Call, Joseph, Private, Company "H", 113th Illinois
Chatfield, Charles A., Lieutenant, Company "E", 113th Illinois
Chatfield, Charles Henry, Captain, Company "D" of the 85th Illinois.
Chatfield, Clark Samuel, Corporal, Company "C", 2nd Illinois Cavalry
Chatfield, Henry E., Sergeant, Company "I", 18th Michigan Volunteers
Chatfield, Isaac Willard, 2nd Lieutenant, Company "E", 27th Illinois

Chatfield, William S., Private, Company "F", 156th **Illinois**
Chester, Frank, Adjutant, Company "G", 20th **Illinois**
Clark, Ezekiel, Private, Company "I", 113th **Illinois**
Clark, George R., Lieutenant Colonel, Company "A", 113th **Illinois**
Cole, Daniel, Private, Company "G", 113th **Illinois**
Cole, Seth R., Private, Company "A", 113th **Illinois**
*Conway, James J., 1*st *Lieutenant, Company "G", 113*th *Illinois*
Cowgill, Aquilla, 2nd **Lieutenant, Company "H", 113**th **Illinois**
Cowgill, Wilder, Private, Company "H", 113th **Illinois**
Daniels, Harrison, Lieutenant, Company "H", 113th **Illinois**
Darly, Thomas, Private, Company "H", 113th **Illinois**
Dashill, Virgil, 1st**. Lt. Company "K", 113**th **Illinois**
Dennison, James H., Sergeant, Company "K", 113th **Illinois**
*Eells, Samuel, Private, Company "F", 6*th *Iowa Cavalry*
Forman, Charles M., Private, Company "F", 120th **Illinois**
Freeman, Daniel H., Wagoner, Company "E", 113th **Illinois**
Friel, Henry, Sgt., Company "G", 113th **Illinois**
Frith, Charles, Private, Company "H", 113th **Illinois, deserted, April 1, 1863**
*Gable, George W., Private, Company "D", 113*th *Illinois*
*Gibbs, Henry T., Private, Company "C", 113*th *Illinois*
Glennon, Edward, 1st **Sergeant, Company "F", 42**nd **Illinois**
Griffin, William, Private, Company "H", 113th Illinois
*Hall, Moses, Private, Company "H", 113*th *Illinois*
Hamblin, Stephen, Sgt., Company "H", 113th **Illinois**
*Harter, Frances, Private, Company "H", 113*th *Illinois*
Harwood, Asa G., Sgt., Company "A", 113th **Illinois**
Hawkins, Jesse, Private, Companies "I", and "E", 12th **Illinois Cavalry,**
deserted,
*Higgins, Maurice, Private, Company "H", 113*th *Illinois*
*Jackson, Henry, Private, Company "E", 113*th *Illinois*
*Jones, Elias S., Private, Company "E", 113*th *Illinois*
Joslyn, Walter S., Orderly, Company "G", 113th **Illinois**
King, George E., Captain, Company "F", 113th **Illinois**
Lamb, Morris, Private, Company "G", 20th **Illinois**
Lintleman, Richard, Sergeant, Company "E", 113th **Illinois, March 17, 1866**
*Martin, James, Private, Company "A", 113*th *Illinois*
Martin, Thomas H., Corporal, Company "A", 113th **Illinois**
McDearmon, John Demster, Corporal, Private, Company "A", 113th **Illinois**
McDearmon, Merrill, Private, Sergeant, Company "A", 113th **Illinois**
*McGreggor, Richard, US Private, Company "H", 113*th *Illinois*
*Miner, Henry August, Private, Company "H", 113*th *Illinois*

Mitchell, William P., 1ˢᵗ Lieut. Company "F", 7ᵗʰ Illinois, Dishonorably Dismissed, Jan. 25, 1865

Moffatt, Joel, Private Joel Moffatt, Company "K", 113ᵗʰ Illinois

Newton, Charles A., Commissary Sergeant, Company "D", 113ᵗʰ Illinois

Nichols, Franklin N., Musician, Company "H", 113ᵗʰ Illinois

Norton, Gould P., Corporal, Company "G", 113ᵗʰ Illinois

Orton, Albert, Private, Company "I", 1ˢᵗ Illinois U.S. Artillery, disabled, May 17, 1865

Paddock, John W., Colonel, 113ᵗʰ Illinois Regiment

Palmer, George, Private, Company "F" 76ᵗʰ Illinois

Parker, Daniel S., Regimental Adjutant, 113ᵗʰ Illinois

Place, Samuel, Private, Company "H", 113ᵗʰ Illinois

Rice, Oliver, Private, Wagoner, Company "H", 113ᵗʰ Illinois

Rodgers, Charles, Corporal, Company "E", 113ᵗʰ Illinois

Rohrer, John, Sergeant, Company "G", 20ᵗʰ Illinois

Runyon, John, Private, Company "E", 113ᵗʰ Illinois

Scotland, Thomas, Private, Company "A", 113ᵗʰ Illinois

Sheldon, George W., Company "A", 113ᵗʰ Illinois, discharged June 9, 1864, disabled

Shufeldt, Theodore, Private, Company "E", 113ᵗʰ Illinois

Smith, Ambrose, Corporal, Company "G", 113ᵗʰ Illinois

Smith, Malcomb F., Sergeant Major, Company "E", 113ᵗʰ Illinois

Squires, Charles, 2ⁿᵈ Lieutenant, Company "K", 113ᵗʰ Illinois

Sutherland, Bliss, Captain, Company "H", 113ᵗʰ Illinois

Sutherland, Mason, Captain, Commander, Company "E", 113ᵗʰ Illinois

Sutton, Peter D,, Sergeant, Company "H", 113ᵗʰ Illinois

Sutton, Smith, Private, Company "H", 113ᵗʰ Illinois

Swortfiger, Edward, Private, Company "K", 120th Ill. (prior svc. in 113ᵗʰ) Sept. 10, 1865

Wainwright, Edward, Private, Company "A"

Walker, Martin, Private, Company "A", 113ᵗʰ Illinois

Warden, William "Billy", 1ˢᵗ Sgt., Co. "F", 76ᵗʰ Ill.; June 27, 1865, after leg amputation

Welch, Thomas, Company "F", 76ᵗʰ Illinois

Westfall, Charles, Corporal, Company "A", 113ᵗʰ Illinois

Wickens, Frank, Private, Company "G" 20ᵗʰ Illinois

Williams, Henry M., Sergeant, Company "A", 113ᵗʰ Illinois

Woodruff, George A., Sergeant, Company "H", 113ᵗʰ Illinois

The Index of this book contains alphabetical listings and page references for all of the boys in Company "B" and all of the other soldiers mentioned by Chatfield.

Diaries from the 113th Illinois

Daily journaling was a widespread practice during the war. Many Civil War diaries were published after the war ended, and today it's not difficult to find complete Civil War diaries on the Internet. The diaries kept by fellow soldiers helped to provide details that filled in the blanks left by Chatfield's own diaries and letters. Three soldiers provided the bulk of the diary-based material.

Sergeant James H. Dennison

Dennison, a sergeant in Company "K" of the 113th Illinois, maintained a diary while in Andersonville, a first-hand account of his experiences there. Dennison's *Andersonville Diary* was published by the Kankakee Historical Museum in 1987.

Orderly John J. Kellogg

Kellogg, of Company "B" of the 113th Illinois, eventually published his diary information in book form: *The Vicksburg Campaign and Reminiscences from Milliken's Bend to July 4, 1863*. Civil War historians frequently reference its lively content. Kellogg served as the company's orderly through April 4, 1864, when he departed Memphis for Springfield to assist in recruiting. Sometime after that, Kellogg was promoted to captain to command a company in the 88th Colored Infantry. Following his discharge, Kellogg settled in Washington, Iowa, where he spoke to a variety of groups over the years, recounting the events of the war. In 1913, he drew upon his diary to write and publish his book.

Riley Vincent Beach

Private Riley Beach, from Limestone Township in Kankakee, was one of Chatfield's friends in Company "B" of the 113th Illinois. Beach became a minister after the war and spoke to many audiences about his war experiences. In 1917, at the age of 74, he made an effort to record his Civil War memories, using a typewriter to manually hammer out his story on 7.5" X 9.5" blue-lined notebook paper. A carbon copy of Beach's memoirs accompanied the collection of Chatfield's letters, its over forty pages bound within a black and red bookkeeper's journal by a single ring—its brass screw fasteners missing. Handwritten on the first page was the title of his unpublished work: *The Recollections and Extracts from the Diaries of Army life of Reverend Riley V. Beach of Company "B", 113th Illinois Infantry Volunteers*. Beach's *Recollections* provided many useful details for *The Chatfield Story*.

Once Beach got behind Union lines in Wilmington, North Carolina, the army placed him on furlough to recuperate for 30 days. He reached his Limestone, Kankakee, home on March 21, 1865, and was still there on April 14 when President Lincoln was assassinated. Returning to duty at Benton Barracks, Saint Louis, Missouri, he was subsequently ordered to Springfield, Illinois, for a short stay, before being sent to Chicago to muster out with the regiment which was on its way north from Memphis. He arrived in Chicago one day after his regiment had arrived and was sent back down to Springfield to muster out. His delay in mustering out cost him an 18-month delay in pay. He finally mustered out on July 1, 1865. Beach arrived back in Limestone on July 8, 1865.

Beach moved around for the next three years before finally settling down. First, he moved to Lynn County, Iowa, 300 miles west of Limestone. Then he moved back to Illinois, only to depart again and go east to Ohio, working briefly as a teacher, before deciding, once and for all, to become a minister. Having made the decision, Beach returned to his home state of Illinois and trained for the ministry in Oswego, just south of where he would eventually marry. He was ordained as a minister at the Methodist Episcopal Church in Oswego, Illinois, in 1868.

Two years later, almost 28, Beach married Melinda Margaret Edwards in Kane County, 27 miles north of Oswego. Immediately after exchanging vows (October 8, 1870) the couple moved to Butler County, Nebraska, where Beach served as a minister for the next 17 years. Beach actively participated in the *Grand Army of the Republic* and gave numerous talks about the war to a variety of audiences. He and Melinda had four children in Butler County, three girls and a boy. In 1887, the Beach family moved 250 miles west to Big Springs (Deuel County, Nebraska) locating on a farm south of the city. Beach continued his ministry and was ordained as a deacon in Orleans, Nebraska, in 1894. Riley and Melinda sold the farm in 1906 and moved to a newly-built residence above the Post Office in Big Springs. Beach was then 64—young enough to continue his ministry, remain active in the G.A.R., and maintain regular correspondence with Chatfield and other Civil War friends. He didn't slow down until his body weakened from the toll of diabetes. He died in his daughter's home in Chappell, Nebraska, on March 4, 1928—almost three years after Chatfield had died. Beach was buried in the Big Springs Cemetery, 198 miles northwest of his departed friend, Ed Chatfield, who lay at final rest in the Littleton Cemetery.

Two Favorite Songs
Along with the Chatfield letters, tucked away in the same shoebox, were the verses, handwritten by Chatfield, of two of his favorite army songs.

Just Before the Battle
Commemorating the battles fought by the 113th—*Chickasaw Bayou, Arkansas Post*, the *May 19 and May 22 Vicksburg assaults*, and *Brice's Cross Roads*—Chatfield preserved lasting memories by recording George F. Root's 1863 composition.

Just before the battle Mother,
I am thinking most of you.
While upon the field, we're waiting.
With the Enemy in view.
Comrades brave, are round me lying.
Filled with thoughts of home and God.
For well they know that on the morrow.
Some <u>may sleep beneath the sod.</u>
Chorus,
Farewell Mother you may never.
Press me to your heart again.
But you will not forget me Mother.
If I'm numbered with slain.—

Oh I long to see you Mother.
And the loving ones at home!
But I'll never leave our "Banner."
Till in honor I can come.
Tell the <u>Traitors</u> all around you.
That their cruel words we know.
To kill our Boys in every battle.
<u>By the help they give the foe.</u>
Chorus

Hark! I hear the Bugle sounding.
Tis the signal for the fight.
Now may God protect us Mother.
As he ever does the right.
Hear the <u>Battle</u> cry of Freedom.
How it swells upon the air.
Oh yes! we'll rally round the standard
Or will perish nobly there.
Chorus.

The Prisoner's Life

The second song preserved with the collection of letters was one of suffering and courage, commemorating Chatfield's experience within the Confederate prisons. Written by George F. Root, *"Tramp! Tramp! Tramp!"* was called *"The Prisoner's Hope"* by many soldiers. Chatfield titled it *"The Prisoner's Life."*

In the Prison Cell I sit
Thinking Mother Dear of you
And our bright and happy home so far away.
And the tears they fill my eyes
Spite of all that I can do
Tho' I try to cheer my comrades and be gay.*

Chorus

Tramp. Tramp. Tramp the Boys are marching
Cheer up Comrades they will come
And beneath the starry Flag
We shall breath the air again
Of the free land of our Beloved home.

In the Battle front we stand
When the fiercest Charge they made
And they swept us off a hundred men or more
But before we reached their lines
They were beaten back dismayed
And we heard the Cry of Victory Oir and Oir [O'er and O'er]

[Chorus]

So within the Prison Cells
We are waiting for the day
That shall come to open wide the Iron door
And the hollow eye grow bright
And the poor heart almost gay
As we think of seeing home and friends once more

[Chorus]

---

*   Chatfield, in recording the lyrics, had omitted this line.

BIBLIOGRAPHY AND RESOURCES

Articles, Books, Manuscripts, Monographs and Unpublished Letters

Bastian, David F. *Grant's Canal: The Union's Attempt to Bypass Vicksburg.* Pennsylvania: Shippensburg, Burd Street Press, 1995.

Beach, Riley V. *Recollections and Extracts from the Diaries of Army Life of Reverend Riley V. Beach of Co. "B" 113th Illinois Infantry Volunteers.* Author's private collection of Beach's hand typed copy, circa 1917.

Bearss, Edwin C., "The Battle of Brice's Cross Roads," in *Blue and Gray Magazine*, Vol. XVI, Issue 6, August 1999.

Bearss, Edwin C., "Forrest's Defense of Mississippi: June-August 1864, Brice's Cross Roads," in Kennedy, Ed. *Civil War Battlefield Guide.*

Bearss, Margie, *Sherman's Forgotten Campaign, The Meridian Expedition.* Baltimore: Gateway Press, Inc., 1987.

Boatner, Mark M. III, *The Civil War Dictionary.* New York: Vintage Books, Revised Ed. 1991.

Blackman, Douglas A. *Slavery by Another Name: The Re-Enslavement of Black People in America from the Civil War to World War II.* New York: Doubleday, 2008.

Carter, Lena M., *Twinsburg, Ohio, 1817 – 1917 Part I, Centennial History of Twinsburg, Ohio.* Columbus, Ohio: The Champlin Press, 1917.

Chatfield, Edward L. *The Diaries of Edward L. Chatfield*, Littleton, Colorado: Littleton Historical Museum, inspection by appointment.

Chipman, General N.P., *The Tragedy of Andersonville; Trial of Captain Henry Wirz, The Prison Keeper*, Published by N.P. Chipman, San Francisco: Blair-Murdock Co., 1911.

Cross, Reverend R.T., *Twinsburg, Ohio, 1817 – 1917, Part II, Genealogies.* Columbus, Ohio: The Champlin Press, 1917

Daily Journal, Kankakee Public Library Historic Archives, Kankakee, Illinois.

Davies, Glyn. *A History of Money from Ancient Times to the Present Day.* Cardiff: University of Wales Press, 1999.

Dennison, Sgt. James H., *Dennison's Andersonville Diary,* Transcription and notes by Jack Klasey, Kankakee, Illinois: Kankakee County Historical Society, 1987.

Department of the Navy, *Civil War Naval Chronology, 1861-1865.* Washington D.C.: Naval History Division, 1971.

DiLorenzo, Thomas J., *The Real Lincoln*, Roseville, California: Prima Publishing, 2002.

Donald, David Herbert. *Lincoln.* New York: Simon and Schuster, 1996.

Drew, Ken: *Camp Sumter, The Pictorial History of Andersonville Prison.* Americus Georgia: Good Image Printers, Inc., ISBN#0-9622714-03, published circa 1990 [date of publication not given].

Faust, Drew Gilpin, *This Republic of Suffering, Death and the American Civil War.* New York: Vintage Civil War Library, Vintage Books, 2008

Fonville, Chris E., *The Wilmington Campaign, Last Departing Rays of Hope.* Mechanicsburg, Pennsylvania: Stackpole Books, 1st Edition, 2001.

Hicken, Victor, *Illinois in the Civil War.* Chicago: University of Illinois Press, 2nd Edition, 1991.

Hills, Parker, *A Study in Warfighting, Nathan Bedford Forrest and the Battle of Brice's Crossroads,* The Papers of the Blue and Gray Education Society. No. 2, Danville, Virginia: November 1, 1995.

Hoehling, A.A. *Vicksburg, 47 Days of Siege.* Mechanicsburg, Pennsylvania: Stackpole Books, 1996.

Jones, Wilmer L., *Generals in Blue and Gray.* Pennsylvania: Stackpole Books, 2004.

Kagan, Neil, Editor, *Eye Witness to the Civil War,* Washington D.C.: National Geographic Society, 2006.

Kantor, MacKinlay, *Andersonville.* Cleveland: The World Publishing Company, 1955.

Kankakee Gazette, Kankakee Public Library Historic Archives, Kankakee, Illinois.

Kellogg, Captain John. J. *The Vicksburg Campaign and Reminiscences from Milliken's Bend to July 4, 1863.* Washington County, Iowa: Washington Evening Journal, 1913.

Kellogg, Robert H., *Life and Death in Rebel Prisons.* Hartford, Connecticut: L. Stebbins (Publisher); Printed by Wiley, Waterman, & Eaton, 1865.

Kennedy, Frances H., Ed. *The Civil War Battlefield Guide.* Boston: Houghton Mifflin Company, 2nd Edition, 1998.

King, Charles, et. al., *The Photographic History of the Civil War.* Vol. 4, Secaucus, New Jersey: The Blue & Grey Press, 1987.

Klement, Frank L. *The Limits of Dissent: Clement L. Vallandigham and the Civil War.* New York: Fordham University Press (1998 Paperback reprint of J. Walter & Co. Edition, 1864)

Lattimer, John K., Lincoln and Kennedy: *Medical & Ballistic Comparisons of Their Assassinations.* New York: Harcourt; 1st edition, October 1980.

LeVert, Suzanne, et. al., *The Civil War Society's Encyclopedia of the Civil War.* Princeton, New Jersey: Wings Books, a division of Random House Publishing, Inc. 1997.

Lincoln, Abraham, *Collected Works of Abraham Lincoln, 1809-1865.* Volume 6, Springfield, Illinois: Abraham Lincoln Association, 1953.

Litwack, Leon F., *North of Slavery: The Negro in the Free States, 1790 – 1860*. Chicago: The University of Chicago Press, 1961.

Locke, John, *Essay Concerning Human Understanding*. London: 1690.

McFeely, William S., *Grant, A Biography*. New York: W.W. Norton and Company, 2002.

McPherson, James M., *Battle Cry of Freedom*, New York, Oxford University Press, 2003.

Memphis Daily Bulletin, Memphis Tennessee, "Execution of T.M. Smith," Volume 9, Number 280, Saturday Morning, p.2, col.2, April 30, 1864 (Microfilm; Tennessee State Library and Archives).

Mitchell, Patricia B., *Union Army Camp Cooking, 1861-1865*. Chatham, Virginia: Mitchell's Publications, Revised Edition, 2006.

National Park Service, Vicksburg National Military Park, *Letter Correspondence from the 113 Illinois Volunteers*, Unpublished collection. (Courtesy of Ranger Matt Atkinson).

- Letter 1: from Col. G.B. Hoge to Captain M. Sutherland, Nov. 21, 1862.
- Letter 2: from Col G.B. Hoge to Captain M. Sutherland, Dec. 30, 1862.
- Letter 3: from Dr. J.M. Mack to the Medical Director Under Gen. McClernand, Undated (Estimated to have been written in mid-January 1862, while at Arkansas Post).
- Letter 4: from G.B. Hoge to wife of Captain Mason Sutherland, following Sutherland's death, January 28, 1863.

Parker, Daniel S., Adjutant, 113th Illinois, *Civil War Letters to Mrs. Parker*, Unpublished letters. Courtesy of Kankakee County Museum, Kankakee, Illinois.

Porter, Jerry O., *The Sultana Tragedy: America's Greatest Maritime Disaster*. Gretna, Louisiana: Pelican Publishing Company, 2nd printing, August 1997.

Shea, William L. and Terrence J. Winschel, *Vicksburg Is the Key: The Struggle for the Mississippi River (Great Campaigns of the Civil War)*. Nebraska: University of Nebraska Press, 2003.

Sneden, Private Robert Knox, *Eye of the Storm — A Civil War Odyssey*, Charles F. Bryan, Jr. and Nelson D. Lankford, Editors, New York: The Free Press, 2000.

Wideman, John C, *The Sinking of the USS Cairo*, Jackson, Mississippi: University Press of Mississippi, 1993.

Williams, David, *A People's History of the Civil War*, New York: The New Press, 2005.

Websites
Ancestry.com:

- *1860 Federal Census Information, Kankakee, Illinois*, accessed through www.Ancestry.com (Last accessed in May 2008)
- Archives of *Yuma Daily Sun*, Yuma, Arizona (Last accessed in June 2008)

Akers, Monte, *The Rebel Yell, the Pibroch of Southern Fealty*: http://www.stonewallbrigade.com/articles.html (Last accessed 01/17/09)

Albany Patriot (Georgia) July 28, 1864 http://www.uttyler.edu/vbetts/albany.htm (Accessed 06/02/08)

American Battlefield Protection Program, National Park Service Websites, *Battle of Paducah,* http://www.nps.gov/history/hps/abpp/battles/ky010.htm (Last accessed 01/17/09)

Biographical Directory of the United States Congress, 1774 to the present: http://bioguide.congress.gov/biosearch/biosearch.asp (Last accessed 01/03/09)

Colorado's Historic Newspaper Collection — www.coloradohistoricnewspapers.org (Last accessed 07/21/08)

- *Basalt Journal*, Eagle County; *Castle Rock*, Douglas County; *Colorado Transcript of Golden*, Jefferson County; *Denver News*, Arapahoe County; *Fair Play Flume, Fairplay*, Park County; *Fort Collins Courier*, Larimer County; *Fort Collins Weekly Courier*, Larimer County; *Jefferson County Republican*, Jefferson County; *Leadville Democrat*, Lake County; *Littleton Independent*, Arapahoe County; *Oak Creek Times*, Routt County; *Record Journal*, Douglas County; *Routt County Sentinel*, Routt County; *Steamboat Pilot*, Routt County; *Summit County Journal*, Summit County; *Yampa Leader*, Routt County

Drake, Rebecca Blackwell, *The Ultimate Grief: William T. Sherman.* "Unknown to most, Sherman faced the ultimate grief in life only months after the Siege of Vicksburg. The story of Sherman is one of military triumph followed by personal tragedy." at: http://www.battleofraymond.org/history/sherman.htm (Last accessed 01/17/09)

528
The Chatfield Story: Civil War Letters and Diaries of
Private Edward L. Chatfield of the 113th Illinois Volunteers

Drew, Troy, *James M. Bryant's Daily Records of Deaths in Andersonville*, abstracted from Chipman, Norton P., *The Tragedy of Andersonville: Trial of Captain Henry Wirz, the Prison Keeper, 1911*, University of Missouri-K.C. School of Law's Seminar in Famous Trials course, daily deaths at Andersonville - http://www.law.umkc.edu/faculty/projects/ftrials/Wirz/deathlog.htm. (Last accessed 01/19/09)

Encyclopedia of Arkansas, History and Culture, *Battle of Arkansas Post*, http://www.encyclopediaofarkansas.net/encyclopedia/entry-detail.aspx?entryID=525 (Last Accessed 02/25/09)

Illinois Roster — *Illinois Civil War Muster and Descriptive Rolls Database* at http://www.ilsos.gov/genealogy/index.jsp (Last accessed 01/02/09)

Littleton Historical Museum:
http://www.littletongov.org/history/biographies/chatfield.asp (Accessed 12/28/08)

Macon Telegraph, October 1, 1864 http://files.usgwarchives.org/ga/bibb/newspapers/mt1864.txt (Last accessed 01/21/09)

National Archives and Records Administration, *Thirteenth Amendment to the U.S. Constitution*, http://www.ourdocuments.gov/ (Last accessed 01/24/09)

National Park Service websites: http://www.nps.gov/ (Last accessed 01/15/09)

New York Times archives website: http://query.nytimes.com/gst/abstract.html?res=9 80DEFDD153FE63ABC4A52DFB566838E679FDE (Last accessed 01/24/09)

O'Dea, Thomas, *Description of the O'Dea Andersonville Lithograph*, from an original pamphlet accompanying the lithograph, a part of the private collection of Kevin Frye, transcribed to the internet by Kevin Frye at http://www.angelfire.com/ga2/Andersonvilleprison/odea.html (Last accessed 11/22/08)

Official Records —

- *The Official Records of the Civil War*, eHistory at OSU Online Books: Referenced in footnotes and endnotes as *Official Records*. http://ehistory.osu.edu/osu/sources/records/ (Last accessed 01/15/09)
- *The War of the Rebellion* in Cornell University's Making of America, *Official Records*, Cornell University: Referenced in footnotes and endnotes as *Official Records*. http://cdl.library.cornell.edu/moa/browse.monographs/waro.html (Last accessed 04/10/09)

- *Official Records of the Union and Confederate Navies,* in Cornell University's Making of America (ORN, Cornell University) Referenced in footnotes and endnotes as *ORN.* http://cdl.library.cornell.edu/moa/browse.monographs/ofre.html (Last accessed 04/10/09)

Ohio History Central Website, *Land Act of 1820,* http://www.ohiohistorycentral.org" (Accessed 05/31/08)

Project Gutenberg's On Line Book Catalogue: http://www.gutenberg.org/catalog/ (Last accessed 01/24/09)

- Abraham Lincoln: *Collective Writings*
- John McElroy: *Andersonville, A Story of Rebel Military Prisons*
- Ulysses S. Grant: *Memoirs*
- William T. Sherman: *Memoirs*

San Francisco Museum Website: Dickson, Samuel, *Adah Isaacs Menken (1835-1868),* http://www.sfmuseum.org/bio/adah.html (Last accessed 01/17/09)

Sullivan, Megan. *"African-American Music as Rebellion:* "From Slavesong to Hip-Hop," http://www.eatmos.com/johnnyotis/juba.sullivan.pdf (Last accessed 01/16/09)

Tate, Garvin, *A Day at Holly Springs,* http://www.d-a-c.com/HollySprings/town.htm (Last accessed 01/15/09)

Thompson, E. R., *Pioneer and General History of Geauga County, with Sketches of Some of the Pioneers and Prominent Men.* Chardon, Ohio: Geauga County Courthouse, 1880, http://www.heritagepursuit.com/Geauga/GeaugaMiddlefield717.htm (Last accessed 01/15/09)

INDEX

536
The Chatfield Story: Civil War Letters and Diaries of
Private Edward L. Chatfield of the 113th Illinois Volunteers

The Chatfield Story: Civil War Letters and Diaries of
Private Edward L. Chatfield of the 113th Illinois Volunteers
550

ENDNOTES

1   E.R. Thompson, *Pioneer and General History of Geauga County,* p. 731
2   Ibid.
3   Ibid.
4   Ohio History Central Website, "Land Act of 1820"
5   Glyn Davies, *A History of Money,* 479
6   *Daily Journal,* February 1, 1951 p. 22, courtesy of Kankakee Public Library Archives
7   Kennedy, *The Civil War Battlefield Guide,* 48-52
8   Riley V. Beach, *Recollections and Extracts,* 1
9   Kennedy, 52-56
10 *Daily Journal,* Ibid.
11 1860 Federal Census Information, Kankakee County, Illinois
12 See, for example: Leon F, Litwack, *North of Slavery.*
13 *Official Records,* Series II, Vol. 4, 265-268
14 Shea and Winschel, *Vicksburg is the Key*
15 John J. Kellogg, *The Vicksburg Campaign,* 10
16 Ibid., 14
17 Charles King, et. al., *Photographic History of the Civil War,* 47
18 *Official Records,* Series I, Vol. 17, Part 2, 741
19 William S. McFeely, *Grant, A Biography,* 62
20 Daniel S. Parker, *Civil War Letters,* December 4, 1862
21 Ulysses S. Grant: *Memoirs,* Events of December 12, 1862

22 William T. Sherman, *Memoirs,* H. W. Halleck's 12/07/1862 letter to Sherman at College Hill

23 John C. Wideman, *The Sinking of the U.S.S. Cairo, 31*

24 Ibid., 29-30

25 National Park Service Information, Vicksburg

26 Wideman, 32 - 33

27 Ibid., 34-35

28 Parker, December 13, 1863

29 Ibid.

30 See Garvin Tate's account, *A Day at Holly Springs,* at www.d-a-c.com/HollySprings/town.htm

31 Parker, December 20, 1862

32 Sherman, *Memoirs,* Events on Christmas Day, 1862

33 Ibid. Events on December 26, 1862

34 Ibid. Events of December 27-29, 1862

35 Parker, December 30, 1862

36 Sherman, *Memoirs,* Events on December 30-31, 1862

37 Parker, January 3, 1863

38 Kennedy, 156

39 Parker, January 3, 1863

40 Parker, January 4, 1863

41 Sherman, *Memoirs,* Events of Jan. 4-8, 1863, and *Official Records,* Series 1, Vol. 17, part 2, p. 536

42 Ibid., January 10-11, 1863.

43 Encyclopedia of Arkansas, *Battle of Arkansas Post,* website reference

44 Grant, *Memoirs,* Events of January 17-18, 1863

45 Ibid.

46 David Bastian, *Grant's Canal,* 1-7

47 Bastian, 8-49

48 Ibid., 3 and 55

49 Ibid., 22

50 National Park Service, Vicksburg, *Letter Correspondence,* Letter 4

51 Ibid., Letter 3

52 *Illinois Roster* record for Captain Mason Sutherland

53 Grant, *Memoirs,* Events of January 29, 1863

54 Suzanne LeVert, et. al. *Encyclopedia of the Civil War,* 235

55 *ORN,* Series 1, Vol. 23, 403, and Vol. 24, 697

56 Mitchell, *Union Army Camp Cooking,* 18

57 Ibid.

58 S.M. Fox, *Story of the Seventh Kansas,* Kansas State Historical Society, *Transactions,* Vol. VIII (1903-1904) p. 46, in Mitchell, 19

59 Mitchell, 19

60 Bastian, 41-44

61 *Official Records,* Series 1, Vol. 24, Part 1, 386-390

62 *Official Records,* Series 1, Vol. 24, Part 3, 134

63 Ibid., 21

64 Ibid., 119

65 ORN, Series 1, Vol. 24, p. 477

66 Ibid., 486-487

67 *ORN,* Series 1, Vol. 20, 763

68 *Official Records,* Series 1, Vol. 24, Part 1, 488

69 Ibid., 491

70 Ibid., 490-492

71 Ibid., 436

72 *ORN,* Series 1, Vol. 20, 6-18

73 *ORN,* Series 1, Vol. 20, 8

74 *Official Records,* Series 1, Vol. 24, Part 1, 475

75 Ibid., 19-22

76 Sherman, *Memoirs,* Events for April 3 and 4, 1863

77 Beach, 5

78 *ORN,* Series 1, Vol. 20, 137-138

79 Grant, *Memoirs,* Events of January 29, 1863

80 *ORN,* Series 1, Vol. 24, 552 - 554

81 Beach, 5

82 Sherman, *Memoirs,* Events for April 16, 1863

83 Boatner, *Civil War Dictionary,* 359-360

84 Beach, 22

85 *Official Records,* Series 1, Vol. 24, Part 3, 212-213

86 *ORN,* Series 1, Vol. 24, 604-605

87 Ibid., 605-606

88 *Official Records,* Series 1, Vol. 24, Part 3, 240

89 *Official Records,* Series 1, Vol. 24, Part 1, 49

90 *Official Records,* Series 1, Vol. 24, Part 3, 827

91 *Official Records,* Series 2, Vol. 6, 657

92 DiLorenzo, *The Real Lincoln,* 36 and 145

93 See: Frank L. Klement, *The Limits of Dissent*

94 *Official Records,* Series 1, Vol. 24, Part 2, 254-255

95 J.J. Kellogg, 21

96 Beach, 6

97 J.J. Kellogg, 21

98 Beach, 7

99 J.J. Kellogg, 22

100 Ibid., italics added.

[101] Megan Sullivan, *African-American Music*, Website reference

[102] *Official Records*, Series 1, Vol. 24, Part 1, 736-739

[103] *Official Records*, Series 1, Vol. 24, Part 3, 300

[104] *Official Records*, Series 1, Vol. 24, Part 2, 255

[105] J.J. Kellogg, 23

[106] Ibid.

[107] *Official Records*, Series 1, Vol. 24, Part 3, 870

[108] Ibid., 876

[109] Ibid., 879

[110] Kennedy, 164-167

[111] David Williams, *A People's History*, 173 -174

[112] *Official Records*, Series 1, Vol. 24, Part 3, 313

[113] J.J. Kellogg, 24

[114] *Official Records*, Series 1, Vol. 24, Part 2, 255

[115] Grant, *Memoirs,* "Battle of Big Black River Bridge," Chapter XXXVI

[116] *Official Records*, Series 1, Vol. 24, Part 2, 256

[117] J.J. Kellogg, 25

[118] *Official Records*, Series 1, Vol. 24, Part 2, 257

[119] J.J. Kellogg, 28-30

[120] *Official Records*, Series 1, Vol. 24, Part 2, 259

[121] J.J. Kellogg, 33

[122] Ibid., 37

[123] Ibid., 37-38

[124] *ORN*, Series 1, Vol. 25, 21-22

[125] J.J. Kellogg, 38-39

[126] Official Records, Series 1, Vol. 24, Part 2, 258

[127] J.J. Kellogg, 41-43

[128] Ibid., 43

[129] Sherman, *Memoirs*, Events for May 22, 1863

[130] Ibid.

[131] J.J. Kellogg, 44-46

[132] Ibid., 47

[133] William H. Tunnard, "The History of the Third Regiment" in
A. A. Hoehling, *Vicksburg, 47 Days of Siege,* 48

[134] Sherman, *Memoirs,* Events from May 22-May 31, 1863

[135] J.J. Kellogg, 49

[136] Tunnard, in Hoehling, 70

[137] J.J. Kellogg, 49-51

[138] *Official Records*, Series 2, Vol. 5, 723

[139] *Official Records*, Series 2, Vol. 6, 657

[140] Mary Ann Loughborough, *My Cave Live in Vicksburg*, in
Hoehling, 101

141 Kennedy, 173-175
142 *Official Records*, Series 1, Vol. 24, Part 1, 161
143 Wilmer L. Jones, *Generals in Blue and Gray*, 134
144 J.J. Kellogg, 55
145 *Official Records*, Series 1, Vol. 24, Part 1, 103
146 Ibid.
147 *Official Records*, Series 1, Vol. 24, Part 1, 103-104
148 J.J. Kellogg, 57-58
149 *Official Records*, Series 1, Vol. 24, Part 2, 372
150 *Official Records*, Series 1, Vol. 24, Part 1, 109
151 *Official Records*, Series 2, Vol. 6, 59
152 Hoehling, *Vicksburg, 47 Days of Siege,* 239
153 *Official Records*, Series 1, Vol. 24, Part 2, 377-378
154 *Official Records*, Series 2, Vol. 6, 72
155 J.J. Kellogg, 61-62
156 Beach, 10-11
157 Ibid., 11
158 Ibid.
159 *Official Records*, Series 2, Vol. 6, 183-184
160 Beach, 13
161 Ibid.
162 *Official Records*, Series 2, Vol. 6, 232
163 Ibid., 237-238
164 *Official Records*, Series 3, Vol. 3, 817
165 Rebecca Blackwell Drake, *The Ultimate Grief: William T. Sherman*
166 Abraham Lincoln, *Collected Works*, 1809-1865, Vol. 6, October 3, 1863 (Project Gutenberg's Website)
167 See: Margie Bearss, *Sherman's Forgotten Campaign*
168 Jerry O. Porter, *The Sultana Tragedy*, 28
169 *Official Records*, Series 1, Vol. 30, Part 2, 752 and 756
170 *Official Records*, Series 1, Vol. 31, Part 1, 767
171 Beach, 20
172 Ibid.
173 Ibid.
174 Ibid.
175 Ibid., 21
176 Ibid.
177 Ibid.
178 *Official Records*, Series 1, Vol. 32, Part 2, 135-136
179 Kennedy, 261
180 *Official Records*, Series 2, Vol. 8, 810
181 *Official Records*, Series 1, Vol. 32, Part 1, 173

[182] *Biographical Directory of the United States Congress, 1774 to the present,* Search: Ralph P. Buckland

[183] Boatner, p 95

[184] Kennedy, 261

[185] Official Records, Series 1, Vol. 32, Part 1, 202

[186] Kennedy, 261

[187] Ibid., 262

[188] Ibid.

[189] Beach, 23-24

[190] Boatner, 367

[191] *Official Records,* Series 2, Vol. 6, 1035

[192] San Francisco Museum Website: "Adah Isaacs Menken" and T. Allston Brown, *A History of the New York Stage.*

[193] Sgt. James H. Dennison *Andersonville Diary*

[194] American Battlefield Protection Program, National Park Service Website, "Battle of Paducah"

[195] Beach, 24

[196] Boatner, 359-360

[197] American Battlefield Protection Program, National Park Service Website, "Battle of Paducah"

[198] Boatner, 296

[199] Ibid.

[200] Williams, 366

[201] *Memphis Daily Bulletin,* April 30, 1864

[202] *Official Records,* Series 1, Vol. 39, Part 1, 221-222

[203] Edwin C. Bearss, "The Battle of Brice's Cross Roads," 14

[204] *Official Records,* Series 1, Vol. 39, Part 1, 118

[205] Beach, 29

[206] *Records,* Series 1, Vol. 39, Part 1, 118

[207] Ibid.

[208] Kennedy, 346

[209] E.C. Bearss, 13

[210] Ibid.

[211] *Official Records,* Series 1, Vol. 39, Part 1, 222

[212] Ibid., 90

[213] E.C. Bearss, 14

[214] *Official Records,* Series 1, Vol. 39, Part 1, 87, 128

[215] Ibid., 90, 118

[216] Ibid., 118-119

[217] Ibid., 128

[218] Ibid., 91

[219] Ibid., 222

220 E.C. Bearss, 17
221 *Official Records*, Series 1, Vol. 39, Part 1, 119
222 Ibid., 222
223 E. C. Bearss, 19
224 Ibid., 20
225 Ibid., 19
226 Ibid., 20
227 *Official Records*, Series 1, Vol. 39, Part 1, 92
228 *Official Records*, Series 1, Vol. 39, Part 1, 119
229 E.C. Bearss, 44
230 Beach, 29
231 E.C. Bearss, 44
232 Ibid.
233 Ibid.
234 Beach, 29
235 Ibid.
236 Ibid.
237 Ibid., 29-30
238 Parker Hills, *A Study in Warfighting*, 35-37
239 Ibid.
240 Monte Akers, "The Rebel Yell."
241 Beach, 30
242 Ibid.
243 Ibid.
244 Ibid.
245 Hills, 42
246 E.C. Bearss, 49
247 Hills, 42
248 E.C. Bearss, 49
249 *Official Records*, Series 1, Vol. 39, Part 1, 120
250 Beach, 31
251 Ibid.
252 Ibid.
253 Ibid.
254 Ibid.
255 Dennison, 41
256 Williams, 366
257 Kennedy, 347
258 E.C. Bearss, 50
259 Boatner, 85
260 *Official Records*, Series 1, Vol. 39, Part 1, 120
261 Dennison, 41, and Beach, 33

262 Beach, 32

263 Dennison, 38

264 Beach, 32 and Dennison, ibid.

265 Beach, 32

266 Ibid.

267 Ibid., 32-33

268 *Official Records*, Series 2, Vol. 7, Part 1, 381

269 Boatner, 85

270 Dennison, 39

271 Beach, 33

272 Dennison, 39

273 Beach, 33

274 Ibid.

275 Ibid.

276 Robert H. Kellogg, *Life and Death in Rebel Prisons*, 246

277 MacKinlay Kantor, *Andersonville*, 155

278 Victor Hicken, *Illinois in the Civil War*, 348

279 Troy Drew, *James M. Bryant's Daily Records of Deaths in Andersonville*, Deaths on 06/19/1864

280 Beach, 38

281 R.H. Kellogg, 59

282 *Official Records*, Series 2, Vol. 7, 381

283 Beach, 34

284 Chipman, *Tragedy of Andersonville*, 55

285 LeVert, et. al., 289

286 *Official Records*, Series 2, Vol. 7, 606

287 General N. P. Chipman, *The Tragedy of Andersonville*, 77

288 Ibid., 53

289 Ibid., 153

290 Ibid., 154

291 Beach, 38

292 Chipman, *Tragedy of Andersonville*, 53

293 Private Robert Knox Sneden, *Eye of the Storm*, p. 203

294 Chipman, *Tragedy of Andersonville*, 54

295 Ibid., 258

296 Ibid., 264

297 Ibid., 76

298 Ken Drew, *Camp Sumter*, 28

299 Beach, 37

300 Ken Drew, 35

301 Ibid., 38

302 Ken Drew, 13

303 Ibid.
304 Beach, 37
305 Ibid.
306 Ibid.
307 Ibid., 36
308 Ibid.
309 Ibid.
310 Sneden, 242
311 Beach, 36
312 John McElroy, *Andersonville*
313 R.H. Kellogg, 171-172
314 Ken Drew, 15
315 Beach, 36
316 Ken Drew, 15
317 Official Records, Series 2, Vol. 7, 499
318 Beach, 35
319 Ibid.
320 R.H. Kellogg, 140
321 Ken Drew, 16
322 Beach, 34
323 Ken Drew, 16
324 Ibid.
325 *Official Records*, Series 2, Vol. 7, 517
326 Ken Drew, 16, and R. H. Kellogg, 87
327 Ken Drew, 21
328 R.H. Kellogg, 210
329 Ibid.
330 Beach, 36-37
331 Ibid., 37
332 John K. Lattimer, *Lincoln and Kennedy, Comparison of Assassinations*, 59
333 Williams, 85 - 88
334 *Official Records*, Series 2, Vol. 7, 708
335 Ibid., 763
336 Dennison, 67
337 Ken Drew, 23
338 Beach, 38
339 Dennison, 65-71
340 *Official Records*, Series 2, Vol. 7, 879
341 Beach, 38
342 Ken Drew, 28
343 Troy Drew, *Bryant's Daily Records*

344 *Official Records*, Series 1, Vol. 39, Part 2, 411-413
345 Macon Telegraph, October 1, 1864
346 Albany Patriot — July 28, 1864, 3
347 R.H. Kellogg, 283-284
348 Beach, 38
349 Ibid.
350 R.H. Kellogg, 285
351 Ken Drew, 24
352 Beach, 39
353 Ibid.
354 R.H. Kellogg, 330
355 Beach, 39
356 *Official Records*, Series 2, Vol. 7, 1113-1114
357 *Official Records*, Series 2, Vol. 8, 765
358 Dennison, 83
359 *Official Records*, Series 2, Vol. 8, 765
360 *Official Records*, Series 1, Vol. 39, part 2, 364-365
361 Boatner, 509
362 Dennison, 84
363 *Official Records*, Series 2, Vol. 7, 1160
364 Beach, 39
365 Dennison, 84
366 *Official Records*, Series 2, Vol. 7, 976-977
367 Ibid.
368 Ibid.
369 Ibid.
370 Ibid., 1150
371 Ibid., 1099
372 R.H. Kellogg, 341
373 Beach, 40
374 *Official Records*, Series 2, Vol. 7, 1197
375 Ibid., 979
376 Dennison, 86-88
377 *Official Records*, Series 2, Vol. 7, 1219-1221
378 Ibid., 979
379 *Official Records*, Series 1, Vol. 42, Part 3, 782
380 *Official Records*, Series 1, Vol. 44, 274
381 Ibid., 611
382 Kennedy, 401
383 Dennison, 90
384 *New York Times*, January 17, 1865
385 *Official Records*, Series 1, Vol. 53, 46

[386] Williams, 239

[387] *Official Records*, Series 2, Vol. 8, 139

[388] Ibid., 160

[389] National Archives and Records Administration, *Thirteenth Amendment to U.S. Constitution*

[390] Douglas A. Blackman, *Slavery by Another Name*

[391] Sherman, *Memoirs,* in his December 12, 1864 letter to General Halleck

[392] *Official Records*, Series 2, Vol. 8, 86

[393] Ibid., 126

[394] Dennison, 94

[395] *Official Records*, Series 2, Vol. 8, 766

[396] Ibid.

[397] Ibid., 451

[398] Ibid., 205

[399] Ibid., 422

[400] Ibid., 453

[401] Dennison, 97

[402] Ibid., 7, 97

[403] Beach, 40

[404] *Official Records*, Series 2, Vol. 8, 244

[405] Ibid., 263

[406] Beach, 40

[407] *Official Records*, Series 2, Vol. 8, 317

[408] Beach, 40

[409] Ibid., 41

[410] *Official Records*, Series 2, Vol. 8, 268

[411] Beach, 40-41

[412] Ibid., 41

[413] Chris E. Fonville, *The Wilmington Campaign*, 446-447

[414] Beach, 43

[415] *New York Times* archives website

[416] David Herbert Donald, *Lincoln,* 597-599

[417] *Official Records*, Series 1, Vol. 29, Part 2, 529

[418] Blackman, *Slavery by Another Name*

[419] Thompson, *Pioneer and General History of Geauga County,* 731

[420] Littleton Historical Museum, http://www.littletongov.org/history/biographies/chatfield.asp

[421] Ibid.

[422] State of Colorado, Arapahoe County Records, Book A3, p. 426

[423] State of Colorado, Jefferson County Records, Vol. L, p 544

[424] State of Colorado, Arapahoe County Records, Book A2, p 62

425 Ibid.
426 Ibid.
427 Ibid.
428 Ibid., Book A15, p. 27
429 Ibid., Book 12, p. 18
430 Ibid., Book A62, p. 53
431 Ibid., Book A-52, p. 423
432 Ibid., p. 424
433 Ibid., p. 436
434 Ibid., p. 461

3652531

Made in the USA